STEPHEN CRANE'S CAREER:
PERSPECTIVES
AND
EVALUATIONS

Edited
With Introductions
And Notes
BY
Thomas A. Gullason

New York University Press
New York 1972

To
Harput and Adana
And Old Armenia
For Two Great Gifts:
My Father
Sarkis Gullason (1895-1969)
And My Mother
Rebecca Sahagian Gullason

PREFACE

I

I have brought together this volume to celebrate the centennial of Stephen Crane's birth (November 1, 1871); to provide a serviceable source for students, scholars, and general readers; and to encourage a review-reappraisal of Crane as a writer (his biography and his journalism are touched upon only briefly), and of his position in America's literary history, where he has long been regarded as limited and minor. I have included views of Stephen Crane and his art from many perspectives. The volume contains different types of criticism with different emphases—from the 1890s to the present—so that one can trace the history of Crane scholarship and more readily identify its forms, directions, and its "growth."

It should be a truism that no one critic is argus-eyed enough to achieve total understanding of a writer's art, meaning, and worth. But a knowledge of the critics or critical systems—in combination— leads one closer to the ideal of total comprehension.

In his volume of essays, *Toward a Pluralistic Criticism* (1965), Professor Oscar Cargill proposes that the reader-critic can synthesize all the existing scholarship on a writer and his work, to which he may contribute his own particular interpretation or assessment. Though a seemingly mechanical kind of routine, this approach is most rewarding. It helps any reader-critic to bring order out of chaos; to see relationships and patterns that an individual critic or critique cannot reveal; and to sharpen and expand meanings. In his summary of a second approach, that of the more creative, highly individualized,

v

and all-encompassing pluralistic critic, Professor Cargill encourages the student of poetry—and really any student of imaginative litera-ture—to

> approach the work of art with every faculty, with every tech-nique, with every method he can command, for he must know not only what the poem probably meant to its creator but also what it probably means to several different kinds of readers in his own generation if he is to communicate his appreciation and delight to them. In a word, he must have the keenest sense of time to deal with the pluralistic values of any given work of art; he must himself be a pluralist, athletically able to keep receding values in view, willing to embrace new values as they come on, in order to dispense in acceptable language an appre-ciation appropriate to the sensibilities of the youngest of his generation as the purest form of judgment. His role, if prop-erly understood, is neither that of ambassador of the old nor ambassador of the new, for each is a partisan, but of liaison officer between the two. It is the role of both scholar and critic.

To help the reader approximate these ideals, I have in this selection of Stephen Crane criticism tried to include a wide range of varying interpretations (within the limits of available and sensible criticism of Crane). In one way, though, I have set up an arbitrary pattern in order to encourage the reader to focus first on the estimates-reminiscences; then to study closely the various qualities and issues discussed in the essays on Crane's poems, novels, and short stories; and finally to make his own reevaluations about Crane's worth as an artist. Moreover, after reviewing the entire body of Stephen Crane scholarship, I have tried to *save* the "classic" critics (such as Edward Garnett) and to *recover* some critical viewpoints (such as the essays by Elbert Hubbard and Jonathan Penn, and O. Henry's parody) which, though not widely known, deserve attention. And I have also presented some critics (such as Robert Hough and Clark Griffith) who have *discovered* new departures in Crane criticism.

Because this is the centennial of Stephen Crane's birth, I have included the section, "A Family Portfolio." Here I present several "firsts": an engraving of the Reverend Jonathan Townley Crane (Stephen Crane's father), and extracts from two volumes of his Jour-

nal; a biographical sketch of the Reverend Crane by his wife, Mary
Helen Peck Crane, along with one of her newspaper articles; and an
article by Stephen Crane's talented brother, J. Townley. The three
short stories by the Reverend Crane and the three sketches by Stephen
Crane, included in this section, make their first appearance in a
volume; I originally published them in *American Literature* (May,
1971) and in the *Southern Humanities Review* (Winter, 1968). The
brief sketch by Cora Crane was first published in 1901; it was not
until 1960 that Lillian Gilkes reproduced it in part in her *Cora Crane;*
here it is reprinted in full.

II

The essays in this volume that first appeared individually in
magazines or books probably made isolated impacts. Brought together
in this volume and placed alongside complementary essays, they
should present a broader and more cohesive view of the problems in
Stephen Crane scholarship, as well as the variety of perspectives
needed to appreciate Crane's artistry and value. Essays which study
one specific quality in Crane's work are placed alongside those which
present other strands from his work or are more general in perspective. Independently and collectively, all of these essays should make
the reader look more closely at Crane before making any generaliza
tions about him. Some qualities in Crane, his comedic sense for
example, have to be explored further; they should prove him to be
more valuable and more complex than has been presumed.

III

In summary, I have tried within the limits of this volume to en
compass the range of response to Stephen Crane's work and to suggest
new directions. Any editor, however, has to bridge some obvious gaps.
First, I present two essays of my own, which go beyond the individual studies on Crane's novels and short stories included in this
volume. I attempt to make fresh remarks about Crane as novelist and
short-story writer. Second, in the general introduction, and the brief
introductions to each section of this volume, I have placed Crane in
the context both of his times and of the stream of modern American
literature and have suggested further areas for research.

Hopefully, the future course of Stephen Crane criticism is reflected in this volume. All the critics represented serve an important function. Critics are necessary gadflies who prod, annoy, frustrate, stimulate, and warn the easily satisfied reader, the secure scholar, and the fact-crammed literary historian to forsake their "final" positions and reenter the lifetime creative-critical act of appraisal and reappraisal.

*   *   *   *   *

The assistance and services provided by many libraries and universities throughout the United States enabled me to achieve the variety and scope necessary for this type of volume. I want to thank in particular the libraries at Princeton, Dartmouth, Amherst, Yale, Harvard, and Columbia, and at the Universities of Pennsylvania, Maine, New Hampshire, Vermont, and Connecticut; the Boston Public Library, the New York Public Library, and the Free Library of Philadelphia. I also wish to thank the Interlibrary Loan Department at the University of Rhode Island and Mrs. Kathleen Schlenker; Kenneth A. Lohf, Librarian for Rare Books and Manuscripts at the Butler Library, Columbia University; and Roger Merola, of the Audiovisual Services Center at the University of Rhode Island.

I am grateful to the various authors and publishers who kindly allowed me to reprint material in this book. I want to pay special thanks to Professor Walter Sutton of Syracuse University; Professor Joseph X. Brennan of the University of Notre Dame; and Professor Eugene Current-García, of Auburn University, who helped me locate the O. Henry parody of Stephen Crane. Special thanks are also due to Anthony Meisel, Diane Girling, and Chris Kentera, Director of the New York University Press.

I wish to acknowledge the constant aid and advice of my wife, Betty, and the good humor of my son, Edward, who "teasingly knocked" Stephen Crane's elbow and mine.

I am indeed gratified to be able to express my deep appreciation to Oscar Cargill, former Chairman of the Department of English at New York University and now Professor Emeritus, for his remarkable patience, kindness, and support.

Thomas A. Gullason
University of Rhode Island
Kingston, Rhode Island

CONTENTS

I

STEPHEN CRANE: "INFANT PRECOCIOUS"

"Writing in America must have been pretty dead then. . . . There was literary prohibition in Steve Crane's day all right. . . . What that man knew he never got said. . . . He said a lot. He was an explosion all right. It's about time people began to hear the explosion." Sherwood Anderson made these rhapsodic statements in 1926, and they generally reflect the response of a small but vocal band of young writers of the 1920s who worshipped Stephen Crane's unorthodox life and literature. A handful of admirers worked diligently during this period to rediscover him: Vincent Starrett with his anthology, *Men, Women and Boats* (1921); Edward Garnett with his remarkable summary of Crane's art in *Friday Nights* (1922); Thomas Beer with a colorful biography, *Stephen Crane* (1923); and Wilson Follett with his twelve-volume edition, *The Work of Stephen Crane* (1925-1927).

At the same time, Anderson and others never really understood what Crane had accomplished in the 1890s. True, Crane's age was not fully prepared for him; as an "infant precocious" he would have been more at home in the iconoclastic 1920s. Yet without the pressures and conflicts of the 1890s, Crane might never have taxed his energies enough to produce his original work. And he was able to produce it before his untimely death in 1900 at the age of twenty-eight.

During his own lifetime, Stephen Crane received some unusually favorable response, despite his sardonic comments on almost everything his age represented. His literary fathers, William Dean Howells and Hamlin Garland, encouraged and helped him in the first stages of his career. *The Red Badge of Courage* (1895) won him a national reputation in America and even in his soon-to-be adopted country, England. His contacts with established and upcoming artists, newspapermen, reformers, and publishers were legion: Joseph Conrad, Henry James, Ford Madox Ford, H. G. Wells, Harold Frederic, S. S. McClure, Edward Marshall, Jacob Riis, and many others. Yet shortly after his death he was almost completely forgotten. This same pattern of rapid decline occurred in the 1930s and 1940s, following the short-lived enthusiasm during the 1920s.

Thanks to the gathering momentum of the criticism published during the 1950s and 1960s, it seems that with the opening of the present decade Stephen Crane no longer needs to be rediscovered. He is popular with academic critics and with the general public. Reprints of his works, additions to his canon, a new critical edition of his writings (being prepared by the University Press of Virginia), a newsletter, numerous essays, anthologies, volumes of biography, bibliography, and criticism already published or scheduled for publication—these are clear evidences of Crane's burgeoning reputation, which is thrusting him into the forefront as a major writer.

Yet why has Stephen Crane's literary reputation always been plagued with brief rises and long falls? His rises can be attributed partly to his bohemian biography, which makes him seem even more glamorous when various "myths" are highlighted. His life is a classic study of the romantic writer-hero: He often went hungry; he was racked by disease (tuberculosis); he was unappreciated by the genteel publishers of the day and oppressed by his age, which falsely accused him of drunkenness, dope addiction, and liaisons with prostitutes; he was never to have any peace but, with courage and fortitude, was still able to win some wars; and he died young.

But this is the fad response to Crane's biography. The public at large, especially after his death, reacted unfavorably to Crane because of his "bad" life and because so little was really known or understood about him. The critics and the public responded similarly to Crane's literary work. They admired *The Red Badge,* but little else. His handful of great short stories was lost in a stockpile of journalistic materials. If the poetry attracted, it was mainly due to its shock value—"God is cold." As a rebel and as an "infant precocious" he was highly appealing for a time, but in terms of his life and his art many people thought that he did not have any lasting value as a major writer. The fact that his literary writings were largely unavailable until the 1950s did not help matters.

Despite these periodic rises and falls, Stephen Crane has survived because of his extrinsic importance. Literary histories have rightly acknowledged that Crane passed on the legacies of naturalism and impressionism; that he wrote the first modern novel of the slums, *Maggie* (1893), and the first modern novel of war, *The Red Badge;* that he was the forerunner of the Imagist movement in poetry; and that he helped to create the modern American short story.

With all this, Stephen Crane is still at a crossroads today. We need to know much more about his life, though crucial letters and manuscripts are harder to come by. His life in America—at Port Jervis, Claverack College, Lafayette College, Syracuse University, Asbury Park, Ocean Grove, and New York City—is still vague and shadowy; his life in England is similarly sketchy. Moreover, the available record of Crane's family heritage is limited and misleading. R. W. Stallman's bulky biography of 1968 was inadequate, adding very little in the way of relevant materials that would have humanized and completed Crane's portrait. The earlier biographies are still useful: Thomas Beer's work clearly displays some unsolved mysteries; it is also one of the most cryptic biographies on record; John Berryman, in his biography of 1950, is almost as cryptic, though he is more sensitive to Crane's art than either Beer or Stallman. More recent scholarship has recovered a lost period of Stephen Crane's life, that of his schooling at Pennington Seminary (1885-1887), which suggests that he was surrounded with educational opportunities that were substantial and useful to his development as a writer. The recent discovery of the Reverend Jonathan Townley Crane's two-volume Journal and four of his short stories can now be used to correct his narrow portrait found in the *Dictionary of American Biography*, on which scholars depend. *The Stephen Crane Newsletter*, begun in 1966 and edited by Joseph Katz, steadily adds new materials and information on many areas of Crane's biography.

This same lack of knowledge hinders a real understanding of Stephen Crane's literary worth. Some valuable inroads have been made into special areas of his art, such as his parodistic and mock-epic techniques. But it was not until 1962 that Robert Hough provided solid evidence about Crane's color aesthetics, proving that he was not just a sensational writer full of pyrotechnics. Hough's essay exposes the incomplete understanding of Crane's aesthetics that frustrates Crane scholarship. The exaggerated attention given to Crane's naturalism has obscured his unique and varied qualities. Only with the recent additions (and hopefully more) to Crane's canon, with further studies into the theory and practice of his writings, and with more biographical evidence, can scholars provide a fuller and fairer portrait of the artist and the man.

Instead of looking ahead, some of Stephen Crane's critics have been looking backward and repeating the charges of others. For all his genius and precocity, is Crane really limited and superficial, a writer without power? Or is he vastly underrated, and really one of America's most ambitious and electric talents? *In toto* Crane does satisfy the demands of William Faulkner, who rated authors on their splendid failures "to do the impossible," on their never being satisfied to stay within what they knew. A major short-story writer, and more than moderately successful as a novelist and as a poet, Crane made spectacular breakthroughs in art and theme which affected the course of modern American literature.

II

A FAMILY PORTFOLIO

A. INTRODUCTION

Stephen Crane was descended from talented and distinguished people: lawyers, jurists, military leaders, politicians, statesmen, and ministers. Yet very little is known about Crane's family heritage or how it influenced him. The present scholarship on Crane's father, the Reverend Jonathan Townley Crane, is incomplete and inaccurate. The Reverend was supposedly hostile to fiction, yet he himself wrote fiction, for example the three newly discovered stories reproduced in this section. Moreover, the extracts from the Reverend's Journal (unknown to Stephen Crane scholarship) reveal more closely the qualities of his character, besides adding important biographical information. The new pieces by Mrs. Crane give further insight into her husband's nature, as well as her own. The new article by J. Townley sheds more light on Stephen Crane's newspaper experience and on his sojourns in Asbury Park. The three new sketches by Crane himself present unusual examples of his fascination with American history, folklore, and local color. Crucial gaps still exist in our knowledge of Crane's relationship with Cora Taylor. Exactly how good or how bad was Cora's influence on Crane's literary work? Her sketch, "What Hell Might Be," raises some interesting literary questions, beyond the obvious biographical ones.

1. *A Recently Discovered Engraving of the
Reverend Jonathan Townley Crane, D. D.*

Reprinted from: *Pennington Seminary Review*, I (June 1889), opposite p. 1.

2. *Extracts from the Reverend Crane's Newly Discovered Two-Volume Journal*

Tues., January 24, 1865

Met Dr. C. S. Stockton, with whom I went on to Mt. Holly, where I delivered my lecture on the war for religious liberty in Holland.

Fri., January 27, 1865

In P.M. preached the funeral sermon of Weir, a soldier who was lately released from Andersonville, but was too far gone to recover. He died, aged 30, leaving a wife, and one or two children. This makes seven funerals of soldiers, which I have attended since Conference.

Sat., February 4, 1865

Rec'd letter from T. H. Landon, inclosing a tract intended to prove the annihilation of the impenitent. It seemed a weak document to me.

Wed., February 8, 1865

At 8 o'c. went to Washington Hall, and lectured on the war between Holland and Spain to a very good audience.

Tues., March 14, 1865

Received a long letter from Bro. Landon in regard to the "extinction theory" of Storrs. Answered it.

In the afternoon, went with Mrs. Crane to take tea at Bro. Freeman's. Home at 9 1/2 o'c.

Mon., April 3, 1865

News of the fall of Richmond and Petersburg, which creates universal excitement and joy. Worked a little in the garden. In the evening, general class, attended by about 25 persons, in all. Perhaps the popular commotion lessened the number.

Tues., April 4, 1865

Letter from Scranton, which I answered. Worked in the garden. In the evening, went to the meeting assembled to rejoice over the fall of Richmond. Made the first speech. . . .

Sat., April 8, 1865

Wrote the outline of a Sermon on National affairs, Ecc. 7.14.

Mon., April 10, 1865

Official news this morning of the surrender of Lee and all his army, and the town is full of joy.

Sat., April 15, 1865

News comes that the President was mortally wounded by an assassin last evening, and died this morning. The whole place rings with the startling rumor. How cheering the thought that God lives.

Sun., April 16, 1865

A day of gloom, and excitement. Church full of people. Preached a sermon (Psa. 146. 3-4.) designed to be suitable to the occasion, but felt wholly unfitted to preach at all.

Sun., April 23, 1865

Preached for the colored people at 3 ½ o'c. on national affairs. Visited the Sunday School also. In the evening, preached on the Sixth Commandment, to a full house.

Fri., April 28, 1865

Rose at 5 ½ o'c. and worked in the garden till 11 o'c. when I found myself "demolished" for the day. Mrs. Crane, M. Helen,

Aggie, and my sister arrived from Newark. Leaders and Stewards met in the evening.

Sat., May 6, 1865

Rain. Made out my returns for the Income Tax, reporting $1,310.31 above the $600. exempted.

Thurs., May 11, 1865

Heard the Hon. Geo. Thompson, M. P. speak in the hall on American affairs, and the attitude of England toward us. He represented the aristocracy as being unfriendly, but the masses as devoted to the cause of freedom. His speech was decidedly able, and left a good impression on the audience.

Mon., June 5, 1865

In the evening, held our General Class meeting. There were few present. I feel discouraged about our evening meetings. Our Sabbath congregations are good. Our Sunday School is flourishing beyond all former times. My own class of little people are models of faithfulness. But our prayer meetings, or weeknight classes, are poorly attended.

Mon., August 28, 1865

Spent the day at home. About 4 1/2 o'c. in the afternoon, our fourth daughter and tenth child [Myra Blanche] was born.

Tues., September 12, 1865

Went with Bro. Eddy to Lake Hopatcoug. Arrived at noon. After dinner tried "trolling" for pickerel; and caught nine, the largest of which weighed three pounds. The scenery is beautiful, the transparent water, the green hills that surround the place, and the clouds gliding above, and mirrored below. I was so much interested in the changing views, as our skiff glided along, that I almost forgot the fish. We put up at the hotel of Mr. Philips.

Tues., October 17, 1865

Called at the Jail and had an interview with Cucnel, who is under sentence of death for the murder of his wife. He was reading the Bible when I entered his cell. He talks slowly, and is quite deaf, and gives indications of feeble intellect.

Sun., October 22, 1865

In the afternoon, preached in the Jail: to about 16 or 18 prisoners, about half of whom are going to state's prison. At the close of the service, they gathered around me, and wanted me to promise to come again. They were very attentive, and I hope that good was done.

Fri., November 24, 1865

Wrote an article on Negro Suffrage. . . .

Sun., November 26, 1865

Preached in the evening from Rom. 6.23. to a crowded congregation, a sermon suggested by the execution of Cucnel.

Thurs., November 30, 1865

Went to New Brunswick to attend the State Temperance Convention. Quite a large number of delegates were present. We organized a permanent State Society, to hold an annual meeting on the last Wednes. of September.

Mon., January 8, 1866

Completed an article on Mexico and the Monroe Doctrine, and sent it to the State Gazette at Trenton.

Fri., January 12, 1866

In the evening, lectured again on Astronomy.

Mon., January 15, 1866

I have written a supplement to our election laws. This is my own in originating the idea, and preparing the bill. According to it, every man who accepts a bribe for his vote, is declared not to be entitled to vote at that election. Every man suspecting another of accepting a bribe may challenge him, and put him on his oath, and in case he refuses to take the oath, his vote is to be rejected. It seems to me that this will stop bribery, if any law can do it. I wonder if it will pass.

Thurs., January 18, 1866

This morning, considering the matter of singing at our social meetings, it struck me that our choruses, good as many of them are, are not as largely endowed with the devotional element as it seems to me desirable that they should be. The idea of writing a chorus occurred to me, and I wrote this, to indicate what I mean.

> We praise thee, we bless thee; we hallow thy name,
> Ascribing Salvation to God and the Lamb,
> We praise thee, we bless thee; in songs we adore,
> Hosanna, we'll praise thee, when time is no more.

Sun., February 25, 1866

Held a general class meeting. The basement was full, and all spoke who could get an opportunity, some 50 of them. Preached from Psa. 130.4. to a crowd. Received 36 on probation, who came and stood together around the pulpit. It was a famous time of rejoicing. To God be all the glory.

Met my class at 2 o'c. There were over fifty present. Went with Bro. I. Searing to the School House on the Mendham road, and preached from Psa. 85.6. In the evening preached on the parable of the Prodigal son. The house was crowded. Sixteen came forward, several for the first time, among them Capt. Winslow. The good work progresses, convictions multiply, the whole church seems alive with divine power. Thus ends a day of victory.

Wed., February 28, 1866

Wrote an article for the Gazette, denouncing the project of the Morris and Essex R. Road to take the Sabbath to make a certain alteration of their track. Called at the shop of Greenwood and Hays, and invited the workmen to seek Christ. Wrote an article for the Banner, on the Railroad business. Prayer meeting in the afternoon, four seeking religion.

Sat., April 21, 1866

Spent the day at home, among my books, yet not doing much, as I am not yet recovered from a severe attack of sick headache, which came on last evening. Did not go out at all.

Fri., May 4, 1866

Evening: lectured for my Bible class on *Tobacco.* The lecture room was well filled.

Mon., May 21, 1866

Spent some time this morning in reading Thackeray's *Vanity Fair,* recommended as a true picture of English "Society." If the picture is true, "Society" needs reforming.

Mon., June 25, 1866

In the morning [in Montreal, Canada] occurred the Catholic festival of St. John the Baptist. A procession of societies, schools, etc. marched thro' the streets, to the French Cathedral, where I saw "High Mass" performed for the first time. It was quite an imposing show, but to me, at least, nothing more.

Sat., August 11, 1866

Did nothing all day worth mentioning.

Sun., August 12, 1866

At 2 o'c. was called to visit Mr. Nixon, the tavernkeeper, who is very sick.

Sun., October 14, 1866

Three of our children are sick with what proves to be the dreaded Scarlet fever. Lizzie, Lu. [Luther] and Blanche. Who can foresee the end? Perhaps all will live through it; possibly the time has come when our hitherto unbroken circle shall cease to be such. Well, God reigns, and in his hands we are safe, whatever awaits us.

Mon., October 15, 1866

Another case of scarlatina, Eddy [Edmund] is down with it. Lizzie [Elizabeth] grows worse and the prospect darkens. Two doctors consult, and neither is hopeful.

Our dear little Lizzie, the gem of our circle, died this afternoon just at Sunset. We are no longer an unbroken number. Our colony on the other shore is begun.

Thurs., October 18, 1866

Was called at 5 o'c. The baby is worse; no hope. Thus the fatal stroke is repeated. "Though he slay me, yet will I trust in Him." At eight o'clock and thirty minutes Myra Blanche went from our arms, to those of the Good Shepherd.

Sat., November 24, 1866

Read John Scarlett's ms. poem, describing his early life, his skepticism, his conversion, etc. The poem contains many things of interest to the personal friends of Bro. Scarlett.

Tues., December 4, 1866

Home all day. Heavy storm. In evening, heard Bayard Taylor
lecture on the Russians.

Tues., December 18, 1866

Took tea at the Rev. Wm. Merritt's with the Rev. Dr. Butler,
the returned Missionary at Barcilly, India. Heard him lecture
in the evening, on the Sepoy rebellion.

Sat., January 12, 1867

On my return home, found my sister suffering with a sudden
attack of bleeding at the lungs, and in an apparently very
critical condition.

Tues., January 15, 1867

On my return home, I entered my sister's room, and as soon
as she saw me, she called me to her, and asked me to help her
up. I raised her to a sitting posture, and asked her if that
rested her. She whispered "Yes," with some difficulty, leaned
her head on my shoulder, as I sat with my arm around her,
and in a few minutes, was gone. Thus peacefully and without
pain died my beloved sister, in her 58th year, a faithful con-
scientious christian.

Mon., February 18, 1867

This morning, at half past two, our eleventh child [really
twelfth child, Jesse] was born.

Tues., April 2, 1867

Had a genuine attack of the enemy of my peace in the days of
my youth, sick headache, which for the day, not only disqualified me for taking my share of the final labor of the moving
that I was more a burden than a help, but made my wife so
anxious in my behalf that she took the responsibility of send-

ing for the doctor without my consent. Patience and abstinence rather than medicine, however, cured me of the malady, with no worse result than some 36 hours of exceeding pain and discomfort.

Fri., July 19, 1867

Delivered my first lecture on Astronomy, in the evening, to a pretty good audience.

Thurs., August 1, 1867

Our infant is sick with cholera infantum, and we are not without fears.

Fri., August 2, 1867

Infant better in some respects, but the general state not very encouraging. . . . Sat up a part of the night with the little one.

Tues., August 6, 1867

This afternoon, at 2.20', our little Jesse Peck, aged five months and nineteen days, went to the better home above. Last evening, we thought him better, the worst symptoms of the disease seemed to abate, and we pleased ourselves with the idea that he was recovering. This morning, he appeared as usual, only cold, and all the measures resorted to, to warm him were in vain. . . Thus "he was not, for God took him."

Sun., August 11, 1867

I hear that a dancing school, under the tuition of a colored man, was inaugurated yesterday. So we go. Two or three of our Sabbath School Scholars have joined the dancers, I hear, and among them, the little daughter of Bro. Harvey.

Fri., September 20, 1867

Mr. Hill stated in his speech that on a recent visit to the New Jersey state prison, he learned that of 477 prisoners, 310 were under 25 years of age; that 384 were led into crime by means of drinking alcoholic liquors, and that among these 384, not one was a pledged Temperance man when he fell into crime.

Wed., November 1, 1871

This morning, at 5.30' our fourteenth child was born. We call him Stephen, the name of the ancestor of the Elizabethtown Cranes, who was one of the Company of "Associates" who settled at E. town in 1665: also of S. Crane of Revolutionary times, who was prominent in patriotic labors and counsels for 15 years.

Sat., November 11, 1871

Prostrate all day with a severe attack of sick headache.

Wed., November 29, 1871

Went to Bound Brook, and lectured on Temperance.

Fri., July 5, 1872

Went to the Campground [at Deuville], and found my family well, and the infant [Stephen], especially, much improved by the change from the city to the woods.

Fri., November 1, 1872

Went to Ocean Grove Camp Ground for the first time to choose a lot.

Sat., November 23, 1872

Heard Bro. A. J. Palmer lecture on Rebel Prisons.

Mon., August 25, 1873

Started in the evening Boat "Sunyside" for Saratoga Springs, to attend the National Temperance Convention.

Mon., October 20, 1873

Home at 10 o'c. In the house all day, feeling exceedingly
weary, and half sick. Steven is so sick that we are anxious about
him.

Mon., November 17, 1873

On my return to Bro. Vansant was seized with a severe pain
in the muscles and chords of the neck, which tortured me all
night.

Tues., November 18-22, 1873

Sent for Dr. Hubbard and Mrs Crane. Bro. Vansant made
me a bed in his study, where I remained till Saturday morning, suffering most of the time intensely, and utterly unable
to get home. The physician called it in a general way, the
result of a sudden cold. The symptoms were something 'like
neuralgia, or rheumatism, and as bad as either I presume.

Thurs., January 1, 1874

Spent the day at home, reading Wesley, Foster, Peck, and
others, on the Subject of Entire Sanctification. Wrote to Dr.
Geo. Peck. The state is scriptural, but the theory of the work
does seem to me, at this juncture, unsatisfactory. If I read
aright, all the exhortations, all the promises, refer to truly
regenerated persons as they are. No one of the writers named
but is constantly running the one state into the other, first
distinguishing the two states and then confounding them.

Mon., May 18, 1874

Thirty years ago, today, I went to my first circuit, to begin
my ministry.

Wed., July 15, 1874

In the afternoon, married, in my own house, Joseph Harley, and Emily L. Cooke, of Newark. Dr. G. Peck at the same time baptized our youngest child, Stephen, who was born Nov. 1, 1871.

3. *Three Newly Discovered Fictions by the Reverend Crane, Reproduced in Volume Form for the First Time* *

I

DIDN'T GET IN—A TRUE STORY FOR BOYS **

By Rev. J. T. Crane, D.D.

Once upon a time, not a great while ago, there were three boys in one of the Ward Schools of a certain city. I do not mean to tell their real names, because, if I should, their playmates would tease them about getting into the newspapers. So we will call them Thomas, Richard, and Harry; or, if you boys like it better, Tom, Dick, and Harry. They all sat together in school, Dick's place being in the middle. They read and they wrote together, and studied geography, grammar, and such things. Every week the teachers reported to their parents. They used a printed card, which had on it one column for scholarship, another for deportment, and a third for absences. If a boy did first-rate in his lessons, he was marked 100 in the column for scholarship. If he did poorly, he was marked 80 or 70, and so on. If he behaved well, never breaking the rules, he was marked 100 in the column for deportment. If he broke the rules, he was marked less.

One day the boy, whom we agreed to call Tom, brought home his card. His father examined it, and called out, "See here, Tom, what about your deportment? You have only 85. Why don't you get 100?"

"I get marked down for whispering in school," said Tom.

"What makes you whisper when it is against the rules?"

"O," replied Tom, "the boys will talk a little. The teacher sees it, and asks us about it, and I say, 'Yes, sir,' and get the blame. Some boys say 'No, sir,' and get clear."

"Tom, do you always tell the truth, when the teacher asks you about breaking the rules?"

---

* I first published these fictions, and one other, in *American Literature* (May 1971). They are reprinted by permission of *American Literature* and The Duke University Press. [*Editor.*]

** Reprinted from: *Sunday-School Classmate*, I (April 1873), 4-5.

"Yes, sir, I try to do it," answered Tom.

"Well," said his father, smiling, "I like that. Don't break the rules. But if you should, don't tell lies about it. Tell the truth, if it takes your head off."

Some time afterward, when the weekly report was examined, a low mark was found in the column of scholarship.

"Look here, Tom, you can do better than this. What is the matter?"

"The sums were hard last week," said Tom; "we could none of us do them all."

"And so you all got marked in about this fashion?"

"No, sir," replied Tom, rather slowly. "Dick was marked ahead of the rest of us."

"How was that when you were all deficient?"

"O, Dick borrowed. I did part of the sums. Harry did part. Dick sits between us, and he copied from both our slates, and so beat us both."

"Do you ever copy in this style, Tom?"

"No, sir," said Tom, looking his father straight in the face, with both eyes wide open.

"Well," said his father, "I am glad of that. No matter what happens, don't cheat, even if you get down to the very foot of the class. Don't cheat, Tom. Remember."

Time passed, and the complaints of Dick's cheating, and getting good marks for it, were frequent. Tom was worried. He saw boys above him, who used unfair means, and received honors to which they were not entitled. He felt the injustice, and at times scolded hard about it, and got almost angry. But his father always said, "Hold on, Tom. Stick to the right, no matter what happens. Anyhow, *stick to the right.*"

The end of the school year came, and the boys were examined to see if they were prepared to leave the Ward School, and go up to the city High School. Twenty-five or thirty passed, and were sent up to the High School, to be examined again there, to see if they were fit to be admitted. And this last examination was a scorcher. There was not the ghost of a chance to cheat. The examination took place in a large room, almost like a church; and the candidates were made to sit so far apart that to whisper or copy was impossible. They were required to answer, on paper, without saying a word to any one, the questions put to them. Each did his best, and then rolled up his papers, gave them to the examiners, and went home.

About a week after the examination Tom came running into the study, saying, "Father, I have heard from the High School. We are all right. Harry and I are admitted!"

"That is good. That is grand. How about Dick?"

"Didn't get in!" said Tom.

MORAL.

Stick to the right, and wait till the end comes.

II

THE LIFE OF A POTATO WORM.

By Rev. J. T. Crane, D.D.

In a certain garden there was a plot of ground where potatoes and tomatoes were growing. One evening, no one knew when, a little egg, no larger than a mustard seed, was laid on the leaf of a potato plant, and fastened there with glue, so that it should not fall off and be lost. It was only a little speck, so small that no one saw it. There it stayed some days, and then it burst, and there came out a little worm, so small that no one saw it.

And the worm was blind, and did not know what to do. And there came a spirit and whispered to it to bite the leaf where it was. So it bit the leaf, and finding that it was good, began to eat. Day after day the worm ate and grew. It was still blind. It felt warm at noonday, but saw not the sun, nor knew that there is one. It felt cool at night, but did not know that it was dark, or suspect that the stars were looking down at it. It ate all the leaves upon the stalk where it was born, and then was sad at the thought that there was no more food. But the spirit came again and whispered to it to feel all around. And it swung its blind head about till it touched the leaf of a tomato plant. The worm climbed upon the tomato, and once more was abundantly supplied with food.

And still it grew. And one day there came two children into the garden, and Robbie spied the worm, and said, "Look here, Mary, see what a great horrid green worm; I am going to kill it." But Mary said, "Don't kill it, Robbie. The Lord made it, and perhaps he made

---

Reprinted from: *Sunday-School Classmate*, I (September 1873), 44.

it for something." But the worm did not hear a word of this conversation, or suspect how near death it was.

After a time it ceased to eat and to grow, and seemed to be asleep. And the spirit came and told it to go down into the ground and dig itself a grave. And so it crept down the stalk of the tomato till it reached the earth, where it burrowed down till it passed out of sight. Then it drew itself together till it was only a third of its former length, and its skin became dry and wrinkled, and then it split open, and within was a little case like that of an Egyptian mummy; and the worm was still inside. Again all was silent and still as the tombs in the hearts of the pyramids, and day and night passed on.

And then one day just as the sun was setting the spirit came and again whispered to the worm, and it burst its mummy-case and came forth. And, lo! it was not a worm at all, but a beautiful gray moth with four silver wings and two shining eyes, which glowed in the twilight like those of a cat. And it looked about it and saw the grass wet with dew, and the flowers and the trees, and the evening sky and the stars coming out one by one. And it spread its wings and flew along like an arrow from flower to flower, and sipped their honey, and drank the dew, and was happy in what God had made it.

And then the two children came again into the garden, and when they saw the beautiful moth hovering about the flowers and darting from one to another so swiftly, they laughed and clapped their hands. And Robbie said, "See that pretty moth. How different it is from that great ugly worm that I wanted to kill once and you would not let me." Mary answered, "God made them both," but neither of them knew that the worm and the moth were the same.

III

LETTER FROM A CAT.

By Rev. J. T. Crane, D.D.

Mr. Editor: I hope that you do not believe that dogs alone are entitled to be heard. I may be slightly prejudiced against them, still, let them have justice. Dogs are good in their place. They do very well to hunt rabbits by day, and watch the house by night. But there

---

Reprinted from: *Sunday-School Classmate*, I (November 1873), 59.

are objections to them. Some of them will bite. They all run in the mud and get so dirty that you can hardly invite them into the parlor. I might add, in a whisper, that they sometimes have fleas about them; but that, I suppose, is their misfortune, and an honorable, high-minded cat scorns to upbraid others for what they cannot help.

We cats ask for justice. We, too, have much to plead in our own favor if it were necessary. I may be permitted to say, of my own family, that we have always moved in the first society. Indeed, I was told by my grandmother that her grandmother told her that when General Washington was courting the widow Custis he took her cat up in his lap one evening, and, gently smoothing her back with his hand, said several times, in a distinct voice, "Poor Pussy!" That cat was my ancestor. But you must not suspect that I am proud and haughty because of it. O no; I speak to common cats just the same.

Cats have made some figure in the world. In the history of "Puss in Boots" it is evident that if it had not been for the cat the master would never have married the princess. Nor without her help would Whittington ever have become Lord Mayor of London. Without the cat the bells might have rung themselves hoarse, and the poor boy would have been a poor boy still.

We are slandered. There is a foolish belief in some quarters that if a cat is left alone with the baby the cat will get into the cradle and smother it. What an absurd story. We could not smother the baby if we tried our best. And why should we want to hurt the baby? Babies are among our best friends. When our baby is fed I always contrive to be there; for I know that when it has got all the milk it wants some one will say, "There, give puss the rest."

And some people, who ought to know better, have in their albums a ridiculous picture of a cat grinning from ear to ear, and saying, "Ha, ha, I have eaten the canary!" My friends tell me that this picture was clearly intended to pass for my portrait, and was maliciously contrived for the purpose of accusing me of murder. I did not eat the canary. But I know who started the story. It was Ponto, who has been pouting for the last two weeks because he tried to steal bones from my plate, and got his ears soundly boxed for it. Yet I am sorry to say that some people believe the slander. No longer ago than yesterday, when my mistress was away from home, I heard the rest of the family talking about it at dinner, and one of the boys said that I ought to be drowned for eating that bird. And what do you suppose that they were themselves eating at that very moment? It was a bird! I had seen it often in the barn-yard. I do not know the name of it, but it was a very large bird with a wart on its nose, and a very disagreeable voice, and a great deal of self-conceit, which made it love to parade around in a fussy way with all its feathers set on end. But it was a bird; and the family were eating it at the very time when the boys proposed to drown me, on the charge of having eaten a bird! What sort of justice do you call that? I confess that when I heard the remark, and remembered that Miss Floy was not at home, my feelings were so hurt that I left the room; nor did I come back until I saw my mistress return.

We cats, no doubt, have our little imperfections. We are apt to pride ourselves on our accomplishments, especially our proficiency in music. Still, our superiority in this delightful art is so generally acknowledged that we may well be excused if we are a little vain. We never perform without attracting an audience. Envious dogs, like Ponto, sometimes try to interrupt us; but as we usually select the roof of a shed, or some other elevated spot, as the place of meeting, we are out of their reach, and can afford to look calmly down and pardon their harmless noise. The people around us always listen with great attention. No sooner do we begin our practice than the windows go up, no matter what hour of the night it may be, and we are saluted with cheers, the clapping of hands, and other demonstrations of approval. We wish, however, that our admirers would be a little more careful about one thing. Articles of various kinds are often placed on the window-sill; and when the people, in their eagerness to hear every note, lean over to listen, these articles sometimes get knocked off, and come near falling on our heads. Last night, for example, while we were executing a very difficult piece of music, a bootjack and several geological specimens fell out; and, finally, something of the nature of crockery struck near us with a tremendous crash; and Miss Tabby Whitenose, our soprano, declared that really it made her so nervous that she could not sing another note, and we adjourned without even saying Good-night. How can people be so careless!

Tell the people, then, to be just to us. If they do not want us about the house let them say so. We are able to take care of ourselves. We are no paupers like Ponto and the other dogs. We can go into the fields and catch mice, and find our own living. We protest against cruelty and abuse. We bear pain silently, to be sure, but we feel it, nevertheless. Perhaps if we should cry out as Ponto does when he is hurt we would get more pity. The girls are pretty good, though some of them might improve a little. But a good many boys are cruel, and cruelty to the weak is cowardly. Tell them that for me.

Truly your friend,   FELIS ALBA.

4. *A Newly Discovered Biographical Sketch of the Reverend Crane
by Mrs. Crane*

REV. JONATHAN T. CRANE, D.D.

Jonathan Townley Crane, youngest child of William Crane and
Sarah Townley, was born June 18th, 1819, in a red farm-house at
Connecticut Farms, two miles from Elizabethtown, as Elizabeth was
then called.

He was a merry-hearted child, full of fun and always laughing.
His lint-white locks, blue eyes and blonde complexion, added to a
frail body, gave the lad a delicate appearance which did not promise
the vigorous manhood and earnest life to which he attained.

His parents attended the First Presbyterian Church of Elizabeth.
He was taught the Westminster Catechism and indoctrinated in the
tenets of the Confession of Faith, but the stern doctrines of Cal-
vinism failed to take hold of the thoughtful, sunny-hearted boy.

When but eleven years of age his father died, and two years later
his mother became a victim of cholera.

Thus bereaved, himself and his only sister, Agnes, found a home
with his mother's sister, Mrs. Jonathan Meeker, of New Providence,
whose house was a home for the Methodist ministers of those times.

His sister married the Rev. Curtis Talley, of the New Jersey Conference, and thus providentially the young Jonathan was surrounded
by those Methodistic influences which moulded, in a marked degree,
his whole life. At eighteen years of age he was converted during a
revival in the old church at New Providence, Brother Talley being
the pastor. The young convert ardently embraced the doctrines of the
Methodist Episcopal Church, to which he yielded a loyalty intense
and lasting as his life. Immediately after his conversion the divine call
came to him to preach the Gospel of Christ.

Like the early disciples, it found him at his work. He had been
apprenticed to Judge Smith Halsey, of Newark, a well-known manu-
facturer of trunks, where he earned the esteem of his fellows and of
his employer by his industry and unfailing good nature. There his
evenings were spent in reading and study. He often said that the

Reprinted from: *Pennington Seminary Review*, I (June 1889), 1-5.

present to him of a story for boys, called Jack Halyard, made him a reader.

With the call to the ministry came the conviction that he must obtain the best education possible to equip him for this sacred calling.

His brother Richard bought his time of Mr. Halsey, and he gave himself up to study and preparation. A small legacy from his father's estate was increased by teaching the district school near the old homestead, and also at Morristown.

After eighteen months of preparation he entered the Sophomore class in Princeton College, from which he graduated in 1843, taking a prize for English composition.

He was licensed as an exhorter at Perth Amboy, December 15th, of the same year, and as a local preacher at Franklin Street, Newark, May 13th, 1844, the Rev. J. L. Lenhart being pastor. The Rev. John S. Porter, Presiding Elder of the Newark District, appointed him to Parsippany Circuit. He preached his first sermon in the M. E. Church at Whippany, May 19th.

The following spring he entered the New Jersey Conference and was sent to Asbury Circuit. His labors here were most abundant. At the end of six months he was transferred to a more important point, taking the circuit comprising Quarantine and Port Richmond, on Staten Island. In 1846 he traveled Hope Circuit, and in 1847 he was stationed at Belvidere. His labors on that charge were blessed with a glorious revival and large accessions to the church.

During the revival a dance was gotten up in the town, and the burning question of the hour was, "Should Christians dance?" The young preacher grappled with it, preaching a sermon to a large audience which settled the question so far as his church was concerned. This sermon was so much commended that he enlarged it and published his "Essay on Dancing" the following year. This little book has run through nine editions.

January 18th, 1848, he was married to Mary Helen Peck, the only daughter of Rev. George Peck, D.D., then editor of the *Methodist Quarterly Review*, to which Mr. Crane was a contributor. In the spring of that year the young couple removed to Orange, to which station he was returned the following year.

In June, 1849, he was elected Principal of Pennington Seminary. He entered upon this work with the industry, zeal and untiring energy which characterized all his labors. The institution, which was a stock concern, had not been a financial success, and this fact had not enhanced the patronage.

When the new Principal shouldered his responsibilities he found the institution like the proverbial sinking ship,—well nigh deserted. Nothing daunted, he spent his vacation traveling in search of young people who ought to be educated and in urging their parents to educate them; and yet, in spite of his strenuous efforts, his first term was opened with only twenty-six students, only five of them being boarders. Among these was a young man, a former student, who boasted of being an incorrigible. Without reporting himself at the office, he proceeded to inform himself as to the promised discipline of the new Principal, and endeavored to sow the seeds of insubordination among the students. Mr. Crane called him into the office and informed him that under *his* rule there was no room for those who were not there for purposes of self-improvement. The young bully departed with his baggage by the morning stage. This strike in behalf of good discipline had a wholesome effect on those who had formerly been dominated by this young man.

During this first year of the new *régime* the Seminary was purchased by the New Jersey Conference. A new interest was awakened in behalf of the institution among the members of that body, and the new administration being found satisfactory, confidence was restored and the number of students increased so that all the rooms were filled before the close of the school year. Mr. Crane wrote in his diary, January 1st, 1851: "My term of office opened under the most discouraging circumstances. The best friends of the institution were fearful; those who were indifferent declared 'the location bad and that it could not be made to prosper.' But it has prospered; we have more students than we can accommodate. All is peace and harmony, and we are exceeding the hopes of our most sanguine friends."

At the watchnight, held in the village church, December 30, 1850, a revival commenced which swept with mighty force among the students of the Seminary. Its manifestations reminded one of the joyful shouts and *"power"* of the old-time Methodism. Prayer and praise broke the stillness of the morning hour. For three days recitations were suspended and the time given to the work of soul-saving.

Mr. Crane made himself the friend and counsellor of his *"boys,"* and won them to him by his ready sympathy and his happy faculty of seeing the bright side of life and minifying its difficulties. An omnivorous reader, and an indefatigable student, he never failed them when they went to him for help or information.

The new Principal was an advocate of co-education, and by his efforts a female department was arranged for, the building put up,

and opened May 19, 1853. At the close of the first day sixty boarders
were registered.

During the nine busy years that Mr. Crane was Principal of the
Seminary, he preached almost every Sabbath, lectured on temperance
and other topics. He was ever ready to help weak and struggling
churches or causes, without fee or reward, seldom receiving more than
his traveling expenses, and often not that.

He delivered a course of lectures to his students on Sabbath after-
noons on the Ten Commandments, which he afterwards published
under the title "The Right Way."

Bishop Hurst said of this book that it was the best ever written
on that subject.

His books were, in all cases, the outgrowth of his studies and
preparation for the pulpit.

Dickinson College conferred on him the degree of D.D. in 1856.

He was a pioneer in the temperance cause in New Jersey, serving
as corresponding editor of the *Reformer,* a temperance sheet published in Trenton. During his vacations, while canvassing for students,
he lectured and preached on the subject from Haverstraw to Cape
May. In company with other brethren, he went annually before legis-
lative committees to plead for prohibitory laws, and used often to
express himself in favor of woman being given the ballot that she
might better protect her home.

That Dr. Crane was a success as an educator is evidenced by the
men and women trusted and honored in Church and State, who revere
his memory as an able and efficient instructor, one who brought the
best culture of heart and brain to his work, and whose aim was to
stimulate them to the highest possible attainments.

Dr. Crane was pre-eminently a minister of the Gospel of Christ.
To proclaim the *Riches of His Grace* was his highest ambition. During his Seminary career he often longed for the pastorate, but felt
under obligation to remain at his post until the success of the female
department was assured. At the close of the school year of 1858 he
felt that this mission had become an accomplished fact, and so he
tendered his resignation, which had been under consideration for over
two years. The way was prepared for him to do this, as the trustees
desired him to take the entire responsibility of the boarding department and finances, and he did not feel called upon to "secularize"
himself as such an arrangement would necessitate. He afterwards made
the same decision when urged to become a candidate for a much
higher position.

He then became pastor of Trinity Church, Jersey City. In 1860

he was assigned to Haverstraw, New York. There the war found him.
Dr. Crane was an anti-slavery man before, but the news of the firing
on Fort Sumter reaching him, just as it did that Sunday morning as
he was going into his pulpit, fired his soul. He preached, made
speeches and ardently labored for the Union cause with a patriotism
that was uncompromising. He was a member of the Christian Commission, and went to the front to look after the soldiers. With the
blood of a revolutionary grandsire in his veins, he was unflinching in
his love for his country. His great grandfather, Stephen Crane, was an
influential member of the Continental Congress, making himself very
useful in those troublous times.

Dr. Crane was appointed to Central Church, Newark, in 1862. To
Morristown in 1864, where he remained three years.

The splendid church there was projected and well under way
during his pastorate. Here a memorable revival occurred, resulting in
a largely increased membership.

Thence to Hackettstown. From here he was taken up at the
close of his first year and made Presiding Elder of the Newark district.
He served in this office four years and then was transferred to the
Elizabeth district.

He became pastor of the Cross Street Church, Paterson, in the
spring of 1876. There he delivered the centennial oration, July 4th,
amid scenes of rejoicing and lofty patriotism.

In 1878 he was appointed to Port Jervis, where his useful life
closed, Monday, February 16th, 1880.

Sunday, the 15th, he preached twice and conducted his Bible
class. His last sermon was characterized by wonderful power and made
a profound impression upon the large audience. His theme was "What
Infidelity must do before it can destroy Christianity," from the text:
"Woe unto him that striveth against his Maker."

The summons came to him suddenly. With the manuscript of an
unfinished book before him, he was seized with paralysis of the heart.
Summoning me to his relief, all efforts to alleviate his sufferings
failed, and in less than an hour he was gone, before physician or
friends could reach his bedside.

Dr. Crane was a man without an evil habit. Pure in thought,
word and deed, he exemplified in his life the religion which he pro-
fessed, and commended it to all with whom he came in contact. He
loved all mankind. His charity covered every human weakness, yet
he never compromised with sin. Patient and persevering in search of
truth, quick to discriminate, he was fearless in attacking error.

He could disarm an opponent with a shaft of wit that left no sting, and could differ with his brethren, firmly maintaining his own views without a touch of bitterness.

As a pastor he was indefatigable, visiting the sick, caring for the children (who all loved him), and hunting up the wanderers. As a preacher he was clear, forcible and eminently practical, aptly illustrating his points.

As a writer he took a wide range of topics, writing for the *Methodist Quarterly,* the *Christian Advocate, The Methodist,* and contributing articles for the *Sunday-school Times* for a period of twenty years.

Besides the "Essays on Dancing" and the "Right Way; or, Practical Lectures on the Decalogue," he wrote "Popular Amusements," "Arts of Intoxication," "Holiness, the Birthright of all God's Children," and "Methodism and Its Methods." The "Birthright" had passed through two editions. He was rewriting it when he died, and he expressed the hope that he would be able to "re-state his views in a manner that would commend them to those who differed from him theoretically." That brethren should so differ was painful to him. He was an independent thinker, but the one question to which he brought all the fruits of his research and labor was—"Is it Scriptural?" That settled, he would have died for the truth.

The discussions elicited by the publication of "The Birthright," he considered, had shed light upon the subject of which it treated, and had been healthful to the church. Dr. Crane took great satisfaction in the fact that many eminent ministers and others endorsed the doctrinal views set forth in the book, notably Bishops Janes and Scott. The former said of the book, "Whatever else dies, that book will live."

Dr. Crane was an honored representative of the Newark Conference in four General Conferences.

The morning that he died, of the ambitions of life he said to me, "I want nothing higher than to be a minister of Christ." In his last prayer meeting he said: "I am willing to trust all I am and hope for on the Atonement of the Lord Jesus Christ." He fell with the harness on. He went direct from the family altar, where he had prayed so fervently for his church, especially for the young, for our absent children and for us who knelt with him there.

That day a great sorrow fell upon the church and his family. The trusted counselor, the loving friend and father, "was not, for God took him."

The whole community was startled by the suddenness of his departure, for he was universally beloved. Over fourteen hundred people passed reverently by, to look upon him for the last time in the Port Jervis Church. A second service was held in St. James' Church, Elizabeth, where a large part of the Newark Conference assembled to pay a last tribute to their departed friend and brother.

And so we laid his body away under the evergreens, amid the scenes of his childhood, as a flood of golden sunshine burst upon the scene.

MRS. HELEN CRANE.

5. *A Newly Discovered Newspaper Article by Mrs. Crane*

CHANGE OF BASE.

By Mrs. M. H. Crane.

The insidious wiles of the adversary of all good are made manifest by the strategy employed to switch human souls off the right track. In this beautiful place it is not the avowed skeptic, the open grog-shop, or the gambling hell that Christians are called upon to combat, but it is the growing taste for worldly amusements which keeps the young from the house of God, dissipating religious convictions and makes the commands of God of no effect. In this category we may count card playing, dancing and theatre going. These frivolous amusements have little to recommend them. They are good as devices to "kill time," which means to waste the precious hours given us for holier uses. But says one, "young people must have innocent amusement." Just so, but cards have ever kept bad company. The young man, fearing death on board the ill fated *Columbus,* could not pray until he had parted company with the pack of cards in his pocket. Dancing and theatre going lead to late hours, unsafe companionship and a dissipation of mind which unfits one for the serious work of life.

In the little back room in the drug store our young men may be initiated into drinking habits, and take their places just as surely among the moderate drinkers ultimately to swell the great army one hundred thousand strong, who go to a drunkard's death every year, as in the open saloon. "No drunkard shall enter the kingdom of heaven."

The pool and billiard rooms, with their obscenity and profanity, are the training schools in which our boys may take the first steps in vice, and becoming infatuated with gaming, render themselves victims to a passion which is soul destroying, and from whose toils few ever escape. Surely Christians here need to remember that "eternal vigilance is the price of liberty."

Reprinted from: Ocean Grove *Record,* March 15, 1884, p. 3.

6. *A Newly Discovered Newspaper Article by J. Townley Crane*

ASBURY PARK AS A NEWS CENTRE

By J. Townley Crane

I have had several hundred persons ask me during the last nine years why I lived at Asbury Park when I had charge of the Long Branch department of the *Tribune* and the Associated Press. Everyone that thinks about the matter naturally entertains the opinion that I ought to live at Long Branch. The reason I make my headquarters in the Park is easily explained. There is more news to be found in Asbury Park in one week, year in and year out, than is to be found in the Branch in a month. This little seaside town of ours is the best news centre on the entire New Jersey coast. The first two years I spent on the coast I lived at Long Branch but I became convinced that if I wanted to keep up with the procession I must move here. That my judgment was sound has been shown by the fact that nearly all of the men who come down to the coast to represent the big papers of the country make their headquarters in our bustling town. It is not a remarkable thing that the most remarkable town on the Atlantic coast should be "chock full" of news. Then it must be remembered that there is but one James A. Bradley [founder of Asbury Park] and that he belongs to our town and to us. Mr. Bradley can be safely relied upon to give the newspaper men plenty of news to write up, as he is constantly breaking out in new advertising schemes. That the newspaper men do not always agree with Mr. Bradley when he starts out in one of his new moves is not to be wondered at as Mr. Bradley does not always agree with himself. When he tries one of his unique schemes and finds that he has made a mistake he can "take a tumble" to himself about as quickly as any man I have met since I entered journalism. Sometimes he does not drop his mistaken move as quickly as one expects him to, but all of a sudden he gives it up and no one hears any more about it. When he is criticized by the newspaper men some of his friends are ready to

Reprinted from: *The Daily Press* [Asbury Park], August 22, 1892, p. 11.

batter the heads of the scribes with brick bats. The most unconcerned man over the affair is Mr. Bradley himself. He never cares for the attacks that are made upon him when they are honestly made. Telling the truth about him will never injure Mr. Bradley or any other honest man. I know that he likes to have the newspapers express honest opinions on his work in behalf of the town which he founded and in which he takes such justifiable pride. He always means right but if he makes a blunder the newspapers have the right to say so.

The work here is about as pleasant as it is in any other town. Of course there are some people here who claim that the correspondents have no right to say anything about the town excepting in the way of praise and when articles are published that they do not like they are very bitter in remarks about the writers. I have been terribly blackguarded by persons that took exception to articles that have been published in some of the papers that I write for and yet I had nothing to do with the ones that were declared objectionable. This kind of warfare while often annoying, is also amusing.

One of the funniest things that we meet with in newspaper work is the wonderful "smarty" who can always tell the difference between special dispatches and those furnished by the Associated Press, the United Press and the half hundred other concerns and bureaus that are sending news to the journals of the country from this section of the coast. I have been reviled like a pickpocket over an alleged Associated Press dispatch that was never seen by any person in the employ of the great news gathering corporation until it was published. Even the most experienced New York editor can not tell by picking up a paper exactly where the dispatches came from. In order to give an opinion that would be of any value he would have to compare several papers and then it would not be safe to wager very much cash on his opinion. There are more news agencies now than ever and as many of the papers do not mark their dispatches, it is almost impossible to tell the origin of any of them.

The people of the Park and especially our summer guests are always willing to treat a news-gatherer properly as long as he goes about his work in a quiet and dignified manner. No matter what kind of a story he is at work upon he can always find some one who will give him at least some of the facts in the case. When he finds the case to be a very hard one to work up and is refused all information by those who ought to give it to him then he has to do the best he can with the information furnished by those that know at least a part of the story. The efforts that are constantly being made by a certain class of persons to make a personal matter out of any case that a correspondent may have to work up is the result of their narrow mindedness. Half of the time the newspaper man has never heard of the people who figure in the case until he goes to work upon it. Now, why should he have any personal spite against a man or a woman that he never heard of before and whose own actions are the cause of the notoriety given to them. He is employed by the paper he represents to secure *the news* and he does not care anything more about John Smith than he does for William Brown or James Robinson. The corps of writers who make their headquarters at the Park are a hard-working band of men and if they make mistakes it is only natural, as they are made out of the same kind of clay as the rest of the human race and are just as liable to make blunders. They do very hard work, especially in the summer time and are often still at their desks when nearly every other person in the Park is fast asleep. If they were always given perfectly straight statements the people who are concerned in the articles they write would have no cause for complaint. To tell the truth they do not sit up nights worrying about the fact that Tom, Dick and Harry do not like their work. If their labor suits the editors of their papers it would be an excessively foolish thing for them to worry about the opinions of outsiders. When the editors are not suited with their reporters' work they discharge them.*

---

* This news article was published the day after Stephen Crane's "On the New Jersey Coast" (New York *Tribune,* August 21, 1892, p. 22) for which both Stephen and J. Townley were fired; presumably J. Townley was later rehired. [*Editor.*]

7. *Three Recently Discovered Sketches by Stephen Crane,*
    Reproduced in Volume Form for the First Time *

I

NOT MUCH OF A HERO.
EXAMINING THE RECORD OF "TOM" QUICK,
INDIAN SLAYER.
A NOTORIOUS CHARACTER OF PIONEER TIMES IN
PENNSYLVANIA—HIS MONUMENT DISCREETLY
SILENT AS TO HIS VIRTUES **

Milford, Penn., April 4.—It is supposed to be a poor tombstone
that cannot sing praises. In a thousand graveyards the prevailing
sentiment is: "Here lies a good man." Some years ago the people of
this place erected a monument which they inscribed to "Tom Quick,
the Indian Slayer, or the Avenger of the Delaware." After considerable speechmaking and celebrating, they unveiled the stone upon
which was inscribed the following touching tribute to the life and
character of the great Delaware Valley pioneer: "Tom Quick was the
first white child born within the present borough of Milford."

As he has long been known in history as a righteous avenger inflamed with just wrath against his enemies, the silence of the marble
upon those virtues which nearly all dead men are said to have possessed is astonishing. Why the worthy gentlemen who had the matter
in hand failed to mention any of those qualities or deeds by which
"Tom" Quick made fame, but simply mentioned a fact for which he
apparently was quite irresponsible, is, possibly, an unintentional rebuke to those who have delighted to honor those qualities of pitiless
cruelty which rendered him famous. His exemplary character has
made his memory popular in many parts of the valley. A local writer
in Port Jervis some years ago was asked to dramatize a life of "Tom"
Quick. He agreed and began a course of reading on his subject. But
after much study he was compelled to acknowledge that he could not

---

* I first published these sketches, and several others, in *The Southern Humanities
Review* (Winter 1968). They are reprinted by permission of *The Southern Humani-
ties Review* (Auburn University), and the Editors. [*Editor.*]
** Reprinted from: New York *Tribune*, May 1, 1892, part II, p. 15.

make Quick's popular qualities run in a noble and virtuous groove. He gave up the idea of making Quick the hero and introduced him as a secondary character, as a monomaniac upon the subject of Indians. The little boys living about Milford must be much agitated over the coldness of the monument's inscription, for Quick was a boys' hero. He has been a subject for the graphic and brilliant pens of the talented novelists of the dime and five-cent school. Youths going westward to massacre the devoted red man with a fell purpose and a small-calibre revolver always carry a cheap edition of Tom Quick's alleged biography, which is, when they are at a loss how to proceed, a valuable book of reference. In these volumes all the known ways to kill Indians are practically demonstrated. The hero is pictured as a gory-handed avenger of an advanced type who goes about seeking how many Indians he can devour within a given time. He is a paragon of virtue and slaughters savages in a very high and exalted manner. He also says "b'ar" and "thar" and speaks about getting his "har riz." He is a "dead shot" and perforates Indians with great rapidity and regularity, while they, it seems, persist in offering themselves as targets with much abandon and shoot at him with desperate wildness, never coming within several yards of their aim.

Historians are, as a rule, unsentimental. The aesthetic people, the lovers of the beautiful, the poetic dreamers, have always claimed that Quick during his lifetime killed one hundred Indians. The local historians stoutly assert that he only killed fifteen at the most. But certainly there must be some glory in fifteen Indians and when the manner in which the historians say Quick killed his Indians is taken into consideration it is not surprising that Quick occupies a unique place in history. He was born in Milford as above-mentioned, where his parents had settled in 1733. His father built mills and owned other valuable real-estate in the town, but "Tom" loved the woods and the mountains and chose rather to spend his time wandering with red companions than staying in or near the settlements. He became a veritable Indian in his habits. Until the French and Indian War he lived in perfect amity with the savages, sharing their amusements and pursuits. During this war, however, some savages shot "Tom's" father from ambush. His friendship turned immediately to the deadliest hatred and he swore that he would kill every redskin that crossed his path; he would hunt them as long as one of them remained east of the Alleghanies. The first Indian to be killed by Quick was named Muskwink. After the French and Indian War this Indian returned to the Valley of the Neversink. One day Quick went to a tavern near the junction of the Neversink and Delaware rivers. There he met Muskwink, who was, as usual, intoxicated. The Indian approached "Tom" and told him with great glee that he was of the party that killed Quick's father. He said he had scalped the old man with his own hand. He described laughingly the dying agonies of Quick's father, and mimicked his cries and groans. "Tom" was immediately worked up to the convulsive fury of an enraged panther. He snatched an old musket from the wall and pointing it at Muskwink's breast, drove him out of the house in advance of himself. After proceeding with his prisoner about a mile from the tavern, he shot him in the back, dragged the body into the bushes and left it.

At another time "Tom" and two other white men went into ambush in a thicket which overlooked some rocks where Indians often fished. Three Indians came to the rocks and were attacked by the white men. One was killed by a blow on the head with a club. Another was shot through the head and through the hand, while the third jumped into the river to save his life.

On one occasion Quick and a number of other white hunters sought shelter for the night in the log cabin of a man named Showers. An Indian arrived later and asked permission to stay all night. Showers agreed and the Indian, rolling himself in his blanket, lay down among the white hunters. In the middle of the night there was an explosion. When the hunters hastily struck a light they discovered Quick with a smoking rifle in his hand standing over the body of the Indian, who had been shot dead in his sleep.

Some time after the killing of Muskwink, an Indian with his squaw and three children was paddling down the Delaware River in a canoe. When the family was passing through Butler's Rift "Tom" Quick rose from where he lay concealed in the tall reed-grass on the shore and aiming his rifle at them commanded them to come ashore. When they had come near he shot the man, tomahawked the woman and the two eldest children and knocked the babe's brains out against a tree.

Quick made a statement to his nephew that he had killed an indefinite number of Indians. He said he would lie in the woods and wait until he heard a rifle go off. Then he would creep stealthily in the direction of the sound and would often find an Indian skinning a deer or a bear. He said that it was an easy matter then to put a ball through the red man's head or heart.

Another tale told of him smacks somewhat of the impossible and yet should be recognized as a unique method of fighting Indians. It

seems that the tribes used to send small parties of their young warriors to kill this implacable hater of their race. A party of these Indians once met Quick in the woods. He was splitting a long log. They
announced to him their intention of killing him. He parleyed with
them for some time. Finally he seemed to agree to their plan, but requested that he be allowed, as his last act on earth, to split that log.
They agreed for certain reasons only known to themselves. He drove
a wedge in the end and then he begged as another favor that they
assist him in splitting the log. Again they innocently and guilelessly
agreed. Arranging themselves in a long line down the side of the log,
the imbecile redskins placed their fingers in the crack held open by
the wedge and began to heave. "Tom" then calmly knocked out the
wedge, the log closed up and their fingers were all caught tight and
fast. They, of course, danced about like so many kittens whose claws
were caught in balls of yarn. "Tom" enjoyed their peculiar gyrations
and listened to their passionate comments for a while and then proceeded to cut them up in small pieces with his axe. It is a notable fact
that no one in the history of the country has ever discovered that kind
of an Indian except "Tom" Quick in this alleged adventure. Quick
finally died from old age in his bed quietly.

Apparently, if these adventures of his can be taken as examples,
"Tom" Quick was not an "Indian fighter." He was merely an Indian
killer. There are three views to be taken of "Tom" Quick. The deeds
which are accredited to him may be fiction ones and he may have
been one of those sturdy and bronzed woodsmen who cleared the path
of civilization. Or the accounts may be true and he a monomaniac
upon the subject of Indians as suggested by the dramatist. Or the accounts may be true and he a man whose hands were stained with
unoffending blood, purely and simply a murderer.

II

A REMINISCENCE OF INDIAN WAR.
BRANDT'S MURDEROUS VICTORY AT LACKAWAXEN FORD.

Lackawaxen, Pike County, Penn., June 10.—In July, 1779, a red
wave of savages, with crest of bloody steel, swept down the Delaware
Valley. The settlers fled before it to the crowded stockades and block-

Reprinted from: New York *Tribune*, June 26, 1892, Part II, p. 17.

houses where a legion of colonels and majors wrote letters and dispatched them to each other. The savages were led by Brandt. They burned and pillaged, while the colonels indited epistles. One wrote: "An express is just this moment come from Colonel Stroud's, bringing the melancholy account that the Tories and Indians in the upper part of the Minisink, in York Government, are burning and destroying all before them. It is said the enemy are six hundred strong and that the Tories join them every hour. It is not to be doubted that they will be in this State very soon, and the inhabitants above are all moving, and in the greatest distress and confusion. By a letter I have seen this morning from Captain Alexander Patterson, at Colonel Stroud's, stationed as quartermaster, it is mentioned that they have neither military stores or provisions, so that if they should suddenly attack that part of this country, destitute of help as they are, the country must fly before the enemy."

He was too busy with Indians to bother with pronouns. Another wrote: "Brant is Doing the mischief att [*sic*] Peainpack, and to my sorrow I acquaint you it has struck the People in general with such fear that they are moving away from the upper end of the Minisink very fast. If there is not some Means Taken To Stop the Enemy, the whole of the Inhabitance will move from this Place, and if so, pray what will be the Consiquence? Ruin and Destruction will Emediately Follow."

When the first of the fugitives reached Goshen, in Orange County, N. Y., Colonel Tusten who commanded the local militia, rallied his forces, with as many volunteers as could be raised, and held a council of war. The Indians, having devastated the valley and gorged themselves with plunder, had begun a retreat. Colonel Tusten said in the council that he doubted the expediency of a pursuit at that time, for the Indians outnumbered the whites two to one. But one man cried:

"Let the brave men follow me. The cowards may stay behind."

It was impossible for the prudent to say more. So they set out. They were joined by Colonel Hathorn, of the "Warwick Regiment," who had a few men with him. He, being the senior officer, took command. Thirty-four miles from their starting point they held another council of war, where the leaders were blistered by the words of valiant subordinates. So Colonel Hathorn decided to try to intercept Brandt at the Lackawaxen Ford of the Delaware, where they understood he was going to cross the river. Hathorn and his men made a bold dash for the ford, hoping to reach it first. But Brandt reversed his column, passed down a ravine and came upon the patriot force in the rear.

The battle of the Minisink followed. The scene of the fight is a little over a mile from this town, across the river, in Sullivan County, N. Y.

The Americans were caught like a lot of kittens in a bag, but Hathorn was a gallant officer and a sagacious leader. He made a stout-hearted fight. On a plateau near the river the Americans took their position. They threw up an irregular breastwork of stones and logs. They used every crevice and boulder possible as a means of protection, and lay close to the earth. Ninety men, without water and with no provisions, held this position from 10 o'clock until sundown, on a sultry July day.

Before a shot was fired Brandt appeared in full view of the Americans and requested them to surrender. He said his force was superior to theirs, and he had them penned in. If they surrendered, he would protect them. He was interrupted by a bullet. He retired, and the Indians immediately began a furious fire. The little plateau was covered with black powder smoke, from which the little red flames leaped at the Indians like tongues of snakes. Brandt opened the battle with his usual cautiousness. His men made no targets of themselves, but crept warily toward the Americans, taking advantage of every feature of the ground and firing at every hand, head or shoulder which appeared above the rocks on the plateau. But they could not make the patriots yield an inch, though the Indian dead lay thickly on the slope. The panting, powder-grimed whites on the height held their ground. The Indians were repelled at every point. The band of Americans on the plateau had grown to manhood with rifles in their hands. They were of that bronzed and sturdy race who were hewing their way through the matted forests and making homes in the dense jungles of an American wilderness. If a part of the line flinched even for a moment, they would all die. Each man felt his responsibility as a link in the chain of defence, and yielded not an inch. The powder ran short, of course, and they had to make every bullet find a red, howling mark.

As the day worn on, and one after another of his whooping minions was bowled over without making any gap in the American line, Brandt grew disheartened. It is said that there was one brave hunter who held the key to the American position. It is not explained by any one how this could be. A careful investigation of the battlefield as it appears to-day fails to discover any spot where one man could hold the key to the plateau against nearly 300 Indians. Or, if there was such a key, why leave it to the guardianship of one man, unsupported by the fire of his comrades, and with no reinforcing body?

But, at any rate, the tradition runs that way. Near sundown the Indians shot this man, and Brandt with a body of warriors sprang through the gap. Immediately the Americans became demoralized. They began a retreat. Where the noble red man shines out in transcendent lustre is as a pursuer. The scalping-knife and the tomahawk took the place of the rifle. The Americans made a frantic rush for the river. The Indians sank their hatchets in the body of every white man they could overtake. Captain Vail, of the militia, being wounded in the battle, was unable to retreat. While seated upon a rock, bleeding, he was slaughtered by the Indians. Seventeen wounded Americans and a surgeon were found behind a ledge of rocks. They were all killed. The Americans, scattered and broken, worn out with fighting against overwhelming numbers, fled madly. Many threw themselves into the Delaware and endeavored to escape by swimming as much as possible under the water. A small and decrepit band of those who had fought arrived home safely. There were thirty-three widows in the Presbyterian congregation at Goshen.

Fifty men had been cut off from the main body by Brandt's sudden attck. They took no part in the battle at all. It is said that they were led by the man who made the valorous oration at the council of war.

III

TWO MEN AND A BEAR.
A LIVELY SPARRING MATCH.

Hartwood, N.Y., July 12.—The bear as a pugilist is a new discovery. He has never been associated with the phrases, "Break away" or "Go to your corner." He has no fame as a professional. Yet the oldest and most experienced hunters about here claim that the bears are the best boxers in the world. They say that an axe or a crowbar is perfectly useless in the hands of a man against the paws of a big bear. Sometimes when a bear is attacked by dogs he simply rears himself upon his haunches and strikes out with his forepaws deftly, swiftly and with tremendous force. He can hold his position against any number of dogs unless the smaller animals get around in the rear

---

Reprinted from: New York *Tribune*, July 24, 1892, Part II, p. 17.

and make a desperate charge there. Every time a dog is hit by one of the powerfully swinging paws of the bear he topples over with broken ribs or a crushed skull. The bear deals swift blows right and left, straight from the shoulder, and he creates speedily a great mourning among the owners of the dogs. But it is happily a fact that there are few canines who are stout-hearted enough or foolish enough to wade in and attempt to grapple with the bear. Their general plan is to form a circle just without the reach of the mighty claws. From this safe position they keep up a prodigious barking and howling as if they were valiantly assaulting a regiment of Indians. The bear makes a little advance upon a certain portion of the circle and the uproar grows terrific as the dogs retreat hastily. Mayhap there may be a heavy dog among the crowd who is made of stern stuff. He watches his chance and bolts in at a vulnerable point. If he passes the bear's guard and gets a good grip, he encourages other dogs, who make a combined attack while the bear is engaged in wrenching loose the jaws of the first dog. The bear then has a bad quarter of an hour, but many of the dogs must weep and wail and gnash their teeth, for the bear crunches them and crushes them as if they were papier-mache images. But this plan is not the general one used by the dogs. As before mentioned, their forte is to sit around and howl. Then, if the bear starts to make off, they are snapping at his heels like so many fiends, and the great creature is speedily forced a make a halt. He rears himself up and makes a number of fierce dabs at the more courageous dogs. In this manner, they have occasionally been known to delay the bear until the hunters arrive, but in the very few cases in which numbers of dogs have come up with a bear, it has been a bad year for dogs in that part of the country.

The tale-tellers say that once upon a time, two men chopping logs in these woods, discovered a bear very close to them, engaged in stripping some bushes of huckleberries. They cautiously approached him with up-lifted axes. He discovered them and started slowly over the rocks. They rushed upon him. He sat up on his haunches, squared off and wacked [sic] at the foremost man with a swiftness that nearly took their breaths away. The paw struck the axe-helve and completely shivered it. The bear then made a pass at the second man, clipped him along side the head and knocked him, head over heels, over a fallen log with the blood starting from his nose and mouth, and a nice contusion that fitted the side of his head like a hat. By this time, the first man was up a tree. The bear went over and smelt of the man behind the log, and evidently satisfied himself that he was dead. He then turned about with the apparent intention of climbing the tree, but the first man sat on a branch and was very meek and quiet, so the bear changed his mind and shambled off over the ridge. He was watched out of sight by the man in the tree, who then climbed down and carried his unconscious companion on his back to a house one mile and a half away.

8. *A Fictional Sketch by Cora Crane*

WHAT HELL MIGHT BE

There was a woman—young, world-worn, selfish, floating on the swift stream of desire, never able to reach the smooth sea of satisfaction—until one day—

He came, and with him came once again melody in the notes of birds. A fragrance of incense overspread the earth and the flowers clothed themselves afresh in gay attire, while over all the sun poured down a rain of golden light so glorious, so dazzling that it blinded the woman, and with the man she sought the sweetness of shade found only in that valley which is invisible to the common eye. Out of the glare they went into a quiet spot touched tenderly by sun-fingers stretched down through leaves of ancient oaks, that spread their arms protectingly as if in benediction as the two walked in the shade on a carpet of blossom-studded green.

Life, to this man and woman, was a sweet, perfect thing.

He was a painter and his canvas glowed with colors that only love's brush may mix. He was pure of heart and soul, and he loved the woman. Under this gentle tutor her nature changed, softened, grew. She became gentle, firm, seeking to do good.

They looked into each other's eyes, and the woman said: "This is heaven," and the man replied: "This is heaven indeed."

Then the man was taken from the woman to do his appointed work in the unknown life beyond, saying to her: "Be patient; work and wait as I shall wait until we meet again, dear heart."

And the man passed and the woman did as he had bade her. She was patient, she worked, she waited. At times she sank into that fathomless depth of woe known only to the lonely heart; then she would remember that *he was waiting for her,* and she was patient and worked again.

Years passed and the woman's golden hair silvered; the dark eyes that *he* had loved faded and closed in dreamless sleep. Greedily grasping the ferryman's hand, she, too, passed into the shadow land.

But he was not waiting for her! Ages, cycles she wandered far and

Reprinted from: *The Smart Set,* V (November 1901), 48.

far away through the unknown land, peering into each passing face, grasping flowing robes only to see strange faces; vainly calling his name aloud, and weeping, weeping, always weeping; never resting; ever seeking the love of her life.

At last she saw him. "Yes, it is he, my beloved!" she cried, holding out her arms to him.

He did not know her.

C. H. CRANE
(Mrs. Stephen Crane.)

III

ESTIMATES-REMINISCENCES OF STEPHEN CRANE: THE 1890s TO THE 1960s

A. INTRODUCTION

Whether written by professional and academic critics, practicing authors, a publisher's reader, close friends, or members of his family, the estimates-reminiscences of Stephen Crane serve several useful purposes. They save pertinent factual material; reflect the taste and response of different generations; keep the author alive, by at least talking about him; sum up his achievements and failings; and can influence the attitudes of later critics and readers. They also encourage critics and readers to go back to Crane's literary work. However, it is a tragic fact that Stephen Crane is known secondhand by many, through a handful of critical readings of his works. Over the years, few really far-ranging and sound estimates-reminiscences of Stephen Crane have been written.

Several of the critics included in this section attempt to get down to the central issues relating to Stephen Crane's life and art; they try to see Crane as a whole, something explicators, who usually dissect parts intensively, are often unable to do. Among Crane's contemporaries, William Dean Howells, Hamlin Garland, and Edward Garnett come closer in some ways to the nature and spirit of Crane's talent. They have saved intimate details relating to his literary sources, writing habits, and psychological makeup that bring the reader of the 1970s into a living participation with the drama and frustrations surrounding Crane, his work, and its acceptance. The more distant and more "objective" critics, such as H. L. Mencken, wrote with a broader understanding of Crane's tragic struggle to write in the midst of the "literary prohibition" of the 1890s.

Stephen Crane was very easy prey for the parodists. His poetry has received the most sustained attack, and his fiction has not escaped some adverse comment. Kindly or destructive, the parodies starkly expose what some of Crane's peers felt were flaws in his work; they bring into relief the conflict between Crane's modernism and the traditionalism of the 1890s; and they show the risks he took as he struggled to be original and individual. Undoubtedly, the parodies were damaging to Crane's short literary career and to his posthumous reputation.

The writers of estimates-reminiscences sometimes draw upon one another so closely that they tend to make rigid certain evaluations of an author. Also, because a critic is anxious to cover a good deal of ground, he is often too sweeping in his remarks. A careful balance between specific facts and generalizations is necessary so that the writers of estimates can avoid the pitfalls of overstressing a particular thesis, of superficiality, cliché, and contradiction.

The essays which are more reminiscences than estimates have special problems. They can be overly biographical and factually inaccurate, as is the case with Hamlin Garland's essay, which has been, in many ways, a negative influence on Crane's reputation. Garland's factual unreliability is especially clear when one compares the essay reprinted in this volume with its several other versions, and with the corroborated facts of Crane's biography.* Ford Madox Ford is also inconsistent and unreliable with his materials in his reminiscences of Crane. Sometimes those who knew Crane intimately, like Joseph Conrad, run the risk of being apologetic or sentimental as they review his life; at other times, they strive so hard to be impartial that they become unreasonably critical and demanding. A full portrait of Stephen Crane by any of those who knew him personally is an impossible ideal.

A few estimates-reminiscences pose other dangers. At times, critics who are also good writers are more committed to clever phrasing and dramatic interest, and therefore sacrifice fairness to achieve these ends. This was a major flaw in Thomas Beer's biography, *Stephen Crane* (1923), and is often true of parodists. Other writers of estimates pounce upon Crane's "sins"—his real and mythic scandals—and almost totally forget his artistic life.

It is important, then, to weigh carefully the various estimates-reminiscences included in this volume. The estimates by Howells and Garland might have been the most illuminating and the most perceptive, but they are not. Both followed Crane's career almost from its inception. They immediately recognized his genius, and they encouraged and aided him in every conceivable way during the initial phases of his writing life. Yet both "literary fathers" abandoned Stephen Crane, even before his death in 1900. For both Howells and Garland had a limited and provincial sense of art and aesthetics and never recognized his genius as a short-story writer. Presumably

---

* For a careful study of some of the confusions in the Garland-Crane chronology, see Donald Pizer, "The Garland-Crane Relationship," *The Huntington Library Quarterly*, XXIV (November, 1960), 75-82.

Howells called "The Monster" the "greatest short story ever written by an American," though he did not include nor mention Crane in his anthology, *The Great Modern American Stories* (1920). Both Howells and Garland made too much of Crane's human weaknesses. In some ways, the little-known "estimates" by Rupert Hughes ("Chelifer") show far more understanding and respect for Crane's artistry.

One can speculate on why there was an almost total lack of comment on Stephen Crane between 1900 and 1920 in America. Even more surprising is the fact that so little attention was given to him during the 1930s, for his novels and sketches, like *Maggie,* "An Experiment in Misery," "The Men in the Storm," and "An Ominous Baby" would have appealed strongly to the depression critics, who were to make much of John Steinbeck's *The Grapes of Wrath* (1939). One obvious reason for this situation was that Crane's writings were not readily available. Certainly *The Work of Stephen Crane* (1925-1927), published in twelve volumes, in a limited edition of 750 sets (at $90 a set), was not enough to generate a real and sustained interest in Crane.

The English critics included in this section may not have fully understood the American character of his work; but they had already reacted favorably to Rudyard Kipling, who influenced Crane, and they responded enthusiastically and intelligently to Crane himself. From the 1890s to the present, American critics have been embarrassed and angered by the English claim that they discovered Crane first. Though this is not true, the most sensible early estimates of Stephen Crane are English, not American. The English discovered more and respected more about Crane before the American critics.

As the present decade opens, Stephen Crane is receiving greater critical attention than ever before, the kind reserved for major writers. Even French, Italian, Russian, Scandinavian, and Japanese critics have been attracted to him. Yet if V. S. Pritchett's and Warner Berthoff's views are accepted as representative of the 1960s, and go unchallenged in the 1970s, then Stephen Crane is a minor writer all over again.

For Pritchett and Berthoff bring to mind the deadly and narrow stereotypes that have long been associated with Crane, and that have been fostered in part by the estimates-reminiscences. Presumably, Crane is *only* an impressionist, or *only* a naturalist, or *only* an ironist. He is novel and exciting, but he is also limited, superficial, and without power. He came into literary life "fully armed," but then he really had very little equipment—a sporadic education, little interest in reading, and less intellectual stamina. He was amazingly original, but then he was an imitator, borrowing from many sources, especially Tolstoy. He was good only when he relied on his demon—his imagination; he was prosaic and dull when he mirrored everyday reality. His single theme was fear, or was it war? And so on.

1. *American Estimates-Reminiscences*

a. *Rupert Hughes ("Chelifer") on Stephen Crane*

I

THE JUSTIFICATION OF SLUM STORIES.

Literature is the greatest of all democratizing forces. The liberation of man from despotries and serfdom has found its most tireless and skillful architect in literature. It will not stop now with the foundation of a few republics and constitutional monarchies. The freedom of man is not yet consummated. Nor will it be till the boundary-lines between the castes of to-day, social if not electoral, are blended into indistinguishable gradations of congeniality and luck in accumulating money. When Mrs Croesus realizes in the depth of her soul that the only difference between her daughter and her maid is the individual equation and certain accidental effects of environment; when Croesus, Jr., acknowledges to himself that the young street-car driver is in all essentials his equal, and may twenty years hence occupy a higher social plane and a nobler place in his country—when these two consummations are reached—mote I be there to see!—then actual democracy will assume the earth. It is inevitable that deep students of humanity should feel a keen sympathy for the denizens of "low life, and that they should send novels, like tracts, out a-proselyting. A critic is only trying to dam Niagara with a goose-feather when he resists the tendency.

It is usually taken as one of the premises of devotion to beautifully purposeless art, that all stories of low life must be harrowing, pessimistic, dank with despair. Critics should keep off these premises. The sun shines for all. . . . Down in the tenements laughter is not an unheard thing. Sometimes it is punctuated with hiccups, sometimes it is more boisterously crude than the wont of Fift' Avnoo; but it is

Reprinted from: *Godey's Magazine*, CXXXI (October 1895), 430-432.

just as enjoyable and more hearty. In these recent studies of low life this is especially noticeable.

*   *   *

I regret to see that America cannot show the equal of these two [English] books [*Tales of Mean Streets,* by Arthur Morrison; and *Neighbors of Ours,* by Henry W. Nevinson] in its own studies of low life. But the cosmopolitan population of the country should offer the best field in the world, and doubtless competent tillers will not long be wanting.

Mr. J. W. Sullivan has written a volume of "Tenement Tales of New York," which contains much well-selected, well-observed material. The style in which they are told, however, is so baldly crude, there is so little verisimilitude in the talk of the characters and such complete lack of color and chiaroscuro in the narration, that they cannot be granted high value. Occasional bits of philosophizing are the best things in the book.

No better proof of the comedy possible in works on low life could be asked for than the writings of Mr. Edward W. Townsend, whose "Chimmie Fadden" has become a household familiar, and whose vivid language has infected the nation. Of course "Chimmie" figures principally in a scenery of high life, but the character-drawing is perfect and there are not a few visits to that seventh paradise, the "Bow'ry." Any writer who realizes the picturesqueness and charm of such a character deserves all he can realize on it.

But probably the strongest piece of slum writing we have is "Maggie," by Mr. Stephen Crane, which was published some years ago with a pen-name for the writer and no name at all for the publishers. But merit will out, and the unclaimed foundling attracted no little attention, though by no means as much as it deserves. The keenness of the wit, the minuteness of the observation, and the bitterness of the cynicism resemble Morrison's work. The foredoomed fall of a well-meaning girl reared in an environment of drunkenness and grime is told with great humanity and fearless art, and there is a fine use of contrast in the conclusion of the work, where the brutal mother in drunken sentimentality is persuaded with difficulty to "forgive" the dead girl whom she compelled to a harsh fate by the barren cruelty of home-life.

The subjects chosen by all these writers compel an occasional plainness of speech which may give a shock to spasmic prudishness, but there is nothing to harm a healthy mind, and they all should have the effect of creating a better understanding and a wiser, more active sympathy for the unfortunates who must fill the cellar of the tenement we call life. To do this is far better even than to be artistic.

CHELIFER.

II

THE RISE OF STEPHEN CRANE.

So sudden a bound into fame as that of the young Mr. Crane has not been permitted to an author for many a weary year. To call his ascent rocket-like is not to overlook his previous and terrestrial efforts, because even a rocket must atract a certain local attention by its vigor preparatory to the abrupt leap at the clouds. But when a youth whose acquaintance with the Twenties is only of short standing is suddenly sct about with a mob of "indolent reviewers" grown sud denly violent, and when he is tossed to their shoulders as the superior of Tolstoi and Zola and all other war-painters in spite of the fact that the war he pictures ended long before he began—when all these unusual things happen in the literary china-shop, one is justified in likening Mr. Crane to a rocket.

Whether Mr. Crane himself admits his alleged superiority to Zola and Tolstoi or not; after all this riotous praise, it is impossible that he should not take himself seriously. It is to be hoped that he does—seriously enough to look with anxious eye at his future. It cannot be denied that he has arrived. But the rocket arrives, too, and then drops back into oblivion, the profounder for its flaring swan song. But literary rockets have wings, and often need only to preen them and train their erratic swoops into steady exaltation to hold their sky-place. Of all the writers in real renown, Mr. Crane has the most manifest faults to correct. So glaring are they, indeed, that many cannot see beyond them into the virtues that justify Mr. Crane's place in contemporary repute. Without presuming on patronage, it is self-evident that Mr. Crane's future is now in its most critical stage. Hard work, merciless self-criticism, and vigilance that the value of a marked individuality may not warp off into the nagging of a mere eccentricity are now vital to his sustained success.

The best writers nod into grammatical errors that their own greatness cannot authorize, but of all the authors with any claim on

Reprinted from: *Godey's Magazine*, CXXXIII (September 1896), 317-319.

serious attention that I have ever read, Mr. Stephen Crane is the most flagrant desecrator of the memory of Sts. Lindley and Dionysius Thrax. Many of these errors are such as no conceivable proofreaders—those obscure protectors of many an orthographical and grammatical reputation—would have let pass without positive instructions. And such instructions are as inconceivable as such proofreaders.

In the book of poems [*The Black Riders*], No. VII., addressed to a "Mystic Shadow," queries "Whence come ye?" though, of course, "ye" is only a plural pronoun. The use of "who" and "which" in restrictive clauses where "that" should be used is a bit of slovenliness in which Mr. Crane goes along with too much otherwise goodly company to deserve special attention.

The misuse of the solemnities approaches illiteracy in a case like "If thou can see," which fault is further magnified by the addition of the words "In*to* my heart *that* I fear thee not" (LIII.). In LVIII. there is a so-called "sage" who says, "This one is me." In LXI. it is reiterated that "There was a man and a woman who sinned."

The famous "Red Badge of Courage" bristles more with false grammar than with bayonets. It may be priggishly nice to object to speech about "men who *advocated that* there were," etc. (p. 3), or the use of "made fun *at*" (p. 10), or the misuse of the reflexive "himself" for "him" (p. 27), or "he felt carried along by the mob" (p. 35), or the manneristic placing of "too" at the beginning of a sentence (pp. 124, 163), or to object to the cleft infinitives of pp. 13, 74, 157, etc. But there can surely be no justification for "he wished that he was at home again" (p. 27, cf. p. 165). "There was perspiration and grumblings" with no punctuation to save the construction; "the din became crescendo" (p. 45); "he could not flee no more than a little finger can commit a revolution from a hand" (p. 56); "—the emblem. They were like beautiful birds" (p. 63); "as if he was wearing invisible mittens" (p. 67), and "as if the regiment was" (p. 68, cf. also p. 102); "the majesty *of he* who," etc. (p. 68); "some sort of a bundle" (p. 80); "his feet caught aggravatingly," which does not seem to mean that they swelled (p. 80); "beginning to act dumb and animal-like" (p. 104); "He would have liked to have used" (p. 109); "a soldier would arouse and turn" (p. 135, cf. 139); the continual dialectic abbreviation of "of" into "a'" instead of "o'"; the use (p. 191) of "epithets" to refer to the noun "mule-drivers"; "whom he knew to be him" (p. 216); "There was, apparently, no considered loopholes" (p. 219), and "brutalities liable to the imagination" (p. 224). "George's

Mother," too, though short on inspiration, is long on errors, like the continued misuse of "aggravation" (p. 34), "liable" (p. 61), and "aroused" (p. 175).

Mr. Crane, in his remarkable aptitude for bold and striking effect, is not only led into a frequent neglect of the time-hallowed rights of certain words, but is so tireless in the pursuit of color and vividness that he falls occasionally into almost ludicrous mishap, like the mention of Henry's mother's cheeks as "scarred" by tears ("Red Badge," p. 7), or the reference to a "dauntless statue" (p. 25), as if a statue could be either dauntless or dauntful; on p. 106 we have "terror-stricken wagons"; on p. 195 smoke is "lazy," which one can understand; but it is more, it is "ignorant." Page 211 gives us human auricles as "perched ears," and compels one to wonder if their noses had gone home to roost. Having run on the words "sputtering of musketry" (p. 154), I wrote in the margin, "We have had 'spattering,' and 'splattering,' and now 'sputtering.' The next must be 'spluttering.'" On 189 I could cry "Eureka!" nay, more, the word occurred twice after that, and on p. 215 we got "gluttering." What this unrecorded thing may mean one can only guess. It must be one of Wonderland Alice's "portmanteau words," formed from "gutter" and "leaking," perhaps. If the book had been a three-volume edition, the etymologist might perforce have turned entomologist and picked up strange lavender creatures like schruttering, phthuttering, bjuttering, and mnuttering. Mr. Crane is prone to repetition, too—a sort of self-encoring that always saps the reader's former enthusiasm. It gets on one's nerves, and one is afraid to approve some novel expression for fear that Mr. Crane also dotes on it and will bring it back like a music-hall performer in reply to a deafening silence of applause. One character in the "Red Badge" is called "the loud soldier" a dozen times; one hears of "a blue demonstration," till he becomes part of it. At least two times Henry expects the corpses to start up and "squawk" at him; smoke is "slashed" by fire more than once; there is a "*mêlée*" of noise twice in five pages. Everything is "like" something or other till the little word takes on the torment of the waterdrops of the Japanese torture-chamber.

Mr. Crane is much noted for his color-scheming. Psychologists and a few of us laymen have met people that see the whole language prismatically, each letter of the alphabet having a definite permanent color that tinges all the words it is part of. Then there are musicians that do not speak of the colors of music merely analogically or rhetorically, but have definite and permanent hues for every chord.

A friend of a friend of mine could play you any picture or paint you any sonata you could produce. With such people dispute is impossible for the more blear-eyed of us. . . . But Mr. Crane goes further than alphabets and triads. Actions are rainbows to his unscaled eyes. Red is his favorite color. He began painting literature with it in his first book, "Maggie." The first thousand reds give a bizzare effect and a notable vividness. Thereafter a stack of reds has not the cheer we once imputed to it. We have "a crimson roar" ("Red Badge" p. 82), "crimson fury" (p. 81), "red rage" (p. 57), "the red sickness of battle" (p. 232), "a yellow light on . . . his ambitions" (p. 6), "black words" (p. 201). We have all shades of red oaths except crushed strawberry and peachblow. In "George's Mother" a man "fell with a yellow crash" (p. 93); there is "a gray stare" (p. 150); and things go on so luridly that so harmless a thing as "crimson curtains" (p. 173) makes the badgered reader believe himself a bull and Mr. Crane a picador and all the other -dors of the arena. There must hereafter be a "Red Badge of Crane-age."

Mr. Crane has, most of all writers, the defects of his qualities. But the good thing and the rare thing is to have the qualities. These he has. His work is distinctive and his attitude his own. For the sake of these fine things much can be forgiven.

His first book, "Maggie," is now reissued. Its original appearance brought no crimson royalties, though it won reddish praise from the few that examined it. In our issue of November [October], 1895, we praised it as the strongest representative of American slum-fiction. It has the inevitableness of a Greek tragedy, and the reader that grants to the fate of Euripides's fanciful "Medea," an import and significance he refuses to see in the predestined ugliness of the end of this well-meaning "Maggie," has an outlook on life that is too literary to be true. Indeed, he has misread his classics, if the woes of their creatures leave him uneducated into sympathy with the miseries of the miserables of his own town.

As for style, this story is by far the best-balanced thing Mr. Crane has done. It makes no lunge at oddity, and is yet full of fearlessness and vigor. Its truth is patent to any one that knows the life it transcribes. In the new edition one notes many revisions, all of them unimportant and almost all of them ill-advised.

It was "The Black Riders" that brought Mr. Crane his first notice. The book was received with wild howls of derision, tempered by an occasional note of abashed praise. That it is neither rimed nor metrical should not excite an admirer of Oriental poetry. That its "lines" were uniformed with small caps, is a matter of little moment. This eccentricity was doubtless only a desire to get out from under the overshadowing mountain of Walt Whitman; and novelty is always a partial excuse. Some of these little chunks of sentiment are mere drivel; most of them are full of marrow.

Take this example (VIII.):

"I LOOKED HERE;
I LOOKED THERE;
NOWHERE COULD I SEE MY LOVE.
AND—THIS TIME—
SHE WAS IN MY HEART.
TRULY, THEN, I HAVE NO COMPLAINT,
FOR THOUGH SHE BE FAIR AND FAIRER,
SHE IS NONE SO FAIR AS SHE
IN MY HEART."

That is to say that things that are identical are not the same with themselves. Where is the Daniel to translate the latter half of XVI.? But Mr. Crane has been thinking—that is the main thing—and if in his thought-experiments he sometimes lands in a blind alley, so do the greatest scientists.

The work of the thinker that dares to be unconventional is always beer and skittles for the parodist. The keenest of the Crane parodies is probably this from *Town Topics*:

"A BAT ON A CHURCH STEEPLE.
A GRAY CAT ON A WALL.
WA-A-OW!

DO YOU HEAR THE CAT?
YOU ARE A LIAR!
THE GRIM WAIL WAS THE YAWP
OF GREEN-DEAD HOPES—
DEAD AND DECAYED.
TAG! YOU ARE IT."

But the individuality that, in its excess, gave justice to such a parody, gave birth, too, to a neat thought, or a big thought, here and there; and much of it that is not new is made new by the new way of its expression. Two of the most effective are X. and XXXVII.:

"SHOULD THE WIDE WORLD ROLL AWAY,
LEAVING BLACK TERROR,
LIMITLESS NIGHT.
NOR GOD, NOR MAN, NOR PLACE TO STAND
WOULD BE TO ME ESSENTIAL,
IF THOU AND THY WHITE ARMS WERE THERE,
AND THE FALL TO DOOM A LONG WAY."

"ON THE HORIZON THE PEAKS ASSEMBLED;
AND AS I LOOKED,
THE MARCH OF THE MOUNTAINS BEGAN.
AS THEY MARCHED, THEY SANG,
'AYE! WE COME! WE COME!' "

But it remained for "The Red Badge" to aggravate the flutter caused by "The Black Riders" into a literary sensation. The American reviewers were excited; the English fairly lost their heads with enthusiasm. His faithfulness to the actuality of war was proclaimed above that of Tolstoi's "Sebastopol" or Zola's "La Débâcle." All these books forsake the traditional beauty of battle and go into a devoted study of dead bodies and carnage generally. Mr. Crane is chiefly different in the Yankee irreverence for solemnity that aids in giving realism to the book. Its verisimilitude is marvellous. Mr. Crane must have interviewed many a veteran with the truth-reaching powers of the trained reporter he once was. The work is of the modern school in that even the most heroic things are done with studied awkwardness and innobility. The tone is kept down always where one anticipates a height, as in Henry's farewell to his mother and to his sweethearts. Even in the charges men do not forget to be plebeian and timorous. After the standard-bearer falls, two youths struggle for the flag in the midst of flying bullets; and yet down in their hearts each wishes the other to get it. The psychological value of the book is great. The development of a country gawk who goes to war for no particular reason, and runs away in the first battle, but is finally developed into a brave soldier, is a theme of much dignity, handled with devout earnestness. The book is frankly a study of the details of battle from the limited scope of a private. The scenes with the cowards, with the wounded, and with the victorious are all filled with touches of most intense humanity. The language is frequently of amazing strength and suggestiveness, and one gets from the whole book a view of war that is new, and has every evidence of truth. The episode of the tall spectral soldier who is mortally wounded, but stalks grimly in search of a fit "rendezvous" with death, is one of the most gruesome incidents in our literature, and on a footing with some of Poe's best work. The final charge is a triumph for the book as well as for the army, and the work ends with calm nobility. It fills a niche previously unattempted in our war-romance, and is so fine where it is good that its many errors cannot harm it much.

In the "Red Badge" Mr Crane was a slapdash impressionist. In "George's Mother" he attains the very peak of the realistic inconsequential. The book has one good scene, Kelcey's first intoxication. It has a few bits of neat observation. But on the whole, it is not worthy of mention in the same breath with the three other books.

All in all, Mr. Crane's vigor is so great and his individuality so distinct that he takes a hardly disputed place at the very head of the American story-writers of the younger school.

CHELIFER.

III

MR. CRANE'S CRAZYQUILTING.

What manner of joke Stephen Crane and his illustrator, Will. Bradley, had in mind when they got up their new book [War Is Kind] has not leaked out. It is in effect more Mr. Bradley's in the matter of superfices than Mr. Crane's, but Mr. Blank—(an inferential collaborator) has more in the book "War is Kind" than either. It is Mr. Crane's purpose to tell us that war is not kind in a thirty-line Walt Whitmian lyric, so why mislead us? To be ironical is all right, but why drive the iron in so far? We all know that war was brutal, that it killed lovers, husbands and sons, but we never thought of telling

Reprinted from: The Criterion, XXI (June 3, 1899), 26-27.

the sweethearts, wives and mothers that war, therefore, was kind. The burglar held the old lady on the red-hot stove. Oh, he was a kind man! That is the apparent recipe. It is very original. You will remember Mr. Crane's phrase if ever you go to war and eat canned beef, and if you have Mr. Bradley's pictorial idea of war (when it is kind) on the retina of your memory, you will think you are dining in Delmonico's, and the lady is the carver. Through the courtesy of Frederick A. Stokes & Co. [publisher of *War Is Kind*] we are enabled to copy Mr. Bradley's figure on the cover as a clue to the enigma. It is a pity that we can give only that half of the cover, for our readers would surely have enjoyed the treat of seeing the other half with its cheery coffin-lid, weeping willow, floral piece ("Gates Ajar" probably on the portion hidden by the coffin), and its harp of seven strings all beautifully Beardsleyized. We must, however, leave something for the buyers of the book to gloat over. In the same way one refrains from quoting Mr. Crane's poem beyond a sample line or two:

> Mother, whose heart hung humble as a button
> On the bright, splendid shroud of your son,
> Do not weep;
> War is kind.

Confound the fellow with his "humble as a button." That will stick in your memory, too. You will scoff at it, of course, but it will come back at you, and you will fancy that you see her, her poor head, some gray hairs maybe in it, bending over that army coffin covered by the flag. What is that? You thought I started out to make fun of this book of decadent affectations. Well, so did I, and I had bitter thoughts about the posing of the author as well as the drearily deliberate saltimbanque of an artist, but there you are—a big tear or· something splashing on the paper, and an aching thought of that mother-love and mother-heart "humble as a button on the bright splendid shroud of her son."

Crane, you see, is an artist. (I wish to explain: don't think I am taking anything back.) He is frugal of words and has the magic of style and the wizardry of effects. Something of that in him which Alfred Lord Tennyson found in Monsieur Victor Hugo when he wrote the line:

French of the French and Lord of human tears.

Tennyson, of course, found it in Hugo's prose, and that is where you will find it in Crane, for it is precisely in the line that is so prosy that Crane gives the supreme touch. Yes, Mr. Capenbells, it is there you touch the button, and the five anapoests on which you gallop off in diminuendo are regular as the hoofbeats of the erl-king's black stallion when he bore off the boy to the halls of night.

With some apt bits of color in the rest of the slim book there goes much of the cynicism that affects the sad eye and the world-glance, yet cannot see beyond the foothills of a sick-headache. It is the kind that grows up around the cheap table d'hôte.

> A man said to the universe:
> "Sir, I exist!"
> "However," replied the universe,
> "The fact has not created in me
> "A sense of obligation."

Surely he and Mr. Bradley were in evil case the night that Mr. Crane wrote "Woe Is Me," and Mr. Bradley induced the former Countess of B——— (everybody at Parrotini's said she was a countess before she married Schafwurst, the dilapidated baritone, whom she beats) to sit for the lady's portrait which, again through the courtesy (copyrighted) of Stokes & Co. we faithfully reproduce.

> Thou art my love,
> Let these sacred love-lies choke thee,
> And thou art a wretch.
> For I am come to where I know your lies as truth,
> And your truth as lies—
> Woe is me.

Well, looking at the wobble of it and the likeness of it, we have no objection. We get to the surely maudlin stage a little further on—

Ah, God, the way your little finger moved
As you thrust a bare arm backward
And made play with your hair
And a comb, a silly gilt comb.
—Ah, God—that I should suffer
Because of the way a little finger moved.

Prithee, Mr. Crane, let a friend beckon you with a little finger and whisper in your ear: You have rare gifts that you squander: quit fooling. The sins of moral flabbiness and flatulence that you mock us with are past endurance from a man of your calibre, and are not to be condoned by a Bradley cover, rough edges, green-gray paper, even if the stuff be doled out a line to the page as

The chatter of a death-demon from a tree-top.

Read Whitman's essay, "Poetry To-day in America."

                                                                    C.

IV

THE GENIUS OF STEPHEN CRANE.

That Stephen Crane is a genius I have been convinced ever since I read that little fatherless yellow-covered book "Maggie, a Tale of the Streets, by Johnston Smith." To this belief I have clung in spite of many jolts and jars, for the retainer of this author must hang on like the watcher in the crow's nest of a ship, which ploughs splendidly forward, but with much yawing and buffeting and many a career.

Mr. Crane's faults are not surreptitiously stowed away; they are carried aboveboard like a defiant figurehead or a pirate's black flag. For instance, there's his grammatical carelessness; he takes the natural liberty of a writer handling so elastic a language as ours and carries it to license, to criminal excess, for which there is no excuse. First, you blame the proof-reader; then you realize that no proof-reader

_____

Reprinted from: *The Criterion,* XXII (January 6, 1900), 24.

could live and let slip the things that get into Mr. Crane's books unless his hands were tied behind him by definite orders. Of all the writers I have ever read with respect, Mr. Crane makes the greatest number of solecisms. Many of them bear the look of absolute illiteracy; they are as inconsistent with his capabilities for discriminating and *récherché* composition as Wordsworth's off-hours are with his inspirations. That superb work, "The Red Badge of Courage," and the later, "Active Service," fairly bristle with these things.

Then he is wont to take it into his head to send his glorious argosy on some fool's errand of wanton affectation, and triviality. These outlandish junketings marked many, though not all, of his "Black Rider" lines, much of "George's Mother," the general idea (though, strangely, not the detail) of "The Third Violet," and almost all of that crazy nightmare, "War is Kind."

Yet, withal, Mr. Crane seems to me to be the most definite and individual of all our book-writers; and I credit him with having written some of the best pages America has contributed to literature, in "Maggie," "The Red Badge," certain of the "Black Rider" lines, "The Open Boat," and in the two books just published from his hand.

"Active Service" enambers some of Mr. Crane's impressions of Greece, which he saw as a war correspondent. The hero is far from ideal; he stumbles into heroism more or less unintentionally; he takes good and ill fortune with a bad grace generally; he is in short a hero by accident, an average flawful character, peevish and irritable at worst and not very good at best. But because he is like the great average of humanity, he is the more worthy of consideration. Though the book drags a bit at first, it later enchains and hales along the interest unflaggingly, and this without sacrificing probabilities.

The heroine is a fine study, an American girl, whose deep emotions are held in strict leash by a sturdy self-respect. Her frumpish and shallow mother and her petty and professorial father are well characterized, and an actress is brought in to mix things up. As a psychological study of motives the book is keen; as a piece of narrative construction, the latter half of it shows an ability Mr. Crane has given little evidence of before.

But, chiefly, the book is worthy for its details. There is an abundance of that minute observation that distinguishes Mr. Crane's manner. There is, furthermore, a warmth of amorous life that is unusual in his prose; the love of the heroine for the man is beautifully painted, and when, after many misunderstandings, they reach the great understanding in a crisis of danger, there is a nobility of situation. All is petty again when a silly contretemps cuts the Gordian knot of love. There is a deep and faithful pathos in the scene where the heroine, so strong in public, is found, by her foolish old father, alone in the dark and crying over her broken heart. Then, when the man of text-books becomes for the nonce a man of action and re-unites the lovers, there is a new height of power, all is ecstatic, rose-colored and blissful. Now Mr. Crane writes like a lover, with just the right luxury and extravagance. Leaving the accepted lover, the girl gives him "a star-like beseeching glance,"

"and this glance expressed in its elusive way a score of things which she had not yet been able to speak. It explained that she was loth to leave him, that she asked forgiveness for leaving him, that even for a short absence she wished to take his image in her eyes, that he must not bully her, that there was something now in her heart which frightened her, that she loved him, that she was happy—"

The last page of the book is simply a ravishment of beauty.

A most notable feature of Mr. Crane's style is the hunt for the one fit word. Always with him it is the unexpected, the unusual, the vivid epithet. How fine is this of Athens:

it was as if in the white dust which floated across the old-ivory face of the palace, there were the souls of the capable soldiers of the past.

What better phrase for a deployment could there be than this:

horsemen fanning out in all forward directions.

The hero, being a Yankee, was eternally annoyed by the Greek character, for he was not born in a country laved by the childish Mediterranean.

There is a deal of excellent philosophy sprinkled about these pages, particularly in the observations on the war correspondents, those "lone wolves," and the studies of conduct and emotion in danger.

From this worthy book to the collection of three shorter stories, headed by "The Monster" is a far cry. The three short stories are in themselves curiously unlike in every way. The first is gruesome and homely; the second is strenuous and picturesque; the third is a graceful account of a little child's running away.

"The Monster" is an incursion into the realms of the horrible without once losing sight of realism or plausibility. There is no strain on credulity, no mysticism of any sort. The plot bluntly told is this: An amiable negro, in saving a child from a burning laboratory, has his face burned into such a ghastly and featureless horror that he becomes innocently a terror to the people of his town. The gratitude of the physician, whose son he has saved, stands in the way of citizens who would lock the monster up, and in consequence the physician and his wife are ostracized by the village. That is all that there is to it; its sickening qualities are mitigated by the indirectness of their suggestion, its trivialities are redeemed by the psychological dignity of the physician's problem. The characters are all discriminatingly and vividly drawn, from the helpless and well-meaning monster to the cynical old spinster who is thus presented:

Martha Goodwin was single, and well along into the thin years. She lived with her married sister in Whilomville. She performed nearly all the housework in exchange for the privilege of existence. Everyone tacitly recognized her labor as a form of penance for the early end of her betrothed, who had died of small-pox, which he had not caught from her. * * * She had adamantine opinions upon the situation in Armenia, the condition of women in China, the flirtation between Mrs. Minster, of Niagara avenue, and young Griscom * * * and many other colossal matters. * * * She contended that all the Turks should be pushed into the sea and drowned. * * * This woman of peace, who had seen only peace, argued constantly

for a creed of illimitable ferocity. She was invulnerable on
these questions, because eventually she overrode all opponents
with a sniff. This sniff was an active force. It was to her antagonists like a bang over the head. * * * In regard to social
misdemeanors, she, who was simply the mausoleum of a dead
passion, was probably the most savage critic in town. * * *
One reason that she was formidable was that she did not even
imagine that she was formidable.

The scene of the fire in the laboratory is a most gorgeous study
in high colors, that ought to be quoted for its high beauty. The
second story, "The Blue Hotel," is a wonderful thing in its way,
full of stirring action and most subtly motived.

A big genius; this young fellow Crane!   *Chelifer*.

b. *Elbert Hubbard on Stephen Crane*

Stephen Crane is a genius. Just what genius is the world has not determined, for, like the ulster, the word covers a multitude of sins. But if pushed for a definition, I would say that genius is only woman's intuition carried one step further. It is essentially feminine in its attributes, and the men of genius (as opposed to men of talent) have always been men with marked feminine qualities. The genius knows because he knows, and if you should ask the genius whence comes this power, he would answer you (if he knew) in the words of Cassius; "My mother gave it me."

* * *

When in 1891 Stephen Crane wrote a tale called *Maggie of the Streets,* Mr. Howells read the story [in 1893], and after seeing its author, said, "This man has sprung into life full-armed;" and that expression of Mr. Howells fully covers the case. I can imagine no condition of life that might entangle a man or woman within its meshes that Stephen Crane could not fully comprehend and appreciate. Men are only great as they possess sympathy. Crane knows the human heart through and through, and he sympathizes with its every pulsation. From the beggar's child searching in ash barrels for treasure, to the statesman playing at diplomacy with a thought for next fall's election, Stephen Crane knows the inmost soul of each and all. Whether he is able to translate it to you or not is quite another question; but in the forty or more short stories and sketches he has written I fail to find a single false note. He neither exaggerates nor comes tardy off.

The psychologists tell us that a man cannot fully comprehend a condition that he has never experienced. But theosophy explains the transcendent wisdom of genius by saying that in former incarnations the man passed through these experiences. Emerson says: "We are bathed in an ocean of intelligence, and under right conditions the soul knows all things." These things may be true, but the essence of Crane's masterly delineation is that he is able to project himself into the condition of others. He does not describe men and women— *he is that man.* He loses his identity, forgets self, abandons his own

Reprinted from: "As to Stephen Crane," *The Lotos,* IX (March 1896), 674-678.

consciousness, and is for the moment the individual who speaks. And whether this individual is man, woman, or child, makes no difference. Sex, age, condition, weigh not in the scale.

During the latter half of the year 1895 no writing man in America was so thoroughly hooted and so well abused as Stephen Crane. I have a scrap-book of newspaper clippings that is a symposium of Billingsgate mudballs, with Crane for the target. Turning the leaves of this scrap-book I find these words used in reference to a plain little book called *The Black Riders:* idiocy, drivel, bombast, rot, nonsense, puerility, untruth, garbage, hamfat, funny, absurd, childish, drunken, besotted, obscure opium-laden, blasphemous, indecent, fustian, rant, bassoon-poetry, swell-head stuff, bluster, balderdash, windy, turgid, stupid, pompous, gasconade, gas-house ballads, etc., etc.

There are also in this scrap-book upward of a hundred parodies on the poems. Some of these are rather clever, but they differ from Crane's work in this, that there is not a molecule of thought in one of them, while there is a great moral truth taught in each of Crane's poems. Usually, people—even sensible people—will not take time to find it. But one might as well accuse Aesop of idiocy when he has a fox talk to a goose. Of course, we could truthfully swear that no fox ever carried on a conversation with a goose since the world began. But to assume that Aesop was therefore a fool would be proof that the man who made the assumption was a fool and not Aesop.

Personally I do not greatly admire *The Black Riders,* but I have no quarrel with the book. I simply accept it, and give thanks. But granting for argument's sake that *The Black Riders* is "rot," it then must be admitted that it was a great stroke of worldly wisdom. For Stephen Crane now has the ear of the world. Publishers besiege him with checks in advance, and the manuscript of a story he has just completed has been bid on by four different firms, with special offer for the English copyright. The forty-six short poems in *The Black Riders* were all written in the space of two days and a night—in a time of terrible depression. The work was then handed to a dear friend. This friend thought he saw the deep burning thought of a prophet in the lines, and he conceived the plan of publishing them. A thousand copies were printed and sold inside of six months. If you want a first edition of *The Black Riders* now, it will cost you five dollars, and if you can pick up *A Maggie of the Streets* for twice that, you'd better do it—and do it quick.

Stephen Crane attended Lafayette College for a time in his nineteenth year. The teachers there write me that they only remember him as "a yellow, tow-haired youth, who would rather fight than study." They advised him to "take a change," so he went to Syracuse University—his guardian being anxious he should be "educated." His fame at Syracuse rests on the fact that he was the best short-stop ever on the University baseball team. He soon became captain, this on account of his ability to hold his own when it came to an issue with certain "scrapping" antagonists.

Once when he was called upon to recite in the psychology class, he argued a point with the teacher. The Professor sought to silence him by an appeal to the Bible: "Tut, tut—what does St. Paul say, Mr. Crane, what does St. Paul say?" testily asked the old Professor.

"I know what St. Paul says," was the answer, "but I disagree with St. Paul."

Of course no Methodist college wants a student like that; and young Crane wandered down to New York and got a job reporting on the *Herald*.

Since then he has worked on the editorial staff of various papers. He is now, however, devoting his whole time to literature, living at Hartwood, Sullivan County, N. Y. Hartwood has a store, a blacksmith shop and a tavern. When the train comes in all of the citizens go down to the station to see 'er. Should you ask one of these citizens who Stephen Crane is, he would probably answer you as he did me:

"Mr. Crane, Mr. Crane! you mean Steve Crane?"

"Yes."

"Why, he's—he's Steve Crane an' a dern good feller!"

Mr. Crane is now in his twenty-fifth year. He is a little under the average height, and is slender and slight in build, weighing scarcely one hundred and thirty pounds. He is a decided blonde: his eyes blue. His handsome, boyish face and quiet, half-shy, modest manner make him a general favorite everywhere with women. And to me, it is rather curious that women should flock around and pet this sort of a man, who can read their inmost thoughts just as that new German invention can photograph things inside of a box, when a big, stupid man with a red face and a black mustache they are very much afraid of. I don't understand it a bit.

At a recent banquet * given at the Genessee Hotel, in Buffalo,

---

* This is the Society of the Philistines banquet of December 19, 1895, whose chief sponsor was Elbert Hubbard. [*Editor.*]

in honor of Mr. Crane, thirty-one men sat at the feast. These men had come from Chicago, New York, Boston, and elsewhere to attend the dinner. Several lawyers, one eminent physician, and various writers were there. Crane was the youngest individual at the board, but he showed himself the peer of any man present. His speech was earnest, dignified, yet modestly expressed. His manner is singularly well poised, and his few words carry conviction.

Still he can laugh and joke, and no man has a better appreciation of humor. He loves the out-doors, and in riding horseback by his side across country I have admired his happy abandon, as he sits secure, riding with loose rein and long stirrup in a reckless rush.

In the New York *Times* for January 26 [1896] is a two-column letter from London, by that distinguished critic, Mr. Harold Frederic. The subject of the entire article is Stephen Crane.

*   *   *

There is a class of reviewers who always wind up their preachments by saying: "This book gives much promise, and we shall look anxiously for Mr. Scribbler's next." Let us deal in no such cant. A man's work is good or it is not. As for his "next," nobody can tell whether it will be good or not. There is a whole army of men about to do something great, but the years go by and they never do it. They are like those precocious children who stand on chairs and recite "pieces." They never make orators. So, as to Crane's "future work," let us keep silent. But if he never produces another thing, he has done enough to save the fag-end of the century from literary disgrace; and look you, friends, that is no small matter!

c. Jonathan Penn on Stephen Crane

If it were the office of literary criticism to give absolutely candid and cynically practical advice to aspirants seeking literary glory in our day, I should say, "Cultivate the bizzare." We are compelled, however, by the traditions of the Trade, to blink at the realisms of contemporary writers, and we pretend to discuss their psychology and their art when we all know very well that the bulk of this current, popular firework fiction is not literature at all, but like the latest whirlwind dance of another sensation, that has been cleverly "boomed."

The art of getting up a "boom" is the great art of contemporary literature, as of all other arts which aim to please at any cost of decency, dignity, and sanity. If one really wants "points" on how to succeed in literature, we should throw all the misleading classic examples of steadfast genius into the kitchen fire, and consult an expert on advertising. As this is obviously beyond the means of sane worthy writers, I deviate from the strict tradition of criticism to put before the reader a concrete example of a cleverly nursed little "boom" that a bright and deserving young man has recently pulled off. I hope he has made enough out of it to secure his old age in a good life insurance policy annuity, for it is the irony of our bustling day, so eager for the new, that a "boom" seldom comes to any man more than once in a lifetime.

The Stephen Crane "boom" is being insidiously undermined by the efforts of Stephen Crane, and it can now be considered in the lurid red light, as Crane would say, of bitter and inexorable fact.

Here is a young man who owes his amazing success in literature to his keen power of introspection and intuition. As a youth at school, he had the impatience of dull routine so characteristic of genius, and he completed his course of studies with a distinctly individual conception of the significance of the English language, though one that can only wreak injury to the genius of literature if such latitude is widely imitated. An apprenticeship on a certain New York newspaper, which has made a profound study of revising and reorganizing the body of the language so as to bring it within the comprehension

Reprinted from: "A Little Study of Stephen Crane," The Lotus, II (October 1896), 208-211.

of the largest circulation on earth; completed Mr. Crane's preparation for his momentous career in "poster" literature. A period of effort and introspection revealed to him a certain strain of vague illogic in his mental constitution, which he realized at once could either ruin or make him. Too many strive to overcome such a defect, when they have enough power of self-criticism to detect it. When they succeed, they are reduced to the common crowd of writers who respect the language and are careful and painstaking, but unremarkable. It is the mark of genius to recognize in one's mental constitution a strong vein of illogic. If it is given full swing, it results in the most startling presentations of all the ideas and observations within one's ken. This perception, with perfect satisfaction in it as originality of mind, releases the imagination, so that it plays the very deuce with language, and easily commands attention. It is to literature what the spectacular is to the mechanic-made drama. A rhetorical exuberance, with certain knotty predilections, is an ordinary accompaniment of an uncertain acquaintance with one's mother tongue.

Mr. Crane has lost no time in his short life—for he is still very young in years. He realized at an extremely early age, in that tender budding time of innocence and influences which most unsophisticated aspirants devote to the study of good examples, the immense sensational value of the bizarre in this epoch of literary cocktails. He recognized the power of the ludicrous and irrelevant in immediately arresting attention. The recipe for the successful mixing of the new mysticism is a furious scepticism of all the old orthodoxies, with an unlimited credulity for all the bogies of the nursery. This puts one upon a familiar footing with the Almighty, and Mr. Crane's first success was achieved in this foggy region, where the soul of man encounters God in the palpable diminution of a Shape, and spits scorn upon the mechanical horrors of the universe. "The Black Riders, and Other Lines" deals almost exclusively with great moral questions. It is lunacy revealing the irony of sanity, and its goblin atmosphere admirably suits the literary epicure who has enough catholicity to thoroughly enjoy the surprises of folly. It is a book of horrors for the tea-table; and for all who love the meaningless and mysterious rhapsodies of an intellectual booze it is an inspired book. It is filled with the ludicrous sobriety of a sincere lunatic or a "wanton cynic," and so deserves its decided success as a genuine curiosity of literature, with those who have a greater craving for what is curious than for what is really literature. On the other hand, criticism declares: Here is originality of design and expression without significance or merit; audacity of conception without real and sincere thought—in a word, a mere farce of literary chicane. "A new Boozy Prophet," I thought—but he has turned out better.

I spent one wild night of hilarity with "The Black Riders, and Other Lines," and the profound sagacity of this literary delirium at once convinced me that the author was a genius in his unerring perception of his own gift of illogic and confusion, and of the public's susceptibility to any startling bait of lunacy. A writer without any sense of humor is relieved of all fatal hesitancy, and he is sure of a public, for the sense of humor is very rare. This is one of Mr. Crane's strong qualities. He writes completely incomprehensible jangles of words with the rapt sobriety of Saint John. With such a talent he cannot fail of achieving pre-eminence and the sympathy of a large audience.

I bartered my copy of "The Black Riders" for a tin of the Arcadian smoking mixture, so I cannot quote any of the lines. But, for the benefit of readers who have not seen the originals, I print a verse of my own, written at the time, which is very fairly representative of Mr. Crane's style and the whole body of his thought:

I heard a man mumbling in the horrid silence of the night.
He was chattering aloud with the good God;
But God in the darkness vouchsafed no sign.
And I asked him, scoffing, what he desired of the Omnipotent.
"I am rich, I am Plutos," answered he, angrily,
"And I am bargaining for the moon."
"And why do you want it?" asked I, in amaze.
"Because I am tired of all my other toys."
"And the price?" asked I, scoffing, for I bore the badge of Lazarus
"Untold millions, heaped up to Heaven's gate."
"Fool!" I cried in bitter derision,
"Offer the good God your corrupt soul."

This is one phase of Mr. Crane. If it were the only one, he would scarcely have engaged so much attention as he has done in literary circles. In an entirely different mood, he achieved his one real success in literature—"The Red Badge of Courage." This is a sort of prose epic of war, from the consciousness of the private soldier in the thick of action. It is a strong and fascinating conception, worked out with unfailing power and unity, to complete illusion. It is good work of an unusual kind, and it is all the more interesting and valuable as a psychological study when it is remembered that it is written by a young man who never saw a battle nor served in the army. It seems at first incongruous that the author of "The Black Riders" should have written this story, but a second and careful reading reveals some of the same characteristics of sacrificing clearness of style and language to effectiveness, and despotically using words out of their proper relevance and significance. If every writer did this for the mere sake of appearing original, we should soon forfeit our heritage of a clear comprehension of the best thoughts of the best minds in our language. This is a wanton mischief in literature to which many contemporary writers seem prone, and it cannot be too severely condemned. Even true originality of conception cannot atone for such a trespass upon what is not simply the treasure-trove of any one writer, but the common property of our race to be handed from one generation to another in its integrity. Therefore every writer owes it to his readers and critics to attempt to master the niceties of the language. Mr. Crane has openly set them at defiance in order to turn the language to impressionistic uses of his own devising.

This book shows Crane in his highest mood of insight and imagination. It is doubtful if he will ever reach the same high plane again, for he shows a decided weakness in his tendency to persist in mannerisms that become familiar upon a second acquaintance, and so lose their effectiveness. The extraordinary success of "The Red Badge of Courage" in England, where every American writer since Hawthorne has been dismissed with contempt, has awakened a general belief that Crane is to be America's young hopeful in letters. But, unfortunately, Crane, like many other young hopefuls, does not apparently realize the truth of Lowell's saying, that a naive thing repeated is naive no longer. The fondness Mr. Crane shows for chromatic effects—a sort of "poster" commentary—cannot be such a consistent passion with all his readers.

We cannot accept the rather grotesque characters and descriptions of East Side life in "Maggie" and "George's Mother" as equally veritable and valuable pictures of the human consciousness as the convincing psychological pictures of the war. These are written in the unmistakable staccato style of the "star" reporter on a newspaper of "the largest circulation in the cosmos." The stories as simple fiction are unsatisfactory, and as studies of real life they seem a little fatuous. They are both concerned mainly with a series of minutely described drinking feats, ending in certain little unpleasantnesses. The story of "George's Mother" consists entirely of the history of a protracted "jag." But it is to be doubted whether the guzzling bouts of the canaille can really occupy an unequivocal place in literature. Considering their insignificant claims, on esthetic grounds, to the consideration of intelligent people, it is becoming a matter of serious moment whether the inarticulate lower classes do not occupy altogether too much prominence in fiction. This is especially to be deplored since our sentimental epoch has relegated all literature but the novel to ignominy and oblivion.

A careful and impartial, though not at all unappreciative, reading of all of Mr. Crane's published work leads the writer to the conclusion that here is another clever writer who will take his place among the other popular and prolific entertainers of current literature. But to claim for him, as has been done by English and American critics, an assured pre-eminence as a writer of genius, is an extravagance of the cordiality that lacks judgment. Of course this is all a matter of individual judgment, and this opinion is offered as quite tentative, with all proper diffidence—though the diffidence happens to come last, like a kiss in a love-letter.

d. Parodies of Stephen Crane's Poetry in The Philistine

I

THE SPOTTED SPRINTER.

After The Manner of Mr. Steamin' Stork.

I saw a man making a fool of himself;
He was writing a poem,
Scratch, scratch, scratch went his pen,
"Go 'way, Man," says I; "you can't do it."
He picked up a handful of red devils and
Threw them at my head.
"You infernal liar," he howled,
"I can write poetry with my toes!"
I was disquieted. I turned and
Ran like a Blue Streak for the Horizon,
Yelling Bloody Murder.
When I got there I
Bit a piece out of it
And lay down on my stomach and
Thought.
And breathed hard.

Reprinted from: *The Philistine,* I (July 1895), 70.

II

In
Praising poetry of William Morris
And Stephen Crane
Were you poking fun?
I hope 'twas so:
For
You must perceive
That those slashed and mangled lines
Do no more resemblance bear
To true poetry
Than hacked and shattered corpse
On battle field
Bears
To a perfect man,
Whose form divinely fair
Fitly enfolds feelings consummate
Against such lines—
And in fact 'gainst all your verse,
I do
Protest.

NELSON AYRES.

NEW ORLEANS, Aug. 15, '95.

Reprinted from: *The Philistine*, I (September 1895), 136.

III

I saw a man tugging at his Boot-Straps.
"It is futile," I said,
"You can never lift yourself that way."
"You lie!" he cried,
And tugged on.

Reprinted from: *The Philistine,* VIII (February 1899), back cover.
This parody was inspired by poem XXIV of *The Black Riders.* [*Editor.*]

e. O. Henry Parodies Stephen Crane's Fiction

BLUE BLOTCH OF COWARDICE.

Life.

(An incident of the Pursuit of the Insurgents, with Profuse Apologies to Mr. Stephen Crane.)

I.

Above, the air hung like a custard pie, in a burnt blanket. A Spanish cavalier, muttering mild green curses, stood near. He was stewing the last dish of leeks which his mother had given him before he left home. From a clump of sordid trees two miles off came the happy cackling of muskets.

"There will be death today," said the youth. "Dark brown death." At this point the cavalier's chameleon curse turned to a light yellow, owing to the proximity of a pot of Spanish mustard.

II.

Slowly the baby's rattle of rifles opened into a Fourth of July. The youth gradually awoke, being kicked violently in the stomach by a baby-faced lieutenant.

"Get up, you," said the latter, with a small blue black curse. "The insurgents are retreating in our direction."

"I presume this is what they call war," muttered the youth, stupidly, with his chin in his hands. "We have been chasing the insurgents for three months, and we haven't had a thing but our backs to 'em the whole time."

He looked over his stock of oaths, but could find none of the precise shade that he wanted.

Reprinted from: The Houston *Post*, May 24, 1896, p. 4.

III.

Shapeless chunks of rifle smoke were kicking about in the grass. The regiment had been fighting like demons. Here and there were men squirming horribly in the grass. This was because sundry red ants had found lodgment between their shoulder blades.

"The terrible loss to the insurgents in this battle," said a Spanish officer, who was preparing news for the press, "can not be less than three killed and four wounded."

IV.

With frantic leaps a horse, bearing a huge Spanish general, came down upon them, each jump biting off large sections of the horizon. Behind him, on foot, came a small dark man, waving a machete.

The regiment ran and ran, intuitively, with mouths closed, and long, practiced strides.

An undreamt of frenzy seized the youth. He deliberately stopped and looked back—then ran on.

"I have seen an insurgent," he burbled, triumphantly. "I need no longer feel upon my heart the blue blotch of cowardice."

He was still running when far off on the chin of the horizon dimpled the smile of the next morning.

f. Frank Norris Parodies Stephen Crane's Fiction

THE GREEN STONE OF UNREST.

By S——N CR——E.

A Mere Boy stood on a pile of blue stones. His attitude was regardant. The day was seal brown. There was a vermillion valley containing a church. The church's steeple aspired strenuously in a direction tangent to the earth's center. A pale wind mentioned tremendous facts under its breath with certain effort at concealment to seven not-dwarfed poplars on an un-distant mauve hilltop.

The Mere Boy was a brilliant blue color. The effect of the scene was not un kaleidoscopic.

After a certain appreciable duration of time the Mere Boy abandoned his regardant demeanor. The strenuously aspiring church steeple no longer projected itself upon his consciousness. He found means to remove himself from the pile of blue stones. He set his face valleyward. He proceeded.

The road was raw umber. There were in it wagon ruts. There were in it pebbles, Naples yellow in color. One was green. The Mere Boy allowed the idea of the green pebble to nick itself into the sharp edge of the disc of his Perception.

"Ah," he said, "a green pebble."

The rather pallid wind communicated another Incomprehensible Fact to the paranthine trees. It would appear that the poplars understood.

"Ah," repeated the Mere Boy, "a Green Pebble."

"Sho-o," remarked the wind.

The Mere Boy moved appreciably forward. If there were a thousand men in a procession and nine hundred and ninety-nine should suddenly expire, the one man who was remnant would assume the responsibility of the procession.

The Mere Boy was an abbreviated procession.

Reprinted from: "Perverted Tales," San Francisco *Wave*, XVI (December 25, 1897, Christmas Supplement), 5.

The blue Mere Boy transported himself diagonally athwart the larger landscape, printed in four colors, like a poster.

On the uplands were chequered squares made by fields, tilled and otherwise. Cloud-shadows moved from square to square. It was as if the Sky and Earth was playing a tremendous game of chess.

By and by the Mere Boy observed an Army of a Million Men. Certain canon, like voluble but non-committal toads with hunched backs, fulminated vast hiccoughs at unimpassioned intervals. Their own invulnerableness was offensive.

An officer of blue serge waved a sword, like a picture in a school history. The non-committal toads pullulated with brief red pimples and swiftly relapsed to impassivity.

The line of the Army of a Million Men obnubilated itself in whiteness as a line of writing is blotted with a new blotter.

"Go teh blazes b'Jimminey," remarked the Mere Boy. "What yeh's shooting fur. They might be people in that field."

He was terrific in his denunciation of such negligence. He debated the question of his ir-removability.

"If I'm goin' teh be shot," he observed; "If I'm goin' teh be shot, b'Jimminy—"

*   *   *

A Thing lay in the little hollow.

The little hollow was green.

The Thing was pulpy white. Its eyes were white. It had blackish-yellow lips. It was beautifully spotted with red, like tomato stains on a rolled napkin.

The yellow sun was dropping on the green plain of the earth, like a twenty-dollar gold piece falling on the baize cloth of a gaming table.

The blue serge officer abruptly discovered the punctured Thing in the Hollow. He was struck with the ir-remediableness of the business.

"Gee," he murmured with interest. "Gee, it's a Mere Boy."

The Mere Boy had been struck with seventy-seven rifle bullets. Seventy had struck him in the chest, seven in the head. He bore close resemblance to the top of a pepper castor.

He was dead.

He was obsolete.

As the blue serge officer bent over him he became aware of a something in the Thing's hand.

It was a green pebble.

"Gee," exclaimed the blue serge officer. "A green pebble, gee."

The large Wind evolved a threnody with reference to the seven un-distant poplars.

*g. Charles Battell Loomis Parodies Stephen Crane's War Correspondence**

ST—PH—N CR—N—

Brindisi [Italy], April 24. Able students of the art of war who read my "Red Badge of Courage" said that beyond a doubt I must have borne arms in our Civil War but as a matter of fact, I wasn't even borne in arms until a year or so after it was finished. Now, if I could write so graphic and convincing an account of a conflict, the varying colors of which had faded and gone before I came upon the scene, it follows that I ought to be able to write an account of the present Graeco-Turkish war that shall be at least as highly colored as any other man's and that too from a point where I am able to give my whole attention to writing and mixing my colors and am in no danger from stray bullets. From what the critics say, I know all about war without ever having been near one. What have I to expect by being on the scene except an incapacitating wound? It is more fair to those who sent me out as war correspondent that I stay here in Italy. So I will give my imagination free play and sling in lots of color, and there's not one man in a million can tell where I'm wrong if I am.

I have just received the following despatch:—"Athens, April 24. It is learned here that a desperate battle was fought at Mati yesterday."

The fight must have been between the Greeks and the Turks and so it was full of my favorite color, red—Turkey red. The Turkish and Greek troops lay encamped before Mati. A huge and laborious fog wallowed and pirouetted by turns, shutting out the operations of the armies from the knowledge of my contemporaries, Richard Harding Kipling and Rudyard Davis. Now and again a Greek youth filled with patriotic fire of an exceedingly effective shade of scarlet would swear volubly in Greek, but as I am not a linguist I am unable to spell his conversation either phonetically or after my own system. The effect of the Greek fire which is of course in constant use in the

---

* This parody was first reprinted in E. R. Hagemann, " 'Correspondents Three' in the Graeco-Turkish War: Some Parodies," *American Literature*, XXX (November 1958), 339-344. [*Editor.*]
Reprinted from: "Our Correspondents in the East," *The Critic*, n. s. XXVII (May 1, 1897), 297-298.

army was to color the fog beautifully and make Richard Harding think he was at a pyrotechnic display at Coney Island. Shortly after four o'clock the Turks were ordered to win the battle and they pressed forward with religious frenzy, waving their bundles of shoe-strings, just as they do on Broadway. A giant Turk stubbed his toe and fell to sobbing piteously, but unmoved at the sight the rest swept on uttering huge yellow oaths that it would tax even my ingenuity to spell. One Turk who had been in business in New York and had returned to fight for his country ran along crying irrelevantly, "This is a heluva note. Wanta shoestring? This is a heluva note. Wanta shoestring? Five cent."

At half-past four the Greeks heard a pale green rumble and they knew that the Turks were upon them. The Greek youth remembered that other youth who fired the Ephesian dome, and he spoke of it to a tall Greek who stood next to him, but he received no response. A squirrel sat upon a cannon and cracked cannon balls with saucy gibberings, unspellable. Red and brown and green ants hurried this way and that as if scenting the coming danger. The Greek youth remembered his mother. She would be making doughnuts full of grease about this time and he cried silently. A short Greek by his side looked blue for a minute, and then at a remark from the youth he changed color. The fog as if rejoiced at balking the efforts of Davis and Kipling wallowed at intervals of five minutes.

Then there was a Turkish crash, cream color with a selvedge of red and the ants and the youth and the squirrel were gone and the Turks had won the battle of Mati.

h. *William Dean Howells on Stephen Crane*

In several times and places, it has been my rare pleasure to bear witness to the excellence of what [Frank] Norris had done, and the richness of his promise. The vitality of his work was so abundant, the pulse of health was so full and strong in it, that it is incredible it should not be persistent still. The grief with which we accept such a death as his is without the consolation that we feel when we can say of some one that his life was a struggle, and that he is well out of the unequal strife, as we might say when Stephen Crane died. The physical slightness, if I may so suggest one characteristic of Crane's vibrant achievement, reflected the delicacy of energies that could be put forth only in nervous spurts, in impulses vivid and keen, but wanting in breadth and bulk of effect. Curiously enough, on the other hand, this very lyrical spirit, whose freedom was its life, was the absolute slave of reality. It was interesting to hear him defend what he had written, in obedience to his experience of things, against any change in the interest of convention. "No," he would contend, in behalf of the profanities of his people, "that is the way they *talk*. I have thought of that, and whether I ought to leave such things out, but if I do I am not giving the thing as I *know* it." He felt the constraint of those semi-savage natures, such as he depicted in "Maggie," and "George's Mother," and was forced through the fealty of his own nature to report them as they spoke no less than as they looked. When it came to "The Red Badge of Courage," where he took leave of these simple aesthetics, and lost himself in a whirl of wild guesses at the fact from the ground of insufficient witness, he made the failure which formed the break between his first and his second manner, though it was what the public counted a success, with every reason to do so from the report of the sales.

The true Stephen Crane was the Stephen Crane of the earlier books, the earliest book; for "Maggie" remains the best thing he did. All he did was lyrical, but this was the aspect and accent as well as the spirit of the tragically squalid life he sang, while "The Red Badge of Courage," and the other things that followed it, were the throes of an art failing with material to which it could not render

---

Reprinted from: "Frank Norris," *The North American Review*, CLXXV (December 1902), 770-771, 777.

an absolute devotion from an absolute knowledge. He sang, but his
voice erred up and down the scale, with occasional flashes of brilliant
melody, which could not redeem the errors. New York was essentially
his inspiration, the New York of suffering and baffled and beaten life,
of inarticulate or blasphemous life; and away from it he was not
at home, with any theme, or any sort of character. It was the pity
of his fate that he must quit New York, first as a theme, and then
as a habitat; for he rested nowhere else, and wrought with nothing
else as with the lurid depths which he gave proof of knowing better
than any one else. Every one is limited, and perhaps no one is more
limited than another; only, the direction of the limitation is different
in each. Perhaps George Douglas, if he had lived, would still have
done nothing greater than "The House with the Green Shutters," and
might have failed in the proportion of a larger range as Stephen
Crane did. I am not going to say that either of these extraordinary
talents was of narrower bound than Frank Norris; such measures
are not of the map. But I am still less going to say that they were
of finer quality because their achievement seems more poignant,
through the sort of physical concentration which it has. Just as a
whole unhappy world agonizes in the little space their stories circum-
scribe, so what is sharpest and subtlest in that anguish finds its like
in the epical breadths of Norris's fiction.

*   *   *

Personally, the young novelist [Frank Norris] gave one the
impression of strength and courage that would hold out to all lengths.
Health was in him always as it never was in that other rare talent of
ours [Crane] with whom I associate him in my sense of the irretrieva-
ble, the irreparable. I never met him but he made me feel that he
could do it, the thing he meant to do, and do it robustly and quietly,
without the tremor of "those electrical nerves" which imparted itself
from the presence of Stephen Crane. With him my last talk of the
right way and the true way of doing things was saddened by the
confession of his belief that we were soon to be overwhelmed by the
rising tide of romanticism, whose crazy rote he heard afar, and
expected with the resignation which the sick experience with all
things. But Norris heard nothing, or seemed to hear nothing, but
the full music of his own aspiration, the rich diapason of purposes
securely shaping themselves in performance.

i. H. L. Mencken on Stephen Crane

The revolt of the eighteen nineties, in America, was an echo of the simultaneous English revolt, and it showed a good deal of warmed-over feebleness. One turns back today to such things as "Songs from Vagabondia" (1893), and marvels that they ever fluttered the academic elms. The chief rebels, seen in retrospect, take on an almost ludicrous respectability. They fired their stinkpots at Richard Watson Gilder, James Whitcomb Riley, and Thomas Nelson Page, and began whooping for—James Lane Allen and Maurice Maeterlinck! The struggle was slow as well as feeble. It was the last year of the decade before Frank Norris set off the great bomb of "McTeague"; it was the first year of the next before Theodore Dreiser sprung the mine of "Sister Carrie." What is apt to be forgotten is that there were casualties among the rebels as well as among the armed detectives and *agents provocateurs* of God. For one William Vaughn Moody who renounced the decorous imitation of Shelley for the harsh limning of the native fauna there was many a discreet fellow who succumbed to the New England miasma and became a literary Epworth Leaguer, and a score of Richard Harding Davises who yielded themselves to the lascivious approaches of the family magazines and newspaper syndicates. Of all these dead, I have a feeling that Davis, in more ways than one, was the most pathetic. His country remembers him as he was at the end: an elderly Beau Brummell of letters, read only in crowded street-cars and in the more archaic varieties of finishing schools. But there was a day, *circa* 1891, when he was on the battlements, a hero if not a leader, and I have a suspicion that his padded shoulders and towering form brought in more recruits than any other bait.

Is Stephen Crane to be credited to him? Thomas Beer hints that it is so. If it is, then Davis was more important to the movement than all those who mocked him after he had gone down, for Crane was unquestionably the one genuinely solid figure that it produced —Crane was the centre and forefront of it while he lived, and remains its chief glory, in memory, to this day. I am old enough to remember the blast that THE RED BADGE OF COURAGE made in 1895. It was an

Reprinted from: "Introduction," *The Work of Stephen Crane*, X *(Major Conflicts)*, ed. Wilson Follett. New York: Alfred A. Knopf, Inc., 1926, pp. ix-xiii.

episode not matched in American letters, before or since. "Leaves of Grass" sneaked in quietly and almost furtively; "The Spy" had been prepared for by "Precaution"; Mark Twain was already a national figure when he published "Huckleberry Finn"; "McTeague" had forerunners and was expected. But THE RED BADGE OF COURAGE came like a flash of lightning out of a clear winter sky; it was at once unprecedented and irresistible. Who was this astonishing young man? A drunken newspaper reporter in New York! One of Davis's heroes! The miracle lifted newspaper reporting to the level of a romantic craft, alongside counterfeiting and mining in the Klondike. More, it gave the whole movement of the nineties a sudden direction and a powerful impulse forward. At one stroke realism was made its goal—not the old flabby, kittenish realism of Howells's imitators, with its puerile labouring of trivialities, but the sterner, more searching realism that got under the surface—the new realism that was presently to flower in "McTeague," and then in "Sister Carrie," and then in a whole procession of books, some of them good and some of them bad, but all of them alike marked by an honest endeavour to depict human life as men and women were actually living it in the world. THE RED BADGE OF COURAGE, of course, was not Crane's first attempt to achieve that revolution. He had tried two years before with "Maggie," and Howells had been duly sympathetic and Gilder had been duly shocked. But "Maggie," in 1896, remained an almost unknown book; it existed only in an obscure and shabby edition, bare of Crane's name; it was not until after THE RED BADGE that it was to come out between covers. The latter made Crane; not "Maggie." And more, perhaps, than any other book, it made the thing we call American literature to-day.

Crane never wrote another long story as good as THE RED BADGE. Compared to it, "The Third Violet" and ACTIVE SERVICE are flaccid and infirm, and even "Maggie" and "George's Mother" seem almost conventional. His method, in truth, was grossly ill-adapted to the novel, properly so-called. He had, so to speak, no literary small talk; he could not manage what the musicians call passage work. His superlative skill lay in the handling of isolated situations; he knew exactly how to depict them with a dazzling brilliance, and he knew, too, how to analyse them with penetrating insight, but beyond that he was rather at a loss: he lacked the pedestrian talent for linking one situation to another. This weakness threw him naturally into the short story, and there he was instantly at home. The short story gave him all the room he needed—and no more. Better, perhaps, than any other of his stories, "The Blue Hotel" reveals his singular capacity at its best. The episode there related is obviously the last scene in a long drama: the life of a nobody. The Swede's grotesque and sordid death is by no means a phenomenon *in vacuo;* we somehow feel that it is the fit and foreordained climax to a long series of obscure events, all bound together by chains of occult causation. A novelist would have tried to describe those events, to account for them, to relate them intelligibly. But to Crane they were all visible in the climax. He depicted that climax with a few strokes of outline and flashes of colour, and at once the whole drama was revealed, its beginning as well as its end, its inner meaning as well as its overt shape. The story is superlative among short stories. There is in it the austere economy of "The Taking of Lungtungpen," there is in it the brilliant dramatic effect of "The Mark of the Beast," and there is in it, too, something that Kipling has never been able to achieve: the profound dignity and epic sweep of "Youth," "Falk," and "Heart of Darkness" [by Joseph Conrad].

Crane put his name to stories that are well worthy to be mentioned after "The Blue Hotel" and stories that fall far below it. Like most of the men of the nineties, he suffered sorely, not from neglect, but from too much appreciation. The magazines bombarded him with orders, and he was also beset by the newspaper syndicates, then on a high tide of prosperity, and more often than not he succumbed to them. The result was a great deal of hurried and third-rate work. There was no time to ponder and revise; sometimes there was not even time enough to get an idea firmly by the tail. Had he lived to middle age, I dare say, he would have rewritten some of his earlier stories, and perhaps expunged others from the minutes altogether. But it is a testimony to his solid worth that, even presented haphazard and uncritically, unsorted and uncombed, he yet holds the attention and respect unflaggingly—that he is always obviously the true artist, even when he is playing the artisan. The short story in America owes more to him than he has got credit for. He loosened and extended its form, he quickened its tempo, and he greatly enriched its substance. The drive of a powerful originality was in him. He was, within his limits, one of the noblest artists that we have produced.

*j. Hamlin Garland on Stephen Crane**

I

In July of 1891, I gave a series of lectures at Avon-by-the-Sea in a summer school managed by Mr. and Mrs. Alberti of New York. Among other of my addresses was one upon "The Local Novel," and I remember very distinctly the young reporter for the *Tribune* who came up to me after the lecture to ask for the loan of my notes.

He was slim, boyish, with sallow complexion, and light hair. His speech was singularly laconic. "My name is Crane," he said. "Stephen Crane," and later I was told that he had been a student in a school near by, but had left before graduating to become a newspaper writer in New York. As I recall it, his presence at Avon was due to the Albertis, who knew his family—anyhow, he was reporting for the assembly.

Although not particularly impressed with him in this short interview, the correctness of his report ["Howells Discussed at Avon-by-the-Sea," New York *Tribune*, August 18, 1891, p. 5.] of my lecture next day surprised me. I recognized in it unusual precision of expression and set about establishing a more intimate relationship. We met occasionally thereafter to "pass ball," and to discuss the science of pitching, the various theories which accounted for "in-shoots" and "outdrops," for he, like myself, had served as a pitcher and gloried in being able to confound the laws of astronomy by making a sphere alter its course in mid-air.

In the middle of my second week he turned up at my boarding house in a very dejected mood. "Well, I've got the bounce," he said with a sour twist of his mouth. "The *Tribune* doesn't need me any more."

Not taking him seriously, I laughingly said, "They're making a mistake."

---

* Because of Hamlin Garland's lapses of memory concerning his meetings with Stephen Crane, the reader should consult Donald Pizer, "The Garland-Crane Relationship," *The Huntington Library Quarterly*, XXIV (November 1960), 75-82. [*Editor.*]
Reprinted from: "Stephen Crane," *Roadside Meetings.* New York: The Macmillan Company, 1930, pp. 189-200, 202-206.

"That's what I told them," he answered. "But you see I made a report of a labor parade the other day ["On the New Jersey Coast," New York *Tribune,* August 21, 1892, p. 22.], which slipped in over the managing editor's fence. When he read it in print he sent for me, made a little speech, and let me out."

"I should like to see that report," I remarked.

Thereupon he took from his pocket a clipping from the *Tribune* and handed it to me. It was very short, but it was closely studied and quite merciless in its realism. It depicted that political parade of tailors, house painters, and other indoor workers exactly as they appeared—a pale-faced, weak-kneed, splay-footed lot, the slaves of a triumphant civilization, wearing their chains submissively, working in the dark for careless masters, voting for privilege, seemingly without the slightest comprehension of their own supine cowardice; but it was Crane's ironical comment, his corrosive and bitter reflection upon their servility, and especially their habit of marching with banners at the chariot wheels of their conquerors, which made his article so offensive to the party in power.

Handing the article back to him I asked, "What did you expect from your journal—a medal?"

He smiled again in bitter reflection. "I guess I didn't stop to consider that. I was so hot at the sight of those poor, misshapen fools shouting for monopoly that I gave no thought to its effect upon my own fortunes. I don't know that it would have made much difference if I had. I wanted to say those things anyway."

He went away a few days after this, and I forgot all about him till in the winter of 1892 when I met his friends, Mr. and Mrs. Alberti, with whom he kept in touch in New York City.

My brother Franklin was playing at this time in [James] Herne's famous New England play, "Shore Acres," and I, busied on some unimportant book, was "baching it" with him in a small apartment, when there came to us through the mail a yellow, paper-bound volume called "Maggie, a Girl of the Streets." The author's name was given as "Johnstone [Johnston] Smith," and across the cover in exquisite upright script were these words: "The reader of this book must inevitably be shocked, but let him keep on till the end, for in it the writer has put something which is important."

The first sentence of the story had not only singular comprehension and precision, it threw over its sordid scene a somber light in which the author's tiny actors took on grandiose significance. "A very small boy stood on a heap of gravel for the honor of Rum

Alley. He was throwing stones at howling urchins who were crowding madly about the heap and pelting him. His infantile countenance was livid with fury. His small body was writhing in the delivery of great crimson oaths. His features wore the look of a tiny insane demon."

In another paragraph the bully appears. "Down the avenue came boastfully sauntering a lad of sixteen years, although the chronic sneer of an ideal manhood sat already upon his lips. His hat was tipped with an air of challenge over his eyes. Between his teeth a cigar stump tilted at the angle of defiance. He walked with a certain swing of the shoulders that appalled the timid." This was Pete.

Such were the principal male characters. Maggie was the sister of one, the victim of the other, and the heroine of the book. On her fell all the tragedy, all the disgrace of a life in the East Side slums. Frail flower of the muck, she went early to her decay and death.

It was a bitter story, but it interested me keenly. I secured Crane's address from Mrs. Alberti and wrote at once to him, accusing him of being the author of the book. I gave my own address and asked him to come and see me. Soon afterward he came to our little apartment and confessed his authorship of the book.

" 'Maggie,' " he said, "has been only privately half published and therefore remains entirely unsold." (A sample copy of this edition of "Maggie" sold recently for over two thousand dollars, illustrating once again the unpredictable trend of literary taste.)

He was living at this time with a group of artists or art students ("Indians," he called them), in an old building on East Twenty-third Street. According to his acridly humorous description of their doings, they all slept on the floor, dined off buns and sardines, and painted on towels or wrapping paper for lack of canvas. He complained of the noise and confusion of these "savages, all dreaming blood-red dreams of fame."

He was distressingly pale and thin at this time, and appeared depressed, but no sooner had he filled his "crop" with the meat and coffee which my brother served, than he gave out an entirely different expression. He chortled and sang as he strolled about the room, comically like a well-fed hen, and for an hour or two talked freely and well, always with precision and original tang.

He interested me more than he did my brother, and although his change of mood was very flattering to Franklin's skill as a cook, he never offered to assist in washing the dishes. I did not ascribe this to laziness; on the contrary, he always appeared to my brother and me as one remote from the practical business of living. We were amused rather than irritated by his helplessness. He never mentioned his kin and I assumed that he was estranged from them.

One day late in March he arrived, reeking as usual with stale cigarette smoke, with a roll of manuscript in the side pocket of his long, shabby gray ulster.

"What have you there?" I asked, pointing accusingly at his conspicuous burden. "It looks like poetry."

He smiled sheepishly. "It is."

"Your own?"

"Yes."

"Let me see it!" I commanded, much amused by his guilty expression. Handing the roll to me with a boyish gesture, he turned away with pretended indifference, to my brother. Upon unrolling the manuscript, I found it to be a sheaf of poems written in blue ink upon single sheets of legal cap paper, each poem without blot or correction, almost without punctuation, all beautifully legible, exact and orderly in arrangement. They were as easy to read as print and as I rapidly ran through them, I was astounded by their power. I could not believe that they were the work of the pale, laconic youth before me. They were at once quaintly humorous and audacious, unrhymed and almost without rhythm, but the figures employed with masterly brevity were colossal. They suggested some of the French translations of Japanese verses, at other times they carried the sting and compression of Emily Dickinson's verse and the savage philosophy of Olive Shriner [Schreiner], and yet they were not imitative.

"Have you any more?" I asked after I had come to the end of the roll.

"I have four or five up here," he replied, pointing toward his temple, "all in a little row," he quaintly added. "That's the way they come—in little rows, all ready to be put down on paper. I wrote nine yesterday. I wanted to write some more last night but those 'Indians' wouldn't let me do it. They howled so loud over the other lines that they nearly cracked my ears. You see we all live in the same box," he explained with sour candor, "and I've no place to write except in the general squabble. They think my verses are funny. They make a circus of me."

I was greatly interested in his statement that the verses were composed in his mind all ready to be drawn off. "Do you mean to say that these lines are arranged in your head, complete in every detail?"

"Yes, I could do one right now."

"Very well. Take a seat at my desk and do one for me." Thereupon with my pen he wrote steadily, composedly, without a moment's hesitation, one of his most powerful poems. It flowed from his pen like oil, but when I examined it, I found it not only without blot or erasure, but perfectly correct in punctuation. I can not be sure of the poem but I think it was the one which begins:

God fashioned the ship of the world carefully

and goes on to tell how "a wrong called," God turned His head and this ship without rudder slipped down the ways, and as a result has ever since wandered helplessly, going foolish journeys, doubling on its track, aimlessly drifting through the universe.

It appealed to me with enormous force at the moment. Coming from this hungry, seedy boy, written in my commonplace little study on a sunlit winter morning without premeditation—so he said—it wrought upon me with magical power. I understood a part of the incredulity of "Those Indians" who could not take their fellow "Indian" seriously. He declared that it had never been on paper before and that he had not consciously arranged its words in his mind. He just knew in a general way that it was there to be drawn off.

After he went away I read the poems aloud to my brother, pausing to exclaim over their ironic humor, their brevity, their originality of phrases. "What has the fellow been reading? If they are wholly the work of this unaccountable boy, America has produced another genius as singular as Poe," I concluded.

I confess that I took these lines very seriously. I hastened to show them to my most scholarly friends in order to detect the source of their inspiration. They remained original. I could not say that Crane had imitated any other writer.

He continued for some weeks to "precipitate" others but in diminishing flow. I recall that he came into Herne's dressing room at the theater one night to tell me that he had drawn off the very last one. "That place in my brain is empty," he said, but the poem he showed me was not a cull—it was tremendous in its effect on Herne as well as on me.

Later, much later, he wrote to say that he had gained the power to "turn the poetic spout on or off," but my interest in his verse was momentarily weakened by another and still more amazing demonstration of his subconscious endowment.

One day he turned up just in time for luncheon with another roll of manuscript, a roll so large that it filled one of the capacious pockets of his ulster. "What have you there," I demanded, "more lines?"

"No, it is a tale," he said with that queer, self-derisive smile which was often on his lips at this time.

"Let me see it," I said, knowing well that he had brought it for that purpose.

He handed it over to me with seeming reluctance, and while he went out to watch my brother getting lunch I took my first glance at the manuscript of "The Red Badge of Courage," which had, however, no name at this time. The first sentence fairly took me captive. It described a vast army in camp on one side of a river, confronting with its thousands of eyes a similar monster on the opposite bank. The finality which lay in every word, the epic breadth of vision, the splendor of the pictures presented—all indicated a most powerful and original imagination as well as a mature mastery of literary form.

Each page presented pictures like those of a great poem, and I experienced the thrill of the editor who has fallen unexpectedly upon a work of genius. It was as if the youth in some mysterious way had secured the coöperation of a spirit, the spirit of an officer in the Civil War. How else could one account for the boy's knowledge of war?

I spoke of this and in his succinct, self-derisive way, he candidly confessed that all his knowledge of battle had been gained on the football field! "The psychology is the same. The opposite team is an enemy tribe!"

At the table, while he applied himself with single-hearted joy to my brother's steak, I brooded over his case, and looking across at him, sallow, yellow-fingered, small, and ugly, I was unable to relate him in the slightest degree to the marvelous manuscript which he had placed in my hands. True, his talk was vivid, but it was disjointed and quaint rather than copious or composed.

Upon returning to my little study I said to him very seriously, "Crane, I daren't tell you how much I value this thing—at least not now. But wait! Here's only part of the manuscript. Where's the rest of it?"

Again he grinned, sourly, with a characteristic droop of his head. "In hock."

"To whom?"

"Typewriter."

"How much do you owe him or her?"

"Fifteen dollars."

Plainly this was no joking matter to him, but my brother and I were much amused by his tragic tone. At last I said, "I'll loan you the fifteen dollars if you'll bring me the remainder of the manuscript to-morrow."

"I'll do it," he said as if he were joining me in some heroic enterprise, and away he went in high spirits.

He was as good as his word, and when I had read the entire story I set to work to let my editorial friends know of this youngster. I mailed two of his completed sketches* to B. O. Flower of the *Arena*, asking him to be as generous as he could, "for the author is hungry"; and I suggested to Crane that he call upon Irving Bacheller, who was then running the Bacheller Syndicate, and say to him that I had advised Crane to make certain studies of East Side life in New York City and that I hoped the Syndicate would commission the writing of them.

Crane seemed grateful for the little I was able to do, but was not at all confident of earning a living with his pen.

I remember talking with him about "the bread lines," which regularly formed each night at certain bakeries which gave away their stale bread, and at my suggestion he went down one winter's evening, joined one of these lines, and made a study which he afterwards called "The Men in the Storm," a fine sketch which syndicated, I believe, along with others of somewhat similar character. And yet in spite of my aid and these promising activities, he remained almost as needy as ever. Thin and seedy, he still slept on the floor—according to his own story, smoking incessantly and writing in any possible corner.

One day when he was particularly depressed I said to him, "You'll be rich and famous in a year or two. Successful authors always look back with a smile on their hard times."

"You may be right," he replied soberly, "but it's no joke now. I'd trade my entire future for twenty-three dollars in cash."

Without claiming too much for my powers as a fortune teller, I could not believe that this boy would long remain obscure. He had

---

* Here Garland probably refers to "An Ominous Baby" and "The Men in the Storm," both later published in the *Arena*. [*Editor*.]

too much to give the reading world. His style was too individual, his imagination too powerful, to fail of winning the applause of those who count originality among the most desired qualities of American literature. Some of his phrases were to me quite inevitable for their condensation and clarity.

He had a genius for phrases. For example: in speaking of a truck driver he said, "In him grew a majestic contempt for those strings of street cars that followed him like *intent bugs.*" As for Maggie, "To her the world was composed of hardships and insults." Of the mother, "It seems that the world had treated this woman very badly and she took a deep revenge upon such portions of it as came within her reach. She broke furniture as if she were at last getting her rights."

Of course I am aware that the character of these books did not make for popularity, but I was sure that the marvelous English which this boy had somehow acquired would compensate for his street loafers, birds of the night, beggars, saloon keepers, drunken tenement dwellers, and the like.

"Your future is secure. A man who can write 'The Red Badge of Courage' can not be forever a lodger in a bare studio."

He replied, "That may be, but if I had some money to buy a new suit of clothes I'd feel my grip tighten on the future."

"You'll laugh at all this—we all go through it."

"It is ridiculous, but it doesn't make me laugh," he replied smilelessly.

In the *Arena* for June, 1893, I reviewed a novel by Bourget and "Maggie" under the caption, "An Ambitious French Novel and a Modest American Story." So far as I knew this was the earliest review of Crane's first book. . . .

II

Shortly before I left for the West he called to tell me that he had shown his verses to Mr. John D. Barry and that Mr. Barry had "fired them off to Copeland & Day."

"I am sorry—I was on the point of interesting a New York publisher in them."

The poems appeared soon after in a form which too strongly emphasized their singularities. With the best intention in the world, Messrs. Copeland & Day gave a leading to the critics who quite generally took the "Black Riders" as a cue for laughter.

I saw nothing of him during 1894, but in May of that year he wrote me from Chicago a letter in which he mentions the poem he read to Herne and me. . . .

* * *

The serial publication of "The Red Badge of Courage" brought him an admirer in the person of Ripley Hitchcock of Appleton's, who made him an offer for the book at "customary royalty." He accepted, glad of the chance. This helped him somewhat, but as royalties are only paid annually and as the book sold very slowly, he continued to suffer need.

At this point his affairs took a sudden turn upward. He became the figure I had hoped to see him become two years before. Some English critics wrote in highest praise of "The Red Badge," and the book became a critical bone of contention between military objectors and literary enthusiasts. Crane was accepted as a man of genius.

Some time in the summer of 1896 he called at my New York hotel and, not finding me, left the following note:

"Just heard you were in town. I want you to dine to-night with me at the Lantern Club, sure! Roosevelt expects to be there. He wants to meet you. Don't fail. I will call here at six, again."

He also left a book, "George's Mother," in which he had made this characteristic inscription, "To Hamlin Garland of the great honest West, from Stephen Crane of the false East."

This dinner at the Lantern Club was important in several ways. I do not recall meeting Roosevelt, but Irving Bacheller was there and we had much talk about Crane and other matters. The club met in a very old building, in its loft, as I recall it, on Williams Street and the walls of the dining room were covered with the autographs of so many distinguished writers that I hesitated to add mine. It was a bit of the Colonial New York which had perilously survived, I say perilously, because it gave way soon after to a modern building, and remains but a pleasant memory to the older newspaper men of to-day.

I saw Crane several times during his troubles with the New York police, and while I sympathized with him in his loyalty to a woman [Dora Clark] whom he considered had been unjustly accused of soliciting, his stubborn resolve to go on the stand in her defense was quixotic. Roosevelt discussed the case with me and said, "I tried to save Crane from press comment, but as he insisted on testifying, I could only let the law take its course."

The papers stated that Crane's rooms had been raided and that an opium layout had been discovered. Altogether it was a miserable time for him. The shady side of his bohemian life was turned to the light.

Meeting him in McClure's office one day, I said to him very earnestly, "Crane, why don't you cut loose from your associations here? Go to your brother's farm in Sullivan County and get back your tone. You don't look well. Settle down to the writing of a single big book up there, and take your time to do it."

Impulsively thrusting out his hand to me, he said, "I'll do it." Alas! He did not. He took a commission to go to Greece and report a war. On his return from Greece he went to Cuba.

Long afterward Louis Senger, one of his companions on this mission, wrote to me, conveying the information that just before they went to Cuba Crane told him to write to me in case anything happened to him down there.

*   *   *

After the Cuban war, Crane married and went to England, where he lived till he was ordered into Germany for his health. I have only one letter from him while he was in England, and in that he told me nothing of himself. It was all about a new writer he had discovered, a certain Joseph Conrad. "Get his 'Nigger of the Narcissus,' " he wrote. "It is a crackerjack. Conrad knows your work. You should meet him when you come to England."

It was more than twenty years later when I met Conrad in Bishopsbourne and talked of "The Nigger" and of Crane. "A wealthy admirer turned over to the Cranes a great, half-ruined manor house not far from here," said Conrad, "and Stephen kept open house there. The place was so filled with his semi-bohemian associates in London that I seldom went there—I didn't enjoy his crowd, but I liked him and valued his work. I went over to see him when he was brought to Dover on his way to the Black Forest. He wore a beard and was greatly emaciated. The moment I looked into his eyes I knew that he was bound for a long voyage—and that I should not see him again. He died soon after in Bavaria."

In an article written soon after Crane's death,* I said:

"He was too brilliant, too fickle, too erratic to last. He could not go on doing stories like 'The Red Badge of Courage.' The weakness of such highly individual work lies in its success by surprise. The

---

* Garland is referring here to his "Stephen Crane: A Soldier of Fortune," *Saturday Evening Post*, CLXXIII (July 28, 1900), 16-17. [*Editor.*]

words which astonish, the phrases which excite wonder and admiration, come eventually to seem tricky. They lose force with repetition and come at last to be distasteful. 'The Red Badge of Courage' was marvelous, but manifestly Crane could not go on repeating a surprise. When he wrote in conventional phrase his power diminished. If he continued to write of slum life, he repeated himself. It seems now that he was destined from the first to be a present-day Poe, a singular and daring soul, irresponsible as the wind. We called him a genius, for he had that quality which we can not easily measure or define.

"His mind was more largely subconscious in its workings than that of any man of my acquaintance. He did not understand his own processes or resources. When he put pen to paper he found marvelous words, images, sentences, pictures already formed in his brain, to be drawn off and fixed on paper. His pen was 'a spout,' as he himself says. The farther he got from his own field, his inborn tendency, the weaker he became. Such a man can not afford to enter the dusty public thoroughfare. His genius is of the lonely wood, the solitary shadowland.

"To send him to report actual warfare was a mistake His genius lay in depicting the battles which never saw the light of day, and upon which no eyes but his own had ever gazed. He was a strange, willful, irresponsible boy, one that will not soon be forgotten out of American literature."

I see no reason to change this estimate of him.

k. Alfred Kazin on Stephen Crane

Out of this welter of enthusiasms that gave so many different clues to the future, there now emerged at the end of the century the one creative artist who sounded the possibilities open to his generation, though he fulfilled so few of them himself. In his day Stephen Crane stood as the "marvelous boy" in the tradition of Chatterton, Keats, and Beardsley—the fever-ridden, rigidly intense type of genius that dies young, unhappy, and the prey of lady biographers. Everything that he wrote in his twenty-nine years seemed without precedent. Before him Harold Frederic and Hamlin Garland had displayed the opportunities for an American naturalism, but their outlook was confined to local grievances and was expressed through a local temper. Frank Norris was still finding his way and was still dependent upon topical issues and the ideas of others. But no conventional background or stimulus explains Crane's disposition to naturalism; neither the depression of the nineties, which never troubled him, nor the classic texts of European naturalism, by which he was generally bored. He was a naturalist by birth, so to speak; but there is nothing in the placid Jersey parsonage of the Reverend Jonathan Crane that explains the grim finality of mind, in its way an astounding capacity for tragedy, that devoured his fourteenth child. Sentimental critics have charged that Crane had a secret disaffection born out of his father's martyrdom in the service of Methodism and its apparent futility in the face of world events, but the surest thing one can say about Crane is that he cared not a jot which way the world went. No one was ever less the reforming mind; revolutions were something foreigners attempted that Hearst would pay good money to report. He accepted the world always, hating it always, plotting his way through it alone with a contempt that was close to pain.

Thomas Beer, who understood him best, hit at the secret of Crane's career when he wrote of a ruthless literary courage possible only to those who are afraid. Life tossed him up and down like a cork. To his last days he was tormented by disease and insecurity,

---

Reprinted from: *On Native Grounds: An Interpretation of Modern American Prose Literature.* New York: Reynal & Hitchcock, 1942, pp. 67-72. By permission of Harcourt Brace Jovanovich, Inc. Copyright, 1942, renewed, 1970, by Alfred Kazin.

greedy friends and witnesses of his genius who thought him a strangely convivial freak, stupid editors and pristine reviewers, the doltish open mouth of the public, pointing, giggling, and retailing stories. Crane never had a juvenile period, a time of test and error, of sentimental amplitude and human indirection. The hard, fixed boundaries which hold his books were iron clamps which were set early. All through that miserably unhappy life, even in the first days of glory when *The Red Badge of Courage* fell out of the heavens, he was the stricken boy Conrad saw at the end in Brede Place in England, sitting in a baronial pile eating his heart out in hack work, devoured by syco-phants, always in some portentous torment, with the suffering eyes and the absurd mustache that fell over his face like the mask of old age.

The world was a ship, he wrote in one of his poems, that God had fashioned and let slip.

> God fashioned the ship of the world carefully.
> With the infinite skill of an All-Master
> Made He the hull and the sails,
> Held He the rudder
> Ready for adjustment.
> Erect stood He, scanning his work proudly.
> Then—at fateful time—a wrong called,
> And God turned, heeding.
> Lo, the ship, at this opportunity, slipped slyly,
>
>   .   .   .   .   .   .
>
> Making quaint progress,
> Turning as with serious purpose
> Before stupid winds.
> And there were many in the sky
> Who laughed at this thing.

And no more than God could he hope to reclaim it. "I cannot be shown," he said once, "that God bends on us any definable stare, like a sergeant at muster, and his laughter would be bully to hear out in nothingness." He would not appeal against wrong, and he thought it monstrous to complain. Essentially uneducated, his resources lay in his physical senses, which he exploited with an intensity dispro-portionate to his strength and yet unequal to the fervor of his spirit.

He read very little, and nothing surprised him more than when people who read his work condescendingly discovered his debt to Zola or to Tolstoy. *War and Peace,* which he knew, stimulated him to the boyish cockiness that flared at rare instances and was one of his more charming traits. "Tolstoy could have done the whole business in one-third of the time and made it just as wonderful," he laughed. "It goes on and on like Texas." He thought of writing a book entitled *Peace and War,* which would do "the job" better and be an answer to Tolstoy. It was perhaps because he had read so little, as Willa Cather suggested, that he felt no responsibility to be accurate or painstaking in his transcription of common events. Like every sensuous artist, he was a magnificent guesser, and nothing proved how deeply he had imagined the psychology of battle in *The Red Badge of Courage* than his experience as correspondent in the Greco-Turkish War. *"The Red Badge* is all right," he said when he came out of it.

Yet the stark greatness of the novel did grow in part out of his instinctively intimate knowledge of American manners and character. As Carl Van Doren observed, the verisimilitude of the book testified to Crane's knowledge of the popular memory and authentic legends of the war. One side of him was the local village boy who never quite lost his feeling for the small talk and the casual pleasures of the American town, and it showed not only in the campfire talk of the men in *The Red Badge,* but in the charming little-boy stories in *Whilomville Stories* and the extraordinary transcriptions of Negro speech in *The Monster.* What kept Crane alive, in one sense, was just that feeling; without it his despair might have seemed intolerable and, for an artist of his sensibility, incommunicable. He baited the universe but never those village citizens who are as benign in his work as small-town fathers in the *Saturday Evening Post.* They were his one medium of fraternity, and his strong, quiet affection for them testifies to the unconscious strength of his personal citizenship.

In this sense even the most astonishing effects in *The Red Badge of Courage* reflect Crane's background, for its soldier-hero might have been any Amrican boy suddenly removed from the farm to fight in a war of whose issues he knew little and in which his predominating emotion was one of consummate perplexity and boredom. As a novelist of war Crane anticipated the war studies of the future; he had no palpable debt to Stendhal and Tolstoy, on whom he was supposed to have modeled his realism. Waterloo in *La Chartreuse de Parme* and Austerlitz in *War and Peace* are scenes against which the hero of sensibility enlarges his knowledge of life; but the novelists of social protest after the First World War, from Henri Barbusse to Humphrey Cobb, indicted the morality of war for its assault on the common citizen. Crane's hero is Everyman, the symbol made flesh upon which war plays its havoc; and it is the deliberation of that intention which explains why the novel is so extraordinarily lacking, as H. L. Mencken put it, in small talk. Scene follows scene in an accelerating rhythm of excitement, the hero becomes the ubiquitous man to whom, as Wyndham Lewis once wrote of the Hemingway hero, things happen. With that cold, stricken fury that was so characteristic of Crane—all through the self-conscious deliberation of his work one can almost hear his nerves quiver—he impaled his hero on the ultimate issue, the ultimate pain and humiliation of war, where the whole universe, leering through the blindness and smoke of battle, became the incarnation of pure agony. The foreground was a series of commonplaces; the background was cosmological. Crane had driven so quickly through to the central problem that everything else seemed accessory in its effect, but he was forced to describe emotions in terms of color because the pressure behind so wholly concentrated a force drove him to seek unexpected and more plastic sources of imagery. Often he revealed himself to be a very deliberate tone-painter, as calculating and even mechanical a worker in the magnificent as Oscar Wilde or Richard Strauss. He aimed at picture qualities and he synthesized them so neatly that, like the movement of the hunters and the hunted in a tapestry of the medieval chase, they illustrated a world whose darkness was immensity. "In the Eastern sky there was a yellow patch, like a rug laid for the feet of the coming sun; and against it, black and pattern-like, loomed the gigantic figure of the colonel on a gigantic horse."

Yet for all its beauty, Crane's best work was curiously thin and, in one sense, even corrupt. His desperation exhausted him too quickly; his unique sense of tragedy was a monotone. No one in America had written like him before; but though his books precipitately gave the whole esthetic movement of the nineties a sudden direction and a fresher impulse, he could contribute no more than the intensity of his spirit. Half of him was a consummate workman; the other half was not a writer at all. In his ambitious stories of New York tenement life, *Maggie* and *George's Mother,* the violence seemed almost celestial, but it was only Crane's own, and verbal; both stories suffer from excessive hardness and that strangely clumsy diction that Crane never learned to polish. In a great show piece like *The Open Boat* (drawn from an almost direct report of experiences in the Caribbean in the days when he was reporting the Cuban insurrection for New York newspapers) he proved himself the first great pyrotechnician of the contemporary novel; but the few superb stories are weighed down by hack work. The man who wrote *The Blue Hotel* also wrote more trash than any other serious novelist of his time. Even in buffooneries like his unfinished last novel, *The O'Ruddy,* there is the sense of a wasted talent flowing over the silly improvisation in silent derision. He had begun by astonishing the contemporary mind into an acceptance of new forms; he ended by parodying Richard Harding Davis in *Active Service* and Stevenson in *The O'Ruddy.* Yet it was not frustration that wore him out, but his own weariness of life. His gift was a furious one, but barren; writing much, he repeated himself so joylessly that in the end he seemed to be mocking himself with the same quiet viciousness with which, even as a boy, he had mocked the universe. An old child, it was not merely by his somberness that he anticipated the misanthropy of the twentieth-century novel. Pride and a fiercely quaking splendor mark his first and last apotheosis: he was the first great tragic figure in the modern American generation.

l. John Berryman on Stephen Crane

Since Dr. Johnson observed that a century was the term commonly fixed as the test of literary merit, authors have crowded each other out of sight more and more rapidly. The term cannot be now so long. An English critic says the present point is to write a book that will last just ten years; but a decade must be too short—fashion can catch up older trash than that. For Johnson, remember, the "effects of favour" must have ended. Under our industry of literary scholarship, having to be kept supplied with subjects, "survival" is a more ambiguous condition than it used to be: one may stand to gain by overvaluing his author however meager, or his author's toe. Other conditions make a term difficult to fix. But Crane has been dead half a century, academic interest has avoided him as both peculiar and undocumented, and some of his work is still decidedly alive. This is long enough. We are not dealing with absolutes: the questions of interest with regard to an author remembered at all are how, and what part, and why, and whether justly. Perhaps a question more general arises too in connection with Crane. American genius has not been literary. The executive idealism of a few men like Washington represents our spirit at a higher level, probably, than can any of our literary masters. It may be merely our failure so far to have produced a national author that creates this impression, though we have to reckon also with a kind of national commitment as different as possible from, say, French cultural commitment. At any rate the fact is certain: we have had little genius in literature. The question is this: whether we have not in Stephen Crane a genius very formidable indeed, an artist of absolute and high vision—the sort of writer before whom most of our imposing earlier authors utterly shrivel away—a national glory, if the nation cared.

Let us lay aside at the outset matters of influence. Enough has been mentioned in passing, of influences felt by Crane (Tolstoy, Mark Twain, Goethe, Emerson, Whitman, Olive Schreiner, others), to rescue him from the status of a "sport." He concentrates tendencies and powers already tentatively in play. At the same time these influ-

Reprinted from: "Crane's Art," *Stephen Crane*. New York: William Sloane Associates, 1950, pp. 263-269. By permission of William Morrow & Company, Inc. Copyright © 1950 William Sloane Associates.

ences certainly tell us very little about him; Crane was perhaps as original as an author can be, and be valuable. We shall have to study him by himself. More interesting by a good deal is the influence he exerted, great and distinct upon Conrad, Willa Cather, Ernest Hemingway, very decided upon others of his contemporaries and then upon Theodore Dreiser, Sherwood Anderson, Carl Sandburg, even Sinclair Lewis, as well as T. E. Lawrence, F. Scott Fitzgerald, more recent figures. Strong and lasting despite interruptions in his fame and availability, this influence is part of his importance. "The stones he put in the wall"—as Anderson said it—"are still there. . . ." But critics have read him so little that the source of this whole aspect of recent English and American literary art has gone mainly unrecognized and must remain matter for special study. Crane's influence will be found no simple affair, traced through these authors: it affected vision, technique, material. Whether, however, it has ever been commensurate with the degree of revolution Crane effected is doubtful. I think it has not, and look for an explanation to the fact that his work of characteristic power has not yet been isolated from his inferior, ugly, and trivial work.

I ought to say where this power is. It is in "The Open Boat" above all, and "The Blue Hotel"; in the single long work *The Red Badge of Courage* and short war-studies from "A Mystery of Heroism" through "Death and the Child," "The Price of the Harness," "Virtue in War," to "The Clan of No Name," "An Episode of War," "The End of the Battle," "The Upturned Face"; in the early and late companion studies of society's ferocity, *Maggie* and *The Monster;* in two singular visions of happiness, "The Pace of Youth" and "The Bride Comes to Yellow Sky"; in other prose constructions delicate, dreadful and humorous, from "A Dark Brown Dog," "The Reluctant Voyagers," "An Experiment in Misery," through "The Veteran" to "Shame" and "An Illusion in Red and White"; in two dozen poems from "Once I Saw Mountains Angry" through the title-poem of *War Is Kind* to the posthumous marvelous "A Man Adrift on a Slim Spar." The list by no means exhausts Crane's excellence—very little behind some of this work come a number of other stories, such as "The Little Regiment" and "Three Miraculous Soldiers," the three Mexican stories, chapters even in *George's Mother* and "War Memories," passages scattered everywhere. But at any rate not much less than this list will do in instance of where this author remains vivid, living.

You need very little to live. With *Wuthering Heights* and some verses one woman is with us always. But my display of Crane's work will certainly surprise both in bulk and variety most readers and critics. The truth is that Crane sprang into fame amid a storm of excited bewilderment and has passed into permanence in almost perfect silence. The occasional critic or historian who looks at him is just puzzled. A few are not comfortable yet about his being here at all, and among the majority who accept him there is no agreement about what kind of author he is. The most considerable attempts to account for him are still those by two of his English friends: first the very able ten pages written by H. G. Wells for the *North American Review* just after Crane's death in 1900. . . . Meanwhile Edward Garnett, whose "Appreciation" in *The Academy* (December 17, 1898) was the most acute view taken during Crane's lifetime, added some remarkable sentences when he extended it in 1921 for *Friday Nights.* . . .

There is first the question, baffling to most of his friends, his critics, and his age, of whether Stephen Crane did not write almost entirely from *inspiration*. His work seemed to come from nowhere, prose and poetry alike. The word "dream" is recurrent in comment on him—even Hemingway, vouching for the authority of *The Red Badge,* uses it when he calls that book "a boy's long dream of war." When Crane told an interviewer that it was a product of labor, the man was not less but more astonished, that Crane should have "kept this story in hand for nearly a year, polishing and bettering it. Perhaps this is the most amazing thing about a thoroughly amazing book. If he had said he wrote it in three days (as he wrote the 'Black Riders') one might understand such a *tour de force.*" Crane's rejection of the notion of "inspiration" is irrelevant. Of course he *did* write from inspiration, and of course he wrote also from close long observation, inquiry, study, and then he rewrote. He was like other men of genius, in short, often inspired and immensely deliberate. Yet this double explanation does not really account for the impression his work has always given, which might be put as follows: one is surprised that it exists at all—and one's surprise, if it diminishes, does not disappear with familiarity. Hamlin Garland tells us indeed that Crane just "tapped" his brain for his poems. He certainly went through no apprenticeship in poetry; he just began—began, we shall see, at a very high level—and if *The Black Riders* was not, evidently, written in three days, it was written abruptly and with effortless rapidity. As for prose, we have discovered an early development there, but so early and masterly that the prodigy remains. All this is thoroughly exceptional.

At the same time, Crane looks like a polar type of modern self-consciousness. He copied into his notebook—whether as program or as confirmation is unknown—a sentence from Emerson which comprehensively defines one effect of this art which lighted the 'nineties: "Congratulate yourselves if you have done something strange and extravagant and have broken the monotony of a decorous age." Literary ambition unusually deliberate and powerful is manifest all through his early life. "I began the war with no talent but an ardent admiration and desire. I had to build up." Readers and critics have recognized an effort in his work, and it forms a large basis for critical objection. They see affectation, strain. A word applied nearly as frequently as "dream" is its converse: "trick." Just before his death, a feminine critic put the objection as established: "Men of intelligence yawn. The trick is too easily seen through."

Impressions more contradictory are hard to imagine, and a third must be mentioned. Crane's work ever since it appeared has struck readers as "barbaric." His poems were "crazy," and they still—in standard anthologies—look very weird. The ferocity of his prose, whether intended or casual, seems primitive. His animism is like nothing else in civilized literature. Mountains, trees, dogs, men, horses, and boats flash in and out of each other's identities. The sun "had its hat over one eye" and one man's voice makes another man "wish that he was a horse, so that he could spring upon the bed and trample him to death." This is characteristic and frequent. A disappointed boatman has a "face like a floor." If Crane lulls you into safety for a minute, wait only. He is examining the electric chair in Sing Sing: "the comfortable and shining chair . . . waits and waits and waits" for "its next stained and sallow prince . . . an odor of oiled wood, a keeper's tranquil, unemotional voice, a broom stood in a corner near the door, a blue sky and a bit of moving green tree at a window so small that it might have been made by a canister shot." The sentence concludes like an electrocution, and when the keeper is quoted he might be a friendly aesthetician describing Crane's effect on the reader: "We calculate that the whole business takes about a minute from the time we go after him." These images come all from early, negligible, unreprinted newspaper stories; assaults in his important work may be more violent still. Crane's humor, finally, and his irony are felt as weird or incomprehensible. When he began a book of poems with the line,

> Do not weep, maiden, for war is kind,

the reviewers treated him, reasonably, as an *idiot*.

A dream, a trick, a savage or imbecile attack: any account of his work which hopes for assent will have to try to reconcile these views with each other, and with still other views. All we need agree yet is that it seems to display an essential, *obvious* coherence, originality, and authority, such as will justify any care we may take to appreciate it.

m. Warner Berthoff on Stephen Crane

In Stephen Crane's fiction, too, where the violences of war or of slum life and the dumb suffering of the insulted and injured provide the main occasions, the formulas of naturalism are called into service; they do not, however, determine what is presented. Crane's motive was not to diagram conditions or assert universal truths but to produce a certain kind of composition, a vivid showbox of serial impressions in an appropriate style. A passage late in one of his best-known stories, "The Blue Hotel," is in fact as compact a statement of the naturalist point of view as can be imagined, but its effectiveness is all in its placing and timing; what is impressive is not the point of view but the ironic poise and discretion with which the essential commonplaceness of the point of view is overcome and perhaps transfigured. With the narrative sentences framing it, this passage offers a fine instance of the expressive tact and virtuosity which are at the center of Crane's achievement and which led first Garland and Howells and then Joseph Conrad and Henry James to accept him at once into the company of the elect. In it the doomed Swede of the story—the swaggering, quick-eyed outsider who will soon, in ironic fulfillment of his own gratuitous prediction, be haphazardly murdered—is seen struggling across town at night through a prairie blizzard:

> He found a street and made travel along it, leaning heavily upon the wind whenever, at a corner, a terrific blast caught him.
>
> He might have been in a deserted village. We picture the world as thick with conquering and elate humanity, but here, with the bugles of the tempest pealing, it was hard to imagine a peopled earth. One viewed the existence of man then as a marvel, and conceded a glamor of wonder to these lice who were caused to cling to a whirling, fire-smitten, ice-locked,

Reprinted from: *The Ferment of Realism: American Literature, 1884-1919.* New York: The Free Press, 1965, pp. 227-235. By permission of The Macmillan Company. Copyright © 1965 by The Free Press, a Division of The Macmillan Company.

disease-stricken, space-lost bulb. The conceit of man was explained by this storm to be the very engine of life. One was a coxcomb not to die in it. However, the Swede found a saloon.

In front of it an indomitable red light was burning, and the snowflakes were made blood-color as they flew through the circumscribed territory of the lamp's shining. . . .

Coming as it does just before the story's theatrical climax, the passage serves like a chorus or a reflective soliloquy; it brings the whole rising occasion into a more brilliant focus. But within this focus the naturalist view of life is applied not differently from the rays of the red lamp: not to explain or interpret but to spotlight and transfigure.

The passage is not faultless. The quick changes and contrasts in perspective and in grammatical voice, though achieving the ironies they aim at, only just miss being disagreeably affected; and "coxcomb" does seem a lapse into the kind of Kiplingesque smartness of diction that Willa Cather later identified as the period mannerism Crane had chiefly to overcome.[1] A certain susceptibility to lapses of this kind and in general a continuous brittleness of improvisation are characteristic of the best of Crane's work. They have become less obtrusive in *The Red Badge of Courage* (1895), the Civil War fantasia of frontline terrors and sublimities that established his reputation overnight, and in the psychologically acute novella of city life, *George's Mother* (1896), than in the journalistic ironies of his first novel, *Maggie, A Girl of the Streets* (1893); and they are most steadily under control in certain stories of the later '90s. But nothing Crane wrote is entirely free of the quality of the *tour de force*. On the other hand there is something of his virtuoso inventiveness in his slightest and most perfunctory work; nothing he wrote is altogether unrewarding. The shortness of his career and that ripeness of individual sensibility evident in his style from the first—the basis of Howells's remark that Crane had sprung into life "fully armed"—make chronology and questions of development nearly immaterial in his case. Toward the end of his hurried life we do note an increase of potboilers: *The Third Violet* (1897), *Active Service* (1898), the local-color collection *Whilomville Stories* (1900), the unfinished parody-romance *The O'Ruddy* (1903, completed by Robert Barr). Surer now of a market for his work and needing income, Crane was writing too much and too fast, to the point of becoming, like one of the young artists in *The Third Violet,* "a trained bear of the magazines." But between 1896 and 1899 there is also the assured narrative mastery of his admirable longer stories, "The Little Regiment," "The Blue Hotel," "The Open Boat," "The Monster," "The Price of the Harness," and (even if we grant H. G. Wells's reasonable objection that it overinsists upon its message) "Death and the Child."

Flaws in Crane's work are easy enough to spot; it is the peculiar integrity of his art, at its best, that has escaped definition. Criticism has been clearer about what he did without, among the traditional procedures of English fiction, than about what exactly took their place. There is, in short, a Crane problem, and it is as well stated as it has ever been in the puzzled excursus Joseph Conrad wrote into a letter to Edward Garnett in 1897. "His eye is very individual and his expression satisfies me artistically," Conrad remarked of Crane, but then asked:

> Why is he not immensely popular? With his strength, with his rapidity of action, with that amazing faculty of vision— why is he not? He has outline, he has colour, he has movement, with that he ought to go very far. But—will he? I sometimes think he won't. It is not an opinion—it is a feeling. I could not explain why he disappoints me—why my enthusiasm withers as soon as I close the book. While one reads, of course, he is not to be questioned. He is the master of his reader to the very last line—then—apparently for no reason at all—he seems to let go his hold.

Can the broad truth of this be disputed? Crane's work is artful, original, concentrated, indistractible sometimes to the point of a mesmerizing intensity. Nevertheless it lacks mass, moment, tenacity; it has no power of imposing itself beyond reversion on our fully extended consciousness of experience. The themes it appears to carry —in *The Red Badge,* for example, the young soldier's encounter with the gods of battle and, so it has been claimed, his "growth into manhood"—dissolve to fantasy as we try to trace out their actual progression. It is understandable why most recent commentary on Crane has got diverted into biographical and psychoanalytic speculation. So it has been argued that Crane lacked "culture," that he had no training besides yellow journalism to guide his highly individual talent, that in any event the principal coordinates of his understanding of life were drawn from the conventional ethos of his parents' Methodism or else from the Oedipal dilemmas inflicted on him as the youngest of their ten children. These probabilities are all relevant. But they do not confront the specific problem Conrad defines, which is that Crane possesses as a writer an irresistible authority that is nevertheless transient, provisional, uncompelling.

Conceivably it is in Crane's very artfulness, what he does at his best, that we must look for explanations. To explain the frailness of his hold on our attention as resulting from that "impressionism" of style and of notation by which his work has been identified from the first—"He is *the only* impressionist, and *only* an impressionist," Conrad declared—is still not enough, however. For Crane's work presents itself not as a record of impressions and observations drawn from life but as a barrage of self-generating images and inward conceits whose essential function is to rival life, perhaps supplant it. He is, at his best, a visionary writer (Conrad is at the edge of saying so), and his authority is a visionary authority. It is visionary in a peculiar way, however, in that the images it presents refer to nothing equally authoritative beyond themselves, no clear pattern of understanding, no really coherent structure of imaginative experience. Except by a kind of parodic mimicry, they scarcely even refer to each other or to the narrative events they coexist with. *The Red Badge of Courage* is the fullest demonstration of Crane's special power; again and again particular gestures or moments of consciousness are given a dream-like autonomy. But these visionary flashes are as fleeting as they are brilliant. The emotions, the dramatic convergences, that contribute to their making somehow do not survive their crystallization in words. As they thus form no proper succession, neither can they be made to yield up a coherent narrative theme or argument. There is a gap between the story and the concrete demonstration that would be disastrous to the work as a whole if the story was anything more than a moving screen for the author's vision-generating eye to project its inventions upon. Much the same view may be taken of Crane's abrupt, laconic little poems, despite his claiming to have written them, in contrast to his stories, in order "to give my ideas of life as a whole." If anything about them persuades, it is not their epigrammatic parable-arguments, and certainly not their "philosophy," which is mostly the second-hand agnosticism and ironic fatalism of the period, but rather the absoluteness of certain free-floating images now and then projected in them. Nothing quite like this naked magic-lantern work exists elsewhere in our literature. Even Poe's inventions carry a more consistent reference to common experience or to some stable conception of it. The nearest parallels to Crane's best manner are to be found, rather, in the work of certain graphic artists—in Daumier, perhaps, or above all in Goya, the rapt, strict master of the *Tauromaquia* and the *Disaster of the War*—work of a kind, moreover, that for all its transcendent purity of composition is like Crane's in being continuous with the documentary concerns of nineteenth-century journalism.[2]

The test of seriousness in visionary expression, which is always radically simplifying, is a peculiar one: purity of specification, undivided attentiveness to the real presence of the projected subject. Representations of divinity do not have to be theologically accurate or complete; they only have to eliminate everything that is not numinous. We would not think of asking whether Goya's record of the Peninsular War is, as a record, comprehensive or symbolically coherent or universally valid with respect to the order of experience contemplated. We only notice its terrifyingly consistent apprehension of actual terror and outrage, its reduction of all contingencies to that one overmastering perception. Yet we do not hold the whole of it in mind as we can the formal order of dramatic tragedy. There is a passivity of observation about it; in each new instance it seeks only to dissolve itself into the occurrence that calls it forth. It tells us simply, "I saw this—and this, too." Crane had some such consciousness of his own essential effort as a writer. "I go ahead," he writes in a letter of 1898, "for I understand that a man is born into this world with his own pair of eyes, and that he is not at all responsible for his vision—he is merely responsible for his quality of personal honesty. To keep close to this personal honesty is my supreme ambition." And it may be said that everything convincing in Crane's work turns on visionary images which have, as they succeed one another, the hallucinatory serenity and intactness of dream images. So the conventional village ironies in "The Monster" about the practice of charity and common decency draw what force they have from the strange, self-animating flame-blossoms and chemical serpents in the burning laboratory where the Negro stableman saves his employer's son and is himself deformed; without these actual terrors we are left with a sentimental parable more outlined (though it is brilliantly outlined) than told.

Crane's poems offer even purer instances of his puzzlingly inconclusive power. They come to life as they manage to convey the sense of some self-contained and irreversible apprehension; otherwise they offer remarks. The opening lines of *The Black Riders* (1895), Crane's first collection, are characteristic:

> Black riders came from the sea.
> There was clang and clang of spear and shield,
> And clash and clash of hoof and heel. . . .

—a setting out of autonomous images which the inert closing lines of this first poem ("Thus the ride of sin") simply has no necessary contact with. These transfiguring lines from the volume, *War Is Kind* (1899), are less spectacular but have the same visionary autonomy:

> In the morning
> A noise of men and work came the clear blue miles
> And the little black cities were apparent.

Even the many poems about God and faith divide according to the same general measure. There are those that make assertions, and there are those (or passages in them) that compose incontrovertible images. The significant difference between, on the one hand,

> God lay dead in heaven,

or,

> Well, then, I hate Thee, unrighteous picture;
> Wicked image, I hate Thee,

and, on the other,

Withal there is One whom I fear;
I fear to see grief upon that face,

is a difference not primarily of argument or emotion but of imaginative realization.

Crane's is not in any case a religious sensibility, the subject of these poems notwithstanding. He himself is not possessed in consciousness by the images his poems articulate. The visionary is rather his way of reporting, of proving his presence on the scene of this world. He seems unable to verify his awareness of phenomena except by turning them into something rich and strange, forcibly removing them from the familiar continuum of life and consciousness, imputing to them the fixity of the legendary, the already translated. What results is of course a kind of idealization. The real itself is not real until it has been glazed into purity. "One feels," V. S. Pritchett remarks, "that Crane stands apart from his scene and that a great skill has taken the place of an innured contemplation of the subject." It is hardly literature that he is involved in. It is rather a way of living by means of words and phrases; Crane is our first Action Writer, our New Jersey, Protestant, newspaper-office Rimbaud. Though his writing frequently reproduces certain general patterns of subjective experience—violation, abandonment, the defensive effort to survive, the overwrought sequences of deprivation, yearning, and despair—what it regularly lacks is the inward organization that gives the structures of developed art their power to coerce, and hold, attention, and that comes into them dialectically, by way of some renewed encounter with the material occasion or with other possibilities of statement or simply with their own formal advance. That is why in the general development of modern Anglo-American writing Crane's remarkable achievement is marginal and diversionary, but at the same time—a little like that of Hemingway, and for like reasons—disproportionately influential. At certain moments achievement of this kind can be a liberation. For whatever else one may decide about Crane's work, the best of it must be granted that minimal integrity of voice and registered perception the securing of which, in the general slackness of the '90s, was bound to be a precedent of genuine value.

NOTES

1. Crane himself was aware of the general danger in this quarter. In a letter of 1894 he speaks of having "renounced the clever school in literature," along with the "clever Rudyard-Kipling style" he had begun with.

2. It is of interest that one important influence on *The Red Badge* appears to have been the richly illustrated series, *Battles and Leaders of the Civil War* (4 volumes, 1884-1888).

2. *English Estimates-Reminiscences*

a. H. G. Wells on Stephen Crane

The untimely death at thirty [twenty-eight] of Stephen Crane robs English literature of an interesting and significant figure, and the little world of those who write, of a stout friend and a pleasant comrade. For a year and more he had been ailing. The bitter hardships of his Cuban expedition had set its mark upon mind and body alike, and the slow darkling of the shadow upon him must have been evident to all who were not blinded by their confidence in what he was yet to do. Altogether, I knew Crane for less than a year, and I saw him for the last time hardly more than seven weeks ago. He was then in a hotel at Dover, lying still and comfortably wrapped about, before an open window and the calm and spacious sea. If you would figure him as I saw him, you must think of him as a face of a type very typically American, long and spare, with very straight hair and straight features and long, quiet hands and hollow eyes, moving slowly, smiling and speaking slowly, with that deliberate New Jersey manner he had, and lapsing from speech again into a quiet contemplation of his ancient enemy. For it was the sea that had taken his strength, the same sea that now shone, level waters beyond level waters, with here and there a minute, shining ship, warm and tranquil beneath the tranquil evening sky. Yet I felt scarcely a suspicion then that this was a last meeting. One might have seen it all, perhaps. He was thin and gaunt and wasted, too weak for more than a remembered jest and a greeting and good wishes. It did not seem to me in any way credible that he would reach his refuge in the Black Forest only to die at the journey's end. It will be a long time yet before I can fully realize that he is no longer a contemporary of mine; that the last I saw of him was, indeed, final and complete.

Though my personal acquaintance with Crane was so soon truncated, I have followed his work for all the four years it has been known in England. I have always been proud, and now I am glad, that, however obscurely, I also was in the first chorus of welcome

Reprinted from: "Stephen Crane: From An English Standpoint," *The North American Review*, CLXXI (August 1900), 233-242.

that met his coming. It is, perhaps, no great distinction for me; he was abundantly praised; but, at least, I was early and willing to praise him when I was wont to be youthfully jealous of my praises. His success in England began with "The Red Badge of Courage," which did, indeed, more completely than any other book has done for many years, taken the reading public by storm. Its freshness of method, its vigor of imagination, its force of color and its essential freedom from many traditions that dominate this side of the Atlantic, came—in spite of the previous shock of Mr. Kipling—with a positive effect of impact. It was a new thing, in a new school. When one looked for sources, one thought at once of Tolstoi; but, though it was clear that Tolstoi had exerted a powerful influence upon the conception, if not the actual writing, of the book, there still remained something entirely original and novel. To a certain extent, of course, that was the new man as an individual; but, to at least an equal extent, it was the new man as a typical young American, free at last, as no generation of Americans have been free before, of any regard for English criticism, comment or tradition, and applying to literary work the conception and theories of the cosmopolitan studio with a quite American directness and vigor. For the great influence of the studio on Crane cannot be ignored; in the persistent selection of the essential elements of an impression, in the ruthless exclusion of mere information, in the direct vigor with which the selected points are made, there is Whistler even more than there is Tolstoi in "The Red Badge of Courage." And witness this, taken almost haphazard:

"At nightfall the column broke into regimental pieces, and the fragments went into the fields to camp. Tents sprang up like strange plants. Camp fires, like red, peculiar blossoms, dotted the night. * * * From this little distance the many fires, with the black forms of men passing to and fro before the crimson rays, made weird and satanic effects."

And here again; consider the daring departure from all academic requirements, in this void countenance:

"A warm and strong hand clasped the youth's languid fingers for an instant, and then he heard a cheerful and audacious whistling as the man strode away. As he who had so befriended him was thus passing out of his life, it suddenly occurred to the youth that he had not once seen his face."

I do not propose to add anything here to the mass of criticism upon this remarkable book. Like everything else which has been abundantly praised, it has occasionally been praised "all wrong;" and I suppose that it must have been said hundreds of times that this book is a subjective study of the typical soldier in war. But Mr. George Wyndham, himself a soldier of experience, has pointed out in an admirable preface to a re-issue of this and other of Crane's war studies [*Pictures of War*], that the hero of the "Red Badge" is, and is intended to be, altogether a more sensitive and imaginative person than the ordinary man. He is the idealist, the dreamer of boastful things brought suddenly to the test of danger and swift occasions and the presence of death. To this theme Crane returned several times, and particularly in a story called "Death and the Child" that was written after the Greek war. That story is considered by very many of Crane's admirers as absolutely his best. I have carefully re-read it in deference to opinions I am bound to respect, but I still find it inferior to the earlier work. The generalized application is, to my taste, a little too evidently underlined; there is just that touch of insistence that prevails so painfully at times in Victor Hugo's work, as of a writer not sure of his reader, not happy in his reader and seeking to drive his implication (of which also he is not quite sure) home. The child is not a natural child; there is no happy touch to make it personally alive; it is THE CHILD, something unfalteringly big; a large, pink, generalized thing, I cannot help but see it, after the fashion of a Vatican cherub. The fugitive runs panting to where, all innocent of the battle about it, it plays; and he falls down breathless to be asked, "Are you a man?" One sees the intention clearly enough; but in the later story it seems to me there is a new ingredient that is absent from the earlier stories, an ingredient imposed on Crane's natural genius from without—a concession to the demands of a criticism it had been wiser, if less modest, in him to disregard —criticism that missed this quality of generalization and demanded it, even though it had to be artificially and deliberately introduced.

Following hard upon the appearance of "The Red Badge of Courage" in England came reprints of two books, "Maggie" and

"George's Mother," that had already appeared in America six years earlier.* Their reception gave Crane his first taste of the peculiarities of the new public he had come upon. These stories seem to me in no way inferior to the "Red Badge;" and at times there are passages, the lament of Maggie's mother at the end of "Maggie," for example, that it would be hard to beat by any passage from the later book. But on all hands came discouragement or tepid praise. The fact of it is, there had been almost an orgie of praise—for England, that is; and ideas and adjectives and phrases were exhausted. To write further long reviews on works displaying the same qualities as had been already amply discussed in the notices of the "Red Badge" would be difficult and laborious; while to admit an equal excellence and deny an equal prominence would be absurd. But to treat these stories as early work, to find them immature, dismiss them and proceed to fresher topics, was obvious and convenient. So it was, I uncharitably imagine, that these two tales have been overshadowed and are still comparatively unknown. Yet, they are absolutely essential to a just understanding of Crane. In these stories, and in these alone, he achieved tenderness and a compulsion of sympathy for other than vehement emotions, qualities that the readers of "The Third Violet" and "On Active Service," his later love stories, might well imagine beyond his reach.

And upon the appearance of these books in England came what, in my present mood, I cannot but consider as the great blunder and misfortune of Crane's life. It is a trait of the public we writers serve, that to please it is to run the gravest risk of never writing again. Through a hundred channels and with a hundred varieties of seduction and compulsion, the public seeks to induce its favorite to do something else—to act, to lecture, to travel, to jump down volcanoes or perform in music halls, to do anything, rather than to possess his soul in peace and to pursue the work he was meant to do. Indeed, this modern public is as violently experimental with its writers as a little child with a kitten. It is animated, above all things, by an insatiable desire to plunge its victim into novel surroundings, and watch how he feels. And since Crane had demonstrated, beyond all cavil, that he could sit at home and, with nothing but his wonder-

---

* The original *Maggie* was privately printed in 1893 in the United States. The revised *Maggie* and *George's Mother* were first published in 1896 in both the United States and England. [*Editor.*]

ful brain and his wonderful induction from recorded things, build
up the truest and most convincing picture of war; since he was a
fastidious and careful worker, intensely subjective in his mental habit;
since he was a man of fragile physique and of that unreasonable
courage that will wreck the strongest physique; and since, moreover,
he was habitually a bad traveller, losing trains and luggage and
missing connections even in the orderly circumstances of peace, it
was clearly the most reasonable thing in the world to propose, it
was received with the applause of two hemispheres as a most right
and proper thing, that he should go as a war correspondent, first
to Greece and then to Cuba. Thereby, and for nothing but disappointment and bitterness, he utterly wrecked his health. He came
into comparison with men as entirely his masters in this work as
he was the master of all men in his own; and I read even in the
most punctual of his obituary notices the admission of his journalistic
failure. I have read, too, that he brought back nothing from these
expeditions. But, indeed, even not counting his death, he brought
back much. On his way home from Cuba he was wrecked,* and he
wrote the story ["The Open Boat"] of the nights and days that
followed the sinking of the ship with a simplicity and vigor that
even he cannot rival elsewhere.

"The Open Boat" is to my mind, beyond all question, the crown
of all his work. It has all the stark power of the earlier stories, with
a new element of restraint; the color is as full and strong as ever,
fuller and stronger, indeed; but those chromatic splashes that at
times deafen and confuse in "The Red Badge," those images that
astonish rather than enlighten, are disciplined and controlled. "That
and 'Flanagan'," he told me, with a philosophical laugh, "was all
I got out of Cuba." I cannot say whether they were worth the price,
but I am convinced that these two things are as immortal as any
work of any living man. And the way "The Open Boat" begins, no
stress, plain—even a little gray and flattish. . . .

* * *

From that beginning, the story mounts and mounts over the
waves, wave frothing after wave, each wave a threat, and the men
toil and toil and toil again; by insensible degrees the day lights

---

* Crane was on his way to Cuba from Florida, not on his way home from Cuba.
[*Editor.*]

the waves to green and olive, and the foam grows dazzling. Then as the long day draws out, they come toward the land.

* * *

"The Open Boat" gives its title to a volume containing, in addition to that and "Flanagan," ["Flanagan and His Short Filibustering Adventure"], certain short pieces. One of these others, at least, is also to my mind a perfect thing, "The Wise Men." It tells of the race between two bar-tenders in the city of Mexico, and I cannot imagine how it could possibly have been better told. And in this volume, too, is that other masterpiece—the one I deny—"Death and the Child."

Now I do not know how Crane took the reception of this book, for he was not the man to babble of his wrongs; but I cannot conceive how it could have been anything but a grave disappointment to him. To use the silly phrase of the literary shopman, "the vogue of the short story" was already over; rubbish, pure rubbish, provided only it was lengthy, had resumed its former precedence again in the reviews, in the publishers' advertisements and on the library and book-sellers' counters. The book was taken as a trivial by-product, its author was exhorted to abandon this production of "brilliant fragments"—anything less than fifty thousand words is a fragment to the writer of literary columns—and to make that "sustained effort," that architectural undertaking, that alone impresses the commercial mind. Of course, the man who can call "The Open Boat" a brilliant fragment would reproach Rodin for not completing the edifice his brilliant fragments of statuary are presumably intended to adorn, and would sigh, with the late Mr. Ruskin for the day when Mr. Whistler would "finish" his pictures. Moreover, he was strongly advised—just as they have advised Mr. Kipling—to embark upon a novel. And from other quarters, where a finer wisdom might have been displayed, he learned that the things he had written were not "short stories" at all; they were "sketches" perhaps, "anecdotes" —just as they call Mr. Kipling's short stories "anecdotes;" and it was insinuated that for him also the true, the ineffable "short story" was beyond his reach. I think it is indisputable that the quality of this reception, which a more self-satisfied or less sensitive man than Crane might have ignored, did react very unfavorably upon his work. They put him out of conceit with these brief intense efforts in which his peculiar strength was displayed.

It was probably such influence that led him to write "The Third Violet." I do not know certainly, but I imagine, that the book was to be a demonstration, and it is not a successful demonstration, that Crane could write a charming love story. It is the very simple affair of an art student and a summer boarder, with the more superficial incidents of their petty encounters set forth in a forcible, objective manner that is curiously hard and unsympathetic. The characters act, and on reflection one admits they act, *true,* but the play of their emotions goes on behind the curtain of the style, and all the enrichments of imaginative appeal that make love beautiful are omitted. Yet, though the story as a whole fails to satisfy, there are many isolated portions of altogether happy effectiveness, a certain ride behind an ox cart, for example. Much more surely is "On Active Service" an effort, and in places a painful effort, to fit his peculiar gift to the uncongenial conditions of popular acceptance. It is the least capable and least satisfactory of all Crane's work.

While these later books were appearing, and right up to his last fatal illness, Crane continued to produce fresh war pictures that show little or no falling off in vigor of imagination and handling; and, in addition, he was experimenting with verse. In that litle stone-blue volume, "War is Kind," and in the earlier "Black Riders," the reader will find a series of acute and vivid impressions and many of the finer qualities of Crane's descriptive prose, but he will not find any novel delights of melody or cadence or any fresh aspects of Crane's personality. There remain some children's stories [*Whilomville Stories*] to be published and an unfinished romance [*The O'Ruddy*]. With that the tale of his published work ends, and the career of one of the most brilliant, most significant and most distinctively American of all English writers comes to its unanticipated *finis.*

It would be absurd, here and now, to attempt to apportion any relativity of importance to Crane, to say that he was greater than A. or less important than B. That class-list business is, indeed, best left forever to the newspaper plebiscite and the library statistician; among artists, whose sole, just claim to recognition and whose sole title to immortality must necessarily be the possession of unique qualities, that is to say, of unclassifiable factors, these gradations are absurd. Suffice it that, even before his death, Crane's right to be counted in the hierarchy of those who have made a permanent addition to the great and growing fabric of English letters was not only assured, but conceded. To define his position in time, however, and in relation to periods and modes of writing will be a more reasonable undertaking; and it seems to me that, when at last the true proportions can be seen, Crane will be found to occupy a position singularly cardinal. He was a New Englander of Puritan lineage,* and the son of a long tradition of literature. There had been many Cranes who wrote before him. He has shown me a shelf of books, for the most part the pious and theological works of various antecedent Stephen Cranes. He had been at some pains to gather together these alien products of his kin. For the most part they seemed little, insignificant books, and one opened them to read the beaten *clichés,* the battered outworn phrases, of a movement that has ebbed. Their very size and binding suggested a dying impulse, that very same impulse that in its prime had carried the magnificence of Milton's imagery and the pomp and splendors of Milton's prose. In Crane that impulse was altogether dead. He began stark—I find all through this brief notice I have been repeating that in a dozen disguises, "freedom from tradition," "absolute directness" and the like as though he came into the world of letters without ever a predecessor. In style, in method and in all that is distinctively *not* found in his books, he is sharply defined, the expression in literary art of certain enormous repudiations. Was ever a man before who wrote of battles so abundantly as he has done, and never had a word, never a word from first to last, of the purpose and justification of the war? And of the God of Battles, no more than the battered name; "Hully Gee!"—the lingering trace of the Deity! And of the sensuousness and tenderness of love, so much as one can find in "The Third Violet!" Any richness of allusion, any melody or balance of phrase, the half quotation that refracts and softens and enriches the statement, the momentary digression that opens like a window upon beautiful or distant things, are not merely absent, but obviously and sedulously avoided. It is as if the racial thought and tradition had been razed from his mind and its site ploughed and salted. He is more than himself in this; he is the first expression of the opening mind of a new period, or, at least, the early emphatic phase of a new initiative—beginning, as a growing mind must needs begin, with the record of impressions, a record of a vigor and intensity beyond all precedent.

---

* Most of the earlier Cranes first settled in New Jersey, though one branch of the family settled, for a time, in Connecticut. [*Editor.*]

b. *Joseph Conrad on Stephen Crane*

My acquaintance with Crane was brought about by Mr. S. S. Pawling, partner in the publishing firm of Mr. William Heinemann.

One day Mr. Pawling said to me: "Stephen Crane has arrived in England. I asked him if there was anybody he wanted to meet and he mentioned two names. One of them was yours." I had then just been reading, like the rest of the world, Crane's *Red Badge of Courage.* The subject of that story was war, from the point of view of an individual soldier's emotions. That individual (he remains nameless throughout*) was interesting enough in himself, but on turning over the pages of that little book which had for the moment secured such a noisy recognition I had been even more interested in the personality of the writer. The picture of a simple and untried youth becoming through the needs of his country part of a great fighting machine was presented with an earnestness of purpose, a sense of tragic issues, and an imaginative force of expression which struck me as quite uncommon and altogether worthy of admiration.

Apparently Stephen Crane had received a favourable impression from reading the *Nigger of the Narcissus,* a book of mine which had also been published lately. I was truly pleased to hear this.

On my next visit to town we met at a lunch. I saw a young man of medium stature and slender build, with very steady, penetrating blue eyes, the eyes of a being who not only sees visions but can brood over them to some purpose.

He had indeed a wonderful power of vision, which he applied to the things of this earth and of our mortal humanity with a penetrating force that seemed to reach within life's appearances and forms the very spirit of their truth. His ignorance of the world at large—he had seen very little of it—did not stand in the way of his imaginative grasp of facts, events, and picturesque men.

His manner was very quiet, his personality at first sight interesting, and he talked slowly with an intonation which on some people, mainly Americans, had, I believe, a jarring effect. But not on me. Whatever he said had a personal note, and he expressed himself

---

Reprinted from: "Stephen Crane: A Note Without Dates," *The London Mercury,* I (December 1919), 192-193.
* The "individual," Henry Fleming, was not left nameless, nor were the other characters of *The Red Badge.* Conrad repeated this error in other places. [*Editor.*]

with a graphic simplicity which was extremely engaging. He knew little of literature, either of his own country or of any other, but he was himself a wonderful artist in words whenever he took a pen into his hand. Then his gift came out—and it was seen to be much more than mere felicity of language. His impressionism of phrase went really deeper than the surface. In his writing he was very sure of his effects. I don't think he was ever in doubt about what he could do. Yet it often seemed to me that he was but half aware of the exceptional quality of his achievement.

This achievement was curtailed by his early death. It was a great loss to his friends, but perhaps not so much to literature. I think that he had given his measure fully in the few books he had the time to write. Let me not be misunderstood: the loss was great, but it was the loss of the delight his art could give, not the loss of any further possible revelation. As to himself, who can say how much he gained or lost by quitting so early this world of the living, which he knew how to set before us in terms of his own artistic vision? Perhaps he did not lose a great deal. The recognition he was accorded was rather languid and given him grudgingly. The worthiest welcome he secured for his tales in this country was from Mr. W. Henley in the *New Review* and later, towards the end of his life, from the late Mr. William Blackwood in his magazine. For the rest I must say that during his sojourn in England he had the misfortune to be, as the French say, *mal entouré*. He was beset by people who understood not the quality of his genius and were antagonistic to the deeper fineness of his nature. Some of them have died since, but dead or alive they are not worth speaking about now. I don't think he had any illusions about them himself; yet there was a strain of good-nature and perhaps of weakness in his character which prevented him from shaking himself free from their worthless and patronising attentions, which in those days caused me much secret irritation whenever I stayed with him in either of his English homes. My wife and I like best to remember him riding to meet us at the gate of the Park at Brede. Born master of his sincere impressions he was also a born horseman. He never appeared so happy or so much to advantage as on the back of a horse. He had formed the project of teaching my eldest boy to ride and meantime, when the child was about two years old, presented him with his first dog.

I saw Stephen Crane a few days after his first arrival in London. I saw him for the last time on his last day in England. It was in Dover, in a big hotel, in a bedroom with a large window looking on to the sea. He had been very ill and Mrs. Crane was taking him to some place in Germany, but one glance at that wasted face was enough to tell me that it was the most forlorn of all hopes. The last words he breathed out to me were: "I am tired. Give my love to your wife and child." When I stopped at the door for another look I saw that he had turned his head on the pillow and was staring wistfully out of the window at the sails of a cutter yacht that glided slowly across the frame, like a dim shadow against a grey sky.

Those who have read his little tale, *Horses,* and the story, *The Open Boat,* in the volume of that name, know with what fine understanding he loved horses and the sea. And his passage on this earth was like that of a horseman riding swiftly in the dawn of a day fated to be short and without sunshine.

c. Edward Garnett on Stephen Crane

A short time ago I picked up on a London book-stall, the first edition of "The Red Badge of Courage." Its price was sixpence. Obviously the bookseller lay no store by it, for the book had been thrown on the top of a parcel of paper-covered novels among the waifs and strays of literature. Chancing to meet a young American poet I asked him, curiously, how his countrymen esteemed today that intensely original genius, Crane, the creator of "The Open Boat," "George's Mother," "Maggie," "The Black Riders." He answered, "One rarely hears Crane's name mentioned in America. His work is almost forgotten, but I believe it has a small, select circle of admirers." I confess I was amused, especially when a little later a first edition of "Almayer's Folly," the first Conrad, was sold at auction for five hundred times the amount of the early Crane. And Conrad was also amused when I told him, and we suggested a title for an allegorical picture yet to be painted the Apotheosis of an Author crowned by Fashion, Merit and Midas. For we both had in mind the years when the critics hailed "The Nigger of the Narcissus" as a worthy pendent to the battle-pictures presented in "The Red Badge of Courage," and when Sir, then Mr. Arthur Quiller-Couch spoke of "The Nigger," as "having something of Crane's insistence."

We talked together over Crane and his work and cast our memories back over twenty years when we were both in touch with "poor Steve," he more than I. And we agreed that within its peculiar limited compass Crane's genius was unique. Crane, when living at Oxted, was a neighbour of mine, and one day, on my happening to describe to him an ancient Sussex house, noble and grey with the passage of five hundred years, nothing would satisfy him but that he must become the tenant of Brede Place. It was the lure of romance that always thrilled Crane's blood, and Brede Place had had indeed, an unlucky, chequered history. I saw Crane last, when he lay dying there, the day before his wife was transporting him, on a stretcher bed, to a health resort in the Black Forest, in a vain effort to arrest

Reprinted from: "Stephen Crane And His Work," *Friday Nights: Literary Criticisms and Appreciations* [First Series]. New York: Alfred A. Knopf, Inc., 1922, pp. 201-217.

the fatal disease, and I see again his bloodless face and the burning intensity of his eyes. He had lived at too high pressure and his consumptive physique was ravaged by the exhausting strain of his passionate life, and sapped by the hardships of the Cuban campaign, which he suffered as a war-correspondent. Crane's strange eyes, with their intensely concentrated gaze, were those of a genius and I recall how on his first visit to our house I was so struck by the exquisite symmetry of his brow and temples, that I failed to note, what a lady pointed out when he had left, the looseness of his mouth. Yes, the intensity of genius burned in his eyes, and his weak lips betrayed his unrestrained temperament. Crane's genius, his feeling for style were wholly intuitive and no study had fostered them. On first reading "The Red Badge of Courage," I concluded he had been influenced by the Russian masters, but I learned when I met him, that he had never read a line of them. Would that he had! For Crane, as Conrad reminded me, never knew how good his best work was. He simply never knew. He never recognized that in the volume "The Open Boat," he had achieved the perfection of his method. If he had comprehended that in "The Bride Comes to Yellow Sky" and in "Death and the Child" he had attained then, his high water mark, he might perhaps have worked forward along the lines of patient, ascending effort; but after "The Open Boat," 1898, his work dropped to lower levels. He wrote too much, he wrote against time, and he wrote while dunned for money. At first sight it appears astonishing that the creator of such a miracle of style as "The Bride Comes to Yellow Sky" should publish in the same year so mediocre a novel as "On Active Service." But Crane ought never to have essayed the form of the novel. He had not handled it satisfactorily in "The Third Violet," 1897, a love story charming in its impressionistic lightness of touch, but lacking in force, in concentration, in characterization. My view of Crane as a born impressionist and master of the short story, I emphasized in an Appreciation in 1898,* and since it is germane to my purpose here, I reprint the criticism:—

---

* This appeared in *The Academy* [London], LV (December 17, 1898), 483-484. [*Editor.*]

MR. STEPHEN CRANE

AN APPRECIATION

"What Mr. Crane has got to do is very simple: he must not mix reporting with his writing. To other artists the word must often be passed: rest, work at your art, live more; but Mr. Crane has no need of cultivating his technique, no need of resting, no need of searching wide for experiences. In his art he is unique. Its certainty, its justness, its peculiar perfection of power arrived at its birth, or at least at that precise moment in its life when other artists—and great artists too—were preparing themselves for the long and difficult conquest of their art. I cannot remember a parallel case in the literary history of fiction. Maupassant, Meredith, Mr. James, Mr. Howells, Tolstoy, all were learning their expression at the age where Mr. Crane had achieved his, achieved it triumphantly. Mr. Crane has no need to learn anything. His technique is absolutely his own, and by its innate laws of being has arrived at a perfect fulness of power. What he has not got he has no power of acquiring. He has no need to acquire it. To say to Mr. Crane, 'You are too much anything, or too little anything; you need concentration, or depth, subtlety, or restraint,' would be absurd; his art is just in itself, rhythmical, self-poising as is the art of a perfect dancer. There are no false steps, no excesses. And, of course, his art is strictly limited. We would define him by saying he is the perfect artist and interpreter of the surfaces of life. And that explains why he so swiftly attained his peculiar power, and what is the realm his art commands, and his limitations.

"Take 'George's Mother,' for example—a tale which I believe he wrote at the ridiculous age of twenty-one. In *method* it is a masterpiece. It is a story dealing simply with the relations between an old woman and her son, who live together in a New York tenement block. An ordinary artist would seek to dive into the mind of the old woman, to follow its workings hidden under the deceitful appearances of things, under the pressure of her surroundings. A great artist would so recreate her life that its griefs and joys became significant of the griefs and joys of all motherhood on earth. But Mr. Crane does neither. He simply reproduces the surfaces of the individual life in so marvellous a way that the manner in which the old woman washes up the crockery, for example, gives us the essentials. To dive into the hidden life is, of course, for the artist a great temptation and a great danger—the values of the picture speedily get wrong, and the artist, seeking to interpret life, departs from the truth of nature. The rare thing about Mr. Crane's art is that he keeps closer to the surface than any living writer, and, like the great portrait-painters, to a great extent makes the surface betray the depths. But, of course, the written word in the hands of the greatest artist often deals directly with the depths, plunges us into the rich depths of consciousness that cannot be more than hinted at by the surface; and it is precisely here that Mr. Crane's natural limitation must come in. At the supreme height of art the great masters so plough up the depths of life that the astonished spectator loses sight of the individual life altogether, and has the entrancing sense that all life is really one and the same thing, and is there manifesting itself before him. He feels that, for example, when he watches Duse at her best, or when he stands before Leonardo da Vinci's 'La Joconda' in the Louvre and is absorbed by it. I do not think that Mr. Crane is ever great in the sense of so fusing all the riches of the consciousness into a whole, that the reader is struck dumb as by an inevitable revelation; but he is undoubtedly such an interpreter of the significant surface of things that in a few strokes he gives us an amazing insight into what the individual life is. And he does it all straight from the surface; a few oaths, a genius for slang, an exquisite and unique faculty of exposing an individual scene by an odd simile, a power of interpreting a face or an action, a keen realizing of the primitive emotions—that is Mr. Crane's talent. In 'The Bride Comes to Yellow Sky,' for example, the art is simply immense. There is a page and a half of conversation at the end of this short story of seventeen pages which, as a dialogue revealing the whole inside of the situation, is a lesson to any artist living. And the last line of this story, by the gift peculiar to the author of using some odd simile which cunningly condenses the feeling of the situation, defies analysis altogether. Foolish people may call Mr. Crane a reporter of genius; but nothing could be more untrue. He is thrown away as a picturesque reporter: a secondary style of art, of which, let us say, Mr. G. W. Steevens is, perhaps, the ablest exponent of today, and which is the heavy clay of Mr. Kipling's talent. Mr. Crane's technique is far superior to Mr. Kipling's, but he does not experiment ambitiously in various styles and develop in new directions as Mr. Kipling has done. I do not think that Mr. Crane will or can develop further. Again, I do not think he has the building faculty, or that he will ever do better in constructing a perfect whole out of many parts than he has arrived at in 'The Red Badge of Courage.' That book was a series of episodic scenes, all melting naturally into one another and forming a just whole; but it was not constructed, in any sense of the word. And further, Mr. Crane does not show any faculty of taking his characters and revealing in them deep mysterious worlds of human nature, of developing fresh riches in them, acting under the pressure of circumstance. His imaginative analysis of his own nature on a battlefield is, of course, the one exception. And similarly the great artist's arrangement of complex effects, striking contrasts, exquisite grouping of devices, is lacking in him. His art does not include the necessity for complex arrangements; his sure instinct tells him never to quit the passing moment of life, to hold fast by simple situations, to reproduce the episodic, fragmentary nature of life in such artistic sequence that it stands in place of the architectural masses and co-ordinated structures of the great artists. He is the chief impressionist of our day as Sterne was the great impressionist, in a different manner, of his day. If he fails in anything he undertakes, it will be through abandoning the style he has invented. He may, perhaps, fail by and by, through using up the picturesque phases of the environment that nurtured him, as Swinburne came to a stop directly he had rung the changes a certain number of times on the fresh rhythms and phrases he had created. But that time is not yet, and every artist of a special unique faculty has that prospect before him. Mr. Crane's talent is unique; nobody can question that. America may well be proud of him, for he has just that perfect mastery of form which artists of the Latin races often produce, but the Teutonic and Anglo-Saxon races very rarely. And undoubtedly of the young school of American artists Mr. Crane is the genius—the others have their talents."

On the above criticism Conrad wrote me at the time, "The Crane thing is just—precisely just a ray of light flashed in and showing all there is."

II

But when I wrote that criticism, that journalistic novel "On Active Service" was yet to be published, and I did not fully comprehend Crane's training and his circumstances. I sounded a warning note against "reporting," but though he had emerged from journalism, he was still haunted by journalism and was encircled by a—well! by a crew of journalists. I remarked, "I do not think Mr. Crane can or will develop further," but pressing him were duns and debts and beckoning him was the glamour of the war-correspondent's life, and before him were editors ready for ephemeral stuff, while they shook their heads sadly over such perfect gems as "The Pace of Youth." Crane had seen much for a man of his years, but he was still thirsting for adventure and the life of action, and he had no time to digest his experiences, to reflect, to incubate and fashion his work at leisure. In the two or three hurried years that remained to him after the publication of "The Open Boat," he created some notable things, but the dice of fate were loaded by all his circumstances against his development as craftsman.

We must therefore be thankful that his instinct for style emerged when his psychological genius broke out and so often possessed him in the teeth of the great stucco gods and the chinking of brass in the market place. He had written his best things without advice or encouragement, urged by the demon within him, and his genius burned clear, with its passionate individuality, defying all the inhibitions and conventions of New England. Was that genius ever appreciated by America? I doubt it, though Americans were forced to accept him, first because of the fame which "The Red Badge of Courage" brought Crane in England, and secondary because his subject was the American Civil War, a subject that could not be disregarded. On re-reading "The Red Badge of Courage" I am more than ever struck by the genius with which Crane, in imagination, pierced to the essentials of War. Without any experience of war at the time, Crane was essentially true to the psychological core of war —if not to actualities. He naturally underestimated the checks placed by physical strain and fatigue on the faculties, as well as war's malignant, cold ironies, its prosaic dreadfulness, its dreary, deadening tedium. But as Goethe has pointed out, the artist has a license to ignore actualities, if he is obeying inner, aesthetic laws. And Crane's subject was the passions, the passions of destruction, fear, pride, rage, shame and exaltation in the heat of action. The deep artistic unity of "The Red Badge of Courage," is fused in its flaming, spiritual intensity, in the fiery ardour with which the shock of the Federal and Confederate armies is imaged. The torrential force and impetus, the check, sullen recoil and reforming of shattered regiments, and the

renewed onslaught and obstinate resistance of brigades and divisions
are visualized with extraordinary force and colour. If the sordid
grimness of carnage, is partially screened, the feeling of War's cumulative rapacity, of its breaking pressure and fluctuating tension is caught
with wonderful fervour and freshness of style. It is of course, the
work of ardent youth, but when Crane returned from the Graeco-
Turkish war he said to Conrad, "My picture of war was all right!
I have found it as I imagined it." And his imaginative picture he
supplemented, four years later, in that penetrating, sombre, realistic
piece "Memories of War" ["War Memories"] in "Wounds in the
Rain," his reminiscences of the Cuban campaign that in fact had
set death's secret mark already on him. I may note, too, how Crane,
sitting in our garden, described that on questioning Veterans of the
Civil War about their feelings when fighting, he could get nothing
out of them but one thing, viz., "We just went there and did so
and so."

III

And here I must enlarge and amend my criticism of 1898 by
saying that two qualities in especial, combined to form Crane's
unique quality, viz. his wonderful insight into, and mastery of the
primary passions, and his irony deriding the swelling emotions of
the self. It is his irony that checks the emotional intensity of his
delineation, and suddenly reveals passion at high tension in the clutch
of the implacable tides of life. It is the perfect fusion of these two
forces of passion and irony that creates Crane's spiritual background,
and raises his work, at its finest, into the higher zone of man's tragic
conflict with the universe. His irony is seen in its purest form in
"Black Riders," 1896, a tiny collection of *vers libres*, as sharp in their
naked questioning as sword blades. These verses pierce with dreadful
simplicity certain illusions of unregarding sages, whose earnest com-
mentaries pour, and will continue to pour from the groaning press.
In "Maggie," 1896, that little masterpiece which drew the highest
tribute from the veteran, W. D. Howells, again it is the irony that
keeps in right perspective Crane's remorseless study of New York slum
and Bowery morals. The code of herd law by which the inexperienced
girl, Maggie, is pressed to death by her family, her lover and the
neighbours, is seen working with strange finality. The Bowery inhabitants, as we, can be nothing other than what they are; their human

nature responds inexorably to their brutal environment; the curious habits and code of the most primitive savage tribes could not be presented with a more impartial exactness, or with more sympathetic understanding.

"Maggie" is not a story *about* people; it is primitive human nature itself set down with perfect spontaneity and grace of handling. For pure aesthetic beauty and truth no Russian, not Tchehov himself, could have bettered this study, which, as Howells remarks, has the quality of Greek tragedy. The perfection of Crane's style, his unique quality, can, however, be studied best in "The Open Boat," 1898. Here he is again the pure artist, brilliant, remorselessly keen, delighting in life's passions and ironies, amusing, tragic or grimacing. Consider the nervous audacity, in phrasing, of the piece "An Experiment in Misery," which reveals the quality of chiaroscuro of a master's etching. No wonder the New York editors looked askance at such a break with tradition. How would they welcome the mocking verve and sinister undertone of such pieces as "A Man and Some Others," or the airy freshness and flying spontaneity of "The Pace of Youth"? In the volume "The Open Boat" Crane's style has a brilliancy of tone, a charming *timbre* peculiar to itself. As with Whistler, his personal note eschews everything obvious, everything inessential, as witness "Death and the Child," that haunting masterpiece where a child is playing with pebbles and sticks on the great mountain-side, while the smoke and din of the battlefield, in the plain below, hide the rival armies of pigmy men busy reaping with death. It is in the calm detachment of the little child playing, by which the artist secures his poetic background; man, pigmy man, watched impassively by the vast horizons of life, is the plaything of the Fates. The irony of life is here implicit. Perfect also is that marvel of felicitous observation "An Ominous Babe," where each touch is exquisitely final; a sketch in which the instincts of the babes betray the roots of all wars, past and to come. This gem ought to be in every anthology of American prose.

The descent of Crane in "On Active Service" 1898 [1899], to a clever, journalistic level, was strange. It was a lapse into superficiality; much stronger artistically was "The Monster," 1901, a book of stories of high psychological interest, which might indeed have made another man's reputation, but a book which is ordinary in atmosphere. The story "The Blue Hotel" is, indeed, a brilliant exploration of fear and its reactions, and "His New Mittens" is a delightful graphic study of boy morals, but we note that when Crane breathes an everyday, common atmosphere his aesthetic power always weakens. One would give the whole contents of "Whilomville Stories," 1902 [1900], for the five pages of "An Ominous Baby"; and the heterogeneous contents of "Last Words," 1902, a volume of sweepings from Crane's desk, kick the balance when weighed against the sketch "A Tale of Mere Chance," the babblings of a madman, which Dostoevsky might be proud to claim. The companion sketch "Manacled" (in "The Monster") bears also the authentic stamp of Crane's rare vision.

To conclude, if America has forgotten or neglects Crane's achievements, above all in "Maggie" and "The Open Boat," she does not yet deserve to produce artists of rank. Crane holds a peculiar niche in American literature. Where it is weak, viz. in the aesthetic and psychologically truthful delineation of passion, Stephen Crane is a master. And masters are rare, yes how rare are masters, let the men of Crane's generation, looking back on the twenty years since his death, decide.

d. H. E. Bates on Stephen Crane

But long before O. Henry's first volume, *Cabbages and Kings* (1904), America had thrown up a writer who may well have learned something from him, who was realist and humorist, who felt the same attraction for the life of East Side New York and Latin America, who handled vernacular joyously, and who possessed in a high degree the final quality that O. Henry lacked—for "here came a boy," says Mr. Thomas Beer,[1] "whose visual sense was unique in American writing, and whose mind by some inner process had stripped itself of all respect for those prevalent theories which have cursed the national fiction"—here, in short, arrived an ironist and a poet, Stephen Crane.

In the very early nineteen-twenties, as a boy of sixteen or seventeen, I picked up a story of Crane's called *Five White Mice,* and was electrified and troubled by that curious feeling, which you get sometimes on hearing a piece of music, of renewed acquaintance, of having taken the thing out of the storage of my own mind. I have no doubt now that this was purely the result of a certain quality of inevitability in Crane, a quality found less in prose literature than in poetry and music, where again and again the order of words and sounds has the air, most notably in Shakespeare and Mozart, of having been preordained. "An artist," says Miss Elizabeth Bowen in a study of Jane Austen,[2] "can never be fully conscious," but in Stephen Crane, author of some of the most remarkable short stories in American literature, you have an example of an artist who was really not conscious at all. "An artist, to be effective," says Miss Bowen again, "has to be half-critic. Fancy and reason ought to have equal strength." Crane's genius, on the other hand, was entirely intuitive. He apparently never knew, as Conrad once remarked, how good his best work was. He arrived (and the phenomenon is by no means rare in American literature) fully equipped; he had no need to improve, to work "forward on the lines of patient, ascending effort"; it was his tragedy that he began at the highest point of his achievement and thereafter could only descend.

Reprinted from: *The Modern Short Story: A Critical Survey.* London: Thomas Nelson and Sons Ltd., 1941, pp. 64-71. By permission of Laurence Pollinger Limited, Authors' Agents.

Crane's life and work have, in fact, all the picturesque and tragic qualities of the story of genius. In 1892 he wrote, in two days, a long-short story called *Maggie*. It is the story of a prostitute. Never, perhaps, in the history of the American short story has a story of a prostitute been written at a more inopportune moment. Fearlessly honest, almost cruelly realistic, without a touch of "visible sentiment," it gave both Crane's friends and the editors of the day an attack of the horrors. Up to that moment no one in American literature had done anything like it. Crane simply cut off from life—or rather the section of it called the Bowery—a lump of raw meat and slapped it down on the pages with neither dressing nor garnish, asking later of horrified editors, "You mean the story's too honest?" Crane, like all writers who desire simply to set down what they see as truthfully as possible, must have been inexpressibly shocked to find that there was any other viewpoint or standard. What he had done must have seemed to him, as to most rebel writers, a very natural thing. The Bowery was full of drunks, prostitutes, crooks, loafers, and everything else; they talked a strong unacademic language ("Look at deh dirt what yeh done me. Deh ol' woman 'ill be trowin' fits"); they lived a life of saloons and debt, violence and stench, tears and trouble. Crane simply set it down, doing more or less what someone else forty years later was to do, and be applauded for, in *Dead End*. To-day *Maggie*, though its essential qualities and naturalism and truth remain completely undated, has little power to shock. In 1892 Crane took it from publisher to publisher as if it were a bomb. Finally, in despair and with astonishing ignorance, Crane borrowed a thousand dollars and paid for the publication of the book himself. "The bill for printing eleven hundred copies was $869, and Appletons tell me that the printer must have made about $700 out of me. . . . A firm of religious and medical printers did me the dirt." A year after *Maggie* was written Crane had succeeded in disposing of a hundred copies of his mustard-covered volume at 50 cents a time, and thereafter entered "that period of starvation so much admired in the history of artists by comfortable critics."

It is now, of course, an old story that W. D. Howells went "sedately mad" over *Maggie,* and proceeded to champion Crane. This helped to make Crane's future, but it was not until Crane, partly it seems out of a bravado to do better than Zola and partly out of a worship of *War and Peace*, wrote *The Red Badge of Courage*, that things began to happen. That short novel is a picture, as realistic in its way as *Maggie,* of the American Civil War. It has some of the sardonic, brilliant, and embittered quality of Bierce; but what makes it exceptional is that though the Civil War was legally if not emotionally ended in 1865, Crane was not born until 1871. By an intensified imaginative approach Crane wrote a novel that could scarcely have been more real if he had fought in the conflict. It seemed like a piece of factual reporting inspired by memory. It had great success —but, what is more significant, Crane's only success in the novel-form. Subsequently his very great natural gift of visual writing was to express itself in the form for which it was inevitably adapted. In a couple of dozen stories Crane was to impress on the short story of his time, and indeed of all time, a new poetic irony.

What was Crane's method? Sometimes I doubt if he ever had a method, except that of direct transposition. Forty years after Crane's death Mr. Christopher Isherwood is expressing many a writer's feeling and attitude with the significant words, "Some day all this will have to be developed, carefully printed, fixed." [3] From that method Crane's method differed only in the speed of the recorded performance; there was no "some day," no sort of recollection in tranquillity. Long before the motion-picture camera shot the Bowery or the cacti of Mexico, Crane had shot them with an eye mounted on a swivel, so that his stories are made up, like a film, of a series of selected illuminatory shots, often of startling metaphorical vividness. But like the camera, Crane reflected the surface of things; the eye was so swift in its reflexes that the mind behind it apparently had no time to check, re-direct or re-shape the image it recorded. Such a powerful natural gift inevitably imposed its own limitations; the moment it ceased to function, for whatever reason, Crane's art became, as in the later novels and stories, as commonplace as calico:

> Although Whilomville was in no sense a summer resort, the advent of the warm season meant much to it, for then came visitors from the city—people of considerable confidence —alighting upon their country cousins. [4]

The method—if there is a method—is that of any tenth-rate provincial reporter without the wit to determine whether what he is doing is good or bad. To go back to almost any early sentence of Crane is to discover incredible contrast:

The sun swung steadily up the sky, and they knew it was broad day because the colour of the sea changed from slate to emerald green, streaked with amber lights, and the foam was like trembling snow.[5]

The sharp colouring, the vivid, awakening effect, are qualities that touch every page of this volume, *The Open Boat,* with a strange brilliance of personal tone. Here the Mexican stories are like flashes of sombre, tropical paint; *The Pace of Youth* is a perfect gem of comic spontaneity; in *Death and the Child* all the malignant terror and stupidity of war is shown up in a way that seems even more bitterly true to-day than when it was written; in *The Bride Comes to Yellow Sky* one is irresistibly reminded of certain well-directed Westerns, notably passages of *Stage-Coach,* in which a quality of poised and sinister tension is remarkably handled. In all these stories, and their companions, Crane is working with pictures; he is painting rather than writing; and no other writer in the whole of American literature, up to the end of the nineteenth century, can challenge his natural gift of swift impressionism.

Indeed Crane, like Bierce, belongs to to-day rather than to the day before yesterday. His method is closely aligned with the method now more and more in contemporary use; the method by which a story is told not by the carefully engineered plot but by the implication of certain isolated incidents, by the capture and significant arrangement of casual, episodic moments. It is the method by which the surface, however seemingly trivial or unimportant, is recorded in such a way as to interpret the individual emotional life below. Crane handed the basic point of that method to a generation that was not ready for it. Dying at the turn of the century, exhausted by disease, by over-work as a war-correspondent, and by a curious romantic passion for living grandly, Crane seems for a moment to mark the end of an age. In reality, I think, he anticipates one. He anticipates a generation of prose-writers who, in another age, would have found a more natural expression in lyric poetry and who now find, in the short story, their nearest working medium; he is the forerunner of writers who replace the use of the artificially concocted situation with the record of life seen at first hand, the picture "developed, carefully printed, fixed" and unmarred by the professional touch-up of the studio.

NOTES

1. Thomas Beer: *Stephen Crane: A Study* (Heinemann)
2. Derek Verschoyle: ed. *English Novelists* (Chatto and Windus)
3. Christopher Isherwood: *Good-bye to Berlin* (Hogarth)
4. Stephen Crane: *Whilomville Stories* (Harper and Orn, 1900)
5. Stephen Crane: *The Open Boat* (Heinemann, 1898)

e. V. S. Pritchett on Stephen Crane

Stephen Crane is one of those writers who, after one startling *tour de force,* burn themselves out. American journalism seized him, labelled him, thrust him into 'real life' as a war correspondent and annulled his imaginative talent and health. At 28 he was dead. Fittingly he has become a legend, a symbol of the misused artist. It is natural to compare Crane with his Scottish contemporary Stevenson, even though Crane disliked the comparison. The two looked astonishingly alike; they shocked and they charmed. Crane's Methodist background is matched by Stevenson's Calvinist upbringing and both men, we notice, moved to an ironical, unbelieving, moral dandyism which affected their prose. They believe in the word and not the Word and are constantly surprising us with phrases that come to an ear trained by the pulpit and the Bible. (In *The Red Badge of Courage,* Crane will refer to 'the remonstrance of the guns.') Crane is a very literary writer and he was compared, as he complained, to everyone from Tolstoy to Loti and Conrad. We get near his essence in H. G. Wells's remark that Crane's writing suggested Whistler rather than Tolstoy; Wells is the only European critic to have kept in mind the distinguishing American character of Crane's work.

The fact is that Crane was as profoundly American in his disposition for writing fable or poetic romance, as were Hawthorne, Poe, Melville, and Henry James. *The Red Badge of Courage* is not simply one of the earliest realistic novels about war written in Tolstoy's sceptical and anti-romantic spirit; it is a poetic fable about the attempt of a young man to discover a real identity in battle. The case becomes stranger when we remember that Crane wrote this book before he had had any real experience of war at all. (It was only after writing *The Red Badge of Courage* that he became a war correspondent.) A study of Tolstoy and a number of Memoirs of the American Civil War were his principal guides for a book that is a distillation for special ends; we are not told where the battle is, for what reasons, or, indeed, what the military situation is. In other novelists who write about war, from Vigny to Tolstoy, from Tolstoy to Hemingway and

Reprinted from: "Introduction," *The Red Badge of Courage and Other Stories.* London: Oxford University Press, 1960, pp. vii-xii. By permission of Oxford University Press.

Jules Romains, we *know* because they immerse us in what they lived. Crane, by an astonishing bound of imagination, has created battle as the simple and confused soldier sees it, but for reasons that are psychological, i.e. he is describing an interior battle, a battle of the spirit. The battle itself is compared at times with a mad religion, a sectarian conflict. The story might well be an artist's transposition of a dilemma of religious conscience; he has been romantically committed to 'fight the good fight,' is frightened into running away, and then has to reassemble his self-respect out of fear, doubt, and lies and learn how to live with his experience. It is quite true that all Crane's stories are concerned with fear, but with fear as a moral ferment, fear as the question put to the American dream of toughness, the emotion natural to the lonely uncertainty about who or what one is. The desire of all the Crane heroes is to find an identity by belonging to something. The theme is at the heart of *Maggie,* in the early Bowery Tales; in *The Red Badge of Courage,* and even in short, half-comic stories like *The Bride Comes to Yellow Sky, The Blue Hotel,* and the dramatic report of *The Open Boat.*

In his psychological observation and in his ear for speech Crane is one of the founders of American realism as we have known it since his time. In him it moves towards the fabulous and poetic; occasionally it sprawls and becomes rhetorical—see the end of *Maggie.* He appears to have been bedevilled by the theory that a writer must know from personal experience the thing he is writing about—a theory he certainly did not stick to in *The Red Badge of Courage* except in an esoteric sense, and did stick to in *The Open Boat* and his war reporting. The feeling for 'life' is related to anxiety about toughness and to the American approval of aggressiveness and to fighting as an initiation rite. Here is an excellent portrait of a barman from the Bowery:

> He sat on a table in the Johnson home, and dangled his check legs with an enticing nonchalance. His hair was curled down over his forehead in an oiled bang. His pugged nose seemed to revolt from contact with a bristling moustache of short, wire-like hairs. His blue double-breasted coat, edged with black braid, was buttoned close to a red puff tie, and his patent leather shoes looked like weapons. His mannerisms stamped him as a man who had a correct sense of his personal

superiority. There was valour and contempt for circumstances in the glance of his eye.

Shoes like weapons! Crane's feeling for fighting, temper, rage, and pride is innate. (He said he learned about battle on the football field.) Sticks, stones, rifles, artillery, dray horses—and once—a fire engine bashing its way along, became valued symbols. In the Bowery Tales the fighting, drunken slum characters occasionally suspect that there is something else in life besides brawling but they are not quite sure what it is. When Maggie's drunken mother becomes morally indignant at her fate and maudlin about her death, a dim, perverse light has been lit. Crane always sharpened the irony of his writing and rigorously censored what there was in him of the didactic. He is not cynical but his view of life is a hard one: we must fight to live but we shall get nothing out of it. We live and die alone. No one will ever know the secrets that both shame us and keep us going. Maggie is alone, the absurd Swede in *The Blue Hotel* is alone on his fatal see-saw of fear and bravado, the anonymous young man in *The Red Badge of Courage* is alone.

Crane was a brilliant impressionist and has strong affinities with the Impressionist painters. As they sought to record infinitesimal particles of light, he sought to record the innumerable glints of significant natural and psychological detail in the prolonged battle scene of *The Red Badge of Courage*. It is a search sustained by a poetic fervour which usually subsides before it becomes rhetoric, and then rises again with a sealike motion as it meets the next incident. He is always simple and explicit, alert for the random irony. He is aware of the ironical disparity between what imagination and tradition suggest and what in fact is seen. Jim Conklin, dying of his wounds, walks with his court of mourners like a spectre seeking a place to die. When he does fall down to die, Crane will notice that his left shoulder hits the ground first and that he gives 'a little commonplace smile.' The death of Conklin is tragic; but it is horrible, too, because in its final agonies it is grotesque. So grotesque that another dying soldier starts boasting that he himself will not die with such a lack of dignity. Death exposes; it is the final betrayal in lives which—one now sees—have been most mercifully protected by shames, concealments, and lies:

> The youth could see that the soles of his shoes had been worn to the thinness of writing paper and from a great rent in one of them the dead foot projected piteously. And it was as if fate had betrayed the soldier. In death it exposed to his enemies that poverty which in life he had perhaps concealed from his friends.

The irony is relentless; the red badge of courage itself is a soldier's wound and the young man does indeed win it. But it is false. For the boy gained his badge when, in a panic, he struggled with one of his own panic-stricken fellows and was clubbed by him. Crane, the lapsed Methodist, could not have been more thoroughly lost to his faith; and one can see in this poem, if one cares to do so, that he is outside, reduced to man's primitive state, in the older, madder religion of war.

With his gift for metaphor—a gift which is not without its affectations—Crane once described a woman going in black to a prayer meeting 'like a limited funeral.' When we sit back and reflect on the importance of *The Red Badge of Courage,* this phrase comes to mind. The tale *is* a *tour de force,* but it is a minor work. As a novel about war it is itself a 'limited funeral.' If we compare his work with Tolstoy's—which was his direct inspiration—we see that Tolstoy's reflections on war and his war narratives are not derived at second hand from literature in order to enact a drama of personal salvation; they are the work of a man who had been a soldier and one who has the sense of campaign and of the complete military life. Wars do not occur for the purpose of providing private moral tests. We would not gather from Crane's little masterpiece that he was describing a battle in a civil war—the most dreadful of all wars, but sometimes called the purest—where large, public moral issues profoundly affecting the growth and spirit of a nation were being decided. The war appears to be meaningless. We have no strong impression that the soldiers he describes are really civilians. The result is that the tale has length, very much in the manner of picaresque writing, but no depth—or at any rate no more than a bias towards privacy. His tale is a marvellous one for a very young man to have constructed out of nothing, but it remains a brilliant collection of impressions and surfaces. Perhaps he felt a romantic guilt in not having known the real thing, a guilt not uncommon among post-war generations. Romantic, restless, dipping into 'life' all over the world, a journalist-*voyeur* with his own Hamlet-like train of guilts and scruples, killing a frail body in the search for a physical justification, Crane is a writer who is arrested at the stage of personality. Achieving it, his talent declined. We might now be saying his life as a writer was tragic, had he lived out the normal span.

IV

THE SOURCES/RESOURCES
OF STEPHEN CRANE'S ART

A. INTRODUCTION

Far more attention has been paid to Stephen Crane's biography than to his literary craft. This situation has arisen partly because most critics have not found enough richness and variety in Crane's poetry and fiction; moreover, there are still important questions in his life that need answers. Some critics have taken literally William Dean Howells' pronouncement that Crane came into life "fully armed." Stephen Crane, a good many insist, presents the puzzling case of an artist who began writing at the height of his powers, and who wrote for ten hurried years; consequently, there was not much to explore in terms of his art.

During the 1890s and later, Stephen Crane may have gained a certain reputation as the genius who was "fully armed." At the same time, critics and readers have had many doubts and misgivings. If, according to some critics, Crane had no sources and no antecedents, he wrote only *tour de forces*, like *The Red Badge of Courage*. The term *tour de force* was meant as a "compliment," suggesting a stroke of genius or luck, or great cleverness. Other critics considered Crane as a vastly overrated writer because he was presumably uneducated, little read, and anti-intellectual. These critics thought that because Crane had few or no antecedents or sources, he could never be relevant and substantial enough, even as a social critic or satirist. For many, a writer's richness and variety can be corroborated by his sources and resources.

However, numerous critics have searched for sources of Crane's works. They have most often settled on the influences that molded *Maggie* and *The Red Badge*. The bewildering number of sources for *The Red Badge* does not really clarify Crane's writing. What these source studies often suggest unintentionally is that Crane must have borrowed more than we presume, and therefore created less. In the end, Crane seems to have lost both ways—as the original genius, and as the writer with his sources/resources.

The study of sources—literary, religious, historical, biographical, cultural—can be of real value in bringing the critic and the reader closer to the writer and his creation. A legitimate source can show how a writer utilizes, distills, and alters his basic materials. At the same time, a source can illuminate the writer's tone and point of view toward his art and its expression. Sources can also reveal the reasons for the success or failure of a writer's work. For example, because Crane was psychologically troubled by his ambivalent relationship with his mother, which he drew upon in *George's Mother* (1896), he lost the proper aesthetic distance needed to capture the humanity and variety in George Kelcey, Mrs. Kelcey, and the novel's evolving themes. With the aid of sources, then, one can reconstruct the artist's creation, measure the intended aim and real achievement in his work, and therefore make a more careful assessment of it.

There are limits to source studies. They are useful as *means,* never as *ends.* They form only part of an evolving creation, and they are often remarkably transformed by the creative writer. A legitimate source can be obscured by illegitimate ones, which a critic can use to distort what a writer has done. Parallel sources or analogues are usually interesting means of comparing writers who may never have known one another's work, but this kind of source study often degenerates into an irrelevant catalogue of names. Source studies can also be overemphasized. Critics generally have so scrutinized the sources for *The Red Badge* that they have forgotten or minimized other larger and meaningful areas in the novel itself: style, tone, the function of the grotesque, and the mixing of tragic and comic materials.

The source studies included in this section demonstrate how Stephen Crane drew from the reality of his everyday life whatever he needed or whatever interested him. These studies do not cover all possible facets of Crane's borrowings; much more still needs to be done. Crane's newspaper experience played a vital part in his literary development, and only recently has his reportage become widely available. Particular locales like Port Jervis, Asbury Park, and Ocean Grove stimulated Crane's imagination in special ways; they have been superficially treated thus far. Literary sources need to be explored further; Kipling, for example, was both a positive and a negative influence on Crane's art and themes. More can be done with Crane's borrowings from Garland, Howells, and others. The impact of painting and the American social scene are also fruitful areas for further study. For all the talk of Crane's link with naturalism as a source, little has been done to fully explore it. Most surprising is the general neglect of a most obvious influence on Crane's life and work —the Bible.

1. *The Newspaper Experience of Stephen Crane*
By Joseph J. Kwiat

The significance of newspaper work for the literary careers of Stephen Crane, Frank Norris, and Theodore Dreiser has not been widely recognized, although this experience was invaluable in formulating many of their unconventional attitudes toward life, their selection of subject matter, even their techniques. It is true that newspaper writers were compelled to devote their time, energy, and interest to the loud and ephemeral demands of the city room; and while, at first glance, this atmosphere may seem stifling, it was actually a richly rewarding and fertile one for the men who were to lead the revolt against the ideals of the genteel tradition. No doubt the bohemian nature of newspaper life in the 'nineties contributed to this opposition to bourgeois values. But more important, probably, was the intimate relationship with life, the variety and contrast, which a newspaper assignment made necessary.

James L. Ford, a seasoned newspaperman, indicated in 1894 the value of newspaper work for a literary career. "There are," he wrote, "young men working in newspaper offices now who will one of these days draw true and vivid pictures of modern New York as it appears in the eyes and brains of those who know it thoroughly, and very interesting fiction it will be, too." [1] Ford protested the "literary quarantine" of the most picturesque section of the city, the lower-class life stretching below Cooper Union, "in which may be found a greater and more interesting variety of human life and customs than in any other region that I know of." The quarantine, he felt, was imposed by the half-educated and quarter-bred audience which disliked the "low" and "vulgar" and admired only the "genteel." And then, addressing himself to the young newspapermen who held the promise of a living and honest American literature, Ford offered words of encouragement and advice.

Reprinted from: "The Newspaper Experience: Crane, Norris, and Dreiser," *Nineteenth-Century Fiction* VIII (September 1953), 99-108, 116-117. By permission of The Regents of the University of California and the author. Copyright © 1953 by The Regents of the University of California.

The enduring novel of New York will be written not by the man who, knowing his audience of editors rather than his subject, is content with a thin coating of that literary varnish known as "local color," but by this very young man from Park Row or Herald Square. . . . When this young man sits down to write that novel, it will be because he is so full of his subject, so thoroughly in sympathy with his characters—no matter whether he takes them from an opium-joint in Mott Street or a ball at Delmonico's—and so familiar with the various influences which have shaped their destinies, that he will set about his task with the firm conviction that he has a story to tell to the world.[2]

It is almost as if Ford knew the ambitions of the younger generation of the 'nineties—their desire to get at the facts, wherever they were to be found, and their determination to understand the "various influences" underlying city life. His words suggest with prophetic force, for example, Stephen Crane's intentions, and also his well-known difficulties in publishing *Maggie: A Girl of the Street* and *George's Mother*. Yet these books were the "true and vivid pictures of modern New York" to come out of the 'nineties.

Crane began writing for newspapers in 1888, when he was sixteen. He assisted his brother Townley, manager of a news bureau, in reporting the summer news at Asbury Park and other New Jersey resorts, selling much of his material to the New York *Tribune*. For the remainder of his life he was sporadically a newspaper writer. . . .

One of the first lessons the novelists learned from their newspaper work was the discovery that a writer's value depended to a considerable extent upon the ability to *see* as well as upon his ability to cultivate memory, speed, and deftness in capturing the human-interest angle of an assignment. Dreiser's first published feature was for a Sunday issue of the Chicago *Daily Globe*. A description of Chicago's slum section, it was commended by his copyreader, John Maxwell, for its evidence of ability to observe. "A hell of a fine novel," said Maxwell, "is going to be written about some of these things one of these days." Crane's dispatches to the New York *World* in 1898—"The Red Badge of Courage Was His Wig-Wag Flag" (July 1) and "Stephen Crane's Vivid Story of the Battle of San Juan" (July 14)—were considered by Richard Harding Davis and other correspondents to be two of the most valuable contributions to literature that the war produced. Both were, of course, written under extreme pressure of time. "The best correspondent," wrote Davis, "is probably the man who by his energy and resource sees more of the war, both afloat and ashore, than do his rivals, and who is able to make the public see what he saw." [3] Of Crane's ability to "make the public see what he sees," Davis concluded, "it would be impertinent to speak."

The second lesson these men learned from newspaper work was the awareness that life was not all serene, well-ordered, genteelly beautiful. Their experience was, by and large, city experience, a chronicling of success and failure, pretense and violence. The newspapermen could hardly fail to be impressed by the enormous contrast between the world of wealth and fashion and the world of the slums. They could not ignore the dramatic implications of life, and they could hardly fail to wonder about its meanings. It is no accident, therefore, that the novelists developed social and philosophical attitudes which to some degree conflicted with their responsibilities as reporters.

* * *

For this generation "color" was, on the whole, in lower-class life, the life of the streets and the slums. Undoubtedly setting down the facts was of first importance. Crane's stint as summer correspondent for the New York *Tribune* demanded the ability to collect facts and gossip, although the young writer frequently insisted upon interpreting them in ironic fashion. . . .

* * *

Social and philosophical judgments, of course, had no significant place in the newspaper medium, a fact which worked hardship on all three of these writers. Perhaps Crane's difficulties best suggest the nature of the conflict between reportage and serious fiction.

Crane's dispatches to the *Tribune* before 1892 were apparently competent but unworthy of special notice. In 1891 the day editor, W. F. Johnson, was shown the Sullivan County sketches and the first draft of *Maggie,* and recommended five of the sketches for publication. Crane's journalistic future appeared, if not spectacular, at least promising. He had several years of experience on newspapers behind him, his fiction had found a market, and he had received the day editor's nod of recognition. But a more critical attitude and skeptical tone were evident in Crane's routine dispatches in the summer of

1892. A report of a meeting of ministers at Ocean Grove, for example, reflects in the lead paragraph the correspondent's tongue-in-cheek attitude toward the guardians of moral righteousness.

> The sombre-hued gentlemen who congregate at this place in summer are arriving in solemn procession, with black valises in their hands and rebukes to frivolity in their eyes. They greet each other with quiet enthusiasm and immediately set about holding meetings. The cool, shaded Auditorium will soon begin to palpitate with the efforts of famous preachers delivering doctrines to thousands of worshippers. The tents, of which there are hundreds, are beginning to rear their white heads under the trees.[4]

There is observation here, but there is also editorializing, of a kind not likely to be universally well received. Another item reports the address of a reformed convict who "went considerably into the details when describing the lives and methods of 'crooks,'" and who evidently stirred Crane's special interest in low-class life.

The objective and the subjective are curiously mingled in the reports of that crucial summer. The construction of a "razzle dazzle" is reported on with a gratuitous comment on the desperate search of the middle class for respectable pleasures. "Just what this will be is impossible to tell. It is, of course, a moral machine."[5] Yet, in the same column, Crane could write straightforwardly and even respectfully of the professional fighter, James J. Corbett, then training at Asbury Park. The pugilist's "gentlemanly bearing and quiet manners" were apparently in contrast with the behavior of the ordinary run of noisy and vulgar pleasure seekers at the resort. Three weeks later Crane took obvious delight in reporting the suppression of the "Observation Wheel" on the complaints of the residents of Ocean Grove; they said, he noted, "that the steam organ disturbed their pious meditations on the evils of the world."[6] Reporting an illustrated lecture by Jacob Riis, author of *How the Other Half Lives,* Crane prefaced his news item with this comment: "The thousands of summer visitors who have fled from the hot, stifling air of the cities to enjoy the cool sea breezes are not entirely forgetful of the unfortunates who have to stay in their crowded tenements."[7]

Crane's contempt for the hypocritical twinges of middle-class consciences is so apparent that a final blow-up with his editor might reasonably have been predicted. It came on August 21, when the *Tribune* printed his account of the American Day parade of the New Jersey councils of the Junior Order of United American Mechanics. The parade, Crane wrote,

> was a deeply impressive one to some persons. There were hundreds of the members of the order, and they wound through the streets to the music of enough brass bands to make furious discords. It probably was the most awkward, ungainly, uncut and uncarved procession that ever raised clouds of dust on sun-beaten streets. Nevertheless, the spectacle of an Asbury Park crowd confronting such an aggregation was an interesting sight to a few people.
>
> Asbury Park creates nothing. It does not make; it merely amuses. There is a factory where nightshirts are manufactured, but it is some miles from town. This is a resort of wealth and leisure, of women and considerable wine. The throng along the line of march was composed of summer gowns, lace parasols, tennis trousers, straw hats and indifferent smiles. The procession was composed of men, bronzed, slope-shouldered, uncouth and begrimed with dust. Their clothes fitted them illy, for the most part, and they had no ideas of marching. They merely plodded along, not seeming quite to understand, stolid, unconcerned, and, in a certain sense, dignified—a pace and bearing emblematic of their lives. They smiled occasionally and from time to time greeted friends in the crowd on the sidewalks. Such an assemblage of the spraddle-legged men of the middle class, whose hands were bent and shoulders stooped from delving and constructing, had never appeared to an Asbury Park summer crowd, and the latter was vaguely amused.
>
> The bona fide Asbury Parker is a man to whom a dollar, when held close to the eye, often shuts out any impression he may have had that other people possess rights. He is apt to consider that men and women, especially city men and women, were created to be mulcted by him. Hence the tan-colored, sun-beaten honesty in the faces of the members of the Junior Order of United American Mechanics is expected to have a very staggering effect upon them. The visitors were men who possessed principles.[8]

So far as the *Tribune* was concerned, this was the end of Crane's employment. For Whitelaw Reid, owner and publisher of the paper, was also the Republican candidate for the vice-presidency. Ironically, strenuous objections to Crane's report came, not from the Asbury Parkers who were the real target for Crane's barbs, but in behalf of the marchers who were supposed to have been grossly insulted. This jeopardy to Reid's political ambitions in a year of economic tension caused the temporary dismissal of Townley Crane and the permanent dismissal of Stephen, who was recognized as the real villain of the piece. There is evidence that the *Tribune* not only dismissed him, but that its management attacked and maligned him as well.[9]

It was two years and more before Crane was again working for a newspaper; and it was several more years before, as a war correspondent, he served as a regular staff reporter. Meanwhile as a free-lance writer he contributed sketches and feature articles to various newspapers. As literary reporter of the manifold life of New York City, Crane found a role in which he was free from a city editor's deadeningly insistent demands for facts. A number of Crane's sketches show clearly the kind of experience which interested him.

"An Experiment in Misery" originally appeared in the New York *Press* for April 22, 1894. An account of the submerged and defeated lives in the midst of the impersonal life of the city, it opens with a description of the "glowing life" of Chatham Square on a cold and storming night—cable cars, people tramping in the mud, elevated trains, and corner saloon. The scream of a flop-house habitué is interpreted as "giving voice to the wail of a whole section, a class, a people." The final scene depicts the young man of the sketch on a bench in City Hall Park. And the sight and sound of the buildings and the roar of the city in the background were for him, Crane says, "The voice of the city's hopes, which were to him no hopes."

The same theme appears in "Stories Told by an Artist in New York," which appeared in the *Press* for October 26, 1894. It reveals a wry humor born of its author's observation of the artistic struggle for existence within the jungle of the city. Another sketch, "The Silver Pageant," with its similar background, names of characters, and fundamental problem, was very probably written for newspaper publication at the same time. The situation centers upon Gaunt, a slow and absent-minded artist, who discovers that he must make drawings for book publishers in order to earn a living. When he announces to his artist friends that he intends to paint a picture, they pay him a visit and find him a suicide in his studio. Like the young man in "An Experiment in Misery," Gaunt had discovered that the voice of the city's hopes were for him, the artist, hopeless. For both sketches, Crane obviously drew on his recent experiences with his artist friends, the "Indians," at the old Art Students' League building.

A number of other sketches for newspapers between 1894 and 1896 show how Crane earned his living by exploiting his special knowledge and understanding of New York City. The morbid and stupid animal curiosity of pedestrians at the sight of an Italian who had collapsed on the street is presented in "When a Man Falls a Crowd Gathers" (New York *Press,* December 2, 1894). Paralleling this street drama are Crane's impressions of the inanimate sounds and activities of the city itself, a display of cosmic indifference to the private little tragedy being enacted in its midst.

The street cars jingled past this scene in endless parade Occasionally, down where the elevated road crossed the street, one could hear sometimes a thunder, suddenly begun and suddenly ended. Over the heads of the crowd hung an immovable canvas sign: "Regular Dinner twenty cents." The body on the pave seemed like a bit of debris sunk in this human ocean.

Bowery dialect and some tough dialogue are rendered with remarkable authenticity in "The Duel That Was Not Fought" (New York *Press,* December 9, 1894) which has for its setting a saloon on lower Sixth Avenue. An amusing sketch of undaunted love as seen against the background of a beach and amusement park is presented in "The Pace of Youth" (New York *Press,* January 18, 1895). Another sketch, "The Roof Gardens and Gardeners of New York: A Phase of New York Life as Seen by a Close Observer" (Washington *Post,* August 9, 1896), is concerned with the problem of survival in an environment which appears to be the organized enemy of its inhabitants. Crane presents with compassion and irony the desperation of human beings who are attempting to make a virtue out of the unnatural life of the city.

Here is a vast city in which thousands of people in summer half stifle, cry out continually for air, fresher air. Just above their heads is what might be called a country of unoccupied land. . . . Down in the slums necessity forces a solution of problems. It drives the people to the roofs. An evening upon a tenement roof with the great golden march of the stars across the sky, and Johnnie gone for a pail of beer, is not so bad if you have never seen the mountains nor heard, to your heart, the slow, sad song of the pines.

A description of a picturesque section of Greenwich Village, "Minetta Lane, New York" (Philadelphia *Press,* December 20, 1896), shows Crane as more interested in achieving the pictorial effects of the artist working in chiaroscuro than in conveying the reporter's kind of information.

Minetta Lane is a small and becobbled valley between hills and dingy brick. At night the street lamps, burning dimly, cause the shadows to be important, and in the gloom one sees groups of quietly conversant negroes, with occasionally the gleam of a passing growler. Everything is vaguely outlined and of uncertain identity, unless, indeed, it be the flashing buttons and shield of the policeman on his coast.

* * *

Crane, obviously, was no ordinary reporter. He found it impossible to refrain from comment on the life he saw, but that it "brought him out" is clear enough. It might be possible to overestimate the importance of his newspaper work in his literary development, and yet there is obvious error in minimizing it. For it gave him, at the very least, vital subject matter, an attitude which reinforced his respect for honesty and integrity, and a medium for expressing himself when other opportunities were not immediately available. . . .

All three, Crane, Norris, and Dreiser, discovered that their value to a newspaper depended upon the cultivation of technical facility and an awareness of the human interest angle. All three attempted to be "detached" observers who accepted life as it was for its facts and drama. All three focused their attention on the city scene and the problems of the common man, the spectacle of business and political power, war, and the hypocrisy of moral professions. And, finally, all three were strengthening and sharpening their talents for their more serious creative work when they incorporated these valuable lessons from their newspaper "apprenticeship" into their imaginative efforts as writers of fiction.

NOTES

1. *The Literary Shop* (New York, 1894), p. 154.
2. *Ibid.*, pp. 127-128.
3. Richard Harding Davis, "Our War Correspondents in Cuba and Puerto Rico," *Harper's New Monthly Magazine*, XCVIII (May, 1899), 941.
4. "Meetings Begun at Ocean Grove," New York *Tribune*, July 2, 1892.
5. "Crowding into Asbury Park," New York *Tribune*, July 3, 1892.
6. "On the New-Jersey Coast," New York *Tribune*, July 24, 1892.
7. *Idem.*
8. New York *Tribune*, August 21, 1892.
9. See Melvin Schoberlin's Introduction to *The Sullivan County Sketches of Stephen Crane* (Syracuse, New York, 1949), p. 10

2.   *The Origins of Stephen Crane's Literary Creed*
By James B. Colvert

Literary source hunters have experienced little difficulty in suggesting influences upon Stephen Crane's early novels and stories. But
where such study should ideally throw light upon the genesis and
processes of Crane's art, too often the claims and surmises about his
literary origins are so general or so tenuous that they serve more to
endarken than enlighten. Spiller, in the *Literary History of the
United States,* fairly states the whole case:

> The appearance of an original artist, springing without
> antecedent into life, is always illusion, but the sources of
> Crane's philosophy and art are as yet undeciphered. Neither
> the cold-blooded determinism of his belief nor the sensuous
> awareness of his writing can be without source, but nowhere
> in the scant record he has left is there evidence that he, like
> Garland, read widely in the current books on biological science.
> A direct influence of Darwin, Spencer, Haeckel, or their
> American popularizers cannot be established. Rather he seems
> to have absorbed these influences at second hand through
> Russian and French writers.[1]

The problem of the "cold-blooded determinism of his belief"
aside for the moment, how can the literary historian account for the
"illusion" of Crane's appearance as an "original" artist and the amazing rapidity of his apparently untutored growth? In the spring of
1891 he was a Sophomore at Syracuse University, ambitiously planning to end his college career in order to become a writer; by the
fall of 1892 he had already formulated the creed of art by which he
was to be guided for the remaining eight years of his life and was
presumably writing his first novel; by the spring of 1893 the author
of *Maggie: A Girl of the Streets*[2] had won the attentions of two of

Reprinted from: *The University of Texas Studies in English,* XXXIV (1955), 179-
188. By permission of *Texas Studies in Literature and Language* and the author.

the most influential literary men of his time, Hamlin Garland and William Dean Howells.

Two theories are commonly advanced to explain this phenomenal literary development. First is the popular and persistent notion, perhaps inevitable in view of his unusual literary rise, that Crane had no origins at all, that he was a "natural" genius who had no need for a literary situation in which to develop. An informed contemporary, Howells, could only say that the young author of *Maggie* "sprang into life fully armed," [3] and Garland, Crane's patron for a time after 1893, propagated for almost twenty years the idea that his protégé was an inexplicable genius, a sort of unconscious recorder of whatever came to him from the outer reaches of a ghostly world. This belief is commonly found in history and criticism even today. He was, a critic wrote in 1941, "an artist who was really not conscious at all. He arrived . . . fully equipped. He had no need to improve." [4] And as late as 1952 a historian asserted that Crane was an artist of "amazing, almost miraculous prescience," and thus "that despair of the academic critic, a highly 'original' writer." [5]

The other view, accepted in part at least by Spiller in the *Literary History of the United States,* is that Crane sprang directly from the tradition of the French and Russian naturalists, a thesis extensively argued in Lars Ahnebrink's study of *The Beginnings of Naturalism in American Fiction.*[6] Ahnebrink attributes Crane's basic concept of fiction and the writer to the European naturalists, particularly Zola, whose *L'Assommoir* and *La Débâcle* he regards as important sources for Crane's first three novels, *Maggie, George's Mother,* and *The Red Badge of Courage.* Turgenev's *Fathers and Sons,* Ahnebrink thinks, probably influenced *George's Mother,* and Ibsen's *An Enemy of the People* perhaps suggested Crane's novelette, *The Monster.*

But there are serious objections to both of these views. The notion that Crane had no literary antecedents contradicts the fundamental principle that every writer is at first dependent upon his times and its traditions, however widely he may later deviate from them in the process of creating something new out of the old. Nor is the second theory much more acceptable. The chief difficulty with the idea that Crane adopted the doctrines and methods of the naturalists is that it assumes, without much evidence, that he read and imitated the writers of this school, an assumption which does not at all square with the fact that Crane's work and the naturalists' differ in many important respects. There are reasons to doubt seriously that the American ever read Zola or the Russians. When Ahnebrink asserts that "even before the composition of *Maggie,* he [Crane] was familiar with some of Zola's work," he ignores the fact that Crane read *Nana* —the only novel by Zola he ever commented on—more than five years after he started writing *Maggie.*[7] No evidence exists that he ever read *L'Assommoir,* and *La Débâcle* he threw aside, according to Thomas Beer, after reading only a few pages.[8] There is no external —and no convincing internal—evidence that he knew either Turgenev or Ibsen.

On the contrary, there is good reason to believe that Crane was unusually ill-read. John Barry, the editor of *The Forum* who read Crane's *The Black Riders* in manuscript in 1894, referred to the young poet as "woefully ignorant of books,"[9] and Berryman, who thinks Crane's reading has been underestimated, can nevertheless assert that "it is not easy to think of another important prose-writer or poet so ignorant of traditional literature in English as Stephen Crane was and remained."[10] All his life he denied, sometimes with considerable irritation, any connection with the naturalists. "They stand me against walls," he complained about his English acquaintances to James Huneker in 1897, "with a teacup in my hand and tell me how I have stolen all my things from de Maupassant, Zola, Loti, and the bloke who wrote—I forget the name."[11] Except for a reference to the brief period in 1891 when, as a student at Syracuse, he was studying intensely with a view to forming his style, there is little evidence that he ever read much at all, an omission he once defended on the ground that in this way he avoided the risk of unconscious imitation.[12] Unlike Frank Norris, who once referred to himself as "Mr. Norris, Esq. (The Boy Zola)!" Crane seems to owe little, if anything, to nineteenth-century French and Russian naturalism.[13]

How, then, can the literary beginnings of this precocious (but, one supposes, hardly supernatural) young writer be accounted for? "Here came a boy," Beer wrote of the twenty-year-old ex-college student who went into the East Side slums in the spring of 1891 for material for Maggie, "whose visual sense was unique in American writing and whose mind by some inner process had stripped itself of all respect for these prevalent theories which have cursed the national fiction. He was already an ironist, already able to plant his impressions with force and reckless of the consequent shock to a public softened by long nursing at the hands of limited men."[14] But what had stimulated to action his natural rebelliousness and what were the "inner processes" that turned him to slums for the subject of his painfully realistic *Maggie?* From whom had he learned the use of irony, and to whom was he indebted for his interest in painting and his characteristic use of color imagery? What was the origin of his belief that direct personal experience is the only valid material for the writer, and what led him to emphasize so strongly his belief that absolute honesty is a prime virtue of the artist? These questions, it would seem, define the problem of Crane's literary origins, and the answers are to be found in the period of his almost incredibly brief apprenticeship to the craft of fiction in the years 1891-92.

Crane left one of the most important clues to his artistic origins in a letter of 1896 to Lily Brandon Munro, a lady he was once in love with in his Syracuse student days. "You know," he wrote, "when I left you [in the fall of 1892] I renounced the clever school in literature. It seemed to me that there must be something more in life than to sit and cudgel one's brains for clever and witty expedients. So I developed all alone a little creed of art which I thought was a good one. . . . If I had kept to my clever Rudyard-Kipling style, the road might have been shorter, but, ah, it wouldn't be the true road." [15] The significant point here is not so much Crane's rejection of Kipling as a literary mentor as his implicit admission that the Englishman had served him as a model sometime between 1891 and 1892. It seems more than likely that the young American owed to Kipling the basic principles of his artistic beliefs, for Crane's theory of literature matches precisely the esthetic credo of Dick Heldar, the young artist-hero of Kipling's *The Light That Failed,* a novel Crane read sometime before 1892, probably during the spring semester of 1891 at Syracuse University.

Few young writers in a rebellious mood were likely to escape the attraction of Kipling in the first years of the nineties. At the time *The Light That Failed* was appearing in *Lippincott's Magazine* in January of 1891, Kipling was already a best-selling author whose fiction was considered new and unorthodox. His amazing popularity had in fact become a subject for reviewer's verse:

> No matter where I go, I hear
> The same old tale of wonder;
> It's some delusion wild, I fear,
> The world is laboring under.

> Why every friend I've met today
> (I couldn't help but note it)
> Has asked me "Have you read 'Mulvaney'
> Rudyard Kipling wrote it." [16]

Immediately following this is a review of *The Light That Failed* which emphasizes the unorthodoxy of his realistic tale of an artist's adventures as a war correspondent and suggests something of the appeal it must have had for the youthful Crane, then a cub reporter for his brother Townley's Asbury Park news agency: "Bohemian and unconventional as the characters are," the reviewer states, "no one who has seen much of the two classes whence they are chiefly drawn —newspaper correspondents and lady art students—can say they are grossly exaggerated." [17]

There is convincing evidence that Crane not only knew this novel before 1892, but that it indeed made a profound impression upon him. S. C. Osborn notes that Crane's famous image at the end of Chapter IX in *The Red Badge of Courage*, "The sun was pasted against the sky like a wafer," occurs in Kipling's *The Light That Failed* and concludes that the younger writer unconsciously incorporated the idea into *The Red Badge*.[18] There are strong reflections, moreover, of Kipling's early manner—the impressionistic "modern" imagery, the sententious, often flippant, dialogue, and a keen sense of the ironic—in Crane's earliest fiction, *The Sullivan County Sketches*, written in the summers of 1891 and 1892. In these pieces, which comprise all that may be properly called apprentice work, if the first drafts of *Maggie* and a story published in the Syracuse school paper are excepted, Crane put into practice the basic theories of Dick Heldar, the rebellious and unorthodox artist in *The Light That Failed*.

Dick Heldar must have been the apotheosis of all that the nineteen-year-old Crane hoped to become. Dick is an Impressionist painter in revolt against the canons of nineteenth-century respectability. He chooses Bohemian life for the freedom it gives him in his enthusiastic pursuit of fame, and with great determination he seeks the truth about life in the slums of London and on the battlegrounds of remote deserts. He is proud, independent, and free in the expression of iconoclastic opinions.

Crane's orientation was remarkably similar. As a boy he was in perpetual revolt against the respectability of his conventional, middle-class Methodist home life, and at Claverack College, Lafayette, and Syracuse, an indifferent student at all three places, he incurred the displeasure of the faculty for expressing "angular" opinions. He was asked to withdraw from Lafayette at the end of his first semester for refusing to conform to academic regimen. "Away with literary fads and canons," he exclaimed to a friend in the late spring of 1891,[19] and about the same time he began making trips to New York to study life on the Bowery and in the slums. In the fall of 1892, after he was dismissed from the *Tribune* for writing an ironic account of an Asbury Park labor parade, Crane moved into the East Side more or less permanently, where he remained, observing and writing in wretched poverty, for more than two years.

This way of life he led by choice like Kipling's Dick Heldar, from whom he probably got the idea that this privation was valuable, perhaps even indispensable, to his development as an artist. "There are few things more edifying unto Art than the actual belly-pinch of hunger," Kipling explains when he puts Dick into the London slums to starve and paint within walking distance of an affluent friend. "I never knew," Dick says in explaining the value of his experience with poverty, "what I had to learn about the human face before." [20] When he is at last paid for some art work, Dick calls upon his friend and explains that he could not have asked for help because "I had a sort of superstition that this temporary starvation—that's what it was, and it hurt—would bring me more luck later." [21] Crane, as his way of life during this period shows, was of the same belief. One of his nieces, recalling her uncle's misery in the New York slums, was puzzled by his conduct: "We still wonder why he went through such experiences when he was always so very welcome at both our house and Uncle Edmund's. Perhaps he was seeking his own 'Experience in Misery' . . . altho doubtless it came also through his desire to make his own way independently." [22] To these views Crane himself assented, but a more significant explanation lies in his persistent notion that great art is born of the "belly-pinch of hunger":

It was during this period [he wrote to the editor of Leslie's Weekly about November, 1895] that I wrote "The Red Badge of Courage." It was an effort born of pain—despair, almost; and I believe that this made it a better piece of literature than it otherwise would have been. It seems a pity that art should be a child of pain, and yet I think it is. Of course we

have fine writers who are prosperous and contented, but in
my opinion their work would be greater if this were not so.
It lacks the sting it would have if written under the spur of
a great need.[23]

The remarkable kinship in temperament and attitude between
Kipling's protagonist and Crane strongly suggests that Dick's ideas
about art deeply impressed the young writer. Dick may have inspired
Crane in the use of color images for special effects, a stylistic feature
which blazes forth in the Sullivan County tales of 1892. For *The
Light That Failed* bristles with artist talk about color. Heldar exclaims
with sensuous enthusiasm about the scenery of Sudan: "What color
that was! Opal and amber and claret and brick-red and sulphur—
cockatoo-crest sulphur—against brown, with a nigger black rock
sticking up in the middle of it all, and a decorative frieze of camels
festooning in front of a pure pale turquoise sky." [24] Crane's interest
in painting, it is true, probably originated in his associations with
his sister, Mary Helen, who taught art in Asbury Park in the late
eighties and early nineties, and with Phebe English, a young art
student with whom he fell in love when he was a student at Claverack
College.[25] But in *The Light That Failed* he had before him not only
an enthusiastic appreciation of the expressive potentialities of color,
but also a striking example, in Kipling's "wrathful red disk" images,
of how color could be used by the writer to evoke mood and emotional atmosphere.

More important in Crane's literary credo, though, are the principles governing the selection of materials, their treatment, and the
attitude of the artist toward them. In *The Light That Failed* Kipling
advances and defends the position that real life furnishes the only
valid materials for art. "How can you do anything," his hero exclaims,
"until you have seen everything, or as much as you can?" [26] Like
the blind and ruined Heldar, who met his death following wars to
the far corners of the earth, Crane, ill with tuberculosis, wandered
away his energies—in the West, Mexico, the Florida swamps, Greece,
and Cuba—in quest of experience in the world of action. "I decided,"
he wrote once in reference to his literary creed of 1892, "that the
nearer a writer gets to life the greater he becomes as an artist," [27] and
in 1897, when his career was drawing to a close, he wrote from England
to his brother William: "I am a wanderer now and I must see
enough." [28] Both Crane and Kipling's hero expressed and acted upon

the firm belief that the artist's material is necessarily drawn from personal experience.

Important corollaries for the realist are the convictions that all experience, ugly and unpleasant though it may be, must be faithfully and truthfully reported if the artist is to maintain his integrity. Around this idea Kipling builds one of the key scenes in *The Light That Failed*. Heldar, disappointed because one of his realistic war sketches has been rejected by all the magazines, decides to alter it to conform to the conventional idea of what the soldier is like:

> I lured my model, a beautiful rifleman, up here with drink.
> . . . I made him a flushed dishevelled, bedevilled scallawag,
> with his helmet at the back of his head, and the living fear
> of death in his eye, and the blood oozing out of a cut over
> his ankle-bone. He wasn't pretty, but he was all soldier and
> very much man. . . . The art-manager of that abandoned paper
> said that his subscribers wouldn't like it. It was brutal and
> coarse and violent. . . . I took my "Last Shot" back. . . . I
> put him into a lovely red coat without a speck on it. That is
> Art. I cleaned his rifle—rifles are always clean on service—
> because that is Art. . . . I shaved his chin, I washed his hands,
> and gave him an air of fatted peace. . . . Price, thank Heaven!
> twice as much as for the first sketch.[29]

"If you try to give these people the thing as God gave it," Dick argues when his friend Torpenhow reprimands him for this practice, "keyed down to their comprehension and according to the powers he has given you . . . half a dozen epicene young pagans who haven't even been to Algiers will tell you, first that your notion is borrowed and, secondly, that it isn't Art!"[30] But Torpenhow destroys the repainted picture and delivers Dick an impassioned lecture on truth and integrity in the practice of art, after which the penitent Heldar concludes, "You're so abominably reasonable!"[31]

This idea Crane was expounding as early as the spring of 1891, about the time he read Kipling's novel. "I became involved," he wrote again in reference to his creed of 1892, "in the beautiful war between those who say that art is man's substitute for nature and we are the most successful in art when we approach the nearest to nature and truth, and those who say—well, I don't know what they say. Then they can't say much but they fight villainously." [32] On another occasion he stated Dick's idea more explicitly: "I cannot see why people hate ugliness in art. Ugliness is just a matter of treatment. The scene of Hamlet and his mother and old Polonius behind the curtain is ugly, if you heard it in a police court. Hamlet treats his mother like a drunken carter and his words when he has killed Polonius are disgusting. But who cares?" [33]

Writing in 1898 about his literary aims, Crane reasserted his belief in this principle and showed how largely it had figured in his career: "The one thing that deeply pleases me in my literary life— brief and inglorious as it is—is the fact that men of sense believe me to be sincere. . . . I do the best that is in me, without regard to cheers or damnation." [34] This echoes the principle oratorically preached to Dick upon the occasion of his moral lapse: "For work done without conviction, for power wasted in trivialities, for labor expended with levity for the deliberate purpose of winning the easy applause of a fashion-driven public, there remains but one end,— the oblivion that is preceded by toleration and cenotaphed with contempt." [35]

These striking parallels in the artistic aims and attitudes of Dick Heldar and Crane strongly suggest that Kipling's novel provided the young American with his basic conception of the art of fiction. Since the evidence for the influence of the naturalists upon Crane's literary theory is unconvincing, and since he knew neither Howells nor Garland's theories of realism and veritism until after 1892, before which time he had read *The Light That Failed,* it seems likely indeed that Kipling is Crane's chief literary ancestor. This belief is further strengthened by the fact that Crane read Kipling's book at the most impressionable period of his literary life. As a rank novice, rebellious against social and literary conventions and searching for a rationale for a new fiction, Crane must have found Kipling's ideas immensely stimulating. "For short, scattered periods Crane read curiously," Berryman states, "and instinct or luck or fate led him early to what mattered." [36] Later, it is true, he found support for his creed in the ideas of Howells, Garland, and the Impressionist painters with whom he was in constant association during his Bohemian New York period. But the book which laid the basic principle was *The Light That Failed.* Here is developed explicitly a whole literary credo which exactly parallels Crane's. In advocating and following closely the principles that art is grounded in actual experience, that absolute honesty in the artist is an indispensable virtue, that all experience, including the ugly and the unpleasant, is material for the artist, Crane, through Kipling, anticipated the "cult of experience" in American fiction which reached its full development in the literary renaissance of the twenties.[37]

NOTES

1. Robert E. Spiller and others, eds., *Literary History of the United States* (3 vols., New York, 1948), II, 1021.
2. The book, Spiller writes (*ibid.*, 1022), with which "modern American fiction was born."
3. Thomas Beer, *Stephen Crane: A Study in American Letters* (New York, 1923), 96.
4. H. E. Bates, *The Modern Short Story* (New York, 1941), 65.
5. Edward Wagenknecht, *The Cavalcade of the American Novel* (New York, 1952), 212.
6. University of Uppsala *Essays and Studies on American Language and Literature*, IX (1950).
7. Beer, *Stephen Crane: A Study in American Letters*, 148.
8. *Ibid.*, 97.
9. John D. Barry, "A Note on Stephen Crane," *The Bookman*, XIII (1901), 148.
10. John Berryman, *Stephen Crane* (New York, 1950), 24.
11. Robert W. Stallman, ed., *Stephen Crane: An Omnibus* (New York, 1952), 674. All references to Crane's letters are to this source.
12. Barry, "A Note on Stephen Crane," 148.
13. This view is in harmony with that of Albert J. Salvan, a student of Zola who concludes in his study of the naturalist's influence in the United States: "Dans la question toujours délicate d'établir un rapport d'influence définie entre Zola et Stephen Crane, nous sommes forcés de rester sur une note évasive. Il n'est guère douteux que l'auteur de Maggie manquait d'une connaissance très entendue de la littérature française du XIX⁰ siècle en général." *Zola aux États-Unis* (Providence, 1943), 163.
14. Beer, *Stephen Crane: A Study in American Letters*, 77.
15. Stallman, *Stephen Crane: An Omnibus*, 648.
16. "The Light That Failed," *The Literary News*, XII (1891), 29.
17. *Ibid.*, 19.
18. Scott C. Osborn, "Stephen Crane's Imagery: 'Pasted Like a Water,'" *AL*, XXIII (1951), 363. Osborn notes only one occurrence: "The fog was driven apart for a moment, and the sun shone, a blood-red wafer, on the water." *The Writings in Prose and Verse of Rudyard Kipling* (New York, 1897), IX, 63. The image occurs in variations twice more: "A puddle far across the mud caught the last rays of the sun and turned it into a wrathful red disc" (p. 13), and again: "The sun caught the steel and turned it into a savage red disc" (p. 31). See n. 37.
19. Arthur Oliver, "Jersey Memories—Stephen Crane," *New Jersey Historical Society Proceedings*, n.s., XVI (1931), 454-55.
20. Rudyard Kipling, *The Light That Failed*, in *The Writings in Prose and Verse of Rudyard Kipling* (New York, 1897), IX, 41.
21. *Loc. cit.*

22. Edna Crane Sidbury, "My Uncle, Stephen Crane, As I Knew Him," *Literary Digest International Book Review*, IV (1926), 249.
23. Stallman, *Stephen Crane: An Omnibus*, 591.
24. *The Light That Failed*, 53.
25. Joseph J. Kwiat, "Stephen Crane and Painting," *The American Quarterly*, IV (1952), 331.
26. *The Light That Failed*, 105.
27. Stallman, *Stephen Crane: An Omnibus*, 627.
28. *Ibid.*, 663.
29. *The Light That Failed*, 55-56.
30. *Ibid.*, 49.
31. *Ibid.*, 56.
32. Stallman, *Stephen Crane: An Omnibus*, 648.
33. Berryman, *Stephen Crane*, 21.
34. Stallman, *Stephen Crane: An Omnibus*, 679-80.
35. *The Light That Failed*, 67.
36. Berryman, *Stephen Crane*, 24.
37. When this article was in page proof, I saw R. W. Stallman's "The Scholar's Net: Literary Sources," *College English*, XVII (1955), 20-27, in which Mr. Stallman states that Scott C. Osborn, who first pointed out the similarity between Kipling and Crane's wafer image, "failed to explore the related images for what they mean and how they are used. . . . Nor is there any other point of correspondence between *The Light That Failed* and *The Red Badge of Courage*—only this single image (p. 20)."

3. *Stephen Crane and Painting*
By Joseph J. Kwiat

Stephen Crane, John Berryman flatly states in his recent book,[1] "owes nothing whatever, apparently, to painting." Berryman denies H. G. Wells's claim that the novelist was influenced by painters in his use of color, and he informs us that Crane "knew, by the way, few real painters—Linson, Jerome Myers, later Ryder; mostly illustrators." [2] These statements may be challenged on several counts.[3] It is doubtful what Mr. Berryman means by "real painters." It is not possible to differentiate sharply between painters and illustrators in that period; Corwin K. Linson, for example, was an illustrator as well as a painter. And it is not clear what Berryman's general sources are or how much information he possesses concerning Crane's knowledge of Myers and Ryder.

There is evidence, however, that Crane knew graphic artists very early in his career and that this experience was reflected in his newspaper writings in two ways: in his utilization of the image of the artist as subject and in his "painterly" stylistic devices. Crane, furthermore, discussed how important it was for the writer to be "honest" and "independent," and he associated these attitudes with graphic artists and with the problems of what he considered to be a closely allied art form. Finally, Crane explicitly compared his own general literary intentions with the technical and philosophical implications of what the French Impressionists, as he conceived them, were attempting in color.

I

One of Crane's sisters, Mary Helen, was an artist and taught art classes in Asbury Park in the late eighties and early nineties. While attending Claverack Academy from 1888 to 1890, Stephen fell in love with Phebe English, an art student, who gave him some of her paintings. They remained friends to about 1892.[4] Crane scholars

Reprinted from: *American Quarterly*, IV (Winter 1952), 331-338. By permission of The Trustees of the University of Pennsylvania and the author. Copyright, 1952, Trustees of the University of Pennsylvania.

generally mention his "innate sensitivity to color" and even his reading in Goethe's theories on color while at Syracuse University. But it is plausible to assume that Crane's interest in color had an early indebtedness to his artist sister and artist friend.

After his dismissal from the New York *Tribune* in 1892 and the disappointment following the publication of his novel, *Maggie,* in 1893, Crane lived and spent a great deal of time during the next two years in the old building of the Art Students League, then located on East Twenty-Third Street. Most of the inhabitants were struggling artists. These "Indians," as Crane called them, included R. G. Vosburgh, David Ericson, Nelson Greene, Frederick Gordon, W. W. Carroll, Edward S. Hamilton, and a Wolfrom.[5] This setting and several of these men appeared in *The Third Violet* and in many of Crane's sketches. He was also associating with other cliques of artists. One of these centered around Corwin K. Linson,[6] and another was a kind of dining-club which included Henry McBride, Gustave Verbeek, and Edward S. Hamilton.[7]

After his dismissal from the *Tribune,* Crane contributed sketches and feature articles to various newspapers as a free-lance writer. And it was as literary-reporter on the manifold life of New York City that Crane found a rôle freer and more congenial than a city editor's insistent demands for facts rather than impressions would have permitted. Many of these sketches reveal how he was stimulated by the kind of experience which interested him intensely, namely the difficulties of the graphic artist within the city's impersonal life. There can be little doubt that Crane identified his own miserable fate as a writer during this period with the misfortunes of his artist friends.

Crane drew upon his recent experiences with the "Indians" at the old Art Students League building in "Stories Told by an Artist in New York."[8] The sketch, born of its author's observation of the artistic struggle for existence within the jungle of the city, reveals a wry humor. A magazine illustrator, Pennoyer, works on a pen-and-ink drawing and hopes for payment from the *Monthly Amazement.* Corinson (Corwin K. Linson?), another artist, deserts the precarious existence of art for the relative security of turning out crayon portraits at fifteen dollars per week and is, therefore, in a position to stake his less fortunate friends to a Thanksgiving dinner. Great Grief does a comic section and dreams of renting an expensive studio and buying second-hand curtains and plaster casts. And Purple

Sanderson, when his opinion differs from that of every art dealer in New York, eats regularly by working at the gasfitter's trade.

Because of its similarity in background, in names of characters, and in its fundamental problem, "The Silver Pageant" [9] was probably written for newspaper publication at much the same time as "Stories Told by an Artist in New York." The situation centers upon Gaunt, a slow and absent-minded artist, who discovers that he must make drawings for book publishers in order to earn a living. When he announces to his artist friends, Grief, Pennoyer, and Wrinkles, that he intends to paint a picture, they pay him a visit and find him a suicide in his studio.

Crane's newspaper work indicated that he not only utilized the image of the artist as subject for his sketches but that he also made use, as a writer, of the techniques of the artist. Several of his early dispatches for the New York *Tribune* were characterized by an impressionistic manner which may well have been formed by his familiarity with the method of the graphic artist. For the "impressionistic" method, as Hamlin Garland pointed out in *Crumbling Idols* in 1894, was "a complete and of course momentary concept of the sense of sight" and that it should be "the stayed and reproduced effect of a single section of the world of color upon the eye." For Crane, however, the method was not only useful as a way of "seeing" the world but for "feeling" its anonymity and indifference as well. It gave, in effect, another dimension to his ironic attitude toward life.

Crane's report of a meeting of ministers at Ocean Grove, New Jersey, reflected in the lead-paragraph the correspondent's tongue-in-cheek attitude toward the guardians of moral righteousness. But it also conveyed an ironical effect achieved through the contrasting use of black and white: "The sombre-hued gentlemen who congregate at this place in the summer are arriving in solemn procession, with black valises in their hands and rebukes to frivolity in their eyes. . . . The tents, of which there are hundreds, are beginning to rear their white heads under the trees." [10] Crane's final dispatch for the *Tribune* was his impressionistic account of the American Day parade of the Junior Order of United American Mechanics. "Asbury Park," he wrote, "creates nothing. It does not make; it merely amuses. . . . The throng along the line of march was composed of summer gowns, lace parasols, tennis trousers, straw hats and indifferent smiles. The procession was composed of men, bronzed, slope-shouldered, uncouth and begrimed with dust." [11] The manner of such American impressionistic painters of the period as John Twachtman, Childe Hassam, Theodore Robinson, and J. Alden Weir as they, in turn, understood the "new disintegrations" from Monet and Sisley may possibly be seen in Crane's technical handling of the scene.

Crane later wrote a newspaper sketch, "An Experiment in Misery," which was an account of the submerged and defeated lives in the midst of the impersonal life of the city. The flophouse scene, for example, is written with the feeling of a painter for the nightmarish effects of figures in shadows and gaslight upon a room:

> The youth sat on his cot and peered about him. There was a gas-jet in a distant part of the room, that burned a small flickering orange-hued flame. It caused vast masses of tumbled shadows in all parts of the place, save where, immediately about it, there was a little grey haze. As the young man's eyes became used to the darkness, he could see upon the cots that thickly littered the floor the forms of men sprawled out, lying in death-like silence, or heaving and snoring with tremendous effort, like stabbed fish.[12]

The beach and amusement park scene in "The Pace of Youth" is a brilliant illustration of Crane's affinity to the graphic artist in his skillful handling of the problems of perspective, composition, and color for the purpose of capturing a mood and an "impression":

> There was a vista of sand and sky and sea that drew to a mystic point far away in the northward. In the mighty angle, a girl in a red dress was crawling slowly like some kind of spider on the fabric of nature. A few flags hung lazily above where the bath-houses were marshalled in compact squares. Upon the edge of the sea stood a ship with its shadowy sails painted dimly upon the sky, and high overhead in the still, sunshot air a great hawk swung and drifted slowly.[13]

And Crane's description of a picturesque section of Greenwich Village, in "Minetta Lane, New York," reveals the writer striving for the pictorial effects of a painter working in chiaroscuro:

Minetta Lane is a small and becobbled valley between hills and dingy brick. At night the street lamps, burning dimly, cause the shadows to be important, and in the gloom one sees groups of quietly conversant negroes, with occasionally the gleam of a passing growler. Everything is vaguely outlined and of uncertain identity, unless, indeed, it be the flashing buttons and shield of the policeman on his coast.[14]

II

Crane's involvement in the writer's obligation to be honest, esthetically as well as in every other way, was closely linked with his feeling that the writer should maintain his individuality in thought and style. And it is important to see that Crane's attitude was identified with graphic artists and with the problems of what he considered to be an allied art.

David Ericson, Crane's artist-friend, recalled that when the young novelist was writing *Maggie* he went down to the slums with an artist: "They were gone about a week. . . . Steve said nothing, but Carroll told me it was a horrible experience. Crane only smiled about it for to him it was the cream of life. He got what he was after." [15] Still another artist-friend, R. G. Vosburgh, remembered that soon after Crane completed *The Red Badge of Courage* he received a commission to write a story about New York lodging houses. "Crane and one of his friends in the studio spent a night and two days as tramps on the Bowery and East Side, about the lodging houses. This was the kind of work that pleased him best, for, he said, it was in such places human nature was to be seen and studied. Here it was open and plain, with nothing hidden. It was unvarnished human nature, he said." [16]

Recalling the period around the publications of *The Sullivan County Sketches,* a transitional phase between his early newspaper reporting days of resort gossip and his more serious literary work, Crane wrote to his intimate friend, Lily Brandon, on February 29, 1896:

You know, when I left you [shortly after the completion of these sketches], I renounced the clever school in literature. It seemed to me that there must be something more in life than to sit and cudgel one's brains for clever and witty expedients. So I developed all alone a little creed of art which I thought was a good one. Later I discovered that my creed was identical with the one of Howells and Garland and in this way I became involved in the beautiful war between those who say that art is man's substitute for nature and we are the most successful in art when we approach the nearest to nature and truth, and those who say—well, I don't know what they say.[17]

And in *The Third Violet* (1897)—a story which Wilson Follett, editor of Crane's works, considers chiefly valuable as a chapter of autobiography—Crane satirized the false notion that genuine art must be divorced from the life which holds greatest significance for the artist, the life that is most immediate and intense. One of the indigent painters in the story carries on a dramatic monologue in which only "quaint" and "foreign" subject matter is interpreted as legitimate for the artist. The portrayal of American subject matter is to be shunned, he says, for two reasons: it is "hard to find" and, since it is absent from the work of previous "respectable" artists, it would damn the artist for his "originality":

"Here is a little thing I did in Brittany. Peasant woman in sabots. This brown spot here is the peasant woman, and those two white things are the sabots. Peasant woman in sabots, don't you see? Women in Brittany, of course, all wear sabots, you understand. Convenience of the painters. I see you are looking at that little thing I did in Morocco. Ah, you admire it? Well, not so bad—not so bad. Arab smoking pipe, squatting in doorway. This long streak here is the pipe. Clever, you say? Oh thanks! You are too kind. Well, all Arabs do that, you know. Sole occupation. Convenience of the painters. Now, this little thing here I did in Venice. Grand Canal, you know. Gondolier leaning on his oar. Convenience of the painters. Oh yes, American subjects are well enough, but hard to find, you know—hard to find. Morocco, Venice, Brittany, Holland —all oblige with colour, you know—quaint form—all that. We are so hideously modern over here; and, besides, nobody has painted us much. How the devil can I paint America

when nobody has done it before me? My dear sir, are you
aware that that would be originality? Good heavens! we are
not aesthetic, you understand. Oh yes, some good mind comes
along and understands a thing and does it, and after that it
is aesthetic. Yes, of course, but then—well—Now, here is a little
Holland thing of mine; it—" [18]

A novel, Crane explained in another place, "should be a succession of . . . clear, strong, sharply-outlined pictures, which pass before
the reader like a panorama, leaving each its definite impression." He
fully realized that the problem of knowing about life was accompanied by the difficulty of telling about it, and he stated that his
chief desire was "to write plainly and unmistakably, so that all men
(and some women) might read and understand." But he was also
compelled to admit that the ability to write "plainly and unmistakably" was a difficult feat. "The complex interwoven mesh of life,"
Crane deplored in The O'Ruddy, "constantly, eternally, prevents
people from giving intelligent explanation." He frankly admitted
the limitations of the writer's art in "War Memories": "I bring this
to you," he wrote, "merely as an effect—an effect of mental light and
shade, if you like; something done in thought similar to that which
the French Impressionists do in colour; something meaningless and at
the same time overwhelming, crushing, monstrous."
Since, as Crane indicated in "War Memories," he was attempting
in words what the French Impressionists were striving for in color,
he prefaced his statement of his artistic intentions with his "impression" of a scene in which a church had been converted into a hospital:

The interior of the church was too cavelike in its gloom for
the eyes of the operating surgeons, so they had had the altar-
table carried to the doorway, where there was a bright light.
Framed then in the black archway was the altar-table with
the figure of a man upon it. He was naked save for a breech-
clout, and so close, so clear was the ecclesiastic suggestion that
one's mind leaped to a fantasy that this thin, pale figure had
just been torn down from a cross. The flash of the impression
was like light, and for this instant it illumined all the dark
recesses of one's remotest idea of sacrilege, ghastly and wanton." [19]

Underlying Crane's concern with the technical problem of presenting the qualities of his special vision, notably the mental effects of light and shade, was his deterministic attitude toward his materials. This concept of literary "impressionism" was reflected in much of his fiction.

It is almost impossible to "place" Crane as a member of a literary school. But a key to Crane's literary principles may be found in his frequently expressed admiration for Joseph Conrad's artistry. Conrad's artistic credo, as expressed in the preface to *The Nigger of the Narcissus,* was essentially a visual and pictorial approach to "life" and "truth." For the artist's task was to snatch "a passing phase of life" and, above everything else, "to make you *see.*" Conrad continued: "It is to show its vibration, its colour, reveal the substance of its truth . . . the stress and passion within the core of each convincing moment." Crane, undoubtedly, would have also agreed with Henry James's assertion that the novelist had a great deal in common with the painter.

This is not to say that Crane was solely indebted to the graphic arts and artists for his literary genius.[20] But it is equally false to say, as Mr. Berryman says, that Crane "owes nothing whatever . . . to painting." Robert E. Spiller expressed the difficult problem of the student of Crane when he observed, "The appearance of an original artist, springing up without antecedent into life, is always illusion, but the sources of Crane's philosophy and art are as yet undeciphered." [21] This paper attempts to decipher, in a preliminary manner, one of those sources. It seems apparent that an understanding of the relationship between Crane's knowledge of graphic artists and his awareness of certain of the specific problems of their art, particularly that of the "impressionists," will give valuable critical insights into the theory and practice of Crane's own literary art.[22]

NOTES

1. John Berryman, *Stephen Crane* (New York: W. Sloane Associates, 1950).
2. *Ibid.,* p. 289.
3. Robert E. Spiller, in his review of Berryman's book, has also expressed a questioning attitude: ". . . the fact that Crane lived and talked with painters and in several of his stories identified himself with a fictional painter might offer the scholar more suggestive connections with French impressionism than the summary 'opinion': 'He owes nothing whatever, apparently, to painting.'" *Saturday Review of Literature,* XXXIV (January 27, 1951), 11.
4. I am indebted to Mr. Melvin H. Schoberlin's letter to the writer, January 1,

1949, for information on this phase of Crane's life. According to another letter from Schoberlin, Crane's room at Syracuse University had several "impressionistic" paintings by Phebe English hanging on the wall. Schoberlin to the writer, October 22, 1951.

5. Schoberlin letter to the writer, January 1, 1949. The art discussions in which Crane participated were, according to Schoberlin, mainly concerned with what these painters called "Impressionism."

6. Ibid.

7. Henry McBride, "Stephen Crane's Artist Friends," Art News, XLIX (October 1950), 46.

8. Stephen Crane, Last Words (London: Digby, Long & Co., 1902), pp. 133-45. The sketch originally appeared in the New York Press, October 26, 1894.

9. There is no record of newspaper publication. It was collected under the heading of "New York Sketches" in Last Words, pp. 145-48.

10. New York Tribune, July 2, 1892.

11. Ibid., August 21, 1892.

12. The Work of Stephen Crane, ed. Wilson Follett (New York: Alfred A. Knopf, 1925-26), XI, 26-27. Hereinafter this set will be referred to as Work of Crane. The sketch originally appeared in the New York Press, April 22, 1894.

13. Ibid., pp. 61-62. The sketch originally appeared in the New York Press, January 18, 1895.

14. Last Words, pp. 154-55. The sketch originally appeared in the Philadelphia Press, December 20, 1896.

15. David Ericson letter to Ames W. Williams, November 4, 1942; courtesy of Mr. Williams.

16. R. G. Vosburgh, "The Darkest Hour in the Life of Stephen Crane," The Criterion, I (February 1901), 27.

17. Quoted in Introduction to The Sullivan County Sketches of Stephen Crane, ed. Melvin Schoberlin (Syracuse: Syracuse University Press, 1949), p. 19.

18. Work of Crane, III, 220-21.

19. Anglo-Saxon Review, III (December 1899), 34.

20. Crane's awareness of the advantages of the novelist's craft over that of the painter's is revealed amusingly in the statement made by his artist-friend, David Ericson, when the writer had drifted into his studio: "He was at that time writing 'The Red Badge of Courage.' I remember one time when he was lying in a hammock of his saying 'That is great!' It shocked me for the moment. I thought how conceited he is. But when he read me the passage, I realized at once how wonderfully real it was, and said that the writer had that advantage over us painters in that he could make his men talk, walk and think, whereas a painter can only depict a man in one position at a time. He seemed very pleased with this compliment." David Ericson letter to Ames W. Williams, November 4, 1942; courtesy of Mr. Williams.

21. Robert E. Spiller, "Toward Naturalism in Fiction," in Literary History of the United States, ed. by Robert E. Spiller, Willard Thorp, Thomas H. Johnson, and Henry Seidel Canby (New York: The Macmillan Co., 1948), II, 1021.

22. An examination of Crane's fiction in these specific terms is the subject of a forthcoming study.

4. *Crane and Goethe: A Forgotten Relationship*
By Robert L. Hough

One of the few explicit references to influences on Stephen Crane occurs in a letter from his classmate and fraternity brother at Syracuse University, Frank Noxon, who in 1926 remarked that Crane's use of the word "red" in the title *The Red Badge of Courage* "was part of a program":

> After the book appeared he and I had somewhere a talk about color in literature. He told me that a passage in Goethe analyzed the effect which the several colors have upon the human mind. Upon Crane this had made a profound impression and he had utilized the idea to produce his effects.[1]

Noxon's statement, though noted by previous critics, has never been investigated. This fact is surprising when one realizes that Crane's color-impressionism has been one facet of his writing that has engrossed critics and reviewers since 1895 and the first reviews of *The Red Badge of Courage*. Most of the comment has centered around Crane's relationship to the just-emerging French impressionistic painters—Monet, Renoir, Pissarro, and others.[2] What is interesting is that none of the writers after 1926 have explored what Crane himself indicated to be one source of his ideas on color: Goethe. The question of Crane's relationship to the impressionists has so captured critics that the German poet-philosopher has been forgotten, and yet a study of Goethe's color theories is a rewarding field of investigation because it offers answers to some of the questions arising from Crane's dramatic and skillful handling of color.

The book by Goethe which influenced Crane is not difficult to isolate because the only extensive comments on color made by the earlier writer appear in his lengthy anti-Newtonian dissertation on light, *Farbenlehre,* published in 1810 and translated into English as

Reprinted from: *Nineteenth-Century Fiction*, XVII (September 1962), 135-148. By permission of The Regents of the University of California and the author. Copyright © 1962 by The Regents of the University of California.

Goethe's Theory of Colors by Sir Charles Eastlake in 1840.[3] In this work Goethe reserves one short section for the topic "Effect of Color with Reference to Moral Associations" in which he speaks specifically to painters and discusses the "aesthetical ends" of color.[4]

From Noxon's description, it is almost assuredly this section that Crane read. In his introduction to this section, Goethe writes:

> [We] shall not be surprised to find that its [color's] effects are at all times decided and significant and that they are immediately associated with the emotions of the mind. . . . Hence color considered as an element of art may be made subservient to the highest aesthetical ends. . . . From some of our earlier observations we can conclude, that general impressions produced by single colors cannot be changed, that they act specifically and must produce definite, specific states in the living organ.
>
> They likewise produce a corresponding influence on the mind. Experience teaches us that particular colors excite particular states of feeling.[5]

Following this introduction Goethe describes the effects gained from the three primary colors, red, yellow, and blue, and their intermixtures (red-yellow, yellow-red, red-blue, and blue-red). He then discusses complementary colors, harmony and contrast, color combinations, tone, and chiaroscuro; and ends the section with a short series of paragraphs entitled "Allegorical, Symbolical, Mystical Applications of Color" that implicitly invite readers to make their own subjective approach to symbolic applications of color phenomena, a suggestion any writer with a penchant for color would have relished. After making a Christian interpretation of the three primary colors that merge into each other, Goethe concludes, "If our doctrine of colors finds favor, applications and allusions, allegorical, symbolical, and mystical will not fail to be made, in conformity with the spirit of the age." [6]

Undoubtedly Goethe was influenced by certain of the associationist doctrines of Locke, Hume, and Hartley in his interest in the interaction between color and emotion. For Goethe a certain color called to mind certain feelings and sensations, and there was a constant interrelationship between sense impression and emotion. But

Goethe leaves the associationists when he explains the emotions physiologically rather than psychologically. For the associationist certain reactions to specific impressions are often common to a large group of people because of common experiences. Red becomes associated with blood or the church or a rose, and from these alliances grow specific reactions. Goethe believed in a different sequence. Emotional reactions to colors were caused by physiological changes in the eye which brought about changes in the mind. Thus one was physically conditioned to certain responses of color and light, not psychologically conditioned. Churchmen, kings, painters simply took advantage of these responses when choosing and using color; they knew their own reactions and projected these to other people.

In his section on moral associations Goethe places particular stress on the emotional effect of color. He believed first there should be a scientific study of light and its components, then a study of the physiological reaction of the eye, then a study of the psychological reaction of the mind. Too many artists, Goethe felt, painted without real knowledge of the emotional response to color. They did not select their detail carefully enough. They tended to paint what they saw (without closely observing) or what others had seen before them. There was a dread of theorizing on the impact of color, and in some pictures color was general rather than specific or "characteristic." Goethe was fond of donning different colored glasses and reporting his response to landscapes tinged with red or yellow or blue. Usually he found that painters did not completely understand light and shade. Shadows were often blue, he claimed, and illuminated objects were yellow. Too many times, he concluded, artists did not know the essential element of their craft.

Before proceeding with Goethe's remarks, let us look for a moment at Crane's usual treatment of color. Obviously the young writer was fascinated by color throughout most of his early writing career.[7] *The Red Badge of Courage,* "The Black Riders," "A Gray Sleeve," "A Dark-Brown Dog," "A Silver Pageant"—his titles alone suggest this. But in looking through his work, one discovers that though he made great use of color, Crane employed it for specific and limited ends. Never, for example, does he utilize it for a massed tableau or lengthy descriptive effect such as one might find in Cooper. Nor does he primarily employ it for depiction of character or clothing. What Crane tends to do is to use his color dramatically, dealing with it metaphorically or psychologically and often using it to give a sudden flash of insight into a particular situation or physical setting.

Here it is best to distinguish between a descriptive use of color and a metaphoric use. There is obviously a different purpose in using "red" to describe boots and mittens and using it to describe "cheers" and "oaths." In the first the emphasis is on the description, the color of the object; in the second the emphasis is on the emotional effect, the connotation of the adjective. It is in examples of the second type that Crane makes his important contribution. Sometimes the metaphors are synesthetic, usually involving the senses of sight and sound ("red cheers," "a crimson roar," "a yellow crash"), but more often they are simply quick color-images. In *The Red Badge of Courage,* a charging army is a "red and green monster," boughs are "green doors," a dying man's face is "gray paste," war is a "red animal," curses create a "blue haze," shells explode in "crimson fury."

There is, of course, a crucial middle ground between pure description and pure connotation. In this area the description has a dual purpose: it must both depict and symbolize, tell and suggest, and often it takes a great writer to achieve both goals. Henry James is a master here; Crane, in his best stories, is not far behind. But in Crane's case it is the color that does the real work, and again Crane is more occupied with his suggestion than with his description. The color sets a mood, defines a situation. Here is the depiction of daybreak as seen through the eyes of the fearful, anxious Henry in *The Red Badge of Courage:*

> In the gloom before the break of the day their [the men's] uniforms glowed a deep purple hue. From across the river the red eyes of the enemy campfires were still peering. In the eastern sky there was a yellow patch like a rug laid for the feet of the coming sun; and against it, black and patternless, loomed the gigantic figure of the colonel on a gigantic horse.[8]

Here through the use of color Crane vividly suggests the feelings of a sensitive youth facing his first battle. From this example and others one perceives that Crane's impressionism is largely visual, that color is a key element, and that the purpose is to convey emotion (rather than panorama or spectacle) through quick, vivid description.[9]

This kind of technique, though undoubtedly refined by Crane's own sensibility and experience, might well have been suggested by Goethe, who, as we have seen, was interested in color for its emotional impact and who constantly referred to the sensation (*empfindung*), the impression (*eindruck*), the effect (*wirkung*) of color. What probably interested Crane the most was Goethe's emotional evaluation of the various colors. For Goethe the cold colors were blue, red-blue, and blue-red. These had an affinity to black and thus to darkness and produced a "restless, susceptible, anxious impression." These colors, however, might give a "soft" impression if used in the proper lightened shade. The warm colors (and it is these that Crane most often used) were yellow, red-yellow (orange), and yellow-red (vermillion). These were basically attractive to the human eye and excited feelings that were "quick, lively, and aspiring." In discussing yellow, Goethe writes:

> In its highest purity it always carries with it the nature of brightness, and has a serene, gay, softly exciting nature. . . . We find from experience, again, that yellow excites a warm and agreeable impression. . . . The eye is gladdened, the heart expanded and cheered, a glow seems at once to breathe toward us.[10]

But yellow is "extremely liable to contamination" and when sullied produces a "very disagreeable effect":

> When a yellow color is communicated to dull and coarse surfaces, such as common cloth, felt, or the like, on which it does not appear with full energy, the disagreeable effect alluded to is apparent. By a slight and scarcely perceptible change, the beautiful impression of fire and gold is transformed into one not undeserving the epithet foul; and the color of honor and joy reversed to that of ignominy and aversion. To this impression the yellow hats of bankrupts and the yellow circles on the mantles of Jews may have owed their origin.[11]

Both these effects of yellow are employed by Crane. The cheery gay impression is usually associated with sunlight or dappled shade and is most often found in scenes of the early morning. Here is the morning march from *The Red Badge of Courage:*

> The rushing yellow of the developing day went on behind their backs. When the sunrays at last struck full and mellowingly upon the earth, the youth saw that the landscape was streaked with two long, thin, black columns. . . . Some ardor of the air which was causing the veteran commands to move with glee—almost with song—had infected the new regiment. . . . The company wags all made their best endeavors. The regiment tramped to the tune of laughter.

Later, after the battle, Henry imagines his public deeds passing in review:

> Those performances which had been witnessed by his fellows marched now in wide purple and gold, having various deflections. They went gayly with music. It was a pleasure to watch these things. He spent delightful minutes viewing the gilded images of memory.[12]

Yellow is more prominently used, however, to connote ugliness, ominousness, or disaster. Very often Crane's reference is to a sickly yellow or a pale yellowish light (the color not appearing with "full energy"). In *Maggie*, for example, the death waters which receive Maggie's body are illumined by the "yellow glare" of a factory which lights "for a moment the waters lapping oilily against the timbers." The saloon where Pete tends bar "shed a yellow glare" and "called seductively to passengers to enter and annihilate sorrow or create rage." The unhappy girls who work with Maggie in the sweatshop wear "various shades of yellow discontent." In *The Red Badge of Courage* the color of the corpse's mouth "changed to an appalling yellow." Henry's mother throws "a yellow light . . . upon the color of his ambitions." In *George's Mother* both the tenement rooms occupied by the Kelceys and by Bleecker shine with a "yellow glare." The drunken Kelcey falls "with a yellow crash." A "pale flood" of sunlight streams over Mrs. Kelcey when George tells her he has been fired. In truth, Crane's early work almost radiates with pale and ominous yellows.

A second similarity between the two writers exists in their attitudes toward red. This was a color that Goethe placed in a special category. Not only was it the "acme," the "culmination" of the spectrum, but because it "includes all the other colors" (Goethe believed red was all-inclusive rather than white), its effect was "peculiar." All colors, Goethe held, increased in energy and power as they approached red, and for this reason yellow which in its pure state produced an agreeable, cheerful sensation created "an intolerably powerful impression" when it became yellow-red.

> The active side [of color] is here in its highest energy, and it is not to be wondered at that impetuous, robust, uneducated men, should be especially pleased with this color. Among savage nations the inclination for it has been universally remarked, and when children, left to themselves, begin to use tints, they never spare vermilion and minium. . . . It produces an extreme excitement, and still acts thus when somewhat darkened. . . . I have known men of education to whom its effect was intolerable if they chanced to see a person dressed in a scarlet cloak on a grey, cloudy day.[13]

This same heightening effect also occurred with blue except that it, being a cold color, produced a progressively disturbing rather than enlivening sensation as it became blue-red. Curiously enough, pure red, the epitome of power, produced a "feeling of satisfaction" because it represented an equilibrium between "two contrasted extremes which have gradually prepared themselves for a union." But this feeling of satisfaction resulted partly from the impression of power, and of all the colors red and its variant tints were the most volatile in their emotional impact, capable of inspiring such diverse sentiments as awe, dread, dignity, grace, and majesty. Goethe leaves no doubt about the effectiveness and potentiality of red, when properly used, in furthering an artist's intentions. He writes, "Whoever is acquainted with the prismatic origin of red, will not think it paradoxical if we assert that this color, partly *actu,* partly *potentia,* includes all other colors . . . [and is the] highest of all appearances of color. . . ."[14]

Crane's fascination with red is so obvious and so frequently exemplified in his stories, particularly his early ones, that it needs little extensive comment. Berryman believes that as a small boy Crane was inordinately attracted to the color, and articles of clothing

—boots, hoods, mittens, cloaks—are often red in Crane's stories of childhood. But the stories of childhood come late in Crane's writing career, and here, as in other late stories, red is purely descriptive, whereas in the earlier stories, *Maggie,* the Sullivan County sketches, and *The Red Badge of Courage,* red is usually metaphoric, sometimes synesthetic, and almost always used to heighten emotion or to imply violence. In *Maggie,* Jimmie's teen-age years are the "red years," he has "blood-red dreams at the passing of pretty women," and red is the color constantly associated with Maggie's brutal and drunken mother. In *The Red Badge of Courage,* the title itself is a metaphor of violence, and war is symbolized throughout by red, crimson, or flame color. Indeed Crane was almost obsessed with red in this novel, using some aspect of the color sixty times in the story. The fear, the rage, the annihilation of war—all are presented in shades of crimson and carmine. In the beginning Henry and the men "were going to look at war, the red animal—war, the blood-swollen god"; and at the end Henry knew he "had been where there was red of blood and black of passion and he was escaped. . . . He had rid himself of the red sickness of battle."

Another color technique that distinguishes Crane's work, most noticeably in *The Red Badge of Courage,* is the constant juxtaposition of light and color against darkness and shade, or conversely (though less often), a foreground of darkness or cloud framed by light or color. This technique of contrast which both describes and suggests intensifies the emotion generated by the scene, and Crane used it time and again. Red quills of rifle-fire flash out against black battle clouds, dark horsemen loom against the coming sun, the red eyes of hostile campfires glare in the blackness of night, perspectives are mingled white and dark as sunlight and smoke shift and filter. Note the contrasts in this description of early evening:

> When another night came the columns, changed to purple streaks, filed across two pontoon bridges. A glaring fire wine-tinted the waters of the river. Its rays, shining upon the moving masses of troops, brought forth here and there sudden gleams of silver or gold. Upon the other shore a dark and mysterious range of hills was curved against the sky.[15]

R. W. Stallman, who first commented on Crane's use of contrast, believes it definitely links the author with the nineteenth-century impressionistic painters who employed similar devices of juxtaposition and perspective.[16] But it is quite possible that Crane first studied this technique while reading Goethe, who discusses at considerable length both the physiological and psychological effects of light and dark on the human eye. Goethe believed that depending on the effect he wished to achieve, the painter could heighten or subdue the force of his colors by judicious placement against light or dark. Goethe's judgment is explicit. "The colors of the active side [that is, the warm colors] placed next to black gain in energy, those of the passive side [the cold colors] lose. The active conjoined with white and brightness lose in strength, the passive gain in cheerfulness." [17] Thus if one wished to accentuate or dramatize, he used yellow, orange, and bright red with black, and blue, purple, and dark red with white. This is exactly what Crane does. Again note the contrasts.

> The level sheets of flame developed great clouds of smoke that tumbled and tossed in the mild wind. . . . The clouds were tinged an earthlike yellow in the sunrays and in the shadow were a sorry blue. The flag was sometimes eaten and lost in this mass of vapor, but more often it projected, sun-touched, resplendent.[18]

Later, Goethe remarks that pictures in black and white have little attraction for the viewer. The human eye demands color and then complementary color:

> If the artist abandons himself to his feeling, color presently announces itself. Black no sooner inclines to blue than the eye demands yellow, which the artist instinctively modifies and introduces. . . . All kinds of *camayeu*, or color on color, end in the introduction either of a complemented contrast, or some variety of hue.[19]

In several parts of this section, Goethe stresses the value and "satisfaction" gained from contrast and complementarism. He produces a color wheel and draws lines from color to complement.

"Yellow," he writes, "demands red-blue, blue demands red-yellow, red demands green, and contrariwise." [20] With such statements before him Crane could have learned the entire principle of contrast and worked out what Goethe calls elsewhere "the law of desired change."

Near the end of his remarks Goethe summarizes the effect of color on the human eye. He divides color-impressions into three categories or "rubrics": "the powerful, the soft, and the splendid."

> The first is produced by the preponderance of the active side, the second by that of the passive side, and the third by completeness, by the exhibition of the whole chromatic scale in due balance.
>
> The powerful impression is attained by yellow, yellow-red, and red, which last color is to be arrested on the plus side. But little violet and blue, still less green, are admissible. The soft effect is produced by blue, violet, and red, which in this case is arrested on the minus side; a moderate addition of yellow and yellow-red, but much green may be admitted. . . . the harmonious effect [the splendid] only takes place when all the colors are exhibited together in due balance.[21]

From earlier examples we have seen Crane's attempt at a powerful effect with yellows, oranges, and reds. His personal view of the universe as an uncaring, sometimes hostile world encouraged the use of these colors while it discouraged the employment of soft colors, except for use in irony or relaxation of tension. The end of *The Red Badge of Courage* when Henry turns "with a lover's thirst to images of tranquil skies, fresh meadows, cool brooks—an existence of soft and eternal peace" is a good example of Crane's use of soft imagery, whether one decides the tone is serious or ironic. Other instances of Crane's employment of soft colors can be found in his descriptions of nature, particularly in his skies which are "light blue," "fairy blue," "pure blue," and "enameled" blue, and which usually symbolize nature's indifference to the plight of man.

Much the same situation exists in the case of the "splendid," which again Crane uses sparingly. It is usually connected with nature and utilized ironically, as in "The Open Boat," where the beauty of the sea contrasts sharply with the misery and anxiety of the men. Crane writes, "It was probably splendid, it was probably glorious, this play of the free sea, wild with lights of emerald and white and amber." Later

> When the correspondent again opened his eyes, the sea and the sky were each of the gray hue of the dawning. Later, carmine and gold was painted upon the waters. The morning appeared, finally, in its splendor, with a sky of pure blue, and the sunlight flamed on the tips of the waves.
> On the distant dunes were set many little black cottages, and a tall white windmill reared above them.[22]

Here one has almost the entire spectrum in a view which the men ironically cannot enjoy.

When these facts are considered together, the influence of Goethe on Crane is clear. Certainly the symbolic use of color derives from the German writer, who felt that a perfect symbolic application was one in which

> color would be employed in conformity with its effect and would at once express its meaning. If, for example, pure red were assumed to designate majesty, there can be no doubt that this would be admitted to be a just and expressive symbol.[23]

Crane did not use his red to designate majesty, but he did use it "in conformity with its effect." If war was Crane's metaphor for life, whether on the battlefield or in the slums, then red and its close allies were his colors for that metaphor—and this is as Goethe would have it.

But one cannot completely separate a symbolic use of color from other uses or from impressionism. In fact, in studying Crane, one keeps coming back to Hamlin Garland's definition of impressionism, "the stayed and reproduced effect of a single section of the world of color upon the eye," [24] and Goethe's comment about color being used "in conformity with its effect." A window glows "a deep murder red" during battle, shells explode "redly" flinging "the brown earth," a house stands "white and calm amid bursting shells." Color is here both symbolic and impressionistic, and its use is in perfect keeping with Crane's statement on impressionism made in his late story, "War Memories":

> I bring this [impression of a wounded man] to you merely as an effect, an effect of mental light and shade, if you like; something done in thought similar to that which the French impressionists do in color; something meaningless and at the same time, overwhelming, crushing, monstrous.[25]

From this comment it seems clear that Crane saw the effectiveness of combining the symbolic and the chromatic, and he worked hard at integrating the two. In fact, these quick, momentary images of color and meaning become a conscious device in the early stories, and Crane was perfectly aware of the critical excitement caused by his technique, one which H. G. Wells called Crane's "force of color," his "chromatic splashes."

I think too that though Crane knew the work of the impressionists and may have profited from their ideas, especially in his technical handling of scene,[26] some of the influence usually credited to them probably originated with Goethe. Critics in linking Crane and the impressionistic painters most often mention Crane's careful selection of detail, his emphasis on color, his use of suggestiveness, and his concern for the fleeting effect of light and contrast. Yet, as we have seen, every one of these ideas is specifically mentioned by Goethe, and the last three are dealt with at length.

The question whether Crane knew Goethe or the impressionists first has not been definitely decided, but in all likelihood Crane read Goethe at least a year or so before he knew the impressionists, most probably coming on the German writer while still at Syracuse University in 1891. *Maggie*, begun in the spring of that year, shows the same color techniques as those specifically credited to Goethe when Crane discussed *The Red Badge of Courage* with Noxon. Yet Crane probably had no real knowledge of the impressionists until the fall and winter of 1892-1893 when he lived with "the Indians," a group of young struggling artists with whom he discussed life, art, and "impressionism." [27]

What seems most likely is that Crane grafted on to what he knew of Goethe the impressionistic ideas that he found congenial.

Certainly Crane would have had some knowledge of the principles found in the French painters from his reading in Goethe, for the German writer clearly adumbrates many impressionistic concepts. The stress on the emotional reaction to color, the concern with contrast and complementarism, the interest in light and shade, and the whole concept of a scientific approach to the problems of light may be found in both Goethe and the French painters. Here is Goethe, writing in 1810, explaining an impressionist concept used seventy years later:

> Color combinations [that is, combinations of primary colors and intermixtures] have also the common quality of producing the intermediate color of our colorific circle by their union, a union which actually takes place if they are opposed to each other and seen from a distance. A surface covered with narrow blue and yellow stripes appears green at a certain distance.[28]

In conclusion, it does not seem too much to say that if Crane knew Goethe, he knew something about impressionism before he knew the impressionists. In Goethe lay the essential raw materials for an experiment, whether literary or artistic, in the psychological and impressionistic use of color, and Crane, seeking some way to break away from the stereotypes of the nineteenth-century novel, availed himself of such material. It is quite possible, I think, that much of the argument over whether or not Crane is indebted to the impressionists is primarily academic. He did know Goethe, and this accounts for many of his color techniques. In truth, Noxon's comment concerning Goethe's "profound impression" upon Crane does not seem exaggerated when one considers the scope and potentialities inherent in the ideas of the German writer and the uses to which Crane put them. All in all the ore was there, and Crane, sensitive genius that he was, had the talent and imagination to refine it into his own peculiar gold.

NOTES

1. *Stephen Crane: Letters*, ed. R. W. Stallman and Lillian Gilkes (New York University Press, 1960), p. 336. Noxon did not know when or how much Crane knew of Goethe's book, but Crane's metaphorical use of color certainly antedates *The Red Badge of Courage*, going back at least to *Maggie* (begun in 1891), which reveals considerable use of the technique.

2. The question of Crane's relationship to the French painters has a long history and has recently become a controversial issue. H. G. Wells in 1900 and J. D. Barry in 1901 were two early writers who believed Crane's work definitely showed the influence of the impressionists, and later Harry Hartwick bolstered this position. (See respectively Wells' "Stephen Crane from an English Point of View," reprinted in Edmund Wilson's *The Shock of Recognition;* Barry's "A Note on Stephen Crane," *Bookman*, XIII, 148; and Hartwick's *The Foreground of American Fiction*, pp. 21-44). Crane's indebtedness was generally accepted until 1949 when Melvin Schoberlin disputed this interpretation, commenting that Crane's sense of color was "innate" and that he "borrowed nothing" from the impressionists. (See Melvin Schoberlin (ed.), *The Sullivan County Sketches*, pp. 14-15). John Berryman in his *Stephen Crane* (1950) agreed with Schoberlin, holding that Crane's color was "primitive" and "psychological" and not like that found in painting. (See Berryman's *Stephen Crane*, p. 289.) Almost immediately R. W. Stallman and Joseph Kwiat objected; both argued that the influence of the studio on Crane could be demonstrated and that Crane's techniques were too close to those of the impressionists to be accidental. (See Stallman's *Stephen Crane: An Omnibus*, pp. 184-187 and Kwiat's "Stephen Crane and Painting," *American Quarterly*, IV, 331-338.) In 1958 the posthumous reminiscences of Crane's artist-friend Corwin Linson supported the Schoberlin-Berryman thesis. Linson wrote that early impressionism was "an affectation" to Crane and that the impact and understanding of the French artists came too late to influence Crane. (See Linson's *My Stephen Crane*, pp. 46-47.) The topic has also become an item in Ph.D. dissertations on Crane. Both John Bushman's "The Fiction of Stephen Crane and Its Critics" (unpublished dissertation, University of Illinois, 1943), pp. 42-43, and Will Jumper's "Tragic Irony As Form: Structural Problems in The Prose of Stephen Crane" (unpublished dissertation, Stanford University, 1958), pp. 112-141 support the theory of Crane's indebtedness. Jumper's review of the entire problem is the most extensive yet written.

3. Crane did not know German, and it appears almost certain that he gained his information from Eastlake's translation, the only one made of this work in the nineteenth century, rather than from the two or three magazine articles which discussed Goethe's theory of colors. The articles all stress the scientific rather than the aesthetic investigation in the book and probably would not have appealed to Crane. For a typical article see John Tyndall's "Goethe's Farbenlehre," *Popular Science Monthly*, XVII (1880), 215-224, 312-321.

4. In his letter Noxon says that Crane mentioned a "passage in Goethe." This entire section would take about 15 pages in a modern pocket book. It is possible that Goethe's remarks were excerpted or summarized in some contemporary book, but I have not found such a volume. I suspect Noxon meant passage in a general rather than a specific sense.

5. *Goethe's Theory of Colors*, trans. Sir Charles Eastlake (London: J. Murray, 1840), pp. 304-305.

6. *Ibid.,* p. 352.
7. Crane's use of color imagery is much less frequent after 1897. It never completely dies, but none of the later stories contain the color found in the Sullivan County sketches or *The Red Badge of Courage.*
8. *Stephen Crane: An Omnibus,* ed. R. W. Stallman (New York: Knopf, 1952), p. 239.
9. Crane employs some metaphors of sound ("a vast hive of men buzzing in frantic circles") and some of touch ("a voice of cave-damp"), but his usual imagery is visual and chromatic.
10. *Goethe's Theory of Colors,* p. 307.
11. *Ibid.,* p. 308.
12. *Stephen Crane: An Omnibus,* pp. 241-242 and 366 respectively. It is interesting to note that there is no description of sunrise on the second day of battle.
13. *Goethe's Theory of Colors,* pp. 309-310.
14. *Ibid.,* pp. 313-314.
15. *Stephen Crane: An Omnibus,* p. 246.
16. *Ibid.,* pp. 185-187. Stallman gives several examples of Crane's use of contrast between light and dark, warm color and cold color.
17. *Goethe's Theory of Colors,* p. 325.
18. *Stephen Crane: An Omnibus,* p. 267.
19. *Goethe's Theory of Colors,* p. 334.
20. *Ibid.,* p. 318.
21. *Ibid.,* pp. 340-341.
22. *Stephen Crane: An Omnibus,* p. 442.
23. *Goethe's Theory of Colors,* p. 350.
24. Garland, *Crumbling Idols* (Gainsville: Scholars' Facsimiles and Reprints, 1952), p. 122.
25. Stephen Crane, *Work,* ed. Wilson Follett (New York: Knopf, 1925-26), IX, 246.
26. Kwiat, *op. cit.,* cites some excellent examples of Crane's impressionistic use of color and chiaroscuro in his handlng of scene. See pp. 334-335.
27. Kwiat believes Crane may have had some earlier inkling of impressionism from his sister Mary Helen, who was an art instructor in Asbury Park in the late 1880's, and from Phebe English, a young painter-acquaintance whom Crane knew while he was at Claverack Academy. Outside of a sketchy article in *Harpers* in February 1887, there is no literature in American magazines on the impressionists until mid-1892.
28. *Goethe's Theory of Colors,* p. 323.

5. *"That Was at Chancellorsville": The Factual Framework of* THE RED BADGE OF COURAGE *By Harold R. Hungerford*

The name of the battle in which Henry Fleming achieved his manhood is never given in *The Red Badge of Courage*. Scholars have not agreed that the battle even ought to have a name; some have implied that it is a potpourri of episodes from a number of battles.[1] Yet an examination of the evidence leads to the conclusion that the battle does have a name—Chancellorsville. Throughout the book, it can be demonstrated, Crane consistently used the time, the place, and the actions of Chancellorsville as a factual framework within which to represent the perplexities of his young hero.[2]

I

Evidence of two sorts makes the initial hypothesis that Crane used Chancellorsville probable. In the first place, Crane said so in his short story "The Veteran," which was published less than a year after *The Red Badge*. In this story he represented an elderly Henry Fleming as telling about his fear and flight in his first battle. "That was at Chancellorsville," Henry said. His brief account is consistent in every respect with the more extended account in *The Red Badge;* old Henry's motives for flight were those of the young Henry, and he referred to Jim Conklin in a way which made it clear that Jim was long since dead.

This brief reference in "The Veteran" is, so far as I know, the only direct indication Crane ever gave that the battle in *The Red Badge* was Chancellorsville. He appears never to have mentioned the matter in his letters, and his biographers recount no references to it. Such evidence as that cited above must be used with discretion; Crane might conceivably have changed his mind. But there is no good reason why he should have done so; and in any case, the clue given us by "The Veteran" can be thoroughly corroborated by a second kind of evidence, that of time and place.

Reprinted from: *American Literature*, XXXIV (January 1963), 520-531. By permission of The Duke University Press.

No one questions that *The Red Badge* is about the Civil War; the references to Yanks and Johnnies, to blue uniforms on one side and to gray and butternut on the other clearly establish this fact. If we turn now to military history, we find that the evidence of place and time points directly to Chancellorsville.

Only three actual place-names are used in the book: Washington, Richmond, and the Rappahannock River.[3] Henry Fleming and his fellow-soldiers had come through Washington to their winter quarters near the Rappahannock River, and their army was close enough to Richmond that cavalry could move against that city. Such a combination points to northern Virginia, through which the Rappahannock flows, to which Union soldiers would come through Washington, and from which Richmond would be readily accessible. Chancellorsville was fought in northern Virginia.

Furthermore, the battle was the first major engagement of the year, occurring when the spring rains were nearly over. The year cannot be 1861; the war began in April, and soldiers would not have spent the winter in camp. Nor can it be 1862; the first eastern batle of 1862, part of McClellan's Peninsular Campaign, in no way resembled that in the book and was far removed from the Rappahannock. It cannot be 1864; the Battle of the Wilderness was fought near the Rappahannock but did not end in a Union defeat. Its strategy was in any case significantly different from that of the battle in *The Red Badge*. Finally, 1865 is ruled out; Lee had surrendered by the time the spring rains ended.

If we are to select any actual conflict at all, a *reductio ad absurdum* indicates the first eastern battle of 1863, and that battle was Chancellorsville. Moreover, 1863 marked the turning-point in the Union fortunes; before Gettysburg the South had, as Wilson remarked in *The Red Badge,* licked the North "about every clip" (p. 255). After Gettysburg no Union soldier would have been likely to make such a statement; and Gettysburg was the next major battle after Chancellorsville.

Like the evidence of "The Veteran," the evidence of time and place points to Chancellorsville, and it is therefore at least a tenable hypothesis that Chancellorsville and *The Red Badge* are closely connected. In the next three sections I shall present independent proof of that hypothesis by showing that the battle in Crane's novel is closely and continuously parallel to the historical Chancellorsville.[4]

II

The events preceding the battle occupy the first two chapters and part of the third (pp. 238-258). The opening chapter establishes the situation of the Union army. As winter passed into spring, that army was resting in winter camp across a river from a Confederate army. It had been there for some time—long enough for soldiers to build huts with chimneys, long enough for a new recruit to have been encamped for some months without seeing action. ". . . there had come months of monotonous life in a camp. . . . since his regiment had come to the field the army had done little but sit still and try to keep warm" (p. 244). Such was the situation of the Army of the Potomac in April, 1863; it had spent a cold, wet winter encamped at Falmouth, Virginia, on the north bank of the Rappahannock River opposite the Confederate army. The army had been inactive since mid-December; its men had dug themselves into just such huts, covered with folded tents and furnished with clay chimneys, as Crane describes (p. 240). Furthermore, the arrival of a new Union commander, General Joseph Hooker, had meant hour after hour of drill and review for the soldiers; and Henry was "drilled and drilled and reviewed, and drilled and drilled and reviewed" (p. 245).

To this monotony the "tall soldier"—Jim Conklin—brought the news that "The cavalry started this morning. . . . They say there ain't hardly any cavalry left in camp. They're going to Richmond, or some place, while we fight all the Johnnies. It's some dodge like that" (p. 247). He had earlier announced, "We're goin' t' move t'-morrah—sure. . . . We're goin' 'way up th' river, cut across, an' come around in behint 'em" (p. 238). Of course Jim was "the fast flying messenger of a mistake," but the mistake was solely one of dates; the infantry did not move at once. Many soldiers at Falmouth jumped to Jim's conclusion when eleven thousand cavalrymen left camp April 13 for a raid on the Confederate railroad lines near Richmond. No one in the book denied that the cavalry had left; and Jim's analysis of the flank movement was to be confirmed at the end of the book when another soldier said, "Didn't I tell yeh we'd come aroun' in behint 'em? Didn't I tell yeh so?" (p. 373). The strategy Jim had predicted was precisely that of Chancellorsville.

The Union army at Falmouth did not leave camp for two weeks after the departure of the cavalry, and such a period accords with the time represented in the book; "for days" after the cavalry left, Henry fretted about whether or not he would run (p. 249).

Finally Henry's regiment, the 304th New York, was assembled, and it began to march before dawn. When the sun rose, "the river was not in view" (p. 252). Since the rising sun was at the backs of the marching men, they were going west. The eager soldiers "expressed commiseration for that part of the army which had been left upon the river bank" (p. 253). That night the regiment encamped; tents were pitched and fires lighted. "When another night came" (p. 257), the men crossed a river on *two* pontoon bridges and continued unmolested to a camping place.

This description fits aptly the march of the Second Corps. Many of its regiments were mustered before dawn on April 28, and then marched west and away from the Rappahannock. The Second, unlike the other corps marching to Chancellorsville, was ordered not to make any special secret of its whereabouts and was allowed fires when it camped. The Second crossed the Rappahannock on *two* pontoon bridges the evening of April 30 and camped safely near Chancellorsville that night; all the other corps had to ford at least one river, without the convenience of bridges. Furthermore, by no means all of the army moved at once; two full corps and one division of the Second Corps were left behind at Falmouth to conduct a holding action against Lee.

It is clear from the text that at least one day intervened between the evening on which Henry's regiment crossed the bridges and the morning of its first day of fighting (pp. 257-258). If Crane was following the chronology of Chancellorsville, this intervening day of pensive rest was May 1, on which only the Fifth and Twelfth Corps saw fighting.

III

Action began early for Henry's regiment the next day, the events of which parallel those at Chancellorsvile on May 2. The statements (pp. 258-279) about what Henry and his regiment did are clear enough. He was rudely awakened at dawn, ran down a wood road, and crossed a little stream. His regiment was moved three times before the noon meal, and then moved again; one of these movements took Henry and his companions back, for in the afternoon they proceeded over the same ground they had taken that morning and then into new territory. By early afternoon, then, Henry had seen no fighting. At last a brigade ahead of them went into action; it was routed and fled, leaving the reserves, of which Henry's regiment was a part, to withstand the enemy. The regiment successfully resisted the first charge, but when the enemy re-attacked, Henry fled.

It might seem that tracing the path of Henry and his regiment before his flight would not be impossible, but it has proved to be so. The regimental movements which Crane describes loosely parallel the movements of many regiments at Chancellorsville; they directly parallel the movements of none.[5] Nevertheless, broad parallels do exist. Many regiments of the Second Corps moved southeast from Chancellorsville on May 2; many of them first encountered the enemy in midafternoon.

Furthermore, it can be demonstrated that the 304th, like the regiments of the Second Corps, was near the center of the Union line. In the first place, the "cheery man" tells Henry, and us, so (p. 312). His testimony deserves some credence; anyone who can so unerringly find a regiment in the dark should know what he is talking about. Moreover, the conversation of the soldiers before the assault (pp. 266-267) makes it clear that they were not facing the rebel right, which would have been opposite the Union left. Nor were they far to the Union right, as I shall show later.

The evidence given us by the terrain Henry crossed also points to a position at about the center of the Union line. During the morning and early afternoon he crossed several streams and passed into and out of cleared fields and dense woods. The land was gently rolling; there were occasional fences and now and then a house. Such topographical features, in 1863, characterized the area south and east of Chancellorsville itself. Further east, in the area held by the Union left, the terrain opened up and the dense second-growth forest thinned out; further west the forest was very thick indeed, with few fields or other open areas. But southeast of Chancellorsville, where the Union center was located, the land was cultivated to a degree; fields had been cleared and cut off from the forest by fences. Topography so conditioned action at Chancellorsville that every historian of the battle perforce described the terrain; if Crane knew the battle as well as I suggest he did, he must have known its topography.

Topography also gives us our only clue to the untraceable path of Henry's flight. At one point he "found himself almost into a swamp. He was obliged to walk upon bog tufts, and watch his feet to keep from the oily water" (p. 285). A man fleeing west from the center of the Union line would have encountered swamps after a few miles of flight. The detail is perhaps minor, but it corroborates the path Henry had to follow to reach the place where he received his "red badge of courage." He went west, toward the Union right held by the Eleventh Corps.

Henry's flight led him to the path of the retreating wounded soldiers, among them Jim Conklin. The scene of Jim's death (pp. 289-301) contains no localizing evidence, for Crane was concentrating upon the men, not their surroundings. Nevertheless, it is appropriate to Chancellorsville; the roads leading to the river were clogged with retreating Union wounded in the late afternoon of May 2. There were no ambulances near the battle lines, and many wounded men died as they walked.

By contrast, the scene of Henry's wound can be readily fixed. He received it in the middle of the most-discussed single action of the battle, an action which cost Stonewall Jackson his life and a major general his command, almost surely won the battle for Lee, and generated thirty-five years of acrimonious debate. Even today, to mention Chancellorsville is inevitably to bring up the rout of the Eleventh Corps.

About sunset on May 2, 1863, Stonewall Jackson's crack troops attacked the predominantly German Eleventh Corps. The Eleventh, which was on the extreme right of the Union line and far from the fighting, was taken wholly by surprise, and many soldiers turned and ran in terrified disorder. The result was near-catastrophe for the Union; now that Jackson's men had turned the flank, the path lay open for an assault on the entire unprotected rear of the Union army.

Appropriately enough for such a battle, Jackson's men were halted by one of history's more extraordinary military maneuvers. For in a battle in which hardly any cavalry were used, a small detachment of cavalrymen held Jackson's corps off long enough to enable artillery to be dragged into place and charged with canister. The cavalrymen could do so because the dense woods confined Jackson's men to the road. The small detachment was the Eighth Pennsylvania Cavalry; the time was between 6:30 and 7 P.M. Theirs was the only cavalry charge at Chancellorsville, and it became famous not only because it had saved the Union army—perhaps even the Union—but also because no two observers could agree on its details; any historian is therefore obliged to give the charge considerable attention.

All these elements fit the time and place of Henry's wounding. Night was falling fast after his long afternoon of flight; "landmarks had vanished into the gathered gloom" (p. 308). All about Henry "very burly men" were fleeing from the enemy. "They sometimes gabbled insanely. One huge man was asking of the sky, 'Say, where de plank road? Where de plank road?' " A popular stereotype holds that all Germans are burly, and an unsympathetic listener could regard rapidly-spoken German as "gabbling." Certainly the replacement of *th* by *d* fits the pattern of Germans; Crane's Swede in "The Veteran" also lacks *th*. These might be vulgar errors, but they identified a German pretty readily in the heyday of dialect stories. Furthermore, plank roads were rare in northern Virginia; but a plank road ran through the Union lines toward the Rappahannock.

One of these fleeing Germans hit Henry on the head; and after he received his wound, while he was still dazed, Henry saw the arrival of the cavalry and of the artillery:

> Around him he could hear the grumble of jolted cannon as the scurrying horses were lashed toward the front. . . . He turned and watched the mass of guns, men, and horses sweeping in a wide curve toward a gap in a fence. . . . Into the unspeakable jumble in the roadway rode a squadron of cavalry. The faded yellow of their facings shone bravely. There was a mighty altercation. (pp. 309-310)

As Henry fled the scene, he could hear the guns fire and the opposing infantry fire back. "There seemed to be a great luck of men and munitions spread about in the forest and in the fields" (p. 310).

Every element of the scene is consistent with contemporary descriptions of the rout of the Eleventh Corps. The time is appropriate; May 2 was the first real day of battle at Chancellorsville as it was the first day for Henry. The place is appropriate; if Henry had begun the day in the Union center and then had fled west through the swamps, he would have come toward the right of the Union line, where the men of the Eleventh Corps were fleeing in rout. The conclusion is unavoidable: Crane's use of the factual framework of Chancellorsville led him to place his hero in the middle of that battle's most important single action.

The first day of battle in *The Red Badge* ended at last when the cheery man found Henry, dazed and wandering, and led him back to his regiment by complicated and untraceable paths.

IV

The second day of battle, like the first, began early. Henry's regiment was sent out "to relieve a command that had lain long in some damp trenches" (p. 328). From these trenches could be heard the noise of skirmishers in the woods to the front and left, and the din of battle to the right was tremendous. Again, such a location fits well enough the notion of a center regiment; the din on the right, in the small hours of May 3, would have come from Jackson's men trying to re-establish their connection with the main body of Lee's army.

Soon, however, Henry's regiment was withdrawn and began to retreat from an exultant enemy; Hooker began such a withdrawal about 7:30 A.M. on May 3. Finally the retreat stopped and almost immediately thereafter Henry's regiment was sent on a suicidal charge designed to prevent the enemy from breaking the Union lines. This charge significantly resembles that of the 124th New York, a regiment raised principally in the county which contains Port Jervis, Crane's hometown; and the time of this charge of the 124th—about 8:30 A.M. —fits the time-scheme of *The Red Badge* perfectly.[6]

The next episode (pp. 360-362) can be very precisely located; Crane's description is almost photographically accurate. Henry was about a quarter of a mile south of Fairview, the "slope on the left" from which the "long row of guns, gruff and maddened, denounc[ed] the enemy" (p. 360). Moreover, "in the rear of this row of guns stood a house, calm and white, amid bursting shells. A congregation of horses, tied to a railing, were tugging frenziedly at their bridles. Men were running hither and thither" (p. 361). This is a good impression of the Chancellor House, which was used as the commanding general's headquarters and which alone, in a battle at which almost no cavalry were present, had many horses belonging to the officers and orderlies tied near it.

The second charge of the 304th, just before the general retreat was ordered, is as untraceable as the first. It has, however, its parallel at Chancellorsville: several regiments of the Second Corps were ordered to charge the enemy about 10 A.M. on May 3 to give the main body of the army time to withdraw the artillery and to begin its retreat.

The two days of battle came to an end for Henry Fleming when his regiment was ordered to "retrace its way" and rejoined first its brigade and then its division on the way back toward the river. Such a retreat, in good order and relatively free from harassment by an exhausted enemy, began at Chancellorsville about 10 A.M. on May 3. Heavy rains again were beginning to make the roads into bogs; these rains prevented the Union soldiers from actually recrossing the river for two days, for the water was up to the level of several of the bridges. "It rained" in the penultimate paragraph of *The Red Badge;* and the battle was over for Henry Fleming as for thousands of Union soldiers at Chancellorsville.

V

This long recitation of parallels, I believe, demonstrates that Crane used Chancellorsville as a factual framework for his novel. We have reliable external evidence that Crane studied *Battles and Leaders of the Civil War* in preparation for *The Red Badge* because he was concerned with the accuracy of his novel.[7] He could have found in the ninety pages *Battles and Leaders* devotes to Chancellorsville all the information he needed on strategy, tactics, and topography. A substantial part of these ninety pages is devoted to the rout of the Eleventh Corps and the charge of the Eighth Pennsylvania Cavalry. These pages also contain what someone so visually minded as Crane could hardly have overlooked: numerous illustrations, many from battlefield sketches. The illustrations depict, among other subjects, the huts at Falmouth; men marching in two parallel columns;[8] pontoon bridges; the Chancellor House during and after the battle; and the rout of the Eleventh. With these Crane could have buttressed the unemotional but authoritative reports of Union and Confederate officers which he found in *Battles and Leaders.*

If it is unfashionable to regard Crane as a man concerned with facts, we ought to remember that late in his life he wrote *Great Battles of the World*[9]—hack work, to be sure, but scrupulously accurate in its selection of incident and detail and in its analysis of strategy. One can do far worse than to learn about Bunker Hill from Crane.

VI

Two questions remain unanswered. First, why did Crane not identify the battle in *The Red Badge* as he did in "The Veteran"? One answer is fairly simple: no one called the battle Chancellorsville in the book because no one would have known it was Chancellorsville. No impression is more powerful to the reader of Civil War reports and memoirs than that officers and men seldom knew where they were. They did not know the names of hills, or streams, or even of villages. Probably not more than a few hundred of the 130,000 Union men at Chancellorsville knew until long afterwards the name of the four corners around which the battle raged. A private soldier knew his own experiences, but not names or strategy; we have been able to reconstruct the strategy and the name because Crane used a factual framework for his novel; and the anonymity of the battle is the result of that framework.

Of course the anonymity is part of Crane's artistic technique as well. We do not learn Henry Fleming's full name until Chapter 11; we never learn Wilson's first name. Crane sought to give only so much detail as was necessary to the integrity of the book. He was not, like Zola and Tolstoi, concerned with the panorama of history and the fate of nations, but with the mind and actions of a youth unaccustomed to war. For such purposes, the name of the battle, like the names of men, did not matter; in fact, if Crane had named the battle he might have evoked in the minds of his readers reactions irrelevant to his purpose, reactions which might have set the battle in its larger social and historical framework. It would have been a loss of control.

Why, with the whole Civil War available, should Crane have chosen Chancellorsville? Surely, in the first place, because he knew a good deal about it. Perhaps he had learned from his brother, "an expert in the strategy of Gettysburg and Chancellorsville" (Beer, p. 47). More probably he had heard old soldiers talk about their war experiences while he was growing up. Many middle-aged men in Port Jervis had served in the 124th New York; Chancellorsville had been their first battle, and first impressions are likely to be the most vivid. It is hard to believe that men in an isolated small town could have resisted telling a hero-worshiping small boy about a great adventure in their lives.

Moreover, Chancellorsville surely appealed to Crane's sense of the ironic and the colorful. The battle's great charges, its moments of heroism, went only to salvage a losing cause; the South lost the war and gained only time from Chancellorsville; the North, through an incredible series of blunders, lost a battle it had no business losing. The dead, as always, lost the most. And when the battle ended, North and South were just where they had been when it began. There is a tragic futility about Chancellorsville just as there is a tragic futility to *The Red Badge*.

Finally, Chancellorsville served Crane's artistic purposes. It was the first battle of the year and the first battle for many regiments. It was therefore an appropriate introduction to war for a green soldier in an untried regiment.

The evidence of this study surely indicates that Crane was not merely a dreamer spinning fantasies out of his imagination; on the contrary, he was capable of using real events for his own fictional purposes with controlled sureness. Knowledge of the ways in which he did so is, I should think, useful to criticism. For various cogent reasons, Crane chose Chancellorsville as a factual framework within which to represent the dilemma of young Henry Fleming. Many details of the novel are clearly drawn from that battle; none are inconsistent with it. Old Henry Fleming was a truthful man: "that was at Chancellorsville."

NOTES

1. Lyndon Upson Pratt, in "A Possible Source for *The Red Badge of Courage*," *American Literature*, XI, 1-10 (March, 1939), suggests that the battle is partially based upon Antietam. Lars Ahnebrink denies his arguments and favors elements from Tolstoi and Zola in *The Beginnings of Naturalism in American Fiction*, "Upsala Essays and Studies in American Language and Literature," IX (Upsala, 1950). Both argue from a handful of parallel incidents of the sort which seem to me the common property of any war; neither makes any pretense of accounting for all the realistic framework of the novel.

2. This study developed from a class project in English 208 at the University of California (Berkeley) in the spring of 1958 and 1959. I am grateful to those who worked with Crane in these courses; and I am particularly grateful to George R. Stewart, who was unfailingly helpful to me in many ways and to whose scholarly acumen and knowledge of the Civil War I am deeply indebted.

3. All references to the novel are to *The Red Badge of Courage and Selected Prose and Poetry*, ed. William M. Gibson, Rinehart Editions (New York, 1956); page references will be included in the text. Although this edition contains the manuscript passages excised from the first edition, I have based no conclusions upon them. For Washington, see p. 244; for Richmond, p. 247; for

the Rappahannock, p. 329. Henry's reference to the Rappahannock may be
an ironic twist on a journalist's cliché, but the twist itself—the original was
Potomac—seems to me to be the result of conscious intent on Crane's part.

4. The literature on Chancellorsville is substantial. The most useful short study
is Edward J. Stackpole, *Chancellorsville: Lee's Greatest Battle* (Harrisburg,
Pa., 1958). The definitive analysis is John Bigelow, Jr., *The Campaign of
Chancellorsville: A Strategic and Tactical Study* (New Haven, 1910). Orders,
correspondence, and reports are available in *The War of the Rebellion: A
Compilation of the Official Records of the Union and Confederate Armies*,
ser. I, vol. XXV, parts 1 and 2 (Washington, D. C., 1889). See also *Battles and
Leaders of the Civil War* (New York, 1884), III, 152-243. The parallels pre-
sented below are drawn from these; all are in substantial agreement.

5. So flat a statement deserves explanation. I have read with great care all of the
307 reports of unit commanders in the *Official Records*. I have also studied
more than a dozen histories of regiments which first saw action at Chancellorsville. Many show general parallels; none show parallels with the novel
which I consider close enough to be satisfactory.

6. See Cornelius Weygandt, *History of the 124th New York* (Newburgh, N. Y.,
1877).

7. Thomas Beer, *Stephen Crane* (New York, 1923), pp. 97-98. Corwin Knapp
Linson, *My Stephen Crane*, ed. Edwin H. Cady (Syracuse, 1959), pp. 37-38,
corroborates Beer's account.

8. Here the illustration seems to explain the otherwise inexplicable description
in the novel (p. 252); Civil War soldiers rarely marched thus.

9. Philadelphia, 1901. *Great Battles* is not in the collected edition, *The Work of
Stephen Crane*, 12 vols. (New York, 1925-1926), and apparently has never been
discussed by scholars. It includes no Civil War battles, although Crane at one
time considered an article on Fredericksburg, the battle immediately preceding
Chancellorsville; see *Stephen Crane: Letters*, ed. R. W. Stallman and Lillian
Gilkes (New York, 1960), p. 98.

V

APPROACHES TO STEPHEN CRANE'S ART

A. INTRODUCTION

Source studies suggest the various possible materials Stephen Crane consciously or unconsciously drew upon for the preparation and development of his creative work. Approaches to Crane's art are determined by the critics, the literary historians, and the readers who view the finished individual work, a representative cross section of works, or the author's total canon. For good or ill, the acknowledged and unacknowledged sources Crane may have used often determine the approach taken. If Rudyard Kipling is a most important source, Crane can be made to read like an American Kipling. The literary history of the 1890s has been used to show that in his art Crane was a disappointing protégé of Howells and Garland on the one hand and an ambitious student of Zolaesque naturalism on the other. Philosophies of other periods have also been applied to make Crane read like a lost generation writer of the 1920s, or a social critic of the 1930s. He has also been read as a symbolist in the 1950s, and an existentialist and parodist in the 1960s.

The object of an approach study is to suggest a valid way in which Stephen Crane's work can be read, evaluated, and appreciated. Unfortunately, the particular approach of "naturalism" has for years been accepted as the only way to approach Crane. This has minimized and limited his strengths as an artist. One cannot ignore the various qualities in Crane—his impressionism, irony, comedy, parody, satire, naturalism, and symbolism; his grotesque character creations, and his tragicomic view of life; his tone, rhythm, style, and imagery; the episodic, dramatic, cinematic, and musical structure of his stories —all of which subtly enrich and deepen the value of his writing. Crane was continually shifting ground and experimenting with forms, genres, themes, and styles. When he is approached solely as a naturalist in *Maggie, George's Mother,* and *The Red Badge,* his later work, like *Whilomville Stories,* may seem to be totally irrelevant or work really written by someone else. If Crane is read as the anti-romantic writer in *The Red Badge,* then *The O'Ruddy,* an historical romance, is often wrongly read as a signal of his literary collapse and/or surrender, a weak echoing of Robert Louis Stevenson. Stephen Crane cannot be forced to fit precise and imposed categories.

Because Crane was so long approached via naturalism, his art

suffered for many years. Compared to Émile Zola, the leading writer
of the naturalistic school, whose novels were epic in scope and full
of raw power, Crane seemed narrow and anemic. If, like Zola, he was
concerned about social problems, he was too cryptic and too arty.
Moreover, many critics thought that Crane's creative work was much
like his naturalistic-journalistic writing (the same could be said of
other naturalists-journalists, such as Zola and Theodore Dreiser),
which they considered was hastily composed, second-rate, and of no
lasting value. A few critics have recently stated that Crane, Zola, and
Dreiser are fundamentally poets, not naturalists.

Today, Stephen Crane is still read narrowly and is not fully
understood or respected, even though more attention than ever before
is being given to his literary techniques. Only by understanding the
true dimensions of his themes and arts, only with a real appreciation
of his varied craft, can one come to respect Crane's individual talent,
and make intelligent evaluations.

1. *Stephen Crane as Social Critic*
By Russel B. Nye

I

The wave of humanitarianism and social reform which swept over the United States after the post-Appomattox period of expansion encompassed in its breadth some widely disassociated strains of thought. A crusade against a laissez-faire philosophy materialized in religious, political, economic, and social thought, and the last quarter of the old century saw sharply defined groups of liberal and conservative set one against the other. The historical significance of the liberal movement of the 1890's, and its effects in literature and socio-political thought, need no review or interpretation here.[1] The opponents of the individualistic, Spencerian doctrine, numbering among them the familiar names of Howells, Bellamy, Garland, Riis, Woolsey, Root, La Follette, Henry George, Veblen, many others in equally widely distributed fields, criticized in one way or another existing conditions, each attempting to find a more or less collectivistic way out of a naturalistic chaos. The attention of thinkers in every field was turned toward society, and literature too began to take on social meaning. We do not ordinarily classify Stephen Crane among these social critics, but his interest in poverty, crime, maladjustment, and other problems of an urban society, led him, as well, to search for a solution to the social riddle.

Critics of Crane seem to have agreed upon two aspects of his mind and art worth emphasis, his technical contributions to the short story, and his naturalistic philosophy.[2] Both of these approaches to Crane are real and valuable, but there seems to have been more or less overlooked what is perhaps the essential portion of his work, that is, his social thought and criticism, his extreme awareness of life around him, his consciousness of a class struggle. A great deal of attention has been paid to Crane's realistic method, but little to what problems he presented realistically—the problems of society.

This sociological interest on Crane's part is evident in numerous

Reprinted from: *The Modern Quarterly: A Journal of Radical Opinion*, XI (Summer 1940), 48-54.

incidents given by Thomas Beer in his biography of the man.[3] Crane talked sympathetically and interestedly to New York street-walkers, wandered through the Bowery, slept in flophouses, talked with drifters, pried stories out of breadlines and loiterers, and kept himself out of money by responding too readily to a hard luck story. Crane knew the lower levels of New York life as well as, if not better than, any other literary man of his day. This social consciousness is a major portion of his interest and of his art, one which we cannot afford to overlook.[4]

Around this interest in and observation of society, Stephen Crane built an important part of his work. His novels and novelettes, *The Red Badge of Courage, Active Service, The O'Ruddy, The Third Violet,* and his war sketches, *Tales of Two Wars, Wounds in the Rain,* are no doubt familiar to many readers. A survey of his interest in the submerged tenth, however, of his interest in the Bowery he knew, opens an area comparatively unexplored.[5]

II

It is significant that Crane's first book, *Maggie, A Girl of the Streets,* 1893, deals with a social problem.[6] What are the causes, he argues, which lie behind delinquency? The sweatshop, poverty, society and its false standards, tenement life—these things, all remediable by intelligent reform, cause Maggie's fall. In nearly all of the *Midnight Sketches, An Experiment in Misery, A Street Scene in New York, A Self-Made Man, An Ominous Baby, The Monster, The Auction, George's Mother, Whilomville Stories, A Desertion,* and a few others, we find the continuation in prose of his discussion of the problems which lay before him in society.[7]

An Experiment in Misery Crane wrote after spending a night in a Bowery flophouse. A youth, standing penniless in the city, sees

"... a multitude of buildings, of pitiless hues and sternly high, emblematic of a nation forcing its regal head into the clouds, throwing no downward glances; in the sublimity of its aspirations ignoring the wretches who flounder at its feet."

To the youth

> ". . . social position, comfort, the pleasures of living, were unconquerable kingdoms."

Representative of an impersonal and unheeding society, the city wrings from him

> ". . . the protest of the wretch who feels the touch of the imperturbable granite wheels, and who then cries with an impersonal eloquence, with a strength not from him, giving voice to the wail of a whole section, a class, a people." [8]

In the face of this terrible and impersonal cruelty of society, weak men quail, and this lack of courage, this giving up of personal aim, is to Crane one great cause of social illness.[9] Courage, then, is one answer, but it is not the complete solution to the problem of social dereliction. Aside from the personal equation, and what is more important, society in the aggregate must reform and realign itself. In the series called *Midnight Sketches*, Crane, with his scrupulous honesty, set down conditions as he saw them in lower New York, conditions which intelligent reform and social rehabilitation could easily wipe out. Not only is institutional reform needed, but a revolution in social psychology. In *The Monster*, as has but been pointed out,[10] Crane attacks the hypocrisy and injustice of the mob mind, choosing as its most representative figure the gossipy, small-minded old maid.[11] The cruelty of society to the individual indicated to Crane that psychological as well as institutional reform was necessary for society.[12]

Turning once more to the personal equation in society, Crane wrote *George's Mother*, in which lack of opportunity, lack of initiative, and, ironically enough, mother-love, combine to replace a young man's ambition with frustration and defeat—the defeatism and cowardice which Crane saw as an important cause of the individual's maladjustment to society. This story and *An Experiment in Misery* may be bracketed together as studies in the evolution of a Broadway drifter.

The closest approach found in Crane's work to economic criticism as a part of social theory appears in the stories *A Self-Made Man* and *An Ominous Baby*. The former is a satiric sketch of a man's rise in the world,[13] while the latter, upon closer examination, gives an important key to this aspect of his social thinking. Given two children, the one poor, the other rich and pampered. The child of wealth has a toy which the other desires, so the poor child takes it by force and runs away. How shall we interpret the act of this *ominous* child? Is Crane here merely placing in simple terms an argument for a more equal distribution of wealth and property? Is he advocating or anticipating a class revolt? Some such interpretation is fairly clear—at least, he comes perilously close to an almost anarchistic conception of a solution for economic inequality.

The interest in children displayed in *An Ominous Baby* Crane carried into his *Whilomville Stories*. Rather than being humorous sketches, these stories are significant in an analysis of his social thought. Crane studied the world of the child because it contained in little the world of adults;[14] the child's society was to him a microcosmic representation of the greater society he probed in his other stories; it was man's society reduced to simplest terms, with all the ills of that society present in miniature. How did these things come to be in children? was Crane's question—are social ills and their causes born in man? No, he feels, they develop only as the child begins to merge his individuality with the greater pattern of society, as the individual clashes with the group. Man is not innately evil; he rather learns and adopts. This, I think, is the real social significance of the *Whilomville Stories,* that in them Crane is searching in the child's society for the answers to the questions of an adult society. They seem to show that the origin of social evil is without rather than within mankind, and thus may be escaped.[15]

After a survey of Crane's social thought, we are faced with a seeming contradiction, a lack of alignment, in his larger philosophy. How can the dichotomy between social reform and humanitarianism on the one hand, and a naturalistic fatalism on the other, as expressed in *The Open Boat* and *The Red Badge of Courage,* be explained? If we live in a universe of blind forces, how can we hope to better man's condition in society, when we are at the mercy of these forces, beyond our power to control? [16] The answer is, of course, that Crane was not wholly a naturalist. He did not let a naturalistic view of the universe lead him into an amoral social philosophy of survival of the fittest, of life as a state of war on the social level. It is important to note that he at no time condoned the Frank Cowperwoods, the Wolf Larsens, or the Jadwins of his day. The cleavage in Crane's philosophy seemingly is explained thus: the forces of destiny are blind and impersonal and cannot be conquered, as we see in *The Open Boat;* but the forces of society, those which lead to the social evil seen in *Maggie* and other of his stories, are man-made forces, and can be controlled by man, who set them in motion. The world of nature we can only face with stoicism; the world of society, however, can be reshaped—progress is possible on the human and social level. The individual, then, Crane feels, must adjust himself to two spheres of life, nature and society. In relation to the former he is powerless; his relation to the latter ought to be one of humanitarianism, tolerance, and justice. He seems to feel that man in the aggregate, after his individuality has been lost in the crowd, is cruel, or rather, needlessly inhumane and unintelligent.[17] If men will try to improve, both individually and collectively, as they are free to do so, their social state, and if they will avoid the hypocrisy and cowardice which lie at the root of social evil, the world and its society will be a better place in which to live.[18] This is, in essence, the core of Stephen Crane's social philosophy, ideas which place him as a critic squarely in the liberal realistic, humanitarian tradition of his day.

III

Crane's conceptions of evil, freewill, and progress perhaps need further clarification and summary. As previously explained, freewill and progress are co-existent on the social, human level, but not existent in relation to the forces of outside, physical nature. Evil, to Crane, seems to mean specifically social evil, as in the stories already discussed, which evil finds its origin not in individual man but in institutions, in society (which is man collectively), in the friction which arises from the necessity of individualities living in relation with one another. Reform, rehabilitation, and a new system of social ethics and psychology can of course avert this type of evil. On the other hand, there intrudes often into man's society the forces of nature, causing incidents which can more easily be called fatalistic than evil, since the naturalistic physical world knows neither good nor evil, nor volition. Here, of course, there is neither escape nor solution, as we see in *The Open Boat* and *The Blue Hotel*. This latter story, when contrasted with *Maggie*, illustrates this double aspect of evil especially well. The death of the Swede is the logical result of a series of happenings which were harmless in themselves. It is caused by fate, the blind force of a naturalistic universe, which in this case has invaded the world of society. Nothing could have been done to avert this culmination or collaboration of events. But the death of Maggie, conversely, was not such—her end is the result of a set of social conditons, remediable and removable by society. In the world of man, then, natural law need not hold completely, and the suicides of future Maggies can be averted. To study and observe these conditions, and to find perhaps a solution, was the objective of Stephen Crane's social criticism.

NOTES

1. V. L. Parrington, "The Beginnings of Critical Realism," Vol. III of *Main Currents in American Thought*, 1930, gives a most complete account of the period, from an economic and social viewpoint. The political revolt of the 90's is well explained in J. M. Jacobson, *The Development of American Political Thought*, 1932, Chapter VII, 497-539.

2. See, for example, the varying emphases of F. L. Pattee, *Development of the American Short Story*, 1923, and of Harry Hartwick, *The Foreground of American Fiction*, 1934.

3. Beer, Thomas. *Stephen Crane*, 1923. Introduction by Joseph Conrad.

4. Further evidence for Crane's interest in social problems is seen in the fact that in 1894 he wrote an essay on charities in the slums which Elbert Hubbard bought for *The Philistine*, but never published. See Beer, p. 110. Crane had little sympathy for slum missions, feeling them useless. See his letter to Catharine Harris, 1896, quoted by Beer, p. 140, and poems XVI and LX of *Black Riders*, for his opinion of charities.

5. Thomas Beer seems to have first recognized the importance of this aspect of Crane's work. See both his biography of Crane and introduction to *The O'Ruddy*, in *Works*, Vol. VII, 1925-26, edited by Wilson Follett. See also W. L. Phelps' introduction to Vol. V, *Works*, and Edith Wyatt, quoted in the introduction to *The Red Badge of Courage*, edited by M. J. Herzberg, 1926, for notes on Crane's social criticism.

6. "Maggie had represented the terror of an environment tinged by social judgment." Beer, *Stephen Crane*, p. 117.

7. In another connection, these stories are important. They mark the discovery of New York as a local-color city, several years before O. Henry's popularization of "Bagdad-on-the-Subway." Crane's presentation of Bowery speech paved the way for Townsend's *Chimmie Fadden*, 1895. Further, they anticipate startlingly the modern so-called "plotless" short story. An interesting comparison can be made between Crane's "A Street Scene in New York" and Thomas Wolfe's "Death the Proud Brother," or Crane's "The Snake" and William Saroyan's "Snake."

8. *Works*, Vol. XI, pp. 27-34.

9. Of this story Crane said, "In . . . 'An Experiment in Misery' I have tried to make plain that the root of Bowery life is a sort of cowardice." Quoted in Beer, *Stephen Crane*, p. 140.

10. Wilson Follett, introduction to Vol. III, *Works*, and Thomas Beer, *Stephen Crane*, pp. 162-3.

11. Crane renewed this attack in *The Third Violet*, in *The O'Ruddy*, and in a

lost short story mentioned by James Huneker. Beer, *Stephen Crane*, p. 206.

12. See "The Auction," ". . . the auctioning of their household goods, the sale of their home,—this financial calamity lost its power in the presence of the social shame contained in the crowd's laughter." *Works*, Vol. VI, p. 81.

13. The same satire is found in poems XVI and XX of *War is Kind*. Crane had little use for the entrepreneur.

14. Joseph Conrad mentions Crane's absorbing interest in the Conrad child, and his observation of and companionship with the boy. See Conrad's introduction to Beer's biography, pp. 20-1.

15. Capable of being interpreted as Rousseauistic, Crane's interest in children displayed here is really not carried to any such length. It s noticeable that he does not imply that a return to a simple, childlike society is an improvement, nor does he seem to feel that children are socially better situated. For a Rousseauistic interpretation see Hartwick, *The Foreground of American Fiction*, p. 32.

16. Parrington, *op. cit.*, p. 325, remarks of the naturalist turning reformer, "From concern over a devastating milieu he may end in desiring to change that milieu to the end that men may achieve happiness." However, as soon as the thinker admits of the possibility of a change by man's own will, he ceases being a pure naturalist, since he admits man's ability to shape at least part of hs own life and environment. As Parrington indicates, this shift of view is seen in London, Herrick, and Norris.

17. In *The Third Violet*, Crane has Hollanden say, "No, I like people. But, considered generally, they are a collection of ingenuous blockheads." *Works*, III, p. 167.

18. This ethic, with its emphasis on mercy, justice, sincerity, and social brotherhood, is strikingly parallel to the basic doctrines of the Social-Gospel movement in religion, of Crane's time. Cf. C. M. Sheldon's *In His Steps*, 1897, and Walter Rauschenbusch's *Christianizing the Social Order*, 1912. Despite Crane's reputation as a blasphemer, there is no doubt but that he had in mind justice and mercy as parts of both man and deity. Cf. poems XXIX, LXV of *Black Riders*.

2. *Stephen Crane's* Homo Absurdus
By William Bysshe Stein

"The night of the jungle" is the dark metaphor of Crane's sensibility. Like the *Weltnacht* of modern existentialism, it controls his vision of human destiny. Beginning with *Maggie,* his requiem for the God of Christianity, he commits himself to record the anxiety, the frustration, the despair, the irrationality, and the absurdity of existence. In this perspective both life and death are emptied of meaning, and, as a consequence, man is denied the catharsis of tragedy. He is always doomed to play the role of a clown, but most of the time without the self-awareness of the clown. This fact perhaps explains why the occurrence of death in Crane's fiction is always touched with macabre humor. It may seem on occasions that some of his heroes or characters, after a crisis of experience, achieve an understanding of themselves in terms of acceptable ideals and values. But in cases like these—the terminal vows of Henry Fleming in *The Red Badge of Courage* serve as a good example—the reader must ask himself whether the individual has reached his new wisdom through an assimilation of the contradictions that he discovered in his thoughts, feelings, and actions in the course of a specific ordeal. If he has not, then we must conclude that he is the victim of self-deception. In line with Crane's belief that "Preaching is fatal to art in literature," his stories tell themselves. One does not find the theme crystallized in isolated episodes or images; the total report of a pattern of action is the meaning of a story. If there are moral lessons to be learned, they are defined ceremonially, in the sequence of connected events that constitutes a hero's initiation into the ludicrous "pathos of his situation." (This phrase from "The Open Boat" has, one cannot deny, at least a verbal similarity to the existential lamentation, "the pathos of existence.")

The absurdity immanent in Crane's nihilistic world, appropriately, is found in "the night of the jungle" associated with his artistic sensibility. The epithet occurs in "The Monster," and it directs attention to the frustration and despair that accompany Doctor Tres-

---

Reprinted from: *Bucknell Review*, VIII (May 1959), 168-174, 182-186, 188. By permission of the *Bucknell Review* and the author.

cott's attempts to reconcile his conduct to the chaos of values underlying the community's hypocritical pretensions to a Christian view of
human affairs. Crane, consistent with the purpose I assign to his
fiction, roots the hero's conflict in an utterly absurd contradiction.
Acting in accordance, though somewhat pompously, with traditional
ethical values, he commits "a blunder of virtue." His charitable
treatment of Henry Johnson, a Negro whose face is horribly mutilated
in the rescue of Trescott's son in a fire, is adjudged a crime against
the people. In general, they agree that he went beyond the call of
Christian duty in preserving the life of the now demented monster.
While Trescott can accept this reaction as a manifestation of public
hysteria, he is confounded when Judge Hagenthorpe, the civil custo-
dian of justice and reason, concurs with this verdict. In this reduction
of the rational to the irrational and of the irrational to the rational,
the hero discovers his own and the world's absurdity. In the last scene
of the story Crane dramatizes the advent of the immitigable solitude
of the individual lot when man perceives his plight to be the incongruous truth of existence. Making an effort to explain to his wife
the logic of their social ostracism, he first lapses into dumb pity,
then into ridiculous silence:

> Glancing down at the cups, Trescott mechanically counted
> them. There were fifteen of them. 'There, there,' he said.
> 'Don't cry, Grace. Don't cry.'
> The wind was whining round the house, and the snow
> beat aslant upon the windows. Sometimes the coal in the
> stove settled with a crumbling sound, and the four panes
> of mica flashed a sudden new crimson. As he sat holding her
> head on his shoulder, Trescott found himself occasionally
> trying to count the cups. There were fifteen of them.

Is it wrong to say that Trescott is estranged from the God of his
culture, from nature, from other men, from his wife, and, worst of
all, from himself? Has not he lost his sense of identity with his
environment, the test of being in the existential view of humanity?

We must, I believe, answer these questions in the affirmative.
But this is not to be considered a unique resolution of action in
Crane's fiction. Parallels to it are found, paradoxically, in those works
which have, of late, been so persistently connected with the theme

of moral regeneration—"The Open Boat" and *The Red Badge of Courage*. The first work, I contend, objectively registers the absurdity that envelops any encounter with contingent death. It filters into man's thoughts, it dominates man's feelings, and it informs the world of man's existence. The men in the boat, particularly the correspondent, try desperately to justify their survival in the struggle against the sea, but the value categories of their culture fail to serve them in their predicament. The idealistic virtues of bravery, fortitude, and integrity possess no meaning in a universe that denies the importance of man. And Crane, like a Sartre or a Camus, traces this condition to the withdrawal of God from the province of humanity. In His absence or death His place has been usurped by the idiot forces of nihilism:

> . . .'if I am going to be drowned, *why,* in the name of the seven mad gods who rule the sea, was I allowed to come thus far to contemplate sand and trees? Was I brought here merely to have my nose dragged away as I was about to nibble the sacred cheese of life? *It is preposterous.* If this old ninny-woman, Fate, cannot do better than this, she should be deprived of the management of men's fortunes. *She is an old hen who knows not her intention.* If she has decided to drown me, *why* did she not do it in the beginning and save me all this trouble. *The whole affair is absurd.'* (Italics mine.)

Crane here asks the same questions implicit in Trescott's enumeration of the cups. Pathetically, they are all negative in content, for they cannot be answered. In effect, man cannot construct a rational picture of the world out of his own experience. He knows only that he is the victim of forces beyond his control, that he suffers without apparent justification, that he confronts the reality of nothingness. As opposed to the abstract and the possible, this is the real and the concrete—the existence that defies understanding in terms of essence.

Crane next carries this phase of the correspondent's subjective dialect to its logical conclusion, applying the lesson of divine treason to a redefinition of the meaning of good and evil. How ridiculous it is, he argues, to fret about the transcendent realm of values if these are not to be realized here and now under the stress of human problems:

It represented in a degree . . . the serenity of nature amid the
struggles of the individual—nature in the wind, and nature
in the vision of man. She did not seem cruel to him then,
nor beneficent, nor treacherous, nor wise. But she was indifferent, flatly indifferent. It is, perhaps, plausible that a man in
this situation . . . should see the innumerable flaws of his life,
and have them taste wickedly in his mind, and wish for another
chance. *A distinction between right and wrong seems absurdly
clear to him,* then, *in this new ignorance of the grave-edge,* and
he understands that if he were given the opportunity he would
mend his conduct and his words, *and be better and brighter
during an introduction* or at tea. (Italics mine.)

In addition to parodying the old wives' tale that man, on the brink
of death, is involuntarily forced into an audit of his spiritual resources,
Crane debunks the moral function of the categories of good and evil.
Since the world has been stripped of causality, there is no one to
whom man is responsible for his individual behavior. Only the gods
of the properties have any visible existence, and to these the correspondent turns in burlesque adoration. Here, ostensibly, society has
learned to distinguish between right and wrong in a manner that
touches human needs and desires, however petty and futile they are.
This *reductio ad absurdum* of moral authority, interestingly enough,
has its analogue in Camus's *The Stranger.* Meursault cannot feel
sorry for himself or for the man whom he murdered, for he is beyond
good and evil. He is the unregenerate "outsider" who has lost his
identity in the world. Any effort at all to combat this state of affairs
would be wasted. Hence he passively accepts the rule of chaos. This
knowledge, it would seem, is not unlike the correspondent's "new
ignorance."

At least one gathers this impression from Crane's description of
the correspondent's sudden immersion in the sea. The latter, in his
alienation from God and nature, finds himself hopelessly confused.
His sense of being is disjointed, for he cannot coordinate thought,
feeling, and action. Instead of worrying about drowning, he bewails
the temperature of the water: "The coldness of the water was sad;
it was tragic. The fact was somehow mixed and confused with his
opinion of his own situation, so that it seemed almost a proper reason
for tears. The water was cold." And instead of concerning himself
with the necessity of preserving his strength, he hails his weariness

as a chance to make a truce with his fear of physical pain: "he reflected that when one gets properly wearied drowning must really be a comfortable arrangement . . . ; and he was glad for it, for the main thing in his mind for some moments had been horror of temporary agony; he did not wish to be hurt." These contradictory responses to the crisis of death parallel a basic premise of existential philosophy. The sense of the absurd originates in the human mind, and it grows directly out of the irrationality of experience. In the process an irreconcilable conflict between consciousness and reality is engendered. For, as in the behavior of the correspondent, man cannot adjust himself to the conditions of existence.

Significantly, these incongruities of experience contrast with his earlier convictions about the meaning of the collective ordeal. I refer to "the subtle brotherhood of men" that the correspondent predicates for the group in the boat. This fleeting apprehension, I submit, is merely self-deception—man torturing his imagination to find purpose in purposelessness, nobility in ignobility, dignity in degradation. This supposition of meaningful human unity, if one is to accept its validity, must be correlated with the outcome of the experience. The brief comradeship is unpityingly dissolved by contingent circumstance, for the oiler perishes in the turbulent waters. Is not this the message of "the great sea's voice" that the survivors are left to interpret? Is not this what Sartre calls the triumph of the absurd—the appalling realization that "every existing thing is born without reason, prolongs itself out of weakness and dies by chance"? This is the pathos of existence that the correspondent first discovers in his memory of the soldier dying at Algiers: "it was an actuality—stern, mournful, fine," and he "was moved by a profound and perfectly impersonal comprehension." Related to the terminal episode of the story, the respective fates of the men are as inexplicable as the death of the soldier. To die is simply to die. To live is to be absurd—in chilled solitude to watch all trusted hopes and anticipations dissipate. This idea is, I believe, firmly crystallized in the correspondent's comical theophany just a few minutes before he discovers that his companion in the ordeal has died: "he was naked—as naked as a tree in winter; but a halo was about his head, and he shone like a saint." If, as some readers insist, this vision of one of the rescuers is a symbol of moral regeneration, then Crane is here leaping the void of the absurd, hand in hand with Kierkegaard.

In any event, at least as I look at it, a similar inappropriateness

attaches to the moral resolution of "The Blue Hotel." The point
at issue is the Easterner's belief in a law of causality that operates
behind the commission of human evil: "Every sin is the result of
collaboration. We, five of us, have collaborated in the murder of
this Swede. Usually there are from a dozen to forty women really
involved in every murder, but in this case it seems to be only five
men . . . ; the fool of a gambler came merely as a culmination, the
apex of a human movement, and gets all the punishment." This
ethical stand, ignoring the preposterous reference to the role of the
female in this crime (incidentally, contradicting Crane's notoriously
romantic attitude towards women), is basically Christian. It assumes
that man is a moral agent because he possesses free will; it likewise
takes for granted that man can control the forces of chaos which
continually threaten the spiritual balance of the universe. Unfortunately, this kind of reasoning does violence to Crane's development
of the antecedent action, for the Swede, literally, is depicted as his
own *reductio ad absurdum.* When he projects his distorted fantasies
upon an existent disorder of reality (the conflicting attitudes of the
characters with whom he is thrown into immediate relationship), he
surrenders his fate to a world rendered irredeemably absurd. In this
perspective the Easterner's rational approach to the Swede's wholly
irrational predicament represents an intellectualistic arrogance. This
negative outlook, in turn, makes his moral sympathies sterile and
abstract. His contemptuous treatment of the cowboy in the last scene
of the story bears witness to this depersonalization of values. In his
retrospective guilt, which he obviously does not feel, there is every
indication of spiritual self-deception. Only the failure to act saves
him from the disillusionment of Trescott. In the final analysis, then,
the Easterner is no less ridiculous than the Swede.

Crane's narrative strategy, it seems to me, supports this interpretation. For each character directly associated with the Swede in the
story is hopelessly self-absorbed and, like the latter, lost in contemplation of some private vision of his personal role in the universe.
Crane dramatizes this idea in the progression of the plot: the infatua-
tion of Mr. Scully with a misconception of ingratiating hospitality;
of Johnnie with a muddled image of a confidence man; of the cowboy
with a juvenile code of bravado; of the Easterner with an illusion
of intellectual self-reliance; of the bartender with a pose of indifference; of the townspeople with a mask of pride; of the gambler with
a delusion of self-importance. We preceive in this state of affairs the

incredible disunion of the human family. Each individual is pathetically estranged from the world in which he seeks to enact a particular role; for his aspirations and desires are completely uncoordinated with any common goal in life. In this confusion of purposes no one, not even the Easterner, can define the nature of the so-called sin of collaboration. His deterministic ethic is a dream of order in a reality ruled by the forces of chaos. And Crane, I would guess, uses the enveloping fury of the snowstorm to counterpoint this brutal truth. The howling blizzard swallows up the petty tempests of human feeling. It drowns out man's frustrated cries of anger and hate, challenging the significance that he attaches to his Lilliputian struggles. It ignores the absurd prerogatives of honor and pride that he claims for himself under the authority of his frail ego. Nature, or more properly her surrogate, disdains to acknowledge the self-importance of the stranger in her midst. Though this elucidation may perhaps seem intentionalist, these symbolic overtones parallel the more overt narrative dialectic of "The Open Boat." Moreover, Crane provides a clear rubric for these observations in the obtrusive metaphor of the blue hotel. The grotesquely painted hostelry is as out of place on the prairies as man is in the universe.

*   *   *

Like Kierkegaard and Kafka, Crane finds the absurd in every walk and in every stage of life. It manifests itself in the contradictions of social experience independent of class and position. We find this in "The Monster," in "The Blue Hotel," and in "The Bride Comes to Yellow Sky." It also occurs in the crises of love and death, and, as in the writings of the other men, it is intimately allied to the incongruities of religious faith in the world. *Maggie* and *The Red Badge of Courage,* for instance, cannot be properly understood without considering the role of God (or the Devil) in the universe. Though "The Open Boat" touches on man's estrangement from the divine, this today, like "Five White Mice" and "A Mystery of Heroism," is concerned more with man's contingent status in life, a position that no human code of conduct can ease or mitigate. But regardless of the individual plight, the various characters share one common experience always; all of them are led to question the self-identity that allegedly gives them a place in the order of things.

This latter perspective, I think, illuminates the problem of the hero in *George's Mother,* though it is also connected with an implicit comedy of religious faith. The young man's mother, a doting, ignorant woman whose social and moral principles have been shaped by a devotion to the mission evangelicalism of her Bowery environment, warps the self-image of her only son by extravagant flattery and excessive attention. But since this illusion of self-identity is not recognized by the outside world, George encounters a series of frustrations which encourage him to daydream and finally to drink. In each case he seeks to live up to those expectations for himself that are confusedly impressed upon his mind by the conflicting opinions of his mother and of the world. When the perfections his mother finds in his personality fail to consummate a romance, he turns upon her in thwarted fury, suddenly realizing the alienation of his ideals from existent reality: "Kelcey suffered from his first gloomy conviction that the earth was not grateful to him for his presence upon it. When sharp words were said to him, he interpreted them with what seemed to be a lately acquired insight. He could now perceive that the universe hated him. He sank to the most sublime depths of despair." These sentiments are not, of course, expressive of assimilated knowledge. They spring from self-pity. He does not as yet perceive that he is his own *reductio ad absurdum* and that his follies are rooted in himself. This realization comes when he attempts to evaluate human experience in accordance with his personal conception of values. Through a chance meeting with an old friend of the family, he is introduced to a convivial group of tavern frequenters whose alcoholic congeniality give him the illusion of self-importance. In achieving a momentary faith in himself, he proceeds to stake the entire meaning of life upon the permanence of this brotherhood of mirth and pleasure. This assumption parallels the rationalizations of Fleming and the correspondent in similar crises of estrangement. In the passage which follows there are verbal echoes of the two other stories, particularly of *The Red Badge of Courage* in the profane secularization of religious imagery:

> He was all at once an enthusiast, as if he were at a festival of a religion. He felt that there was something fine and thrilling in this affair isolated from the stern world, from which the laughter arose like incense. He knew that old sentiment of brotherly regard for those about him. He began to converse tenderly with them. He was not sure of his drift of thought,

but he knew that he was immensely sympathetic. He rejoiced
at their faces, shining red and wrinkled with smiles. He was
capable of heroisms.

But, as in other instances, Crane merely employs this transitory
self-deception to herald the advent of existential disillusionment. For
when George awakens from a drunken stupor at the scene of the
party in question, nauseated by the noxious "odors of tobacco, men's
breaths, and beer half filling forgotten glasses," he sickens at his
own absurdity: "As he lay pondering, his bodily condition created
for him a bitter philosophy of life, and he perceived all the futility
of a red existence. He saw his life's problems confronting him like
granite giants, and he was no longer erect to meet them. He made
a calamitous retrogression in his war. Specters were to him now
large as clouds." This betrayal of hope is a short time later accentuated in the circumstances attendant upon the death of his mother.
Called to her sickbed, he is unable to establish any kind of emotional
rapport with her sympathetic neighbors, with the "plump young
clergyman," or with his own dying mother: "[He] began to stare
at the wall-paper. The pattern was clusters of brown roses. He felt
them like hideous crabs crawling upon his brain." This tableau, I
think, cannot be separated from Trescott's identical dissociation of
sensibility. However, on another level of reference, the horrifying
image of the last line is an anticipation of Kafka's terrifying vision
of reality; and, in another coincidence. George's emotional paralysis
is not wholly unrelated to the attitudes of Camus's Meursault at the
side of the coffin of his dead mother.
    But Crane's revelations of existential absurdity are not always
so desperately futile. In "The Bride Comes to Yellow Sky," for
example, he subjects the brittle substance of human identity to serio-
comic scrutiny. Yet it would be unwise for any reader to discount
the significance of Jack Potter's fears that an unannounced marriage
in another city will deprive him of his established position in the
small town in which he is a marshal. Like the masses of mankind,
Crane implies, Potter has no inward sense of selfhood. He is what
people believe him to be, and he has modeled his personality on
their expectations. In effect, he has so completely merged himself
with his persona that he is unaware of his own individuality, the
sudden impulse that precipitated the marriage. As a consequence,

apart from his self-conscious behavior on the train returning him
to Yellow Sky, all his meagre store of ego awareness is sapped of its
strength; and he feels that his rash matrimonial venture is equivalent
to a forfeiture of the self-image by which the world knows him:

> Of course people in Yellow Sky married as it pleased
> them, in accordance with a general custom; but such was
> Potter's thought of his duty to his friends, or their idea of
> his duty, or of an unspoken form which does not control men
> in these matters, that he felt he was heinous. He had com-
> mitted an extraordinary crime. Face to face with this girl
> in San Antonio, and spurred by his sharp impulse, he had
> gone headlong over all social hedges.

While in the preceding stories the apprehension of estrangement
from the community has, for the most part, brought on unbearable
pathos, Crane in this instance softens the impact of this realization
in a bizarre twist of humor. He apparently recognizes that the quality
of individual sensibility determines the nature of the response to
an experience with absurdity. Thus it would be preposterous to
exhibit Jack Potter in the throes of bitter despair and frustration.
His emotional and intellectual faculties, at least as the reader glimpses
them, would preclude any kind of radical discomposure. For this
reason, probably, Crane focuses on the external effect of the marshal's
derelict marriage, that is, its confounding influence upon Scratchy
Wilson, a drunk who goes on periodical shooting sprees. The latter
is the first one to encounter the couple after they alight from the
train in Yellow Sky, and he, oblivious to existential contingency,
immediately assumes that Potter is armed and ready to deal with him
as he has in the past. When he discovers that the social status of
Potter has changed, he, in his narrow, illiterate conception of life,
reacts to this sudden expression of the world's irrationality in hilarious
bewilderment: " 'Well, I 'low it's off, Jack,' said Wilson. He was looking at the ground. 'Married!' He was not a student of chivalry; it was
merely that in the presence of this foreign condition he was a simple
child of the earlier plains. He picked up his starboard revolver, and,
placing both weapons in their holsters, he went away. His feet
made funnel-shaped tracks in the heavy sand." But however grotesque

this dénouement, its implications are nevertheless darkly foreboding, for they linger in the memory, haunting intimations of the forces of chaos that underlie the inscutable flux of the universe.

* * *

Bafflement and frustration crowned by an oath: this is the substance of the life that Crane re-creates in his best stories. Whether or no the imprecation is sounded in the text, it is subsumed in the cloud of despair that shrouds the noblest efforts of man under a blanket of futility. Or perhaps sometimes the curse is transformed into the diabolic laughter of mockery and negation. One or both, they belong to Crane's vision of reality, for they are extensions of "the night of the jungle," the pessimistic metaphor of his sensibility. This existential disillusionment hardly varies from work to work. When he first perceived that

> God lay dead in heaven;
> Angels sang the hymn of the end;
> Purple winds went moaning,
> Their wings drip-dripping
> With blood
> That fell upon the earth

there was no recourse to any truth except that of the absurdity of human life.

3. *The Importance of Tone in Stephen Crane's Fiction*
By Gorham B. Munson

So much has been said about *le mot juste* and so little about
le ton juste! Yet failure or success in writing depends more upon the
latter than upon the first. By an edifying accident, in the collection
of Stephen Crane's short stories known in the Modern Library series
as *Men, Women and Boats,* his greatest short story, "The Open
Boat," was immediately followed by his worst failure, "The Reluctant
Voyagers."

The plot of "The Reluctant Voyagers" was good. Two men
bicker with each other at the seaside; they swim out to a raft and
bask there; in their semiconscious loafing they fail to notice that
the raft has drifted too far from shore; during the ensuing night
they are picked up by a schooner and taken to New York Bay; as
they, still in their bathing costumes, are being transported by row-
boat to the wharf, they quarrel anew and capsize the boat; they are
rescued by another boat and landed but for a time it appears as
though their oarsman had been drowned.

Such a plot is at once seen to be amenable to a variety of treat-
ments; Crane himself wished to present it humorously, to write a
comic story. But he spoiled his intention as soon as he started the tale.

> "Two men sat by the sea waves.
> " 'Well, I know I'm not handsome,' said one gloomily.
> He was poking holes in the sand with a discontented cane
> "The companion was watching the waves play. He seemed
> overcome with perspiring discomfort as a man who is resolved
> to set another man right.
> "Suddenly his mouth turned into a straight line.
> " 'To be sure you are not,' he cried vehemently." [1]

No light touch here! The sparseness of the diction, the brief
rhythm, the heavy tone, cause one to expect something tense, as in

Reprinted from: "Prose for Fiction: Stephen Crane," *Style and Form in American
Prose.* New York: Doubleday, Doran & Company, Inc., 1929, pp. 159-160, 167-170.

"The Open Boat": yet what follows is obviously meant to be diverting. In fact, throughout the entire tale Crane never found the right tone for it, and consequently the reader is continually misled. Therefore, "The Reluctant Voyagers" seems unreal, forced, bad in every respect, whereas it is bad in only one: wrong tonality.

Indeed, an erratic sense of tone was one of Crane's besetting sins as a craftsman. He strikes his tone right in "The Open Boat," but even in that powerful story there are little stumbles into negligent journalese.

*   *   *

One can, to be sure, study the form of "The Open Boat" as one pores over the moves in a chess game, but in what ensues remember that the difference between an art and a game is this: art is a means, whereas the game itself is the end. Anatomically considered, here is the outline of the plot of "The Open Boat." But the reader is asked to take this skeleton and clothe it with the functions that each member performs in the story, for, to repeat, form is a plot functioning.

(1) There is a description of the situation that makes the story: a frail boat, four men in it, and the heavy waves continually charging at the little cockleshell.

(2) The conversation of the cook, the oiler, and the correspondent ending on a note of grim doubt: "We're not there yet."

(3) The conversation of the cook, the oiler, and the captain revolving about the terrible question: "Do you think we've got much of a show now, boys?"

(4) The omen of the sea gull.

(5) The sighting of the lighthouse.

(6) The subtle brotherhod that springs up in the boat.

(7) Raising of the sail and the sighting of land.

(8) The smoking of the four dry cigars.

(9) The ominous exchange of home addresses by the four men as they near the surf.

(10) The reflections of the men as they approach the danger of the surf.

(11) The turning back from the shore and the rowing out to sea.

(12) The running man on the beach and the disappointment that follows.

(13) Out to sea again and the gripping of hunger.

(14) The feeling between the oiler and the correspondent voiced in the meek question, "Will you spell me for a while?"

(15) While the men take turns sleeping in the bilge water of the boat, a roving shark appears.

(16) The growth of a feeling of indifference toward human fate on the part of nature.

(17) Dawn comes and the suspicion of nature's aloofness is enhanced.

(18) The men take their boat into the surf and it is swamped.

(19) Swimming in the surf and the additional dangers of an unfavorable current and the wild swamped boat.

(20) Rescue.

(21) The death of the oiler.

(22) The terse conclusion.

REMARKS ON THE OUTLINE

The problem, which I am for the most part handing over to the reader, is to assign functions to each one of these items. It is easy to see from the outline that the story moves on two planes. On the physical plane it is developed by reiterated descriptions of the hugeness and might of the waves and the smallness of the boat. On the emotional plane the development proceeds by alternation, the alternation of hopefulness and despair.

In the end I believe all who study the story will concede that it is itself wavelike in form. The reader's sympathy is firmly attached to the four men because of their utmost exertions in fighting the sea, and because of this sympathy the reader shares their suspense and is carried by hope up to the crest of an emotional wave only to tumble into the trough of despair as some new hostile element enters. Finally, in a surf of excited feelings, the story grounds on the shore of its conclusion.

Here then is an exercise which, if completed, should reveal better than any full account by a critic how organic literary form is. But while engaged in that, do not overlook our many other technical concerns with this story. Notice how limited the vocabulary is to words that denote sensible objects and to words that denote emotions. Notice the particularization of the circumstances of the struggle,

Crane's much applauded sense of the telling detail. And notice the tone of the story—a tone of seriousness and anxiety. *Le ton juste!*

NOTES

1. Reprinted from *Men, Women and Boats,* by Stephen Crane, copyright 1921, by and with the permission of and special arrangement with Alfred A. Knopf, Inc., authorized publishers.

4. *Parody and Realism in Stephen Crane's Fiction*
By Eric Solomon

Far from being a reporter, or a war novelist, or an uneducated genius, Stephen Crane was, I contend, that most conscious of literary artificers, a parodist. In the fullest sense of the term, Crane parodied the familiar themes of fiction, but not always, nor even primarily, for comic effect. Harry Levin well defines this type of serious parody: "Fiction approximates truth, not by concealing art, but by exposing artifice. The novelist finds it harder to introduce fresh observations than to adapt the conventions of other novelists, easier to imitate literature than to imitate life. But a true novel imitates critically, not conventionally; hence it becomes a parody of other novels. . . ." [1] The finest parody can retain the force of the original while criticizing it. Rosemary Freeman calls this a kind of parody that is not primarily directed toward satire even though using some satiric techniques; it is "parody based upon literary samples in which the aim is creating a meaning that is positive and constructive, not absurd." [2] We should recall that in its seventeenth-century sense parody was a neutral term for simple substitution of new words to familiar music, without any satiric implications. For an early novelist like Henry Fielding, parody is "like a *burlesca* movement in music, with brilliantly exaggerated clichés of meretricious style followed by extended movements which rework the themes, no longer merely cliché or parody, but something new: passionate, sympathetic, wise, and always willing to be as ridiculous as life itself." [3]

Crane worked in many traditional or contemporary genres: the slum novel, the war novel, the fiction of childhood, the sea story, the Western tale, the small-town novel, the love story. In all these forms, he came to grips, and in some cases to grief, with modes of fiction that were familiar to a literate public, and he made of each something different—"made it new," in Ezra Pound's phrase. As James Agee understood when he wrote movie scenarios of "The Bride Comes to Yellow Sky" and "The Blue Hotel," Crane accepted the tradition of the Western tale, in the first story comically deflating

---

Reprinted from: *Stephen Crane: From Parody to Realism*. Cambridge, Mass.: Harvard University Press, 1966, pp. 4-18. By permission of Harvard University Press. Copyright, 1966, by the President and Fellows of Harvard College.

the cliché of the duel in the streets, familiar in Western fiction from *The Virginian* to *High Noon,* and in the latter story both deepening and excoriating the Western myth by showing how it could destroy one who believed in it too much—or not enough. In Thomas Beer's phrase, Crane refuted Western melodrama in melodrama's terms.[4] *The Red Badge of Courage* helped, along with the work of Stendhal, Zola, and Tolstoy, to supply a counter to the tradition of dashing, courageous heroes in war fiction. Because they eschew buffoonery and irreverence, Crane's parodies of romantic and sensational fiction differ from the usual parodies produced by such vigorous antiromantics as Bret Harte, Mark Twain, and Frank Norris—for parody was a major form of nineteenth-century American humor, a taut attack on flaccid and obsessive writing.

Crane sliced away the traditional excrescences, and reclaimed what was of artistic value in the familiar genres by applying his own stark techniques of style and setting to such overwrought themes as heroism in battle or such sentimental themes as loss of innocence in the big city. Crane, as Erich Auerbach has said of a much greater parodist, Cervantes, was not simply a destructive critic but the continuer of literary tradition. Thus, just as Mark Twain parodied some aspects of the official culture while taking others seriously, Crane throughout his work combined the comic with the serious. He often used a vocabulary of clichés that he restored to their original force, as he found new and deeper uses for the idiom, by refracting a serious view of life through traditional plots. Like Henry James and William Dean Howells, Stephen Crane concentrated on character and motivation; yet by dealing with the stuff of romance—the physical activities of strong men—and at the same time avoiding excesses by means of intense selectivity, Crane wrote subtle adventure tales. The parodist's pen selected, the adventurer's spirit vivified, and the artist's intelligence discovered the serious view. In the midst of his pastiches, moreover, often appeared the finest passages ever produced in the traditional form. These passages showed Crane moving forward from the parodic base as he discovered the aesthetic potential in the familiar.

As we shall see, Stephen Crane wrote parodies of every genre in which he worked, scoffing at the formulae of each while retaining its emotive power. Sometimes he was satisfied with simple burlesque. One of his very earliest satiric pieces, "The Camel" (1891), caricatures travel literature; Crane describes the adventures of a traveler who gorges a camel with whiskey in order to smuggle the liquor into the dry state of Maine. Duels, romantic love, millionaires' clubs, and excessively tall stories also come under Crane's ironic view, for he was always a humorist, even in his early journalism; but his best short parodies take aim at the French novel, the stage melodrama, and the mystery story.

In "Why Did the Young Clerk Swear? Or, The Unsatisfactory French" (1893) a bored clerk in a haberdashery store seeks excitement by reading a "French novel with a picture on the cover." [5] The reading is interrupted by a series of customers—a man seeking a hand laundry, an elderly gentleman who wants a nightshirt that opens front and back, a woman who must have a certain brand of shirt, a tough in search of a barroom—none of whom the clerk can satisfy. But neither can he find satisfaction in the French novel that Crane lampoons. The book is in part a story of heated romantic passion. Silvere swoons with love for the "fresh, fair, innocent" Heloise. "Silvere burst into tears. 'I love her! I love her! I shall die.' " Crane derides the rarely fulfilled prurient expectations of this type of vaguely pornographic fiction. With one hand Heloise lifts her skirts, and, "Silvere leaning forward, saw her"—the clerk's salacious thoughts are interrupted by a customer and disappointed by the author—"handkerchief fall in a puddle" (p. 110). Crane's distortion of naturalism, quite clearly in this instance Emile Zola's brand, is acute. "A baker opposite was quarreling over two sous with an old woman. A grey-haired veteran with a medal upon his breast and a butcher's boy were watching a dogfight. The smell of dead animals came from adjacent slaughterhouses. The letters on the sign over the tinsmith's shop on the corner shone redly like great clots of blood" (p. 110 a dash of self-mockery in the last phrase?). Crane pinpoints the naturalist's technique of editorializing by juxtaposition—a technique he often employed himself: the veteran and the butcher's boy, the baker and the dead animals, the medal and the dogfight. The parody of the scientific brutality of Zola's prose is combined with a mimicry of Balzac's passion for detail as the clerk skips "some seventeen chapters descriptive of a number of intricate money transactions, the moles on the neck of a Parisian dress-maker, the process of making brandy, the milk-leg of Silvere's aunt, life in the coalpits, and scenes in the Chamber of Deputies" (p. 111). The sensual passages of the burlesqued novel are full of images of nature and animal life, but the novel ends, to the clerk's disappointment, with Heloïse's virginity intact. The short parody ticks off, with accuracy and wit, the fraudulent aspects of popular, teasingly lurid fiction. In his later work

Crane would learn how to join the realistic interruptions and the parodied readings, which here he splits asunder. But he would never lose his contempt for the "tiresome platitudes," "commonplace narratives," and "mildewed phrases" that a friend of this period remembers Crane castigating.[6]

Crane's fiction is dappled by ironic thrusts against stage melodrama; he insists upon the distance between a real-life poker game and a theatrical one, finds in real situations of stress "none of that magnificent fortitude, that gorgeous tranquility amid upheavals and perils which is the attribute of people in plays."[7] In "Some Hints for Playmakers" (1894) Crane lampoons the kinds of popular drama that offend him: the romantic melodrama, the society play, the foreclosed-mortgage play, and the musical that has to contort the story to make room for songs. The cast of Crane's society play, which looks forward to the best nonsense plays of Robert Benchley or Ring Lardner, consists of "The Duchess; Her Niece; A Nice Man; and Intriguing, Spiteful, Contemptible, Malicious, Well-bred, and Devilish Men and Women." The play ends when the niece and the young man come together (" 'Lucy!' 'Albert!' ") as she finishes reading a note and says, "Oh! then, he is really the pink of perfection, and not an odious pig, as I thought. Dottie Hightights, at the Tinsel Theatre, is his own grandmamma, and not a bad, wicked woman, as I thought."[8] One wishes that Crane had given us the words to one of the numbers in his musical, entitled "In the Wrong Room, or, When She Turned Up the Gas, He Jumped from an Eighth-story Window" (p. 39). Many of Crane's dark sketches, like "Manacled" (1900), impugn stage melodrama. Here the hero, in prison garb and handcuffs because of the cruel machinations of his enemies, responds to the villain's sneers, " 'Tis well, Aubrey Pettingill. . . . You have so far succeeded; but, mark you, there will come a time—."[9] The mood of this sketch shifts quickly, however, from humor to horror as the stage burlesque gives way to the realization that an actual roaring fire is engulfing the theater, trapping the speaker, who is deserted by the other actors. In miniature, this piece exemplifies Crane's best technique; what starts as caustic humor shades into black reality.

"A Tale of Mere Chance" (1896) takes off the Poe school of mystery, horror, and detection. Told in the first person, the story reviews the ghastly career of an insane murderer. The narrative method is a burlesque of "The Cask of Amontillado" as the speaker addresses the reader in a reasonable tone, and of "The Tell-Tale

Heart" when the murderer believes that he is followed through the streets by a crowd of bloodstained white tiles that advertise his guilt. One other element of Poe's mysteries, the ingenious detective Dupin, is ridiculed when the narrator explains that a detective need not be particularly clever to discover a man in a spotted orange coat followed by shrieking, bloody tiles. Stephen Crane clearly enjoyed the practice of parody. He indulged in this rather parasitic form of literary criticism, however, most often as a prelude to literary creation where he carried his art far beyond the immediate occasion. Thus his best parodies are encapsulated in his novels and stories. According to T. S. Eliot, immature poets imitate, mature poets steal; Crane wrote parodic imitations, then took over, annexed the forms, and created what parody meant to the Greeks: parallel song.

In his major fiction, as we shall see, Stephen Crane worked in familiar genres and transmuted them into the products of his special sensibility, forming in his best works at once incisive criticisms of traditional styles and entirely fresh fictional creations.[10] No matter what Crane's particular setting happened to be, whether his story took place in an open boat on a wild sea or in the quiet streets of a small town, whether he was portraying toughs or innocents, mothers or children, grotesques or victims, he worked from certain basic assumptions about man and society. For Crane the chain of being was only too clear: at the top was a harsh, uncaring, Hardyesque god; at the bottom was a basically good, weak, striving man. Somewhere in the middle, both dominating man and on occasion being conquered by him, was society. Crane's poetry, for the most part, was dedicated to the metaphysical problems raised by man's relation to his god. His fiction, on the other hand, portrayed man struggling to survive in his society. All fiction of course is a re-forming of life, a differentiating of raw, chaotic experience according to the author's particular vision (as Crane said, an author "is not at all responsible for his vision—he is merely responsible for his quality of personal honesty"),[11] and in Crane's work we find a thoughtful and often angry view of man as a social animal.

We must not look to Stephen Crane, however, for polemics or manifestoes in the manner of his earliest mentors, Hamlin Garland and William Dean Howells. For Crane, immediacy obviated the need for explanations. In the hard and exact diction of ordinary speech, in particulars instead of generalizations, his clear, concentrated prose (self-indulgent only in his literary overuse of metaphor) established an ironic stance. As a parodist, Crane did not need the kind of fully developed philosophy with which some recent interpreters have sought to supply him. According to David Worcester, the writer of parody poses as a passive agent, letting the condemnation come by analogy so that the reader seems to be drawing his own independent conclusions.[12] The controlling tone in Crane's fiction was humorous, ironic, darkly serious, experiential, self-conscious.

Employing either mocking overstatement or grim understatement, Crane criticized traditional views of life and art. If we should seek an archetypal plot for Stephen Crane's fiction, the plot would be something like this: a youth, innocent and contemplative (in the later work, a man, nervous and apprehensive), ventures into a world of violence and rage (unleashed by war, by external nature, and by society itself); he is buffeted, and his existence is jeopardized; he runs, and perhaps he escapes, probably losing something of value. He doesn't really grow, but ends with a whimper. Yet he has looked upon evil, and survived.

Some development of this basic formula occurred in the eight years of Crane's writing life. For example, his concepts about the nature of courage changed and became more complex. *Maggie* and *George's Mother* are largely studies in cowardice; *The Red Badge of Courage* draws the narrow line between fear and bravery; "A Mystery of Heroism" portrays the enigma of a brave action; and the later war stories reflect the stolid acceptance of danger displayed by the professional. In "The Open Boat" courage is a necessity; in "The Five White Mice" it is foolish; in "The Bride Comes to Yellow Sky" it has become comic; and in *The Monster* true courage appears as moral strength.

The question of Stephen Crane's development is a difficult one. His most famous and in some ways his best work came early, which has been the case with many—perhaps most—American authors. Indeed, Howells remained convinced that Crane's earliest work, *Maggie,* was his finest. Although there is always some justification for a chronological study of an author's work, in Crane's case a thematic study seems more rewarding. By a close reading of his fiction, we may discover that what might appear to be generally loose and perverse in Crane's work is actually an artful pattern of burlesque, a reinterpretation of action in the perspective of past fiction. We will examine his writings consecutively within each genre in order to discover how he polished and complicated the form, but it does not seem fruitful to move year by year through Crane's career. As man and artist he was too inconsistent to fit into an easy pattern of development from youthful brilliance to mature competence. When an author dies before thirty, his work is still plastic, in flux.

One approach to Stephen Crane's fiction of parody, as I call it, is the consideration of his work in connection with the methods of two of his near-contemporaries, Ezra Pound and T. E. Hulme. As they aimed to "desuetize" poetry, Crane in his fiction stripped bare the bones of the traditional genres, anatomized the skeletons, and then presented what seemed a defense of realism. Like Hulme, Crane believed in a dry hardness of art, and mocked the vague and eloquent. In the short, almost elliptical quality of his best prose, Crane echoed the imagist concept that one perfect image might be better than a lengthy work. To be sure, Crane was inconsistent. He padded some of his work because he needed money to support his establishment at Brede Place in Surrey. Yet even his hack work—with the exception of *Great Battles of the World*—retained the parodic vision.

At the end of his life—literally on his deathbed—Stephen Crane returned to straight parody. In the unfinished *The O'Ruddy* (completed by Robert Barr, published 1903), Crane sought to write an extended burlesque of the romantic novel as it was practiced by Alexander Dumas, Robert Louis Stevenson, and Crane's own friends Arthur Quiller-Couch, H. B. Marriot-Watson, and A. E. W. Mason— or, since *The O'Ruddy* has a wild Irishman as the hero, of the kind of high-spirited adventure novels produced by Charles Lever earlier in the century. Many of the conventions of a Lever novel such as *Charles O'Malley, The Irish Dragoon* (1840) are mocked in Crane's pages as the O'Ruddy pursues his love through duels, dangerous night journeys, thickly plotted mysteries.[13]

Whatever Stephen Crane was attempting, *The O'Ruddy* is a botch. Only rarely can parody extend for four hundred pages. And Crane knew this well, for in his major works he shifted at the proper moment from burlesque to realism. *The O'Ruddy* makes no such shift, and as a consequence its pages proliferate with repetitive accounts of the hero's adventurous sallies and brave confrontations. As one of his friends asserted, Crane "had begun it, scoffing at some of us who were writing that sort of romantic tale, but, as he went on with it, he got bitten by the theme and the treatment and the period, and was enjoying himself writing it."[14] This enjoyment precluded sensitivity. Where in his serious stories the parodic humor sets in sharp relief the often grim core, here the humor is rambling and overdone. A few bits in *The O'Ruddy* nevertheless remind us of what brilliant travesty Crane could invent at his best. The novel has some wickedly effective scenes. There is a fine slapstick rendering of code duello punctiliousness, and a delightful portrait of a mock highwayman who is a coward and only in the business because his venal mother insists: "I would be thinking only of the ballads, and how honourable it is that a gallant and dashing life should be celebrated in song" (VII, 51). O'Ruddy's Irish servant—a staple in Lever's novels—bewails, in another fine passage, the caste assumptions of romantic fiction: "What? A servant dead? Pah! Send it down the back staircase at once and get rid of it. . . . I have only heard of great fighters, blackguards, and beautiful ladies, but . . . there must be plenty of quiet decent people somewhere" (p. 150).

As Stephen Crane commenced with burlesques of hunting tales, he closed with a lampoon of adventure novels. Although his first parodies were crude and his final one showed a sick man's failure of intensity, the start and finish of Crane's short writing career were given over to the parody form. (Indeed, it could be argued that his trenchant, black poems, were also parodies.) Marcel Proust once insisted that the novelist must first make intentional pastiche in order to avoid later writing involuntary pastiche. The possibility that parody would lead into realism was inherent in Crane's fiction, whatever the setting. As readers, we must remain conscious of what Crane sought to parody, of the forms to which he gave a distorted image. We must understand the place of Crane's tales within the historical continuity of American fiction in order to grasp what his work meant to himself and to his contemporaries.

The realistic movement generally attempted to undercut traditional, sentimental, romantic clichés that marked most popular nineteenth-century American fiction. From early realists like Joseph Kirkland and Edward Eggleston to grim naturalists like Theodore Dreiser, novelists tried to avoid what was stereotyped and false in the general run of fiction. The operative term here is, it seems to me, "avoid." They avoided the unreal by concentrating on details and aspects of life foreign to, say, the pages of domestic love novels. Stephen Crane, however, did not avoid. He met the stereotyped plot and character head on, as it were, laughed at it, and at the same time universalized it by re-creating it according to his stark and anguished view of the human condition. To clarify this point, one might consider *Zury,* Joseph Kirkland's early realistic novel chronicling the success story of a miserly Midwestern dirt farmer, in which the author calls attention to the fact that he is not writing the usual kind of success story. He quotes a piece of newspaper fiction: "A boy, 'born of poor but respectable parents in the little town of B.' was good and strong and willing and ambitious . . ." The boy runs away to sea, saves the whole ship's company in a wreck, wins the hand of the captain's daughter: " 'For a full account of his shrewd doings and his ingenious contrivances on the island, the rescue of all hands, his education, his marriage, and the glorious height from which he looked back on his early discouragements, the reader must look to our next.' " [15] Having proposed the cliché, Kirkland then declined the gambit and wrote about the way things *really* were—a totally different kind of story. So also Howells' Silas Lapham and Dreiser's Carrie Meeber served to repudiate the usual success novel because their stories were different: more true, surely, but different from the false or sentimental stereotype. Stephen Crane, in his novel *George's Mother*, an anti-success story, followed another, more subtle strategy. Most aspects of the traditional success story—poverty, a mother's love, a first job, a romantic interlude, the temptations of drink—are present in the novel; no cliché is *avoided*. Rather, the tradition is shown up in all its weakness by Crane's characterization of his anti-hero and by the fact that his plot turns the novel into a story of absolute, unqualified failure. Crane simultaneously discriminated and assimilated the conventions.

Again, J. W. De Forest's battle scenes in *Miss Ravenel's Conversion from Secession to Loyalty*, a war novel that preceded Crane's *The Red Badge of Courage* by more than two decades, have received deserved praise because of their realism. De Forest evoked accurate, observed details of combat—such as a resting soldier being shot through a newspaper that he was reading. Stephen Crane's battle scenes, however, were realistic in a different way. Crane's hero goes through all the traditional actions involved in that hoary commonplace of war fiction, the baptism of fire. Yet the author altered the conventional pattern and revitalized the form by making his hero afraid. And after *The Red Badge of Courage,* gay, high-spirited war fiction seemed absurd.[16] Crane's method, then, was to parody the traditional and at the same time, through his deeply serious prose style and shadowy characterizations, to universalize the familiar situations of fiction. The realist chose the best parts of earlier literature and, through the addition of observed detail, made them better; the parodist chose the worst parts and, through irony, transmuted them. Crane's comic vision enabled him, paradoxically, to be less compromising, more savage—more painful perhaps—than the realists who often sold out, at the end, to the romantic conventions of character and plot. Crane frequently managed to extract from the subliterary forms he parodied the archetypal or mythical story that underlay the stereotype. He reached below surface realism toward a view of man's comic and terrible freedom of choice.

Such an approach to Stephen Crane's fiction may make him appear to be a negative artist, a critic rather than a creator. I believe, on the contrary, that Crane's very refusal to accept the traditional and his insistence on remaking it qualify him as a modern artist, along the lines of the current tradition of black humor as exemplified in the work of John Barth, Joseph Heller, or Vladimir Nabokov. Perhaps it would not be pretentious to apply to Stephen Crane some of Erich Auerbach's words on Montaigne. "In him . . . man's life—the random personal life as a whole—becomes problematic in the modern sense. That is all one dares to say. His irony, his dislike of big words, prevent him from pushing on beyond the limits of the problematic and into the realms of the tragic." [17] The fictional approach of Stephen Crane precluded high tragedy but insisted upon an honest appraisal of life's ironic obscurities. And one or twice Crane came very close to the tragic.

We should attempt to keep Stephen Crane's achievement in proper perspective, and to avoid overreading or assuming more than appears in the work. Indeed, early in his writings, Crane himself supplied a warning for the overzealous literary critic. This is Crane's parodic description of a sign painter's art: "His work has an air of philosophic thought about it which is very taking to any one of a literary turn of mind. He usually starts off with an abstract truth, an axiom, not foreign nor irrelevant, but bearing somewhat upon a hidden meaning in the sign—'Keep off the grass,' or something of that sort. . . . He also shows genius of an advanced type and the qualities of authorship in his work. . . . He has those powers of condensation which are so much admired at this day. For instance: 'Modesty of apparel is as becoming to a lady in a bathing suit as to a lady dressed in silks and satins.' There are some very sweet thoughts in that declaration. It is really a beautiful expression of sentiment. It is modest and delicate." [18] Yet, without overinterpreting, we may enhance our enjoyment of Crane's fiction by considering the traditions he inverted and recreated, and the manner in which he employed parody to this end.

NOTES

1. Harry Levin, *The Gates of Horn* (New York, 1963), p. 51.
2. Rosemary Freeman, "Parody as a Literary Form: George Herbert and Wilfred Owen," *Essays in Criticism*, 13 (1963), 307.
3. Maurice Johnson, *Fielding's Art of Fiction* (Philadelphia, 1961), p. 48.
4. Thomas Beer, *The Mauve Decade* (New York, 1961), p. 70. Crane's technique often resembles that of James Joyce as displayed in his version of the sermon in *A Portrait of the Artist as a Young Man*. Like Joyce, Crane will employ and parody the convention in a single passage, both raising and lowering the model. Compare John Loofbourow, *Thackeray and the Form of Fiction* (Princeton, 1964), p. 205: "The analytic requirements of parody trained Thackeray to recognize convention and to treat it with intense awareness; as a result, his synthesis of the literary heritage is purposeful and controlled, his expressive formulations experimental and creative rather than traditional."
5. *The Complete Short Stories and Sketches of Stephen Crane*, ed. Thomas A. Gullason (New York, 1963), p. 109.
6. Corwin Knapp Linson, *My Stephen Crane*, ed. Edwin H. Cady (Syracuse, 1958), p. 30.
7. Crane, "A Christmas Dinner Won in Battle" (1895), *Stephen Crane: Uncollected Writings*, ed. Olov W. Fryckstedt (Uppsala, 1963), p. 108.
8. Crane, "Some Hints for Playmakers," *Uncollected Writings*, pp. 36-37.
9. *The Work of Stephen Crane*, ed. Wilson Follett (New York: Alfred A. Knopf, 1925-1927), XII, 233. Subsequent references to this edition will be identified in the text by volume and page number. Since this edition is still the one most available for readers interested in the fullest body of Crane's work, I use it (except for *The Red Badge of Courage*, where there are important textual changes) despite its occasional minor unreliability and its use of a few of the Knopf house rules for spelling.
10. Harry Levin has set forth the reader's obligations when dealing with this kind of writer: we must reread the conventional works and reconstruct their patterns; then "we can relate them to our comparatively realistic book and specify its new departures more precisely. We can define realism by its context." *The Gates of Horn* (New York, 1963), p. 66.
11. Crane, letter to John N. Hilliard, Jan. 1896? *Stephen Crane: Letters*, ed. R. W. Stallman and Lillian Gilkes (New York: New York University Press, 1960), p. 110.
12. David Worcester, *The Art of Satire* (Cambridge, Mass., 1940), p. 42.
13. Thomas Beer thinks that Crane had *Tom Grogan*, a novel by F. Hopkinson Smith, in mind (Crane, *Work*, vol. VII, p. ix). I find no similarities, however. As Corwin Linson has testified, the young author never had any use for "the old school of romance novelists," particularly Sir Walter Scott and Victor Hugo. *My Stephen Crane*, pp. 31-32.
14. Letter from A. E. W. Mason to Vincent Starrett, Oct. 4, 1945, *Letters*, p. 344.
15. Joseph Kirkland, *Zury, The Meanest Man in Spring County* (Boston, 1887), p. 35.
16. An early review of the novel noticed this effect: "A serio-comic effect seems to be intended throughout," John Borrow Allen, *Academy*, 49 (1896), 135.
17. Erich Auerbach, *Mimesis*, trans. Willard R. Trask (New York, 1953), p. 273.
18. Crane, "On the Boardwalk" (1892), *Uncollected Writings*, p. 27.

5. *Stephen Crane and the Ironic Last Word*
By Clark Griffith

In the often ambiguous fiction of Stephen Crane, there is a central ambiguity which criticism seems not to have noticed. It comes from a split between the view of man that Crane holds generally, and what happens to particular characters as certain of his stories develop.

The view of man is consistent, and may be inferred from the large body of Crane's work. It holds, in effect, that man is a limited creature, whose particular limitation is his inability to learn much—to profit morally or intellectually—from the experiences he undergoes. There are two reasons why this is the case, the first of which is inherent in the experiences themselves. They emerge from (or, more accurately, are imposed by) a world that is at once too complex and impenetrable to be studied closely and too little interested in man to be concerned with teaching him anything. Chiefly, however, man's inaptitudes are due to a defect in his own nature. For Crane, the human being is essentially the overreacher: trivial in fact, but prone to become large and significant in his illusions about himself. Typically, he comes to life with too much ego and too many expectations, with too little taste for seeing things in their proper perspective and too great a reliance upon such doubtful qualities as human logic and human reason. And thereby, in his ignorance and unawareness, he is easily tricked into making the wrong guess, the erroneous assumption, the false and inept interpretation. The truth is that he can learn little because he lacks the sort of realistic and self-critical attitudes which make knowledge possible.

And yet, for all that, Crane consistently presents situations in which his characters do appear to learn. Indeed, many of his most memorable works take the form of initiations into knowledge. The protagonists confront an experience, pass through it, meditate about its implications—and emerge from it wiser and more mature than they were before the events occurred.

Consider, along these lines, "The Open Boat." Step by step, throughout their long ordeal, Crane's four castaways have driven

Reprinted from: *Philological Quarterly*, XLVII (January 1968), 83-91. By permission of The University of Iowa and the author.

home to them a set of irreducible truths about man's place in the cosmos. For one thing, they learn that in the eyes of the universe all lives, including their own, are expendable. They find that nature can be neither kicked nor wheedled into submission, but that the natural order is as remote from man and as unmindful of his needs as is the "high cold star" above him. From the naïve assumption that survival can somehow be earned, they come to see that those who get to shore safely get there not because they have been good or diligent, but solely as the result of chance—the happy accident. At the end of the story, the three survivors are sadder for their experience. But the point is that in their sadness they have also become wiser men. They have had to give up a foolishly sentimental view of themselves, and to replace it with what, in Crane's eyes, would be the scientific view of experience, infinitely more difficult to maintain, but with the virtue of being truer and more credible.

Though the terms of the lesson are different, this same process of learning from experience is not only repeated in "The Blue Hotel"; it appears there with even greater explicitness. Looking back on the events at Ft Romper, the Easterner is appalled by his own guilt. He believes he bears as much responsibility for the murder of the Swede as though he had actually wielded the knife: bears it because, by refusing to say that Johnnie did cheat at cards, he acted as accessory to the fistfight, helped coax the Swede back out into the enveloping and all-destructive darkness, and so sent the Swede off at last to find violence and death in the nearby saloon. Nevertheless, his guilt has a positive side, for out of it the Easterner has wrested a new understanding of what should be one man's moral involvements with his fellow men. Next time a crisis comes, he will know better and behave differently. At least, as he implies to the cowboy, he will know enough next time to stand up and be counted. If the past is beyond redeeming, still with an enlarged comprehension of what it means to be moral and courageous and human, the Easterner can see to it that the disasters of the past never recur in the future.

And in Crane's undoubted masterpiece the business of gleaning knowledge from life assumes truly classical proportions. At the opening of *The Red Badge of Courage*, we are shown in Henry Fleming an example of Crane's man at his misguided worst. Brash and presumptuous, Henry is ceaselessly engaged in attempting to make the world conform to his will and his beliefs. He has illusions about literally everything: pictures in his head that tell him how his mother should say farewell, what the enemy will look like, how

wars ought to be conducted, what the hero feels, and how one will
suffer if one is a coward. When the pictures fail to come true, Henry
reacts with astonishment or with the sort of absurd rationalization
which occurs when, terrified of war and forgetting his eagerness to
be a warrior, he concludes that "he had not enlisted of his free will.
He had been dragged by the merciless government." And of course
the pictures rarely do materialize. Henry is as often wrong about
events as he is prone to prejudge them. Much of *The Red Badge
of Courage* seems designed to show that, given his particular outlook,
he can never hope to interpret correctly. For a long while in the
book, he seems cast to the role of the Great American Boob.

But only for a while. Perhaps the turning point comes with
Henry's repeated exposures to battle, or when he witnesses the
death of Jim Conklin, or during the episode in the woods when he
stumbles upon a decaying corpse. At all events, the youth has his
transformation. The fear and despair he knows in battle teach him
the need for greater modesty in his expectations about himself.
Because he panics and runs away, he accepts the fact that he cannot
always master life, but is only an ordinary man, with man's ordinary
imperfections. Though the Henry who appears at the close of *The
Red Badge of Courage* is more somber and reflective than he was at
the start, his melancholy is compensated for by his having learned
humility, detachment, and a sense of redeeming irony. That war has
given him a soul is Henry's own estimate of what happens. And an
astute critic of Crane, confirming Henry's judgment, adds that

> after intense misgivings and flight, Henry learns something of
> his weaknesses and capabilities. He thus manages to come to
> terms with his small segment of a world at war, and achieves
> a measure of maturity.[1]

With these illustrations before us, it becomes possible to restate
the paradox with which we set out. On the one hand, Crane appears
to say that men can learn next to nothing; on the other, he portrays
specific characters as they apparently master lessons of great value.
How, short of imputing confusion to a writer of genius, can we
resolve the contradiction?

The answer, I believe, involves our scrutinizing a technique that
Crane uses repeatedly. He sets forth circumstances in which there

is only the appearance of learning. A character will seem to profit from his experiences; but we look more closely and find that the character has stood still, or, alternatively, that his new-found knowledge is somehow fraudulent and thus becomes the basis upon which he predicates even grosser errors. In a given story, therefore, ostensible meanings tend to undercut themselves. What we took to be an act of crucial discovery is inverted—and often is inverted at just the point where the discovery has come to seem most meaningful. Crane's method of pulling the rug from beneath us—for this is what his technique does—is a model of craft and slyness. I shall call it his strategy of the ironic last word.

II

"The Open Boat" concludes with this curious sentence:

> When it came night, the white waves paced to and fro in the moonlight, and the wind brought the sound of the great sea's voice to the men on the shore, and they felt they could then be interpreters.

The sentence is puzzling, because one would have supposed that the essential interpretations had all been made earlier. Already, as we have seen, the men on shore have had to face up to the callousness of nature, to the paltry value placed on human life, and to the fact that chance seems to determine every experience and every outcome. Furthermore, the only other important interpretation in the story—that of the correspondent concerning the virtues of brotherhood—also belongs to his two nights in the open boat. Nevertheless, Crane's syntax is insistent. "The men felt they could *then* be interpreters": it is *after* the terror that the evaluations of terror will commence. What shape shall we give to those interpretations which, obviously, are still to be heard?

I propose an hypothesis. Once they are almost ashore, Crane's castaways begin to have second thoughts about the meaning of their situation. It occurs to them even then that their survival will be "a true miracle of the sea"; when a prospective rescuer appears, he strikes them as having been sent straight from Heaven, for "a halo was about his head, and he shone like a saint." And now, safely beyond all danger (brought, indeed, to a place where the sea is only moonlit foam and a distant voice), the three survivors are, I suspect, about to go one step further toward forgetting reality. They are about to decide that the scientific view of their ordeal is inconsistent with what really happened, and, in any case, not nearly flattering enough to their egos. Accordingly, they will soon reject it in favor of the happier, more sentimental explanation. And it is the sentimental version that will cause the men to *re*-interpret—to conclude, each one separately, *well I made it, I survived, didn't I? therefore, my life must be important, somebody or something must have cared for me, I must after all have especially earned the miracle.*

To read the story this way is to find in it more specificity than Crane gives. Yet the reading seems warranted by three points. First, there is Crane's careful, highly subtle preparation for a change in attitude. Second, there is his strategic placing of the word *then.* And finally, and perhaps most decisively, there is the end of "The Blue Hotel," where the term *interpreter* is not used, but an interpreter actually appears and proceeds to make an actual interpretation.

We have already noticed the drift of the Easterner's musings. It now remains to quote certain of the comments he makes to the cowboy, and to catch, if possible, the tone in which they are uttered. "Fun or not," he says

> . . . Johnnie was cheating. I saw him. I knew it. I saw him. And I refused to stand up and be a man. I let the Swede fight it out alone. . . . We are all in it! This poor gambler isn't even a noun. He is a kind of adverb. Every sin is the result of a Collaboration. We, all five of us, collaborated in the murder of this Swede . . . only five men—you, I, Johnnie, old Scully; and that fool of an unfortunate gambler came merely as a culmination, the apex of a human movement, and gets all the punishment.

This is an excited and assertive tone, as befits a speaker who is reasoning out great moral discoveries. In addition, the tone is somewhat ponderous (consider the big word *culmination,* the bigger phrase *apex of a human movement),* and it is more than a little smug (mark well what is being said: *we were awful; yet look at what we did; see how, by actions of ours, the course of events was altered).* And, above all else, it is the tone of a badly mistaken man. For with each word he says—each fresh argument he brings into play— the Easterner demonstrates that he and his whole elaborate analysis could not possibly be more wrong-headed.

Nobody packed the Swede off to be killed, except the Swede himself. In love with death (though all unconscious of this yearning), he arrived at Ft. Romper, as he might have come anywhere, searching for an assassin. His behavior is perfectly consistent, from the moment he first becomes conspicuous at the hotel, through his accusations of Johnnie, down to his annoying the gambler. And the consistency is always that of a man with a strong urge for self-annihilation. When in death he stares fixedly at a cash register, the machine looks back at him with a precise account of the Swede's motivations: " 'This registers the amount of your purchase.' " But if the cash register is right—if the Swede came to buy death and found it—then there is no defending the Easterner's view that " 'We are all in it!' " By acting differently, the five of them might indeed have changed the time or the place or the form of the murder; the fact of the murder, however, they could not have prevented. Consequently, the Easterner's great discovery is, in reality, no discovery at all. For all the intricacies that enter into them, his moral insights turn out to be meaningless. Despite the momentous air with which it is expressed, the sense of guilt he feels is due to nothing more than his excessive self-esteem.

It is while the Easterner's last words still reverberate that Crane compounds the irony of "The Blue Hotel" by adding one word more. We have to agree with the cowboy's indignation: " 'Well, I didn't do anythin', did I?' " But this is not to say of course that we see in the cowboy a figure who has learned something. He is not interpreting, but only peering "blindly" into the Easterner's mysterious theories, and then responding in a defensive rage. The cowboy is right, without having any idea of why he is right. Hence his correctness is in no way impressive.

And what, finally, of Henry Fleming? On the last pages of *The Red Badge of Courage,* we see him as we see the survivors and the Easterner: removed now from the center of violence and attempting to sum up what the violence has signified. But are his summations more perceptive than theirs? Let us look at the evidence of his last words.

It is true that they begin promisingly with Henry's sense that because he has known dismay and flight, his eyes seemed to open to some new ways. He found that he could look back upon the brass and bombast of his earlier gospels and see them truly. He was gleeful when he discovered that he now despised them.

With this conviction came a store of assurance. He felt a quiet manhood, nonassertive but of sturdy and strong blood.

As a repudiation of what one was (and was, so to speak, only yesterday), this may strike us as a shade facile. Nevertheless, it is sound doctrine, just the shrewd, clear-eyed view of the self that Crane would encourage. Were this mood to last, Henry's debt to experience would be certain, his "measure of maturity" beyond disputing.

But now, without warning, his reflections take a different turn:

He knew that he would no more quail before his guides wherever they should point. He had been to touch the great death, and found that, after all, it was but the great death. He was a man.

There is no doubting Henry's seriousness. His emphatic verbs (*knew, was*) and carefully placed modifiers (*no more, wherever, but*) make it clear that he means precisely what he says. What we cannot accept seriously, however, is the presence of such arrogance in one who has renounced all "brass and bombast." And then, of course, we see the point. Already, a new picture is starting to form in Henry's head. It resembles neither the frightened boy he was, nor the man of modesty and moderation he just resolved to be. But it is a more satisfying conception than either, for it images a noble, fearless, larger-than-life Henry, who has triumphed by imposing his will on reality, and who is now free to repeat the triumph at any time he chooses. It is thus as outsized and unwarranted a picture as any that Henry has ever created.

And more picture-making is to come. Next, while the war rages over the nearest hill, Henry's thoughts turn to images of "tranquil skies, fresh meadows, cool brooks—an existence of soft and eternal peace." Nor are these the images of some remote dream. They belong to the immediate present, for even now Henry feels that his "scars faded as flowers. He had rid himself of the red sickness of battle.

The sultry nightmare was in the past." Surely, the blunders here are self-evident. If the scars can fade this quickly, the hurts must never have meant very much. By the casual way he shrugs it off, Henry limits the power of the "red sickness" to endure and to discipline. And, what is most damaging of all, the attitude he takes toward these matters is of a kind with his earlier follies. At another point in the book, he had been pleased to tell himself that "he had not enlisted of his free will. He had been dragged by the merciless government." His shutting out of reality then is in no way different from the easy forgetfulness—the bland, unthinking self-deception— he indulges in now.

Breaking through "leaden rain clouds," the sun shines on a Henry Fleming who believes he is almost totally enlightened. In Henry's eyes, he has passed the moral test of battle, and come away a complete man. But if Henry succeeds in fooling himself (and, apparently, some of his critics), Stephen Crane knows better. What Crane sees is that if Henry has his momentary insight, it quickly trails off into the old delusion that he is a unique being, set apart from the other "bedraggled" troops, and living in a world that is a "world for him." Like the survivors and the Easterner, Henry only seems to have learned from experience. In actuality, he ends up as far removed from truth as ever. As is the case with these other figures, the last words in his story are the youth's undoing, for they become the measure of his continuing ignorance.[2]

III

> Beliefs are bandaged, like the Tongue
> When Terror were it told
> In any tone commensurate
> Would strike us instant Dead
> —Emily Dickinson

Is the ironic last word merely a narrative trick, a game played by Crane to poke fun at his characters and perhaps at the unwary reader as well? Or has this strategy some deeper significance? Since Crane is both a consummate ironist and a profoundly compassionate writer, it seems to me that we are justified in taking the latter view.

What the strategy then underscores is not simply human ignorance; in a way, it justifies the ignorance, for it attests, as well, to the helplessness of man in a naturalistic universe. During his moments of great stress, there are forced upon the individual certain naturalistic facts which are always true enough but, in their accuracy, too dreadful to be borne. When the moments have passed, therefore, and when, at his leisure, the individual has the time to pause and reflect: then, because he cannot help himself, he must try to evade the facts. If his rationalizations and extravagant claims and easy failures of memory seem foolish, they are also the marks of his being intensely human. They mean that man is not readily able to abide the vision of himself that reality presents. Simply to survive, he has to cling to life-giving illusions—to construct some new vision in which he will be larger and more glamorous than reality ever allows for.

Thus it is that no one, least of all Stephen Crane, laughs at Henry or the survivors, or even at the pomposities of the Easterner. The mistakes into which these characters fall are far too poignant and far too psychologically necessary to evoke laughter. Motivating the mistakes is a world that has afflicted the men by according them too few grounds for taking themselves seriously. In their frustration, the men have responded in the only way they know how. They have had no choice except to blot out the bitterest lessons of experience, and to create in their own minds that air of being important and con-sequential which life denies them.[3] Their self-deceptions may indeed be vain and credulous. Yet they are not really to be blamed for practicing the deceptions; for given their fundamental natures, they could hardly do otherwise. That the individual must sooner or later "bandage" his beliefs; that, in order to live at peace with himself, he has to stretch the truth a little and engage in some selective forgetting —this, for Crane, is the sign that he participates in the human condition. And, as "The Open Boat" says in a slightly different connection, it is likewise "the pathos of his situation."

NOTES

1. William M. Gibson, in the introduction to the Rinehart edition of *The Red Badge of Courage and Selected Prose and Poetry* (New York, 1960), p. vii. Except that it is more cautiously phrased, Mr. Gibson's comment is of a kind with most other views of Henry: see, for example, R. W. Stallman's introduc-tion to the Modern Library edition of *The Red Badge of Courage* (New York, 1951), pp. xxii-xxxvii, and John E. Hart "*The Red Badge of Courage* as Myth and Symbol," *University of Kansas City Review*, XIX (1953), 249-56. Of the interpreters I have read, only Charles C. Walcutt, in *American Literary Nat-*

uralism, a Divided Stream (University of Minnesota Press, 1965), holds (pp. 81-82) that Henry has *not* achieved "a lasting wisdom or self-knowledge."

2. In trying to establish Henry's final position I have appealed to the end of *The Red Badge of Courage* as it stands in the published version. The longer manuscript version, which is now available in several sources, shows that Henry's last thoughts have become even more strident: for instance, he not only assumes that he can face the "great death" without qualms; in addition, he apparently claims immortality for himself, since he feels that the "great death" is reserved "for others." I have supposed that Crane deleted this and other similar passages in order to make more subtle and ironic Henry's decline from a momentary insight back into "the brass and bombast of his earlier gospels."

3. If it seems that by acknowledging guilt (no matter how unnecessarily), the Easterner accepts rather than rejects the "bitter lesson" of experience, let the reader re-examine the next to the last paragraph of "The Blue Hotel." Clearly, the attitudes expressed there are more boastful than they are contrite. If, as he keeps insisting, the Easterner is appalled by himself, he also derives a strange sense of satisfaction from what he thinks he has done. The truth is that he cannot imagine anything so dramatic as the Swede's murder occurring in his surroundings, without his being, in some way, responsible for the occurrence.

"The Blue Hotel" is also a useful place for distinguishing between the two kinds of illusions that Crane portrays. When, in his madness, the Swede decides that Ft. Romper is a part of the wild and dangerous west, this is a destructive illusion, since it prompts the pattern of fear-crazed behavior which results in the Swede's death. By contrast, the illusions of Henry, the survivors, and the Easterner about themselves are at least creative, representing as they do man's attempt to claim a little dignity, a little power, and a little status in the face of an indifferent reality. The worst that can be said of the creative illusions is that they are pretentious—though, again, very human in their pretentiousness. Certainly, they do no real harm; and it is even possible to suppose that, just because they have misunderstood themselves, the Easterner will be a better man and Henry a more courageous one.

6. *Stephen Crane and Impressionism*
By Rodney O. Rogers

The question of how French impressionist painting influenced
Stephen Crane's writing has been one of lasting interest. Crane's
friends were quick to imply his indebtedness. H. G. Wells noted his
"persistent selection of the essential elements of an impresion." [1]
Conrad called Crane a "complete impressionist," [2] while R. G.
Vosburgh declared that "impressionism was his faith." [3] These
suggestive though uniformly vague remarks later provoked more
thorough investigations of the subject. The evidence implying Crane's
early knowledge of impressionism was adequately rehearsed,[4] and this
body of fact became the basis for conjectures of an analytical nature.

The standard approach to the question notes similarities between
stylistic techniques in Crane's writing and in impressionist painting.
For instance, Crane's " 'painterly' stylistic devices"—notably his use
of color and chiaroscuro—have been tentatively identified as "impressionistic." [5] R. W. Stallman goes farthest of all when he calls Crane's
style "prose pointillism" because "it is composed of disconnected
images, which coalesce like blobs of color in French impressionist
painting," [6] a remark illustrating how easily such a line of argument
can be made to finesse the question it proposes to address. For unless
Stallman actually means that Crane learned to write a certain way
by conceiving literary images as dots of paint, his statement, however
thought-provoking, suggests not a causal connection but only an
analogy between these two widely divergent art techniques. While
such an analysis is helpful to a point, a more meaningful relation of
Crane to impressionism would seem to await the admission that
painting can exert influences upon writing which do not primarily
depend upon the use of similar stylistic techniques by artists working
in vastly different art media. I will suggest that Crane's sense of the
nature of reality is what most convincingly implies his link with
impressionism. If Crane in fact owes anything substantial to the
French school, it consists mainly in his having adopted the world
view upon which impressionism as a painting style depends.

Reprinted from: *Nineteenth-Century Fiction*, XXIV (December 1969), 292-304.
By permission of The Regents of the University of California and the author.
Copyright © 1969 by The Regents of the University of California.

The French impressionist painters, Wylie Sypher rightly remarks, "brought to the evolution of modern style a new sense of atmosphere and, consequently, a new sense of space." They discovered that light qualifies the value of space and that details in a scene are displaced and different fragments of space combined as the angle of vision shifts. Hence in impressionist paintings atmosphere succeeds scene in importance. Space is not geometric but "apprehensive," and objects are not rendered as distinct shapes so much as they are translated into the essence of a sensation. For the impressionist therefore "the structure of the world is relative . . . three-dimensional space is not an absolute value." [7] The nature of reality, the physical world, according to the impressionist view, depends primarily upon how it is perceived. A corollary to this idea is that a person's psychology affects the way he conceives the world.

While the evidence is by no means conclusive, it seems likely that Crane became aware of the impressionist ontology through Hamlin Garland, probably the most influential upon Crane of the numerous artists, both painters and writers, who were Crane's friends while he was still a literary unknown. Garland was Crane's mentor as well as his sometime companion during the period that the older, established writer was formulating the literary credo soon to be expressed in *Crumbling Idols* (1894). The impressionist style, Garland could have explained to Crane, "indicates a radical change in attitude toward the physical universe. It stands for an advance in the perceptive power of the human eye." The impressionist painter knows "that the landscape is never twice alike. Every degree of the progress of the sun makes a new picture." [8] Impressionism is a realistic style of description precisely because reality is ephemeral, evanescent, constantly shifting its meaning and hence continually defying precise definition.

These ideas, implicit in impressionist painting, are expressed in Crane's writing through certain techniques which he characteristically employs to control narrative point of view. The narrator of his predominantly visual fiction typically registers and simultaneously evaluates the various, frequently contradictory views of the world which define his protagonist's sensibility. In *The Red Badge*, for instance, the narrator repeatedly gives us the visible correlatives of Henry Fleming's fleeting, shifting moods. Now nature assumes the shape, color and gesture of Fleming's dread: "The blue smoke-swallowed line curled and writhed like a snake stepped upon. It swung its ends to and fro in an agony of fear and rage" (I, 148).[9] Now it mirrors his naïve aspirations: the battle standard beckons as "a goddess, radiant, that bended its form with an imperious gesture to him" (I, 164). Through such poetically rendered impressions the narrator's irony cuts relentlessly, suggesting yet other meanings for the reality described. "Absurd ideas took hold upon him. He thought that he did not relish the landscape. It threatened him" (I, 50-51). Crane is acutely responsive to the paradox inherent in the impressionist concept that the nature of reality depends in part upon the psychology of whoever perceives it:

> To the maiden
> The sea was blue meadow,
> Alive with little froth-people
> Singing.
>
> To the sailor, wrecked,
> The sea was dead grey walls
> Superlative in vacancy,
> Upon which nevertheless at fateful time
> Was written
> The grim hatred of nature. (VI, 111)

Like this poem, most of what Crane wrote implores the reader not to accept any one description as final. The sequence of discrete impressions which comprise his fiction continually qualifies the presented view of the world. The time scheme of the narrative method thus becomes in his relatively plotless stories a flow and flux of equivocal points of view which accents the idea that no finite series of statements, however precise each one may be, accurately sums up reality. Indeed the meaning of Crane's fiction, as well as its characteristic irony, depends in the main upon the irreconcilability of these contradictory statements.

Crane modulates between dissimilar points of view in at least three distinct ways: by direct, literal statement; by manipulating narrative focus; and by employing what I call "verbal disparity." While the three techniques tend to overlap each other in practice, certain passages clearly illustrate the principal effects of each. Direct statement, frankly intrusive, is the most frequently remarked though perhaps not the most effective technique Crane employs to qualify an established narrative point of view. At one point in "The Blue Hotel" the Swede, victorious over Johnnie Scully in a fist fight, swaggers triumphantly through a driving blizzard. The narrator suddenly interrupts the story:

> He might have been in a deserted village. We picture the world as thick with conquering and elate humanity, but here, with the bugles of the tempest pealing, it was hard to imagine a peopled earth. One viewed the existence of man then as a marvel, and conceded a glamour of wonder to these lice which were caused to cling to a whirling, fire-smitten, ice-locked, disease-stricken, space-lost bulb. The conceit of man was explained by this storm to be the very engine of life. (X, 124)

In this statement a distancing effect ironically undercuts the Swede's view of man as triumphant in the world. The narrator's intrusion figuratively moves away from the subject toward a point in space from which the perspective makes human life appear minute and inconsequential. The result is an impression far different from that which Crane had maintained by viewing the world primarily through the eyes of his protagonist.

A similar modulation occurs in "The Open Boat," a story where the narrative locus in general is the dinghy walled in by waves:

> As each slaty wall of water approached, it shut all else from the view of the men in the boat, and it was not difficult to imagine that this particular wave was the final out-burst of the ocean. . . . In the wan light the faces of the men must have been grey. Their eyes must have glinted in strange ways as they gazed steadily astern. Viewed from a balcony, the whole thing would doubtless have been weirdly picturesque. (XII, 31)

Here the last sentence accomplishes the same shift of viewpoint which occurs in the passage cited from "The Blue Hotel." In this case however the effect is entirely the result of literal statement and does not depend additionally upon the sort of metaphorical transformation which in the former passage reduces men to insects clinging to a bulb-like earth. The narrator simply imagines himself out of the boat looking down upon it from above. The resulting description of the sea contrasts ironically with the men's impression that they are barbarously and wrongfully imperiled by the waves' snarling crests.

More commonly Crane accomplishes a modulation of point of view without resorting to direct statement. By carefully manipulating his narrative focus he shifts perspective without forcing his narrator to intrude into the story. Near the end of "Flanagan and His Short Filibustering Adventure," the narrator has been seeing his story through the eyes of the doomed, shipwrecked mariners. Suddenly the scene shifts to a dance hall on the nearby beach and he assumes the viewpoint of a group of revelers concerned only peripherally in the sea drama. The irony growing out of such disparate impressions of the same moment—emphasized by the reiteration of the verb "floated" —is tersely summed up in the story's concluding paragraph: "Save for the white glare of the breakers, the sea was a great wind-crossed void. From the throng of charming women floated the perfume of many flowers. Later there floated to them a body" (XII, 200). While similar shifts in point of view in general characterize fiction employing a ubiquitous narrator, Crane's ironic use of the juxtaposition to suggest that man's experience of the world is multifaceted, marks this particular modulation as impressionist in concept.

A related, still less obtrusive kind of viewpoint manipulation involves not an abrupt relocation of the visual locus, but rather a gradual readjustment of the perspective with which a scene is viewed. In the description of Maggie's death scene, a subtle distancing effect is employed to block the reader's potentially sentimental response:

> She went into the blackness of the final block. The shutters of the tall buildings were closed like grim lips. The structure[s] seemed to have eyes that looked over them, beyond them, at other things. Afar off the lights of the avenues glittered as if from an impossible distance. Street-car bells jingled with a sound of merriment.
>
> At the feet of the tall buildings appeared the deathly black hue of the river. Some hidden factory sent up a yellow glare, that lit for a moment the waters lapping oilily against the timbers. The varied sounds of life, made joyous by distance and seeming unapproachableness, came faintly and died away to a silence. (X, 210-211) [10]

Maggie's journey from light into darkness, concluded by this passage, is controlled with great care. The first paragraph, quoted, like those immediately preceding it, presents—not unsympathetically—Maggie's uncomprehending impression of a world cruelly indifferent to her no longer romantic notions of what life ought to be. Through Maggie's eyes we see the buildings at extreme closeup, metaphorically face to face. We hear, as she does, the sound of a paradoxically animated life leaving her behind. The second paragraph, however, modulates away from Maggie's point of view and reasserts the ironic perspective toward Crane's heroine which in general characterizes the novel's narrator. An almost cinematic transition moves the visual locus relatively far away from the death scene. As Maggie, figuratively speaking, shrinks from view, we no longer experience the world through her eyes and ears. Part of the shift is metaphorical. The buildings are no longer threatening faces but whole bodied giants at whose feet Maggie is dwarfed and obscured. In addition the perspective is widened to include, besides the street's end where the unseen suicide presumably occurs, the dimly lighted river, a factory identified by the light its windows emit, and—I think—the sides of tall buildings seen as from above. From this vantage point sound like light dies to a serene nothingness and Maggie's death becomes, to a considerable extent, an event physically insignificant enough to warrant no more than a passing concern.

Besides employing techniques such as these, which depend upon a physical displacement of the narrative locus, Crane also manipulates point of view by means of gradually or suddenly widening the angle of vision originating at a fixed point in space. The resulting impression typically contrasts ironically with the narrower, hence more limited viewpoint which it qualifies. In "The Open Boat," after enduring a night of terror culminating in exhaustion and sleep, the correspondent awakens to a vision which is virtually apocalyptic. In contrast to the situation at the outset of the story, the widened perspective now allows the men to know the color of the sky: "When the correspondent again opened his eyes, the sea and the sky were each of the grey hue of the dawning. Later, carmine and gold was painted upon the waters. The morning appeared finally, in its splendor, with a sky of pure blue, and the sunlight flamed on the tips of the waves" (XII, 55). This somewhat tranquil impression implicitly denies the malignancy which the correspondent previously had attributed to the sea and leads toward his ultimate contention that nature, conceived in its broadest possible perspective, is flatly indifferent to man.

Such an impressionist manipulation occurs so frequently in *The Red Badge* that it becomes virtually a formula for irony. Characteristically the sky in some shade of benignity or indifference is the principal element brought into the impression by the widened angle of vision. For instance, one of Henry Fleming's earliest experiences in actual battle contradicts and broadens his initial narrower impression that the entire world is engaged in a war being waged directly under his nose: "As he gazed around him the youth felt a flash of astonishment at the blue, pure sky and the sun gleaming on the trees and fields. It was surprising that Nature had gone tranquilly on with her golden process in the midst of so much devilment" (I, 70). Earlier an impassive sky had denied Fleming's impression that an animated nature threatened his mortal existence: "But the long serpents crawled slowly from hill to hill without bluster of smoke. A dun-coloured cloud of dust floated away to the right. The sky overhead was of a fairy blue" (I, 40). Here the progression of the three sentences accomplishes an ever widening and hence readjusting angle of vision. Which of the three descriptions of war is more truthful than the other two? Reality, Crane is saying, is not simply what it momentarily seems to be, for one's impression of the world shifts from moment to moment. Considered in this light, the narrator's continually readjusting point of view appears as an effort to tally a sum whose terms increase without limit. That examples of a similar nature can be multiplied at will from Crane's fiction would seem to corroborate such a conclusion:

> From off under the trees came the rolling clatter of the musketry. Each distant thicket seemed a strange porcupine with quills of flame. A cloud of dark smoke, as from smoldering ruins, went up toward the sun, now bright and gay in the blue, enamelled sky. (I, 151)

As in the previous instances, the widening angle of vision from a fixed vantage point reaches to subtend an image of tranquil sky which ironically qualifies the initial impression that nature is brutal and threatening. Interestingly, Crane seems in general to have conceived the sky as symbolic of the idea that nature is indifferent to man.

> If I should cast off this tattered coat,
> And go free into the mighty sky;
> If I should find nothing there
> But a vast blue,
> Echoless, ignorant—
> What then? (VI, 101)

Though one could cite poems by Crane which contradict this implicit definition of God, I think these lines serve admirably to confirm what we sense about Crane's use of sky imagery in *The Red Badge* and elsewhere in his fiction.

In addition to the methods for modulating point of view I have already described, Crane uses verbal disparity to qualify the value of an impression. These metaphorical modulations in effect are metaphysical tropes which, by violently yoking together disparate ideas, change an established point of view suddenly and dramatically. Set into vivid relief by the fairly austere quality of an overall "colloquial" prose style, such metaphors are perhaps the principal means through which a writer like Crane "calculatedly provokes response in his readers by manipulating vocabulary." [11] In "The Blue Hotel" Crane ends the sentence describing the Swede's murder with a simile which wholly contradicts the more sublime impression of man established in the first part of the sentence: "then was seen a long blade in the hand of the gambler. It shot forward, and a human body, this citadel of virtue, wisdom, power, was pierced as easily as if it had been a melon" (X, 129). In "The Open Boat" Crane's choice of domestic imagery at one point momentarily adds a ludicrous aspect to the description of the imperiled mariners: "Many a man ought to have a bathtub larger than the boat which here rode upon the sea" (XII, 29). In "Flanagan" a pastoral metaphor ironically reverses an impression of the sea as cruel which depends upon the viewpoint of a group of seasick Cuban insurgents:

> They were all sick to the limits. They strewed the deck in every posture of human anguish. . . . The patriots were all ordered below decks, and there they howled and measured their misery one against another. All day the *Foundling* plopped and foun-

dered over a blazing bright meadow of an ocean whereon the foam was like flowers. (XII, 187)

In "The Price of the Harness" a domestic trope in which something is cooking reduces the immediate world to the size and perhaps to the shape of a kitchen, qualifying drastically the established impression that a battle of grand proportions is being waged:

> The sun burned down steadily from a pale blue sky upon the crackling woods and knolls and fields. From a roar of the musketry it might have been that the celestial heat was frying this part of the world. (IX, 29)

Less often such verbal disparities are aural rather than imagistic. In the last stanza of "A Man Adrift on a Slim Spar," the ground rhythm as well as the imagery and the use of pleasing sibilants and sonorous vowels, tends to distract attention from the fact that a violent death is taking place:

> The puff of a coat imprisoning air:
> A face kissing the water-death
> A weary slow sway of a lost hand
> And the sea, the moving sea, the sea.
>   God is cold.[12]

In particular, regular meter and the graceful repetition of sound in the penultimate verse construe a not unattractive impression of the sea which argues to a degree successfully against the tentative conclusion expressed by the final line.

Ultimately Crane's impressionist modulations of point of view suggest the idea, crucial to most of what he wrote, that "the final meaning of . . . experience escapes at last into mystery." [13] Despite his own statement to the contrary, Crane rarely is content to present merely a "slice out of life." [14] Rather he must continually qualify what he "sees," and in this endless process of adjustment and redefinition, far more than in conventional narrative statement, reposes the most essential meaning of his art. Crane's typical story presses for its effect through his narrator's ironic modulations between two or more contradictory points of view. In "Death and the Child," for instance, Crane's narrator exists primarily to evaluate the two anti-thetical definitions of man suggested by the protagonist Peza's war experiences. The narrator first states this antithesis, implicitly yet succinctly, in the story's opening paragraphs, employing a compli-cated modulation which incorporates most of the impressionist techniques I have identified:

> The peasants ... were streaming down the mountain trail ... in their sharp terror. ... This brown stream poured on with a constant wastage of goods and beasts. ... It was as if fear was a river, and this horde had simply been caught in the torrent. ... It was a freshet that might sear the face of the tall, quiet mountain   . From it there arose a constant babble of tongues ... sometimes choking, as from men drowning. ...
>
> The blue bay, with its pointed ships, and the white town lay below them, distant, flat, serene. There was upon this vista a peace that a bird knows when, high in air, it surveys the world, a great, calm thing rolling noiselessly toward the end of the mystery. Here on the height one felt the existence of the universe scornfully defining the pain in ten thousand minds. The sky was an arch of stolid sapphire. Even to the mountains, raising their mighty shapes from the valley, this headlong rush of the fugitives was too minute. The sea, the sky, and the hills combined in their grandeur to term this misery inconsequent. (XII, 241-242)

In this passage, condensed here solely for brevity's sake, a sense of physical involvement gives way to a far more encompassing, less engaged outlook. Irony in the main results from the diminution achieved by figuratively "backing away" from what is seen. Physical detail disappears. The metaphorical river of fear is absorbed by the bay's implacable serenity. The perspective gradually widens into an arc subtending sea, mountains and sky, an outlook whose effect is heightened by the bird trope suggesting that a godlike visual com-mand of the world has been achieved. Before sounds of struggle and alarm can reach the figuratively distant locus informing the revised perspective, they have been filtered into silence.

Without effacing either, such an impressionist modulation, like numerous similar ones throughout the story, emphasizes the contrast between two opposed ways of looking at man in the world. These two outlooks, one involved and the other detached, correspond to the two disparate attitudes between which Peza wavers as he attempts to conceive the meaning of his participation in the Greco-Turkish war. Peza believes that joining his father's countrymen in arms against the Turks will assist him in formulating "an active definition of his own dimension, his personal relation to men, geography, life" (XII, 243). His idea that war provides man a backdrop for his heroic gesturing seems substantiated when the battle reflects back to Peza his own intense pride and fear. Shells pass over his head "with the sound of great birds frantically flapping their wings" (XII, 257). The battle seems aware of his approach, endowed "with the intelligence of a barbaric deity" (XII, 256). The landscape confronts him "with the gaze of startled antelopes" (XII, 255). Yet a contrary sense of his relative significance in the overall action from time to time threatens Peza's self-importance. In one lucid instant he modestly wonders if the universe takes "cognizance of him to an important degree." He reflects "that the accidental destruction of an individual, Peza by name, would perhaps be nothing at all" (XII, 248). At another such moment he becomes aware that, amid the roar of fighting, "trees were growing, the grass blades . . . extending, according to their process." He inhales "a deep breath of moisture and fragrance . . . a wet odour" expressing, the narrator tells us, "the opulent fecundity of unmoved nature, marching on with her million plans for multiple life, multiple death" (XII, 249).

Despite these menacing revelations and others like them, Peza's self-esteem, though severely challenged, is not entirely destroyed when the story ends. He flees the battlefield in terror, stumbling in his breathless exhaustion upon a very young peasant child who, unmindful of the war, is playing innocently nearby. Peza's agony illustrates his uncompromising defiance of the idea, epitomized in the child, that life is a birth–death process indifferent to the individual:

> the child repeated his words: "Are you a man?" Peza gasped in the manner of a fish. Palsied, windless and abject, he confronted the primitive courage, the sovereign child, the brother of the

mountains, the sky, and the sea, and he knew that the definition of his misery could be written on a wee grass-blade. (XII, 268)

Here the child's question implicitly asks for an unequivocal definition of man which the narrator is patently unwilling to supply. The story's relentless irony ultimately intends not to deny but only to qualify Peza's romantic view that man is an heroic individual who ought to be supported by the world. Consequently, while Crane is not very subtly challenging Peza's individualism with the symbolic figure of the child representing nature as process, his narrator is giving us a rather detailed description of Peza's pathetic reaction to the confrontation. As a result the overall impression of Peza's anguish before the child in part elicits sympathy for the view of man as a suffering individual:

He breathed as if life was about to leave his body. He was covered with dust; his face had been cut in some way, and his cheek was ribboned with blood. All the spick of his former appearance had vanished in a general dishevelment, in which he resembled a creature that had been flung to and fro, up and down, by cliffs and prairies during an earthquake. (XII, 268)

In particular the last sentence of this description employs a simile which implicitly controverts the idea that nature is wholly indifferent to man. Thus the tableau of the final scene preserves intact, like the rest of the story, the contrasting points of view which from the first suggest two contradictory ways of conceiving the individual's significance in the world.

The struggle of antithetical viewpoints maintained to the very end of "Death and the Child" allows the story a complexity of meaning which a less equivocal conclusion could not support. Which is the more valid explanation of man's relationship with the world: Peza's, or the view suggested by the "primitive" behavior of the peasant child? The answer depends, the story suggests, primarily upon how man is viewed. Neither of the contradictory outlooks, paradoxically, exhausts the other. Crane neither accepts nor rejects Peza's egoism; here as elsewhere he remains "simultaneously at war with the people he creates and on their side." [15] His narrator's hard-headed reluctance to decree an hierarchy of values emphasizes the complexities of a world whose meaning ultimately is declared to be relative, and accounts in this way for the philosophical depth of Crane's "realistic" fiction. Crane's artistic landscape, however true to reality, remains deceptive, fluxional, paradoxical, protean rather than procrustean—in short, impressionistic. The flow of contradictory yet complementary impressions which characterizes his art opens ultimately onto an unrestricted overview of the "real," a comprehensive outlook achieved primarily through his narrator's genuinely noncommittal modulations between various disparate points of view.

I have tried to explicate Crane's careful control of point of view in a way which will make clear his implicit debt to impressionism. Yet impressionist painting itself, with its tacit acceptance of the relativist world view which has become a twentieth-century philosophical commonplace, is perhaps best explained as a late nineteenth-century strain of romanticism, that comprehensive artistic movement which reveals the still urgent modern need to relocate man at the metaphysical center of the universe. Hence the ontological assumptions underlying Crane's fiction illustrate his similarity to the French impressionist painters but do not unquestionably establish his debt to them, since—to borrow Sypher's explanation of art style—the possibility remains that Crane's "authentically contemporary view of the world" results from his being "among those artists who have most successfully intuited the quality of human experience peculiar to their day." [16] Nevertheless, Crane without doubt was familiar with the work of the French impressionists, and it therefore seems entirely likely that their sense of the physical world at least buttressed and strengthened his own metaphysical notions, whatever their origins. Moreover, though ultimately an attempt to link Crane to impressionist painting can be no more than tentatively conclusive, it would seem to be justified if it helps identify and explain Crane's characteristic techniques for modulating point of view, since these techniques in large part are responsible for creating the meaning in his fiction.

NOTES

1. *Stephen Crane: Letters,* ed. R. W. Stallman and Lillian Gilkes (New York, 1960), p. 310.
2. *Stephen Crane: Letters,* p. 154.
3. "The Darkest Hour in the Life of Stephen Crane," *The Book-Lover,* II (Summer 1901), 338.

4. See, e.g., Joseph J. Kwiat, "Stephen Crane and Painting," *AQ*, IV (Winter 1952), 332; and Robert L. Hough, "Crane and Goethe: A Forgotten Relationship," *NCF*, XVII (Sept. 1962), 135, n2.

5. Kwiat, p. 331.

6. *Stephen Crane: an Omnibus*, ed. R. W. Stallman (New York, 1952), p. 185.

7. *Rococo to Cubism in Art and Literature* (New York, 1960), pp. 169-196.

8. *Crumbling Idols*, ed. Jane Johnson (Cambridge, 1960), pp. 109, 98.

9. Page references are to *The Works of Stephen Crane*, ed. Wilson Follett (12 vols.; New York, 1963).

10. My emendation brings Follett's text into accordance with the 1896 edition. For information concerning Crane's revision of this passage, see Joseph Katz, "The *Maggie* Nobody Knows," *MFS*, XXI (Summer 1966), 200-212.

11. Harold C. Martin, "The Development of Style in Nineteenth-Century American Fiction," *English Institute Essays 1958* (New York, 1958), p. 133.

12. *The Collected Poems of Stephen Crane*, ed. Wilson Follett (New York, 1930), p. 130.

13. James Colvert, "Style and Meaning in Stephen Crane: *The Open Boat*," *Texas Studies in English*, XXXVII (1958), 45. Colvert's various articles on Crane suggest my present method for analyzing Crane's style.

14. *Stephen Crane: Letters*, p. 158.

15. John Berryman, *Stephen Crane* (New York, 1950), p. 279.

16. *Rococo to Cubism*, p. xxi.

VI

STUDIES OF STEPHEN CRANE'S WORK

A. STEPHEN CRANE AS POET: AN INTRODUCTION

Many forget that Stephen Crane made his first real impact on the American literary scene through his volume of poems, *The Black Riders and Other Lines* (March, 1895), and not through his prose. The privately printed *Maggie* (1893) was little-known, selling only a handful of copies; and *The Red Badge* was not published in book form until October, 1895.

Several factors relating to the preparation and publication of *The Black Riders* had an adverse effect on Crane as a poet. Copeland and Day, avant-garde publishers of the volume, were wary of Crane's anarchistic thoughts about God, and they gave him an early and bitter taste of censorship, finding seven of his poems "unacceptable." Even though Crane disagreed, the seven poems were not published. This episode was a grim repetition of Crane's earlier battle to find a publisher for *Maggie*. While one can point to his volume of erotic poems, *Cantharides* (never recovered), to show that Crane was not really discouraged by censorship, it probably affected his art in a double way: making him angrier and bolder, more shrill and rhetorical on the one hand, and enigmatic and submissive on the other.

With the front and back covers of *The Black Riders* decorated with a trailing black orchid, with the poems themselves all printed in capitals and identified only by roman numerals, with the poems unrhymed and with no seeming sense of rhythm, with the poems both brief and cryptic, the volume and its author were almost immediately linked with Aubrey Beardsley and with decadence, eccentricity, affectation, and sophomoric cleverness. It was all, as Hamlin Garland sadly admitted, a "cue for laughter." The avalanche of parodies that followed testified to Garland's statement, and to the embarrassment and anger that Crane himself probably felt.

In a second collection of his poetry, *A Souvenir and a Medley* (May, 1896), which also included samples of his prose (along with materials relating to The Society of the Philistines Dinner honoring Crane), all the poems save one were printed in capitals. In a third collection, *War Is Kind* (May, 1899), the poems were printed on dark gray paper, and the macabre, erotic, and esoteric illustrations by Will Bradley were clearly imitative of Beardsley. There was, then, a seeming consistency throughout Crane's entire career as a poet: blackness, suggesting the macabre; eccentricity; and an obsessive desire to shock, an unbecoming quality in one who was always striving to be "sincere." Unfortunately, all these qualities, reflected in the various parodies, were also to be linked to his prose and to his career as a whole.

A goodly portion of Stephen Crane's poetry was originally published under the auspices of Elbert Hubbard. By associating with Hubbard, the "arch poseur" and "sassy" iconoclast who showed bad taste in art (as revealed in his *Philistine* and *Roycroft Quarterly*), Crane was only damaging himself. Although Hubbard encouraged Crane's talents, he also printed parodies of his poetry, and these very parodies helped to create and perpetuate the laughing-stock portrait of Crane as a poet.

Moreover, Crane's capacity to write poetry spontaneously helped to undermine his reputation. The way he turned out poems for Garland proved to others that Crane was only an ingenious student of *tour de force*. He presumably wrote *The Black Riders* in three days, and his method of composition seemed unprofessional. Garland recorded it all in several places. Here is one summary from *Roadside Meetings* (1931):

> I [Garland] was greatly interested in his statement that the verses were composed in his mind all ready to be drawn off. "Do you mean to say that these lines are arranged in your head, complete in every detail?"
>
> "Yes, I could do one right now."
>
> "Very well. Take a seat at my desk and do one for me." Thereupon with my pen he wrote steadily, composedly, without a moment's hesitation, one of his most powerful poems. It flowed from his pen like oil, but when I examined it, I found it not only without blot or erasure, but perfectly correct in punctuation. . . .

But while Garland was awed by Crane's originality, he was still suspicious and thought that Crane must have borrowed from others. In the year of Crane's death (1900), Garland wrote that his mind "was more largely subconscious in its workings," that he "did not understand his own processes or resources." In a way, it is surprising that Crane dedicated *The Black Riders* to Garland, a friend who never really understood the reaches of his "demon."

The fact that Crane referred to his poems as "lines" and "pills" seemed self-denigrating and lowered public opinion of him as a poet. At other times, however, he exaggerated the value of his poetry by claiming that *The Black Riders* was his most ambitious effort, and superior to *The Red Badge*. The critics also helped to discount the importance of Crane's poems. They compared him to Bierce, Whitman, Dickinson, Olive Schreiner, John Bunyan, and the Bible, suggesting that he was much more an imitator than a creator. Anthologists often highlighted his radical poems, which were not his best, and were of only passing interest. Many of the critics valued him only as a link to modern American poetry and to Imagism, as one who merely "anticipated others."

In any evaluation of Stephen Crane's poetry, critics and readers have to take into account T. S. Eliot's concern about the "divided" artist: "I am . . . always doubtful whether any man can so divide himself as to be able to make the most of two such very different forms of expression as poetry and imaginative prose." In addition, the brevity of Crane's poems does present an aesthetic problem. In "The Poetic Principle," Edgar Allan Poe shrewdly stated: "Undue brevity degenerates into mere epigrammatism. A *very* short poem, while now and then producing a brilliant or vivid, never produces a profound or enduring effect."

With all these questions and problems, critics for decades had to rely on *The Collected Poems of Stephen Crane* (1930), a textually inaccurate and incomplete edition, to make any judgments on Crane's poetry. Despite this, a few (like John Berryman and Daniel Hoffman) were able to lead others back to an intrinsic study of Crane's poems. With the recent appearance of *The Poems of Stephen Crane* (1966), there is now available an accurate and full text from which to study Crane's value as a poet. (The one single problem with this new edition is that the volume's diligent editor, Joseph Katz, dispenses with the capitalizations in *The Black Riders*, a conscious design on Crane's part.)

Today's critics generally find Stephen Crane's prose superior to his poetry. They read the poetry to understand the forms and themes of his prose; they use it to make excursions into his life and psychology. Many more studies of the poems themselves, individually

and collectively, need to be made. Crane should be taken more seriously as a poet; he is more than a "breath of adolescence," more than
a poet of ideas. He is more complex than most presume, and he did
develop. But first one has to get beyond clichés, and beyond the
surfaces of his poems, which seem only to mirror fragile and hectic
puzzles.

1. *Stephen Crane and Poetic Tradition*
   By Daniel G. Hoffman

In tracing the evolution of Crane's craft let us begin with a simple allegory. Here character and action are explicit embodiments of moral qualities. Perhaps the most striking of Crane's allegorical poems is this one:

> The wayfarer,
> Perceiving the pathway to truth,
> Was struck with astonishment.
> It was thickly grown with weeds.
> "Ha," he said,
> "I see that none has passed here
> In a long time."
> Later he saw that each weed
> Was a singular knife.
> "Well," he mumbled at last,
> "Doubtless there are other roads."
>   (*War Is Kind* xiii)

This allegorical cameo might well have been modeled on a medieval morality play. As in the best of Crane's poems in this vein, the language is direct and, but for the phrase "a singular knife," uncomplicated by nuance. This is a diction without association or metaphor.

At one remove from such directness are poems in which we find, instead of allegorical personages, actions whose import is in direct correspondence to a state of feeling the poet wishes to evoke. Here the language may be more ornate—in the fifteen lines following there are nine qualifying adjectives, adverbs, and phrases—yet the narrative is still relatively straightforward.

Reprinted from: *The Poetry of Stephen Crane*. New York: Columbia University Press, 1957, pp. 252-264, 278-279. By permission of Columbia University Press.

> A youth in apparel that glittered
> Went to walk in a grim forest.
> There he met an assassin
> Attired all in garb of old days;
> He, scowling through the thickets,
> And dagger poised quivering,
> Rushed upon the youth.
> "Sir," said this latter,
> "I am enchanted, believe me,
> To die, thus,
> In this medieval fashion,
> According to the best legends;
> Ah, what joy!"
> Then took he the wound, smiling,
> And died, content.   (*Black Riders* xxvii)

Mr. Stallman considers this poem "a miniature copy of *The Red Badge of Courage*," the conflict in both being that "between *illusion and reality*." [1] Some of Henry's illusions, it is true, are dreams of medieval glory (he thought of war as a time of "heavy crowns and high castles" [2]) but there is surely a difference between the panic and courage of the novel and the satisfied nihilism of the poem. Stylistically the poem is elaborate, dressed as it were in antique brocade. The youth's glittering apparel is not only his clothing; his mind too is dressed "In this medieval fashion." "Apparel that glittered" of course suggests armor, the function of which is to fend off poised daggers. But this youth longs for death "According to the best legends" and is purposely as defenseless as though he were naked. Although the narrative in this poem is complete in itself, the language is richer in associations than that in the simple allegories.

As Crane moves from a poetry of direct correspondences toward a less discursive, more allusive idiom, his language may take on metaphoric functions simply because the referents of the narrative are undefined, e.g.,

> On the horizon the peaks assembled;
> And as I looked
> The march of the mountains began.
> As they marched they sang,
> "Ay, we come! we come!"   (*Black Riders* xxxvii)

Although much plainer in style than "A youth in apparel that glittered," this is more complex in effect. Crane leaves it to us to infer that the mountains, normally massive and immobile, represent the immitigable force in the natural universe. He does not state that their march is *toward him,* the insignificant human observer, yet we feel this to be so. Although all that is said—and that is precious little—is said in a diction sparse and plain, the tone is hugely ominous. Crane does not say, but we know, that the human protagonist stands awe-stricken, dumb and still as stone while the horizon of peaks chants as it closes in upon him—as would the growling peaked waves in the later poem, "A man adrift on a slim spar."

That poem may be taken to represent the fourth stage in the complexity of Crane's poetic idiom. There ... the discursive narrative element is still further suppressed; by indirect suggestion the purposeful ambiguities and interlocking associations of the metaphoric diction reinforce the development of theme which the inferential narrative supplies.

Thus it is evident that Crane develops distinctive methods of poetic structure, as well as ... several styles of diction. ... This I take to be a refutation of Berryman's assertion that "There is no evidence in the poetry or outside it that he ever experimented in verse." [3] Indeed, it is because Crane was what later generations would call an experimental writer that the sum of his work seems as discontinuous as we have found it to be. This is true to a degree of his prose also—many readers have noted the fantasy and impressionism of *Sullivan County Sketches,* the naturalistic determinism of *Maggie* and *George's Mother,* the irony and dreamlike association of incident and metaphor in *The Red Badge,* the naturalism again in "The Open Boat" but now in combination with a superbly controlled symbolistic style, the frontier humor of "The Bride Comes to Yellow Sky," the sustained combination of tension and suppleness in "The Blue Hotel," the irony undercutting the baroque prose of *The Monster,* and the style "flexible, swift, abrupt, nervous ... with an unexampled capacity for stasis also" which Berryman remarks as the norm for Crane's prose.[4] Although Crane's experimentalism led him to absorb many technical influences that came his way, the unifying quality which makes these stories all unmistakably his own is the sensibility they express. The authority of his style, highly individual despite all these modifications, is the guarantee of the uniqueness of that sensibility.

In verse, too, we find several varieties of excellence, unified

288 Stephen Crane's Career

despite variation by the authority of the style. The four stages of increasing complexity we have just noted actually merge into one another, but on the whole we can distinguish between two generic types of Crane poems, the allegories and the non-discursive symbolistic poems. The former category includes such unadorned allegorical narratives as "The wayfarer / Perceiving the pathway to truth," "There was one I met upon the road," "A man saw a ball of gold in the sky," "In heaven / Some little blades of grass," and "The trees in the garden rained flowers." There are also the parables of simple paradox—"A man said to the universe," "I saw a man pursuing the horizon," " 'It was wrong to do this,' said the angel," "A man feared that he might find an assassin," and "Forth went the candid man."

Subtler than these are the metaphorical parables capable of symbolistic extension, such as "A youth in apparel that glittered," "The patent of a lord," "On the horizon the peaks assembled," and the fable of the heart-eater in the desert.

The symbolistic poems which, by virtue of their more complex organization, the larger commitments they express, and the subtlety and resourcefulness of their language, I take to be Crane's most substantial verse, include "A man adrift on a slim spar," "Do not weep, maiden, for war is kind," and "The Blue Battalions"—these I think his three best; and also "Bottles and bottles and bottles," "The Battle Hymn," "Black riders came from the sea," "Fast rode the knight," "I explain the silvered passing of a ship at night," and the opening lines of "There exists the eternal fact of conflict." But this schematization does not accommodate such other poems worthy of mention as the impressionistic "Each small gleam was a voice," the imagistic "To the maiden / The sea was a blue meadow," or the discursive "A newspaper is a collection of half-injustices."

If we compare the intentions of Crane's most complex verse to those of the French Symbolists we can at once identify the characteristics which isolate Crane from them and which link him to the greater writers of the American Renaissance. Mr. Tindall has conveniently summarized Mallarmé's aesthetic, and it is instructive to juxtapose this to Crane's:

> Without intended reference to external reality, his worlds or poems are "inclosed." Fictions or virtual realities, they exist as a piece of music does, by symmetry, interaction of parts, and what he called "reciprocal reflections" . . . as far as possible

from discourse.... [Mallarmé] said that symbolism consisted in evoking an object little by little in order to reveal a state of mind, or, inversely, choosing an object and from it disengaging a state of mind.... This state, far from being a reminder of anything we have known, is a fresh creation; and this creation is the effect of analogy, not from nature's store but made by the poet. What it is an analogy for must be guessed by the reader as the poem creates his state of mind.[5]

It is evident, if the readings I have proposed of his best poems have any merit, that the means by which Crane's verse creates its intended effects resemble those of Mallarmé. But it is equally clear that despite these similarities in technique there is a basic difference in intention. Crane's poems, autonomous though they are, are never "without intended reference to external reality." When his verse moves "as far as possible from discourse" it is not, as is the case with Mallarmé, to construct an autonomous private universe as an alternative to the world of nature. "The nearer a writer gets to life the greater he becomes as an artist" [6]—this is a constant tenet in Crane's artistic practice. The world of his poems is made with the allegorist's prerogative of providing an imaginary construct to represent the real world, not, as the Symbolist would, to substitute for it.

Crane abandons discursiveness when the truths of life which he seeks to discover and reveal cannot be reached by means so direct. In order to express the complexity inherent to a faithful representation of his own sensibility, Crane felt in his early poems that he must break with the conventions of the genteel verse of his time. Hence the iconoclasm, the repudiation of traditional structure and ornament:

> "Think as I think," said a man,
> "Or you are abominably wicked,
> You are a toad."
>
> And after I had thought of it,
> I said, "I will, then, be a toad." [*Black Riders* XLVII]

Thus in 1893. But two or three years later Crane writes a poem in six regular stanzas, alternating questions with replies: "What says the sea, little shell?" (*WK* 11) first appeared in the *Philistine* in February, 1896. The next month the *Chap-book* printed "In the night," whose three stanzas . . . presented a definite time scheme in consistent metrical form. By April "The Blue Battalions" had been written . . . with still more complicated regular stanzas incorporating internal refrains. "Do not weep, maiden, for war is kind" is perhaps Crane's most complexly organized poem, but this had been written by August, 1895. From that time on Crane was no longer in willful rebellion against such conventional techniques as stanzas and refrains, although he never did adopt rhyme or iambic meter. His best longer poems combine firm stanzaic structure with the allusiveness of controlled metaphor. This parallels the conjunction in his prose, remarked above, of metaphoric richness with the skilled organization of incident.

In these more complexly organized poems, Crane, like the French Symbolists, does demand that we guess at the significance of the states of mind or feeling which his poems little by little reveal. But whereas "a symbolist work," Mr. Tindall concludes, "has no certain meaning," [7] this we do not feel to be the case with Crane. The meaning, complex and ambiguous though it may be, is certain nonetheless. His symbols are not metaphors "detached from their subjects" but metaphors whose relation to their subjects must be inferred. They are metaphors of fixed reference, yet their use takes advantage of the ambiguous and symbolic nature of language itself. Crane retains the certainty of the ethical significance of experience, the assurance of the spiritual significance of natural facts, which made allegory the natural expression of his early work.

In so far as Crane's symbols have assigned though unstated meanings they are much closer to the objective correlative described by T. S. Eliot [8] than they are to either the symbols of Symbolism or the images of Imagism. The image, as Ezra Pound defined it, "is that which presents an intellectual complex in an instant of time. . . . It is the presentation of such a 'complex' instantaneously which gives that sense of sudden liberation; that sense of freedom from time limits and space limits; that sense of sudden growth, which we experience in the presence of the greatest works of art." [9] Crane seems to resemble the Imagist poets because, like them, in many of his poems he uses direct treatment, economical diction, and organic rhythm. Yet he actually conforms to the aesthetic Pound describes in only his simplest verse. The Imagist aims at a static representation of a caught moment of experience; this, by virtue of its associations, elicits in us intellectual and emotional awareness of things outside itself. But almost all of Crane's simple "imagistic" poems are themselves in motion. They have plots as allegories have plots. Granting their governing metaphors, they force attention inward upon themselves, not outward to extrinsic associations. There are no such associations; there are only the poems.

In his more complex verse, however, Crane is more ambitious than the Imagist aesthetic allows. In so far as his verse resembles the work of that movement, it is in his impressionistic pieces; Imagism, after all, attempted merely to expand by association the significance of the impression. While Crane appealed to Pound, Sandburg, Edith Wyatt, and others as a forebear of the then contemporary movement, he had long since gone beyond the limitations of the Imagist aesthetic. This was a journey almost all the Imagists themselves were to make— Eliot moving toward soliloquy and drama, Stevens toward the most Symbolist symbolism in English verse, Fletcher reverting to the lush romanticism of Lanier, Marianne Moore developing a unique combination of moral sensibility and parable derived from Whitman and La Fontaine, Sandburg losing completely the economical control Imagism had imposed on his language as he literally appropriates the idiom of everyday speech for poetry.[10] Of the original Imagists, H. D., William Carlos Williams, and Pound remained most influenced by their own programme of the Little Renaissance. H. D. continues with admirable integrity to chisel verbal cameos, and fails to deal successfully with themes rather than with impressions. Pound and Williams have more omnivorous ambitions, the one Ovidian, the other Whitmanesque, but in the organization of both *The Cantos* and *Paterson* we see the limiting effectiveness of Imagist images connected chiefly by mood. Of the two attempted epics, *Paterson* is the more cohesive, but its flaw is another Imagist limitation: the philosophical naiveté of "no ideas but in things."

Since Crane was heralded as a forebear of the movement in which these important poets participated, why, one wonders, has his actual influence on twentieth-century verse been so slight? One reason . . . is the relative unavailability of his verse during the period when its influence might have been most felt. Neither of his books was reprinted nor, except for Stedman's collection in 1900, did any anthology contain Crane's verse until after his *Work* appeared in 1926. By then Imagism had had its heyday. But a more fundamental

reason for Crane's seeming lack of influence is that despite his anticipation of some techniques later to be widely adopted, he held a
conception of poetry which later poets and critics could not share.

The first tenet of Crane's view of poetry was his notion of the
brevity of poetic form. This may at first seem not incongruous with
Imagist compression; indeed, until quite recently twentieth-century
poetry has been almost without exception based upon compact lyric
techniques, whether of symbolist, imagist, or metaphysical origin.
Yet at the same time modern poets have attempted to move beyond
the brevity of lyric form to vehicles more ambitious: the cycles of
interconnected lyrics of Yeats's Crazy Jane poems; the attempted
epics of *The Waste Land, The Bridge, The Cantos, Paterson, The
People, Yes;* the baroque mock-epic of *The Comedian as the Letter
C;* the extended soliloquys of Senlin and *The Four Quartets;* the
verse drama of Yeats, Eliot, MacLeish, Eberhart, and their younger
emulators. But Crane was intransigently committed to envisaging
the proper dimension of all art as brief. *War and Peace, Anna
Karenina, Nana,* the books of Mark Twain, all seemed to him too
long for the work they set out to do.[11] His own best fiction is either
the novella or the short story. And in poetry we have seen him ruthlessly reduce to their minimal essences the works that influenced
him and attempt to keep his best original composition as tightly knit
and nondiscursive as possible.

This is because Crane seeks the ultimate concentration of experience in art. His valuing of brevity may have derived from Poe's
aesthetic theory, yet Crane's observance of this precept does not
resemble Poe's. Crane seeks the moments of highest intensity not,
like Poe, for the sake of the sensation, but because life experienced
at that pitch will reveal to him the meanings which are otherwise
diffused and rendered indecipherable. That intensity is the result of
the collision of forces which operate upon experience, and the work,
to be true to the life it represents, must contain the forces, the experience, and the intensity all together. This it can do either by
presenting a dialectic or in terms of a plot. Crane's best poems use
both methods; they present the bare outlines of a narrative situation
in which there is a tension between two opposed forces. The tension
may be expressed in terms of antithetical statements, dialogue, description, or the effect upon the observer of an action he witnesses. Crane's
mind is always attuned to narrative, to the dynamic representation
of man in conflict. But in his poems he seeks the most universal
statements possible of the themes which possess his imagination.

Hence he must eliminate from the presentation all the particularities of the conflicts which might restrict his statements only to the described events. By making his human figures faceless and nameless, by pitting them against elemental forces, by describing their ambitions and their plights in simple yet overwhelming metaphors, Crane created for his poetry a symbolical form which represented a great advance in subtlety and flexibility over its allegorical beginnings.

But these considerations lead us to the second tenet of Crane's poetic credo which later writers could not share. Twentieth-century verse has recoiled not only from allegory but from narrative itself, concentrating instead upon lyric and dramatic expression. Even the attempted epics named above have been made in terms of lyric, rather than narrative or allegorical strategy (except for Stevens's *Comedian,* which in no respect resembles Crane). Crane, however, went his own way and made his own styles to do the work to which he had to put them. His diction is intrinsic to the structure of his poems; the one cannot be imitated without the other. And since the combination Crane made of allegory (explicit or implied), assigned symbols, dialectic, direct treatment, brevity, and narrative situation remains his own, his verse remains singular after almost half a century of post-Imagist emphasis on directness and economy. A style such as Crane's is the product both of his extraordinary sensibility and of his cultural situation, which was much more impoverished than that of any twentieth-century American poet of distinction.

* * *

Although Crane's poems are restricted in range, they have the unexampled authority which the work of an original artist who explores the furthest reaches of the human spirit, in whatever direction, rightfully commands.

Only Poe and Hemingway have neared Crane's lonely outpost from which in his verse he views, and makes us feel, the reality of a universe where force is law, where love is doom, where God is cold, where man's lot is fated misery, where hope is narrowed to the possibility of courage, and the reward of courage is self-sacrifice. None has surpassed him in the imaginative expression of this sensibility of isolation. Emerson, with his openness to life, could scarcely have had such an artist in mind when he defined "The Poet," yet we do no violence to either man in applying to Crane these words:

He is isolated among his contemporaries by truth and by his art, but with this consolation in his pursuits, that they will draw all men sooner or later. For all men live by truth and stand in need of expression. In love, in art . . . We study to utter our painful secret. The man is only half himself, the other half is his expression.[12]

What Crane's poems express is partly his private doom. But the sensibility of isolation is a bitter gift which Stephen Crane did not hold alone. In lesser degree than was true of him, it is also a characteristic of his country and his culture. Crane takes his authority to be an interpreter from the very extremity of his commitment so widely shared. In these poems which explore the menaced condition of man in isolation, Crane developed new techniques and made available to poetic expression a further reach of imaginative experience than had any American writer before him. His best poems impose aesthetic form on the stark vision that haunted his imagination. They free us to participate in that vision and to contemplate with deepened understanding a part of ourselves.

NOTES

1. R. W. Stallman, ed., *Stephen Crane: An Omnibus* (New York, 1952), p. 569 (his italics); hereafter cited as *Omnibus*.
2. *Ibid.*, p. 229.
3. John Berryman, *Stephen Crane* (New York, 1950), p. 274.
4. *Ibid.*, p. 284.
5. William York Tindall, *The Literary Symbol* (New York, 1955), pp. 48-49; hereafter cited as *The Literary Symbol*.
6. *Omnibus*, p. 627.
7. *The Literary Symbol*, p. 267.
8. *Selected Essays* (New York, 1950), pp. 124-25.
9. *The Literary Essays of Ezra Pound* (New York, 1954), p. 4.
10. I have traced Whitman's influence upon Miss Moore in some detail in a review of her collected poems in *Antioch Review*, XII (Spring, 1952), pp. 123-25. See also "Sandburg and 'The People': His Literary Populism Reappraised," *Antioch Review*, X (Summer, 1950), pp. 265-78, substantially reprinted in *Paul Bunyan, Last of the Frontier Demigods* (Philadelphia, 1952), pp. 132-43.
11. Thomas Beer, *Stephen Crane* (New York, 1923), pp. 143, 147, 157.
12. *The Complete Works of Ralph Waldo Emerson*, ed. Edward Waldo Emerson (Boston, 1903), III, 5.

2. *Stephen Crane's Poetry: Perspective and Arrogance*
By Max Westbrook

Amy Lowell, writing on Stephen Crane's poetry, concludes that he usually "sees only purposeless effort" [1] in the universe. She believes that the affirmative poems he did write are atypical. They are the product of a temporary mood which Crane, a "boy, spiritually killed by neglect," could not sustain in an alien world.[2] Daniel G. Hoffman, who knows Crane died of tuberculosis and not of neglect, believes that the poems are committed to an "heroic ideal" derived in part from Emerson. Hoffman's conclusion, however, is that Crane

> makes us feel the reality of a universe where force is law, where love is doom, where God is cold, where man's lot is fated misery, where hope is narrowed to the possibility of courage, and the reward of courage is self-sacrifice.[3]

The conclusions of Lowell and Hoffman represent the critical consensus: Crane could not maintain his affirmative beliefs in a universe he found to be, in the final analysis, deterministic. It is granted that his experiments are a significant contribution to the development of modern poetry, but his accomplishment is said to be undermined by his inability to sustain a coherent world view.

All poets, of course, have temporary moods, employ different and even conflicting themes. The critics, however, have not questioned Crane's right to use conflicting themes; they have questioned his coherence. It is my contention that Crane's poetry does cohere, but in a way no one has yet noticed. The practice has been to assume that the poems have a single protagonist—everyman, or perhaps Crane himself—whose experiences represent man's relation to ultimate reality. The hopes and beliefs of this protagonist are sometimes affirmed, sometimes mocked. Values are sometimes real, sometimes illusory. And thus the natural conclusion has been that Crane's world view is arbitrary, unrealized. Crane's readers, however, have failed

---

Reprinted from: *Bucknell Review*, XI (December 1963), 24-34. By permission of the *Bucknell Review* and the author.

to distinguish two quite different voices in the poems. The voice of perspective, with reasonable consistency, is affirmed; the voice of arrogance, without exception, is mocked. Behind both voices lies a single and coherent standard of values.

The differentiation of two voices need not be proscriptive. Crane's vision is not that pat. Nonetheless, it can be shown that Crane uses the voice of perspective and the voice of arrogance to make value judgments that are of structural importance to his poetry. The voice of perspective draws Crane's deepest sympathy; it is characterized by humility, kindness, a quiet determination, and by a consistent belief in a truth which is symbolic, elusive, but always real. The voice of arrogance—representing the values Crane attacked in his prose and fiction as well as in his poetry—is characterized by pride, dogmatism, often by an aggressive manner, and by a stubborn insistence on a literal truth. A study of these voices, the most recurrent ones in Crane's poetry, shows that beneath hope and despair there lies an essential unity.

I

Crane's emphasis on pessimistic themes cannot be denied. The anthologies have rightly made famous *War Is Kind* XXI, in which the universe is indifferent to man; and *Black Riders* VI, in which "the ship of the world" is allowed to wander "for ever rudderless." Also well known are poems on the suffering of common men, the hypocrisy of men of esteem, and the innate wickedness of all men. If these poems constitute a balanced and judicious selection, Lowell and Hoffman are right. Deterministic and naturalistic themes offer no rationale for affirmation. Such poems, however, describe only part of the universe as Crane saw it.

That universe includes *War Is Kind* II, which praises the humanistic values of patience, gentleness, and brotherhood. It includes *War Is Kind* XXV, in which God is expressed by symbolic "Songs of carmine, violet, green, gold." *Black Riders* XL and XLII attack what so many of Crane's critics would have us believe he held sacrosanct: the idea that man's failures should be blamed on environment. There is even a surprising affinity between Crane the realist and Emerson the transcendentalist, an affinity which lies in the religious legacy Crane took over—unconsciously perhaps—from his devout family.[4] Crane often attacks naiveté, sentimentality, and hypocrisy; and it is true that the indifference of nature and the destructive power of environment are favorite themes; but the basic values of his personal creed are love, kindness, and sympathy for human suffering.[5]

Crane's handling of humanistic values is Emersonian, specifically, in that the real cannot be institutionalized.[6] The real, as in *Black Riders* XXVIII, is better approached with sensitiveness and humility than with aggressive confidence:

> "Truth," said a traveller,
> "Is a rock, a mighty fortress;
> Often have I been to it,
> Even to its highest tower,
> From whence the world looks black."
>
> "Truth," said a traveller,
> "Is a breath, a wind,
> A shadow, a phantom;
> Long have I pursued it,
> But never have I touched
> The hem of its garment."
>
> And I believed the second traveller;
> For truth was to me
> A breath, a wind,
> A shadow, a phantom,
> And never had I touched
> The hem of its garment.

The poem offers a convenient means of demonstrating my thesis, for in it we hear both the voice of perspective and the voice of arrogance. The first traveller believes that truth is, metaphorically, a "rock," a "fortress," something man can discover in a fixed shape and identify with certainty. If the first traveller is speaking for Crane, then the charge of incoherence is valid, for the negativism of the first traveller's discovery is clearly incompatible with Crane's affirmative poems. The first traveller, however, is wrong. The truth is, in the metaphor of the second traveller, a "shadow," a "phantom," something man can never discover in a fixed shape, something man can never encompass or exhaust. The truth exists, as suggested by the refrain "The hem of its garment," but it exists as an elusive "shadow," not as a fixed "rock" or institutionalized "fortress." The humble and resolute faith of the second traveller marks him as one who has gained perspective through his awareness of the nature of reality. The first traveller, by contrast, concludes that "the world looks black," a negativism which reveals, not the reality of determinism in Crane's poetic world, but the error of the first traveller's own concept of the real.[7]

Believing that the truth is more accurately described as a "shadow" than as a "rock," Crane places a high value on the virtue of humility. Man cannot be arrogant about the grasp he has on a "shadow." In protesting against false gods and cruel men, the man of perspective may become bitter, but he is always humble before the truth, and for this reason he is never mocked. If he is defeated, his downfall is recorded with sympathy, his efforts have not been without purpose.[8] Crane's irony is used to attack the man whose attitude toward the truth is characterized by aggressiveness, dogmatism, conceit—the man whose efforts, therefore, are futile.

In support of her more customary reading of Crane's poetry, Amy Lowell cites *Black Riders* XXIV:

> I saw a man pursuing the horizon;
> Round and round they sped.
> I was disturbed at this;
> I accosted the man.
> "It is futile," I said,
> "You can never—"
> "You lie," he cried,
> And ran on.

If the distinction between the voice of perspective and the voice of arrogance is valid, then it is a mistake to read this poem as an example of determinism or purposelessness. Crane is not a determinist in "I Saw a Man" and an Emersonian in " 'Truth,' Said a Traveller"; nor is there a shift in world view from one poem to the other. The furious pursuit "round and round" describes one man's gross misconception of the nature of truth and the consequent purposelessness of *his* efforts, not the purposelessness of all human striving after higher values.

The quiet observer in "I Saw a Man" tries to speak, only to be interrupted. The man "pursuing the horizon" will not listen. The quiet observer wants to explain what his counterpart does explain in "'Truth,' Said a Traveller": you cannot chase the truth down mad-dog fashion; you cannot even touch "The hem of its garment." Man must be humble and resolute before a truth that is elusive and symbolic.

II

Recognition of the two major voices in Crane's poetry offers a number of advantages. It suggests a new and I think more convincing interpretation for many poems, especially for poems in which the speaker has not yet achieved perspective but is beginning to learn:

> A man saw a ball of gold in the sky;
> He climbed for it,
> And eventually he achieved it—
> It was clay.
>
> Now this is the strange part:
> When the man went to the earth
> And looked again,
> Lo, there was the ball of gold.
> Now this is the strange part:
> It was a ball of gold.
> Ay, by the heavens, it was a ball of gold.

The poem (*Black Riders* XXXV) has been said to mean that man's belief in ultimate values is a mockery, an interpretation which requires that the last line be taken ironically.[9] The tone of the poem, however, is objective, calm. It is characterized by that perspective Crane associates with an awareness of the elusive nature of truth. Thus a more satisfactory paraphrase is suggested: the value represented by the ball of gold exists, but it must be seen in perspective—

obliquely, from a distance—or else be distorted. It cannot be climbed for in the sky any more than it can be chased to the horizon; man cannot get his hands on a truth which is symbolic.[10]

Recognition of the two voices, furthermore, enables one to include in his reading of Crane certain poems which have been slighted by the anthologies or dismissed by the critics as the product of a temporary mood. Crane's so-called affirmative and negativistic poems can be seen to describe different voices heard in the same universe. *Black Riders* XXXIX is typical of this group:

> The livid lightnings flashed in the clouds;
> The leaden thunders crashed.
> A worshipper raised his arm.
> "Hearken! hearken! The voice of God!"
>
> "Not so," said a man.
> "The voice of God whispers in the heart
> So softly
> That the soul pauses,
> Making no noise,
> And strives for these melodies,
> Distant, sighing, like faintest breath,
> And all the being is still to hear."

If the reader distinguishes the voice of perspective from the voice of arrogance, he sees that the worshipper is made absurd by a flaw in his own concept of the real, not by a flaw in the real itself. Listening for God in thunder is just as futile as chasing truth to the horizon. As shown by "The livid lightnings," the mistaken and therefore futile beliefs of man can exist in the same poem—in the same world—with a meaningful belief in higher values.

Failure to distinguish the two voices has led critics to impose a preconceived theology on Crane's poems, to assume that if God is indifferent then man's pursuit of truth must be without purpose, and the God who "whispers in the heart" must be a comfort merely, not a reality. In Crane's poetic world, however, there are two Gods.[11] One, the Old Testament God, is portrayed unsympathetically as a God of pride who judges man coldly, even cruelly. Crane associates Him frequently with the conventional church, sometimes with a corrupt morality that ignores human suffering, sometimes with the theme of nature's indifference. The second God is an internal conscience, a God who speaks only to the individual. Both Gods are forcefully described in *Black Riders* LIII. The Old Testament God, a "puffing braggart" who stamps "across the sky" with "loud swagger," is threatened with curses. The inner God, by contrast, is treated with reverence: "Ah, sooner would I die / Than see tears in those eyes of my soul."

Crane's coherence here lies in a consistent standard of values in which the Old Testament God is associated with cruelty, while the inner God is associated with love. Those who pursue the horizon "round and round" or seek the "rock" of truth share the standard of values represented by the "loud swagger" of the Old Testament God. Likewise, those who realize the "phantom" nature of truth and revere the individual conscience share the standard of values represented by the God who "whispers in the heart."

Awareness of these two different sets of values reveals an unrecognized relation between Crane's poetry and prose. There is need for the establishment of this relation, for Crane's poetry too long has been considered mysterious, enigmatic. Crane himself liked to talk of his poetry in a cryptic fashion, implying that his poems were not composed but were given to him whole, as if by magic. Critics like John Berryman, stressing the subconscious part of creativity, have added to the air of mystery. It is unsatisfactory, however, to hold that Crane's sensibility was one thing in poetry and another in fiction. Actually, the sensibility is essentially the same. It is the art form that is different. If we allow for this very important difference, a clear analogy can be seen between the two poetic voices and two fictive character types which, for convenience, may be designated *eiron* and *alazon*.[12] The unmistakable mark of heroism in Crane is a calm devotion to duty combined with a complete lack of interest in the trappings of heroics. Crane's admiration for the men who charged up San Juan Hill is as much for their disregarding praise as for their courage. "They were all intent on business," Crane says, and pays them, significantly, the "tribute of the toast of silence."[13] It is significant, also, that a high-ranking officer, an admiral, is praised for precisely the same qualities. His is a "noiseless campaign." There is no "bunting, no arches, no fireworks; nothing but the perfect management of a big fleet."[14]

Crane's treatment of heroism, I think, is generally misunderstood. In "The Open Boat," the oiler rows and rows because he feels devotion to the captain and brotherhood with the men. In "The Monster," Dr. Trescott endures ostracism because he feels obligated to the man who saved his son's life. In *The Red Badge of Courage,* Henry Fleming learns to run into battle instead of away from it because he has come to accept the necessity of following "his guides wherever they should point." [15] The list continues, but not one Crane hero is judged by external values, by practical success or failure. Circumstance neither rewards nor punishes. Crane's emphasis, rather, is on the hero's unassuming devotion to duty and to humanistic values, on his role as *eiron.*

The villainous and the wrong-headed in Crane's fiction are also of a type. Not aware of their own insignificance in a universe indifferent to their welfare, they—like the campers of Sullivan County—"undertake to do things beyond their powers." [16] Not having the hero's humbling awareness of the nature of reality, they mistake their own "pursuit of the horizon," their own "fortress," for the truth itself, and become victims of "pretence, assumption, arrogance, conceit." [17] Like Collins in "A Mystery of Heroism," the hero whose efforts are without purpose is no hero at all. Such mock heroes, as *alazons,* are too conceited to admit that the universe is indifferent to their welfare, too arrogant to discover or accept a truth which is "phantom."

As in the poetry, the implications are metaphysical. To mature, for example, is to change from *alazon* to *eiron.* Wilson, in *The Red Badge,* is not merely a loud-mouthed youth who is humbled by experience. His development, like Fleming's, delineates Crane's world view. The early Wilson is characterized by a brashness typically associated with youth, but he is also the *alazon,* guilty of pride, foolish enough to think himself capable of mastering a truth which is beyond the mastery of human beings. Wilson is too loud to hear a God who "whispers in the heart." Only by becoming quiet and humble can Wilson become a man.

In the poetry, the *eiron* appears as the unassuming voice of the man of perspective, and the *alazon* is represented by the loud voice of the man of arrogance.[18] The analogy reinforces an interpretation suggested earlier. "I saw a man" has been taken to symbolize man's quest for meaning or knowledge and to show that man's efforts are futile. This reading requires us to believe that Crane chose a fanatic to represent man's possibilities, to serve as an emblem of a valid quest for truth. The conceit and arrogance of the "man pursuing the horizon," however, are precisely opposite to Crane's own values, the values he advocated in letters, fiction, and poetry. Pursuit of the horizon does not symbolize mankind's quest for higher values, or delimit man's potentialities, or reveal an ultimate purposelessness in human effort. Fanaticism, to Crane, was always abhorrent. The dogmatic cry "You lie" is the cry of the *alazon*.

III

The power of environment and the indifference of nature, as remarked earlier, are important themes in Crane; but the theme of experience as a discipline, though neglected by critics, is equally important. The false truth, the "fortress" of tradition, is someone else's truth, not the individual's; and to hide within the "fortress" is to avoid an "original relation to the universe." [19] Likewise, to chase the ultimate "round and round" is to reject the lesson experience teaches. The man who pursues the horizon and the man who seeks the "fortress" of tradition make the same mistake: both refuse to see that truth cannot be grabbed by the hands of arrogance or codified by the rules of institutions. It must be approached humbly through the oblique language of symbolic experience.

It is not surprising to find this theme in Crane, for the insistence on an "original relation to the universe" is characteristic of much American literature both before and after Crane. Relevant are Melville's Redburn, who attempts to use his father's guidebook as a substitute for his own initiation into life, and Taji, whose too direct quest for an indirect truth causes him to sail quite literally out of this world. Analogous also are the experiences of Huck Finn and Silas Lapham, who learn that the best guide for moral action is personal experience, not the preconceptions of society. Robert Cohn, who tries to learn about life by reading W. H. Hudson, and the Reverend Gail Hightower, who tries to live another man's life, pay an expensive price for failing to discover the necessity and the discipline of experience.

One of Crane's best poems on the theme is *Black Riders* XXVII, in which a youth announces that he is happy to die "According to the best legends." Hoffman reads the poem as a statement in "satisfied nihilism," [20] and indeed the youth is humble before a being who slays him without purpose. The youth, however, has chosen "legends," not the voice that "whispers in the heart," and chosen them because they are the "best," not because they are in accord with actual experience. He is simply another version of Crane's *alazon,* and his death is without meaning because his values are without meaning. Humility alone is not enough, for a man can be dishonestly humble. The death of those who are never given a chance, as in "A Man Adrift on a Slim Spar," [21] is recorded with restraint and sympathy. Toward those who refuse to see that devotion to the "best legends" or to a "puffing braggart" is a kind of suicide Crane's irony is merciless.

Thus Crane's poems describing purposeless efforts are not incompatible with his poems on affirmative themes. What is purposeless is the *alazon's* pursuit of the horizon "round and round," like a dog chasing its tail; what has purpose—realistically stripped of Emersonian optimism—is the moral struggle of the *eiron* who has the humility and integrity to be content with a truth that is "phantom" in a universe that is indifferent. The honest and the knowing speak with the voice of perspective. The dishonest and the ignorant speak with the voice of arrogance. Behind both voices lies a reasonably consistent standard of values that shapes the essential unity of Stephen Crane's poetry.

NOTES

1. Introduction to Wilson Follett, ed., *The Work of Stephen Crane* (New York, 1926), VI, p. xxii.
2. *Ibid.,* p. xxix.
3. *The Poetry of Stephen Crane* (New York, 1957), pp. 278-279.
4. For an excellent, extensive analysis of the family's religious influence on Crane, see Hoffman, chapter three, "War in Heaven."
5. Crane's formulation of this personal creed may be found in R. W. Stallman and Lillian Gilkes, eds., *Stephen Crane: Letters* (New York, 1960), p. 99. See also, p. 334, the testimony of Frank W. Noxon, a college friend: "One of Stephen Crane's characteristics was a haunting solicitude for the comfort and welfare of other people." The judgment is confirmed by scholars. See, for example, the conclusion of Edwin H. Cady and Lester G. Wells, *Stephen Crane's Love Letters to Nellie Crouse* (Syracuse University Press, 1954), pp. 21, 22. For an example of the creed in Crane's poetry, see *Black Riders* LXI.
6. Truth, to Crane, is always ineffable. See *Black Riders* VII, in which the truth is a "Mystic shadow," and *Black Riders* XXVI, in which the truth lies "at impossible distances."
7. Though Crane was too much of a realist to be optimistic, he had little sympathy with rationalization, pessimism, surrender. His belief in the weakness of man and the power of environment is constant, but not ultimate: "The final wall of the wise man's thought however is Human Kindness of course. If the road of disappointment, grief, pessimism, is followed far enough, it will arrive there. Pessimism itself is only a little, little way, and moreover it is ridiculously cheap. The cynical mind is an uneducated thing." (*Stephen Crane: Letters,* p. 99.) In *Black Riders* LXVIII, denial of the quest

for God causes death. See also "Three Poems" II, where Crane praises the "supple-souled men" who struggle heroically in a world of suffering. See Wilson Follett, ed., *The Collected Poems of Stephen Crane* (New York, 1930), p. 131.

8. The point is developed further in my "Stephen Crane: The Pattern of Affirmation," *Nineteenth-Century Fiction*, XIV (December 1959), 219-229.

9. Hoffman, pp. 201-202.

10. *Black Riders* XXXI, on the theme of the Tower of Babel, demonstrates the futility of a literal quest.

11. Crane's distinction between two Gods has been remarked on, most notably, by John Berryman, *Stephen Crane* (New York, 1950), p. 114; Everett A. Gillis, "A Glance at Stephen Crane's Poetry," *Prairie Schooner*, XXVIII (Spring, 1954), 73-79; and Hoffman, chapter three, *passim*. See also "The Battle Hymn" (Columbia Collection, printed by Hoffman, pp. 158-159) and *War Is Kind* XXVII, which suggest that Crane attempted, with dubious success, to combine the two Gods.

12. My source for the terms *eiron* and *alazon* is Francis Macdonald Cornford, *The Origin of Attic Comedy*, ed., Theodor H. Gaster (Garden City, New York, 1961).

13. *The Work*, IX, p. 238.

14. *Ibid.*, p. 226.

15. From R. W. Stallman's edition of *The Red Badge of Courage* in his *Stephen Crane: An Omnibus* (New York, 1952), p. 369.

16. Cornford, p. 183.

17. *Ibid.*, p. 184.

18. See *Black Riders* XI, XX, XXXVI, and *War Is Kind* XIII. In all four, the man who boasts of knowing the truth is shown to be a fool. These poems may profitably be read in conjunction with *Black Riders* XVIII and XXXIII, examples of the high value Crane placed on the virtue of humility.

19. From the opening paragraph of Emerson's "Nature."

20. Hoffman, p. 253.

21. See Hoffman, pp. 94-99, for text and analysis.

3. *Structure and Irony in Stephen Crane's*
"War is Kind"
By Mordecai Marcus

Robert W. Stallman seems to be the first critic to have applied
the concepts of alternation of mood to Crane's fiction and poetry.[1]
Certainly it is a major technique in the poem "War Is Kind," and
a thorough understanding of the poem requires exploration of its
variety of voices and their relationship to its structure. John
Berryman and Daniel Hoffman, authors of two extended comments
on the poem, observe its use of alternation of mood, though neither
critic uses the term. They do not, however, note the complex structure
of the poem, the subtlety of its ironies, nor the ways in which these
technical features create a persona.

Berryman declares that the poem employs a prose element
working against its "poetic appearance of lament" to create an
agonizing protest. Noting the predominance of *i* sounds, Berryman
claims that they contribute to the apparent lament. Suggesting that
the poet stands close to the reader, Berryman feels that the poem
whispers: "I would console you, how I would console you! *If I
honestly could.*" Berryman, however, misses a key irony connected
to the reverberating irony of the title phrase, and this oversight may
be the cause of his mistaken assertion that the poem is not moving
in the line "On the bright splendid shroud of your son," but rather
(presumably typically) in the preceding line: "Mother whose heart
hung humble as a button." [2]

Daniel Hoffman opens a similar path into the poem by noting
that its irony is based on the juxtaposition of an economical,
dissonantal, and overstated style against a more conventionally lyric
and understated style within which the refrain occurs. Hoffman
notes that the overstated style intrudes in the "bright splendid
shroud" line, but the interaction of styles and tones is more complex
than he recognizes.[3]

Since Crane's structure and irony are very complex, adequate
terms for the two styles are difficult to find. Let us call the first
group of alternating stanzas lamentation and the second group

Reprinted from: *CLA Journal*, IX (March 1966), 274-278. By permission of The
College Language Association and the author.

denunciation, and then observe how the modes modulate within and between themselves. The stanzas of lamentation—one, three, and five—focus on individuals, in parallel situations. Each stanza addresses a protagonist-observer who is confronted with the image of a dying or dead beloved person. The three stanzas form a pattern within which the third stanza acts as a pivot for the whole poem. Although all three relationships: maiden-lover, babe-father, mother-son—are archetypally irreplaceable, intensity does mount, for the last relationship epitomizes the social ideal of loss. Additional patterning is created by placing the first two observers in the world of domestic love and asking them to perceive scenes on the battlefield, which is the immediate world of the denouncing stanzas. In the last stanza the worlds of war and home merge as the mother confronts the ambiguously placed shroud.

The irony in the lamenting stanzas differs from the irony in the denunciation, though both groups combine understatement with overstatement. In the sense that the lamenting stanzas imitate the tone of some conventional poetry and the denouncing stanzas the tone of lurid journalism, they may be described as showing poetic and prose styles, or more precisely as imitating such styles, but since the continuing effect is poetic it is more accurate to classify the styles by their irony. As in much of his verse and prose, Crane uses the language of chivalry to create irony. Thus "maiden-lover," "babe-father," and "mother-son," though not consistently chivalric, suggest the noble, delicate, and eternal. Most distinctly chivalric are the "affrighted steed" and "splendid shroud" of the first and last stanzas. These phrases suggest medieval pictorial art, with that ambiguity one sees within and between works of such art: the ambiguity of beauty and death. Thus these stanzas use overstatement in their imitation glorification of war and understatement in their implication that there is no glory. The "yellow trenches," "raged," and "gulped" of the central stanza unambiguously suggest both physical horror and nineteenth-century warfare. Thus the chivalric and realistic elements of the poem are not isolated in the two stanzaic groups, and the central stanza provides a pivot about which the horrors of the other four stanzas revolve.

The three lamenting stanzas offer comfort to the afflicted, but only the first and fifth clearly suggest why this comfort may actually be found acceptable. The poet chooses the child as protagonist for the central stanza deliberately: the child's unconsciousness of those social values implied by "steed" and "splendid shroud" does make it possible that he will accept the idea of glory, though all appearances of glory are absent. But as a potential observer of actual death the child is the least likely to be deluded. The sight that is offered could only horrify or puzzle him, though a socially distorted image of it might delude him. The contrast of the pivotal stanza to the first and last stanzas creates an additional irony, but its full meaning comes into focus only when the last stanza is examined.

In the first and last stanzas the protagonists are divided between agony and delusion. They are bidden to and seem to grasp at comforting formulas, but they see the terrible reality beneath—or almost see it. In the central stanza the poet's voice bids the child to break through the veil of distance, and so the irony is directed against those who would delude the child. The explicit ugliness of detail makes this stanza approach the irony of the denouncing stanzas and reinforces its role as a pivot. In the final stanza Crane combines structural and verbal irony to achieve his intensest lament and a brilliant climax.

In the two stanzas of denunciation Crane's irony is also directed against both the sufferers and the codes of society that send them to death, but the sufferers are now exclusively on the battlefield and delusion is now a subject for anger against all the deluded. Structural variation between these stanzas is slight, and their repetitive quality serves chiefly to continue the contrast with the lamenting stanzas. Once again understatement is combined with overstatement, but now overstatement imitates journalistic and mass-hysterical praise of war. The unthinking but strangely personal praise of war as noble found in the lamenting stanzas is replaced by unthinking and impersonal praise of war as fiercely glorious. Again understatement implies that the attitude is false. The verse is cacophonous. As in the lamenting stanzas the diction comes from clashing levels, but now more obviously: the crudely scornful "Hoarse booming drums," "Little souls," "corpses"; the strained, deliberate, formal triteness of "unexplained glory," "Eagle with crest," "virtue," "excellence"; and the parody of cynicism in "born to drill and die."

Once more the individual ironies are subtle. The statement that men were born to drill and die implies that life is as futile as death. The unexplained glory is indeed unexplainable, for it is an illusion. The reigning battle-god is the opposite of the Christian god whom society claims: his kingdom is hell, not heaven. The flag which stands for the illusion of glory foreshadows the deceptive glory of the shroud. Thus Crane's frequent contrast between a vindictive external god and an internal conscience is replaced by a contrast between a pagan god and a lost or illusory god of mercy.

In both modes, Crane dramatizes values he condemns and asserts that those values are accepted by the victims of war no less than by the society which causes war. But pity and anger remain the respectively dominant feelings of the contrasting stanzas. As the clashing elements of the denouncing stanzas come into focus, the medieval picture fades into nineteenth-century scenes, though the elements are mixed, and the poet expresses loathing for all who do not see these infernal scenes for what they are, or who see reality cynically. The false prophets are condemned more strongly than the deluded soldiers, but all are deluded. Beneath its irony the poem's refrain becomes an equivalent of the most famous American explicit statement about war, for the poem's ironical insistence on the equation of opposites suggests that human existence, particularly in war, is hell. The forced and hypocritical union of opposites in a world where values are indeterminate and basic desires are taunted is a major factor in many visions of existence as hell.

In the final stanza Crane ties together the threads of the poem. The language of "Mother whose heart hung humble as a button" is only partly understatement; it suggests the mother's real humility, and her status in relation to the war-makers—a condition of helplessness and partially compelled humility. (Could Crane have been recalling Lear's "Pray you, undo this button"? In any case, the similar juxtapositions of commonplace image and agonized heart suggest the invasion of everyday life by almost cosmic agony.) But the next line is equally complex and "passionately moving," the quality Berryman denies it and assigns to the preceding line. The "bright splendid shroud" is the image of what the living son would be (minus the shroud); of the dead hero as society wishes the mother to see him; and of the horrifying reality of the corpse. The mother holds all three attitudes, and this ambiguity or confusion creates the poem's climactic and continuing irony.

For the fifth time, a sufferer is told not to weep because war is kind. Had maiden, babe, and mother taken seriously the poem's chivalric implications, they would indeed have accepted war as kind. Crane's intensely circular irony culminates as the kindness of war is opposed to the agonizing confusion of the mother. The poet is actually bidding her to weep, but the world he has portrayed will try to keep her from weeping. The irony does not yet cease, for Crane knows that without the protection of self-deception, life would sometimes be unbearable—that is, unbearable under the dreadful conditions which he attacks.

Many critics have mistakenly taken the need for self-deception to be a central and unqualified idea in Crane's work. Crane sees and uses irony as both defense and attack. Quite probably he could not envisage a world in which irony would not be needed for both these purposes, but this does not mean that he accepted the world in its bitter reality. Crane scholars are discarding the idea that he was a despairing determinist and many now see him as an affirming humanist. Study of this poem supports this position, and also shows how Crane could manipulate various ironic voices so that a definite viewpoint is expressed through an ironic persona. Crane does not pare his fingernails while the world burns, though he sometimes sees the world as a "whirling, fire-smitten, ice-locked, disease-stricken, space-lost bulb." [4]

NOTES

1. "Stephen Crane: A Revaluation," *Critiques and Essays on Modern Fiction, 1920-1951,* ed. John W. Aldridge (New York, 1952), p. 259. *Stephen Crane, An Omnibus* (New York, 1952), p. 571.
2. *Stephen Crane* (New York, 1950), p. 272.
3. *The Poetry of Stephen Crane* (New York, 1957), pp. 189-190.
4. "The Blue Hotel," *Stephen Crane, An Omnibus,* p. 524.

B. STEPHEN CRANE AS NOVELIST: AN INTRODUCTION

Stephen Crane suggested in various and scattered remarks that he rejected the length and superficial "complexity" of the traditional novel. He thought that even Tolstoy, his favorite author, was too lengthy: *War and Peace* could have been done in "one third the time." Thomas Hardy and Mark Twain overtreated their subjects; Hugo and Dickens could be self-conscious tricksters.

In his volume of poems, *The Black Riders,* Crane revealed his commitment to brevity. During his earlier newspaper days, he displayed a talent for writing feature-type sketches, which he had to make informative and brief in order to keep his readers' attention. His study of the Bible—at home, and at Pennington Seminary and Claverack College—influenced Crane to appreciate the beauty and conciseness of the fable and the parable. His technique of impressionism, a painterly and highly selective art, seemed better suited to the short story and the sketch rather than to the novel. From the first, then, Stephen Crane was consciously and unconsciously training himself for brevity.

Crane had difficulty satisfying his demands for brevity and true "complexity" in his own novels. He thought that *The Red Badge* was too long; and in longer novels, such as *Active Service,* he was straitjacketed by the necessity for elaborate plots, characterizations, and actions. Crane probably considered that "elaborate" did not mean or lead to the truly complex but was a way of padding. However, Crane's reputation still rests with his novels, specifically with *The Red Badge* and *Maggie.*

Why did Stephen Crane write novels? In the 1890s, the novel was the most exciting and the most profitable of the imaginative arts, the one that catapulted a writer from obscurity to fame. Though short stories were becoming increasingly popular (with the rise of the magazines, and with the rise of syndicates that placed short stories in the newspapers), they rarely, when collected, became best-sellers; and they never had the prestige of the novel. Moreover, short stories appearing in magazines and newspapers were read by the entire family, while the novel was generally read by the individual adult reader. This meant that the artist would have more freedom in writing the novel and less in writing the short story, because young readers were usually prohibited from reading novels. Just as important, Crane needed the length of the novel to deal with some of his "causes," which he hoped to present artistically. He spoke of his cause in *Maggie:*

> It is inevitable that you will be greatly shocked by this book but continue please with all possible courage to the end. For it tries to show that environment is a tremendous thing in the world and frequently shapes lives regardless. If one proves that theory one makes room in Heaven for all sorts of souls (notably an occasional street girl) who are not confidently expected to be there by many excellent people.

The short story simply did not have the room to do justice to such an imposing issue.

Despite his anxieties about the novel, Stephen Crane contributed much of historic and artistic significance to the novel form. Given his bent for impressionism, he helped to create the modern American novel by destroying the mold of the traditional novel, with its reliance on plot, action, and character. Crane knew how to structure a work—he never lost sight of a story's "long logic"—but he lessened the value of plot and heightened instead the qualities of mood, image, symbol, and tone, bringing new dimensions of feeling, experience, and reality to the reader. He lessened the romantic embellishments usually associated with the hero. His heroes were average and well-intentioned as they faced destructive abstract forces; they were *real* and *modern*. Crane skirted the histrionic action that the romantic writer depended upon; he depicted everyday situations, another characteristic of the modern writer. By employing irony, naturalism, and impressionism, he gave new dimensions to experiences and truths, and developed a new and functional style. All these qualities were found in his early novels—*Maggie, The Red Badge,* and *George's Mother.* In these three works, Crane was really writing the anti-novels of the day, which were revolutionary enough to inspire impressive changes in the course of American literature.

Stephen Crane was critical of other matters in the traditional novel as he espoused modern tendencies. He was dissatisfied not only with the extravagances of the romance (he despised Robert Louis Stevenson) but with the novel as pure entertainment. He was dedicated to the novel of purpose, though he respected romance as part of reality. He was hostile to the intruding author and to preaching in fiction. The rhetoric of the traditional artist was unsatisfactory; he looked upon phrases like "from time immemorial" as "mildewed." He was not at all averse to swearing in fiction. He was dissatisfied with a complete reliance on the powers of the imagination; he often studied documented information. He pored over *Battles and Leaders of the Civil War* for *The Red Badge,* and lived like the poor to get the proper atmosphere for his breadline story, "The Men in the Storm." In his early novels especially, Crane helped to create the modern spirit of tragicomedy. He had never been satisfied with the "somber" moods of Ambrose Bierce, and in his own work he achieved variety, depth, and humanity by mixing comic and tragic materials. To achieve the effect of tragicomedy, he drew upon the arts of the grotesque, parody, and irony.

Despite all these qualities of modernity in his early novels, Stephen Crane was literally engulfed by the tide of romanticism that was flourishing in the 1890s. Moreover, Crane could only be a "dry twig" next to the new "bonfire" of the day, Rudyard Kipling, whom he imitated for a time. Other factors, besides romanticism and Kipling, hindered Crane's fuller success as a novelist. He was, presumably, only a clever young man, a *tour de force* writer who wrote too hastily to be taken seriously. *Maggie* was supposedly written in two days (Crane worked on it for more than a year); *The Red Badge* in ten (Crane worked on it at least several months). He had too many projects running simultaneously. He wrote his last two novels quickly in order to pay off his mounting debts. His impressionism and irony (Thomas Beer correctly reminds us that irony was a term of "reproach" in the 1890s) were looked upon as a form of madness and cynicism. Some thought he read little, and therefore concluded that he did not know enough about literature and literary tradition. He seemed two confusing writers in one: the realist-naturalist with a purpose in *Maggie, George's Mother,* and *The Red Badge;* and the romancer-entertainer in *The Third Violet, Active Service,* and *The O'Ruddy.* Still, critics and readers in Crane's time were fascinated by an inexperienced nineteen-year-old who could write about the slums and prostitution in *Maggie.* They were even more fascinated that Crane could write about war in *The Red Badge* without ever having seen one. But once the shock wore off, what was left? Mainly his bold art and bold new themes, which were little understood or respected.

The general consensus in 1971 is that Stephen Crane's one

major success in the novel form, *The Red Badge,* weakens at the close. *Maggie* and *George's Mother* are respected as "ambitious" performances, but they are somewhat removed from greatness. The final novels are rarely mentioned. To most critics, *The Third Violet, Active Service,* and *The O'Ruddy* are of minor interest because Crane is solely the conventional romancer-entertainer who has forsaken the serious and thought-provoking subjects of his earlier novels, and his revolutionary art and style. All these issues, and more, deserve closer scrutiny and reexamination.

1. *Maggie*

a. New Testament Inversions in Crane's Maggie
By William Bysshe Stein

The rigid naturalistic interpretations of *Maggie*, so popular in some critical circles today, obscure the universal implications of Crane's dramatic re-creation of Bowery existence. It is not enough, for instance, to say that the novel is the sum of "innocence thwarted and betrayed by environment." [1] Such a categorical statement implies that Crane's view of reality is unalterably objective, concerned only with the transcription of calculable sociological data. Actually his creative imagination is deeply stirred by religious aspects of the setting. This is seen in a recurrent pattern of symbolic moral situations which is inspired by the New Testament.

Here, of course, Crane's background is the point at issue. Reared in a confining religious atmosphere (his father was a Methodist minister and his mother a newspaper reporter of church activities), he unconsciously was trained to think in the ideological framework of Christianity. Even in rebellion against its expression in institutional religion, he could not completely subdue its incontrovertible ethical affirmations. We can see, for example, his patent detestation of mission evangelism in *Maggie*, and we can understand his impatience with its blatant self-righteousness. But, on the other hand, he introduces certain scenes and incidents which, though they do not beg attention, are nevertheless manifestations of an intuitive loyalty to the redemptive love of the Gospels. In the opening chapter of the book there is, I think, evidence of this. His juxtaposition of the violent scuffle in the alley with the tableau of human callousness illustrates what I mean: "From a window of an apartment-house that uprose from amid squat stables there leaned a curious woman. Some labourers, unloading a scow at a dock at the river, paused for a moment and regarded the fight. The engineer of a passive tugboat hung lazily over a railing and watched. Over on the island a worm of yellow convicts came

Reprinted from: *Modern Language Notes*, LXXIII (April 1958), 268-272. By permission of The Johns Hopkins Press, copyright © 1958, and the author.

from the shadow of a building and crawled slowly along the river's bank." (pp. 39-40) These phlegmatic onlookers, so carefully foreshortened against the background of a prison, epitomize the indifference of a society familiar with violence and crime. But at the same time their moral unconcern represents the degradation of the values of love and compassion in their daily lives. This is to say that Crane's visualization of the heartlessness of human relationships in this scene takes note of the paralysis of Christianity in this environment and in the world.

In effect, his scenic logic argues that human nature is depraved; but he counterpoints this attitude with an argument to the contrary which promises a deliverance from this amoral state. The complete title of the novel, *Maggie: A Girl of the Streets,* constitutes an initiation into the function of this device of irony. The name Maggie is deliberately equated with the practice of prostitution, but it is also, in context at least, suggestively proposed as a diminutive of Magdalene. This etymology, of course, is not correct, but here the association is almost instinctive for anyone acquainted with the parables. Since Crane presupposes, as all of us must, that in our culture man has been taught to make sense out of his experience in terms of the Christian myth, then the title should excite our sympathy instead of indignation. The heroine, in other words, is entitled to forgiveness like her counterpart in the New Testament. Crane has in mind, I think, Maggie's quite pardonable sin of assuming that love will redeem all, and at this juncture she metamorphoses into Magdalene: "Wherefore I say unto Thee, Her sins which are many, are forgiven; for she loved much: but to whom little is forgiven, the *same* loveth little." [2] This interpretation may seem to run counter to the opinions about Christ expressed by Crane in his poetry; yet his quick sympathy with prostitutes is an impulse of his moral conditioning—a much sounder gauge of his spiritual values, it seems to me, than the sophomoric heresies which dialectically shape some of his poems. Then, too, the novel was written before he began to connect his aggressive moral impatience with the scientific naturalism which enveloped the literary world of his day.

In any event, without too much difficulty this interpretive approach to the title can be applied to certain crucial episodes in the narrative. Jimmy's attempt to convince his mother that Maggie ought to be permitted to return home after her seduction results in a depressing burlesque of the Prodigal Son. By treating the incident humorously, Crane horrifyingly enhances the sadism of the mother. Unable to explain rationally his instinctive desire to protect his sister, Jimmy can only justify it by disclaiming its connection with Christian morality: " 'Well, I didn't mean none of dis prod'gal bus'ness anyway.' " She, however, triumphantly refutes the validity of this precedent with the crushing rejoinder: " 'It wa'n't no prod'gal daughter, yeh fool.' " And reducing Jimmy to impotent silence, she proceeds to revel in the opportunity for abuse which Maggie's inevitable return promises: "The mother's eyes gloated on the scene which her imagination called before her." (pp. 83-84) This inversion and its implications are obvious, but they lend sanction to my belief that the unvoiced inspiration of the novel is Crane's distressed insight into the abandonment of Christian love by his culture.

This perception is forcefully embodied in another important segment of the action. It involves Maggie's quest for salvation after her rejection by Peter, and is an adaptation of another New Testament motif. The minister's lack of mercy in this case parallels the response of the priest in the parable of the Good Samaritan. Maggie, seeking the "grace of God," decides to accost "a stout gentleman in a silk hat and chaste black coat," but he makes "a convulsive movement and save[s] his respectability by a vigorous side-step." (p. 95) A glance at the circumstances of the parable will suffice to establish their relationship with this episode: "A certain man ... fell among thieves, which stripped him of his raiment, and wounded *him*, and departed, leaving him half dead. And by chance there came a certain priest that way; and when he saw him, he passed by on the other side." [3] Ordinarily one would, I think, tend to limit this parody to Crane's contempt for the clergy and their fastidiously cultivated piety. But the satirical probe strikes deeper. It penetrates to the real cause of the degeneration of love in human affairs—the betrayal of Christ by his ministry.

Still another episode evolves out of the religious matrix of the artist's inspiration, the last scene in the novel. Mary's affected sorrow over Maggie's death is made painfully obvious, but once again Crane assumes that the reader will associate the travesty of bereavement with its archetypal counterpart. I refer, of course, to the conventional representation of the Virgin lamenting over the body of Christ after the crucifixion. Crane's re-creation of the depraved Pietà of the slums is contrived to comment ironically upon the mother's name, but it also functions to cast the black pall of an irredeemable Good Friday upon the culture which he criticizes. For, contrary to the critics who argue that Maggie is a victim of her environment, he dramatizes the key scenes of her pathetic fate against the background of man's defection from the redemptive love of Christianity as it is crystallized in John's record of the Savior's conversation after his betrayal by Judas: "A new commandment I give unto you, That ye love one another; as I have loved you, that ye also love one another." [4] Maggie, in short, is crucified by the same forces of hate in human nature that destroyed Christ. Fittingly the concluding chapter of the novel is characterized by the repetition of the word black in contrast with the violent colors of life in the earlier chapters. In this way Crane emphasizes the advent of the Black Friday which can become Good Friday only when it ensures salvation. But, in his perspective, this miraculous transformation cannot occur. The darkness of hate is fixed for ever in time.

And considering the symbolic function of the names of Maggie and Mary, it may not be farfetched to ascribe a similar meaning to the names of Peter and Jimmy. Simon Peter and James were the two disciples who accompanied Christ on the road to Calvary. Even the young Tommy who dies in his infancy may be a vague reflection of his doubting namesake in the New Testament. His death, in any event, seems to prove that Thomas intuitively foresaw the failure of the law of love as in later history it is interpreted by the new Marys, and Peters, and Jameses. Confirmation of Crane's preoccupation with the nature of human and divine love is sardonically recorded in the name he chooses for the unscrupulous prostitute, Nell. The new Helen of Troy mocks the meaning of love in her scarlet arrogance, reversing the downfall not only of her Greek congener but of the Whore of Babylon in The Revelation, the prototypal scarlet woman. She sheds no tears, she wastes no pity, she shows no remorse. She lives in the spirit of the new law of venal love which Crane proclaims to rule the world.

This conviction, enhanced by immersion in the destructive element of personal experience, perhaps explains why in his later fiction religious images, for the most part, serve as simple correlatives of irony. Crane seems to lose even his provisional faith in the symbolic machinery of Christian salvation. When Maggie's innocent dream of love died, something may be said to have died in his soul.

NOTES

1. *Stephen Crane: Stories and Tales,* ed. Robert W. Stallman (Vintage Books; New York, 1955), p. 7, introduction to the Bowery Tales. All parenthetical page references hereafter are to the edition of *Maggie* in this volume.
2. Luke 7: 47.
3. Luke 10: 30-31.
4. John 13: 34.

b. The Structure of Crane's Maggie
By Janet Overmyer

Stephen Crane's first novelette is often considered worth-while only because its author later went on to write *The Red Badge of Courage.* While *Maggie* has several faults, it also has several virtues which indicate plainly that its author, even at twenty, was a skilled craftsman. One of its most noticeable virtues is the relation of structure to theme.

Maggie's structure is often regarded as being flimsy. John Berryman says, "Crane had to rely on loose, episodic structure." [1] While Robert Wooster Stallman feels that *Maggie* has a definite pattern, he says that "not logic but mood defines the relationship by the images and episodes." [2] It is my contention that the novelette has a decided controlling structure that combines with the theme to form a pleasing whole.

The structure, which serves as an encircling frame for the plot, is that of the familiar "play within a play." The very first scene is Jimmie fighting the Devil's Row children with an audience of "a curious woman," "some laborers," and "the engineer of a passive tugboat." Not one of them moves to interfere; they might as well be an audience at a theater. The same is true, to a heightened degree, of the Johnsons' neighbors. Not only do they not interfere in the family's quarrels, even when bodily injury is imminent, but they crowd into the hall and hurl comments at the combatants, much as spectators at a prize fight cheer on their favorite. Again, the fights serve as entertainment. The final, disgustingly ironic comment of Maggie's mother—"I'll fergive her!"—would not have been uttered at all but for the neighbors' prodding. As they repeatedly ask if the mother will forgive, she senses that it would be a fine gesture to make; it would make her out a martyr. The neighbors have gotten their money's worth.

To emphasize this theatrical unreality still further, three scenes are set in a beer hall that presents stage shows, where Pete takes Maggie on their dates. On their first date (Section 7) Maggie has a fine time; she sees a wonderful world hitherto completely unknown

Reprinted from: *The University of Kansas City Review,* XXIX (Autumn 1962), 71-72. By permission of the *University Review* and the author.

to her. The second beer hall scene (Section 12) takes place after Maggie has left home to be with Pete, and is becoming used to such evenings. The stage show is therefore described in less detail than previously, and Maggie, while enjoying herself, has a less pleasant time. On the way out she prophetically sees two street walkers. The third such scene (Section 14) gives very little description of the entertainment and is saddened for Maggie by Pete's desertion of her. Maggie's downward slide is set against the make-believe backdrop to further emphasize the story's theme.

The theme may be stated as being that an unreal view of life precipitates tragedy, or at least unhappiness. None of the four main characters sees life clearly and honestly. Pete correctly views his affair with Maggie as a pleasant interlude for him and nothing more, but he hopes mightily for a satisfactory relationship with Nell, who sees him as a fool. Jimmie is at a loss to understand his sister's fall and, incapable of seeing any relation between his own seduction of various women and Pete's seduction of his sister, damns his sister mercilessly for thus disgracing the family. Once he "almost came to a conclusion that his sister would have been more firmly good had she better known how," but he discards this idea. Neither he nor his mother can understand Maggie's desire for a better life or see how her environment helped to propel her into Pete's arms.

But it is Maggie's view of reality that proves, finally, the most saddening. She sees life as she wishes it to be; to her, Pete is "the ideal man," and the plays she sees represent "transcendental realism." It is quite proper to her that in the theater the villain is punished and the hero is rewarded; she fails to realize that this is not necessarily the way of the world. She believes her love affair with Pete will last forever; when it does not, she is utterly lost.

The play within a play structure thus reinforces the idea that life must be viewed realistically, even if painfully. It is far more painful to fool oneself. Crane begins and ends his story with the emphasis on unreality, and includes several overt references at intervals throughout. It can thus be seen that structure and theme are firmly and complementarily wedded to give the story unity.

As a postscript, it may be added that *Maggie* is further kept from flying apart by the number of parallel incidents. In the following examples, the first event foreshadows the second:

1. Jimmie's fight as a child and his fight with Pete, his early rescuer.

2. The drunkenness of Mr. Johnson and Jimmie.

3. The death of Tommie, an innocent child, and Maggie, an "innocent" girl.

4. The casual seductions by Jimmie and Pete.

5. Maggie's pulling back from the painted women and the minister's pulling back from her.

In addition, there are the following parallels:

1. Two fallen women, Nell and Maggie.
2. The souls of Jimmie and Maggie.
3. The powerlessness of the mission church and of the minister.

There is also a careful alternation of places and people throughout; scenes in the beer hall alternate with scenes of home as scenes of Maggie and Pete alternate with scenes of Jimmie and his mother. All of which shows that while the structure of *Maggie* may be episodic, it is not loose, but tightly controlled; for all his faults, Crane, even at an early age, knew how to structure a story.

NOTES

1. *Stephen Crane* (New York: William Sloane Associates, Inc., 1950), p. 59.
2. "Crane's 'Maggie': A Reassessment," *Modern Fiction Studies*, V (Autumn, 1959), 251-252.

c. Ironic and Symbolic Structure in Crane's Maggie
By Joseph X. Brennan

Perhaps the most remarkable single characteristic of *Maggie* is
its insistent, and at times even oppressive, ironic tone. In its sustained
and vehement irony *Maggie* was as much without precedent in
American fiction as in its daring subject matter, and even today, in
spite of all that the school of naturalism has produced in this manner,
Crane's short narrative still marks something of the limits to which
that method can go. In *Maggie,* indeed, the irony is so all-pervasive,
ranging from the inversion of a single word or phrase to the thematic
idea itself, that it is at once the most striking and yet most elusive
aspect of the novel. In order to illustrate better how far-reaching this
irony is, I shall proceed generally from its more overt and localized
to its more complex manifestations, from the ironic cast of the single
word or phrase to the ironic manipulation of theme and character.

Of the ironic inversion of the single term one might cite numerous instances; chapter iv, however, provides several of the more
interesting examples. In the second paragraph of this chapter we
read that Jimmie "studied human nature in the gutter, and found
it no worse than he thought he had reason to believe it." Where we
would ordinarily expect "no better" Crane overreaches our expectations to emphasize not only Jimmie's cynicism but the inversion of
his scale of values as well: in his world there is no concept of good
and bad; there is only bad or worse. This ironic twist is reinforced
in the next sentence as well: "He never conceived a respect for the
world, because he had begun with no idols that it had smashed."
And later in this chapter, when Jimmie, by his premeditated indifference, had successfully snarled traffic, we read that "some blue
policeman turned red and began ... to ... beat the soft noses of the
responsible horses." Quite clearly the responsibility was not the
horses'; Crane achieves an ironic effect here, however, not by a mere
arbitrary inversion of the expected but by momentarily abandoning
his usual objectivity and letting, as it were, the policeman's red point
of view prevail. The same might be said for Crane's ironic use of

Reprinted from: *Nineteenth-Century Fiction,* XVI (March 1962), 304-315. By permission of The Regents of the University of California and the author. Copyright
© 1962 by The Regents of the University of California.

the term "reverently" in the last sentence of this chapter: "Nevertheless, he had, on a certain star-lit evening, said wonderingly and quite reverently, 'Deh moon looks like hell, don't it?' " This entire passage, indeed, following immediately upon a terse review of Jimmie's brawlings and seductions, is itself a trenchant ironic commentary upon his soulfulness and sensitivity.

More interesting yet, in chapter xvi, is Crane's use of the word "respectability" as a kind of ironic motif; the term is repeated six times, each with broadening implications and heightened ironic effect. There is a very deliberate progression here from Pete's apprehension lest Maggie should compromise the "atmosphere of respectability upon which the proprietor insisted"—the term being used three times in this association—to his confused impression that the respectability of the barroom now being threatened is really his own respectability. Having driven Maggie away at last, Pete then returns "with an air of relief, to his respectability," so that the psychological transference from the barroom to himself is now complete. In the last paragraph this motif reappears when a picture of benevolence and kind-heartedness to whom Maggie makes a gesture of appeal for help draws back from her convulsively to save his respectability. Thus in the brief course of this scene, by means of an ironic manipulation of the term, Crane reduces respectability to a hypocritical sham, a convenient justification for cruelty, irresponsibility, and indifference.

In the delineation of the main characters, moreover, Crane employs with telling effect a technique of ironically leveling the reader's normal assumptions and expectations. When we first encounter Jimmie in chapter i, for example, he is the "little champion," fighting against overwhelming odds for the honor of Rum Alley. But lest by his initial display of courage he should too seriously engage our sympathies, a short while thereafter he turns his fists with unabated fury upon his defenseless sister. In chapter iii, when the father snatches the can of beer which Jimmie had just bought for the leathery old woman downstairs, he protests as though from a certain sense of justice, "Ah, come off! I got dis can fer dat ol' woman, an' it 'ud be dirt teh swipe it. See?" But a moment thereafter we perceive that he is really more concerned with the difficulties this creates for himself: "Look at deh dirt what yeh done me. . . . Deh ol' woman'll be t'rowin' fits." Similarly one might be led to expect that the mother's objection to Jimmie's fighting springs from some dim instinct of solicitude for his physical well-being, yet, as it turns out, the real reason for her objection is that he tears his clothes. One wonders, too, when the father shouts at Jimmie, "Leave yer sister alone on the street," whether it is to Jimmie's pounding of Maggie or to the publicity of it that he is really objecting. In short, Crane has a real flair for this sort of ironic qualification of proper appearances with improper and unexpected motives; by means of this device he can deeply compromise his characters with one deft economical stroke.

Equally important, but somewhat more subtle, is Crane's device of interlinking his chapters by an ironic inversion of some key phrase or circumstance. In chapter x the incredulity—in itself sufficiently ironic—with which the mother greets Jimmie's statement, "Well, Maggie's gone teh d'devil!" takes on another dimension of meaning when we remember that in the previous chapter, after having cursed and calumniated Maggie sanctimoniously from a position of drunken prostration, the mother had then driven her out with the words, "Git th' devil outa here." The point of it all, of course—and this scarcely needs such insistence—is that it is really the mother who is ultimately responsible for Maggie's seduction by Pete.

More effective is the ironic inversion which interlocks chapters x and xi. Outraged by the news of Maggie's seduction, Jimmie sets out to trounce the culprit Pete singlehandedly; but he does not hesitate, in spite of his claims to superiority, to annex the assistance of a friend whom he encounters on the way. The ironic twist comes at the end of chapter xi when Jimmie escapes and the friend who had sought to dissuade him from his purpose—"What's deh use! Yeh'll git pulled in! ... An' ten plunks! Gee! ... What's d'use?"—is himself hauled off by the policeman, evidently to pay the "ten plunks." Though Jimmie has a momentary urge to run to the rescue, he finally consigns his friend to his fate, ironically with that poor fool's very words, "Ah, what's deh use?" Crane uses this ironic inversion, however, not merely for the verbal sport of it, but in order to give firm emphasis to the essential cowardice that sinews all these boastful characters, and Jimmie in particular.

Also striking is the manner in which chapters xv and xvi are thematically tied together. Within the immediate confines of chapter xv, the initial scene of Jimmie's harsh repudiation of the forlorn woman whom he had brought to ruin serves to highlight ironically his self-righteous repudiation of his own sister shortly thereafter, but this scene functions even more importantly to reduce the next meeting between Pete and Maggie to ironic parody. In particular the dialogue of the one scene directly mimics that of the other. "Ah, don't bodder me!" Jimmie complains to Hattie; "Don' be allus bodderin' me," echoes Pete to Maggie. "But Jimmie," protests Hattie, "yeh tol' me yeh—"; "Why, Pete!" exclaims Maggie, "yehs tol' me—" Jimmie: "Yehs makes me tired, allus taggin' me. See" Pete: "Say, yehs makes me tired! See? What d'yeh wanna tag aroun' after me fer?" Jimmie: "Ain yehs got no sense?" Pete: "Ain' yehs got no sense?" Even Jimmie's parting advice to Hattie, "Oh, go teh blazes!" is echoed by Pete, but with less indirection, "Oh, go teh hell!" By means of this grotesque parody, the author not only magnifies the irony of Maggie's situation, but points more deliberately to the dismal round, the universality, of this kind of viciousness in the moral void of these slums.

Closely connected with this ironic repetition and inversion of a given word or phrase is Crane's use of the ironic, and even symbolic, gesture. The fear of contamination, for example, with which in chapter xv the neighboring women recoil from Maggie is really the ironic reversal of her own gesture, at the end of chapter xii, where she draws back her skirts in revulsion from two painted prostitutes. We have already commented upon Pete's repudiation of Maggie in chapter xvi and his return, after that encounter, to his "respectability," but it is somewhat consoling to note how later in chapter xviii the very women whom Pete has treated royally all evening, prostitutes all apparently, scream in disgust and draw back their skirts when he falls to the floor in drunken insensibility. Thus all the accumulated ironies of that gesture, by now clearly a symbol of self-righteous aversion for moral degeneracy, are heaped with a kind of poetic justice upon the prostrate figure of Pete. In order to understand the full significance of that repudiation, however, it is necessary to look more closely at the previous chapter, for the two are closely connected in symbolism and meaning.

Chapter xvii, wherein Maggie is briefly seen plying her trade as a streetwalker, is certainly one of the most skillfully and economically constructed in the story. Unlike many sections of the book, this one states its meaning and conveys a sense of stark inevitability without any overt insistence. After close study, moreover, one realizes that a mere literal reading of this episode, as an unsuccessful evening's ramble that leads to the waterfront, raises certain difficulties. From the description of her clothes—she sports a "handsome cloak" and her feet are "well-shod"—Maggie has evidently prospered in her activity. Obviously successful after a few months' experience, why on this particular evening should she commit suicide? And if she is really seriously interested in engaging profitable attention, why does she enter into "darker blocks than those where the crowd traveled" to solicit less numerous and less well-to-do customers? Why is it also that after Maggie has left the glittering avenues with their tossing sea of umbrellas, there is no further mention of the rain? And in this connection, are we to take as literal or ironic the laborer's response to her overtures, "It's a fine evening, isn't it?"

Clearly this whole passage makes sense only when this evening's venture is taken as a drastic foreshortening or symbolic telescoping of the inevitable decline and ruination to which Maggie and all the women of her order must come. Especially significant in this respect is the pattern of Maggie's encounters: at first she engages the eye of a tall young man in evening dress, one evidently from the social upper crust, but he passes her by when he notices she is no longer "new"; then in order she meets a stout gentleman, he too apparently well off; a business man, who recognizes her and calls her "old girl" rather patronizingly; a young dandy, who addresses her more disparagingly as "old lady"; a laboring man; a mere boy; a drunk; a man with blotched features; and finally a "ragged being with shifting bloodshot eyes and grimy hands." Concomitant with this deliberate regression from wealth and well-being to poverty and physical degeneration, from the most to the least profitable and desirable prospect, there is also a steady shift in the symbolic light, from the brilliant and gay main avenues to the deadly black hue of the river. To have prolonged Maggie's plight over a much more extensive period of time would have quite obviously destroyed the dramatic impact of her story, but in order to point up the more universal implications of her situation, Crane has astutely focused into the range of this particular evening a panoramic and symbolic view of the prostitute's career. These implications he had strengthened also by identifying the subject of this chapter only as "a girl of the painted cohorts" and never specifically as Maggie.

So construed, this section strongly reinforces the meaning of the next and is in turn reinforced by it. Superficially it would seem that the glimpse we receive of Pete, proclaiming to six rapacious women that he is one fine fellow, functions merely as an ironic contrast to what immediately precedes, but upon closer examination one perceives that in its real meaning and implications this chapter reaches much further. It is significant, first of all, that once Pete falls into drunken paralysis, the women upon whom he has lavished his funds abandon him in the saloon compartment, the exit from which is now obscured by the stifling smoke from the lamps. Looking back to the various beer-hall scenes from this point, one finds that there is a steady retrogression here as well, from the bowery version of the de luxe—the great hall in chapter vii—to the shabbiness of the hall of irregular shape in chapter xii, to the unabashed sordidness of the hilarious hall in chapter xiv. Commensurate with this movement from one level of vulgarity to another lower still, there is also a spatial contraction, an increased density of smoke, and an intensification of drunken hilarity. In the present scene, accordingly, it is surely symbolic that Pete is abandoned by a pack of professionals in a narrow saloon compartment from which the way out becomes progressively less apparent. More important, however, is the last sentence of this chapter, where Crane adumbrates in the posture of Pete's present debasement his inevitable and complete degeneration: "The wine from an overturned glass dripped softly down upon the blotches on the man's neck." In the wine drops upon the blotches, Pete's end in drunkenness and disease, one condition leading to and aggravating the other, is thus pointedly symbolized. This meaning is reinforced if one recalls now the previous section where on the lowest level of her inexorable descent to destruction Maggie encounters first a drunkard, then "a man with blotched features," and finally the "ragged being with shifting bloodshot eyes and grimy hands." Nor is this the only verbal tie-up between the two chapters. Just as Maggie has been addressed earlier in chapter xvii as "old girl" and then "old lady," the woman of brilliance and audacity speaks to Pete in the same patronizing manner: "Never you mind, old boy"; and later, "And we're not goin' back on you, old man." By the end of this chapter, at any rate, Pete has reached the point where even women of no high standing pick up their skirts and recoil from him in disgust. Thus Crane would have us understand that Pete's fate is as inevitable as Maggie's and certainly more pitiless, since unlike Maggie he lacks both the conscience and the objectivity to perceive the hopeless waste of his existence.

In the last few pages we have been concerned with various modes of symbolism whose function is primarily or very largely ironic. Before turning to other aspects of Crane's ironic method, it may be well at this point to examine other symbolic passages whose function is only less pointedly related to that device. One of the most unobtrusive but thematically important of these is the following tightly compressed paragraph which appears in the first chapter:

> From a window of an apartment-house that uprose from
> amid squat ignorant stables there leaned a curious woman.
> Some labourers, unloading a scow at a dock at the river,
> paused for a moment and regarded the fight. The engineer
> of a passive tugboat hung lazily over a railing and watched.
> Over on the island a worm of yellow convicts came from
> the shadow of a grey ominous building and crawled slowly
> along the river's bank.

This passage serves first of all to give a sweeping view of the
dismal environment, the "ignorant stables," in which these brawling
little savages proliferate. But more importantly, it sounds a significant
and pervasive theme of the novel, human indifference to human
suffering: the bloody fight of the back-alley gangs may provide some
momentary distraction for the curious or the bored, but it apparently
touches these human spectators no more deeply than that. Most
important of all, however, in this panoramic sweep of the scene, is
the final focusing of the reader's attention upon the "worm of yellow
convicts" and the "ominous" prison in the distance—the inevitable
destiny, apparently, of a large number of these urchins. That prison
fortress, accordingly, is fitly characterized as "ominous" for it portends
the ultimate desolation and insensate degradation towards which
this abandoned segment of society tends. In this connection it should
be noted that these youngsters are described just before and following
this passage as wearing "the grins of true assassins" and leering
gloatingly at the blood upon Jimmie's face.

More curious is the symbol of the horse-drawn fire engine which
appears in chapter iv. Earlier in this chapter it was said of Jimmie
that "He was afraid of nothing," yet some seven paragraphs later we
learn that the mere sight or sound of a fire engine could strike absolute
panic into his soul:

> As one charged toward his truck he would drive fearfully upon
> a sidewalk, threatening untold people with annihilation. When
> an engine struck a mass of blocked trucks, splitting it into
> fragments as a blow annihilates a cake of ice, Jimmie's team
> could usually be observed high and safe, with whole wheels,
> on the sidewalk.... A fire-engine was enshrined in his heart

as an appalling thing that he loved with a distant, dog-like devotion. . . . Those leaping horses, striking sparks from the cobbles in their forward lunge, were creatures to be ineffably admired. The clang of the gong pierced his breast like a noise of remembered war.

Taken in isolation the fire engine may be regarded simply as a symbol of irresistible brute force, the only fact which Jimmie can either respect or admire, for that alone can touch his soul with fear. The ambivalence of Jimmie's attitude, however, is particularly interesting here, for it brings this passage into close relationship with the previous chapter, where the mother's character is dramatized in all its fright and vehemence.

Especially significant in chapter iii is the extreme and curious terror the mother inspires in Jimmie. Though he stands up with dauntless courage to all the abuse of the neighboring roughnecks, and responds on occasion with kicks and curses to his father's violence, he dodges from his mother in abject terror, screaming more from panic than from pain, it seems, once she takes hold of him. So much in dread does he live of her violent outbursts he has even learned to detect their ominous approach: "He cast furtive glances at his mother. His practised eye perceived her gradually emerge from a mist of muddled sentiment until her brain burned in drunken heat. He sat breathless." Once the outburst comes, though it is immediately directed at Maggie, Jimmie runs out of the flat "shrieking like a monk in an earthquake." When at last the battle subsides and his parents collapse in drunken stupor, the mother in the middle of the floor, the father across the seat of a chair, Jimmie enters the room stealthily, still trembling with fear. What follows upon this is particularly interesting. "A glow from the fire threw red hues over the bare floor," and in this symbolically suggestive light, half hypnotized between dread and fascination, Jimmie studies the grotesque figure of his mother:

> His mother's great chest was heaving painfully. Jimmie paused and looked down at her. . . . He was fearful lest she should open her eyes, and the dread within him was so strong that he could not forbear to stare, but hung as if fascinated over the

woman's grim face. Suddenly her eyes opened. The urchin found himself looking straight into an expression which, it would seem, had the power to change his blood to salt. He howled piercingly and fell backward.

Though the mother sinks again into drunken sleep, Maggie and Jimmie clutch one another and huddle in a corner, to spend an all-night vigil gazing with expectant horror at the mother's prostrate form:

> The eyes of both were drawn, by some force, to stare at the woman's face, for they thought she need only to awake and all the fiends would come from below. They crouched until the ghost mists of dawn appeared at the window, drawing close to the panes, and looking in at the prostrate, heaving body of the mother.

This passage serves to rivet the reader's attention, at the very threshold of the adult histories of these children, upon the drunken figure of the mother, the strongest formative force in their lives, and in that sense the chief symbol of the novel. For symbolically embodied in the mother—brutal yet hopelessly maudlin, irresistibly aggressive and invulnerably self-righteous—are all the evil forces of this society that work Maggie's and eventually its own destruction.

The connection between this passage and that of the fire engine can be more readily perceived now in the pattern of Jimmie's psychology. Towards both his mother and the fire engine his attitude is clearly ambivalent; both command that incontestable brute force which fascinates him because it overawes, and wins his respect because it overwhelms. It is also noteworthy that, whether intentionally or not, the mother is frequently described in terms strongly suggestive of the fire engine: she is "immense," "rampant," "chieftain-like," "crimson," "puffing and snorting," "fervent red," and "inflamed." Nor is it any wonder, when one recalls the scenes of her drunken rampages, that "the clang of the fire gong pierced Jimmie's breast like a noise of remembered war." Like the fire engine, the mother smashes everything in her path once her drunken rage runs wild; but whereas the fire engine symbolizes in Jimmie's psychology an ideal of destructive brute force, her outrageous physical strength betokens something more, the devastating moral and psychological might by which she smashes the minds and the souls of her children. As the fire engine symbolizes overpowering physical force in Jimmie's brutal world, the mother represents its destructive spiritual counterpart. Taken together thus these passages reciprocally enrich each other's meaning.

Another set of symbols worth attention is the lambrequin and blue ribbons with which Maggie rather pathetically attempts to improve the appearance of her home. When we study the several passages in which these items appear, it becomes clear that they are intended as symbols of Maggie herself, of her essentially feminine but somewhat romantically distorted sensibility. Although Maggie has worked upon the lambrequin "with infinite care" in order to attract Pete's attention, he fails completely to look at, let alone admire it: symbolically, Pete cannot even discern, much less value, the real virtues of Maggie's nature. One must have a soul in order to recognize one, and Pete, there can be no doubt, has none. Shortly thereafter we read that the mother "had vented some phase of drunken fury upon the lambrequin. It lay in a bedraggled heap in the corner. . . . the knots of blue ribbons appeared like violated flowers." This passage corroborates symbolically what was said earlier, that it is the mother who is really culpable for Maggie's seduction and ruin, for it is the mother who has most ruthlessly outraged Maggie, who has violated her soul repeatedly and trampled her sensibilities.

In the final use of these symbols in chapter x there are several interesting implications concerning Maggie herself. The night before, in the height of her drunken fury, the mother had driven Maggie out of the house and into the willing arms of Pete. Before leaving her home the next day, however, in order to live with Pete, Maggie first attempts to restore appearances.

> The rooms showed that attempts had been made at tidying them. . . . The floor had been newly swept. The blue ribbons had been restored to the curtains, and the lambrequin, with its immense sheaves of yellow wheat and red roses of equal size, had been returned, in a worn and sorry state, to its place at the mantel. Maggie's jacket and hat were gone from the nail behind the door.

Though repeatedly abused and trampled upon, Maggie constantly picks up the remnants of her life and tries to restore them, even if "in a worn and sorry state," to some semblance of decency. When she leaves home to live with Pete, she does so in the full conviction that under the circumstances what she is doing is expedient rather than immoral; now that she has been driven from her home and seduced, going to live with Pete is, from her point of view, the only decent restoration of her life possible. "She did not feel like a bad woman," we are informed further on: "to her knowledge she had never known any better."

It seems likely too that in the lambrequin's "immense sheaves of yellow wheat and red roses of equal size," Crane is suggesting something further about Maggie: the romantic distortion of her sensibility, which beguiles her into regarding a patent vulgarian like Pete as a "golden sun," a "knight" and "ideal man," the "lover . . . under the trees of her dream-gardens." For Maggie is no more spared by Crane's irony than the rest of his characters. Indeed, however sympathetically in other respects she may be portrayed, her tastes and mental perceptions are sometimes absurd to the point of exasperation. When, for example, Pete shouts at a waiter, "Ah, git off d'eart!" and from this evidence Maggie infers that "Pete brought forth all his elegance and all his knowledge of high-class customs for her benefit," one might well wonder whether any kind of moral light could pierce such density.

But if Crane did not spare Maggie's intelligence, he did at least intend to spare her soul, to depict her as the innocent victim of the brutal forces around her, a flower which "blossomed in a mud-puddle," only to be sullied and broken and trampled back into it. This fact is certainly clear enough in the novel, but it is interesting to note how Crane himself phrased it in an inscription copy he sent to Hamlin Garland:

> It is inevitable that you will be greatly shocked by the book but continue, please, with all possible courage, to the end. For it tries to show that environment is a tremendous thing in the world and frequently shapes lives regardless. If one proves that theory one makes room in Heaven for all sorts of souls, notably an occasional street girl, who are not confidently expected to be there by many excellent people.

Although the story itself, fortunately, is nowhere so explicit about heaven and salvation, it nevertheless dramatizes quite forcefully this central thematic irony: the self-righteous condemnation of a woman who is good by the very society responsible for her downfall. From this thematic center extends the whole labyrinthian structure of particular ironies briefly surveyed above.

Maggie, then, is a much more intricately structured work of art than its more obvious infelicities of style and emphasis might lead one to suspect. Though the vehemence of Crane's ironic vision undoubtedly accounts for much that is excessive in *Maggie,* to that same force, whenever he succeeded in harnessing it to his artistic instincts, is due most of its artistic strength as well. Crane's irony, moreover, is generally more subtle and successful when rendered in large deliberate patterns; when such patterns were also fused into symbol, for which Crane has a much surer instinct, the effects are truly brilliant.

d. Stephen Crane's "Maggie" and American Naturalism
By Donald Pizer

Stephen Crane's *Maggie: A Girl of the Streets* has often served as an example of naturalistic fiction in America. Crane's novel about a young girl's fall and death in the New York slums has many of the distinctive elements of naturalistic fiction, particularly a slum setting and the theme of the overpowering effect of environment. Crane himself appeared to supply a naturalistic gloss to the novel when he wrote to friends that *Maggie* was about the effect of environment on human lives. Yet the novel has characteristics which clash with its neat categorization as naturalistic fiction. For one thing, Crane's technique of an intense verbal irony is foreign to the naturalistic vision; for another, Maggie herself, though she becomes a prostitute, is strangely untouched by her physical environment. She functions as an almost expressionistic symbol of inner purity uncorrupted by external foulness. There is nothing, of course, to prevent a naturalist from using verbal irony and expressionistic symbolism, just as there is nothing to prevent him from introducing a deterministic theme into a Jamesian setting. But in practice the naturalist is usually direct. He is concerned with revealing the blunt edge of the powerful forces which condition our lives, and his fictional technique is usually correspondingly blunt and massive. When Zola in *L'Assommoir* and *Nana* wished to show the fall into prostitution of a child of the slums, his theme emerged clearly and ponderously from his full description of the inner as well as outer corruption of Nana and from his "realistic" symbolism. Crane's method, on the other hand, is that of obliqueness and indirection. Irony and expressionistic symbolism ask the reader to look beyond literal meaning, to seek beyond the immediately discernible for the underlying reality. Both are striking techniques which by their compelling tone and their distortion of the expected attempt to shock us into recognition that a conventional belief or an obvious "truth" may be false and harmful. Perhaps, then, *Maggie* can best be discussed by assuming from the first that Crane's fictional techniques imply that the theme of the

Reprinted from: *Criticism, A Quarterly for Literature and the Arts,* VII (Spring 1965), 168-175. By permission of Wayne State University Press, copyright © 1965, and the author.

novel is somewhat more complex than the truism that young girls
in the slums are more apt to go bad than young girls elsewhere.[1]

The opening sentence of *Maggie* is "A very little boy stood upon
a heap of gravel for the honor of Rum Alley." [2] The sentence introduces both Crane's theme and his ironic technique. By juxtaposing
the value of honor and the reality of a very little boy, a heap of
gravel, and Rum Alley, Crane suggests that the idea of honor is
inappropriate to the reality, that it serves to disguise from the
participants in the fight that they are engaged in a vicious and petty
scuffle. Crane's irony emerges out of the difference between a value
which one imposes on experience and the nature of experience itself.
His ironic method is to project into the scene the values of its
participants in order to underline the difference between their values
and reality. So the scene has a basic chivalric cast. The very little boy
is a knight fighting on his citadel of gravel for the honor of his
chivalrous pledge to Rum Alley. Crane's opening sentence sets the
theme for *Maggie* because the novel is essentially about man's use of
conventional but inapplicable abstract values (such as justice, honor,
duty, love, and respectability) as weapons or disguises. The novel is
not so much about the slums as a physical reality as about what
people believe in the slums and how their beliefs are both false to
their experience and yet function as operative forces in their lives.

Let me explore this idea by examining first the lives of the novel's
principal characters and then the moral values which control their
thinking about their lives. Crane uses two basic images to depict the
Bowery. It is a battlefield and it is a prison. These images appear
clearly in the novel's first three chapters, which describe an evening
and night in the life of the Johnson family during Maggie's childhood.
The life of the family is that of fierce battle with those around them
and among themselves. The novel opens with Jimmie fighting the
children of Devil's Row. He then fights one of his own gang. His
father separates them with a blow. Maggie mistreats the babe
Tommie; Jimmie strikes Maggie; Mrs. Johnson beats Jimmie for
fighting. Mr. and Mrs. Johnson quarrel. Mrs. Johnson beats Maggie
for breaking a plate; Mr. Johnson strikes Jimmie with an empty beer
pail. Mr. Johnson comes home drunk and he and Mrs. Johnson fight—
all this in three rather short chapters. Crane's fundamental point in
these chapters is that the home is not a sanctuary from the struggle
and turmoil of the world but is rather where warfare is even more
intense and where the animal qualities encouraged by a life of
battle—strength, fear, and cunning—predominate. The slum and the

home are not only battlefields, however, but are also enclosed arenas. Maggie's tenement is in a "dark region," and her apartment, "up dark stairways and along cold, gloomy halls" (p. 6), is like a cave. Crane's description of the Johnson children eating combines both the warfare and cave images into one central metaphor of primitive competition for food.

> The babe sat with his feet dangling high from a precarious infant's chair and gorged his small stomach. Jimmie forced, with feverish rapidity, the grease-enveloped pieces between his wounded lips. Maggie, with side glances of fear of interruption, ate like a small pursued tigress (p. 8).

By means of this double pattern of imagery, Crane suggests that the Johnsons' world is one of fear, fury, and darkness, that it is a world in which no moral laws are applicable, since the Johnsons' fundamental guide to conduct is an instinctive amorality, a need to feed and to protect themselves.

Once introduced, this image of the Bowery as an amoral, animal world is maintained throughout *Maggie*. Mr. Johnson dies, Jimmie assumes his position, and the Johnsons' family warfare continues as before. Maggie and Jimmie go to work, and each finds that struggle and enclosure mark his adult world. Jimmie becomes a belligerent truck driver, imprisoned by his ignorance and his distrust. He respects only strength in the form of the red fire engine which has the power to crush his wagon. Maggie works in a prison-like sweat shop where she is chided into resentment by her grasping employer. Theirs are lives of animal struggle and of spiritual bleakness in which they only faintly realize their own deprivation. Maggie sits with the other girls in her factory workroom in a vague state of "yellow discontent," and Jimmie, the brawling teamster, "nevertheless ..., on a certain starlit evening, said wonderingly and quite reverently, "Deh moon looks like hell, don't it?'" (p. 17).

The moral values held by the Johnsons are drawn almost entirely from a middle class ethic which stresses the home as the center of virtue, and respectability as the primary moral goal. It is a value system oriented toward approval by others, toward an audience. In the opening chapter of the novel, Jimmie hits Maggie as Mr. Johnson is taking them home. Mr. Johnson cries, "'Leave yer sister alone *on the street'* " (p. 6; my italics). The Johnsons' moral vision is dominated by moral roles which they believe are expected of them. The roles bring social approbation, and they are also satisfying because the playing of them before an audience encourages a gratifying emotionalism or self-justification. The reaction to Maggie's fall is basically of this nature. She is cast out by her mother and brother for desecrating the Home, and her seducer, Pete, rejects her plea for aid because she threatens the respectability of the rough and tumble bar in which he works. The moral poses adopted by the Johnsons and by Pete have no relation to reality, however, since the home and the bar are parallel settings of warfare rather than of virtue.

The key to the morality of the Bowery is therefore its self-deceiving theatricality. Those expressing moral sentiments do so as though playing a role before a real or implied audience. Crane makes the dramatic nature of Bowery morality explicit in scenes set in dance halls and theatres. In a dance hall, an audience of Maggies, Jimmies, and Petes listens enraptured to a song "whose lines told of a mother's love, and a sweetheart who waited, and a young man who was lost at sea under harrowing circumstances" (p. 26). Later, Maggie and Pete see plays

> in which the dazzling heroine was rescued from the palatial home of her treacherous guardian by the hero with the beautiful sentiments.... Maggie lost herself in sympathy with the wanderers, swooning in snowstorms beneath happy-hued church windows, while a choir within sang "Joy to the World." To Maggie and the rest of the audience this was transcendental realism. Joy always within, and they, like the actor, inevitably without. Viewing it, they hugged themselves in ecstatic pity of their imagined or real condition (pp. 29-30).

The audience identifies itself with maligned and innocent virtue despite the inapplicability of these roles to their own lives. "Shady persons in the audience revolted from the pictured villainy of the drama. With untiring zeal they hissed vice and applauded virtue. Unmistakably bad men evinced an apparently sincere admiration for virtue" (p. 30).

This same ability to project oneself into a virtuous role is present in most of the novel's characters. Each crisis in the Johnson family is viewed by neighbors who comprise an audience which encourages the Johnsons to adopt moral poses. In the scene in which Maggie is cast out, both Jimmie and Mrs. Johnson are aware of their need to play the roles of outraged virtue in response to the expectation of their audience. Mrs. Johnson addresses the neighbors "like a glib showman," and with a "dramatic finger" points out to them her errant daughter (p. 56). The novel's final scene is a parody of Bowery melodrama. Mrs. Johnson mourns over the dead Maggie's baby shoes while the neighbors cry in sympathy and the "woman in black" urges her to forgive Maggie. In the midst of her exhortations, "The woman in black raised her face and paused. The inevitable sunlight came streaming in at the window" (p. 68). Crane in this scene connects the sentimental morality of melodrama and the sanctimoniousness of Bowery religion. Both the theatre and the mission purvey moral attitudes which have no relation to life but which rather satisfy emotional needs or social approval. The heroes and heroines of melodrama cannot be confronted with reality, but the church is occasionally challenged. When it is, as when the mission preacher is asked why he never says "we" instead of "you," or when Maggie seeks aid from the stout clergyman, its reaction is either non-identification with reality (" 'What?' " asks the preacher) or withdrawal from it (the clergyman sidesteps Maggie). It is as though the church, too, were a sentimental theatre which encouraged moral poses but which ignored the essential nature of itself and of its audience.

Both of these central characteristics of the Bowery—its core of animality and its shell of moral poses—come together strikingly in Mrs. Johnson. There is a bitter Swiftian irony in Crane's portrait of her. Her drunken rages symbolize the animal fury of a slum home, and her quickness to judge, condemn, and cast out Maggie symbolizes the self-righteousness of Bowery morality. In a sense she symbolizes the entire Bowery world, both its primitive amorality and its sentimental morality. It is appropriate, then, that it is she who literally drives Maggie into prostitution and eventual death. Secure in her moral role, she refuses to allow Maggie to return home after her seduction by Pete, driving her into remaining with Pete and then into prostitution. Maggie is thus destroyed not so much by the physical reality of slum life as by a middle class morality imposed on the slums by the missions and the melodrama, a morality which allows its users both to judge and to divorce themselves from responsibility from those they judge.

Crane's characterization of Maggie can now be examined. His

description of her as having "blossomed in a mud-puddle" with "none of the dirt of Rum Alley... in her veins" (p. 17) is not "realistic," since it is difficult to accept that the slums would have no effect on her character. Zola's portrait of Nana dying of a disfiguring disease which symbolizes her spiritual as well as physical corruption is more convincing. Crane's desire, however, was to stress that the vicious deterministic force in the slums was its morality, not its poor housing or inadequate diet, and it is this emphasis which controls his characterization of Maggie. His point is that Maggie comes through the mudpuddle of her physical environment untouched. It is only when her environment becomes a moral force that she is destroyed. Maggie as an expressionistic symbol of purity in a mud-puddle is Crane's means of enforcing his large irony that purity is destroyed not by concrete evils but by the very moral codes established to safeguard it.

But Maggie is a more complex figure than the above analysis suggests. For though her world does not affect her moral nature, it does contribute to her downfall by blurring her vision. Her primary drive in life is to escape her mud-puddle prison, and she is drawn to Pete because his strength and elegance offer a means of overcoming the brutality and ugliness of her home and work. Her mistaken conception of Pete results from her enclosed world, a world which has given her romantic illusions just as it has supplied others with moral poses. Her mistake warrants compassion, however, rather than damnation and destruction. She is never really immoral. Throughout her fall, from her seduction by Pete to her plunge into the East River, Crane never dispels the impression that her purity and innocence remain. Her weakness is compounded out of the facts that her amoral environment has failed to arm her with moral strength (she "would have been more firmly good had she better known how" [p. 49], while at the same time it has blinded her with self-destructive romantic illusions ("she wondered if the culture and refinement she had seen imitated... by the heroine on the stage, could be acquired by a girl who lived in a tenement house and worked in a shirt factory" [p. 31]).

There is considerable irony that in choosing Pete Maggie flees into the same world she wished to escape. Like Mrs. Johnson, Pete desires to maintain the respectability of his "home," the bar in which he works. Like her, he theatrically purifies himself of guilt and responsibility for Maggie's fall as he drunkenly sobs " 'I'm good f'ler, girls' " (p. 63) to an audience of prostitutes. And like Maggie herself, he is eventually a victim of sexual warfare. He is used and discarded by the "woman of brilliance and audacity" just as he had used and discarded Maggie. In short, Maggie can escape the immediate prison of her home and factory, but she cannot escape being enclosed by the combination of amoral warfare (now sexual) and moral poses which is the pervasive force in her world.

In his famous inscription to *Maggie,* Crane wrote that the novel "tries to show that environment is a tremendous thing in the world and frequently shapes lives regardless." But he went on to write that "if one proves that theory one makes room in Heaven for all sorts of souls (notably an occasional street girl) who are not confidently expected to be there by many excellent people." [3] The second part of the inscription contains an attack on the "many excellent people" who, like Maggie's mother, immediately equate a fallen girl with evil and hell. Crane is here not so much expressing a belief in heaven as using the idea of salvation and damnation as a rhetorical device to attack smug, self-righteous moralism. The entire novel bears this critical intent. Crane's focus in *Maggie* is less on the inherent evil of slum life than on the harm done by a false moral environment imposed on that life. His irony involving Mrs. Johnson, for example, centers on the religious and moral climate which has persuaded her to adopt the moral poses of outraged Motherhood and despoiled Home.

Maggie is thus a novel primarily about the falsity and destructiveness of certain moral codes. To be sure, these codes and their analogous romantic visions of experience are present in Maggie's environment, and are in part what Crane means when he wrote that environment shapes lives regardless. But Crane's ironic technique suggests that his primary goal was not to show the effects of environment but to distinguish between moral appearance and reality, to attack the sanctimonious self-deception and sentimental emotional gratification of moral poses. He was less concerned with dramatizing a deterministic philosophy than in assailing those who apply a middle class morality to victims of amoral, uncontrollable forces in man and society. *Maggie* is therefore very much like such early Dreiser novels as *Sister Carrie* and *Jennie Gerhardt,* though Dreiser depends less on irony and more on an explicit documentation and discussion of the discrepancy between an event and man's moral evaluation of an event. *Maggie* is also like *The Red Badge of Courage,* for the later novel seeks to demonstrate the falsity of a moral or romantic vision of the amorality which is war.

Crane, then, is a naturalistic writer in the sense that he believes that environment molds lives. But he is much more than this, for his primary concern is not a dispassionate, pessimistic tracing of inevitable forces but a satiric assault on weaknesses in social morality. He seems to be saying that though we may not control our destinies, we can at least destroy those systems of value which uncritically assume we can. If we do this, a Maggie (or a Jennie Gerhardt) will at least be saved from condemnation and destruction by an unjust code.

Writers who seek greater justice, who demand that men evaluate their experience with greater clarity and honesty, are not men who despair at the nature of things. They are rather critical realists. Like William Dean Howells, Crane wishes us to understand the inadequacies of our lives so that we may improve them. Although Crane stresses weaknesses in our moral vision rather than particular social abuses, there is more continuity between Howells' critical realism and Crane's naturalism than one might suspect. This continuity is not that of subject matter or even of conception of man and society. It is rather that of a belief in the social function of the novel in delineating the evils of social life. If one sees such a writer as Crane in this light, the often crude and out-dated determinism of early American naturalism lessens in importance. One begins to realize that American naturalism, like most vital literary movements, comprised a body of convention and assumption about the function and nature of literature which unprescriptively allowed the writer to mold this shared belief into a personally expressive work of art. Crane's fiction is therefore permanently absorbing and historically significant not because he was a determinist or fatalist writing about the slums or about the chaos of war. His fiction still excites because his ironic technique successfully involves us in the difference between moral appearance and reality in society. His fiction is historically important because his expression of this theme within the conventions of naturalistic fiction reveals the relationship between critical realism and naturalism. But his fiction is perhaps even more significant historically because he revealed the possibility of a uniquely personal style and vision within naturalistic conventions. Our writers have responded to the critical spirit and the fictional sensationalism and freedom of naturalism without a sense of being burdened by doctrinaire precepts and forms. And it is no doubt this invigorating freedom within continuity which has been one of the principal reasons for the strength and influence of the naturalistic movement in America, from Crane and Dreiser to our own times.

NOTES

1. The interpretation of *Maggie* which follows has been evolving in criticism of the novel for some years, though it has not been pursued as fully or pointedly as I do here. Both R. W. Stallman, in "Crane's *Maggie:* A Reassessment," *Modern Fiction Studies,* V (Autumn, 1959), 251-59, and Charles C. Walcutt, in *American Literary Naturalism, A Divided Stream* (Minneapolis, 1956), pp. 67-72, touch briefly on the theme of *Maggie* somewhat as I do. I have also been aided by Edwin H. Cady, *Stephen Crane* (New York, 1962), pp. 102-111; Joseph X. Brennan, "Ironic and Symbolic Structure in Crane's *Maggie,*" *Nineteenth-Century Fiction,* XVI (March, 1962), 303-315; and Janet Overmyer, "The Structure of Crane's *Maggie,*" *University of Kansas City Review,* XXIX (Autumn, 1962), 71-72.

2. Stephen Crane, *The Red Badge of Courage and Selected Prose and Poetry,* ed. William M. Gibson (Rinehart Editions: New York, 1956), p. 1. References will hereafter appear in the text.

3. *Stephen Crane: Letters,* ed. R. W. Stallman and Lillian Gilkes (New York, 1960), p. 14.

2.   *The Red Badge of Courage*

a. *Animal Imagery in* The Red Badge of Courage
By Mordecai and Erin Marcus

There is extensive use of animal imagery in Stephen Crane's *The Red Badge of Courage*.[1] This imagery largely takes the form of similes and metaphors. Excluding all of the numerous sunken metaphors which imply animal-like action, this short novel contains at least eighty figures of speech employing animals or their characteristics. These images occur in the narrative itself, in the dialogue, and in the thoughts of the central character. However unaware Crane may have been of the abundance and patterning of this imagery, the consistency with which it is used often furthers his characterization and presentation of ideas, and constitutes a significant method of communicating meaning.

The imagery employs domestic, wild, and imaginary animals, and also makes reference to undefined animal-like characteristics. References to domestic animals occur most frequently. With very few exceptions they are applied to people rather than to things, and they always refer to the enlisted men rather than to the officers. Wild animals, on the other hand, are used to describe things as well as individuals. Imaginary animals and vague animal comparisons tend to be used to describe groups of men.

The Red Badge of Courage is the story of Henry Fleming's initiation into manhood through a resolution of fear, and it is also a bitterly anti-romantic treatment of war—one which shows elements of naturalistic philosophy. Crane's use of animal imagery lends considerable support to the novel's themes and viewpoint. It is frequently used to describe the youth's feelings and actions as he passes through progressive stages of apprehension, terror, conquest of fear, and acceptance of the human situation. During the first thirteen chapters the animal imagery helps to portray his apprehensions about the enemy and his early behavior in battle. During this part of the novel the youth struggles with shame and terror. Feeling that he is

Reprinted from: *Modern Language Notes*, LXXIV (February 1959), 108-111. By permission of The Johns Hopkins Press, copyright © 1959, and the author.

inadequate to cope with the coming battle, he reflects that he and his comrades are all sure to be "killed like pigs." His shame about these feelings will not allow him to "warn" his comrades because he fears that a wrong declaration would "turn him into a worm." The youth's terror determines his perception of certain things. On the march at night he perceives the enemy campfires as "the red eyes . . . of a row of dragons," and with at least a suggestion that the point of view is Henry's, his own regiment and army are several times described as a row of monsters, dragons, and wild horses, and he and his comrades are identified with familiar animals such as terriers and chickens. In the thick of battle Henry becomes a "well-meaning cow," and there is in his eyes the look that can be seen in those of a "jaded horse."

The culmination of his terror comes when he observes a fellow soldier throw down his gun and run "like a rabbit," whereupon Henry's fear makes him like "the proverbial chicken" which runs wildly about in all directions in its efforts to escape from danger. Later in the story of his flight, after many harrowing experiences, Henry pauses to consider his situation, and he realizes that he has acted like a worm and "a craven loon." Nevertheless, he cannot leave the scene of battle because of a "certain mothlike quality" within him. His terror, and the animal imagery which accompanies it, contrast sharply with his romantic feelings about war shown in the opening of the novel, when he saw himself full of "eagle-eyed prowess."

After the youth has begun to overcome his fear of battle, his attitudes about himself and about war alter, and the animal imagery which describes him also changes. After he and his regiment have participated successfully in a battle, they are described by the lieutenant as having fought like "hell-roosters" and "wild cats." Henry plunges at the enemy flag like a "mad horse." He now sees his comrades in a different light. He notices their "vicious wolf-like temper." Wilson, his friend, springs "as a panther at prey." The novel consists of twenty-four chapters: in the first twenty-three Henry has changed from a worm and a chicken to a wild cat; in chapter twenty-four he realizes that he has been an animal all the time that he was fighting, and his new acceptance of his precarious lot as a man is shown by his realization that he is a man and not an animal. "He was a man. . . . He had been an animal blistered and sweating in the heat and pain of war."

Crane's conclusion does not clearly suggest that the youth comes to understand that fear made him act like a terrified animal and new-found pride and courage subsequently helped him to act like a fierce animal. Nevertheless, Crane's attitude toward war, as we see it throughout the novel, suggests that he is critical of both fear and aggression. This critical attitude, and Crane's criticism of war, are partially communicated by animal imagery. As we have noted, much of this imagery appears in the representation of Henry's feelings. Armies are often seen as monsters and serpents, and men at war are shown as the victims of strange and vicious forces which either make them timid and cowardly, or brave and reckless. In addition to these images, war is twice described as "the red animal—war." Although Crane's ironic treatment of Henry's cowardice suggests more approval for Henry's actions when he behaves with courage, Crane still communicates the idea that it is as bad to kill like a beast as it is to run like a rabbit. Thus Crane's animal imagery contributes to his moral judgment of war.

The animal imagery also contributes to Crane's naturalism. This, however, is somewhat complicated by his attitude as shown in a scene rather early in the novel in which Henry seeks to justify his cowardice by comparing his behavior to that of a squirrel who runs when a pine-cone is thrown at it. In the squirrel's flight Henry sees the law of Nature at work. Nevertheless, Crane's intention here seems to be at least partially satirical, which suggests that he is perhaps more critical of cowardice than he is of fierceness. In any case, Henry's assumption of manhood leads from an animal-like cowardice to an animal-like fierceness. Crane's inability to lead Henry to manhood by any means other than a release of contrasting animal-like forces in his soul may account for the charge of failure to convince which has often been made of Henry's assumption of manhood. Yet Crane's consistency may be defended by claiming that he has shown two similar but opposing forces which lead to the hero's realization that he is not an animal but a man. For Henry's manhood consists of a final courage which has stemmed from his earlier terror and wild courage. Nevertheless, Crane does not clearly show that his hero understands the ordeal he has experienced, and the fact that he has passed out of the realm where natural forces rule into a realm where will-power functions. Thus Crane is trapped in the dilemma of the determinist who wishes to assert the existence of will-power, but sees change only as the result of natural forces.

Crane's naturalistic tendency is perhaps most clearly visible in references to the soldiers as sheep. The men are driven about and "nobody knows what it's done for." The officers are like "critical shepherds struggling with their sheep." The "sheep" are controlled by forces they cannot understand, just as—in the determinist's viewpoint —man's life is shaped by forces beyond his comprehension or control.

In addition to conveying certain ideas about man and war, Crane's animal imagery makes a considerable contribution to his impressionistic method of description. Many of the images we have cited add to the colorful and imaginative description which permeates the novel. Two particularly vivid and apt pieces of description employing animal images deserve special notice: "the bugles called to each other like brazen gamecocks," and "the blue smoke-swallowed line curled and writhed like a snake stepped upon."

We have cited only a rather small proportion of the numerous animal images in *The Red Badge of Courage*. More intensive examination of them would reveal additional vivid description, further support of leading ideas, and several ironic juxtapositions. Animal images and animal comparisons are used throughout the novel to convey changes in states of mind and the pattern of their development. Most important is Crane's use of them in presenting the theme of change from cowardice to wild courage, and finally from immaturity to manhood.

NOTES

1. The only other mention of this point is a brief notation by Professor William M. Gibson in his introduction to Stephen Crane, *The Red Badge of Courage and Selected Prose and Poetry* (New York, 1956), viii.

b. Crane's Henry Fleming: Speech and Vision
By Robert L. Hough

Two aspects of Stephen Crane's *The Red Badge of Courage,* previously unnoted, deserve attention because they reflect on Crane's concern for realistic speech and on his use of conversation and imagery to depict differing facets of Henry Fleming's character.

First, a close reading of the novel reveals that there are many discrepancies in Crane's treatment of dialect. This can best be shown by the handling of Henry's speech in the novel, as well as that of other characters. Though Crane achieves both irony and sympathy through Henry's conversation, his artistry should not blind one to the fact that Henry's speech is notably inconsistent. At times Crane has his hero speak a colloquial but generally correct English. Just before battle on the second day, Henry says:

> "Nobody seems to know where we go or why we go. We just get fired from pillar to post and get licked here and get licked there, and nobody knows what it's done for. It makes a man feel like a damn kitten in a bag. Now I'd like to know what the eternal thunders we was marched into these woods for anyhow, unless it was to give the rebs a regular pot shot at us." [1]

At other times the tone of Henry's conversation is different. The words are similar, but his speech is full of contractions and mispronunciations. It is more rural, more countrified. Henry tells Wilson, "Day-b'fore-yesterday . . . you would 'a' bet you'd lick the hull kit-an'-boodle all by yourself. . . . Yer changed a good bit. Yeh ain't at all like yeh was" (pp. 56-57). Later he and Wilson embarrassingly scoff at reported praise, "Huh!" "Yer lyin', Thompson" "Oh, go t' blazes!" "He never sed it" (p. 78).

In addition to this tonal difference, Crane is unheeding in specific words that Henry uses. The boy says both "yesterday" and "yestirday," "get" and "git," "just" and "jest," "whole" and "hull,"

Reprinted from: *Forum* [University of Houston], III (Winter 1962), 41-42. By permission of *Forum* and the author.

as well as " 'a' " and " 've" (for have), "t' " and "to," "an' " and "and," " 'im" and "him," and "th' " and "the." Two sets of word-sounds are almost interchangeable in Henry's vocabulary—" 'a" and "of" and "yeh" and "you." (This latter inconsistency extends to related words; Henry uses both "yer" and "you're" and "yerself" and "yourself.") During Jim Conklin's death agony, for example, Henry says:

> "Yes-yes-I tell yeh—I'll take care of yeh, Jim . . . Jim—Jim, what are you doing—what makes you do this way—you'll hurt yerself . . . Where yeh going, Jim? What you think-about? Where you going?" [2]

Furthermore, there does not seem to be any discernible pattern in Crane's inconsistencies. The two writings of "and" and "the" are interchanged without regard for the first letter of the next word. Henry says both "an' don't" and "and don't" and "th' reg'ment" and "the reg'ment." If Crane's changes had purpose, one might guess that Henry would speak more colloquially, more hurriedly during moments of tension and more correctly during moments of calm. But this is not the case; in fact Henry's variations appear side by side both in the battle scenes and in the respites. These inconsistencies seem to indicate that Crane, despite his interest in colloquial speech and his desire to write "the way men talk," did not have the same impassioned, sometimes obsessive concern for accuracy that other realists such as Twain, Harris, and Eggleston had.

Closely related to the problem of Henry's language is the variance between the conventionality of the boy's speech and the brilliance of his thoughts and impressions. Henry's words rarely rise above the commonplace and often they are banal. "By jiminy," "I swan," "sure as shooting," "mad as blazes," "skedaddle," "oh, shucks," "thunderation," "gosh-dern," "lunkheads"—such words as these characterize Henry's vocabulary. Seldom is his speech striking or original and several times in the novel he is inarticulate and unable to express his feelings.

The plasticity of the boy's mind, however, is another matter. Though Crane employs a flexible point of view and it is sometimes difficult to determine whether some thoughts should be credited to Henry or to Crane as narrator, some of the most vivid impressions in the story are explicitly given to Henry:

> Staring once at the red eyes across the river, he conceived them to be growing larger, as the orbs of a row of dragons advancing (p. 11).
>
> The youth turned quick eyes upon the field. He discerned forms begin to swell in masses out of a distant wood. . . . (the shells) came swirling again, and exploded in the grass or among the leaves of the trees. They looked to be strange war flowers bursting into fierce bloom (p. 27).
>
> He felt vaguely that death must make a first choice of the men who were nearest; the initial morsels for the dragons would be then those who were following him. . . . They (the shells) hurled over his head with long wild screams. As he listened he imagined them to have rows of cruel teeth grinning at him (p. 29).

In essence, what the reader finds in Henry is a kind of mute Milton. The boy has a spirited imagination, but one knows this only through the narration of his thoughts, never through his speech. Henry sees the battle and confusion around him in brilliant imagistic impressions of color, motion, and sound, but at no point does he speak of these. He only conceives them, he only *imagines* them.

What has happened is that Crane, consciously or unconsciously, has presented one facet of Henry's character—his typicality, his representation as the average country lad turned soldier—primarily through Henry's speech and another aspect—his atypicality, his representation as an extremely romantic and sensitive youth—through the boy's imagination.

The advantage of this technique is obvious; it represents an economical and efficient way of portraying necessary parts of Henry's character. But the fact that there is such a discrepancy between word and thought tends to detract from the unity of Henry's personality in that Henry's sensitivity implies an intelligence that his speech never manifests.

NOTES

1. Stephen Crane, *The Red Badge of Courage—Text and Criticism,* edited by Lettis, McDonnell, and Morris, (New York: Harcourt, Brace, and Company, 1960), 62. This text is that of the first American edition published in book form by Appleton and Company in 1895. Page references in parentheses are to this text.

2. *Ibid.*, 38, 39. John Berryman in his *Stephen Crane* attributes the discrepancies of dialect in the shortened and earlier newspaper version of the novel to the newspaper editors and their "normalizing Crane's dialect until they tired of the job midway" (page 95). But in the complete version published by Appleton, the discrepancies still appear, despite the fact that the proofs were taken from Crane's own manuscript and that he corrected the proofs himself. This leads one to suspect that some of the earlier errors were not those of the editors.

c. The Cyclical Structure of The Red Badge of Courage
By Thomas M. Lorch

The dominant structural principle which organizes the plot action in *The Red Badge of Courage* is the cycle. The cycles in the work include the alternations in Henry Fleming's thoughts and actions, chapters which repeat with variations the actions of previous chapters, the basic juxtaposition of the first and second days' battles, and the cycle inherent in the book's single action. Crane employs the cycle as a method of comparison and contrast which enables him to define the changes and developments in the novel and to dramatize their thematic significance. In this paper I wish to delineate certain of the more significant cycles and to discuss their contribution to our understanding of the novel.

I

Henry Fleming alternates between two states of mind. The first is self-centered; when in it, his pride and extreme consciousness of himself lead his thinking into rationalization and his imagination into exaggeration. In the second state Henry forgets himself and either acts instinctively (animal imagery is usually used to describe this type of action) or observes and interprets the action and his part in it accurately. Before the battle he is in the first state, and feels isolated and defeated. But one morning, "before he was entirely awake, he found himself running" (p. 40).[1] "He strenuously tried to think" (p. 40), but he cannot and does not like it. Nevertheless, as he approaches the battlefield, "the youth forgot many things as he felt a sudden impulse of curiosity" (p. 42). For a moment Henry forgets himself. But, he does not go directly into battle. Instead he encounters a dead man and "had opportunity to reflect. He had time in which to wonder about himself and to attempt to probe his sensations" (p. 44). His warped thoughts and twisted imaginings return; he fears that the woods will sprout rifles and concludes that the generals are "stupids" (p. 45).

This cycle immediately repeats itself. Self-importantly Henry de-

---

Reprinted from: *CLA Journal*, X (March 1967), 229-238. By permission of The College Language Association and the author.

cides, "He would die; he would go to some place where he would be understood" (p. 51). But gradually he is caught up in the happenings around him. Watching another regiment flee, he has an impulse to join them which testifies to the influence of the group on the individual. But out of curiosity, he stays: "The composite monster . . . had not then appeared. He resolved to get a view of it, and then, he thought he might very likely run" (p. 60). Yet when the battle begins, "He suddenly lost concern for himself, and forgot to look at a menacing fate" (p. 64). In this state he passes his first test. But he gradually regains his self-awareness, and as soon as he begins to think about himself his pride and illusions return. The second attack comes at this moment and his response while concerned with himself is the opposite of his previous reaction. He runs.

The cycle which Crane establishes reveals why Henry fails, and how he may succeed. He fails whenever he isolates himself, exaggerates his own importance, gives himself over to self-centered thought and imagination, and falls into romantic illusions. He succeeds when he forgets himself, becomes a part of the group, and sees things as they are. It is important to notice that success derives from curiosity as well as instinctive, animal behavior; the individual need not resign his humanity. Crane confirms this distinction on the second day by setting Henry apart as flag-bearer. He no longer fights but observes; he forgets himself and remains a part of the group, yet performs the uniquely human acts of observation and interpretation, and in this way retains his identity (pp. 244-245). Crane criticizes only selfish thought, imagination and isolation; instead he demands participation, brotherhood, humility, and honesty.

Henry's alternations do not end with his flight. In chapter VIII he emerges from the woods still in the strong grip of his rationalizations and imaginings, but gradually his curiosity returns. The war machine "fascinated him. He must go close to see it produce corpses" (p. 98). He is not now, as he had been in chapter III, deterred by dead bodies; instead his curiosity is more than satisfied by the sight of the wounded: "The torn bodies expressed the awful machinery in which the men had been entangled" (p. 101). But Crane shows by explicit contrasts between earlier and later chapters that Henry has made some progress. After some vacillation in chapter XI, he repudiates the main rationalization he had clung to in chapter VI, his belief that his army is being defeated, and to this extent returns "to the creed of soldiers" (p. 134). The advancing regiment in chapter XI directly contrasts the fleeing regiment in chapter IV, and just as the earlier flight of the regiment anticipated Henry's flight, the later regiment's advance foreshadows Henry's return. (In both cases the parallels also reinforce the close relationship between individual and group behavior.)

The manner of Henry's return continues the pattern of his alternations; in fact, it pointedly reverses the manner of his flight. The second attack had caught him contemplating himself, but in chapter XII a new flight reminiscent of both the earlier regiment's and his own (on several occasions Henry is forced to watch his own actions grotesquely repeated before him) draws him out of himself. "He forgot that he was engaged in combating the universe. He threw aside his mental pamphlets on the philosophy of the retreated" (p. 136). Crane calls to mind Henry's flight and his earlier state of mind by virtually repeating a paragraph in which he imagines the enemy as invincible dragons about to consume him (pp. 78, 137). But in chapter XII he acts according to "the creed of soldiers" to which he has just returned: he has "the impulse to make a rallying speech" (p. 137). Resisting the flight, he receives his wound, the badge of honor which balances his flight which he had just called "the sore badge of his dishonor" (p. 132). A struggle ensues as difficult and painful as his previous trials; but his previous problems were mental, they are now physical. He is identified with the wounded, Jim Conklin and the tattered man: he goes "tall soldier fashion" (p. 140) and, where quite recently in chapter X he had deserted the tattered soldier, in explicit contrast in chapter XII, the cheery soldier takes him in hand and leads him home.

Henry's cycle of involvement and withdrawal does not disappear after the first day. Awaiting the start of the next day's battle, his false sense of his own superiority and significance returns when he remembers Wilson's packet; he again reaches the conclusion that the generals are incompetent, and when challenged, he begins to withdraw into himself. We fear that the whole cycle will repeat itself. But it is largely laid aside during the second day; Henry is again immediately caught up in the battle, and in terms of the cycle, he remains involved and concerned otherwise than with himself until he leaves the field. Only in the last chapter does Crane suggest the return of the original pattern, in order to introduce an element of ambiguity into the conclusion. As he once again becomes aware of himself, we are reminded of what happened after his initial success. His mind undergoes a subtle change. It took moments for it to cast off its battleful ways and resume its accustomed course of thought. . . . at last he was enabled to more closely comprehend himself and circumstance. (p. 261)

Earlier "He felt that he was a fine fellow" (p. 74), now "He saw that he was good" (p. 263). Is Henry falling back into similar proud illusions? Will the cycle repeat itself? He has replaced his preoccupation with romantic ideals with a concern for his reputation among his fellows. He remembers the tattered soldier and sees "the brass and bombast of his earlier gospels" (p. 265). The ending seems encouraging; the sun shines. But the sun has shone ironically at the end of several earlier chapters. Henry's continuing youth, character and situation, Crane's suggestion of the cyclic movement once again, and the repeated recurrence of other cycles in the novel combine to make it unlikely that any change drastic enough to end Henry's alternations has occurred.

II

The manner in which the second day repeats and mirrors the first constitutes the most important cyclical structure in the novel. Each day's action contains the same basic pattern of preparation and entrance, confrontation and withdrawal, and return. But the general contrasts are as significant as the similarities. Henry's situation and state of mind are markedly different on the two days. During the first he was isolated and alone, during the second he is a member of the group; previously he withdrew from his friends and even betrayed them, later he forms close bonds, especially with Wilson and the lieutenant. Earlier his thoughts and imagination had run away with him, but during the second day he generally sees things as they are. Eric Solomon has observed that on the second day the regiment undergoes a sequence of experiences similar to those Henry passes through on the first day; [2] in this way Crane establishes a close analogy between Henry and the regiment, and further emphasizes the importance of the relationship between the individual and the group.

Yet it has not been recognized that Crane has worked out the parallels between the two days still more carefully and extensively. To begin with, certain chapters from the first day are remarkably similar to corresponding chapters from the second. The two which most closely resemble each other are V and XVII. In both Henry awaits the beginning of the day's battle, then is caught up, forgets himself, and succeeds. The language of each often echoes the other: he is frustrated by the impotence of his rifle, longs to perform abominable cruelties, and behaves like an animal (i.e. p. 66 vs. p. 190). There are, of course, variations, but Crane uses these to point up the differences between the two days. In chapter V Henry's battle rage and hatred develop during the battle, but in chapter XVII, having already adopted "the creed of soldiers," these emotions arise even before the battle. Even before the enemy attack on the second day he rages against their endurance and relentlessness, whereas similar reactions follow their first attack and help to cause his flight. Also, in chapter XVII he becomes aware of himself much as he did at the beginning of chapter VI, but where earlier he had fallen victim to false pride (pp. 74-75), he now recognizes that his success was unconscious (p. 195). The most obvious difference between the two chapters is that on the second day Henry is recognized as a hero by the regiment. But while the basic action, Henry's unconscious success, remains the same in both chapters, the differences in Henry's state of mind and his relation to the group account for the divergence of the results.

The close similarities in action and movement between chapters VI and XVIII enable Crane to introduce marked contrasts which provide further commentary on Henry's flight and state of mind in chapter VI. Both begin with a lull. But where Henry earlier fled to the rear under a new attack, now he and Wilson go to the rear in search of water (the contrast between his earlier isolation and later companionship, and between his earlier irresponsibility and later social responsibility, is also significant). In both chapters Henry comes upon a general and eavesdrops, and in each case the general fears his lines will break; but whereas in chapter VI the lines held, in direct criticism of Henry's rationalizations and cowardice, the general's pessimism about Henry's regiment in chapter XVIII has a sobering influence on the new hero. Henry's self-centered thoughts and fears are notable by their absence in the later chapter. Throughout chapter VI Henry fears he and the army will be swallowed, yet when another soldier concludes at the end of chapter XVIII that "We'll git swallowed," Henry acquiesces without protest. He now accepts the realities of war he had rejected earlier.

The chapters which follow VI and XVIII form larger units which also balance each other. The first we may call "the Flight";

its dominant symbol is the wound. The second we may call "the Charge"; its symbol, a collective as opposed to an individual emblem, is the flag. The direct correspondences here are largely contrasts, until the ends of the units. In chapter VII Henry retreats into the woods; in chapter XIX he charges (his appearance now resembles the way the charging enemy earlier appeared to him). In chapter VIII Henry starts to return, but then joins the wounded moving rearward; at the beginning of chapter XX the regiment's charge falters and it falls into disordered retreat, but then it recovers and wins a small triumph. Significantly, there is no parallel to the death of Jim Conklin, but Henry's betrayal of the tattered soldier is balanced by the failure of the charge; just as Henry returns to face his inner conflicts in chapter XI, the regiment charges again in chapter XXII; and Henry's return to his regiment parallels the regiment's triumphant completion of the charge.

The chapters during Henry's flight contain nightmarish repetitions of his earlier mistakes. Chapter VII, Henry's attempt to escape into the woods, is a mirror image of his attempts and failures to confront the monstrous war machine directly in chapters IV and VIII. Whereas in the latter he seeks out the monster, in chapter VII he tries to get as far from it and as close to what he thinks is its opposite, nature, as possible. But in both cases he finds the same thing: the wound, the corpse, the appalling products of the machine. We may also view Jim Conklin's mad flight into the woods in chapter IX as a macabre repetition of Henry's earlier attempt to escape in the same way; it too ends with the same result. Lastly, in running away from the tattered man, Henry repeats his earlier flight, although now more explicitly from another individual, from responsibility, and from himself.

Here again, the regiment's efforts to complete its charge, its movements backward and forward and its intermediate battles on the second day run parallel to Henry's movements on the first day, both physical and mental. Both Henry and the regiment hesitate and draw back, suffer from their reluctance, and finally meet their responsibilities.

The groups of chapters which constitute the preparations for each day's battles also form balanced units, but the parallels are looser and there is overlapping between the two days: the preparations for the second day actually begin when Henry receives his red badge. Again Crane uses the parallels for purposes of comparison and contrast. In both cases Henry passes through a dark night of struggle, but his first struggle is mental—he thinks in the darkness—whereas before the second day it is physical—he actually wanders lost in the dark. Wilson's behavior before the first and the second day is also contrasted; in chapter III he gives Henry the packet of letters for his family and in chapter XX he asks for its return. But in touching upon the relationship between Henry, Wilson, Jim Conklin and the lieutenant, we encounter a different cyclical rhythm, one not tied to the two day cycle.

III

These relationships develop in four stages. In the beginning, blustering braggart. At first, even Jim is somewhat contentious (that Henry is isolated, timid and withdrawn, while Wilson is a loud, is, like Wilson), but his true soundness and stability emerge when he talks quietly to Henry and during the marches. He is the first to point out the importance of being a member of the group, he answers Henry's criticism of the generals "with calm faith" (p. 48), and he quells Wilson's violent protests by telling him to shut up. "He accepted new environment and circumstance with great coolness" (p. 50). As a result, he emerges as a father or older brother figure, and both Henry and Wilson look to him for advice.

When Henry returns to the regiment, he finds that Wilson has assumed Jim Conklin's role. He had previously covered his fear with loud blustering, but he has become quiet, mature, and confident; where earlier he had started fights, he now stops them. Wilson also takes over the care and guidance of Henry; now he answers Henry's criticisms "with a voice of calm confidence" (p. 185). At the same time, Henry exhibits certain of Wilson's previous characteristics. His criticisms take on the braggadocio and excessive violence of Wilson's earlier complaints, and the lieutenant tells him to shut up as Conklin had previously told Wilson (p. 185).

The third and fourth stages are reached during the second day's battle. Gradually, after his success in the initial encounter, Henry rises to Wilson's and Conklin's level. Henry and Wilson listen to the general without concern for themselves as individuals, and they return to give the regiment accurate news of the coming attack, a task Jim Conklin tried and failed to perform at the beginning. As the battle is rejoined, Henry and Wilson pass beyond Jim Conklin and rise to the level of the lieutenant. Throughout the novel the lieutenant represents not only the virtues of discipline, dedication to duty, and concern for the group which Conklin possesses, but also the qualities of leadership, heroism, and personal identity. Henry and Wilson come to share in his qualities when they join the lieutenant in leading the men, lead the charge, and capture the flag. Through their interrelationships, these men help each other through the various crises (although Henry fails to help the dying Jim, he later has the opportunity to sooth Wilson and even to tell him to shut up). Thus Crane embodies his emphasis on the necessity of brotherhood in still another cyclical pattern.

IV

Finally, the novel as a whole consists of one single action which is cyclical in nature. In brief, Henry and his regiment enter, fight, and leave the battle. The novel begins with the news that the troops are going to march "up the river, cut across, an' come around in behint 'em" (p. 2), and somewhat later, they do so. In the last chapter, "the regiment received orders to retrace its way" (p. 260), and marches back in the direction of the river. In other ways as well, chapter XXIV balances chapter I. In the first chapter he enters his mental maze, and in the last he seems to emerge from it. Both contain a look backward and a look forward. In each he scrutinizes himself in a highly self-conscious manner, but where in the first he looks to the future only slightly reassured, in the last he feels completely confident about both the past and the future.

The action of the novel is complete. But, have the cycles which Crane set in motion come to an end? The last chapter contains numerous suggestions that they have not. On a broader scale the novel's action of entrance and withdrawal parallels Henry's advance and retreat on the first day and the regiment's on the second, yet both the latter return again. One soldier concludes, "We ain't licked, sonny. We're going down here aways, swing aroun', an' come in behint 'em" (p. 264), asserting his belief that the whole action will be repeated. There is still a war, and Henry is still in the army; it seems certain that he will participate in other battles.

But may not Henry himself have solved his personal problem of courage? The analogy which Crane establishes between Henry and the regiment leads us to question this also. We never learn who has won the battle; can we then be certain that Henry has won any permanent victory? The regiment seems to be returning to its original position; does Henry also? Of course, Henry has now been through the war experience, and to some extent at least, it appears that he has learned to accept the war machine and the warlike mechanistic universe.[3] But we have already observed that Crane incorporates into the conclusion a suggestion that Henry's romantic pride may be returning. Henry is young and ebullient and forgets easi.y. New illusions or new forms of old ones may well replace those seemingly dispelled. The novel ends, but its cyclical structure implies that the problems inherent in the individual's relations to war, to society, and to his own illusions, are endless.

NOTES

1. All page references are to the Modern Library Edition, *The Red Badge of Courage* (New York, 1951).
2. "The Structure of *The Red Badge of Courage*," MFS, V (Autumn, 1959), 224, 231-233.
3. Certain passages which appear in the last chapter of the Folio Society Edition (1951) based on the Clifton Waller Barrett manuscript, particularly one which begins, "He was emerged from his struggle with a large sympathy for the machinery of the universe," state this explicitly. But the issue is not a textual one. My reading of the novel's cyclical structure leads me to conclude that Henry's loss of heroic ideals and his compromised conception of self are temporary rather than deep-seated, fundamental changes.

d. Stephen Crane: The Red Badge of Courage
By John Berryman

The wars of men have inspired the production of some of man's chief works of art, but very undemocratically. Napoleon's wars inspired Goya, Stendhal, Beethoven, Tolstoy; a prolonged bicker of 1100 B.C. inspired the poet of the *Iliad,* who celebrated and deplored three centuries later a little piece of it near its end; the Wars of the Roses resulted in Shakespeare's giant effort, again long afterward; the Athenian empire's ruin was adequately dramatized by a participant, the greatest of historians; Picasso made something of the soul-destroying Civil War in his native country. But what came of Cromwell's war? Or of the atrocious conflict between North and South in the United States?

Thirty years after it ended came a small novel by a very young man, called *The Red Badge of Courage.* The immediate literature of the Civil War has been beautifully studied of late in Edmund Wilson's *Patriotic Gore,* but no one would claim for that literature any such eminence as belongs, after almost seventy years, to Stephen Crane's novel. A critic seems to be faced, then, with alternative temptations: to overrate it, as an American, because it chronicles our crucial struggle, or to underrate it, in the grand perspective of the artists just mentioned, because it appears to assert neither the authority of the experienced warrior nor the authority of the historical artist—Tolstoy having both, Thucydides both. Crane was no scholar and had seen no battle. Yet some authority should be allowed him, and identified, for his work has not only brilliantly survived but was recognized instantly abroad—in England—as authentic; professional military men were surprised to learn that he was not one.

It is hard to see how anyone, except a casual reader, could overrate *The Red Badge of Courage* for patriotic reasons, because, though the book does indeed handle parts of the battle of Chancellorsville, it is not really about the Civil War. For instance, it shows no interest in the causes, meaning, or outcome of the war; no interest in politics; no interest in tactics or strategy. In this book, these failures are a

Reprinted from: *The American Novel: From James Fenimore Cooper to William Faulkner,* ed. Wallace Stegner. New York and London: Basic Books, Inc., 1965, pp. 86-96. By permission of Basic Books Inc., copyright © 1965.

merit, in opposition to the supreme fault of *War and Peace,* which is philosophical and programmatic. Here we have only parts of one minor battle, seen from one ignorant point of view, that of a new volunteer. One would never guess that what has been called the first modern war was being studied. All the same, as from the weird diagrams of Samuel Beckett emerges the helpless horror of modern man, we learn, as we learn from few books, about the waiting, the incomprehension, rumor, frustration, anxiety, fatigue, panic, hatred not only of the enemy but of officers; about complaints of "bad luck" and the sense of betrayal by commanders. This is a losing army. Since every intelligent man has to be at some point afraid of proving himself a coward—which is what the ordeal of Crane's protagonist is about—the story presents itself to us initially as making some claim to universality. The claim is strengthened by Crane's reluctance to divulge the name of the hero (it is Henry Fleming) or the names of the only other two people who matter—the tall soldier (Jim) and the loud youth (Wilson)—or the identity of the regiment, or the geography. By *leaving things out* the author makes his general bid for our trust.

But of course he has put in things too, and our problems are where he got them and how he put them. The main things he put in are reflection and action. Much of the book really is battle. Crane had read *Sebastopol,* Tolstoy's short novel, and declared that he learned what war was like from football; after starring in baseball at the two colleges he briefly attended, he coached a boys' football team in New Jersey. One of the staff at his military academy, a major-general, had seen action at Chancellorsville and liked to talk about it. Crane had played war games as a child, and talked with veterans, and read (with disappointment and contempt) magazine articles on the Civil War. Later, after witnessing substantial parts of the Greco-Turkish War, he said, *"The Red Badge* is all right." I don't know that we can say precisely how he learned what he knew, except to recognize in him an acute visual imagination and an inspired instinct for what happens and what does not happen in conflict. Here is a short passage:

> He expected a battle scene.
> There were some little fields girted and squeezed by a
> forest. Spread over the grass and in among the tree trunks, he

could see knots and waving lines of skirmishers who were running hither and thither and firing at the landscape. A dark battle line lay upon a sunstruck clearing that gleamed orange colour. A flag fluttered.

Other regiments floundered up the bank.

Some of the features of Crane's *style* appear: his convulsive and also humorous irony ("expected," as if he would not see it but he saw it, and "firing at the landscape"), its violent animism ("squeezed"), its descriptive energy ("knots and waving lines"—like an abstract-expressionist painting). But a Tolstoyan sense also of futility and incomprehension is swiftly conveyed, and this is only partly a product of the style. He is inventing, he is experimenting. Crane himself goes in for this language—several times he speaks of "experiment" and says of the youth, "He tried to mathematically prove to himself that he would not run from a battle." In the action, then, the fantastic and the literal cooperate. The reflective aspects of the novel are another matter.

The scene of this extremely simple novel is laid in a single mind. It starts with soldiers speculating loudly about whether there is going to be a fight or not. Then "a youthful private" goes off to his hut: "He wished to be alone with some new thoughts that had lately come to him." This has the effect of understatement, putting so flatly the youth's debate with himself about his honor, but it is literal, besides introducing the theme of intense isolation that dominated Crane's work until a later story, his masterpiece, "The Open Boat," where human cooperation in face of the indifference of nature is the slowly arrived-at subject. In *Red Badge* his youth broods in private, having crawled into his dilemma, or hut, "through an intricate hole that served it as a door"—and the rest of the book provides a workout of the plight. On the first day he does well, and then runs away. A Union soldier clubs him in the panic retreat; Crane's ironic title refers to the "badge" of that wound; the youth is taken for a good soldier. He witnesses the death of his boyhood friend, the tall soldier, a true hero. Returned, by the kindness of a stranger, to his regiment, he is cared for as a combatant by the loud youth, toward whom he is also enabled to feel superior in that, scared earlier, Wilson entrusted him with letters to be sent in the event of his death and has now, shamefacedly, to ask for their return. Next day he fights like a hero or demon. Such is the story. Perhaps many readers take it as a novel of development, a sort of success story, and this view is encouraged by the climactic passage:

> He felt a quiet manhood, non-assertive but of sturdy and strong blood. . . . He had been to touch the great death, and found that, after all, it was but the great death. He was a man. . . .

It is possible to feel very uncomfortable with this way of looking at the book. For one thing, pervasive irony is directed toward the youth—his self-importance, his self-pity, his self-loving war rage. For another, we have only one final semiself-reproach for his cowardice and imposture:

> He saw that he was good. . . . Nevertheless, the ghost of his flight from the first engagement appeared to him and danced. There were small shoutings in his brain about these matters. For a moment he blushed, and the light of his soul flickered with shame.

I find it hard to believe that in this passage Crane is exonerating his hero without irony. Finally, we have very early in the book an indication of his pomposity (his mother's "I know how you are, Henry"), and there is pomposity in his final opinion of himself as a war demon. That would suggest a circular action, in the coward middle of which he appeared to reveal his real nature, or in fact did reveal it, by running. The irony embraces, then, all but the central failure.

It is easy to feel uncomfortable with this view, too—more particularly because the apparent wound of the first day is indeed a real wound, and its silent pretension is later justified. On the other hand, the irony never ends. I do not know what Crane intended. Probably he intended to have his cake and eat it too—irony to the end, but heroism too. Fair enough. How far did he fail?

Again I invoke, as praiseworthy, that which is not done. The youth is frantically afraid of being found out (he never is found out) but except in the passage just quoted he never suffers the remorse one would expect. Intimate as Crane is with his hero psychologically, still the view he takes of him is cold, unsentimental, remote. This certainly preserves him from any full failure (though there have been many reliable readers from the day the book was published to now who have not liked it, because they regarded it as artificial and sensational).

The coldness leads to a certain impersonality, and it is a striking fact that some of Crane's deepest private interests find no place in the novel; in fact, they are deliberately excluded. Three of them are worth singling out. In his earlier novel, or long story, called *Maggie,* laid in New York's Bowery, Crane dramatized a distinct social philosophy—environmentalist, deterministic, and convinced that "the root of slum-life" was "a sort of cowardice." Yet his indifference to society in *The Red Badge* is complete, and it would not do to say "Of course it would be," for an army *is* society.

So with the matter of personal philosophy. We happen to know Crane's views perfectly, because he put them at length in letters to a girl (Nellie Crouse) by whom he was fascinated in 1895-96. He wrote:

> For my own part, I am minded to die in my thirty-fifth year [he died at 28, in 1900]. I think that is all I care to stand. I don't like to make wise remarks on the aspects of life but I will say that it doesn't strike me as particularly worth the trouble. The final wall of the wise man's thought however is Human Kindness of course.

Exceptionally for him, Crane capitalized the two words. Now it might have been supposed that, bringing his hero through to maturity in *The Red Badge,* he would have concentrated in this area. But no. It seems impossible not to conclude that the splendid burst of rhetoric with which the novel concludes is just that, *in part*—a burst of rhetoric—and that Crane retained many of his reservations about his hero. As the wisest of modern British novelists, E. M. Forster, once observed, novels almost never end well: character desires to keep on going, whereas remorseless plot requires it to end. I hardly remember a better instance. Yet the last page is confidently and brilliantly done:

It rained. The procession of weary soldiers became a bedraggled train, despondent and muttering, marching with churning effort in a trough of liquid brown mud under a low, wretched sky. Yet the youth smiled, for he saw that the world was a world for him, though many discovered it to be made of oaths and walking-sticks. He had rid himself of the red sickness of battle.

But *then* comes a sentence in which I simply do not believe. "He turned now with a lover's thirst to images of tranquil skies, fresh meadows, cool brooks—an existence of soft and eternal peace." In short we are left after all with a *fool,* for Crane knew as well as the next man, and much better, that life consists of very little but struggle. He wrote to Miss Crouse of

> ... a life of labor and sorrow. I do not confront it blithely. I confront it with desperate resolution. There is not even much hope in my attitude. [Perhaps I should mention that at this time Stephen Crane was an international celebrity.] I do not even expect to do good. But I expect to make a sincere, desperate, lonely battle to remain true to my conception of my life and the way it should be lived.... It is not a fine prospect.

The shutting out of his hero from his personal thought redeems for me, on the whole, the end of the book.

The absence of interest in religion in *The Red Badge of Courage* is even more surprising than the other indifferences, whether seen in a critical way or in a biographical way. Henry Fleming, orphan of a farm widow, was seminary-trained. What emerges from the training is scanty indeed. "He would die; he would go to some place where he would be understood. It was useless to expect appreciation of his profound and fine senses from such men as the lieutenant." This is a fine and funny passage, not deeply Christian. Then there is the famous passage about the wafer, long quoted as a war cry for modernism in American fictional art. Unutterably wounded, upright, the tall soldier has sought a private ground away from the retreat, in a field mysteriously chosen, followed by the youth and a tattered soldier, for his dance of death:

As the flap of the blue jacket fell away from the body, he could see that the side looked as if it had been chewed by wolves.

The youth turned, with sudden, livid rage, toward the battle-field. He shook his fist. He seemed about to deliver a philippic.

"Hell—"

The red sun was pasted in the sky life a wafer.

Pasting is a failingly temporary operation (for the pagan god of the sky?) handed us here as an overpowering rebuke to the youth's rebellion. A wafer is thick nourishment, too, is it not? Disdain and fury against the prerogatives of majesty seem to be the subject. Even here it is hard to decide just how far Crane is sympathetic with the youth and how far critical of him. Revolt, in a seminary youth, should have been better prepared: one would welcome a *trace* of his Christian history, pro or con; that Crane never provides. Shortly afterward we hear:

He searched about in his mind for an adequate malediction for the inadequate cause, the thing upon which men turn the words of final blame. It—whatever it was—was responsible for him, he said. There lay the fault.

Crane did not here believe in evil. Henry Fleming is not evil, nor is anyone. A strange setup for an ambitious novel. Determinism is in control: "It . . . was responsible for him." Or is it? For the next little words are *"he said"*—which may be a repudiation. Again we are in the seesaw, which is not a bad place to be, so long as one trusts the writer.

Crane's religious history can be treated briefly. He could not help being the son of a clergyman and of a madly missionary woman. He told an interviewer:

That cooled off and when I was thirteen or about that, my brother Will told me not to believe in Hell after my uncle had been boring me about the lake of fire and the rest of the sideshows.

Another time he said:

> I cannot be shown that God bends upon us any definable stare,
> and his laughter would be bully to hear out in nothingness.

I think we may conclude that neither this personal opinion nor
the fierce scorn of Christianity that flashes in many of Crane's brilliant
poems really has anything to do with the purely naturalistic framework—from this point of view—of *The Red Badge of Courage.*

With the word "naturalistic," however, we turn to some consideration of the artistic affiliations of the novel. All the categorical
terms that have been applied to Crane's art are slippery, but let me
deny at once that he was a naturalist. The naturalists—Frank Norris,
say, and Theodore Dreiser—are accumulative and ponderous. Crane's
intense selectivity makes him almost utterly unlike them. Crane
himself, when hardly more than a boy, allied his creed to the realism
preached—in revolt against the slack, contrived, squeamish standards
of popular American fiction in the nineties—by his first admirers,
William Dean Howells, then the country's leading critic, and a
younger writer, Hamlin Garland. But Crane's work does not resemble
theirs, either, and he seems to have meant, in his alliance, only that
art should be "sincere" (one of his favorite words) and truthful. Like
many another young genius, he regarded most writers as frauds and
liars, and in fact perhaps most writers *are* frauds and liars. But epithets
so vague as "sincere" and "truthful" tell us very little. The best term
is undoubtedly that of his close friend, the far greater novelist, Joseph
Conrad (though whether a *better* writer it is probably too soon to
say), who observed in a letter to a mutual friend that "He is *the*
only impressionist, and *only* an impressionist."

If we can accept this charcteristically exaggerated but authoritative judgment, we are in a position to make some reservations.
Conrad and Crane, when they met in England in 1897, immediately
recognized an affinity for one another; Conrad was soon charged by
reviewers with imitating Crane (a charge he denied, to Crane). In
truth, parts of *Lord Jim* are much indebted to *The Red Badge;* yet
Conrad clearly did not regard himself as an impressionist. Next,
there exist in Crane's work obviously realistic and fantastic elements
(as in Conrad's and in that of their friend, Henry James, also

domiciled in the south of England at this time), two Americans and a Pole re-creating English fiction, which was languishing, so far as form was concerned, in the powerful hands of Thomas Hardy and Rudyard Kipling. The power of experiment came from abroad, as later from Joyce and Hemingway and Kafka, and in poetry from T. S. Eliot and Ezra Pound.

Finally, the use of irony enters so deeply into most of Crane's finest work (all five latter authors are ironists) that the simple term "impressionist" will hardly do, and my uncertain feeling is that Crane is best thought of as a twentieth-century author. Authorities date modern American literature, some from *The Red Badge* in 1895, some from the re-issue in the following year of *Maggie*. This critique is not the place for an exposition of the nature of irony in relation to Crane, but perhaps something of that will emerge from a summary study of his style. By way, though, of winding up the impressionist reservations, let me reinforce Conrad's label with a quotation from Crane:

> I understand that a man is born into the world with his own pair of eyes and he is not at all responsible for his vision—he is merely responsible for his quality of personal honesty. To keep close to this personal honesty is my supreme ambition.

Ill, dying indeed, hard-pressed with guests and fame and need for money, working incessantly, he said to a journalist visitor during his last year of life: "I get a little tired of saying, 'Is this true?'" He was an impressionist: he dealt in the way things strike one, but also in the way things are.

This famous style is not easy to describe, combining as it does characteristics commonly antithetical. It is swift, no style in English more so improvisatorial, manly as Hazlitt; but at the same time it goes in for ritual solemnity and can be highly poetic. For example, as an illustration of the speed of his style:

> For a moment he felt in the face of his great trial like a babe, and the flesh over his heart seemed very thin. He seized time to look about him calculatingly.

Here we are already into something like the poetic tone which
is well illustrated in the opening sentence of the novel: "The cold
passed reluctantly from the earth, and the retiring fogs revealed an
army stretched out on the hills, resting." This is a high case of the
animism already referred to. The color of the style is celebrated;
maybe he got it from a theory of Goethe's, but the style is also plain,
plain. Short as it is, it is also unusually iterative; modern and simple,
brazen with medieval imagery; animistic, dehuman, and mechanistic;
attentive—brilliantly—to sound:

> As he ran, he became aware that the forest had stopped its
> music, as if at last becoming capable of hearing the foreign
> sounds. The trees hushed and stood motionless. Everything
> seemed to be listening to the crackle and clatter and ear-shaking
> thunder. The chorus pealed over the still earth.

Adverbs are used like verbs, word order deformed: somebody leans
on a bar and hears other men "terribly discuss a question that
was not plain." But the surest attribute of this style is its reserve, as
its most celebrated is its color. Crane guarantees nothing. "Doubtless"
is a favorite word. The technique of refusal is brought so far forward
that a casual "often" will defeat itself: "What hats and caps were left
to them they often slung high in the air." Once more we hear a
Shakespearean contempt, as in *Coriolanus*. In a paradoxical way, if
he will not vouch for what he tells us, if he does not push us, trying
to convince, we feel that he must have things up his sleeve which
would persuade us if we only knew them. As for color: "A crimson
roar came from the distance" is the mildest example I have been
able to find. His employment of it here is not only not naturalistic
(what roar was ever red?) but is solely affective, that is, emotional,
like his metaphorical use, in the novel, of devils, ghouls, demons, and
specters. Crane made use of a spectrum. A final item is his rueful
humor: "He threw aside his mental pamphlets on the philosophy of
the retreated and rules for the guidance of the damned."

On that note we might end, except for a poem written by
Stephen Crane several years after the novel, called "War Is Kind";
it is one of his major poems, and one of the best poems of the period.
In the novel there is little of the pathos of which he had already
shown himself a master in *Maggie,* and little of the horror informing

his best later war stories. These qualities come to life in the poem.

Crane makes a sort of little bridge between Tolstoy—supreme—supreme?—and our very good writer Hemingway. But these superior gentlemen are not competitors. One of the most cogent remarks ever made about the poet of the *Iliad* is that he shared with Tolstoy and with Shakespeare both a virile love of war and a virile horror of it. So in his degree did Crane, and before he had seen it.

3. *George's Mother*

a. The Imagery and Art of George's Mother
By Joseph X. Brennan

Although there has been a considerable revival of interest, during the last ten years, in the art of Stephen Crane, thus far very few of his several important works have been studied with real care. It would seem to have been generally concluded, in fact, that apart from *The Red Badge of Courage, The Open Boat,* and possibly one or two other stories, very little else of his work deserves the critic's close attention. But inasmuch as Crane was a highly skilled and conscious artist with a restless genius for innovation, it might be assumed more rightly that no adequate appraisal can be made of his contribution to our literature until the whole range of his serious fiction has been studied more searchingly. Especially neglected in the contemporary reassessment of Crane has been the quiet but trenchant short novel, *George's Mother,* which together with *Maggie* and *The Monster* has every claim to being numbered among his literary achievements. Since the time of its first appearance in 1896, however, *George's Mother* has received almost no critical consideration at all, although it is eminently more satisfactory in its realism, more convincing in characterization, and less bizarre in style than *Maggie,* the more popular of these companion studies of life in the Bowery. The depiction of the relationship between George and his mother is not only decidedly superior in its elaboration and psychology to that between Maggie and her mother, but is also Crane's most significant exploration of the relationship between parents and children. On every account, indeed, *George's Mother* deserves to be rescued from critical neglect; for like all of Crane's best fiction, this work too can give us a valuable insight into his remarkable ingenuity as an artist.

George's Mother is rather unusual among Crane's longer works of fiction insofar as it is structured upon an evolving pattern of imagery that is at once coherent and all-pervasive. This is the imagery, in brief, of an intense struggle between disparate "religions" or

Reprinted from: *CLA Journal,* IV (December 1960), 106-115. By permission of The College Language Association and the author.

"creeds," generally depicted with the language of medieval romance. Respecting this imagistic structure, it is interesting to note that Crane had earlier thought of entitling this narrative *A Woman without Weapons*. Though the present title may be rather non-committal in comparison, by its juxtaposition of both characters it at least indicates more nearly the central conflict between mother and son.

It is entirely fitting, therefore, that the imagery of conflict should characterize the whole of this brief and pathetic struggle between mother and son. And since mother and son are representative also of larger opposed forces—the Church versus the city of Mammon, the old morality and conformity versus modern license and amorality—the religious coloration of this imagery is appropriate as well. What is most interesting, however, is the manner in which the specific formulation of this basic image is modulated, from beginning to end, to the prevailing psychological outlook of the characters: as the plot moves from a conflict of romantic illusions to one of savage realities, as the mother and her fond dreams decline and a bitterly disillusioned George takes the ascendency, the language shifts perceptibly from that derived in general from medieval romance to that descriptive of the jungle. Thus this shift in language both coincides with and connotationally underlines the moral degeneration of George, the deterioration of the mother-son relationship, and the subsequent defeat of the mother. Let us now consider in more detail how Crane has rendered his thematic intentions through this pattern of imagery.

At the beginning of the novel, when matters stand at their best between George Kelcey and his mother and while they both harbor extravagant romantic dreams concerning his destiny, George enters upon a street scene blazing with color and readily suggestive, in the second paragraph, of a medieval setting and crusade:

> The lights made shadows, in which the buildings loomed with a new and tremendous massiveness, like castles and fortresses. There were endless processions of people, mighty hosts, with umbrellas waving, bannerlike, over them.... Upon the corners, standing in from the dripping eaves, were many loungers, descended from the world that used to prostrate itself before pageantry.

Although the narrator's point of view is omniscient and detached throughout, the objective scene has been subtly adjusted here to the visionary world of this young man with "a self-reliant poise."

The first view we receive of the mother, on the other hand, shows her "trudging on a journey," wielding her household utensils "like weapons." Then begins the battle of her romantic idealism against the physical world that will eventually victimize her son and through him herself as well:

> There was the flurry of a battle in this room. Through the clouded dust or steam one could see the thin figure dealing mighty blows. Always her way seemed beset. Her broom was continually poised, lance-wise, at dust demons. There came clashings and clangings as she strove with her tireless foes.
>
> It was a picture of indomitable courage. And as she went on her way her voice was often raised in a long cry, a strange war-chant, a shout of battle and defiance, that rose and fell in harsh screams. . . .
>
> . . . Still it could be seen that she even then was planning skirmishes, charges, campaigns. She gazed thoughtfully about the room and noted the strength and position of her enemies.

This parody of medieval romance literature, however, is frequently interrupted by the harsh fact of present reality in the form of a "swaggering nickle-plated clock." When this gives her pause to look out at the real world below, where a drunk and a youth are engaged in a "furious altercation . . . like animals in a jungle," she momentarily regards a distant brewery which both dominates the skyline like some medieval cathedral and looms in her life like some ominous bird of prey:

> In the distance an enormous brewery towered over the other buildings. Great gilt letters advertised a brand of beer. Thick smoke came from the funnels and spread near it like vast and powerful wings. The structure seemed a great bird, flying. The letters of the sign made a chain of gold hanging from its neck. The little old woman looked at the brewery. It vaguely interested her, for a moment, as a stupendous affair, a machine of mighty strength.

At that very moment, unknown to her, George is standing at a bar with his friend Jones, the man who first introduces him to drink and drunkenness. Though vaguely disquieted by this scene, the mother nevertheless returns to her chivalric exploits: "In a moment the battle was again in full swing. . . . The little intent warrior never hesitated nor faltered. She fought with a strong and relentless will." In this scene of parody, even the chromos and cigarette pictures stuck on the wall take on the appearance of "trophies." As the battle continues, the little old lady "hurled herself fiercely at the stove that lurked in the gloom, red-eyed, like a dragon. It hissed, and there was renewed clangour of blows."

This image of the dragon deserves further attention here, because together with its reappearance in chapters 5 and 12 it seems to be related to both the classical myth of Perseus and the medieval myth, especially, of St. George and the dragon. By an ironical inversion, however, it is a helpless old female now who comes to the aid of the hero in distress:

> Her mind created many wondrous influences that were swooping like green dragons at him. They were changing him to a morose man who suffered silently. She longed to discover them, that she might go bravely to the rescue of her heroic son. She knew that he, generous in his pain, would keep it from her.

The specific religious nature of this struggle is underscored by the pious refrain which the old woman sings while at work in chapter 2, but it is not until chapter 3 that this fact becomes explicit. There the mother tries unsuccessfully to persuade George to accompany her to a prayer meeting, but upon his stubborn refusal she sets out alone, looking "martyr-like." George, on the other hand, goes out to join a barroom congregation, which has its own ritual, as we shall see shortly, one of orgiastic self-indulgence. Though he cannot enter into his mother's mystic dreams, George nevertheless needs some belief, some ideology, to which he can swear fervent allegiance and from which he can derive some solace to his ego. His various "religions," however, are all fiercely at odds with his mother's evangelical Christianity.

In chapters 6 and 7 Crane reveals and juxtaposes the several romantic illusions of mother and son respecting his presumed destiny.

The language of romance, naturally, continues to set the tone. The mother, for example, "rejoiced at qualities in him that indicated that he was going to become a white and looming king among men." For himself, however, George has conceived two rather distinct dream-worlds: the one distant and romantic and vaguely idealistic; the other immediate and mundane, torrid with desire and the experience of sin. In his romantic dream-world, where he owns "castle-like houses, wide lands, servants, horses, clothes," he envisions himself as the "sublime king of a vague woman's heart." But after having read some books—sentimental romances, evidently—George fashions this dream woman into the major tenet of his faith in life:

> He was told in them that there was a goddess in the world whose business it was to wait until he should exchange a glance with her. It became a creed, subtly powerful. . . .
>
> Often he saw the pathos of her long wait, but his faith did not falter. The world was obliged to turn gold in time. His life was to be fine and heroic, else he would not have been born. . . . Occasionally he wondered how fate was going to begin making an enormous figure of him; but he had no doubt of the result. A chariot of pink clouds was coming for him. His faith was his reason for existence. Meanwhile he could dream of the indefinite woman and the fragrance of roses that came from her hair.

One day when George encounters Maggie Johnson on the stairway carrying a pail of beer, all his romantic dreams are suddenly and rather amusingly toppled. Unlike the "dream-girl" who would endure his calculated indifference like some patient, grateful Griselda, Maggie gives him a glance "so indifferent and so unresponsive to the sudden vivid admiration in his own eyes that he immediately concluded that she was magnificent. . . ." George hastily reconstructs his dreams with Maggie as the idol of his "new religion," but lacking the courage to speak to her, he can only hope that "she would soon discover his noble character." He is nevertheless apprehensive of the "looming princes who would aim to seize her," and when one of them does appear on the scene (presumably Pete, the dandified bartender in *Maggie*), George immediately despairs and vows vengeance upon the universe. From this moment of naive disillusionment begins his long and wilful plunge into debauchery.

George's vengeance begins on the evening of Bleecker's lavish party, which Crane depicts as some orgiastic religious rite or pagan bacchanal. The beer keg, for example, is described as a kind of pagan idol, the graven image of George's newest "creed":

> ... upon a sidewall the keg of beer created a portentous black figure that reared toward the ceiling, hovering over the room and its inmates with spectral stature.

As the keg is tilted more and more, its black shadow on the wall appears to "retreat and advance, sinking mystically to loom forward again with sudden menace, a high dark figure controlled as by some unknown emotion." Caught up in the "valour, barbaric and wild" of the party, George Kelcey is "all at once an enthusiast, as if he were at a festival of a religion." Subsequently "the laughter arose like incense," the men "drank reverently," and old Bleecker, the host, "sat like a fat jolly god." This bacchanalian enthusiasm is also short-lived, however, for when Kelcey awakens from drunken oblivion in Bleecker's apartment the next morning, he sees his host in the harsh daylight as a "tottering old beast."

Temporarily disillusioned with drink and his drinking companions, George spends the next few evenings virtuously at home. Caught between his discouragement with reality and the disappointment of his hopes to escape it, George finally succumbs in chapter 11 to his mother's entreaties and accompanies her to church. In a sense this is the climactic moment in the struggle for George's soul—the struggle between a traditional, dark, and uncompromising Christian fundamentalism, and an alluring, accommodating, modern paganism. The inevitable failure of the Church to convert George to its teachings is clearly prefigured in the description of the chapel physically besieged on every side by the dynamic, aggressive materialism of the city:

> In a dark street the little chapel sat humbly between two towering apartment-houses. A red street-lamp stood in front. It threw a marvellous reflection upon the wet pavements. It was

like the death-stain of a spirit. Farther up, the brilliant light of an avenue made a span of gold across the black street. A roar of wheels and a clangour of bells came from this point, interwoven into a sound emblematic of the life of the city. It seemed an approaching barbaric invasion. The little church, pierced, would die with a fine illimitable scorn for its slayers.

However intimidated and humbled by the awesomeness of the place, the experience is ultimately a negative one for George, and serves only "to prove to him again that he was damned."

From this point onward George's moral decline is precipitately accelerated. Far from being disposed any longer to work for his own or his mother's romantic ideal—to fight the dragon of evil like his saintly namesake—he becomes fascinated now with the dragon itself: "Drink and its surroundings were the eyes of a superb green dragon to him. He followed a fascinating glitter and the glitter required no explanation." The next time his mother asks him to accompany her to the church-meeting, accordingly, George repudiates her violently and sets out to pledge himself instead to a barroom brotherhood, the order of the "green dragon."

Before long, however, George parts company with this fraternal group—which at least has some pretension to civility and status—to espouse the unabashed cynicism and depravity of a street gang, contemptuously in rebellion against all authority, traditions and decency. Now that all his romantic dreams and ideals have been shattered, the conflict between George and his mother is no longer a struggle between opposed "religions" but a death struggle between an absolute faith and a virulent nihilism. Since only the law of the jungle prevails among these angry young men of the street, the language shifts abruptly in the direction of animal violence. In possession of a "sort of den among some boulders," they live by a fundamentally negative and brute code of life:

Their feeling for contemporaneous life was one of contempt. Their philosophy taught that in a large part the whole thing was idle and a great bore. With fine scorn they sneered at the futility of it. Work was done by men who had not the courage to stand still and let the skies clap together if they willed. . . . They longed dimly for a time when they could run through decorous streets with crash and roar of war, an army of revenge for pleasures long possessed by others, a wild sweeping compensation for their years without crystal and gilt, woman and wine. This thought slumbered in them, as the image of Rome might have lain small in the hearts of the barbarians.

The verbal evidence of their animalism can be found readily on every page where they appear. One member of this gang, for example, is likened to a "savage who had killed a great chief," and Fidsey, the frenzied coward through whom George's entrance into the gang is effected, is variously described as raving "in maniacal fury," raging like a "vanquished animal," and "gibbering like a wounded ape." It is no wonder, then, that having descended to the level of these fierce delinquents "who were superior to mothers," George now begins to confront his mother with a "mechanical scowl."

In spite of his growing sullenness and estrangement, however, the mother continues her valiant struggle to make her son conform to some moral and social standard:

Each morning his mother went to his room, and fought a battle to arouse him. She was like a soldier. Despite his pleadings, his threats, she remained at her post, imperturbable and unyielding.

Though George is already hopelessly lost, and his total depravity only a matter of time, until chapter 14 the mother has never desisted from her heroic efforts to control him. The showdown comes one morning when George "swore a tangled mass of oaths," and the mother, realizing that "it was the time for the critical battle . . . turned upon him valorously." But when George responds with savage contempt and aggressive defiance, "She threw out her hands in the gesture of an impotent one. He was the acknowledged victor. . . . He was now uncontrolled, ungoverned. . . ." Morally broken at last, the mother subsequently goes about with a grey impassive face "as if she had survived a massacre in which all that she loved had been torn from her by the brutality of savages." Completely defeated in her pathetic struggle against the forces of her son's corruption, she soon falls into rapid physical decline.

Once George has lost his job—evidently through some serious fault of his own—he discovers that being without funds he has also lost the respect of the barroom brotherhood: "In them all he saw that something had been reversed." Shortly thereafter he even loses face and acceptance among the street hoodlums when despite their howling and growls of protest he backs away from an imminent fight to attend his mother's deathbed. Having lost successively his mother's slavish adulation, his job, the esteem of the convivial brotherhood and acceptance in the neighborhood gang, George finally realizes in the grotesque agony of his mother's death his own hopeless destiny: "Kelcey began to stare at the wall-paper. The pattern was clusters of brown roses. He felt them like hideous crabs crawling upon his brain." Thus the young man who had once dreamed of an ideal woman "with the fragrance of roses that came from her hair," is awakened at last to the nightmare of the reality before him by his mother's shrieks of hallucinatory terror. As the life ebbs from her spent body, he too becomes "conscious of the ticking of the little clock out on the kitchen shelf"—that constant symbol in this narrative of an inexorable reality.

With this summary of the imagistic structure of *George's Mother* before us, we can discern more exactly now Crane's thematic intentions. In spite of the prominent rôle drink and drunkenness play in this brief narrative, intemperance is not the central thematic issue: alcohol is only the stimulant to, not the rudimentary cause of, George's moral deterioration. As the imagery of the story clearly indicates, the primary cause of George's degeneration may be found in his distorted view of life and in the romantic illusions, particularly, by which he and his mother have hoodwinked themselves to certain inauspicious realities. Added to this basic self-deception is the inability of both mother and son to comprehend and enter into one another's world. In this matter the mother is especially vulnerable to the author's ironic thrusts because of the greater restriction of her experience, interests and aspirations. When, for example, George is absorbed at supper one evening in thoughts of Maggie Johnson, whom he had just seen on the stairway, the mother "observing him apprehensively, tried in vain to picture the new terrible catastrophe. She eventually concluded that he did not like the beef-stew. She put more salt in it." This episode wonderfully epitomizes the mother's doting concern for her son's every move and mood, her pathetic inability to determine the direction of his mind, and her ludicrously ineffectual manner of resolving such difficulties.

It should probably be emphasized, in fact, that however sympathetically Crane may treat the mother, he does not completely exonerate her of blame for George's downfall. For he is always acutely aware of her fatal limitations—her naive, romantic idealism, her narrow religiosity, her shallow intelligence and vainglorious pride. Indeed, her failure to comprehend her son and his psychic needs gives considerable impetus to his determined lunge down the road to ruin. Since her failure, however, is one of intelligence rather than good will, the author spares her as generously as his special interest in such ironic disparities permits. In spite of her shortcomings, George's mother nevertheless emerges as one of the few really sympathetic portrayals, and possibly the most pathetic, in the whole range of Crane's fiction. It is not her helplessness particularly which makes for this effect but her heroic struggle against inevitable defeat and the brutal advantage her son takes of her condition.

On the other hand, it is George's loneliness his inability to enter into his mother's mystic world of heroic self-sacrifice, his longing for understanding, pleasure and companionship—which initially drives him to the barroom and eventually into the gutter. Quite unlike his neighbor in *Maggie,* who was decidedly predisposed to resist her ruination, George is readily susceptible to any good occasion for sin. One does not feel in his case, as one surely does in Maggie's, that Fate has composed another grim drama of ineluctable depravation. However conducive or compelling the circumstances of his environment, George never impresses one as being their unwilling or unsuspecting victim.

In conclusion it can be said that *George's Mother* is one of Stephen Crane's most artfully constructed works of fiction and ought more generally to be regarded as such. Especially noteworthy is the manner in which the prolonged struggle between mother and son is consistently rendered in vivid imagistic language. Though rich and varied in its suggestiveness, this imagery nevertheless coheres into an elaborate evolving pattern, modulated from beginning to end to the prevailing temper of the mother-son relationship. Crane has devised this pattern, moreover, not as a mere verbal flourish but as the principal means of revealing and intensifying both theme and plot movement. No other work of Crane, in fact, shows a more careful assimilation of style and imagery to character psychology and theme. For both the precision of its art and the acuteness of its realism, *George's Mother* decidedly merits far greater recognition.

b. Parody and Passion in George's Mother
By Eric Solomon

One of Stephen Crane's late short stories, "A Self-Made Man"
(1899), provides a clue to his method in *George's Mother*. The story
is a pure parody of the American success story best illustrated by the
books of Horatio Alger. Their titles illustrate the novels' approach:
Brave and Bold, Pluck and Luck, Work and Win; and they are, in
Kenneth Lynn's words, about "adolescent boys who, beginning in
poverty and obscurity, took the fabulous city of New York by storm." [1]
The success novels usually showed how a poor but honest, chaste,
bright, and hard-working boy from the country, through a combination of hairbreadth adventures, good luck, and sustained effort,
conquers the dangers of vice and sloth endemic to city life and wins
through to great wealth, the hand of the banker's daughter, and a
vine-covered cottage for his aged mother. The struggle was always
upward, as the title of an 1886 dime novel indicates: *John Armstrong,
Mechanic; or From the Bottom to the Top of the Ladder. A Story
of How a Man Can Rise in America.*

"A Self-Made Man" scoffs at the Alger stereotype; it derides,
although in a gentle manner compared to Nathanael West's savage
lampoon, *A Cool Million,* the absurdities of the genre. The story
opens upon Tom in poverty, studying a hole in his shoe that he
patches with playing cards. He has not much pluck and less luck—
the day he puts four aces in his shoes he is still refused work. Tom
does have self-assurance, however. He reads for an illiterate old man
a letter saying that his son has been robbing him; then Tom pretends
to be a lawyer in order to face down the embezzler, who has a dia-
mond in his shirt front and a bit of egg on his cuff. By looking
impressive and saying, "Ah," Tom frightens the villain into returning
the old man's money, and Tom "came near being happy ever after"
(XI, 259). Getting to know a man who knows another man helps
Tom thereafter to become Thomas G. Somebody in Crane's cynical
version of the rags to riches story. The object of his parody is made

Reprinted from: "The Failure on the Barroom Floor," *Stephen Crane: From
Parody to Realism.* Cambridge, Mass.: Harvard University Press, 1966, pp. 49-67.
By permission of Harvard University Press. Copyright, 1966, by the President and
Fellows of Harvard College.

clear toward the tale's close. Tom's fame has spread through the land as a man who carved his way to fortune with no help but his undaunted pluck, his tireless energy, and his sterling integrity. Newspapers apply to him now, and he writes long signed articles to struggling young men, in which he gives "the best possible advice as to how to become wealthy" (XI, 259).

When we consider the bare plot of *George's Mother* we can understand Crane's parodic approach that reverses the American type of success saga. Like the Alger hero, George is strong, has a job, is recently from the country, and provides sole support for his widowed mother. There the resemblance ends. Where the Alger hero is usually "longing for the time when he can relieve his mother from work and surround her old age with comfort," [2] George resents his mother and supports her largely because she worships him and labors unceasingly for his comfort. The Alger hero has acumen and luck; George is a fool and unlucky. Where the stereotype abstains from temptation, George hastens to succumb—to drink and sloth and, finally, violence. Where Alger sustains the Protestant ethic, Crane burlesques organized religion. An Alger hero wins, George loses the girl. (An additional ironic twist here: the girl is Maggie, and George loses her to Pete.) Most important, the traditional success novel, naturally, recounts the rise in fortune of the young hero; Crane's failure novel tells of the fall of the young antihero. The plot, then, is plainly parodic.

Within the context of the novel, moreover, Crane seems to laugh at another genre, the temperance novel. George Kelcey's mother is an active and devoted member of the W.C.T.U., and George's revolt and downfall to a large extent result from his drinking habits. While the temperance novel always showed the evil, degrading effects of drink, the novels were marked by turgid passages of moralizing as well as overwhelming sentimental melodrama. The author of a temperance novel leaned heavily on generalization; for instance, Walt Whitman's *Franklin Evans or The Inebriate* (1842) tells us, "The truth is that habits of drunkenness in the head of a family are like an evil influence—a great dark cloud, overhanging all, and spreading its gloom around every department of the business of that family, and poisoning their peace, at the same time that it debars them from any chance of rising in the world." [3] In these novels or, more properly, tracts, the victim takes to drink, destroys his prospects, and ruins his wife and children or his parents, or both, who die of shame or starvation. In *Three Years in a Man Trap* (1872), T. S.

Arthur's sequel to his famous *Ten Nights in a Barroom,* a son's drinking causes bitter and protracted death scenes. The taverns themselves in these works are settings of devilish vileness and shame. "A wretched scene!" wrote Whitman. "Half-a-dozen men, just entering the busy scenes of life, not one of us over twenty-five years, and there we were, benumbing our faculties, and confirming ourselves in practices which ever too surely bring the scorn of the world and deserved disgrace to their miserable victims!" [4] The protagonists, though entrapped by their appetites for alcohol, loudly bewail their fates; thus, the hero of Edgar Fawcett's *A Man's Will* (1888): "He thought of his mother, and the tears rushed to his eyes. Crouched on the floor, he wept passionately. 'How can I look on her face again?' " Why the outburst? "He had been drunk; he had broken his pledge." [5] Most temperance novels, after ringing the last changes on the themes of drunken bestiality, maudlin self-pity, and agonized failure, recount the hero's salvation through the power of the church or, more properly, religion combined with the "glorious temperance pledge." [6]

Although a tract with no pretensions as fiction, the book written by Stephen Crane's father is worthy of mention here. Jonathan Townley Crane's *Arts of Intoxication, The Aim and the Results* (1870) exhorts readers to help those engaged in combat with the deadly enemies, smoking and drinking. The book is generally calm in tone, historical and scientific, logical and argumentative, but it finally works up to an analysis of drunkenness that is similar to the party scene in *George's Mother.* "When a company of men are drinking together they tend, at least for a time, to be talkative and merry, and the feeblest attempt at a jest is greeted with unlimited laughter.... So if one of the company takes it into his bewildered head to try to reason about something, he is, in his own eyes, a veritable Solomon..." "When he is so far gone as to stammer in his speech and totter in his gait, and be helpless in mind and body, his sense of his wisdom, his strength, his greatness, and his goodness is at its highest point." [7]

George's Mother follows some of the traditions of temperance fiction but ridicules most aspects.[8] George does drink and fall from grace; but he never moralizes, and he is not "saved." His mother's W.C.T.U. rigidity is as absurd as George's drinking. Crane's novel opens in a bar where George, having met an old friend from the country, drinks beer to his friend's whiskey. The saloon, as in the temperance novels, is an evil place of temptation—but Crane's diction impugns the familiar descriptions: "a little glass-fronted saloon that sat blinking jovially at the crowds. It engulfed them with a gleeful motion of its two widely smiling lips." [9] George's drinking, even the "one more drink," does not instantly unman him, and he is able to deceive his mother quite easily. Actually, the section describing George's mother at her housework is quite funny when considered in reference to the problem of drink. As she works she sings a hymn in defiance of the drunken curses of a neighbor with a red, mottled face who hurls a bottle crashing down to the courtyard. And as she fights dirt and dust in the tenement, her son is in a bar, and a really ludicrous image comments on this irony. "In the distance an enormous brewery towered over the other buildings. Great gilt letters advertised a brand of beer. Thick smoke came from funnels and spread near it like vast and powerful wings. The structure seemed a great bird, flying. The letters of the sign made a chain of gold hanging from its neck. The old woman looked at the brewery. It vaguely interested her, for a moment, as a stupendous affair, a machine of mighty strength" (pp. 25f). Thus the brewery, symbolizing the enemy of temperance, looms over the tenement much as the eyes of Dr. T. J. Eckleburg hover over the valley of ashes in *The Great Gatsby*.

Despite his mother's warnings about his new friend ("He drinks"), George refuses her plea to go to a prayer meeting and instead returns to the little smiling saloon. As *Maggie* charts the movement of the heroine down to the depths through changing descriptions of the beer halls she frequents, so George's first binge takes place in an elegant saloon, all polished wood and gleaming furniture. Crane very effectively describes the process of intoxication. The men gradually become ridiculously jovial, sentimentally tender, bitterly egoistic. "Each man explained, in his way, that he was totally out of place in the . . . world. They were possessed of various virtues which were unappreciated by those with whom they were commonly obliged to mingle; they were fitted for a tree-shaded land where everything was peace" (p. 35). This passage—indeed, the whole treatment of drinking in *George's Mother*—brilliantly exemplifies Crane's parodic technique. As is clear from his language, which is incongruously overblown, Crane is mocking the pretensions of the drinkers—and, by extension, the genre of temperance fiction that was nothing if not utterly serious. Yet while Crane laughs at his protagonists, he also understands their rather pathetic motivations and the needs to which alcohol ministers. The novel provides both a comic view of the drinking-temperance clash and a serious insight into those who drink.

As always, Crane refuses to moralize. He presents George's opinion that his evening of drinking was delightful, shows him staggering on legs "like willow-twigs," describes his hangover, his "baked eyes," and a mouth that seems to have been sucking a wooden spoon. But the victim of his debauch, his mother, is such a whining paragon that the reader is unable to identify with her.

The second major drinking bout takes place after George has been crushed by his failure to attract a girl. In an adolescent urge for "the delicious revenge of a partial self-destruction" (p. 49—an example of Crane's discrimination of motives in contrast to the absolutes of temperance melodrama), George takes part in a stag affair. Again Crane overwrites, I think consciously. The drinking is a bacchic rite, "a festival of a religion"; the host sits "like a fat, jolly god" (pp. 53f). The party moves from dialect jokes to dancing to fisticuffs. The rich, almost fruity, prose parodies the traditional drunk scenes, as George considers his inebriation to be immense, mighty. Crane treats the awfulness of the morning after with derision, and he deliberately avoids the expected confrontation scene between the drunken youth and his aged mother by letting George deceive her about his activities. But he does go to prayer meeting, only to find this usually climactic event in the rake's progress to be hateful and hypocritical.

While the author does not take George's drinking too seriously, Crane does use the fact of George's increasing alcoholism as a device for the portrayal of his weak, self-justifying character. Crane analyzes George Kelcey's drinking habits with great acumen and irony. "He understood that drink was an essential to joy, to the coveted position of a man of the world and of the streets. The saloons contained the mystery of a street for him." (This passage follows directly upon the narration of the church service's unmysterious lack of appeal.) "Drink and its surroundings were the eyes of a superb green dragon to him. He followed a fascinating glitter, and the glitter required no explanation" (p. 68).

George continues to drink, even after his mother discovers his flaw. He slips down the ladder of failure another rung when he takes up with the streetcorner society of a gang of tough, cynical young hoodlums, all jobless delinquents. "Their feeling for contemporaneous life was one of contempt. Their philosophy taught that in a large part the whole thing was idle and a great bore. With fine scorn they sneered at the futility of it. Work was done by men who had not the courage to stand still and let the skies clap together if they willed" (p. 73). This creed—directly opposed to that of the Alger hero—is attractive to George, who wants to run with these anarchic brawlers. His chance comes when, in still another mockery of the Alger code of sportsmanship, George helps one of the gang beat up another man and is thus accepted into their fellowship. Once in the group, George lets his native sloth prevail, and he loses his job. His mother immediately has a stroke. Crane handles this scene with some sympathetic tenderness, but the irony of the plot device is manifest. And when his mother suffers a second, fatal attack, George is engaged in his crudest binge yet, a jostling, brawling struggle for gulps at a great pail of beer. Intemperance wins, the W.C.T.U. heroine dies, and her son is left to meld into the "endless roar, the eternal tramping of the marching city" (p. 90). If we consider the novel from its success-story source, it is a parodic reversal; from its temperance source, it is a burlesque parallel. The two traditions provide a double perspective, and Crane plays them off against each other in order to make the character of George psychologically valid.

There is another element of parody in the verbal texture of *George's Mother*. Here, as in the first section of *Maggie*, Crane leans heavily on war imagery. To be sure, battle metaphors recur in Crane's work from his earliest *Sullivan County Sketches*, and are a basic vehicle for expressing his sense of the naturalistic struggle for existence. In *George's Mother*, however, there seems to be a crucial difference in Crane's employment of these images, and we may conjecture that he is parodying himself, the author of *The Red Badge of Courage*. The use of war images in the passages dealing with the mother's fight against dirt in the tenement falls into Crane's customary naturalistic verbal pattern. She wields broom and dustpan like weapons, and there is a flurry of battle in the room as the old woman poises the broom like a lance, shows indomitable courage, and raises a "war-chant, a shout of battle and defiance." Even when resting she plans "skirmishes, charges, campaigns," and after her rest, "the battle was again in full swing. Terrific blows were given and received" (pp. 25f). As "a little intent warrior," Mrs. Kelcey later in the novel fights to get George off to work; "She was like a soldier ... she remained at her post, imperturbable and unyielding" (p. 77). When her slothful, alcoholic son wins the "critical battle" between them, her defeat leads quickly to her death.

Crane's treatment of George's debauches, however, contains enough echoes of the war novel's diction to hint at self-parody. As George muses upon his drinking companions, "He looked upon the beaming faces and knew that if at that instant there should come a time for a great sacrifice he would blissfully make it" (p. 35). This reminds us of Henry Fleming's pretentious attitude toward his comrades-in-arms. Later George considers the start of an evening party in language remarkably similar to the phrases applied to Henry's romantic visions of war. "He felt that there was something fine and thrilling in this affair. . . . He was capable of heroisms" (pp. 53f). The drinkers inhabit a "strange land," the wrecked room resembles "a decaying battlefield," and the passed-out inebriates are ghastly as corpses (p. 58). And after his gay dreams of heroism, George now perceives "all the futility of a red existence" (pp. 58f). Just to frost the cake of his parody, Crane gives George a red badge; he falls drunkenly and smashes his head on the floor during the party, and later presents to his mother and to his employer an involved lie about a street accident and gains from them the sympathy due such a wounded victim. The scene and the language help to establish the satire. In addition, the echoes from *Maggie* reinforce the belief that Crane may be laughing at his own work. By gratuitously making Maggie and Pete the actual embodiments of George's daydreams of romantic love, Crane calls attention to his previous fiction. This self-parody is, I think, a gratuitous indulgence on Crane's part, almost a parody of parody.[10]

Another parallel to the parodic technique used in *Maggie* appears in the later slum novel. Crane repeats the device of immersing his characters in daydreams that are absurd but that also reflect the conventions of popular fiction or drama. George's mother makes him into a hero of melodrama; her imagination transforms his hangover into a malignant internal disease of lungs or kidneys, and George, in the best fictional tradition, into a stoic, heroic sufferer. Elsewhere, she dreams the familiar success fantasy that the plot of the novel reverses. In her mind George is "a white and looming king among men" (p. 42), one certain to reach the heights, to be an enormous man who will give charity to the poor. In this way *George's Mother* pays notice to the popular domestic novel in which close family relationships, sincere spiritual struggles, and great triumphs provide the framework for the characters' dreams.

Within the privacy of his own mind, George also holds a version of the success dream. But he has a nearer dream, a sexual fantasy founded on the clichés of popular fiction and its illustrations. "In scenes which he took mainly from pictures, this vision conducted a courtship, strutting, posing, and lying through a drama which was magnificent from glow of purple. [A reference to Edgar Saltus' *The Imperial Purple?*] In it he was icy, self-possessed; but she, the dream-girl, was consumed by wild, torrential passion. . . . She was to him as beseeching for affection as a pet animal, but still he controlled appearances, and none knew of his deep abiding love. . . . In these long dreams there were accessories of castle-like houses, wide lands, servants, horses, clothes" (p. 44). His adolescent dreams form George's self-image as a stern general, a perfect lover for whom his goddess must pine pathetically. George's fantasy of heroism, of fate making him an enormous figure, of "a chariot of pink clouds" (p. 45) that would come for him, while similar to his mother's hopeful dreams, is predicated on romantic fiction, as Crane makes clear. "Later, when he had read some books, it all achieved clearer expression. He was told in them that there was a goddess in the world whose business it was to wait until he should exchange a glance with her" (p. 44). That George's dream should be realized in the Maggie whose reality the reader well knows, increases the irony. The world of Maggie and Pete (and of Mrs. Kelcey, who assumes that George's moonstruck expression indicates distaste for her beef stew) destroys his "grand dramas." Once again, Crane follows contemporary fictional cliché and destroys it by the realism of his own plot and characterization. For all the many elements of parody that mark the structure and tone of *George's Mother*, the novel goes far beyond the parody it encompasses, and the work touches upon tragicomedy. If the little parody "A Self-Made Man" might be called Stephen Crane's *Shamela*, *George's Mother* is his *Joseph Andrews*. The elements of parody still inform the major work, but the novel goes beyond the parody principle and stands also as a serious character study.

The title of the novel is fitting if we consider the overtones. George is the leading figure, not his mother, but Crane carefully delineates both characters, and it is the relationship between the mother and the son that makes *George's Mother* Stephen Crane's most penetrating psychological novel. The book shows the two characters as similar in their fantasies and their egos yet seriously in conflict in their views of the proper life. The love-hate relationship between the Kelceys is hinted at in terms that show remarkable psychological control for an author whose reputation is for only one area of psychological competence, an understanding of the psychology of fear. *George's Mother* touches upon a variety of sexual themes: the Oedipal relationship, adolescent fantasies, and sublimation of sexual drives through alcohol.[11]

Crane characterizes George Kelcey with more care than any other of his characters. Young, strong, egocentric, George dwells in the light of his mother's love and his position as breadwinner in a fatherless household. We learn early in the novel that he is the only male survivor in a family of five sons. His mother idolizes and protects her son, yet is also, naturally, too protective and quick to criticize. With great restraint, Crane evokes the tension between the pair; the fact that the mother is a religious member of the W.C.T.U. and George is a backsliding drunk only makes concrete the more fundamental conflict.

In a superb passage the undercurrent of love and resentment is brought to the surface. George is suffering from his first hangover, and his mother is remonstrating with him for his swearing. His harsh demeanor quickly reduces her to a conciliatory state. " 'George, dear, won't yeh bring some sugar home t'-night?' It could be seen that she was asking for a crown of gold." When he, the "injured monarch," prepares to leave without responding to her woeful request for a kiss, she addresses him in lover's tones: " 'George—George—ain't yeh goin' t' kiss me good-bye?' When he moved he found that she was hanging to his coat-tails." And he turns "with a murmur of a sort of tenderness"; after the kiss she looks at him with "reproach and gratitude and affection" (p. 39).

After this scene, Crane analyzes in some detail the emotions of his two protagonists. Both, as we have seen, have active fantasy lives —she dreams of a heroic, loving, successful son, he of a heroic, charming lover—that focus in quite similar ways on George's future. While different in almost every detail of their lives, they have the same sense of pride. "It seemed to her that she must be a model mother to have such a son." In her fantasy, which is completely at variance with reality, she sees him as the perfect son of a perfect mother. There seems something a bit perverse about the love light that comes into her eyes. "The wrinkled, yellow face frequently warmed into a smile of the kind that a maiden bestows upon him who to her is first and perhaps last" (p. 41). The conflicts between mother and son take place because of her fear that he will become too proud and therefore fail to accomplish the wonders she wants for him—and for herself.

For his part, George bitterly resents her carping criticism, which takes in such minutiae as his failure to hang up his coat, yet he understands her pride in him and the resulting power he has over her. While agreeing with her estimate of his worth—and Crane's ironic stance as narrator here is more subtle than in his account of Henry Fleming's ego—George's dreams are less worldly than those of his mother. The fantasies of mother and son are different in objectives but similar in tone. She can show others her pride in her marvelous son but must drive him along the road of perfection because he is to accomplish all that her dead husband and other sons could not. "Upon the dead altars of her life she had builded the little fires of hope for another" (p. 43).

For all his delight in her appreciation of his wit and charm, George has other romantic dream objects. These localize on Maggie, and his bumbling attempts to make contact with her are in pitiful contrast to his dashing fancies. Maggie with her pail of beer and her barkeeper demon lover are too real for George's fantasy world. Pete actually does what George can only ineffectually dream of, and his fantasies explode as Pete "rescues" Maggie from a tenement squabble. His dream in pieces, George turns on his mother "a face red, seamed, hard with rage. They stared a moment in silence. Then she turned and staggered toward her room. Her hip struck violently against a corner of the table during this blind passage" (p. 48). The mother becomes the victim of his frustrations, and his ensuing drunken spree serves both to punish her and to sublimate his thwarted desires.

The relationship Crane outlines between the Kelceys is intense and painful. Each can hurt the other, yet each is full of love. When George returns home after his debauch, his mother kisses him with a smile reminiscent of her girlhood, but then must force him to accompany her to chapel. The tension between them is extreme. "The waves of her desires were puny against the rocks of his indolence. She had a great wish to beat him" (p. 64). She ends in defeat, "but withered grass," in their duel—"He thrusts out his legs in the easy scorn of a rapier bravo"—but he is capable of shame and some kindness. His agony of embarrassment from her actions at the chapel service, however, increases the distance between them. Crane writes of chapel in the same images of war used earlier, but here the imagery is pompous in its religiosity: "the presence of the army of the unknown," the "dull-hued banners" (p. 67) of his mother's world. George opts for the "superb green dragon" of drink (a play on the lack of sainthood of this George), and the struggle between mother and son, personal and intimate, is objectified in the terms of the novel by the clash between chapel and tavern. She makes attendance at chapel a test of his affection; he makes an evening of drinking a proof of his manliness. Although her pride leads her to defend her son's wild ways before the tenement jury of gossips, she shrinks away from his rowdy drinking mates. His alcoholism destroys her hopes, and he is impervious to her criticisms. The two generations are light-years apart. "She never understood the advanced things in life. He felt the hopelessness of ever making her comprehend. His mother was not modern" (p. 76).

The conflict worsens until the two are openly at war. Crane describes their savage arguments with attention to intimate detail and also with compassion. Driven to say terrible things, they speak "in tones dark with dislike." Crane sensitively analyzes George's motivations when he is cruel to his parent. "He brooded upon his mother's agony and felt a singular joy in it. As opportunity offered, he did little despicable things. He was going to make her abject." Again we are reminded of a duel between lovers, but Crane portrays the workings of compensatory actions with a complexity and control that bring to mind the relationship of Paul Morel to his mother in D. H. Lawrence's *Sons and Lovers.* "Her suffering was all a sort of compensation for his own dire pains" (p. 78).

To punish her, George harms himself, and his loss of employment seems to be her final blow. Her dreams are gone, "torn from her" by the son who has lost his own dreams, and she is bereft. He snarls at her and storms away, leaving Mrs. Kelcey in a pose that reverses the traditional sentimental cameo of the beloved mother. No Whistler portrait, this: "A pale flood of sunlight, imperturbable at its vocation, streamed upon the little old woman, bowed with pain, forlorn in her chair" (p. 79).

Crane then moves outside the consciousnesses of his two characters and reports a brief staccato dialogue between a boy and George to establish the fact of Mrs. Kelcey's illness. Crane emphasizes George's dread sense of doom to indicate his actual dependence upon his mother. Moved by what passes for love, he promises to reform, to get a job, to endear himself to her. Crane lets the reader decide George's motives for this kind treatment of his mother. Through a combination of fear, guilt, and affection, he shows warmth to the old lady, and the end of this section reverses the mood of the previous one. The two sit together by the window. "Her hand rested upon his hair" (p. 82).

This idyll is the last gasp of sentiment in the book. Sharply foreshortening, Crane next shows George attempting to borrow money, drinking beer with his cronies. The reader must assume that George's words about reform were just words. Again a messenger tells George of his mother's attack, and he reluctantly leaves his corrupt pleasures and attends her deathbed. Here all their illusions fail. Her religion does not sustain her in the delirium, and she is in terror of death. Although this scene might have been maudlin, Crane, through toughness of spirit, makes the events dramatic, even tragic. The old woman fights death, is oblivious of her son's whining cries for Mother. She dies hard; her demise is nearly a replica of Jim Conklin's death in the war novel. There is an emotional moment in which, although unable to be reached by the present George, she hallucinates about the child George. "She was at a kitchen door with a dish-cloth in her hand. Within there had just been a clatter of crockery. Down through the trees of the orchard she could see a man in a field ploughing. 'Bill . . . have yeh seen Georgie? Is he out there with you? Georgie! Georgie! Come right here this minnet. Right—this—minnet'" (p. 89). The immediacy and reality of her grudging death forestalls whatever pathos might develop. She becomes querulous and tries to drive away people whose presence in the room she imagines. "Her voice became peevish. 'Go away!'" As tightly confined as a Dickinson poem, the death scene ends in bitter restraint. In the presence of a plump, condescending clergyman and a morbidly cheerful neighbor, George stares at the brown roses on the wallpaper that seem like hideous crabs crawling upon his brain. The conflict is over, and neither side has won. The dreams have failed, and love has died. In a novel that contains many elements of burlesque, the powerful yet tender, violent yet touching relationship between a weak boy-man and his equally weak ambitious mother gives genuine distinction to the narrative. The novel ends like a motion picture as the narrative camera eye focuses on George sitting, staring at the wallpaper, then catches an oilcloth table cover, the blue sky outside the window, the chimneys and roofs of the ever-present city that has provided the harsh setting for the story. The sound of a boy and his mother arguing over a trip to the store counterpoints the ending of the long argument between George and his mother. These tenement voices recapitulate the whole impossible conflict; the only affirmative note comes from the reader's (and author's) partisanship for life itself—indicated tautly by the shift to the outside world where the struggle between generations continues.

The novel starts and ends with the voice of the city sounding, and the future fortunes of the protagonist are not indicated. *George's Mother* is, like Nathanael West's work, a strange mixture of comedy and misery. The novel is not as brilliant an achievement as *The Red Badge of Courage;* the slum book has a narrower theme, more limited implication, and less marvelous prose. *George's Mother,* however, is Stephen Crane's most interesting study of personal conflict influenced by social and literary norms. The book shows how ideals, colored by the sentiments of weak fiction and corrupt society, lead to self-destruction and the destruction of others. Crane's novel renders the nexus of love and hate in moving and powerful terms. The pain of the mother-son conflict darkens Crane's ironic humor, while at the same time his parodic frame preserves the conflict from sentimentality. Thus parody and passion engage in this novel and reinforce each other.

NOTES

1. Kenneth Lynn, *The Dream of Success* (Boston, 1955), p. 6.
2. Horatio Alger, *Strive and Succeed* (Philadelphia, 1872), p. 355.
3. *The Uncollected Poetry and Prose of Walt Whitman,* ed. Emory Holloway (New York, 1921), II, 108.
4. *Ibid.,* p. 146.
5. Edgar Fawcett, *A Man's Will* (New York, 1888), p. 127.
6. Mark Twain, incidentally, wrote but never published a parody, *William Baxter, the Reformed Inebriate, or Saved by Fire,* in which the drunken protagonist murders his wife and children, repents, remarries, does the killing again—three times, before his final reform! "But see what perseverance may accomplish. Thoroughly reformed at last, he now traverses the land a brand plucked from the burning and delivers temperance lectures and organizes Sunday Schools." Franklin Rogers, *Mark Twain's Burlesque Patterns* (Dallas, 1960), pp. 99-100.
7. J. T. Crane, *Arts of Intoxication* (New York, 1870), pp. 142, 145.
8. As a matter of fact, Crane usually enjoyed writing with warm humor about drinking and drunks. See, in addition to his Western tales, "Joys of Pulque Down in Mexico" (1895) or "A Lovely Jag in a Crowded Car" (1895). In *Maggie,* however, the treatment of drinking is thoroughly negative.
9. X, 20. Crane uses the same image in "An Experiment in Misery." "The swing doors, snapping to and fro like ravenous lips, made gratified smacks as the saloon gorged itself with plump men." XI, 22.
10. "Authors are in no position to see themselves; conscious self-parodies lack shape and bite." John Updike, *Assorted Prose* (New York, 1965), p. 242. Crane's references here to his own previous serious statements may be for ironic contrast rather than for self-parody; in any case, they don't quite come off.
11. According to Leslie Fiedler, drunkenness is a symbol for sexual betrayal, the saloon is the anti-home, the refuge for the fleeing, ineffective male. Leslie Fiedler, *Love and Death in the American Novel* (Cleveland, 1960), p. 259.

Stephen Crane: The Novelist at War with Himself
By Thomas A. Gullason

I

The word "war" and the phrase "artist at war" are often associated with Stephen Crane. But little has been made of the private wars Crane had with himself as he tried to perfect his craft as novelist. Crane drew quite freely upon his autobiography when he wrote his novels and became reflective and personal. In parts of *Maggie* and *The Red Badge,* he did rely heavily on his imagination to approximate the little experience he had of prostitution and of war; this led him to employ some extravagant and artificial literary devices. All of these factors disturbed the control, range, depth, subtlety, and power of his writing so that he was never completely successful in the novel form, although he had the necessary skills. Crane also drew upon his autobiography when he wrote his short stories, such as "The Open Boat" and *Whilomville Stories;* but in these works he maintained an objective perspective and could tap the riches of his imagination and his wider experience more successfully.

Crane's first novel, *Maggie* (1893, 1896), is indirectly autobiographical. He drew upon his life in Asbury Park and Ocean Grove, where he lived for some years, and where he was a shore correspondent for his brother's news agency. At these summer resorts, Crane listened to, and heard and read about the well-known preachers and reformers who frequently lectured on poverty, the city slums, the plight of the children of the poor, unwed mothers, prostitution, crime, the terrors of drunkenness and gambling. Then, too, these problems of city life were literally present in Asbury Park and Ocean Grove and discussed in the local newspapers; references were made to an "alleged disorderly house" in Asbury Park, an attempted rape case, slick confidence men, petty robberies, speakeasies, pickpockets, cardsharps, gamblers arrested, cases of forgery, embezzlement, and murder.

Crane's own parents were dedicated reformers and humanitarians and often lectured and wrote about the social ills of the day. In part, the general subject matter of *Maggie* and the specific religious scenes echo the world of Crane's father, who was a Methodist minister, and his mother, who was the daughter of one. Stephen Crane himself was never satisfied with the results achieved by preachers and reformers, and so he wrote his novel with a social purpose. Unfortunately, Crane's attempt to be naturalistic collided with his artistic impulses. The well-known inscription to *Maggie* suggests this conflict:

> It is inevitable that you will be greatly shocked by this book but continue please with all possible courage to the end. For it tries to show that environment is a tremendous thing in the world and frequently shapes lives regardless. If one proves that theory one makes room in Heaven for all sorts of souls (notably an occasional street girl) who are not confidently expected to be there by many excellent people.

As he sought to demonstrate this thesis, Crane unintentionally declared war on his own philosophy of impersonality. Too subjective in writing his novel, Crane lacked the distance to capture meaningfully the humanity, variety, and scope of his subject.

The opening paragraphs of *Maggie* provide the framework for the entire novel. Jimmie is fighting in a gang war, and this scene depicts a narrowing and unchanging world which has no possible exits except death. Crane depicts the whole world of *Maggie* with such hard-biting irony that he limits the portraits of the characters and the development of the theme. Jimmie, Maggie, Pete, and Mary Johnson remain one-dimensional: Crane introduces them separately in the beginning of the novel and shows them only in extreme situations, to which they respond in extreme and grotesque ways. He highlights atmosphere, incident, and plot, while he sacrifices the individual natures and motivations of his characters. Consequently, the characters and moral issues harden into stereotypes. Thus Crane seems to achieve his effects somewhat mechanically by planning the presentation of his material to underscore the destructiveness of the environment and to evoke a certain preconceived response from the reader.

Even though he mocks the sentimental melodramas of the day (note the plays that Pete and Maggie attend), Crane unwittingly turns *Maggie* into a melodrama by his flat portraits: the innocent and sweet girl, Maggie, starved for love and the good life; the chivalric suitor, Pete, who is really a villain; the stern yet "grieving" mother, Mary Johnson; and the well-meaning but stupid brother, Jimmie. The deeper truths of character and environment for which Crane aimed are overshadowed by the melodramatic depictions of emotionalism, sensationalism, and violence.

Crane overdisplayed his style and artiness, new to the traditional novel, and his language and dialogue are somewhat strained. The short sentences of *Maggie* do capture the fast pace of city life, with its overtones of emptiness, indifference, and violence. Unfortunately, though, almost everything in the novel receives similar stress, and this leads to unintended melodramatic effects. There is little contrast in tempo and style. Splashes of color, the dependence on adjectives and adverbs, and the pathetic fallacies make the novel seem artificial and contrived; Crane does not yet fully understand the emotional, psychological, and functional uses of style and imagery. In another way, Crane's naturalistic stress on environment leads to melodrama; the dialogue of the parents and the children is hardly differentiated, and the reader forgets the fundamental difference between them. Periodically, Crane toys with language and produces clever effects; this also contributes to artifice, not to art. In one place, he writes: "She swelled with virtuous indignation as she carried the lighter articles of household use, one by one, under the shadows of the three gilt balls, where Hebrews chained them with chains of interest."

If Crane wanted to achieve the spirit of tragedy, or even tragicomedy in *Maggie,* he did not succeed. Mainly he evokes grim humor, horror, and pity. Relying on a broad style of writing to expose his thesis, Crane remains generalized and repetitious; therefore, the reader is not deeply affected by his humanitarian ideas. The physical scenes of the city (the streets, the saloons) and the ever-present conflicts (the family quarrels) are unnecessarily repetitious; they do not really advance very much the life of the novel and the spiritual nature of the characters. The three beer hall scenes, and Pete's drunken self-pity (see Chapter XVIII) are overdrawn; while they do describe the monotony, insensitivity, and degeneration in the slums, they chart too slowly and incidentally the fall of the heroine Maggie.

Nonetheless, *Maggie* still impresses, not only because it was written by a nineteen-year-old, but because Crane attempts to do new things with the form and content of the traditional novel. One can see this in his style and irony, in his impressionism, symbolism, and naturalism. Though he does not yet fully understand the uses of style, imagery, and color, he is boldly trying to adapt them to his creative work. In *Maggie,* Crane heralds the modern theme, the modern artist, and the modern novel.

II

George's Mother (1896), like *Maggie,* boldly moves in the direction of the twentieth-century novel. Crane deals with his subject matter in a realistic-naturalistic way, develops his story by dramatic scene, mood, tone, image, and symbol—rather than by a closely detailed plot and action—and thus demonstrates his kinship with the modern writer. But some special problems exist in *George's Mother,* for it is not a completely satisfying novel.

The extent to which Crane drew from personal experience for the novel becomes apparent when some extrinsic facts are carefully scrutinized. Recent evidence shows that *George's Mother* was being written in 1892 or earlier, which places it closer to the time of *Maggie* and further away from *The Red Badge* (1895). This is of great autobiographical significance. Many critics have noted that Crane was drawing upon his personal relationship with his mother. Crane's own recollection of a personal experience he was to use in *George's Mother* is recorded in Thomas Beer's biography of 1923:

> Once when I was fourteen an organ grinder on the beach at Asbury [Park] gave me a nice long drink out of a nice red bottle for picking up his hat for him. I felt ecstatic walking home and then I was an Emperor and some Rajahs and Baron de Blowitz all at the same time. I had been sulky all morning and now I was perfectly willing to go to a prayer meeting and Mother was tickled to death. And, mind you, all because this nefarious Florentine gave me a red drink out of a bottle. I have frequently wondered how much mothers know about their sons, after all.

However, no biographer or critic ever uncovered the following facts, which can be corroborated. Mrs. Crane had been ill as early as 1888, even earlier; in January of 1891 she had to resign her post as president of the W. C. T. U. of Asbury Park-Ocean Grove because of "failing health." According to her death certificate, Mrs. Crane suffered for twenty-five days before dying on December 7, 1891; her long period of suffering and eventual death were due to a "malignant carbuncle." In an unpublished letter, a descendant reveals that Crane stayed at his brother's house in Lake View, New Jersey, "so that he would be near his mother [who was in a hospital in Paterson] in her sickness," although he was not present at the hour of her death. And Crane himself once admitted, in a well-known statement to Edward Garnett, that "George's mother was an exaggerated portrait" of his own mother's characteristics.

The parallels to real life in *George's Mother* are indeed very close, especially the parallels to Mrs. Crane's death and her son's remorse. Like Stephen Crane's mother, Mrs. Kelcey is not "modern"; her entire life is devoted to the W. C. T. U. and to religion. She is trivial and overpossessive, though well-meaning. She dreams of a glorious future for her son, but is shocked by his wayward behavior. Her dizzy spells, and her hysteria and terror at the time of her death (when she loses control of her faculties) recall the destructive results of Mrs. Crane's fatal malignancy. Moreover, both the impact of Mrs. Kelcey's death on her son George and his guilt feelings are pinpointed in a terrifying image at the close of the novel: "He felt them [the pattern of the wallpaper] like hideous crabs crawling upon his brain."

The problem that the background to this novel presents is evident. *George's Mother* is Stephen Crane's most painful work. A psychological critic can rightly assume that by writing the novel Crane was admitting his sins against his mother and attempting to serve a period of penance, before hoping for some kind of redemption. Crane, then, was frighteningly close to his materials and therefore unable to remain objective toward the life of George Kelcey and his mother. He could not dramatize fully and sensitively the agonizing psychological battle between mother and son; the mother's growing and pitiful awareness of her son's degeneration; the widening gap between the old generation and the new; and the conflict between alcoholism and religion. Crane presents all these issues in an oblique and abridged manner. Partly because of his omniscient point of view, Crane does not quote directly from the minds of his central characters (he does this indirectly, through the narrator's voice); this takes away from the understanding and feeling one is supposed to have for both mother and son, and their tragic situation.

A second and lesser problem is that Crane carries over materials

from *Maggie*. (Crane does this to a lesser degree in *The Red Badge*.)
This blurs the individual art and vision of *George's Mother*. Maggie
and Pete reappear; so does Blue Billie. George himself assumes Maggie's romantic nature; in this case, he desires Maggie. Like Maggie,
he tries to escape harsh reality; he is "seduced" by alcohol and by
drifters such as Jones, Mr. Bleecker, and the street gang. In borrowing from *Maggie*, Crane prevents himself from exploring and developing actions and scenes arising out of the separate world of *George's
Mother*. *George's Mother* is not, as some critics think, meant as a
companion piece to *Maggie*.

In the end, *George's Mother* remains circular and limited in
movement. Crane is needlessly repetitious and sketches the plot loosely
by means of moods and incidents. Not enough time is given to the
rise and fall of the major characters. There is no careful charting of
George's exhilaration, disillusionment, and degeneration; nor is
George's remorse over his mother's illness and death sufficiently motivated. Scenes, actions, and characters remain too briefly developed.
The potential power and greatness of *George's Mother* scatters and
weakens. The whole experience of this domestic tragedy was too real
for Crane.

III

While it demonstrates the similar modern tendencies of *Maggie*
and *George's Mother*, *The Red Badge of Courage* is far more complex and subtle because Crane views the life of war and the life of
a recruit from a variety of perspectives and with a variety of techniques. He is not a propagandist obsessed with a contemporary social
ill. He has no autobiographical "block"; in fact, he seems inspired by
the military heroics of his own ancestors (one was a general, another
a commodore) whom he mentioned in several of his letters.

Because the art and scope of his novelistic craft are broader and
freer and less propagandistic and autobiographical in *The Red Badge*,
Crane presents his ideas and philosophies of life and war more successfully. The skillful blending of description, narration, and dialogue
heightens the sense of immediacy of the battle experiences for the
reader; this accounts for much of the novel's realism and vigor. The
psychological insights into Henry Fleming, the tall soldier, and the
loud soldier are starkly and deftly portrayed. Henry's streams of
thought, while presented indirectly by the omniscient author, help

to make him the most successfully drawn protagonist in all of Crane's novels. By adroitly drawing from a complex of techniques—from impressionism, symbolism, music, the epic, and elsewhere—Crane achieves much more fluidity, scope, meaning, and purpose in his delineation of characters, actions, and themes. The individual scenes of *The Red Badge* are more full-scaled in sensitivity and development than any in *Maggie, George's Mother, The Third Violet, Active Service,* or *The O'Ruddy.*

Yet *The Red Badge* remains a flawed masterpiece. If *Maggie* has more rage than art, *George's Mother* more bewilderment and pain than insight, *The Red Badge* is more showy and artificial in style, color, and imagery. This may be due to Crane's anxieties about his lack of experience concerning war, and it affects his field of vision and the novel's holding power.

These artistic and stylistic flourishes in *The Red Badge* blur its unity, balance, and development. Even Henry Fleming's rationalizations and guilt feelings are overdrawn, partly due to Crane's artiness. The quick movement of the short sentences in *The Red Badge* suggests the rapid and bewildering worlds of fear and hope; but by consistently relying on this style and rhythm, Crane loses variety, unity, and force. Everything in the novel is not meant to reflect a feverish pace and a high dramatic key. There are not enough mood and tonal contrasts in the novel. The few comic touches, like the scene between the thieving soldier and the maiden, do not relieve the tenseness and the "blistering" pace of the novel, which gradually exhausts the reader. The periodic barrages of colors do not always reflect the subtle shades and hues of the action; they attract attention to themselves, because of their novelty and shock value. These various matters even help to blur the ending of the novel, which is meant to be ironic.

Crane becomes too arty and "poetical" when he relies on pathetic fallacies ("He seated himself and watched the terror-stricken wagons"). Many other images in the novel allude to civilian life: to a babe, a football player, a schoolmistress, a mob, a hunter, and fishwives. On the one hand, these images provide ironic contrasts to the war experience, and they help to translate the foreign condition of war more precisely to the civilian reader. At times, however, image follows image, and this makes scenes and actions forced and artificial. Here is one example: "Here and there were officers carried along on the stream like exasperated chips. They were striking about them with their swords and with their left fists, punching every head they could

reach. They cursed like highwaymen. . . . A mounted officer displayed
the furious anger of a spoiled child." Direct statements would often
have been more effective and natural. Some images—like the classic
"The red sun was pasted in the sky like a wafer"—are striking and
powerful, but Crane is also self-conscious as he overdramatizes:

> Within him, as he hurled himself forward, was born a love,
> a despairing fondness for this flag which was near him. It was
> a creation of beauty and invulnerability. It was a goddess,
> radiant, that bended its form with an imperious gesture to
> him. It was a woman, red and white, hating and loving, that
> called him with the voice of his hopes. Because no harm could
> come to it he endowed it with power. He kept near, as if it
> could be a saver of lives, and an imploring cry went from his
> mind.

IV

The early novels—*Maggie, George's Mother,* and *The Red Badge*
—should be studied as examples of the modern Crane. The last
novels—*The Third Violet* (1897), *Active Service* (1899), *The O'Ruddy*
(1903; completed by Robert Barr)—have to be studied as examples
of the traditional Crane.

What was obliquely present in the early novels comes to the
forefront in the final ones, namely the love theme. Crane is not very
successful with this theme; he never displays any real skill in dramatizing the anguish and beauty of love and lovers. Crane never exposes
closely enough the natures and frustrations of Hawker and Grace
Fanhall in *The Third Violet* and Rufus Coleman and Marjory Wainwright in *Active Service.* Because of his own failures as a suitor in
real life (with genteel women like Nellie Crouse and Helen Trent),
which added to his psychological anxieties, Stephen Crane does not
effectively portray the delicacy and sensitivity of his fictional men and
women in love. His creativity seems thwarted when his fiction is too
close to his own painful experiences.

Another major problem in *The Third Violet* and *Active Service*
is that Crane, as a hopeful dramatist, tries to "stage" his novels.
(There are numerous allusions to the theater in *Active Service.*) This
restricts the flexibility of his art and imagination to an awkward

use of the techniques of the theater. In *The Third Violet,* for example, Crane gives excessive attention to dialogue, making this novel his talkiest. And the dialogues do not reveal very much about the characters. The slick talk and witticisms of Hollanden, the speeches between Hawker and Grace, do not always illuminate or deepen the plot.

In many ways, *The Third Violet* reflects the world of the conventional sentimental romance, with melodramatic overtones. Crane is unable to rise above the clichés of the theater of the 1890s; he takes it all seriously enough to parade stereotyped characters, actions, and themes. (If he were parodying all of this, it would be something else again.) In *The Third Violet,* there are the gossiping old ladies (whom Crane satirizes); the lovers who continually misunderstand one another; the patient and kind-hearted father; the impatient and uneasy mother; the wealthy rival suitor; the good-natured "other" girl whose love is never returned; and the well-meaning but teasing friend. There are also stage properties, like the three violets. The characters and their actions, then, cannot be taken very seriously because they are not fresh, vital, or alive. The novel, as a whole, with its thinly staged double plot, does not lead to any complex or subtle meanings.

A second autobiographical issue—besides the love theme—is given significant place in the final novels. This is the theme of class stratification, the tensions between the reigning "aristocracy" and the lower classes. In presenting this theme, Crane clearly indicates that he wants to be serious, besides entertaining, in his last novels. But he deals with this issue in such an erratic manner that he fails to present it powerfully. In real life, Crane had fallen in love with a socialite, Helen Trent. This brief alliance made him very conscious of his lesser social standing. Following the success of *The Red Badge,* he was toasted by the aristocracy; this made him even more uncomfortable. In his letters to Nellie Crouse (his relationship with this genteel lady did not get very far), he criticized the established rich for their exhibitionism, their moral weakness, their lack of courage, kindness, and intelligence. He yearned for what he termed the "natural aristocrat." In his early fiction, Crane had already shown his concern for the plight of the poor *(Maggie);* his hostility toward the rich because of their indifference toward the sufferings of the underprivileged ("The Men in the Storm," "An Experiment in Luxury"); and his bitterness over class or social stratification ("An Ominous Baby").

Crane relives these social tensions in *The Third Violet.* But he is ambivalent, emotional, and has too many preconceived notions to deal effectively and in a penetrating way with the theme of class stratification. In a few places in the novel, Crane almost shouts his defiance against wealth and status. In one scene, Hollanden tries to convince Hawker that it is foolish to fall in love with an heiress like Grace Fanhall: "She's got lots of money . . . loads of it." He adds that Hawker must have "loose screws" in his character to have such "expectations." Hawker replies, "Only general poverty—that's all." Also Hawker must complete with a rich rival, Oglethorpe; and Hollanden enjoys pointing out Hawker's liabilities: "He is a rattling good fellow, and he has stacks of money. Of course, in this case his having money doesn't affect the situation much."

Active Service carries the theatrical style of *The Third Violet* to extremes. All the flaws of *The Third Violet* are magnified in *Active Service,* Crane's most crowded "play." His characters continually fight for places on the stage. Artifice and coincidences abound. The action and development of the characters are poorly motivated; and college boys act like adolescents. The plot itself is like a weather cock; it is ever-changing and elaborate, but it never leads to anything substantial.

Active Service is a novel made up of miscellaneous parts. It is satirical in poking fun at Marjory Wainwright's parents, and at the wealthy suitor, Coke. It deals with the theme of class stratification. It is a love story. It is an adventure yarn. It includes actual experiences Crane had during his tour of duty in the Greco-Turkish War, where he and Cora Taylor were fellow journalists. There are also melodramatic and artificial stage devices: the "important" letter Rufus receives in the beginning of the novel, and the timed entrances and exits of the haughty Nora Black. Even a comic opera war is included in the story.

None of these parts is fully developed. One of the important themes—class stratification—is simply fitted to a trite and lengthy plot, and therefore is almost buried. The newspaperman, Rufus Coleman, falls in love with his former professor's daughter, Marjory Wainwright. She is in love with Coleman herself, and ready to ignore social convention and marry him. Her parents, however, are duly shocked; they consider Coleman a "wastrel" and "vulgar." Coke, the millionaire's son, becomes Coleman's rival for Marjory's affection. When Coleman rescues the Wainwright party from behind enemy lines, he is revered as a hero, and the professor and his wife come to find him acceptable. Though he lacks social graces, and is not a "model man," he is well-salaried. Unfortunately, as in *The Third*

Violet, the characters in *Active Service* are one-dimensional stereotypes: the lover, who is also a cad; the heroine, innocent and childlike; the "other" woman, Nora Black, a notorious hussy, who tries to
destroy the growing relationship between Rufus and Marjory; and the
rival suitor, Coke.

Crane's last novel, *The O'Ruddy,* has to be taken more seriously,
though it is a comedy, and though Crane wrote only twenty-four of
the chapters. The rest of the novel, approximately nine chapters, was
written by Robert Barr. Although Crane supplied him with ideas for
later scenes, and with the thread of the entire plot, Barr's portion of
The O'Ruddy is decidedly inferior in quality to Crane's.

In *The O'Ruddy,* Crane toys with the traditional historical romance and with the traditions of the picaresque novel. He is satirical,
having fun at the expense of both the Irish and the English. He
carries over into *The O'Ruddy* two themes from *The Third Violet*
and *Active Service,* those of love and class or social stratification.
Though Crane does not treat these themes with much subtlety or
force (as usual), he does treat them with a great deal of humor. Crane
satirizes the whole concept of aristocracy and class stratification. The
novel's hero, The O'Ruddy, is a poor, good-natured, illiterate "natural
aristocrat," and an Irishman. He woos and eventually wins the
English Lady Mary only after doing battle with her deceitful father,
the Earl of Westport, and her mother, who is both vulgar and an
alcoholic. Crane also toys with the theory of interchangeability. The
O'Ruddy's own servant, Paddy, passes himself off as the King of Ireland; other servants easily impersonate and outdo their own masters
in pomp and circumstance.

Crane's part of *The O'Ruddy* is consistently far more entertaining than either *The Third Violet* or *Active Service.* As a satirist,
Crane is competent, though not profound. *The O'Ruddy* is a gay,
irreverent novel, a period piece, in which Crane shows that his individual creative imagination is still at work and that he has a significant and controlling purpose. Crane's talents were not really wearing
out in the final three novels, as some critics think; he was simply
shifting ground and experimenting with new themes and a new
(traditional) manner.

In his last three novels, Stephen Crane is the conventional writer
dealing with conventional themes; and his prose and themes are generally prosaic and pedestrian. As the conventional writer, Crane can
be entertaining. However, he does not come to grips with the serious
themes literally present in the last novels; he is sidetracked by senti-

mental, romantic, and melodramatic flourishes, which make his ideas seem at times frivolous and superficial. Crane is exciting when he is unconventional, individual, and modern, when his prose and themes are richly suggestive and multi-layered.

Stephen Crane's own subjective and personal tensions, his almost literal wars with society (over poverty and class stratification) and himself, his fascination with the sentimental-romantic-melodramatic theater, his artiness and cleverness, and probably his fixation with brevity of style scattered his strengths as a novelist. His early novels, however, were important, vital, and ambitious works, all of which made significant breakthroughs in style and theme, and paved the way for modern American literature. This is reason enough to consider Stephen Crane more than moderately successful as a novelist.

C. STEPHEN CRANE AS SHORT-STORY WRITER:
AN INTRODUCTION

Although literary historians and critics usually applaud a writer's achievements in the short story, they rarely allot much discussion to them; they give more emphasis and time to the writer's plays, poetry, or novels. Even now in the 1970s, there is little appreciation of the aesthetics of the short story. In addition, short-story collections are looked upon as ephemera, odds and ends left over from novels, or trial runs for novels. All this places Crane at a distinct disadvantage, since he showed his skills best when he wrote short stories.

Both Edward Garnett and H. L. Mencken, among others, respected Crane mainly as a short-story writer; while they increased understanding of Crane's art and brilliance, they admitted to his "limitations." To Garnett, Crane was a master of the short story and of impressionism, but his art was "strictly limited." He was the "interpreter of the surfaces of life," and a student of the "fragmentary." Crane, concluded Garnett, should never "have essayed the form of the novel." Mencken respected Crane's "superlative" talent in "handling isolated situations," but his method "was grossly ill-adapted to the novel." To later critics and readers, Garnett and Mencken present weak arguments for the "narrow" scope of Crane's art.

There are other, more specific reasons why Stephen Crane was not taken seriously as a short-story writer. During his very brief literary career— roughly from 1892 to 1900—Crane wrote more than a hundred short stories and fictional sketches. This made him "prolific," a term often associated with carelessness. In his letters from England, Crane indicated that he was anxious about his financial debts; he also said that he wanted to write short stories because he could do them faster, and to postpone beginning a novel because it would take too much time. All of this suggested that he was not deeply concerned about the quality of his writing. In addition to his reporting, many of his short stories appeared in newspapers, so that people connected Crane with journalism more than with fiction. Moreover, so much discussion and focus have been placed on *Maggie* and *The Red Badge* that anything else was given secondary stress. Nor could anyone's career as a short-story writer end so tragically. When Cora Crane put together *Last Words* (1902), a posthumous potpourri of Crane's early and late fiction and journalism, it proved to many that Crane did not mature, and probably never was much of an artist.

But between some of his earliest work in *The Sullivan County Sketches* (1892) and his last stories, like "The Squire's Madness," Stephen Crane wrote some major American short stories. Attention has centered for decades on four of them: "The Open Boat," "The Blue Hotel," "The Bride Comes to Yellow Sky," and "The Monster." Significantly, each of these stories has recently been read in new ways that suggest a greater understanding and respect for Crane's artistry and vision. For years, "The Bride Comes to Yellow Sky" was read as a satiric comedy, or as a hilarious parody; lately, a few critics have challenged these readings by pointing to Crane's fundamental serious-ness in the western tale. One of the charges leveled against "The Monster" was that it lacked unity. Recent studies show that the story is indeed skillfully organized; this new insight into its unity elucidates and extends the thematic meanings and nuances of the work. Each new study of "The Open Boat" and "The Blue Hotel" opens up new complexities, new proofs of Crane's skill as artist and thinker. If Crane could never be identified as a tragic artist because of his sup-posedly naturalistic and deterministic bias, he is now being appreci-ated as a tragedian. The next step is to recognize in his short stories the rich blend of tragedy and comedy, namely tragicomedy.

In his best stories, Crane was the supremely balanced writer, able to rise above nagging problems with cleverness, boyish posturings, and superficial reflections on reality. The newspaper "feature," such as "An Experiment in Misery," taught Crane the value of seriousness and deeper insight into reality; it also proved to him the need for art and imagination in order to get beyond the topical newspaper report. There was a classic wedding in his great short stories between theme and form, realism and romance, and imagination and experience.

Stephen Crane's talent as a short-story writer can be respected more if critics and readers view some of his collections of stories as novels-of-short-stories. (Two classic American examples of novels-of-short-stories are Sherwood Anderson's *Winesburg, Ohio* and Ernest Hemingway's *In Our Time;* European examples include Ivan Tur-genev's *A Sportsman's Notebook* and James Joyce's *Dubliners.*) Crane's first real collection of short stories was *The Little Regiment and Other Episodes of the American Civil War* (1896). By comparing and con-trasting people, places, attitudes, tones, and themes, Crane's work in *The Little Regiment* is much more than "miniature" leftovers from

The Red Badge. It makes up, as the subtitle to the collection suggests, a series of individual episodes or scenes from the Civil War, which give the work as a whole a unity and experience similar to that of the novel form.

The eight short stories in the American edition of *The Open Boat and Other Tales of Adventure* (1898) also accumulate and display the variety and largeness of the novel world through thematic and artistic parallels and contrasts in the stories, though some of the efforts, like "Flanagan and His Short Filibustering Adventure" and "One Dash—Horses" are by themselves lesser works. Note, for example, how "Flanagan" echoes "The Open Boat." The design of *The Open Boat* was somewhat altered in the English edition, to which Crane added a group of New York pieces, *Midnight Sketches.* When viewed together, these New York sketches are even more valuable artistically and thematically, for they make up a novel of city scenes. Even *Whilomville Stories* (1900) becomes more valuable, for by adding up the thirteen separate glimpses into the life of the child, the reader gains a remarkable and panoramic view into the child's everyday world of drama, fun, and pain.

By "collecting" his stories and thereby viewing art and reality from differing perspectives, beginning with *The Sullivan County Sketches,* Stephen Crane gradually learned to distill more into later individual stories. His best works, like "The Blue Hotel," are deeper, richer, and more profound; they have more originality, power, art, and meaning than the earlier tales and sketches.

Critics are just starting to probe the genre of the short story; they are showing more respect for the "episodic" and the "fragmentary" form, which in the past they had considered as poorly structured and containing little to say. Hopefully in the future, critics and readers will find even more life and value in Stephen Crane's short stories.

1. *"The Open Boat"*

a. Interpretation Through Language:
A Study of the Metaphors in Stephen Crane's "The Open Boat"
By Leedice Kissane

Stephen Crane regarded man's physical encounters as fascinating because they were symbolic of his psychic adventures. Though famous for writing the most sensational story of the Civil War (*The Red Badge of Courage*) without ever having seen a battle, he regarded *The Open Boat,* based on actual experience, as a greater achievement. To Crane the little dinghy with its four occupants facing the measureless sea was in itself a metaphor. The boat was small, no larger than a bathtub, the one single oar weak and frail, seeming ready to snap, and the men able to see only imperfectly because bent to their toil. Each succession of waves threatened to swamp the tiny vessel. All human beings, Crane would have said, are adrift in an open boat.

When Crane wrote his newspaper account of the sinking of the *Commodore,* his own escape with three others in the lifeboat, and their rescue thirty hours later,[1] those hours in the boat were pointedly omitted. Said he: "The history of life in an open boat for thirty hours would no doubt be instructive for the young, but none is to be told here and now." Clearly the author was saving this material for what he knew would be a great story—man against the forces of the universe. Though the narrative he later wrote has the elements of adventure, its interest resides more profoundly in the consciousness of the narrator, in his coming to recognize the inequality of the struggle which is the condition of life, in his acceptance of it, and finally in his sensing of the solaces which make life under its inexorable condition endurable.

Laying bare the psyche of his protagonist was equally the author's purpose in *The Red Badge of Courage,* but the language employed in the two works is strikingly different. To describe the human conflict in which Henry Fleming is engaged, with its gunfire, smoke, wounds, loud cursing, fear, and death, Crane's metaphors are out-

Reprinted from: *Rendezvous* (Idaho State University Journal of Arts and Letters), I (Spring 1966), 18-22. By permission of *Rendezvous.*

landish and violent. They convey the strangeness with which the chaos impinged on the sensibilities of the inexperienced young soldier. In *The Open Boat* the metaphors are of another sort. As Emerson wrote in *Nature*, some sixty years before Crane's setting adrift:

> A man conversing in earnest, if he watch his intellectual processes, will find that a material image more or less luminous arises in his mind, contemporaneous with every thought, which furnishes the vestment of the thought. Hence good writing and brilliant discourse are perpetual allegories. The image is spontaneous. It is the blending of experience with the present action of the mind. It is proper creation.

A situation which pits man against the implacable vastness of the sea demands linguistic vestments of a different nature from those used to suggest the confusion of battle.

Take for example such a metaphor as "Canton flannel gulls." Canton flannel was a fabric much used in the time of Crane's boyhood for sleepingwear, undergarments, even sheets. Its texture was fleecy soft, its color gray or white. To attribute the qualities of this material to sea gulls is startlingly evocative, yet touched with irony, for the gulls are actually hard and intrusive with their beady eyes and annoying persistence. Another figure often noted is this: "The waves rippled like carpets on the line in a gale." Carpets as Crane knew them were thin (no doubt woven of household rags) and were frequently hung on the clothesline where they were hand-beaten by means of a heavy wire beater. They had to be this very kind of thin rag-carpet in order to ripple in the fashion Crane, the impeccable observer, ascribes to them. Even the figure showing the riskiness of moving about in the boat has the aptness of real experience: "It was easier to steal eggs from under a hen than to change seats in the dinghy."

These are only a few of the material images that rose in the author's mind as he sought to express the thoughts and sensations of the correspondent during his hours in the boat. Almost without exception they are drawn from domestic routines he knew as a boy. "In *The Open Boat* things viewed by the men at sea are viewed as though they were men on land," says R. W. Stallman.[2] Furthermore, could we not say, things at sea are described in terms of specific experiences the men have undergone on land, blended with present impressions or actions of the mind to achieve what Emerson calls "proper creation." For revealing simultaneously the external situation of the men in the boat and the internal workings of the correspondent's consciousness, these domestic figures are eminently well chosen, their consistency serving as a unifying force in the work.

But Crane's use of metaphorical language in *The Open Boat* performs a function beyond the aesthetic. It reinforces his theme by stressing the puniness of man in contrast to the vastness of the physical universe. Its effect throughout the tale is to reduce man in order to magnify the unevenness of his struggle against nature. Memories of carpets on the line, of the feel of fleecy flannel, of gathering eggs—all are those of childhood. The human being is belittled by these figures into puerility, a state in which he is even less well equipped for his uneven struggle.

He is rendered negligible as well by the lowliness of the metaphors—the ordinariness of the life reflected in them with its commonplace chores, activities of the kitchen (where Stephen as a boy must have spent much of his time), and the many indications of near-poverty and humble household arrangements. This suggestion of paltriness in man's stature and conditions is borne out by the prevalence of understatement or litotes: e.g., "Neither the oiler nor the correspondent was fond of rowing at this time." The trivial mundanity of the cook is revealed by his question: "What kind of pie do you like best?" Even the admirable captain is made to seem faintly ridiculous—"like a man looking over a board fence"—as he floats toward shore clinging to a fragment of the boat.

As if these glimpses of human littleness do not sufficiently reduce man, as a crowning indignity he is equated with lower forms of animal life: "The tower was a giant with its back to the plight of the ants." In the famous outcry "Why was I allowed to come so far and nibble the sacred cheese of life?" the speaker parallels himself by implication with an insignificant mouse.

This is Crane's method of showing the bigness of the forces that encompass man. He never expatiates on the expanse of water surrounding the men in the little boat, characterizing only the waves within the radius of their vision. As an example there is this statement, referring to night at sea: "The two lights were the furniture of the world." The emphasis here is not on the untenanted ocean, but on the two pinpoints of light which are its only visible objects. To designate these transitory and ephemeral glimmers, "furniture" seems an oddly specific term. But in its connotation of being exclusively man-made and used by man, and in its limited and humdrum quality, it points up that contrast between human existence and cosmic regime which is the author's chief concern.

If the conflicting forces engaged in this tale are man and nature, the psychic struggle clearly involves man's attitude toward the forces of nature. In tracing the steps the correspondent takes in reaching a fixed conclusion, the author's figures of speech prove most revealing.

At first the man in the boat looks upon nature as an enemy—maliciously cruel and vengeful. "The waves were most barbarously abrupt and tall" pictures faceless savagery endowed with a killer's ferocity. The mousetrap figure mentioned above demonstrates the most wanton cruelty of all, for just as the timid victim approaches the very stuff of life, the fatal trap is sprung. Though the correspondent cries out against such injustice, as he may have protested the slaughter of mice in his mother's kitchen, his cry is rhetorical and seems to expect no clemency.

As the hours in the dinghy pass and the man rows alone at night, his judgment of nature alters. Not gratuitously cruel, perhaps, but surely nature is irresponsibly, chancily menacing. The shark that flashes through the dark water near the boat is likened to a great, gleaming knife, another household object dreaded for its accidental as well as intentional deeds of blood. This creature appears soon after the correspondent's tirade against Fate—"that old ninny-woman"—as an old hen who knows not her intention. He may be thinking of the one of the three mythical sisters who holds her scissors poised to cut man's tenuous thread of life. The shark is an appropriate cutting agent, and the severing of man's life by its agency is as utterly a matter of chance. When the shark veers away as casually as it came, the hit-or-miss quality of Fate or chance is underscored.

At this point the correspondent arrives at the unwelcome truth that nature really does not care. "She is indifferent, flatly indifferent." She would not regard the disposal of him as maiming to the universe. He longs, in a fit of juvenile frustration, to fling bricks at the temple, but in the watery waste around him there are neither bricks nor temples. "A high cold star on a winter's night is the word he feels that she [nature] says to him."

There is no mistaking the inevitability of this edict. The figure of the star is not only cold and remote; it is not to be questioned, and it will not change. Its message is final. This figure closes a section of the tale, and the next one opens with the literary allusion to the soldier who lay dying in Algiers.

Like other figures of speech, literary allusion jets from deep in the subconscious. Unlike them, it is born not of an actual experience but of an intellectual impression—not a material image as Emerson described it, but a mental one. To the narrator the coming into his mind of this bit of verse was mysterious (for he had even forgotten it) but not irrelevant, for it "chimed the notes of his emotion"—the emotion induced by the word from the high, cold, indifferent star.

The narrator has already recognized as precious the comradeship of the men in the boat as they confront the ruthlessness of their common enemy. "The best experience of his life," he calls it. But as a solace for cold indifference and threatened annihilation, a more cosmic comfort is needed, and this is suggested by the thought of the soldier's plight.

"A soldier of the Legion lay dying in Algiers;
There was lack of women's nursing; there was dearth of women's tears;
But a comrade stood beside him and he took that comrade's hand,
And he said, 'I never more shall see my own, my native land.' "

The correspondent recalls that as a school boy he had been bored at the repetitive sing-song of his classmates as each in turn droned this passage from memory. He had cared little about that far-off lonely death. "Less than the breaking of a pencil point," he remembers. Yet now, pictorially vivid, the scene flashes on his inner eye—the low, square buildings, dry sands, the moribund soldier clutching his bleeding wound. And retroactively, as it were, his sympathy wells up. He is sorry.

Though Crane arrives at this rush of pity in a roundabout way, his purpose is clear enough. Only through his own experiencing of outrageous fortune and the imminence of death has the correspondent gained maturity enough to feel compassion for the universal human condition. To feel warm consideration for those close to one whose plight is identified with one's own is natural enough, but to know pity for suffering in general is a transcendent virtue. And it is comforting to know that such human pity exists, especially when one has just perceived the futility of an appeal to the forces that control the world.

Possibly the reference to the remembered poem has another and deeper meaning. Although it is evident that Crane's metaphors, like all metaphorical language, carry a greater weight of significance than at first seems obvious, more unusual are the indications that this significance may be partly or even wholly unintended by the author. Support for this view can be found in Mark Schorer's fine study of metaphorical language—"Fiction and the 'Matrix of Analogy.' " Emily Bronte, the critic points out, learned from her own metaphors, as her genius operated to uncover images that meant more than she consciously knew. "Her rhetoric altered the form of her intention," says Schorer. "It is her education; it shapes her insight." [3]

The change in attitude toward the suffering Legionnaire may have more to reveal than the correspondent's growth in spiritual stature and the comforting implication that universal compassion exists as a sort of general solace for human misfortunes. The second line in the quotation provides a clue—"There was lack of women's nursing; there was dearth of women's tears."

Crane maintains a jeering attitude toward women throughout his tale (there is his reference to Fate as an old ninny-woman, an old hen who knows not her intention) and this at first would seem to be intensified by the bathos of the quoted line: "there was lack of women's nursing; there was dearth of women's tears," especially as rendered with the customary juvenile inflection. Yet the memory of the stanza *in its entirety* prompts the correspondent's spontaneous pity. The implication is plain: If man must venture into far lands and uncharted seas in his physical and psychic quests, he has need *in extremis* of the comforts of woman and the solace of her tears.

The very quality of the metaphors that Crane employs throughout this work suggests a submerged tenderness for home and mother that the author would have scorned to betray. The figures, as we have seen, are drawn from boyhood activities, mostly bounded by kitchen, backyard, and chicken coop. These are the provinces of the women of the household. Here they dispense the comfort and order which a young boy may resent, only to remember it later with longing.

There is ambivalence as well in the treatment of the middle-aged women with coffee-pots "and other remedies sacred to their minds" who follow in the wake of the male rescuer, a naked man who wears like a saint a halo around his head. These are ninny-women, no doubt—old hens—whose faith in their nostrums is scorned in the phrase "sacred to their minds." Yet the very word *sacred* portrays the author's unconsciously altered intention. *Sacred* parallels the saint-like accoutrements of the man rescuer. It is the very word used repeatedly in the key phrase "the *sacred* cheese of life." The remedies are sacred to a woman's mind because they assist her in her peculiar function—that of soothing, minstering to, and nurturing life. They are sacred to all for that reason. *Sacred* becomes, then, a sort of transferred epithet.

Finally the need of women, their love and tears, is implicit in the manner in which Crane tells of the oiler's tragic end. The land welcomes him, too, though he is dead; he is received with hospitality, only a different (cold) hospitality—that of the grave. Throughout the tale the land is the *desideratum;* glimpsing land and trees is equated with nibbling the sacred cheese of life. There is comfort in the hospitality of even a grave on land (where it can be visited and wept over). Hospitality has feminine overtones.

Though clearly attesting to Crane's deterministic beliefs, this tale of the men in the boat cannot be termed pessimistic. There are human influences that mitigate the admitted indifference of nature to insignificant man. One is the association with one's fellows that Crane joyously proclaims; one is the capacity for universal pity, which he feels can be learned through suffering; and one is the love of women which he yet seems to spurn. But the indication of this love is incontrovertibly present, buried in the language. I. A. Richards lists as one of the values of metaphor its ability to "smuggle in," in a semi-surreptitious way, whatever is needed for the wholeness of experience.[4] It is largely through Crane's inadvertent choice of figures that his readers sense the wholeness of his meaning and along with protagonists, learn to be *interpreters.*

NOTES

1. Stephen Crane, "Stephen Crane's Own Story," *New York Press*, January 7, 1897, p. 1; reprinted in *Stephen Crane, An Omnibus,* ed. Robert Wooster Stallman (New York, 1952), p. 475.
2. *Stephen Crane, An Omnibus,* p. 419.
3. *Kenyon Review*, XI (Autumn 1949), 550.
4. *Principles of Literary Criticism* (New York, 1930), p. 240.

b. Realistic Devices in Stephen Crane's "The Open Boat"
By Charles R. Metzger

One of the most obvious things that a writer can do to make his writing seem true to life is to introduce a considerable amount of factual detail. In *The Open Boat* Stephen Crane does exactly this. He is able to introduce a great deal of factual detail largely because he has chosen to tell the story of *The Open Boat* through the person of an "invisible" character that we might call the omniscient narrator. The omniscient narrator can introduce the other characters; he can tell us facts that the characters do not know; he can tell us facts that we do not know and that the characters would not mention in dialogue simply because they know them so well. The narrator can announce for our benefit certain generalizations that will either explain action that follows or summarize action that has already occurred. The omniscient narrator, once he has introduced us to the scene, can be silent and let us overhear conversation, let us learn facts, opinions, etc., from the characters themselves. Being omniscient, the narrator can know what is going on in the mind of a particular character—what he is thinking—as is the case with Crane's reporter in *The Open Boat,* and he can even allow us to "overhear" such interior monologues.

The danger that attends using an omniscient narrator in order to present large quantities and varieties of factual information to the reader is that this narrator may get in the way of the action; he may impede it by volunteering too many facts, too many opinions. Stephen Crane reduces this danger by doing several things. He limits the amount of factual detail or commentary that is introduced—altogether and at any given time. He does not introduce factual detail that the reader doesn't really need to know. He doesn't tell us the name of the ship that sank; he doesn't tell us the Captain's name or the color of the dingey. He does not try to introduce the factual detail he does present all at the same time and he does not introduce all of it through the narrator; he introduces some of it through dialogue. We learn that the oiler's name is Billie by hearing the Captain address him by name. We learn the crucial difference between

Reprinted from: *The Midwest Quarterly,* IV (Autumn 1962), 50-54. By permission of *The Midwest Quarterly.*

a house of refuge and a lifesaving station by overhearing an argument between the cook and the correspondent. By the time the narrator tells us there is no lifesaving station within twenty miles of the dingey, we have already learned what a lifesaving station is.

Crane is careful not only in restricting his presentation of facts to those that will prepare for or validate action, but he is careful also to present facts in terms of appropriate perspectives. In announcing at the beginning of the story that "None of them knew the color of the sky. Their eyes . . . were fastened upon the waves that swept toward them," he suggests to the reader those facts that would be significant to persons in the situation being described. A person in a small boat threatened by every wave is going to be looking at the waves. Later on in the story Crane repeats the same kind of assertion in a slightly different way. He indicates the approach of dawn by describing a change observable in the color of the waves.

Crane also introduces facts to his characters (and hence to the reader) in versions of the ways in which we apprehend facts in real life. In the scene where the correspondent (who is rowing) sees the shark, the word *shark* is not used until after the evidence that would lead a person to conclude that he had seen and heard a shark has been presented: the correspondent is described as hearing the tearing sound (of the shark's fin cutting the surface of the water), as seeing the phosphorescent flash, as seeing the fin itself. All of these events are described and repeated before the word *shark* is ever introduced. In real life, when an experience is unanticipated, we have it first; then assign the words to it that give it discursive meaning. Conversely, as in the sighting of the house of refuge in this story, we sometimes are able to perceive things that we would not otherwise notice, or perceive them earlier than we would otherwise, because we have them, or the word for them, in mind.

Crane's short story appears realistic to us, his characters seem believable, not only because he presents us with a large number of relevant facts apprehended by the characters and by ourselves in versions of the ways that we apprehend facts in real life; but also, because he allows for, because he presents in his story, multiple perspectives, multiple interpretations, and the commission and correction of error. The correspondent does not know for example that anyone but himself has seen the shark, until the captain mentions that he saw it too. The characters in the boat do not know that there is not a lifesaving station within twenty miles; but they are able, by checking their interpretations of what they see and by correcting for error, to determine that the "lifeboat" on the beach is not a lifeboat, but an omnibus, that the man who appears running, but seems to be going too fast, and with an awkward posture, is actually riding a bicycle. Crane also allows (as in the case of the omnibus) his characters to interpret the things they see hopefully; then he allows them to realize the less hopeful but more accurate interpretation; and then he allows them to be angry. He has his characters do this repeatedly, as we readers do the same things repeatedly in real life.

A word now about repetition, which is a very common and a very effective device for making a fact or an event in fiction seem real. There are actually two main kinds of repetition. The first kind is sometimes called preparation and involves mentioning one or more times the possibility that something is likely to happen (in *The Open Boat* the repeated suggestion that the boat will probably swamp, that somebody is likely to be drowned, etc.). Later on in the story when the event actually takes place it seems credible; it seems real to the reader because he has been prepared for its happening by having been told that it might. Most readers don't notice on the first reading of a piece of fiction that they are being "prepared." They forget in their conscious minds what they have been told. The fact that subconsciously many readers remember what they have been told about action that may transpire, makes the action seem real to them when it finally is presented. Another kind of repetition, one of which the reader is usually quite conscious, is akin to the refrain used in poetry. Crane's refrain in *The Open Boat* that begins "If I am going to be drowned—if I am going to be drowned—if I am going to be drowned," is of this sort. Yet even as a refrain that is repeated grossly, it is psychologically defensible since it reminds the reader of those thoughts in real life that often occur to him repeatedly and over which he has a minimum amount of control, since those thoughts are occasioned by his experience and are expressions of his anxiety in relation to that experience. Even the apparently irrational recollection by the correspondent of the poem memorized in childhood about "the soldier of the Legion dying in Algiers" is of this same sort; for the topic of dying—the meaning of the poem memorized in childhood but not understood until the presence of death has been made real by experience—pervades the whole story—and the poem as fact has the same relevance as any other of the facts presented, only ironically so.

Irony is a device often used by "realistic" writers (even as it is used by Crane) to create the illusion of reality. In one sense irony can be viewed as a special version of multiple perspective. It involves a double or contrasting view of events—a contrast usually stated as opposites, between what is expected and what happens, between illusion and reality, between what man would prefer and what he gets. In some respects irony is one of the weakest of realistic devices, because it is so easy. One of the easiest things in the world to do is to point out the contrast between a particular view of the world (*i. e.*, that nature is our home, our permissive and gentle parent) and the facts (namely that the wind, the sea and the tides do not care about us). When irony is given a broader statistical base, when the writer suggests that his characters do not get exactly the opposite of what they expect or want, but merely something different; when irony is expanded to become chance, it is a stronger device. Notice, for example, that it is not the cook who is wearing the life jacket who drowns. It is the oiler, who, however, is portrayed as a strong swimmer.

Despite the weakness of what amounts to occasional gross irony, *The Open Boat* is a very realistic piece of writing; and it is so because the facts presented, the perspectives employed, the contrasts stated are all joined in the work to describe not only some impressive facts of life, but also to demonstrate some defensible generalizations, not only about human experience, but also about how that experience is apprehended and how, when it is apprehended, we react to it.

c. Naturalistic Fiction: "The Open Boat"
By Richard P. Adams

The question as to what constitutes naturalism in art is a vexed
and vexing one, sometimes asked in such a way as to imply pretty
clearly that in the asker's opinion there can be no such thing as art
in naturalism. Yet, in the art of fiction, at least, there is a generally
recognized naturalistic school, which needs to be related better than
it has been in most literary history and criticism to other tendencies
of its time, particularly those of realism and symbolism, and to the
general romantic tradition in which realism, naturalism, and symbolism have all developed. Stephen Crane's story "The Open Boat,"
which is one of the best as well as one of the best known documents
in the American room of the naturalistic school, seems to me to offer
a particularly favorable ground on which to examine these relations
and the problems they present.

Crane gave this story the subtitle "A Tale Intended to be after
the Fact: Being the Experience of Four Men from the Sunk Steamer
'Commodore' "; and, as far as we know or are likely to know, its
events are quite literally those which Crane, as a newspaper correspondent covering a filibustering expedition to Cuba, together with
Captain Edward Murphy, Steward C. B. Montgomery, and Seaman
William Higgins, experienced after the sinking of their ship off the
east coast of Florida. But "The Open Boat" is obviously fiction, as
Crane's careful wording of the subtitle suggests he intended. The
difference between the experience and the story lies not in any
distortion of the facts, even by rearrangement, but purely in their
selection and their handling. It is a matter, for the most part, of what
we may broadly call style; more specifically, it depends in large
measure on Crane's development of a theme and a structure to give
the facts meaning and on his use of vivid imagery to give them life
and power. The result is in my opinion as much a work of art and
of Crane's imagination as if it had all been invented; or as much, it
might be said, as *The Red Badge of Courage,* which Crane wrote
several years before he saw his first battle.

Crane made a clear distinction between the fact and the fiction,

Reprinted from: *Tulane Studies in English,* IV (1954), 137-146. By permission of
Tulane Studies in English.

not only in his subtitle but in the whole work. He must have seen the story in the experience at once, for in his report to the New York *Press*, published four days and dated only three days after he got ashore, he said, with scant apology, that "The history of life in an open boat for thirty hours," although it "would no doubt be instructive for the young," would not "be told here and now." [1] The story relates just that experience. Its structure is superficially defined by the sequence of happenings from Saturday morning, January 2, when the ship went down, to about noon Sunday, January 3, when the dinghy with the four men came to land near Daytona Beach. Nothing is said in the fictional version about the circumstances of the expedition, and there is only a very brief glimpse of the foundering ship and the seven men who went down with it. Even the names of the four in the dinghy are suppressed, except that William Higgins is called, or miscalled, Billie.

The men in the boat leave the scene of the wreck in the morning, approach the shore and try unsuccessfully to land that evening. They pull back to sea, where they spend the night rowing by turns. They try again the next morning to land, this time successfully, except for Billie, who is killed in the surf. This framework might be abstractly formulated as a loss of safety, an approach to safety, a retreat from safety, and a flawed achievement of safety. On and around its bare bones Crane develops his story to the semblance, inclusively symbolic, of an aspect of human experience that persuades us of its interest, convinces us of its importance, and leaves us with a firm sense of its esthetic value and satisfactoriness. Let us inquire more particularly how this is done.

The meaning of the experience, Crane says explicitly, lies in the realization on the part of the men, or at least the correspondent, that nature is indifferent to their welfare. This indifference of nature is the theme and burden of popular scientific materialism and of much naturalistic literature, especially fiction, written during the past century. In "The Open Boat" this typical attitude is expressed in a dialectic opposition of hope, as the men approach the land, and fear, as they are temporarily forced to retreat from it, resolved in the conviction of a meaningless determinism in which there is nothing for either hope or fear to seize on. This conviction is justified or at least confirmed when, by what may seem sheer luck, three of the men come through alive and the fourth does not. It is emphasized by the ironic circumstance that this fourth man, Billie the oiler, is "a wily surfman," the only competent sailor in the lot (the captain being disabled by an injured arm), and the one who has done more than any other to bring them all safely in. There is nothing malignant in this, nor is there anything friendly, or indeed anything at all resembling a human emotion. To the correspondent, as the decision is made to try for shore on the morning of the second day, nature "did not seem cruel ... nor beneficent, nor treacherous, nor wise. But she was indifferent, flatly indifferent." The gap between *seem* and *be* in this passage expresses the overt point of the story.

There are two main symbols for this "serenity of nature amid the struggles of the individual." One of them, the tower on shore which Crane says "was a giant, standing with its back to the plight of the ants," contains the meaning a little awkwardly, and would seem to represent rather the apparent indifference of the people on land than the supposed indifference of nature. The other, which comes earlier in the story, fits the intended meaning better. Leading up to it is the passage describing the process of a man's (implicitly, the correspondent's) realization "that nature does not regard him as important, and that she feels she would not maim the universe by disposing of him," which displaces an anthropomorphic reflection on "the seven mad gods who rule the sea" and who seem determined to drown him. A man in this plight, Crane says, "at first wishes to throw bricks at the temple, and he hates deeply the fact that there are no bricks and no temples." Then he becomes afraid: "he feels, perhaps, the desire to confront a personification and indulge in pleas." Nature, however, is not a person but an abstraction, as Crane's second symbol indicates. "A high cold star on a winter's night is the word he feels that she says to him. Thereafter he knows the pathos of his situation."

The feeling of extreme coldness and remoteness embodied in this second metaphor is a logical concomitant of naturalism. Hyatt H. Waggoner has shown how characteristic it is of our recent literature, describing it, in a term aptly borrowed from John Burroughs, as "the cosmic chill." It is caused, as Waggoner says, by the conviction that the material world is alien to the desires, emotions, and esthetic needs of the human spirit.[2] This conviction and the chilly feeling that goes with it constitute, in my opinion, the distinguishing characteristic of naturalism. And the naturalistic attitude is brilliantly struck in Crane's "high cold star" metaphor, which is as precise as Burroughs' "cosmic chill" and much more concrete.

But, like most naturalists in literature, Crane treats the situation ironically, adopting for his purpose a strategy of radical inconsistency.

In the very passages where he says that nature is not a person but a thing, he calls it "she," as any sentimental disciple of Wordsworth might do while musing on the flowers of the meadow. He sounds like a frustrated romantic, a man convinced very much against his will that the alien world of popular science is the real one, and still very much involved emotionally and esthetically in the "pathetic fallacy," the earlier belief that nature stands in close relation to man, that, indeed, man and nature are organically interfused in a unity that includes and reconciles all things. I am inclined to think that this inconsistency is fundamental and functional in most if not all naturalistic literature. Much of the energy informing that literature, much of the emotional power that makes it go, can be accounted for only by a submerged but still vital belief in the romantic world of warmth and relatedness, the world of Wordsworth and Emerson.

In "The Open Boat" this inconsistency seems deliberate, and it is certainly systematic. Much of the imagery, for example, is heavily and obviously animistic, implying in dozens of terms that the natural things Crane says are indifferent are full of feeling. Waves are not content to be just "abrupt and tall"; they are "wrongfully and barbarously" so. The boat, like "a bucking bronco," is said to have "pranced and reared and plunged"; going over a wave, "she seemed like a horse making at a fence outrageously high," has a "scramble" to get over, and at last "scornfully" bumps the top. In the trough this marish craft is described as "bobbing and nodding" before the next wave, which is called not a wave but a "menace." The waves are also alive in a living sea; each one seems like "the final outburst of the ocean, the last effort of the grim water," and they have "a terrible grace" and "snarling . . . crests." In a further inconsistency, the boat and the waves together correspond to the naturalistic picture of man's situation in the universe: "The little boat, lifted by each towering sea and splashed viciously by the crests, made progress that in the absence of seaweed was not apparent to those in her. She seemed just a wee thing wallowing miraculously, top up, at the mercy of five oceans." This animistic imagery, which pervades the story if anything too much, points up the ironic contrast between the world as romantic men would like to have it—a friendly, living cosmos full of familiar beings and benign feelings—and the world as the popularizers of science tell us it really is—a dead, alien, blind and indifferent congeries of forces.[3]

This irony works in reverse to heighten the effect when a

harmless and only too friendly gull, attempting comically to land on the captain's head, seems to the men "somehow gruesome and ominous," an image which may owe something to *The Ancient Mariner*. Later the same thing is done even more effectively when a shark, the only other actually animate thing to be seen in the ocean, appears to the correspondent "like a gigantic and keen projectile." Here the image recalls *The Red Badge of Courage*, where the blind forces of the naturalistic universe are symbolized by storms of shot and shell.

It seems to me that Crane's use of color in the story helps, in a less explicit but perhaps more subtle way, to build up the same kind of contrast and tension. I am reluctant to make the risky attempt of assigning particular meanings to particular colors, though it may well be that in some contexts they do have such meanings.[4] The wan light of dawn, for example, in which the faces of the men appear gray, and the lighthouse, a very doubtful aid which looks like "a little gray shadow on the sky," may connote the state of worrisome uncertainty with which the story begins.[5] In general, the contrast between light and darkness corresponds vaguely with such oppositions as knowledge and ignorance, confidence and depression, safety and danger, the stock meanings in romantic literature; but Crane's use of it in this story is hardly very systematic or consistent. There is something perhaps a little more tangible in the association of brilliant phosphorescence with the night vision of the projectile shark. Symbolically the shark embodies both life and danger and like the gull suggests a key passage in *The Ancient Mariner*. However, no one in the dinghy is reported to have blessed it unaware.

But the sheer quantity of color in the story, if nothing else, makes the question of its meaning impossible to ignore. By my count there are nearly a hundred more or less distinct terms referring to some kind or aspect of color; and, as every reader of Crane knows, this concentration is one of his most striking personal traits of style. Color for him, whether it means anything specific or not, is always a thing to be noticed, and this interest is in itself, like any act of attention, a value judgment. To Crane, for some reason, color is unusually important.

There is a clue, though a tenuous one, in a passage where, just after nightfall, a "gold" light in the south and "a small bluish gleam on the edge of the waters" to the north are said to be "the furniture of the world," in contrast to the monotony of the waves in the otherwise complete darkness. The word "furniture" might easily break down under too much weight of interpretation, but it does connote home and the comforts of home. It may be regarded as at least a slight indication that what Crane values in color is its tendency to oppose or partly counteract the bleakness of the "high cold star on a winter's night" which embodies the feeling of alienation, or homelessness, of man in the material world. A properly colored world would perhaps be a furnished, comfortably livable home. If so, Crane's emphasis on color reinforces the meaning of the story in the same way that the animistic imagery does, by heightening the contrast between the world of man's desiring and the world of so-called objective reality.

A completely consistent naturalism presumably requires that everything, including man, be reduced to the terms of material cause and effect, as in the behaviorist psychology. But Crane, like most other more or less declared naturalists in literature, is unwilling, perhaps unable, to pay the price of that reduction for whatever benefits might be supposed to accrue from such narrow and rigid consistency. In "The Open Boat" as in *The Red Badge of Courage* and especially in "The Blue Hotel," his men, through whatever trials of danger, suffering, and blind or willful injustice, remain in possession of their souls. Indeed, as a result of their experience, and quite in the traditional romantic fashion, they find or save their souls; that is, they grow stronger, wiser, broader, and more mature.

In this connection the total structure of "The Open Boat" is meaningful in a way that goes far beyond the abstract formula of safety lost and regained, and becomes one of death and rebirth, a symbolic pattern used in many romantic works to convey the essence of personal development. Its focus in Crane might be defined, or at least paraphrased, as the realization of mortality acting to deepen the understanding and increase the love of life, both within the individual and in his relations to others. Crane seems to be saying, as Whitman said before him, that the central meaning of life can be grasped only in the face of death. In *The Red Badge of Courage* the death of Jim Conklin and in "The Blue Hotel" the collaborative murder of the Swede bring important realizations and other changes for the better to the main characters, contributing decisively to their development as men. In "The Open Boat" the same result is achieved, less specifically but no less impressively, by nature's killing of the oiler. The men, like the boy in "Out of the Cradle Endlessly Rocking," listen at night to "the sound of the great sea's voice," and feel that they can now "be interpreters." In his treatment of this motif Crane is entirely romantic and thoroughly out of harmony with the tenets of scientific materialism.

Crane's handling, to be sure, is less bold than that of many early romantics. "The Open Boat" has no such feeling as Melville conveys in his chapter "The Lee Shore" in *Moby Dick*. Melville's Ishmael maintains that "in landlessness alone resides the highest truth," and therefore he would rather remain in deep water and, if he must, "perish in that howling infinite, than be ingloriously dashed upon the lee, even if that were safety! For worm-like, then, oh! who would craven crawl to land!" One answer is that Crane's correspondent would; he is no Bulkington and will be no Ishmael. He wants the comforts of blankets and coffee after the struggle through the waves, as Crane apparently wants some stable certainty in human character to oppose to the deadly certainties of science. The characteristic aim in the early romantic period was to adventure joyously on the boundless ocean of life, on dangerous but fascinating journeys to more than India, through the innumerable relations of universal sympathy. Crane's attitude, by comparison, is almost desperately defensive.

His feeling for human brotherhood, though it is genuine and strong, is also fundamentally different from Melville's or Whitman's. Instead of saying that men and the elements of nature should and normally do work together for the good of the whole, Crane, like Arnold in "Dover Beach," seems to maintain that because the world is indifferent, because human feelings are in human beings only and not in nature, men should be true to one another, and are most likely to be so when they are most in the grip of impersonal cosmic forces. It is immediately after the occurrence of the "high cold star" image that Crane has the correspondent remember and suddenly, for the first time, sympathize with the soldier whose death in Algiers had only bored him before.

Crane's defensiveness is of course in the best of causes, to guard individual human growth and collective human brotherhood against the brutalizing influences of an anti-intellectual and anti-emotional materialism. But his desperation indicates and exposes the weakness of naturalism as a philosophy and a way of life. The naturalists give up the strongest positions before they begin to fight, when they fight at all. It appears very certain to me that anyone who aspires to be more than a laboratory technician must either adhere, however grimly, to the old-fashioned humanist idealism, deny the reality or at least the importance of matter, and take his licking like a man;

or more boldly and I think with a better prospect of making his point, affirm the faith of most of the early and all the best romantics in a universe where it is not entity but relationship, not the what but the how, that counts. A world divided, as both naturalists and humanists tend to divide it, between the vast impersonal forces of omnipotent nature on one hand and the suffering sensibilities of helpless humanity on the other cannot stand.

It does not follow by any means from this criticism of naturalism as philosophy that it may not contribute effectively to the shaping and to the final worth of a story such as "The Open Boat." The very tensions of an inconsistent or contradictory attitude often seem to generate the power with which the artist springs to his highest achievements. If an author can contain these tensions in a symbolic structure such as Crane's pattern of death and rebirth, and if he can weave a sufficiently rich and weighty texture of subordinate imagery around it, as Crane does by laying metaphors of life across metaphors and explicit statements of death, the result may be an emergent synthesis of great power and beauty.

It is precisely for these reasons, of course, that "The Open Boat" is so obviously a work of fiction and not merely a report of certain facts. The circumstance that it does follow a certain set of events, just as they really happened, seems the least important thing about it; if it did no more than that it would have been buried in the files and forgotten long ago, as many of Crane's newspaper stories have been and as many more would have been if he had not also written fiction. But, because the facts are presented in relation to an important and widely appealing theme, because they have lent themselves to arrangement in a symbolic structure the meaning of which transcends both facts and theme, and because the whole is brought to life and into the feelings of its readers by the use of powerfully congruent imagery, the result has permanent significance. Therein lies the difference between fact and fiction, between the world and the painting, between experience at random and great art.

NOTES

1. New York *Press*, January 7, 1897, p. 1; reprinted in *Stephen Crane: An Omnibus*, ed. R. W. Stallman (New York, 1952), p. 475.

2. Hyatt H. Waggoner, *The Heel of Elohim: Science and Values in Modern American Poetry* (Norman, Oklahoma, 1950), p. 21 *et passim*. Cf. John Burroughs, *The Light of Day* (Boston, 1900), pp. 118-120.

3. Meyer H. Abrams, in *The Mirror and the Lamp* (New York, 1953), pp. 55, 65, points out that among the hallmarks of early romantic literature are its "valid animation of natural objects" and its "attempt to overcome the sense of man's alienation from the world by healing the cleavage between subject and object, between the vital, purposeful, value-full world of private experience and the dead postulated world of extension, quantity, and motion. To establish that man shares his own life with nature was to reanimate the dead universe of the materialists, and at the same time most effectively to tie man back into his milieu."

4. Stallman, pp. 185-187, plausibly proposes several such meanings for colors in *The Red Badge of Courage*, but in his discussion of "The Open Boat," pp. 415-420, he is reticent on the subject.

5. See Richard H. Fogle, "The Monk and the Bachelor: Melville's *Benito Cereno*," *Tulane Studies in English*, III (1952), 162-163, for a similar use of the color gray.

2. *"The Bride Comes to Yellow Sky"*

a. *"The Bride Comes to Yellow Sky" as Comedy*
By A. M. Tibbetts

"The Bride Comes to Yellow Sky" has perhaps been misread
more often than any other story of Crane's. Many critics misread it
because they try to interpret it as serious allegory instead of appre-
ciating it as comedy. R. W. Stallman believes, for example, that the
marshal and the badman "represent two opposite worlds or points of
view: the idealistic world of spiritual values whose force lies in its
innocence, and the non-imaginative world of crass realities" (*Stephen
Crane: An Omnibus*, New York, 1952, p. 484). Robert Barnes states
that the story is a "conflict of the East vs. the West" and that the
marshal's new wife is "the symbol of Eastern civilization, duplicity,
and evil" (Item 39, *The Explicator*, 16, April 1958).

    There are probably two reasons for such misreading of "The
Bride." First, Crane's short-story technique, which was formed by
an arresting mixture of modes and strategies, seems to have been
created on purpose to mislead unwary readers. Like Mark Twain,
Ambrose Bierce, Bret Harte, and others whose writing fell into the
tradition of frontier humor and literary comedy, Crane worked hard
the veins of burlesque, irony, and serio-comic exaggeration and understatement. In his belief that life was a long and bitter trick, Crane
actually seems closest to Bierce. But none of the literary comedies
had Crane's control of metaphor and image. The lines that one
always remembers from a Crane story are those that fuse an ironic
statement of a bitter, terrible, or frightening condition with an
equally strong poetic statement. Here, for instance, is a passage from
"The Open Boat," in which the sea's horizon is described as having
an edge "jagged with waves that seemed thrust up in points like rocks":

    A singular disadvantage of the sea lies in the fact that after

Reprinted from: "Stephen Crane's 'The Bride Comes to Yellow Sky,'" *English
Journal*, LIV (April 1965), 314-316. By permission of the National Council of
Teachers of English, copyright © 1965, and A. M. Tibbetts.

> successfully surmounting one wave you discover that there is
> another behind it just as important and just as *nervously
> anxious to do something effective in the way of swamping
> boats.* . . . There was a *terrible grace* in the move of the waves,
> and they came in silence, save for the *snarling of the crests*
> (italics added).

Many writers of Crane's time could have produced the first of these
two sentences, but few if any of them could have written the second.

A probable second reason why critics tend to misread "The
Bride" is that they are accustomed to read Crane as a writer of
portentous and symbolic tragedies. From the early *Maggie,* to *The
Red Badge of Courage,* to the fine, late stories like "The Monster,"
"The Blue Hotel," and "The Open Boat," Crane worked in poetic
sentences freighted with dark meaning. Superficially, "The Bride"
has a fictional ring similar to the other great stories. But it must be
read differently, for it is nearly pure comedy

In fairness, I should say that a few critics have mentioned comic
aspects of "The Bride," but none has treated the story in detail as
a comedy. G. W. Johnson has referred to "the comic aspects of the
'transaction' which occurs between two different conventions . . ."
(*PMLA,* 78, 1963, p. 254). Edwin Cady calls the story "a hilariously
funny parody of neo-romantic lamentations over 'The Passing of the
West' " (*Journal of English Literary History,* 28, 1961, p. 382). R. B.
West hesitates at calling it a comedy of manners, but adds that "if
it is not, we have no traditional name for such a story" (*American
Literature,* 34, 1962, p. 221). Perhaps the best discussion of the story
is in the few paragraphs that Eudora Welty devotes to it in her "The
Reading and Writing of Short Stories," *Atlantic Monthly,* February,
1949, pp. 57-58. In a sharply accurate phrase, Miss Welty calls "The
Bride" a "playful story, using two situations, like counters."

Structurally, "The Bride" is built like many of Crane's best
stories. It is carefully divided into dramatic scenes, and it could easily
be staged as a play. (In the late nineteen-forties, an excellent short
movie was made from the story.) The first scene presents the town
marshal of Yellow Sky, Jack Potter, and his bride as they sit in the
train waiting for its arrival at the marshal's town, Yellow Sky. They
are honest and simple persons, not young, but too inexperienced to
play the part of newlyweds without great awkwardness.

The second scene is a partial flashback; it begins in time at the same moment as the first scene and its function is exposition: the men in the Weary Gentleman saloon tell a drummer from out of town about the ancient gunman Scratchy Wilson, who is a superb shot but harmless except when he is drinking. "When he's sober," explains the barkeeper, "he's all right—kind of simple—wouldn't hurt a fly—nicest fellow in town. But when he's drunk—whoo!" Scratchy intends to shoot up the town, and the barkeeper boards up his place to ride out the storm.

Crane shows us Scratchy for the first time in the third scene. The old gunman, drunk and blazing away with two six-shooters at various targets, including the saloon, is looking for a fight but cannot find one. He remembers his old enemy, the marshal, and staggers away to the marshal's house, where he yells for Potter to come out. In the fourth and last scene, the paths of the two men meet as Potter and his bride round the corner heading for their new home and come upon Scratchy loading one of his pistols. The gunman waves his weapon angrily at them until Potter introduces his new wife. At the sight of the two together and at the knowledge of their marriage, Scratchy's rage is gone, and he walks sorrowfully away dragging his feet. The comedy is ended.

The language of the story is also that of Crane's best work. His metaphors and images are brilliant and precise. When they first see Scratchy, Potter and his wife are afraid: "Potter's mouth seemed to be merely a grave for his tongue. . . . As for the bride, her face had gone as yellow as old cloth. She was a slave to hideous rites, gazing at the apparitional snake." In Crane's description of the couple's reaction to the Pullman, he employs one of his sharpest images: "He pointed out to her the dazzling fittings of the coach; and in truth her eyes opened wider as she contemplated the sea-green figured velvet, the shining brass, silver, and glass, the wood that gleamed as darkly brilliant as the surface of a pool of oil."

However, Crane's customary dramatic, ironic, and poetic techniques in this story are generally either overridden by comic effects or shaped for the ends of comedy. The marshal and his bride are more than faintly ludicrous on the train. The fear of the men in the saloon is comic, as is the sudden deflation of the bragging drummer who, after ducking behind the bar, has "balm . . . laid upon his soul at sight of various zinc and copper fittings that bore a resemblance to armor plate." Scratchy is made out to be a holy terror, but his actions and appearance imply otherwise. He accurately and purposefully shoots in front of a dog instead of at it, and his major targets consist of pieces of paper and adobe walls. Dressed like a child's idea of a cowboy, in a maroon shirt and red-topped boots "of the kind beloved in winter by little sledding boys on the hillsides of New England," the old gunman is obviously a comic figure playing a childishly attractive game. As Eudora Welty remarks, "the more ferocious Scratchy is, the more we are charmed." Even when he faces Potter and his bride, Scratchy avoids shooting him; he merely talks about it, and although Potter is doubtful of his antagonist's harmlessness, the reader is convinced that the marshal is safe.

Throughout "The Bride" Crane uses comic devices with great sureness. There is tongue-in-cheek understatement in his catalogue of the men drinking in the saloon: "One was a drummer who talked a great deal and rapidly; three were Texans who did not care to talk at that time; and two were Mexican sheep-herders, who did not talk as a general practice in the Weary Gentleman saloon." Crane's favorite device is comic overstatement. The marshal's marriage is called an "extraordinary crime" that was "an important thing to his town. It could only be exceeded by the burning of the new hotel." Scratchy's drunken bellowing is called the "chanting [of] Apache scalp-music." In describing the actions of his characters, Crane uses echoes of and allusions to the epic to attain comic overstatement. The barkeeper becomes "the man of bottles." Jack Potter is not merely Scratchy's enemy; he is "his ancient antagonist." And when no one answers his challenges, Scratchy addresses the universe and calls "to the sky" like a hero out of Homer.

Occasionally Crane employs a sort of visual comedy that is close to slapstick. The marshal and his wife in the Pullman are little better than two hayseeds, the butt of joking throughout the car. They are terribly embarrassed and self-conscious. The Negro porter looks down on and bullies them, laughing at them as they leave the train. Potter's trying to tip the porter without drawing attention to himself is perfectly constructed rustic slapstick comedy: "Potter fumbled out a coin and gave it to the porter, as he had seen others do. It was a heavy and muscle-bound business, as that of a man shoeing his first horse."

All of these devices and scenes either anticipate or support the comedy of the confrontation of the "ancient antagonists" who have been involved in a burlesque of the Western feud. Holding a gun on the brave marshal, who is afraid to face the town when it finds out about his marriage, and who has just been caught skulking around back streets trying to get home without being seen, Scratchy works himself into a rage that disappears like a pricked bubble when the bride is mentioned. "No!" he says. And then in a splendid anticlimax of parodic gallantry, he asks: "Is this the lady?"

The feud that Scratchy has enjoyed so much is over. "I s'pose it's all off now," he says, and like a child who has lost something forever he walks away dragging his feet, making "funnel-shaped tracks in the heavy sand." But "The Bride Comes to Yellow Sky" is a comedy that implies a happy ending. Surely the marshal and his bride will live happily ever after; Scratchy Wilson, now that the object of his feuding attentions is no longer available, will undoubtedly reform and get religion; and even the dreadful *shivaree* that Potter was so frightened of will probably turn out to be no worse than an ice cream social at the Baptist Church.

b. *"The Bride Comes to Yellow Sky": History as Elegy*
By Kenneth Bernard

A recent interpretation of Stephen Crane's "The Bride Comes to Yellow Sky" by A. M. Tibbetts dismisses earlier interpretations as missing the point of the story mostly for two reasons: 1. Critics misread it as a serious allegory instead of as pure comedy; 2. Critics, accustomed to "portentous and symbolic tragedies" like *Maggie, The Red Badge of Courage,* "The Monster," "The Blue Hotel," and "The Open Boat," think that "The Bride Comes to Yellow Sky" must be equally "freighted with dark meaning." All this, Mr. Tibbetts feels, is wrong. The story is "nearly pure comedy," full of "tongue in cheek understatement" and "comic overstatement," with a perfectly happy ending: the sheriff and his wife will live "happily ever after," and Scratchy Wilson, an obviously "comic figure playing a childishly attractive game," will "undoubtedly reform and get religion." [1] This, it seems to me, is a superficial reading of the story, robbing it of its deepest associations with much that is vital in American literature. The story seems to be more humorous than it is. Basically it is an elegy; it laments the passing of the old West and its values and deplores the rise of the new, "civilized" values of the East.

The picture of the returning sheriff with his bride, so fearful of the consequences of his act, might well be comical if it were not so overdone. As comedy it is heavy-handed. Statements like "Jack Potter was beginning to find the shadow of a deed weigh upon him like a leaden slab," "He was bringing his bride before an innocent and unsuspecting community," "he felt he was heinous," "He had committed an extraordinary crime," "It could only be exceeded by the burning of the new hotel," and "His friends could not forgive him," are too extreme to be accepted as comedy. The marriage of a sheriff simply would not be that upsetting to his community; the language is grossly inappropriate to his act, even if we do see the end as comedy. Crane had something else in mind; there are other possibilities.

Sheriff Potter's relationship with Scratchy Wilson is the beginning of an answer. Wilson is "about the last one of the old gang that used to hang out along the river." He is Potter's "ancient antagonist."

Reprinted from: *The English Record,* XVII (April 1967), 17-20. By permission of *The English Record.*

These statements should not be interpreted to mean that Wilson is now an outlaw. They are only meant to *suggest* lawlessness. The most we can say of Wilson is that he is, chronologically, displaced. His periodic outbreaks occur only when he is drunk. When sober, says the bartender to the drummer, he "wouldn't hurt a fly—nicest fellow in town." In fact, however, even when he is drunk he would not hurt a fly. His marksmanship when drunk, as demonstrated by his play with the dog, is amazingly accurate. If Wilson were really on a rampage, he could easily kill or wound. But he does not. No one but the outsider, the drummer, is really worried. If anything, the townspeople feel pleasurable anticipation, as if about to participate in an entertainment.[2] And they are. Their role is that of the frightened community. Scratchy Wilson is the desperado. Sheriff Potter's role in the entertainment is that of the man who always "shoots it out" with Wilson, that is, stops him. Only once does Wilson actually shoot Potter, in the leg—just enough bloodshed to lend an aura of truth to the drama that he and Potter and the town enact. *There is no chance whatsoever that he will ever intentionally kill Wilson* (or that Wilson, for that matter, will ever kill him), though it must always seem possible. For what they are participating in is a ritual in celebration of the old West.[3] What must be seen is that Potter feels that the town takes the ritual with the utmost seriousness, although, as we shall see, it does not. When he has all his fearful anticipations on the train, it is of his new role as "traitor to the feelings of Yellow Sky" that he is thinking. He is withdrawing from his role as hero; he has broken Yellow Sky's last tie with an exciting past.

    Wilson gets drunk, not knowing that Potter is away. He bellows and fumes and sways through the town, shooting it up, venting his rage over what is gone. As Crane says, "The man was playing with the town; it was a toy for him." He is reliving a time now dead the only way he knows how. But it is dead. When he yells, it is "as if the surrounding stillness formed the arch of a tomb over him." Potter, whose return as a married man marks the end of homage to the myth, feels his deed weighing on him "like a leaden slab." And when he meets Wilson later and his "mouth seemed to be merely a grave for his tongue," the words have a double meaning. The ritual was for a time dead and gone. And now the ritual itself is gone, as Wilson realizes when he sees that Potter is married. It is a "foreign condition" in the face of which he reverts to being "a simple child of the earlier plains." He is "like a creature allowed a glimpse of another world." His "funnel-shaped tracks in the heavy sand" suggest that something has drained out, possibly even the top half of an hour glass, the sands of which have fallen through.[4] Sheriff Potter also knows that the addition of a wife interferes with the rigid confrontation. Not only does she make him more vulnerable as a human being (for example, he does not have his guns) and therefore less usable as a symbol, but she is from San Antonio, one thousand miles to the east, and represents an obvious intrusion of "eastern" influences.[5] The town cannot believe in Potter any more in his role. He *is* guilty of an "extraordinary crime." He *has* come as "one announcing death." As Wilson says, "I s'pose it's all off now." And it is.

But all this is only half the story. The other half is about the transition from western to eastern values. There are few indications of time in the story. The drummer and the train do not help much to place the story, but the reference to Scratchy Wilson's shirt does. It is a "maroon-colored flannel shirt, which had been purchased for purposes of decoration, and made principally by some Jewish women on the East Side of New York." It cannot have taken place much earlier than the last decade of the nineteenth century.[6] What is important to see chronologically is that the ritual of Potter and Wilson and Yellow Sky dramatizes a last stand, and Wilson in the end is much the same kind of tragic hero as Cooper's hero dying on the prairie with "civilization" hot behind him, Huck Finn lighting out for a territory which he knows is only temporary, and Steinbeck's old man in "Leader of the People," who doesn't know what to do once he has led his wagon train to the opposing Pacific. One image in the story particularly illustrates the critical moment. Crane describes the train as approaching the "keening" Rio Grande "at an angle, and the apex is Yellow Sky." Two forces (parallel to the ideas of bride and Yellow Sky, and marriage and gunfight in the story) are going to clash at Yellow Sky, the train and the river, obvious representations of East and West. The outcome is equally obvious because the river is "keening," wailing for a death.

Potter himself illustrates this "death." His position in Yellow Sky as last hero of the old West is well established in the story. On the train we see him lose his heroic stature. He is an object of ridicule to the other passengers and to the porter. The decor of the train is mentioned twice in the story. Potter sees the "dazzling fittings," "the sea-green figured velvet, the shining brass, silver, and glass, the wood that gleamed as darkly brilliant as the surface of a pool of oil," "the frescoes in olive and silver," in other words, the garish, meretricious representation of the East—as reflecting "the glory of their marriage" and "the environment of their new estate." The elation in Potter's face makes him look ridiculous to the Negro porter, and he subsequently abuses the couple. This is an ironic reversal because the porter, who is at the lowest level of eastern society, condescends to Potter, who has been at the very top of western society. Later, when Potter leaves the train, he "fumbled out a coin and gave it to the porter, as he had seen others do. It was a heavy and muscle-bound business, as that of a man shoeing his first horse." The irony here is more bitter. Not only is Potter, who *was* an individualist, copying, but his first real act in his "new estate," tipping, an "eastern" corruption, is described in terms traditionally associated with his "old estate." It is a muscle-bound business, but he is learning.[7] When Wilson confronts him later, he at first stiffens and steadies, ready to respond in the old way, but then "somewhere in the back of his mind a vision of the Pullman floated . . . all the glory of the marriage and the environment of the new estate," and he tells Scratchy he is married. Crane makes it quite clear in the opening paragraph that East and West are to clash and that the West is doomed to be swallowed by the East: "The great Pullman was whirling onward with such dignity of motion that a glance from the window seemed simply to prove that the plains of Texas were pouring eastward. Vast flats of green grass, dull-hued spaces of mesquite and cactus, little groups of frame houses, woods of light and tender trees, all were sweeping into the east, sweeping over the horizon, a precipice."

NOTES

1. "Stephen Crane's 'The Bride Comes to Yellow Sky,'" *English Journal*, 54, No. 4 (April, 1965), 314-16. For other interpretations see Ray B. West, "Stephen Crane: Author in Transition," *American Literature*, 34, No. 2 (May, 1962), 215-28, who sees the story as a "small 'comedy of manners'"; Robert Wooster Stallman, ed., *Stephen Crane: An Omnibus* (New York, 1952), 484, who sees Potter and Wilson as representing two opposite worlds, that of "spiritual values whose force lies in innocence, and the non-imaginative world of crass realities"; William Bysshe Stein, "Stephen Crane's *Homo Absurdus*," *Bucknell Review*, VIII, No. 3 (May, 1959), 168-88, an existentialist interpretation of estrangement from the community; Edwin Harrison Cady, "Stephen Crane and the Strenuous Life," *English Literary History*, 28, No. 4 (1961), 376-82, who describes it as "a laboriously funny parody of neo-romantic lamentations over 'The Passing of the West'"; George W. Johnson, "Stephen Crane's Metaphor of Decorum," *PMLA*, 78 (June, 1963), 250-56, who speaks of the "conflict between the claims of idealism and realism . . . a vigorous West and a civilized but effete East"; Robert Barnes, Item 39, *The Explicator*

(April, 1958), who sees the story as a transition from the old West to the new, brought about by a corrupting cultural invasion from the East; and S. C. Ferguson, Item 59, *The Explicator* (March, 1963), who criticizes Mr. Barnes for not seeing the story as "a charming spoof on the 'penny dreadful' literature of the school of Ned Buntline."

2. Mr. Ferguson has, mistakenly I think, described Scratchy as in fact "a vicious, drunken desperado who is terrorizing a small fear-paralyzed town."

3. West, correctly, sees the repeated shoot-outs as a "game." See also James P. Overton, "The 'Game' in Stephen Crane's 'The Bride Comes to Yellow Sky,'" *Xavier University Studies*, IV (March, 1965), 3-11.

4. Cady makes the interesting suggestion that the tracks are "like the tracks of the last dinosaur."

5. It would have been incongruous for Potter to go to the Atlantic seaboard for an "eastern" wife. San Antonio serves the double purpose of being east of Yellow Sky and allowing for the important imagery connected with the train ride.

6. West sees the story as taking place much earlier and in more primitive conditions than is true. Yellow Sky has reached the point where it does not need the frontier sheriff of tradition, who is quick on the draw.

7. Tibbetts sees this incident as "perfectly constructed slapstick comedy." It is quite the reverse.

3. *"The Monster"*

a. *"The Monster" and the Art of Stephen Crane*
By James Hafley

Amid all of the extremely worthwhile attention that has lately
been given to Stephen Crane, whose art has now successfully been
shown to have avoided both the Scylla of naturalism and the
Charybdis of impressionism in its progress from *Maggie* through *The
Red Badge* to the achieved fulfillment of the later stories, there has
gone almost unnoticed one work of his that is not only important
but also as deserving as any other of the distinction of being called
his masterpiece; "The Monster" was written in 1897, two years after
The Red Badge and just before Crane's most famous stories—"The
Open Boat," "The Bride Comes to Yellow Sky" and "The Blue
Hotel"—and. is like all these works concerned with an examination
of American values conducted largely in terms of a paradoxical
handling of the appearance-reality motif. It is with the general design
of this novelette as a Crane art work that I wish to be occupied here.

"The Monster" is primarily concerned with the moral problem
that confronts a rather prosperous and highly respected physician,
Dr. Ned Trescott, when his small son, Jim, is saved from death in
a fire by Henry Johnson, the Trescotts' young Negro stableman. It is
at first supposed by the townspeople of Whilomville that Henry has
lost his life in rescuing Jim from the flames, and he is at once
celebrated as a hero; when, however, it is discovered that Henry has
lost not his life, which Trescott has managed to save, but instead,
quite literally, his face—having been horribly disfigured by acids in
the doctor's laboratory as he struggled out of the burning house with
the boy—and that the experience has cost him his sanity as well,
everyone turns against him to insist upon his being ostracized from
the community as a monster. Dr. Trescott stands midway between
the poles of Henry, who becomes gradually symbolic of "God," and
the townspeople; the story ends with Trescott's own ostracism after

Reprinted from: *Accent*, XIX (Summer 1959), 159-165. By permission of the University of Illinois Foundation and the author.

he chooses to side with Henry rather than with his fellow citizens. The point is simply that Henry—like Gregor Samsa in Kafka's *Metamorphosis*—becomes, once he is understood, a norm according to which it is not he but the whole town that has lost face and gone mad; the townsfolk are the real monsters, but in a society where their mechanical civilization controls values, Henry appears both monstrous and insane for his godlike virtues. If the story comes to stand upon this paradox, it is because Crane can find no other means of reconciling his American sense of civilization with traditional moral values —the two seem to him hopelessly hostile.

As a novelette—that is, a very brief novel rather than a short story in its form—"The Monster" can best be understood as the imitation of an action, the action "to lose face." This action is itself paradoxical: Henry and the others who lose face in the story ultimately save face; and those who try to save face, however sympathetic one must sometimes be with their problems, finally lose face in the light of Henry's significance. Just as the entire story is an imitation of this action, so also it is patterned by means of analogous imitations of the action on the part of almost every character, a method which can best be shown by selective illustration.

Jim, the Trescotts' son, foreshadows and encompasses the entire action in miniature at the outset: playing in the garden with a toy locomotive, he accidentally destroys a peony and is gently reprimanded by his father, who decides that the child must stop playing with the train for the day. "During the delivery of the judgment the child had not *faced* his father, and afterward he went away, with his head lowered, shuffling his feet. . . . It was apparent from Jimmie's manner that he felt some kind of desire to *efface* himself" (the emphasis is mine). At the end of the story, Jim must save face before his little friends—his own society—by going up to the terrifying monster, Henry, who is seated in the sun with a heavy veil about his head, and touching him on the shoulder; Henry's courage in saving Jim is thus weighed against the child's face-saving "courage" as he dares to approach the monster-savior.

Alek Williams, a Negro paid five dollars a week by Trescott to look after the faceless Henry, saves face by demanding an amount of money more appropriate for a man who, with his wife and children, must go through the horror of looking at the monster: *six* dollars a week. It is bitterly ironic that Alek explains, "for this kinder wuk er man oughter git er Salary," because throughout the story the Negroes, including Henry, pattern their own manners after the whites' in a way that shows up both their own ignorance and the shoddiness of the civilization they seek to imitate.

Reifsnyder, the town barber (Crane doesn't miss the opportunity for a comparison between saving face and shaving face, with all the implications of the barber-shop as a gossip center really no more trivial than any other social order in the town), shows a certain degree of sympathy for Henry; "How would you like to be with no face?" he asks a customer who is complaining about Henry. But he is answered with a remark that reverberates to the edges of Crane's meaning: "You're kicking because, if losing faces became popular, you'd have to go out of business"; and another customer adds that losing face will hardly become popular "if it's got to be taken off in the way his was taken off."

Bella Farragut, Henry's friend who had announced their engagement when she thought him dead of his bravery, loses face completely when he returns to court her sociably after his recovery; unable to look at him, she "threw herself face downward on the floor, while the monster sat on the edge of the chair gabbling courteous invitations."

One can continue in this way throughout the story, noticing how even on the simplest linguistic level the losing of face is imitated again and again. At the end of the story Dr. Trescott "kept his face in the shadow" as he refuses to dismiss his feeling of responsibility for Henry; when Henry dresses pseudo-elegantly, he is accused of wanting "to make a front"; while one Hannigan tries to keep Henry from rushing into the flaming house after Jim, "his face was black with rage."

As that last phrase has in a small way suggested, Crane intermingles his face-saving images with light-darkness images that function both realistically and with obvious symbolic value. Here again there is a paradox, for there are two sorts of light: natural light and man-made illumination. The electric light, suggestive of an imitative civilization, is superficial and deceptive: it "glares," and after all there remain "ponderous shadows in back of the electric lamps." Those shadows are, as much as the fearful brilliance of the fire, the real light, and although people wait for "the truth of daylight," they must, like the little girl terrified by a glimpse of Henry's face, become to some degree aware of a reality beyond appearance; the child screams when "she saw the night," for she represents a member of a society that judges everything by appearance, and that blinds itself with its own mechanical lights to what is real. Thus when Henry Johnson passes the barber shop one of the customers inside observes, "I guess that was Henry. It looked like him." Again, the burning house, long after it is ablaze within, appears quiet and peaceful from without; and the fire itself is described as if it were a thing of beauty. The acids that burn Henry's face away are "delicate," "jewels," "marvels"; but they are "red-hot jewels," and they "flowed" snake-like, just as the townspeople, morally acid, "flowed" to the scene of the fire.

This conflict between losing and saving face, between appearance and reality, light and dark, impression and fact, is finally one between social and individual value. That is evident throughout the story, but nowhere more artistically than in the seventeenth section, in which Henry, now faceless, makes a social call upon Bella, and the grotesque horror of society is dramatized by Henry's insane attempts to follow a formal code of etiquette. The monster makes "a low and sweeping bow," and speaks with fractured eloquence in what is a ghastly attempt to fuse moral and social graces; he is a "genial monster" a virtuous man behaving according to the standards of polite society. His effects upon society are revelatory of its true nature: Bella crawls on her hands and knees to evade him; she and her relatives represent a "wreck of a family gathering"; they "bleat," they run, and "at the back of the house, Mrs. Farragut, who was of enormous weight, and who for eight years had done little more than sit in an arm-chair and describe her various ailments, . . . with speed and agility scaled a high board fence." It is urged that Henry be removed from the town, because "you know how a crowd gets"; the prim little children's party in the story is paralleled by the scene in which a "populace," a "mob," of children taunts Henry, who for his part sings hymns, quite unaware of their cruelty. And it is useless to attempt to control the savage mob that society really is: "Even if there are a lot of fools in the world," one of Trescott's friends warns him, "we can't see any reason why you should ruin yourself by opposing them. You can't teach them anything, you know." As he is in "The Blue Hotel"—which might be paraphrased "The Sad Society"—Crane is in "The Monster" convinced that whatever constitutes the goodness of man is not to be found in modern social convention. A factory whistle is what summons the townspeople to the fire, which is significantly shown devouring a painting titled "Signing the Declaration."

Henry, as a perfectly good man, is equated with God rather than with any possibility for strictly human conduct: he is like God totally different from man, veiled from the eyes of man from the time when "the bandages on the negro's head allowed only one thing to appear —an eye, which unwinkingly stared at the judge"; he is simply an "unwinking eye," jeered at for his "black face and shiny eye" both before and after that interval in which he was thought to have died and to be a "saint": the world is not ready for its saints, nor society for the idea of God. Before the fire, Bella remarks to her mother that Henry is "divine"; after his mutilation, however good he may be, the point is that "he *looks* like er devil," as Alek puts it. Cooped up in a small room while Alek is caring for him, Henry is treated rather like the fearful Old Testament God—Alek's wife "adopted the attitude used always in church at funerals. At times she seemed to be upon the point of breaking out in prayer." And finally there is nothing for the monster to do but turn "its black crêpe countenance toward the sky . . . waving its arms in time to a religious chant," while the children who stare at him are "transfixed by the solemnity and mystery of the indefinable gestures." In the same way an indefinable—and therefore horrifying—face has replaced Henry's social mask after his act of selfless love. "Humankind cannot bear very much reality"—that line of Eliot's articulates the theme of this story, and the central theme of all Stephen Crane's work. The very word *monster,* one recalls, is derived from *monstrum,* a divine portent of misfortune; and it is frightening as well as amusing to remember that the editor of *The Century,* rejecting this story for publication, explained that "We couldn't publish that thing with half the expectant mothers in America on our subscription list!"

Thus far I have been trying—using relatively few of the hundreds of illustrations the story affords—to indicate how Crane has characteristically patterned the action of "The Monster" and dramatized its theme. Now I should like to look in somewhat more detail at a few parts of just one section, the first, in order to suggest how Crane everywhere organizes his details into microcosmic patterns that duplicate the over-all pattern which is the whole story. This section concerns, as I have said, little Jim's destruction of a flower with his locomotive. More specifically, "little Jim was, for the time, engine Number 36"—he is identified with the machine, the symbol of senseless power—and the flower that he destroys is a peony. Now the peony, a plant used in medicine, was named for the god of healing: Trescott, who is first described to us simply as "the doctor," is himself broken in the course of the story. Physician heal thyself is especially suggested here when one realizes that later the old judge warns Trescott that the Negro whose life he has managed to save "will be your creation, you understand. He is purely your creation." Trescott answers, "He will be what you like, judge," but what the judge and the townspeople like is hopelessly different from what the doctor must like after Henry has saved his son; Trescott's capacity for moral sensitivity, his response to Henry's act, places him, then, in the position of the peony at the opening of the story; and it is his son, Jim, who is finally responsible for, the engine of, his insoluble problem. Jim tries to revive the peony, "but the spine of it was hurt, and it would only hang limply from his hand. Jim could do no reparation." And neither can the doctor when he has tragically healed Henry and thus paradoxically healed himself.

While Jim is playing, "the doctor was shaving [the] lawn as if it were a priest's chin." That figure pretty well releases its own significance in view of such succeeding events as I have earlier mentioned; but one can notice also that it represents in miniature what later the whole story will represent—the absurd effect of any attempt to fuse social and moral values into a whole, or to reconcile their bases. When Jim calls to his father, the doctor stops his mowing, "and with the howl of the machine no longer occupying the sense, one could hear the robins in the cherry-trees arranging their affairs." Nature has its own order, and yet the true human being, as in *The Red Badge,* is powerless to follow this order, precisely because he *is* a human being. "Nature has very evidently given . . . up" the peculiarly humane qualities of humanity, just as certainly as society has done so, and the solitary man, the private person, is left to deal with them as best he can, either by following them to virtual isolation or by quitting them for his social self—sacificing communion for the sake of community. "I guess you had better not play train any more to day," Trescott says, and at the end of the story he and his wife, Grace, are left to themselves in a room that has been prepared for a party of guests but that is filled only with shadows; it is the gospel feast to which all invited guests sent their regrets, and although we are told of Trescott that "his eyes grew used to the shadows," what he also sees—for he is man not God—are the untouched teacups that surround him.

Yet when one compares "The Monster" with Crane's other works one recognizes that it is not the pessimistic outcry which at first it may seem to be. If Crane believed anything he believed that man's acceptance of social responsibility is the means, and the only means, for his personal fulfillment as individual: In *Maggie,* Maggie's brother Jimmie is himself the social cause of his sister's downfall and death because he waves aside his momentary visions of himself behaving to other girls as Maggie's lover has behaved to her; in *The Red Badge* the battle is unnamed and unimportant in itself, but is at the same time vitally important as the social act by means of which Henry Fleming realizes himself as an individual; similarly, and with a kind of Conradian irony, in "The Monster" Trescott's act of social responsibilty (like Henry's saving Jim) is, at the very time that it destroys him, his one means of becoming fulfilled as an individual human being, as something more than an engine or a chattering robin.

One may suggest finally that Crane's vision of society, a romantic vision, is uniquely American and points toward his important position in the American literary tradition. Crane's fiction is filled with protagonists who declare independence by social acts of no social consequence whatsoever: "You can't teach them anything, you know," the judge tells Trescott. Like the reporter in "The Open Boat"—and, notoriously, like Crane himself—Crane's heroes have to learn through experience only; yet the end of that experience is always a vision of themselves alone, themselves as unique, never a vision of others, or one that is communicable to others. Society, the possibility for experience, is thereby *meant* to be worthless, and valuable only because it is without value.

> A man said to the universe:
> "Sir, I exist!"
> "However," replied the universe,
> "The fact has not created in me
> A sense of obligation."

That man of Crane's famous little poem is each of Crane's heroes; he is Henry Johnson, saving Jim; he is Dr. Trescott, saving Henry— yet each saves only himself—he is the achieved American as Crane came through his art to understand the American; and if his tremendous announcement creates in the listening universe no sense of moral responsibility it is nonetheless both beautiful and supremely important because, wrung only from this meaningless battle he has fought, it is what after all makes him "a man."

4. *"The Blue Hotel"*

a. Stephen Crane's "The Blue Hotel": The Failure of Understanding
By Joseph N. Satterwhite

The theme of "The Blue Hotel" has been obscured, it seems to
me, by all the critical attention paid to the Swede's behavior, the
cash-register image/symbol and the Easterner's theory of social complicity. The Swede is not the protagonist of the story; he is simply
an enigmatic irritant who briefly puzzles and annoys the social milieu
and is destroyed, in turn, by it. The cash-register legend, "This registers the amount of your purchase," is misleading because it implies
the Swede has deliberately sought and deserved his death; actually he
has been destroyed by a social environment which has refused or has
been unable to understand him. The Easterner's theory of social
complicity—the murder of the Swede is "the result of a collaboration,"
"the apex of a human movement"—suggests, but does not specifically
announce, the theme of "The Blue Hotel." The Easterner fails to
make clear to the Cowboy that "the human movement" is the complete breakdown of communication, understanding and sympathy
between the social organization and the Swede. This theme—the
failure to understand—is dramatically and ironically climaxed by
the Cowboy's final bewilderment. Actually "The Blue Hotel" is the
counterpart of "The Open Boat," the theme of which is human
understanding and solidarity, "the subtle brotherhood of men." In
the latter story, four men, pitted against a hostile environment,
develop an uncommon degree of understanding and the correspondent
a heretofore unrealized sympathy for his fellowman. "The Blue Hotel"
develops the obverse side of this relationship, demonstrating how society, by its failure or refusal to understand individuals within it,
can as effectively destroy a man as can the sea. The Swede is as much
a victim of his environment as is Billy the oiler whom the surf
destroys in "The Open Boat."

Two ominous refrains run through the story announcing the

Reprinted from: *Modern Fiction Studies*, II (Winter 1956-1957), 238-241. By permission of Purdue Research Foundation, Lafayette, Indiana, copyright © 1957,
and the author.

dual aspect of theme. The first points out the refusal or inability to understand: early in the story Johnny Scully says to the Swede, "I don't know nothing about you, and I don't give a damn. . . ." Shortly thereafter the Easterner says to the Swede, "I don't understand you." Near the end of the story the Gambler says to the Swede, "My friend, I don't know you." Individually and in context, these remarks signify little; in the repetitive aggregate they announce the dominant theme. A second ironic refrain runs through the story, pointing out that no one except the Easterner ever recognizes a positive responsibility to attempt an understanding of the Swede, to initiate him into "the subtle brotherhood of men." Instead, Johnny and the Cowboy maintain a negative position, that, not having laid violent hands on the Swede, they are guilty of no crime: "Why, good Gawd, I ain't done nothin' to 'im," cries Johnny and later, with the Cowboy, repeats, "Why, we didn't do nothin' to 'im." The Cowboy's last denial of complicity, in which he "cried out blindly" to the Easterner, "Well, I didn't do anythin' did I" is a fitting conclusion to a story which illustrates the negative power of society to destroy those it cannot or will not understand.

Although, according to Thomas Beer, Crane saw the blue hotel in "some dreary junction town" and based the fist fight scene on an actual altercation he tried to stop in Lincoln, Nebraska, "The Blue Hotel" is more nearly a parable than an immediate transcript of experience. Scully's place itself is more symbol than hostelry. Like the lifeboat in "The Open Boat," it represents security and refuge from the "profligate fury" of the world. It has the sacred air of a sanctuary about it, its public room being described as a "proper temple" for an enormous stove which hummed with "godlike violence." Over it all Scully presides "like an old priest" who initiates his guests with a ceremonious, baptismal-like washing ritual, in which, it may be noted, the Swede participated "gingerly and with trepidation." The five men who take shelter in the hotel from the raging blizzard are almost a fraternity banded against an unfriendly cosmos. The symbolic nature of their situation makes the failure of the four to understand the Swede all the more reprehensible. These characters are less individuals than representatives of various reasons for the failure to understand. For Scully, the Swede is less a human than an economic factor, and the host spends his energies in protecting his profit and the reputation of his hotel, not in trying to understand the Swede. Johnny Scully is emotionally disqualified for understanding; he is angry when the Swede first enters the hotel and steadily grows more wrathful. Simple incredulity overwhelms the Cowboy; he is bewildered by the Swede, who represents something completely foreign to his limited knowledge and experience. Habitual restraint and reticence isolate the Easterner and reduce him to the status of reflective observer ... the withdrawn, non-participating social consciousness. In a brief scene which opens section V of the story, Crane makes his parable of the failure to understand unmistakably clear. The hotel guests are at a meal, traditionally the most warmly human of the social acts, but the diners are preoccupied with private concerns which preclude their human interest in the Swede and conspire to force him outside the circle of understanding and acceptance:

> At six-o'clock supper, the Swede fizzed like a fire wheel. He sometimes seemed on the point of bursting into riotous song, and in all his madness he was encouraged by old Scully. The Easterner was encased in reserve; the Cowboy sat in wide-mouthed amazement, forgetting to eat, while Johnny wrathfully demolished great plates of food. The daughters of the house, when they were obliged to replenish the biscuits, approached as warily as Indians, and, having succeeded in their purpose, fled with ill concealed trepidation.

The most effective dramatic development of the failure-to-understand theme comes in the two scenes of parts III and IV which take place simultaneously on two floors of the hotel. Upstairs, Scully, the host, intent on placating a discontented guest, attempts to reassure (but not understand) the Swede, and at the same time, in the public room below, Johnny and the Cowboy attempt to identify and categorize (but not understand) the Swede. Scully's three attempts to communicate with the Swede arrange themselves into an interestingly ironic pattern. First he tries to comfort the Swede by pointing out the civilized, humanized aspect of the town: "Why, man, we're goin' to have a line of ilictric street-cars in this town next spring. . . . Why in two years Romper'll be a met-tro-*pol*-is." When the Swede's apprehension persists, Scully attempts to establish his own humanity. He grows intimate with the Swede, pointing, with an incongruous heartiness, to the event in his own life most calculated to soften and humanize him: "There, that's the picter of my little girl that died. Her name was Carrie. She had the purtiest hair you ever saw. I was that fond of her, she—" This approach too fails, and Scully turns to the universal panacea for communication problems, liquor. In giving him whiskey, Scully perhaps is most overtly responsible for the Swede's death, but it is clear that Scully's failure to understand the Swede and establish satisfactory communication with him, a failure he shares with all the others, is the real, ultimate cause of the Swede's death. The Swede takes Scully's liquor, not as an understood, comfortable man, sealing an agreement with a ritualistic drink, but as a thoroughly frightened man who drinks to obliterate fear. At the same time this muted tragedy is played out upstairs, Johnny and the Cowboy approach the problem of the Swede from another angle. They attempt to identify him, to explain him in terms of his nationality rather than in terms of his bewilderment which should claim their understanding and sympathy. In an ironic exchange with Johnny, the Cowboy dramatizes the provincial, isolated mind as it attempts to explain what it cannot understand. When Johnny, in perplexity, cries, "That's the doddangedest Swede I ever see," the Cowboy explains that "He ain't no Swede." " 'It's my opinion,' replied the Cowboy deliberately, 'he's some kind of Dutchman.' "

After the supper scene the action of the story is devoted to the complete deterioration of communication and understanding and the growing isolation of the drunken Swede. This movement culminates in his fight with Johnny (to accommodate the antagonists, all must forsake the island-like security of the hotel and plunge "into the tempest as into a sea"), his banishment from the hotel and, finally, his murder. If the total refusal or inability of his associates to understand the Swede is the ultimate cause for his death, this view of the situation must be suggested. The only observer qualified to do so is the Easterner, who voices his theory of social complicity in a final scene, which although dismissed by Robert Stallman (*Stephen Crane: An Omnibus*, p. 482) as "à moralizing appendix . . . off key" and "totally irrelevant," is the logical conclusion for the thematic development. The Easterner has, from the first, most nearly understood the Swede, but, because of a disinclination to involve himself, has refused to act on his knowledge. He senses what ails the Swede but passively agrees ("Yes, Mr. Scully, I think you're right") when the host declares, after the discussion upstairs, that the Swede is "all right now" and that he'll not jeopardize the good name of his hotel by allowing the Swede to leave. It is the Easterner who sees the prelude to the brutal fist fight—the combatants hopelessly isolated from one another by misunderstanding—as "a tragedy greater than the tragedy of action," a reference, I believe, to the negative force which is acting to destroy the Swede. It is the Easterner, too, who envisions the victorious Swede in a "splendor of isolation . . . a mysterious and lonely figure." And it is he who, symbolically as well as literally chilled by the blizzard and the sight of a man isolated and doomed by the failure of understanding, rushes to the "god-like" stove "so profoundly chilled that he almost dared to embrace the glowing iron." The fight is a revelation for the Easterner, and it is noteworthy that he takes no part in the savagely angry outburst of the Cowboy and Scully after the Swede leaves the hotel. It seems likely that he is already formulating his theory of social complicity. When, three months later, he states it and prefaces it with the observation that "I refused to stand up and be a man," he refers to more than his failure to expose Johnny's cheating at cards. He refers to his failure to assume his responsibility to understand the Swede and bring him into the human community, "the subtle brotherhood of men," a provision Crane knew to be necessary for survival in a world which he characterized in "The Blue Hotel" as "a whirling, fire-smitten, ice-locked, disease-stricken, space-lost bulb."

b. Stephen Crane as Symbolic Naturalist:
An Analysis of "The Blue Hotel"
By James Trammell Cox

The limitations of labels are less apparent when the term, like *naturalism,* has clearly definable boundaries than when it suffers from an excess of meaning, as in the much discussed omnibus *romanticism.* But they are no less real, and no less critically inhibiting. In the case of *naturalism* I would say this is particularly true, and as it has been applied to the fiction of Stephen Crane the effect has been to encourage a view and a lethargy which Crane hardly deserves. R. W. Stallman is almost alone in perceiving a fundamental difference in the fictional method of Crane and that of other naturalists in American fiction; and the value of his work in the eyes of many of the critics of American literature has been obscured by the set features, like a comic mask, of French naturalism. As articulated by Zola in *Le roman expérimental,* it is a central doctrine that *"le naturalisme, je le dis encore, consiste uniquement dans la méthode expérimentale, dans l'observation et l'expérience appliquees à la littérature"* and that *"la méthode atteint la forme elle-même."* And it is this linkage of form and matter, uncritically accepted since the 1870's as an unalterable constituent of literary naturalism, that is at the root of our failure to recognize significant. distinctions between our own naturalists, such as Dreiser or Norris or Crane. We are too quick to assume that any determinist not only has a certain familiar body of ideas but employs a certain method in the presentation of these ideas, that, of course, of the reporter or mere recorder of life.

With Crane this assumption has indeed been qualified to the extent of recognizing a difference, quantitatively at least, in the cumulation of detail, between Crane, say, and Dreiser. Further, a tendency to render much of his material visually, together with an exaggeration of his well-known haste in composition, has combined to demand some sort of qualification of Crane's naturalism; but all too frequently this qualification appears only in the equally half-safe addition of the adjective *impressionistic,* while the underlying as-

Reprinted from: *Modern Fiction Studies,* III (Summer 1957), 147-158. By permission of Purdue Research Foundation, Lafayette, Indiana, copyright © 1957, and the author.

sumption remains that Crane as a literary naturalist is also a literalist. Emotional perhaps, eclectic perhaps, Crane, a sort of cub "reporter" lives on.

It is consequently my purpose in the following analysis of "The Blue Hotel" to establish first of all that Crane's fictional method is that of the symbolist rather than the naturalist in that he carefully selects his details not as pieces of evidence in a one-dimensional report on man but as connotatively associated parts of an elaborately contrived symbolic substructure. Secondly, I am concerned to arrive at what this substructure means. More briefly, I hope to demonstrate the extent to which Stephen Crane is and is not a naturalist, in the abused sense of the term.

The total conceit, which it seems to me "The Blue Hotel" essentially is, fantastically extended and elaborately interwoven, will perhaps emerge with greater clarity if we begin somewhat undramatically at the symbolic center of the story. This I take to be the stove, with the rest of the story, like the room and the hotel itself, "merely [its] proper temple." Crane centers our attention upon it immediately upon the entry of Scully with his guests "through the portals of the blue hotel." For the room which they enter is described as "merely a proper temple for an enormous stove, which, in the centre, was humming with god-like violence. At various points on its surface the iron had become luminous and glowed yellow from the heat" (287).[1] While tonally a little grandiose as literal description, the language used here in this picture of the stove takes on considerable significance when we have noted more than twenty instances in which man is metaphorically shown to "embrace [this] glowing iron." For instance, the cowboy is referred to as "bronzed" (287). Scully's cap is said to cause "his two red ears to stick out stiffly, as if they were made of tin" (287). Also "The cowboy and the Easterner burnished themselves fiery red with this water, until it seemed to be some kind of metal polish" (287). The picture of Scully's daughter has the "hue of lead" (295). The Swede's eyes and Johnnie's cross "like blades" (300), and again "the two warriors ever sought each other in glances that were at once hot and steely" (302). At the fight the Easterner is pictured as "hopping up and down like a mechanical toy" (305). Scully is the "iron-nerved master of the ceremony" (305). The fight is described as presenting "no more detail than a swiftly revolving wheel" (305), and aside from this picture of the fight as a wheel the Swede is described at supper as having "fizzed like a firewheel"(299). *Wheel* as a verb is also used four times (291, 292, 293, and 299). After the first knock-down the fighters are "actuated by a new caution as they advanced toward collision" (306). The Swede is pictured as "breathing like an engine" (307). And when Johnnie is ready to fight again Scully doesn't tell the cowboy to get out of the way but to " 'git out of the road' " (306).

What these indiscriminantly mechanical and/or metallic references have to do with the stove will become increasingly evident when we have gone on to the first group of symbolically related contrasts, white-red, snow-fire, and fear-anger. For the present, however, the purpose of these equations, to identify man with the stove, is suggested more specifically in the two pictures below, first, of the Easterner and then of Scully. For when the fight is over and the group has come back inside, the Easterner "rushed to the stove. He was so profoundly chilled that he almost dared to embrace the glowing iron" (308). And when Scully follows the Swede upstairs to dissuade him from leaving, it would seem that he *has* embraced the glowing iron— in the sense of enclosed within—: "Scully's wrinkled visage showed grimly in the light of the small lamp he carried. This yellow effulgence, streaming upward, coloured only his prominent features, and left his eyes, for instance, in mysterious shadow. He resembled a murderer" (294). For this "murderer's" visage is the same color as that of the surface of the stove, yellow; and it would thus seem to be the stove, "humming with godlike violence," which Crane has in mind as the "engine of life" in the summarizing passage below wherein the indirect statement and the direct meet: "The conceit of man was explained by this storm to be the very engine of life—" (311). Or, philosophically stated, man's inner nature is egocentric, and it is this egocentrism in contact with environment which creates the storm or fundamental conflict relationship between man and his environment.

Thus by the use of the color yellow for its surface and the central position of the stove, spatially and imagistically, together with the supporting figures of speech equating man and metal, Crane in the symbol of the stove sets up a definition of man's inner nature as burning with elemental aggressions, "humming with godlike violence."

Support for this view of the function of the stove is abundantly evident, as suggested above, in the way Crane relates the contrast clusters white-red, fear-anger, and snow-fire. First let us note three occasions in which whiteness is associated with fear. ". . . It seemed to the Swede that he was formidably menaced. He shivered and turned white near the corners of his mouth" (290). Again when the Swede resolves to leave the room because of his fearful conviction that he is going to be killed, he is described as "the whitefaced man" (293). Similarly, the alarmed Easterner, as the Swede later thrusts his fist into Johnnie's face during the card game, is described as having grown "pallid" (391). As instances of what is often called *natural symbolism,* these repetitions are hardly adequate to establish white as a part of a contrived symbolic structure, but as the contrasting association of red with anger emerges in the material to come and a conflict relationship is insisted upon between the two, it becomes evident that these associations do have such a function. For instance in the first scuffle, Johnnie is pictured with "his red face appearing over his father's shoulder" (303). And the Swede, whose actions on a narrative level exemplify the extremes suggested here, is pictured so: "Upon the Swede's deathly pale cheeks were two spots brightly crimson" (294). The same slightly ludicrous image is repeated during the fight, significantly, I think, attached to the other characters as well as the Swede: "Occasionally a face, as if illumined by a flash of light, would shine out ghastly and marked with pink spots" (303). Again it is not without ironic finality when the gambler "wiped his knife on one of the towels that hung beneath the bar rail" (315), leaving inevitably the red stain of blood on the white towel.

In these instances the associations involve color alone and the connection between this material and the symbolic significance of the stove is hardly apparent, but with the addition of snow and fire to white and red, as linked to fear and anger, the connection becomes not only clear but meaningful in the same terms that the stove is meaningful. For instance, in the Swede's first flush of defiance as he raises Scully's bottle to his lips, he looks at Scully with a glance "burning with hatred" (296). After supper as the Swede claps Scully on his sore shoulder, Johnnie expects his father to "flame out" (300) over the matter. Later when the Swede thrusts his fist into Johnnie's face his eyes are "blazing orbs" (301). And the room, after this scuffle, is said to be "lighted with anger" (302). The corresponding contrast, linking snow with white and fear, may also be seen in this line: "A gatepost like a still man with a blanched face stood aghast amid this profligate fury" (288). And the ultimate fusion of these two together in imagery that is loaded with dramatic tension is especially apparent in the passages following: "When the party rounded the corner they were fairly blinded by the pelting of the snow. It burned their faces like fire" (308). Also the earth, in the crucial paragraph mentioned above containing the reference to the "engine of life," is described as a "fire-smitten, ice-locked ... bulb" (311). And in front of the saloon

when the Swede reaches the town "an indomitable red light was burning, and the snowflakes were made blood-colour as they flew through
the circumscribed territory of the lamp's shining" (311). Thus symbolically through the fire, fear and anger are brought into relationship
with the stove, so that we may now see it—or man—as burning not
only with elemental aggressions but also with elemental fears and the
stove with its yellow surface as the same sort of tension-bursting
symbol as that of its opposite, the snow that "burned . . . like fire."

And with man's inmost nature represented by the stove, inside
this "proper temple," this "den . . . now hideous as a torture chamber"
(301), the following description of the storm outside as a sea is not
surprising: "the two little windows presented views of a turmoiling
sea of snow" (288). For if the stove is "the engine of life," or the
inmost point of his inner nature, the snow and the outside would
almost have to be his environment, or the sea of life. And again such
is the implication, with a comment on man's essential isolation, of
this line: "No island of the sea could be exempt [from the fury of
the storm] in the degree of this little room with its humming stove."
And this metaphor is repeated as the men go out to fight: "The men
lowered their heads and plunged into the tempest as into a sea" (304).
Again as the Swede leaves the hotel and starts toward town he "tacked
across the face of the storm as if he carried sails" (310).

At this point, looking upon the blue hotel almost in the sense of
the Anglo Saxon *banhus* (with its "two little windows" presenting
only the view of a "turmoiling sea of snow" and its "enormous stove"
within "humming with godlike violence," we need only to consider
the reflections of the Easterner during the fight outside to fix these
major symbols to Crane's most explicit statement of this conflict,
which is both within man in the conflicting relationship between the
elemental forces of fear and anger and outside in the conflicting
relationship between this inner nature and his environment. For as
the Easterner watches the preparations for the fight outside—or the
narrative objectification of the condition we are concerned with—it
seems to him that "the entire prelude had in it a tragedy greater than
the tragedy of action . . ." (305). And that this tragedy *is* his condition
seems confirmed in the Easterner's thoughts a few moments later
when the fight has started: "To the Easterner there was a monotony
of unchangeable fighting that was an abomination. This confused
mingling was eternal to his sense . . ." (306).

Now, retaining this concept of man's inner nature as central, we
are in a position to follow the really amazing number of ironic con-

trasts by which Crane adds to this hub of his definition. And if we keep in mind Crane's own description of the Swede as a "firewheel," it will seem that these contrasts are the spokes of that wheel which, when spun, fizzes with such a dazzling, bewildering array of confused and blended contradictions, historically, psychologically, and culturally.

The first of these contrasts is that between animal man, represented by the characters of the story and the West, and civilized man, represented by the Easterners, who pass through Fort Romper on the train and who, used to "the brown reds and the sub-divisions of dark greens of the East" and possessed of "opulence . . . splendor . . . creeds . . . classes . . . [and] egotisms," have "no colour in common" with the "citizens of this prairie town" (286) who paint their hotels blue. And to draw such a contrast seems to be the purpose of Crane's twenty-one references in which his characters are likened to animals. Just to note a few: the Swede casts a "wolfish glare upon Scully" (300); Scully turns "panther-fashion" (304) upon the Swede; their calm as Johnnie and the Swede prepare to fight has "elements of leonine cruelty in it" (305); and the cowboy is pictured as holding forward "with the speed of a broncho" (306). It should not be overlooked in this contrast, however, that both the Swede and Mr. Blanc are from the East themselves, so that in effect the action of the story reveals their "civilization" to be but a thin veil over their essential nature and they, like the Easterners on the train, have more colors in common with these citizens of Fort Romper than they suspect.

In much the same way an historical contrast emerges from the language surrounding the fight, for terms and figures appropriate to both the combat of Celtic and Roman and that of modern warfare are used. For example, the return of Scully and the Swede from upstairs is the "entry of two roisterers from a banquet hall" (297). The supper later is a "feast" to which the domination of the Swede gives "an appearance of a cruel bacchanal" (299). And as Johnnie and the Swede first begin to fight inside, they are "two warriors" (302). When they all join in the scuffling and shouting they are a "riotous band" (302). And the cowboy at the end of this is sweating "from his efforts to intercept all sorts of raids" (303). After the scuffle a change is said to have come over Scully's now "Celtic visage" (303). During the fight outside his face is "set in the severe impersonal lines that are pictured on the countenances of the Roman veterans" (305). Inside again after the fight he mutters to himself with "Celtic mournfulness" (308). And the women like some tribal group fall upon Johnnie "amid a chorus of lamentation" (308). All of this language suggestive of the Roman invasion of England in the first century BC is actually devoted to the description of a fist-fight in Fort Romper in the late nineteenth century, so that an historical contrast is sufficiently established in this fact; however a good portion of the language is also appropriate to modern warfare. Shortly after they have washed up, for example, the new guests are pictured as having "trooped heavily back into the front room" (288). After supper they "filed toward the other room" (300). During the scuffle Johnnie is described as trying to break through the "rank formed by Scully and the Easterner" (302). As the group go outside "the snowflakes are streaming southward with the speed of bullets" (304). And during the fight outside the cowboy is caught up in a "holocaust of warlike desire" (305). The cheer from the others as the Swede falls is like "a chorus of triumphant soldiery" (307). And the consequence of language like this is again to emphasize man's fundamentally unchanging nature, whether from East or West, whether his combat be with the mace, the fist, or bullets.

A further contrast of considerable significance in Crane's cumulative definition of man and his universe is to be found in his notion of heaven and hell, again incorporated in the story indirectly, through the imagery, which depicts the blue hotel as alternately the House of God and Hell, while Scully, the proprietor, figures both as God (or one of his many representatives) and as Satan. First, for instance, Scully is pictured reading his newspaper as "curiously like an old priest" (300). And the first "ceremony" (287) performed by this "old priest" for his new guests is to conduct them to three basins of the "coldest water in the world" where the cowboy and the Easterner burnish themselves a "fiery red" and the Swede only dips his fingers "with trepidation" (287)—in the travesty of an ironic baptism, by fire and by fear. The Swede's place in this context—before his "conversion" upstairs by Scully's bottle of "firewater"—is clearly indicated in the picture of him making "the gesture of a martyr" (291). And the three basins referred to here might be overlooked except for the repetition of these three circles in the account of the Swede's effort to pay Scully, when "they both stood gazing in a strange fashion at three silver pieces on the Swede's open palm" (295). For the total being 75¢, these three silver pieces must have been quarters or three equal circles, symbol of the Trinity; and the implication would be that in Scully's house the true god is money—god in three pieces. The presence of the Holy Ghost is also suggested in the subtle effect of the abrupt transition and the use of the reflexive *himself* in the following: "The wind tore at the house, and some loose thing beat regularly against the clapboards like a spirit tapping. A door opened, and Scully himself entered" (291). Nor is the Son missing from the imagery, for in the following account of the Son's sacrifice to man, in the person of the Swede, who has knocked him down, the failure to use *His son* or *Johnnie* rather than *The son* seems deliberately contrived to echo a religious extension: " 'Are you any good yet, Johnnie?' asked Scully in a broken voice. The son gasped and opened his eyes languidly" (307). And it is also the father-son relationship called to our attention here: "by his glance the cowboy could tell that this man was Johnnie's father" (306). And finally it is in these terms that Scully's apparently rhetorical question in his effort to quiet the quarrel becomes meaningful: " 'What do I keep? What do I keep? What do I keep? ... I keep a hotel, do you mind? A guest under my roof has sacred privileges' " (299).

And on the other side of these three coins, there is to be found a certain amount of reference devoted to Scully as Satan and his house as hell, which, together with the above, serves to establish the same sort of defining contrasts we have seen working all the way through the story. First, the fire symbolism already treated is everywhere applicable to a view of the hotel as hell. And the room which is originally a "proper temple" is also a "little den [that] was now hideous as a torture-chamber" (301). It is also significant that the only profanity in the entire story is the word *hell*, which takes on, for example, nicely ironic overtones in Johnnie's reply to the Swede's speculation concerning the number of men killed in this room: " 'what in hell are you talking about?' " (290). Again it is ironic when the Easterner explains that " 'he [the Swede] thinks he's in the middle of hell' " (297). And turning from the hotel to its proprietor, it is not unmeaningful to find that Scully's shoulder "was tender from an old fall" (300) or that he had "red ears" (287) and a sort of Mephistophelean "nimble [ness]" (287). Finally the somewhat forced association, which would put a snake in the middle of the floor in mid-winter in the Midwest, serves also to identify this "torture-chamber" with hell: "The Swede sprang up from the card game with the celerity of a man escaping from a snake on the floor" (291). Thus as another spoke in the cultural, historical, psychological firewheel that is man, we must add his concepts of God, the function of these contrasting references being to suggest that all of heaven and hell are actually here on earth ironically in the *banhus* of man's own mind, which is essentially egocentric and animalistic.

The mind's consciousness of this condition appears, as we have

already seen, on the occasion of the fight outside, in the reflections of
the Easterner, Mr. Blanc—or, anglicized, White—whose awareness as
opposed to Johnnie's and ultimately the Swede's is as different as
white and black. And it is this awareness, which sees life as a grimly
serious, eternal struggle, and the blindness of those who see it as a
mere game that is the subject of a further contrast symbolized in the
game of cards. The first hint that the game of cards is representative
of life and/or an "eternal conflict" comes in the Swede's response to
the invitation to join in: "He asked some questions about the game,
and learning that it wore many names, and that he had played it
when it was under an alias, he accepted the invitation" (289). And
seen as the game of life, this card game is well described by the cowboy,
who remarks, " 'Yes, this is a queer game' " (297). Similarly meaningful
in these terms is the Easterner's repeated cry during the first scuffle:
" 'What's the good of fighting over a game of cards?' " (303). Tech-
nically the irony here is brilliant, for it is the Easterner alone who
recognizes the significance of the fight as life itself, "a monotony of
unchangeable fighting that is an abomination . . . eternal to his sense"
and who knows that life is hardly a game and a game of cards *is*. It
is thus again ironic that Johnnie jumps up from the game with an
"instinctive care for the cards and the board" (301), for in his blindness life is a game and this game is almost his life. For the Swede,
it is. The card game, thus, like the hotel in being both heaven and
hell, is both life and ironically literal a game of cards. And the "fat
and painted kings and queens" of the following passage are symbolically those who blindly view life as a game without understanding
the seriousness of this struggle between the elemental forces of life
"waging above them," or over their heads: "Of course the board
had been overturned, and now the whole company of cards was
scattered over the floor, where the boots of the men trampled the fat
and painted kings and queens as they gazed with their silly eyes at
the war that was waging above them" (302).

If at this point we turn for a moment from our consideration
solely of man's nature as represented by the firewheel and the hotel
to a look at his universe, the deterministic character of which is
represented by the wind, it will be seen in what happens to these
cards that this matter of awareness is of ultimate importance. For
when Scully throws open the door to go out for the fight, these "fat
and painted kings and queens" are "caught up from the floor and
dashed helplessly against the farther wall" (304). And it is ultimately
this fate which awaits the Swede, the least conscious and most instinc-

tive of the characters, when he has been swept by the wind "as if he carried sails" (310) southward in the direction of town and the "low black railway station." That it is the wind as fate or a vast, indifferent, deterministic force which drives man before it from the cradle to the grave, its wail at once a reminder of the one and a promise of the other, seems to be the implication of these lines also: "The entire prelude had in it a tragedy greater than the tragedy of action, and this aspect was accentuated by the long, mellow cry of the blizzard, as it sped the tumbling and wailing flakes into the black abyss of the south" (305). Or these: "The Easterner was startled to find that they were out in a wind that seemed to come direct from the shadowed arctic floes. He heard again the wail of the snow as it was flung to its grave in the south" (307). Here, in other words, is a spatial analogy for a life span, with birth not illogically represented in the white floe, or sheet of floating ice broken off and launched upon the sea, in the north and with death as the "black abyss" or "grave" in the south, the wind providing the wailing, irresistible connection between the two. And the fact that it is southward toward the station, which is all that can be seen of the town from the hotel, that the Swede is driven before the wind, and the fact that the station itself is described as "the low black railway station—which seemed incredibly distant" (304) supports this interpretation of the wind. Similarly, in these terms, it is possible to see in the following a symbolic microcosm of the main action of the story: "Scully threw open the door. Instantly a terrific wind caused the flame of the lamp to struggle at its wick, while a puff of black smoke sprang from the chimney-top" (303). Here in short is the whole story: the fated arrival of the Swede in a train drawn by a "snow-crusted engine" (286), the conflict between himself and his environment, and his sudden death. As suggested before, the emphasis upon black in its relation to the wind and the Swede is equally significant in terms of the previous contrast in awareness, Mr. White, the Easterner, at one pole and Mr. Black, the Swede, at the other. Thus, while it is "conceit," the "very engine of life," that spins this Swede, this firewheel, it is a deterministic force that flings it from white to black, from north to south, from birth to death.

That this deterministic force is indifferent to man's futile concepts of moral value, his "creeds . . . classes . . . [and] egotisms," is implicit in the fact that the Swede was morally right: Johnnie was cheating. Yet it is the Swede who is swept into the "black abyss of the south"—not Johnnie, not the Easterner, who was aware that

Johnnie was cheating and aware too of the graver issues in this conflict over the cards, and not the cowboy, who wanted to fight only through ignorance of the issues and the outcome. Support for this essentially amoral universe appears, furthermore, in a consistently meaningful play upon the valuative terms *good* and *square*. The fact that this play is also consistently ironic, often bitterly so, would suggest further that his naturalism did not come altogether naturally to Stephen Crane. Consider, for example, the deeper irony than that already discussed in the Easterner's cry: " 'What's the good of fighting over a game of cards?' " If instead of the literal leg, as before, we take this game to be the game of life, then the question is profoundly cynical—what, in other words, is the moral value to be found in life that is worth fighting for? More bitter still is the use of *good* in Scully's inquiry, " 'Are you any good yet, Johnnie?' " For the question here is what has been the use or value of Jesus Christ, and for an answer we have only the senseless death of the Swede. And it is also as a woeful instance of the cowboy's unawareness that an ironic interpretation of *good* affords us in this observation: " 'If the bartender had been any good,' observed the cowboy thoughtfully, 'he would have gone in and cracked that there Dutchman on the head with a bottle in the beginnin' of it and stopped all this here murderin' ' " (316).

In the same way, Crane plays upon the word *square* in several ironically meaningful instances: in the Easterner's conclusion, for example, that "the Swede might not have been killed if everything had been square" (316). Also the judgment and the values of society are severely questioned in Fort Romper's opinion of the gambler as "the kind known as 'square' " (312). Less meaningful but equally ironic is the insistence upon *square* in the pictures of the card players, who "formed a square, with the little board on their knees" (300) and who "sat close to the stove, and squared their knees under a wide board" (289). Perhaps, most meaningful of all is the Swede's lusty comment on the supper as he claps Scully "ruthlessly on the shoulder. 'Well, old boy, that was a good, square meal' " (300). For since there is no surface irony here in that we have nothing to indicate that it wasn't a good meal and since all seven instances in which the word *good* is used in the story, as well as six of *square,* are ironic, it would seem safe to assume that there is an irony here too, the implication being that a full belly is the only criterion that can finally be depended upon as a means of knowing what is good and what is square.

To return now to the Swede, his nature as defined by the fire-wheel, one further essential aspect of his nature or condition that is to be found symbolically stated remains—his isolation. And it is from the blue of the heron's legs which causes it to "declare its position against any background" (286) that the initial association of this color with isolation is established. It is confirmed in the fact that the hotel or symbolic *banhus,* which is painted the same color, arouses only "shame, pity, and horror" (286) in the Easterners who pass through Fort Romper on the transcontinental express and who know only "the brown-reds and subdivisions of dark greens of the East" (286). Further, as a symbol, the color blue is developed exactly in the manner of the metaphysical conceit, objectifying and commenting on the relation of isolation to fear. For on two significant moments of crisis in the Swede's relation to the others the snow is described as blue also. For instance, when he is backing away, frightened by the whack the cowboy has given the board, Crane pauses in the account of the action to note that "through the windows could be seen the snow turning blue in the shadow of dusk" (291). In the same way, when he is going outside with the others for the fight and expresses his fear that all of them will "pitch on" him, it is again noted that "the covered land was blue with the sheen of an unearthly satin" (304). It is thus a part of the effectiveness of this symbol that it not only establishes this link between isolation and fear (blue and white) but also comments on this relation in that on both occasions cited above the Swede's fears are revealed by the action to be imaginary. The cowboy was not going to attack him; he only stretches "his long legs indolently" and "puts his hands in his pockets" (291); and he is not pitched on by the others—he fights only Johnnie. The comment, then, is to suggest a reciprocally causal relation: the fear is caused by the isolation as well as the isolation is caused by the fear. And the inability to communicate, which is the result of his isolation, is dramatically reinforced.

Since this isolation is an essential aspect of the Swede's relation to the others, or man's relation to society, in the same way that ego-centrism is the essential feature of his inner nature represented by the stove, the two make up a contrast relationship like the others; but in being central or binding rather than additional, they would have to take their place on the firewheel as a blue rim and a yellow hub. Diagrammatically, then, the firewheel consists of a yellow hub, a blue rim, and the following spokes, successively related by a ribbon of contrast woven through the whole: white, fear, red, anger, snow, fire, red-brown and dark green, blue, East, West, civilized man, animal man, Scully as God, Scully as Satan, hotel as heaven, hotel as hell,

Celtic and Roman warfare, modern warfare, life as a game, and life as eternal conflict. It is no wonder that the Swede in action "fizzes like a firewheel." For seen thus, the firewheel becomes an alternate symbol, with the hotel, of man, as he exists in an amoral, deterministic universe, spinning with the contradictions of his nature and his past before the wind which flings him from north to south, from birth to death.

It remains now only to ask ourselves if this man, so defined, is the one who, in the Easterner's pseudo-naturalistic summation, shares in the responsibility for the Swede's death, when he says: " 'We are all in it! . . . Every sin is the result of collaboration. We, five of us, have collaborated in the murder of this Swede' " (316). And our answer must be no, not really, For this man in this universe, as they are symbolically defined, is totally doomed; the Swede's death is the inevitable result of his condition—or his nature in his universe—so that none of the characters of the story, rather than all, may be said to be responsible. Consequently, the real strength, the ruthless honesty this story possesses is not to be found in the literal surface but in the symbolic substructure, where by means of a fictional method still denied to Crane—recently by Philip Rahv—the author of "The Blue Hotel" has unmistakably contrived a complex but consistently related statement of a severely naturalistic *Weltanschauung*. And to supplement the beginning made by Stallman in his re-examination of Stephen Crane as a symbolic naturalist would seem to remain a much more urgent task for contemporary criticism than to argue with it, before the evidence is fully investigated.

NOTES

1. All page references are to R. W. Stallman, ed., *Stephen Crane: Stories and Tales* (Vintage Books, 1952).

c. Stephen Crane: Tragedian or Comedian,
"The Blue Hotel"
By Marvin Klotz

How shall Stephen Crane be read? The approach engendered by
R. W. Stallman in 1951 has gained many converts who have made
of Crane an incredibly subtle and sophisticated symbolical writer—
downright allegorical—a crafty writer whose metaphors and images
need to be examined with the intensity required in an examination of
Kafka, or Joyce, or Faulkner. The ingenuity of these critics is surpassed only by their proliferation and their refusal to take correction.

The violence which such symbolical readings of Crane has worked
on "The Blue Hotel" is lamentable. For instance, one modern critic[1]
asserts that the stove in the lobby of the hotel is the central symbol
in the story and that various characters are identified with the stove
(which is a kind of God) by more than twenty separate metaphorical
references. To mention a few, he cites the "bronzed" cowboy, Scully's
protruding, red, tin-like ears, the "hue of lead" in the picture of
Scully's daughter, the crossing of the Swede's eyes with Johnnie's
"like blades," and "hot and steely glances." Somehow this critic
finds that even the Easterner's "hopping up and down like a mechanical toy" and Scully's "iron nerves" are significantly related to
the God-stove in the lobby of the Palace Hotel.

Citation of this article reveals, perhaps, the process through which
Crane is made a symbolist. Crane has been noted in the past (and, it
is to be hoped, will be in the future) for his impressionistic language.
He was recognized almost from the very outset as an author particularly interesting for his fresh metaphor, for his unusual imagery
What, however, could be more tempting to modern mythopoeic critics,
drunk on the subtle vapors of Joyce's odyssey and wake, on Faulkner's
bear in the wilderness, on Kafka's penal colony, on Bellow's rain-
maker, on Malamud's grocery clerk, than the rich and suggestive
metaphor of Stephen Crane? The imagery and metaphor remain
imagery and metaphor no longer; they become symbolism. And
these critics replace what is clearly imaginative facility in language—
the intent of which has to do with that part of the definition of art

Reprinted from: *The University of Kansas City Review*, XXVII (Spring 1961),
170-174. By permission of the *University Review* and the author.

involving aesthetics—with a symbolic structure which they claim is persuasively suggested by the metaphor and imagery. That the allegory is forced (to be charitable) and clearly out of step with the time and personality of the author (if so old-fashioned a comment may yet be made) is ignored.

Furthermore, the symbolical Crane has made necessary as a matter of course, the generation of a "philosophy" of Crane, for if an author is going to be symbolical, it follows that he has to have something to symbolize. Inevitably, the first symbolee which occurs to modern critics is Christianity. The next problem is whether the symbolist is "for or against." Well, Crane and Christianity have been worked to a fare-thee-well, though the rebuttal is not as complete as it might be. The difficulty of making either a Christian or an anti-Christ out of Crane has not dampened the enthusiasm of others among the indefatigable critics who have found that Crane is what we always expected he'd be, an existentialist.[2] Unquestionably Crane considered man to be somewhat "absurd," and he doesn't use the word *absurd* in a pejorative sense—this has provided the bellows for the flame of the critical categorizers. That he has been forged into an existentialist is not surprising. But it is reasonably clear that had Crane been aware that he had been frustrated in his attempt to dissociate himself from philosophical characterization (by demonstrating that the absurdity of man makes his philosophical pretensions ridiculous) he would have been furious at even so innocuous a philosophical designation as existentialist.

Well, then, if "The Blue Hotel" is neither symbolical, nor a document in the movement of literary existentialism, what is it? Readers feel that the macabre events of the story and the final section, which Stallman condemns as a "moralizing appendix," surely signify something, perhaps something symbolical or philosophical. What?

A brief glance into some of Crane's letters, where he casually expressed feelings on a variety of subjects might provide suggestions for a reading of the story neither symbolical nor philosophical. In one letter of 1896 to Nellie Crouse he fulminated at some length and asserted, "I detest dogma." [3] In another letter to John Hilliard, he announced that "preaching is fatal to art in literature. I try to give to readers a slice out of life; and if there is any moral or lesson in it, I do not try to point it out. I let the reader find it for himself. The result is more satisfactory to both the reader and myself. As Emerson said, 'There should be a long logic beneath the story, but it should be kept carefully out of sight.' " (158-159) This sentiment, if it was taken at all seriously by Crane as a matter of credo, seems to answer adequately Stallman's objection to the final section of "The Blue Hotel." It may *seem* that the final section is a tacked on moral appendix, but Crane's statement and his method in other tales belie this easy condemnation. Crane's remark to Hilliard should lead us to search for the "long logic beneath the story," though it is certainly not to be found by twisting Crane's metaphors into symbols.

"The Blue Hotel" appeared in *Collier's* in 1898, at the height of the naturalistic wind-storm which the French novelists in conjunction with irate American reviewers had generated. That Crane knew all about naturalism as a literary credo is indisputable. *Maggie* (1893) is a classic working out of one of the more popular modern definitions of naturalism—pessimistic determinism.[4] It even fits Zola's prescription in "The Experimental Novel" (1880, translated 1893) for clinical observation. Crane's acquaintance with Howells and his admiration of Garland make certain his awareness of contemporary literary theorizing. But Crane hated dogmatic systems—they were the absurdities of men, formalized. Furthermore, in a letter from England written late in 1897 to James Gibbons Huneker, particularly interesting in that it was probably written about the time he was working on "The Blue Hotel" (which was finished by February 7, 1898), Crane commented on British manners. "You Indians have been wasting your wind in telling me how "Unintrusive" and "DELICATE" I would find English manners. I don't. It has not yet been the habit of people I meet at Mr. Howells or Mr. Phillips or Mrs. Sonntag's to let fall my hand and begin to quickly ask me how much money I make and from which French realist I shall steal my next book. For it has been proven to me fully and carefully by authority that all my books are stolen from the French. They stand me against walls with a tea cup in my hand and tell me how I have stolen all my things from De Maupassant, Zola, Loti and the bloke who wrote—I forget the book." (160)

Consider what effect these experiences in English drawing rooms might have on a man who was to a large degree, though this aspect of him has almost completely escaped significant critical comment, a humorist. I suggest that his demonstrated scorn of human presumption and his nature as a humorist, taken together with the raging literary struggle over naturalism (a method he had been accused of imitating), make profitable a reading of "The Blue Hotel" as a deliberate burlesque of literary naturalism.

Consider the mocking and sardonic Crane setting about to impale both the drawing room critics and the dogmatic literary naturalists. What might be the most absurd working out of the doctrine (familiar from *Maggie*) of pessimistic determinism? How about a man, determined to die, who surmounts all the obstacles to the achievement of his predetermined end? If we could but be less somber and solemn when reading Crane. The humorous aspects of the story are frequently relegated to a position of critical insignificance while the humorously couched metaphors often take on the stature of ponderous symbolism. Isn't it funny that the heron's-leg blue Palace Hotel is always screaming and howling against the Nebraska landscape? Isn't Pat Scully's masterful propriety strategy funny? And if Pat's heavy fur cap caused his two red ears to stick out stiffly, as if they were made of tin, can't we laugh rather than identify Pat darkly with the God of the stove in the lobby of the hotel?

And so it goes. Is the Swede's ludicrously expressed fear of the "wild west" darkly symbolical, so much so that one critic goes so far as to assert that he, for one, doesn't quite know what the Swede is afraid of?[5] The remarkably funny card games, the card-thumping in turn of the cowboy and the drunken Swede, the "three terrible words," all of these belly laughs are made sober and deep by the symbolic critics. The humor could be cited at length; not a page goes by without two or three chuckles. Yet, nothing daunted, the symbolical critics ignore the humor of the story altogether when they do not pervert it to serve their own ends. And the *reductio ad absurdum* of naturalism—the sardonic motto, "This registers the amount of your purchase"—sums up the career of the dead Swede. Is further evidence still necessary, or can Crane be fathomed at last? Determined to be clear, Crane gives us still another section.

When the Easterner and the cowboy discuss the events at the end of the story, the tone is still clearly humorous, not symbolical—and humorous precisely in that it twits naturalism. " 'This poor gambler isn't even a noun. He is a kind of an adverb. Every sin is the result of a collaboration. We, five of us, have collaborated in the murder of this Swede. Usually there are a dozen to forty women really involved in every murder, but in this case it seems to be only five men—you, I, Johnnie, old Scully; and that fool of an unfortunate gambler came merely as a culmination, the apex of a human movement, and gets all the punishment.'

"The cowboy, injured and rebellious, cried out blindly into this fog of mysterious theory, 'Well I didn't do anythin', did I?' "

An adverb, indeed. Forty women, indeed. Fog of mysterious

theory, indeed. The theory is not at all mysterious; it is a classic statement of naturalism in literature, and the tone of the whole passage,
the whole story is mocking, the effect, first-rate humor. But it is not
man who is mocked—it is theory.

Is the story stretched to fit this reading? Is the ending not at all
funny, but deadly serious? Should we painfully note that the cowboy
doesn't "understand," and build another construct about the nature
of understanding? Should we be astounded that Crane uses the color
white in conjunction with fear and snow, and red in conjunction
with anger and fire, and assert that this reveals a symbolical thread?
Shall the hotel and the saloon be symbolical of two worlds with
different cultural constructs? Shall the blizzard be made the basis
of a dizzy series of different symbolical intentions? Shall the lines from
the story quoted in almost every article on "The Blue Hotel" ever
published—"these lice which were caused to cling to a whirling,
fire-smitten, ice-locked, disease-stricken, space-lost bulb"—shall these
lines be interpreted as a philosophy—or relished as a succulent twit?

In a letter to Beer in 1922, Crane's friend John Northern Hilliard
warned Crane's biographer away from the critical evaluation of Ford
Maddox Hueffer because "he has no humor. And no one without at
least a modicum of humor ought to write about Crane, for Crane
was bubbling over with fun and . . . was always playing. He didn't
have wit, but he had a great gift of fun and a sardonic humor." (326)

NOTES

1. James Trammel Cox, "Stephen Crane as Symbolic Naturalist: An Analysis
   of 'The Blue Hotel,'" *Modern Fiction Studies*, III (1957), 147-158.
2. Peter Buitenhuis, "The Essentials of Life: 'The Open Boat' as Existentialist
   Fiction," *Modern Fiction Studies*, V (1959), 243-250; William B. Stein, "Stephen
   Crane's *Homo Absurdus*," *Bucknell Review*, VIII (1959), 168-188.
3. *Stephen Crane: Letters,* ed. R. W. Stallman and L. Gilkes (New York, 1960),
   p. 116. Page references are given to this volume after subsequent excerpts
   from the letters.
4. Crane spoke of the determining effect of environment in several of the in-
   scriptions he wrote in presentation copies of *Maggie*.
5. Russell Roth, "A Tree in Winter: The Short Fiction of Stephen Crane,"
   New Mexico Quarterly, XXIII (1953), 188-196.

Stephen Crane's Short Stories: The True Road
By Thomas A. Gullason

> *These sounds, near and remote, de-*
> *fined an immense battleground, de-*
> *scribed the tremendous width of the*
> *stage of the prospective drama.*
>   *From "The Little Regiment"*

I

Many will always look upon *The Red Badge of Courage* (1895) as Stephen Crane's magnum opus, but this classic work does not fully reveal the diversity and maturity of Crane's art and vision, which can be found in his short stories. Unfortunately, any reader coming to Crane's short stories has to pick through a good deal of second-rate work before he can arrive at and appreciate some genuine master-pieces. Simple chronology helps one to chart Crane's artistic growth, but it is no final indicator. Anyone, for example, would be foolhardy to accept *Last Words* (1902) as Crane's "last" words as an artist. Put together by Cora Crane, this curious collection includes early sketches ("Four Men in a Cave"); hack journalism ("The Assassins in Modern Battles"); fragile allegories ("The Victory of the Moon"); historical pieces (*Wyoming Valley Tales*); and unfinished last stories ("The Squire's Madness," completed by Cora Crane), among others. But beginning with the publication of "The Open Boat" in June, 1897, and ending with *Whilomville Stories* in 1900, Stephen Crane reached the pinnacle of his craft as a writer of short stories.

It is therefore ironic that Stephen Crane did not take the world of the short story very seriously. As late as July, 1896, he told an inter-viewer: "It seems to me that short stories are the easiest things we write." In February of the same year, Crane confessed to Willa Cather that "he led a double literary life; writing in the first place the matter that pleased himself, and doing it very slowly; in the sec-ond place, any sort of stuff that would sell." Some of his more than one hundred short stories and fictional sketches were "any sort of stuff," and he turned them out easily. With "The Open Boat," Crane translated ease into greatness.

For several reasons, Stephen Crane's newspaper training was detrimental to his short-story writing; and he was involved with journalism from 1888 until his death in 1900. A number of his early writings resembled feature articles; they often echoed the topical issues of the day; they were one-dimensional and superficial. Crane had an especially hard time conquering the bugaboo of cleverness—in style and plot devices—mainly because cleverness was a byword among newspapermen. Moreover, working for newspapers like the New York *Press,* which were diligently crusading against poverty and injustice, Crane focused more and more on social problems. This adversely affected his creative imagination in crucial ways. For one, he became angry, and editorialized in fiction, something he later recognized as a weakness in his writing. Secondly, his themes were journalistic, so that his writings were at times thin and insubstantial. Then, due to the enormous success of *The Red Badge,* he was in great demand; this made him produce hastily written work, a habit carried over from his newspaper training.

Yet gradually and in an erratic manner, Stephen Crane revealed his true bent in the short story. First, there are the four major stories —"The Open Boat," "The Blue Hotel," "The Bride Comes to Yellow Sky," and "The Monster"—where his themes and techniques are brilliantly conceived and carried out. Then a "novel" of episodes, *Whilomville Stories,* to which should be added "His New Mittens." Finally, a group of more-than-workmanlike stories that testify to Crane's substantial talent: "A Mystery of Heroism," "An Episode of War," "The Price of the Harness," "The Upturned Face," "The Five White Mice," "The Wise Men," "Death and the Child," "The Men in the Storm," and "An Experiment in Misery."

A good place to begin a study of Crane's short stories is with *The Sullivan County Sketches,* some of which were published in 1892 in the New York *Tribune;* others appeared years after his death. They all show that he had much to correct, and a need to expand and deepen his skills. All these sketches are slim anecdotes, skeletal in terms of character, action, and theme. Characters do not develop; they simply react. Crane sacrifices narrative and tone, on occasion, for striking effects which he presumed to be clever and mature.

Various terms found in the subtitles to *The Sullivan County Sketches*—"story," "sketch," "study," "episode," "tale"—reveal Crane's early leaning toward the short form. Several reasons why Crane wanted to "sketch" a story were that it allowed him to get beyond the traditions of plot and narration; and it allowed him to draw on the selective details of impressionistic painting in order to explore visual and suggestive qualities such as mood, tone, imagery, and symbol. Nonetheless, Crane still seemed anxious to provide the entertainment of the conventional newspaper tale. All the sketches are brief and uncomplicated, with fast-moving plots, and an almost patented series of ironic reversals. With this structuring, Crane achieves his "cruel" jokes and "terrible" comedies. This plotting also exposes his annihilating irony, which flattens rather than deepens and extends effects and meanings; further, it indicates Crane's early pessimistic and naturalistic bias. Only in his later work does Crane see irony as an expanding and liberating device, which adds new dimensions to the experiences he wanted to portray from life. Crane develops a simplistic moral or point in his sketches—like the sin of vanity—to show again his penchant for preaching in fiction.

Certain subtitles to the sketches point to the mood and atmosphere Crane wanted to develop, and reveal his own emotional and intellectual attitude toward his materials. "Nocturne," "a night of spectral terror," "a winter tragedy," and "a dim study" clearly reveal Crane's attraction to the serious, to melodramatic and gothic situations and adventures, which were popular with the reading public of the 1890s. More specifically, "nocturne" suggests painting and music. All the sketches show Crane trying to adapt impressionistic painting techniques by using color and by sketching in his plot. Musical overtones are suggested by the way Crane counterpoints characters, themes, actions, moods, and tones, and by the rhythms and sounds of the words themselves. While satisfying the reader's hunger for traditional gothic fare, Crane was also experimenting with the art of fiction. Though still the beginning writer, he had already touched upon some of the themes of his later work: the conflicts between Nature and Man, primitivism and civilization.

Up to a point, Crane's art succeeds in *The Sullivan County Sketches*. The short sentences in "Four Men in a Cave" help to establish the moods of drama, suspense, and mystery. The short sentences also suggest Crane's early attraction to understatement or irony. But in places Crane toys with language and with rhetorical devices. He stuffs sentences in "Four Men in a Cave" with extravagant adjectives and adverbs, which break the illusion of reality he was trying to create. When he writes "traitorous rocks," "roared thunderously," "sulphurous words," "seething sentence," Crane shows that he is developing his world in an artificial, not a natural way. In the end, the writing in "Four Men in a Cave" is hard and unpoetical, forced and self-conscious, overly dramatic, and unintentionally a self-parody.

These and other flaws are found in the sketches as a whole. When Crane has native American characters speak in the proper British manner ("Oh, I say, you fellows, let's go back!"), he is a devoted imitator of Kipling. The repetitious and cryptic "Ho!" (used also by the children in *Whilomville Stories*) is another example of artificial dialogue. Crane was often unable to humanize and individualize his characters. Part of his intent is to caricature, to ridicule, and so he creates grotesques. The four men, most often the "little man," suffer; but they are never fully realized as human beings, and their victories or games become only briefly entertaining. In a few places, Crane anticipates his later understanding of the psychology of character. In "The Black Dog," he writes: "Upon the countenance of the pudgy man appeared conceit for an approaching triumph over the little man, mingled with apprehension for his own safety."

In his use of color, Crane is still the dauber and not the skillful impressionist painter. His fascination with parody and the mock epic appear alongside his supernatural themes. Crane tries to mix comedy and tragedy, and descends into melodrama instead. Besides, for a writer who wanted to create a new and revolutionary language and to kill "mildewed" Victorianisms, he relies periodically on the archaic "smote" and "ever and anon." His use of the pathetic fallacy, personification, and the refrain shows that Crane is trying to poeticize his stories; but thus far the results are contrived and rhetorical.

Nonetheless, the sketches are useful literary exercises. In a piecemeal way, they point to the future Crane in terms of structure, style, mood, tone, character, and theme. They also reveal some of Crane's firsthand experiences with war in the woods. The terrain, the forest, the individual's conflict with nature, the noises, the swamp, the fog, the campfire, the animal and war imagery were to become very important to his imaginative creation of the Civil War in *The Red Badge*.

These many evidences clearly prove that Stephen Crane drew much more from his native American scene, and far less from the foreign sources the critics have cited over the years. But Crane has far to go; his work still lacks control and scope. While sound dominates sense in *The Sullivan County Sketches*, each sketch is part of a panoramic study, a "novel" of camping life. This manner of extending his materials prepared Crane for the structuring of his novels, and eventually led him to do more in his later individual short stories, and in his collections of sketches.

The Sullivan County Sketches are tales *after* the fact. They are based on Crane's own camping trips into Sullivan County, New York, where he went each August with three friends, beginning in 1891. In another early fiction, "The King's Favor," Albert G. Thies was a singer whom Crane heard as a student at Claverack College; and King Cetewayo [Keshwayo] was a king of Zululand, captured and imprisoned by the British. "A Foreign Policy in Three Glimpses" draws upon the British plunderings in the Fijis in 1874; the 1884 quarrel between Great Britain and Russia over the annexation of Afghanistan; and the U. S. S. *Baltimore* incident of 1891 in Chile. "The Camel" reflects a current news topic, the prohibition of whisky in Maine. In all these works, and during this early phase of his career, Stephen Crane remains close to the literal "real thing." He tries to combine the real, the satiric, and the fantastic; but he is often only clever and exuberant. Certainly, his newspaper training temporarily frustrated the rich potential of his creative imagination.

II

In his first published volume of short stories, *The Little Regiment and Other Episodes of the American Civil War* (1896), Crane presents a series of sketches or vignettes on the rivalry between two brothers in a regiment; studies of the strained relations between the North and the South; a dramatic picture of the paradoxes of heroism; the plight of the elderly and the children who are some distance from the war zone; and a touching incident of a veteran's sacrifice in peacetime. Added together, these sketches approximate the life and scope of a novel, for they present a variety of perspectives on war and its effects. The whole of *The Little Regiment,* like *The Sullivan County Sketches,* is stronger than its parts; only one episode can be considered outstanding, namely "A Mystery of Heroism." What Crane demonstrates in *The Little Regiment* is his growing awareness of larger possibilities for the single story, as well as for a collection of stories.

In terms of length, the title story, "The Little Regiment," is Crane's longest attempt thus far in the short-story medium. But here Crane overwrites, intrudes into the action, and weakens the effect of the story by editorializing. Nor does he have the proper focus to highlight the rivalry between the brothers in the midst of battle;

he does not really develop the agonizing relationship between them. There is no real movement or thrust to the action, and no fully successful development of the story's theme, because of faulty counterpointing between the men and the regiment. And for a writer craving to be modern, Crane falls back on "anon."

Another story, "Three Miraculous Soldiers," highlights a special feature in Crane's early work, which has long been overshadowed by his supposedly rigid naturalistic point of view. "Three Miraculous Soldiers" not only creates the theatrical and melodramatic world of *The Sullivan County Sketches,* it also reveals Crane's sentimental side. Amid melodrama and the sentimental romance, Crane creates conventional dialogue, conventional characters, and a conventional plot. Individual scenes in "Three Miraculous Soldiers" are painful because Crane wants them to be accepted very seriously, though they are in fact silly. A maturer Crane would have parodied all of this; here he does not. The "philosophic" stance at the tale's end is an unwarranted case of preaching. "A Gray Sleeve" complements "Three Miraculous Soldiers." Here, too, Crane employs many of the trappings of the sentimental romance, and the long descriptions are out of proportion to the developing action. The melodrama, the sentiment, the clichéd plot, and mildewed words like "bethought"—none suggest an individual and modern Crane. The captain's declaration of love, and the heroine's "noble" statement at the close of the story are embarrassing echoes from traditional romance.

"The Veteran" shows that when Crane emphasizes incident and plot, as he did in *The Sullivan County Sketches,* character and "life" are insufficiently developed. The only real value of "The Veteran" is in its depiction of Henry Fleming, the hero of *The Red Badge,* as an aging civilian. No real tragedy can be felt for him as he dies trying to save his animals. "An Indiana Campaign" lacks control and balance between comic and serious themes; and the explicit moral of the story repeats the flat "wisdoms" of *The Sullivan County Sketches.*

Only "A Mystery of Heroism" fully reveals the highly creative, modern Crane. In this story, there is a remarkable balance and counterpointing between the casual, trivial world of Collins and his thirst, and the deadly destruction of war. Already in this story, we can observe Crane's cinematic technique of isolating Collins, then losing him into the chaos of the larger world, and again focusing on him; in this way, Crane heightens the relationship between man and war. Just as important, Crane captures the subtle paradoxes of the situation by portraying the hero and his actions as in a drama and shows keen psychological penetration in his analysis of Collins' rationalizations. (In "An Indiana Campaign," Crane sketches well the psychology of the crowd, anticipating his greater success in "The Monster.") The moods in the story change; and Crane's own tone is at once ironic, satiric, compassionate, and tragic. While the limitations of his naturalistic point of view are apparent, Crane manages to capture the truth of a human situation with a variety of artistic skills. "A Mystery of Heroism" is Crane's first major story, and his first complex one.

As a whole, however, *The Little Regiment* is full of the confusions and cross purposes found in the earlier sketches. Crane is still unable to reconcile his conflicting melodramatic, sentimental, romantic, and naturalistic biases, or to control and balance his ironic, comic, and serious styles. Yet these are more substantial portraits in *The Little Regiment;* they reveal Crane's technical development as well as the larger role of his own imagination in their creation.

III

In moving to New York City, Stephen Crane journeyed closer to the modern and the "now." He left behind the rural and innocent games of *The Sullivan County Sketches* and the imaginary and generally romanticized "battles" of *The Little Regiment.* Crane first visited New York City as early as 1891, but he was not profoundly moved by it until he worked for the newspapers and wrote his social protest stories.

This new phase of Crane's short-story career includes a body of work brought together in nine "Midnight Sketches," which were collected only in the English edition of *The Open Boat and Other Tales of Adventure* (1898). In these sketches, individually published between 1894 and 1896 (there are other "Midnight Sketches" which were not included in *The Open Boat*), Crane abandons the sentimental romance, melodrama, conventional dialogue, and clichéd plots of the stage, and now faces life directly with the seriousness and humanitarian impulses of the dedicated writer. His travels in New York City gave Crane deeper insight into urban life and into contemporary reality; the earlier *Maggie* was not really a part of this experience because Crane first wrote it at Syracuse University. In fact, in much of his fiction up to 1897, and even thereafter, Crane worked by extremes. With the *Midnight Sketches,* he is sincere, but he lacks the distance to achieve a proper objectivity. In these sketches, Crane is partly a naturalist, whose forte is experience, documentation, and precision; and he is partly the developing impressionist, seeking out small yet telling details, moods, and tones.

The *Midnight Sketches* display Crane's Balzacian sense of the physical milieu and the spirit of a place, which he had shown earlier in *The Sullivan County Sketches*. But in neither work does he fully relate the spirit of man to the physical and spiritual sense of place. The *Midnight Sketches* are like journalistic features. Crane draws on contemporary social problems. He captures some delicate nuances and subtleties of city life. But the final effects of these sketches are small and brief, not large and profound. In some ways, this is due to the dominance of Crane's didactic purpose, which limits his imaginative potential. He editorializes in "The Men in the Storm," thereby damaging an otherwise strong sketch. He is heavy-handed in "An Ominous Baby" and "An Experiment in Misery," both of which are solid studies of social problems. In "A Great Mistake" and "A Detail," Crane reveals his amazing feeling for particulars, but he never explores the broader implications of these two tragic sketches.

One of the sketches, "The Pace of Youth," is not a city sketch; it is set in a summer resort, and it shows Crane's continuing interest in comedy, sentimental romance, and melodrama. Another sketch, "The Duel That Was Not Fought," also avoids a theme of social protest; it creates the same sort of mood as "The Blue Hotel," without its tragic awesomeness.

When viewed as a group, these various sketches add up to another panoramic "novel" of reality—this time of city life, with its sights and sounds, its poverty, violence, terror, indifference, hopelessness, and alienation. As Crane learns more about depicting the physical milieu, the spirit of place, and the spirit of people and their dialects, he becomes an enraged writer with a limited and fixed purpose. This blunts his vision and his art. (It is interesting to note that at one time Crane was dissatisfied with capitalism, and became a two-week socialist.) Moreover, most of these sketches first appeared in the New York *Press,* the *Arena,* and the *Philistine,* which suggests once again a journalistic bias. As a newspaperman-writer, Crane could quickly adapt to his audience, though he was never a slave to it.

In *Midnight Sketches,* Crane further develops his impressionistic skills. "A Detail" shows his gift for dramatic presentation, for the sketch is like a playlet; as in his other early sketches, Crane here by-passes the traditional plot and foreshadows the modern American short story. In "The Men in the Storm," he effectively utilizes the

Greek dramatic device of stichomythia. With his characters as play-things of larger forces, Crane probes more deeply into general and broader conditions like poverty. Crane thus becomes more philosophic as he confronts everyday reality, though in the *Midnight Sketches* he does view things with the fatalism and irony of a grim naturalist. At least his extravagant imagination and his dream fantasies, found in the melodramatic and gothic wonder of *The Sullivan County Sketches* and in the artificial and stagelike sentiment and romance of *The Little Regiment,* are now countered with the harsh realities of city life.

IV

One of Stephen Crane's most ambitious collections is the American edition of *The Open Boat,* which omits the nine "Midnight Sketches." The title story and "The Bride Comes to Yellow Sky" are masterpieces of their kind, and they will be discussed along with "The Blue Hotel" and "The Monster," both of which were published later. Some of the other stories in *The Open Boat,* such as "The Five White Mice" and "The Wise Men," are good yarns, told with direct-ness and vigor, and touch upon deeper philosophical issues like chance and fate. "A Man and Some Others" would be considered an im-portant effort by some other writer, but for Crane it is an average tale, somewhat overlong (especially when one remembers Crane's in-tent in the story), lacking in focus and ending weakly, and without sufficient motivation. Tensions and ominous forebodings exist in "One Dash—Horses," a well-structured tale. There are some effective psy-chological touches, and a spirited chase; but in the end "One Dash—Horses" is not a rich story. "Flanagan and His Short Filibustering Adventure" is similar in background to "The Open Boat"; but it winds up as a topical study of the filibustering industry. "Death and the Child" points toward the deeper vision of "The Open Boat." But the story's hero, Peza, is not totally convincing, nor is the tragedy as fully realized as it should be. A story with strong possibilities, "Death and the Child" recalls the finest kind of Biercean allegory.

Stephen Crane's period of true greatness as a short-story writer is unmistakable. With remarkable suddenness, he is able to fuse a variety of haltingly developed skills from his earlier work to create more powerful effects and meanings. In this period, Crane goes be-yond the mold of the literal and traditional story. He relies less on simple narration, and less on the beginning, middle, and end of plot. He strikes a delicate balance between naturalistic accuracy and flights of imagination. "The Open Boat," though another tale *after* the fact, is a richly allusive work. The variety of experiences that Crane isolates in the story expands and deepens its meaning. Thematically, Crane presents far more than the "subtle brotherhood of men." He depicts the terrifying indifference of Nature, man's (the correspondent's) cynicism toward life, and the agonizing process of rebirth. The story's true center recalls Greek tragedy, in its dramatization of the limits of man's suffering, and the quality of his endurance.

Besides the several thematic levels, a variety of techniques are used to enrich the story. The incremental refrain reinforces the story's poetic quality, and its rhythm and movement prepare for and underline the inevitable tragedy. Color imagery functions in an organic way, conveying the passage of Time and making more apparent the beauty and terror of Nature. The scenes of dialogue are perfectly keyed to humanize the four men, to individualize them, and to relate them to the developing tragedy which, together, they reveal. The blunted dialogue, the choric effects (an entire scene is made up of stichomythic lines), the refrain, and the physical setting create the effects of a drama, a literal and immediate experience staged for the private reader. The moods and tones are complex; the men are optimistic, pessimistic, cynical, bored, indifferent, arrogant, fearful, and courageous. Comedy and tragedy, so awkwardly present in his earlier fiction, are here neatly fused as tragicomedy. There are symbolic overtones; the gull and the shark, for example, heighten the sense of danger and imminent death. Sound and sense are carefully fused. Crane's style reflects the natural world and the responses of the men to it. There is no cleverness; there is simple statement growing out of the experience of the story.

"The Open Boat" is at once a great poem, painting, drama, and tragicomedy. It is also an epic in miniature, for the story is broad and sweeping like the ocean. Thomas Mann rightly saw the "spiritual identity" between these two elementary experiences, the ocean and the epic: "The epic, with its rolling breadth, its breath of the beginnings and the roots of life, its broad and sweeping rhythm, its all-consuming monotony—how like it is to the sea, how like to it is the sea! It is the Homeric element I mean, the story going on and on, art and nature at once, naive, magnificent, material, objective, immortally healthy, immortally realistic!"

Though it lacks the epic beauty, power, and profundity of "The

Open Boat," "The Bride Comes to Yellow Sky" is Crane's most perfectly structured story. But so much attention has been focused on its structure that the real experiences and meanings of the story have been minimized. Critics have lately made much of comedy and parody in "The Bride Comes to Yellow Sky." Crane does give disproportionate attention to both comedy and parody in the beginning of the story, but gradually this tone is countered by pathos and tragedy. For the central action of the story deals with a poignant theme: the inevitable confrontation between the past, the present, and the future—the tragedy of Time. The literal action builds toward a confrontation as the community of Yellow Sky, the visiting drummer, the returning married couple, and Scratchy Wilson converge.

The physical sense of open space, the geography of Texas, mirrors the spiritual poverty of the characters and their lives. The sparse dialogue perfectly reflects peace and restfulness, and yet it suggests the ominous, and the imminence of war. The characters together reveal the emotional and intellectual life of the town. When the primitive Scratchy confronts the Potters and their new-found "estate" (i.e., encroaching civilization) the reader becomes aware of the larger war in the story. As a witness to the entire dramatic situation, the reader, in the end, senses both the note of expectation for the future, and that of loneliness and resignation for the past. The movements toward "civilization" are painful and tragic.

As in "The Open Boat," Crane creates effects in "The Bride Comes to Yellow Sky" which are cinematic, dramatic, poetic, and musical. The moods and tones are varied, giving more substance to the tale. With great art, Crane achieves the aura of immediacy, as he gets to the very core of this deceptive and seemingly simple-minded western shoot-up.

The darkest of Crane's tragedies is "The Blue Hotel," and it contains some of his most brilliant writing. As with "The Open Boat" and "The Bride Comes to Yellow Sky," the simple plot lines of "The Blue Hotel" are deceptive, for they gradually sound a variety of chords: parody, satire, comedy, and tragedy. The story focuses on character and action. Crane's portrait of the Swede is almost Dostoevskyean in its psychological penetration. The Swede's fear and bravado, his loneliness and need for camaraderie are dramatically captured.

The web of circumstances which surrounds, traps, and destroys the Swede recalls the world of inevitability in Greek tragedy. Then there is the Greek chorus—the secondary characters like the cowboy, the Easterner, Johnnie, and Scully—all of whom foreshadow the coming events and help to establish the various moods of the story. The themes are subtle and several. On the simplest level, "The Blue Hotel" is a close study of the birth and growth of fear, along with its consequences. It also exposes the myths of the West, and the confrontation between primitivism and civilization.

Mainly, "The Blue Hotel" is a tragedy of inaction; this is ironically underscored by the rationalizing talk of the cowboy and the Easterner in the important coda to the story. Natural events, such as the snow and the tempest, and the smaller actions, such as the fight between the Swede and Johnnie, cloak the spiritual paucity and terror in life, where man's meaning and being can only be found in material objects (playing cards) and physical deeds (the fistfight, the knifing). The tragedy of inaction is felt even more deeply because of the initial comic picture of both Scully and the Swede. This comedy temporarily relaxes the developing tensions, though the relief it provides is false. It helps to develop the characters of the men and their relation to the story's theme. By showing that men can laugh violently in the presence of horror or approaching death, the comedy prepares for the tragedy of the story, where civilized man faces his own most primitive instincts.

The last major story by Stephen Crane—"The Monster"—happens to be the longest he ever wrote, and the one that is least frequently praised. On the surface, it is unexciting because it lacks the boldness of imagery and freshness of style one usually associates with Crane's best work. But its prosaic quality perfectly fits the prosaic world Crane depicts. Only during the scene of the fire does he introduce appropriately vivid images and colors. In every respect, "The Monster" fully represents Crane's mature skills and his complex insights into people and the nature of reality.

One of the reasons for "The Monster's" success is its psychological penetration, not only in terms of individuals like Dr. Trescott and Judge Hagenthorpe, but more important, in the actions of the crowd —the spectators at the fire; and the whole town's reaction to the "monster." Another reason for the story's power is its complex and paradoxical theme, which is not restricted, as many presume, to ostracism. For "The Monster" is not a simplistic story. Besides showing *how* and *why* a "monster" can develop anywhere, Crane also grapples with related problems: the eternal battles between reason and passion, the material and the spiritual. Judge Hagenthorpe's reasonable approach to the "monster" is unreasonable. The compassion of Dr. Trescott does not solve anything; it only escalates problems. Nor can the businessmen of the town "buy up" Dr. Trescott's "monster," which is also theirs. The ending of the story, like a coda, offers no real solution. Though the Trescotts are ostracized, the "monster," paradoxically, still remains.

The story's tempo makes believable the world of a small town, and dramatizes a series of events, which on the surface seem trivial and inconsequential. For the most part, the tempo is slow and tortuous, like the invisible monster that develops from nowhere. Henry Johnson, the literal "monster," helps the reader to feel and see the figurative one. The pedestrian talk of the men in the barber shop; Martha Goodwin's petty yet sharp criticisms; the crowd at the concert; the children and their cruel game with Henry—all these contribute to the portrait of the town and the "monster." The tempo thus creates the sense of an idyllic community, and sets the stage for the introduction of the unusual and its effect on that community. The story also has a comic dimension in Henry Johnson's courtship of Bella Farragut, and Alek Williams's career as "businessman."

Crane brings the reader closer to the experience of "The Monster" by his use of theatrical techniques. Each episode, in fact, is a dramatic scene; each contributes to the growing web of inevitability. Crane also humanizes the drama by successfully rendering the talk of the people, and the dialect of the Negroes. "The Monster," though, is not a Greek tragedy of character; Dr. Trescott and Henry Johnson are not tragic heroes. Mainly, Crane is studying an evolving tragic situation from a variety of perspectives.

Individual scenes in the story are also cinematic. Like a roving camera, Crane focuses on individual characters, then he views them collectively, or in certain pairings. By repeatedly isolating and regrouping characters, Crane shows the unity of small town life, and also the terrible isolation and spiritual inaction of the entire community.

By relying on a loose plot, Crane captures the rhythm and pattern of small town life. With the aid of epic and dramatic techniques, Crane can treat a large theme in an immediate, direct manner. As an ever-widening circle of characters becomes involved in the crisis, Crane tightens the web of the tragedy, and makes the reader feel the presence of a huge, abstract, uncontrollable, and terrifying force.

V

While none of the *Whilomville Stories* is individually superior, Crane does succeed with the collection as a whole in creating a vibrant and full world. Although essentially a study of childhood, the book also studies the reactions of parents. These are mainly domestic or family tales, purposely low-keyed and simple, without the grandiose sweep of the four major stories. A classic of its kind, *Whilomville Stories* demonstrates further Stephen Crane's range and versatility.

The thirteen episodes illuminate a number of universal truths about children, family life, and one's former home town. Crane dissects the child's daily rituals (Jimmie is used as a focal point), his contradictory behavior, and the comedy, bewilderment, pain, and tragedy he often brings upon himself. Crane handles the psychology of both child and adult with sensitivity, precision, and humor.

Each episode contributes to the emerging significance of the "novel." In several stories, Crane suggests his intent. In "Showin' Off," he reflects on the "meanings of boyhood." In "His New Mittens" (part of *Whilomville Stories,* though not included in the collection), he writes: "They sang these lines to cruel and monotonous music which is as old perhaps as American childhood, and which it is the privilege of the emancipated adult to completely forget." In "Shame," he poses a similar idea: ". . . but that was a matter for the jungles of childhood, where grown folk seldom penetrated." *Whilomville Stories* is mainly *about* children, but it is all meant *for* adults. Critics and readers have often missed this important fact.

Crane's subdued and plain style is adapted to the halting and frustrating reactions of children to children, parents to children, and parents to parents. His informal and intrusive "I" point of view adds more literalness and realism to the episodes, and more important, brings to life the sense of one's former home town.

Generally, the episodes are comic, pathetic, and tragic. They become especially poignant when the adult reader recollects his past; sees how he *was* and now *is*. One of the points that Crane makes is that parents continually lack the imagination and sensitivity to understand and sympathize with children and their games. Many scenes from childhood unfold before the adult reader, giving him repeated shocks of recognition. He relives the dares and threats, the boredom, the bragging, the sarcasm, the follies and "wisdoms" of his youth. Once again he feels the pangs of the generation gap, the spiritual hypocrisies, the frustrations of puppy love, the social shame, the pain of adjustment to a new neighborhood. The truths that Crane utters are plain but forgotten, and he presents them with keen psychological understanding. They include such wisdoms as: "Being a boy himself, he did not understand boys at all"; "He gave no thought to the terrors of the next Friday. The evils of the day had been sufficient, and to a childish mind a week is a great space of time"; "The long-drawn animosities of men have no place in the life of a boy. The boy's mind is flexible; he readjusts his position with an ease which is derived from the fact—simply—that he is not yet a man."

VI

Wounds in the Rain (1900) is the last body of short fiction that Stephen Crane prepared for publication during his lifetime. It has only occasional scenes of power, mainly because Crane returns to his newspaper experiences and the work shows many of his earlier flaws. On the other hand, these war sketches anticipate modern fiction in several ways. Crane's prose is quite flat and low-keyed (compare the subdued impressionism in *Wounds in the Rain* with *The Red Badge*), a direct antecedent of Hemingway's style. The grimly realistic pictures of violence and death were to become the trademark of many writers of the 1920s and later.

Though loosely arranged, the volume is organized. Each sketch creates an impression of a particular "wound"—an aggravation, a complaint, a shock—that becomes clearly manifest by the story's end, and sometimes "dressed." The word "rain" colors the themes with the bleakness, the agony, the futility, and the confusions of war. A panoramic study of the Spanish-American War, *Wounds in the Rain* is of considerable historical interest.

But the sketches themselves do not have great literary value. Several of them read like topical journalistic reports. In fact, newsmen play an active part in "The Lone Charge of William B. Perkins," "God Rest Ye, Merry Gentlemen," and "The Revenge of the *Adolphus*." Crane based "The Lone Charge of William B. Perkins" on the real-life misadventures of a fellow correspondent. "Marines Signalling Under Fire at Guantanamo" seems to be an eyewitness account of bravery under fire, and "War Memories" is a thinly disguised autobiographical reminiscence. "The Second Generation" deals with a problem much discussed in the newspapers of the day. The story's hero, Casper Cadogan, a well-to-do young man with political influence, secures a commission in the Army, though he is grossly incompetent. Crane treats this theme with "sharp acid," and the tale dwindles into a fragile allegory.

Only one sketch in the entire collection is of high quality, "The Price of the Harness," in which Crane transforms the facts of real war into fiction; the characters, scenes, and actions are entirely convincing and both the monotonous and the tragic aspects of war are touchingly rendered. The one flaw in the story is its ending, where Crane adds an unnecessary and obtrusive bit of irony.

VII

As a master of short fiction, Stephen Crane cannot be simply categorized as ironist or naturalist. He was a grand experimenter, who perpetually drew from other arts to enrich his own. In his great short stories, he is poet, musician, painter, dramatist, tragicomedian, and epic artist. He draws from romanticism, realism, naturalism, and symbolism to deepen his view of man and reality. "The Open Boat," for example, is simultaneously a rich blend of realism, naturalism, and romanticism. Crane is a master constructionist, who is also very aware of the organic values of pace (tempo), rhythm, imagery, tones, moods, and styles. His best short stories seem almost artless; yet they are not simple, as many critics have made them out to be.

Partly because of his newspaper training, Crane moved awkwardly from the anecdote and the traditional tale to the modern story; from telling of scenes to revealing them; from propagandistic truth to art. Gradually Crane also learned balance and control, and by drawing from both fact and fancy, achieved a proper aesthetic distance. From his earlier attempts at writing collections of stories he learned to do "much in little" in his later individual stories. Nor did Crane's art weaken when he dealt with the homely atmosphere of the *Whilomville Stories;* he brought new life to age-old, even commonplace ideas. He moved from the brief medleys of *The Sullivan County Sketches* to the symphonic "Open Boat."

Sherwood Anderson once said that a story wants "telling and singing," that one should present not only the tale but the "song of it." This is what Stephen Crane sought to do. His successes are still classics of their kind. His innovations in the art of the short-story genre are still modern today.

APPENDIXES

A. STEPHEN CRANE: A CHRONOLOGY

Though three biographies of Stephen Crane have been written—
by Thomas Beer, John Berryman, and R. W. Stallman—and though
many scholars have prepared chronologies of his life in a variety of
anthologies, none of them are fully accurate or complete. The following Chronology adds new biographical information about Crane;
it does not, however, pretend to be totally comprehensive. There are
still too many problems in dating precisely significant events in
Crane's life. Crane was so active during his brief life and career that
there are numerous "lost" facts and periods which have to be accounted for before anyone can propose the word "definitive."

1819   Jonathan Townley Crane (Stephen Crane's father) born in
       Connecticut Farms (two miles from Elizabethtown, later Eliza-
       beth, New Jersey) on June 18. Ancestors include Stephen Crane,
       member of Continental Congress (1774-1776); Jasper Crane, one
       of founders of Newark; General William Crane; and Commo-
       dore William M. Crane.
1827   Mary Helen Peck (Stephen Crane's mother) born in Forty Fort,
       Pennsylvania, on April 10, the only daughter of Methodist
       minister George Peck, editor of the *Methodist Quarterly Re-
       view*, and later of the *Christian Advocate*. Rev. Peck's four
       brothers also Methodist ministers, including Jesse Peck, who
       helps to found Syracuse University.
1843   Jonathan Townley Crane graduates from College of New Jer-
       sey (later Princeton University), taking a prize in English
       composition.
1844   Converted from Presbyterianism to Methodism at eighteen,
       Jonathan Townley Crane begins career in ministry by assign-
       ment to Parsippany Circuit. Preaches first sermon on May 19.
       In following years, holds pastorates in Jersey City, Paterson,
       Morristown, Hackettstown, and elsewhere. For a time, Rev.
       Crane is also presiding elder of Newark district and later of
       Elizabeth district.
1848   Rev. Crane marries Mary Helen Peck in New York City on
       January 18. Publishes *An Essay on Dancing*, which wins him
       wide respect.

1849 Rev. Crane appointed principal of Pennington Seminary in June; remains in post until 1858.

1856 Rev. Crane receives honorary degree, Doctor of Divinity, from Dickinson College.

1858 Rev. George Peck publishes *Wyoming; Its History, Stirring Incidents, And Romantic Adventures.* Stephen Crane to draw upon this volume for his own *Wyoming Valley Tales.*

1865 Cora Howorth born on July 12 in Boston.

1869 Rev. Crane publishes *Popular Amusements.*

1870 Rev. Crane publishes *Arts of Intoxication.*

1871 Stephen Crane born on November 1 at 14 Mulberry Place, Newark, New Jersey, the fourteenth and last child of Rev. and Mrs. Crane.

1872 Family purchases lot in Ocean Grove, New Jersey. Rev. Crane, a pioneer in temperance cause, lectures in Ocean Grove as early as 1875 and 1876. Mrs. Crane active in mission and temperance work, later becoming President of W.C.T.U. in Port Jervis and in Asbury Park-Ocean Grove. Child Stephen brought up by sister Agnes.

1873 Rev. Crane publishes fiction—"Didn't Get In—A True Story for Boys," "Letter from Ponto," "The Life of a Potato Worm," "Letter from a Cat"—in *Sunday-School Classmate.*

1874 Stephen baptized by Rev. George Peck on July 15 in Newark.

1878 Rev. Crane begins last pastorate at Drew Church, Port Jervis, New York, in April. In September, Stephen begins public school education; his health too delicate for him to attend school earlier. Agnes teaches school in Port Jervis until the end of 1882. Port Jervis, Hartwood, and Monticello to become locales for *The Sullivan County Sketches, The Third Violet,* "The Monster," and *Whilomville Stories.*

1880 Death of Rev. Crane on February 16 from "paralysis of the heart." Mrs. Crane moves temporarily to Roseville, suburb of Newark; returns to Port Jervis in 1881, where she lives until early 1883. Mrs. Crane writes for Methodist papers, the New York *Tribune,* and Philadelphia *Press.*

1883 Mrs. Crane purchases home at 508 Fourth Avenue, Asbury Park, New Jersey, in June. Fresh evidence that "Steven" enrolls at Asbury Park School for academic year 1883-1884; Stephen listed as having year's average of "85 or above" (and less than 90) as a student of the Grammar School Department C Class. Sister Agnes teaches at same school.

1884   Death of Stephen's favorite sister, Agnes, in June, of "cerebro-
        spinal meningitis."
1885   Stephen writes first-known story, "Uncle Jake and the Bell-
        Handle," never published during his lifetime. Enrolls at Pen-
        nington Seminary (Pennington, New Jersey) on September 14;
        last term, fall, 1887, and leaves without graduating.
1888   In January, Stephen transfers to Claverack College and Hudson
        River Institute (Claverack, New York) probably because of his
        "fondness for everything military." Remains here until June,
        1890. Publishes his first sketch, "Henry M. Stanley," in school
        magazine *Vidette* (February, 1890), and is promoted to captain
        in military drill. Probably hears Civil War tales from history
        teacher, retired General John B. Van Petten. In summers, from
        1888 to 1892, Stephen works for brother J. Townley's news
        bureau in Asbury Park. Townley recognized as one of most
        popular and most experienced reporters on Jersey Coast.
1890   Stephen enrolls at Lafayette College on September 12 as min-
        ing engineering student. Prefers boxing to study, and at the
        close of the school term is advised to "leave because of scholastic
        delinquencies."
1891   Stephen transfers to Syracuse University in January. Corre-
        spondent for New York *Tribune* in Syracuse and claims he sells
        sketches to Detroit *Free Press*. Publishes his first story, "The
        King's Favor," in May issue of Syracuse *University Herald*.
        Begins writing *Maggie,* and plays varsity baseball. Formal edu-
        cation ends in June, with only one grade recorded (an "A"
        in English literature). In August, meets Hamlin Garland for
        first time in Avon-by-the-Sea, New Jersey, and reports his
        lecture on William Dean Howells (August 18). In love with
        Helen Trent. In New York City in the fall. Death of Mrs.
        Crane in Paterson, New Jersey, on December 7 after long ill-
        ness, from "malignant carbuncle." Stephen says he writes *Mag-
        gie* in "two days before Christmas."
1892   Crane works for New York *Herald* (later does free-lance work
        for many New York newspapers, including *Press* and *Journal*).
        Briefly employed by a mercantile house. *Maggie* rejected by
        Richard Watson Gilder of the *Century* in March, and by others
        in April. First substantial publication of Crane's short fiction;
        five of his *Sullivan County Sketches* appear in New York
        Tribune (July 3, 10, 17, 24, 31). Other recently recovered non-
        fiction sketches published this same year. First of Crane's New

York City sketches published, "The Broken-Down Van" (July 10). New evidence that he begins *George's Mother*. Fired as reporter by *Tribune* for writing sardonic article on parading Junior Order of United American Mechanics in Asbury Park (August 21); J. Townley also fired for this article, though he is presumably rehired later. Crane in love with Lily Brandon Munroe. In November, Crane borrows money from brother William to publish *Maggie* privately.

1893   Eleven hundred copies of *Maggie: A Girl of the Streets* printed (publisher unknown) under pseudonym Johnston Smith. Though supposedly circulating in January, the novel is published in February or March. Composes a version of *The Red Badge of Courage* in ten nights in late March. Crane meets Howells for first time in April. Receives encouragement from Garland (who reviews *Maggie* favorably in June *Arena*) and Howells (who tries to secure a "legitimate" publisher for *Maggie*).

1894   S. S. McClure to buy *The Red Badge* in February or March, but delays until November because he is too "broke to buy it." Crane's short stories and sketches on social issues appear in the *Arena* and New York *Press*. In May, Crane presumably working on novel about a boy prostitute, *Flowers of Asphalt;* manuscript lost. Sells abridged version (18,000 words) of *The Red Badge* to Bacheller-Johnson Syndicate for ninety dollars in November; it appears first in the Philadelphia *Press* (December 3-8), and then in numerous other newspapers. D. Appleton and Company purchases full-length *Red Badge* in December.

1895   In January, Crane meets and falls in love with Nellie Crouse. This same month he begins his trip to the American West and Mexico, writing special features for the Bacheller-Johnson Syndicate. Meets Willa Cather in Lincoln, Nebraska, in February. Publishes volume of free verse in March, *The Black Riders and Other Lines* (Copeland and Day; William Heinemann, 1896), which influences later Imagist poets. To accept post as literary and dramatic critic of Philadelphia *Press* in September; does not materialize. The complete version (50,000 words) of *The Red Badge* published by Appleton in October and by Heinemann in England the last week of November; it becomes a best seller in the U.S. (fourteen editions by 1897) and wins a large following in England. Starts *The Third Violet* in October and sends manuscript to publisher in December. McClure tries to persuade Crane to cover Venezuelan crisis.

1896   In Washington in March for background on political novel suggested by McClure but gives up project, for "Washington pains me." Publishes poems (in *A Souvenir and a Medley*) and *George's Mother* (Edward Arnold) in May. Story "Dan Emmonds" confused for *George's Mother;* new evidence that besides short story "Dan Emmonds" Crane is preparing novel *Dan Emmonds* (now lost). Revised version of *Maggie* (Appleton; Heinemann) published in June. In September, Crane defends Dora Clark, arrested for "soliciting"; incident makes him continual target of New York City police. This same month he is planning (partly at the suggestion of McClure) to "publish a new series of stories, or a long story . . . in which will be presented the life of the metropolitan policeman"; abandons project. *The Third Violet* serialized by McClure's syndicate; in Chicago *Sunday Inter Ocean* (October 25-November 15). In November, publishes his first collection of stories, *The Little Regiment and Other Episodes of the American Civil War* (Appleton; Heinemann, 1897), his "last thing dealing with battle." Meets Cora Taylor (Howorth) in November in Jacksonville, Florida, at her establishment, Hotel de Dream.

1897   Shipwrecked off Florida coast on January 2 on *Commodore,* while carrying contraband to Cuban insurgents; incident becomes source of "The Open Boat," which appears in June. In England in March, where he meets Harold Frederic. With Cora Taylor he covers short-lived Greco-Turkish War (April-May) as correspondent for New York *Journal* and *Westminster Gazette.* Publishes *The Third Violet* (Appleton; Heinemann) in May. Beginning in June, resides at Ravensbrook (Oxted, Surrey) in England with Cora; no evidence that they were ever legally married. Travels to Ireland in September. Meets Joseph Conrad in October, and forms friendships with Henry James, Ford Madox Ford, and others. Mentions *Active Service* (to be based on his Greek experiences) in October, yet novel still not started in December.

1898   Crane leaves England in April to go to Cuba to cover Spanish-American War as correspondent for Joseph Pulitzer's New York *World* and later William Randolph Hearst's New York *Journal;* first dispatches in April, and last in November. Richard

Harding Davis names him best of the war correspondents in Cuba. Publishes major collection of stories, *The Open Boat and Other Tales of Adventure* (Doubleday & McClure; Heinemann edition adds nine "Midnight Sketches"), in April. Plans a novel, *The Merry-Go-Round,* first mentioned in letter of May 29; to be adventure story of a wandering carousel in the Southwest and along the Atlantic shore; probably inspired by earlier tale, "The Pace of Youth" (1893). Reaches the peak of his short-story craft with the appearance of "The Bride Comes to Yellow Sky" (February), "Death and the Child" (March), "The Monster" (August), and "The Blue Hotel" (November-December). Completes a draft of *Active Service* in Havana in November; journeys to New York this same month.

1899   Returns to England and to Cora in January. Lives at Brede Place (Sussex), legend-filled castle, beginning in February. In March, August, and October refers to new novel on the American Revolution; story to be set in New Jersey and to draw on his famous ancestors. Publishes *War Is Kind* (Frederick A. Stokes), last collection of poems, in May. In June, suggestion that Crane try writing political novel again, but he finds "the hypocrisy of politicians too sickening. . . ." *Active Service* (Stokes; Heinemann, November) published in October. To Ireland this same month for background material for last novel, *The O'Ruddy.* Publishes *The Monster and Other Stories* (Harper & Brothers, 1899; 1901). Writing at feverish pace to pay off many debts.

1900   Periodic recurrence of Crane's earlier tubercular attacks from January until his death on June 5 in a sanitorium in Badenweiler, Germany. Buried in Hillside, New Jersey. Robert Barr to finish *The O'Ruddy;* earlier Crane had outlined the entire plot to him. Chapters XXIV and XXV (incomplete?) of *The O'Ruddy* last to be sent to agent by Crane on March 31. Delays by Barr, and others (Rudyard Kipling and A. E. W. Mason) invited to finish the novel; even Cora tempted to complete it. Appearance of *Whilomville Stories* (Harper & Brothers) and Cuban war stories, *Wounds in the Rain* (Stokes; Methuen & Co.).

1901   Publication of Crane's non-fictional historical sketches (researched by Kate Frederic), *Great Battles of the World* (J. B. Lippincott; Chapman & Hall). Cora plans to work on novel of the American Revolution in which "she will introduce personages from whom Stephen Crane was directly descended."

1902   Publication of *Last Words* (Digby, Long & Co.), which includes much of Crane's earliest work; at least two stories, "The Squire's Madness" and "The Man from Duluth" completed by Cora.

1903   *The O'Ruddy: A Romance* (Stokes; Methuen, 1904) published in October, completed by Barr.

1910   Death of Cora Crane on September 4 in Jacksonville, Florida.

B. SELECTED BIBLIOGRAPHY: STEPHEN CRANE
AND HIS WRITINGS

The following bibliography is highly selective. It presents those notes, essays, and volumes from past and present scholarship that anyone should be familiar with for a balanced view of Crane's life and career. A sampling of scholarship in English by Japanese, French, Italian, and Scandinavian critics is also included.

Some useful bibliographical guides to Crane include Ames W. Williams and Vincent Starrett, *Stephen Crane: A Bibliography* (Glendale, Calif.: John Valentine, 1948); Joan H. Baum, *Stephen Crane (1871-1900): An Exhibition of His Writings Held in the Columbia University Libraries September 17-November 30, 1956* (New York: Columbia University Libraries, 1956); Maurice Beebe and Thomas A. Gullason, "Criticism of Stephen Crane: A Selected Checklist with an Index to Studies of Separate Works," *Modern Fiction Studies,* V (Autumn 1959), 282-291; the *Stephen Crane Newsletter,* ed. Joseph Katz (see "Quarterly Checklist" in each issue); and "A Bibliography of Stephen Crane Scholarship: 1893-1969," *Thoth* (Department of English, Syracuse University), XI (Fall 1970, Special Supplement), 3-38. A new guide is forthcoming: Theodore L. Gross and Stanley Wertheim, *Hawthorne, Melville, Stephen Crane: A Critical Bibliography* (New York: The Free Press, 1971).

For present and future bibliographical information and research on Crane, the reader should consult *Abstracts of English Studies* (each issue); *American Literary Scholarship: An Annual* (edited by James Woodress, and published yearly since 1965); *American Literature* (each issue); *MLA International Bibliography,* I (usually published in June); *Modern Fiction Studies* (exclusive of Special Numbers); *Stephen Crane Newsletter* (each issue); *Studies in Short Fiction* (each Summer issue); and the annual Crane bibliography, started in 1963, in *Thoth.*

I. General: Biography and Criticism

Åhnebrink, Lars. *The Beginnings of Naturalism in American Fiction: A Study of the Works of Hamlin Garland, Stephen Crane, and Frank Norris with Special Reference to Some European Influences,*

1891-1903. Uppsala, Sweden: Almqvist & Wiksell, 1950, pp. 89-104, 150-155, 249-276, 328-332, 343-360, 378-381, *et passim*.

Anderson, Sherwood. "Introduction." In *The Work of Stephen Crane*, XI, ed. Wilson Follett. New York: Alfred A. Knopf, Inc., 1926, pp. xi-xv.

Andrews, Allen. *The Splendid Pauper*. Philadelphia and New York: J. B. Lippincott Co., 1968, pp. 194-196, 212.

Bacheller, Irving. *Coming Up the Road: Memories of a North Country Boyhood*. Indianapolis: The Bobbs-Merrill Co., 1928, pp. 276-283, *et passim*.

————. *From Stores of Memory*. New York: Farrar & Rinehart Inc., 1938, pp. 110-112, *et passim*.

Barry, John D. "A Note on Stephen Crane." *The Bookman*, XIII (April 1901), 148.

Bassan, Maurice. "Misery and Society: Some New Perspectives on Stephen Crane's Fiction." *Studia Neophiloligica*, XXXV (1963), 104-120.

————. "Stephen Crane and 'The Eternal Mystery of Social Condition.'" *Nineteenth-Century Fiction*, XIX (March 1965), 387-394.

————, ed. and introd. *Stephen Crane: A Collection of Critical Essays*. Englewood Cliffs, N. J.: Prentice-Hall, Inc., 1967.

Bates, H. E. *The Modern Short Story: A Critical Survey*. London: Thomas Nelson and Sons Ltd., 1941, pp. 64-71, *et passim*. Reprinted by The Writer, Inc., Boston, 1961.

Beer, Thomas. *Stephen Crane: A Study in American Letters*. New York: Alfred A. Knopf, Inc., 1923.

————. "Mrs. Stephen Crane." *The American Mercury*, XXXI (March 1934), 289-295.

Berryman, John. *Stephen Crane*. New York: William Sloane Associates, 1950. Reprinted by Meridian Books [The World Publishing Company], Cleveland and New York, 1962.

Berthoff, Warner. *The Ferment of Realism: American Literature, 1884-1919*. New York: The Free Press, 1965, pp. 227-235, *et passim*.

Brennan, Joseph X. "Stephen Crane and the Limits of Irony." *Criticism*, XI (Spring 1969), 183-200.

Bridgman, Richard. *The Colloquial Style in America*. New York: Oxford University Press, 1966, pp. 137-140, *et passim*.

Brooks, Van Wyck. *The Confident Years: 1885-1915*. New York: E. P. Dutton & Co., Inc., 1952, pp. 133-143, *et passim*.

Cady, Edwin H. "Stephen Crane and the Strenuous Life." *ELH*, XXVIII (December 1961), 376-382.

――――. *Stephen Crane.* New York: Twayne Publishers, Inc., 1962.

Cargill, Oscar. *Intellectual America: Ideas on the March.* New York: The Macmillan Co., 1941, pp. 84-89, *et passim.*

Carmichael, Otto. "Stephen Crane in Havana." *Prairie Schooner,* XLIII (Summer 1969), 200-204.

Cather, Willa. "When I Knew Stephen Crane." *The Library* [Pittsburgh], I (June 23, 1900), 17-18. Reprinted in *Prairie Schooner,* XXIII (Fall 1949), 231-236.

――――. "Introduction." In *The Work of Stephen Crane,* IX, ed. Wilson Follett. New York: Alfred A. Knopf, Inc., 1926, pp. ix-xiv.

Cazemajou, Jean. *Stephen Crane.* Minneapolis: University of Minnesota Press, 1969.

Chase, Richard, ed. and introd. *The Red Badge of Courage and Other Writings.* Boston: Houghton Mifflin Co., 1960, pp. vii-xxi.

"Chelifer" [Rupert Hughes]. "The Rise of Stephen Crane." *Godey's Magazine,* CXXXIII (September 1896), 317-319.

Colvert, James B. "The Origins of Stephen Crane's Literary Creed." *The University of Texas Studies in English,* XXXIV (1955), 179-188.

――――. "Structure and Theme in Stephen Crane's Fiction." *Modern Fiction Studies,* V (Autumn 1959), 199-208.

――――. "Stephen Crane's Magic Mountain." In *Stephen Crane: A Collection of Critical Essays,* ed. Maurice Bassan, pp. 95-105.

Conrad, Joseph. "Stephen Crane: A Note Without Dates." *The London Mercury,* I (December 1919), 192-193.

――――. "Introduction." In Beer, *Stephen Crane,* pp. 1-33.

Crane, Helen R. "My Uncle, Stephen Crane." *The American Mercury,* XXXI (January 1934), 24-29.

Davis, Robert H. "Introduction." In *The Work of Stephen Crane,* II, ed. Wilson Follett. New York: Alfred A. Knopf, Inc., 1925, pp. ix-xxiv.

Denny, Neville. "Imagination and Experience in Stephen Crane." *English Studies in Africa,* IX (March 1966), 28-42.

Dickason, David H. "Stephen Crane and *The Philistine.*" *American Literature,* XV (November 1943), 279-287.

Elconin, Victor A. "Stephen Crane at Asbury Park." *American Literature,* XX (November 1948), 275-289.

Ellison, Ralph. "Introduction." In *The Red Badge of Courage and Four Great Stories by Stephen Crane.* New York: Dell Publishing Co., Inc., 1960, pp. 7-24. Reprinted in Ralph Ellison, *Shadow and Act.* New York: Random House, 1964, pp. 60-76.

Follett, Wilson. "The Second Twenty-Eight Years: A Note on Stephen Crane, 1871-1900." *The Bookman,* LXVIII (January 1929), 532-537.

Ford, Ford Madox. "Techniques." *The Southern Review,* I (July 1935), 26, 29, 31-32, *et passim.*

———. *Portraits from Life.* Boston: Houghton Mifflin Co., 1937, pp. 21-37.

Fox, Austin M. "Stephen Crane and Joseph Conrad." *The Serif,* VI (December 1969), 16-20.

Fryckstedt, Olov W. "Stephen Crane in the Tenderloin." *Studia Neophilologica,* XXXIV (1962), 135-163.

———, ed. and introd. *Stephen Crane: Uncollected Writings.* Uppsala, Sweden: Almqvist & Wiksell, 1963.

Garland, Hamlin. *Roadside Meetings.* New York: The Macmillan Co., 1930, pp. 189-206, *et passim.*

Garnett, Edward. *Friday Nights: Literary Criticisms and Appreciations* [First Series]. New York: Alfred A. Knopf, Inc., 1922, pp. 201-217, *et passim.*

Geismar, Maxwell. *Rebels and Ancestors: The American Novel, 1890 1915.* Boston: Houghton Mifflin Co., 1953, pp. 69-136, *et passim.* Reprinted by Hill and Wang, New York, 1963.

Gibson, Donald B. *The Fiction of Stephen Crane.* Carbondale and Edwardsville: Southern Illinois University Press, 1968.

Gibson, William M., ed. and introd. *The Red Badge of Courage and Selected Prose and Poetry: Stephen Crane,* 3rd ed. New York: Holt, Rinehart and Winston, Inc., 1968, pp. v-xxiii.

Gilkes, Lillian. *Cora Crane: A Biography of Mrs. Stephen Crane.* Bloomington: Indiana University Press, 1960.

———. "Stephen Crane and the Harold Frederics." *The Serif,* VI (December 1969), 21-48

———. "Stephen Crane and the Biographical Fallacy: The Cora Influence." *Modern Fiction Studies,* XVI (Winter 1970-1971), 441-461.

Gillis, Everett A. "A Glance at Stephen Crane's Poetry." *Prairie Schooner,* XXVIII (Spring 1954), 73-79.

Gordan, John D. *"The Ghost* at Brede Place." *Bulletin of the New York Public Library,* LVI (December 1952), 591-595.

Grabo, Carl H. *The Art of the Short Story.* New York: Charles Scribner's Sons, 1913, pp. 161-164.

Greenfield, Stanley B. "The Unmistakable Stephen Crane." *PMLA,* LXXIII (December 1958), 562-572.

Gregory, Horace, and Marya Zaturenska. *A History of American*

Poetry, 1900-1940. New York: Harcourt, Brace and Co., 1946, pp. 133-137.

Greiner, Donald J. and Ellen B., eds. *The Notebook of Stephen Crane.* Charlottesville: The Bibliographical Society of the University of Virginia, 1969.

Griffith, Clark. "Stephen Crane and the Ironic Last Word." *Philological Quarterly,* XLVII (January 1968), 83-91.

Gullason, Thomas A. "New Light on the Crane-Howells Relationship." *The New England Quarterly,* XXX (September 1957), 389-392.

————. "Stephen Crane: Anti-Imperialist." *American Literature,* XXX (May 1958), 237-241.

————. "Stephen Crane's Private War on Yellow Journalism." *The Huntington Library Quarterly,* XXII (May 1959), 201-208.

————. "The Significance of 'Wounds in the Rain.'" *Modern Fiction Studies,* V (Autumn 1959), 235-242.

————. "Thematic Patterns in Stephen Crane's Early Novels." *Nineteenth-Century Fiction,* XVI (June 1961), 59-67.

————. "The Jamesian Motif in Stephen Crane's Last Novels." *The Personalist,* XLII (Winter 1961), 77-84.

————, ed. "Introduction." In *The Complete Short Stories and Sketches of Stephen Crane.* New York: Doubleday & Co., Inc., 1963, pp. 19-45.

————, ed. "Introduction." In *The Complete Novels of Stephen Crane.* New York: Doubleday & Co., Inc., 1967, pp. 3-97.

————. "The Cranes at Pennington Seminary." *American Literature,* XXXIX (January 1968), 530-541.

————. "The Last Will and Testament of Mrs. Mary Helen Peck Crane." *American Literature,* XL (May 1968), 232-234.

————. "A Stephen Crane Find: Nine Newspaper Sketches." *Southern Humanities Review,* II (Winter 1968), 1-37.

————. "Stallman's Crane." *The CEA Critic,* XXXI (May 1969), 8-9.

————. "The Fiction of the Reverend Jonathan Townley Crane, D.D." *American Literature,* XLIII (May 1971), 263-273.

Hagemann, E. R. "Crane's 'Real' War in His Short Stories." *American Quarterly,* VIII (Winter 1956), 356-367.

————. "Stephen Crane Faces the Storms of *Life,* 1896-1901." *Journal of Popular Culture,* II (Winter 1968), 347-360.

Hallam, George W. "Some New Stephen Crane Items." *Studies in Bibliography,* XX (1967), 263-266.

Harriman, Karl. "A Romantic Idealist—Mr. Stephen Crane." *The Literary Review* [Boston], IV (April 15, 1900), 85-87.

―――. "Last Days of Stephen Crane." *The New Hope* [New Hope, Pa.], II (October 1934), 7-9, 19-21.

Hartwick, Harry. *The Foreground of American Fiction.* New York: American Book Co., 1934, pp. 21-44, *et passim.*

Hicks, Granville. *The Great Tradition: An Interpretation of American Literature since the Civil War,* rev. ed. New York: The Macmillan Co., 1935, pp. 159-163, *et passim.* Reprinted by Quadrangle Paperbacks, Chicago, 1969.

Hitchcock, Ripley. "Preface." In *The Red Badge of Courage.* New York: D. Appleton and Co., 1900, pp. i-viii.

Hoffman, Daniel G. "Stephen Crane's New Jersey Ghosts: Two Newly-Recovered Sketches." *Proceedings of the New Jersey Historical Society,* LXXI (October 1953), 239-253.

―――. *The Poetry of Stephen Crane.* New York: Columbia University Press, 1957.

―――. "Stephen Crane's First Story." *Bulletin of the New York Public Library,* LXIV (May 1960), 273-278.

―――. "Stephen Crane's Last Novel." *Bulletin of the New York Public Library,* LXIV (June 1960), 337-343.

Hoffman, Frederick J. *The Twenties: American Writing in the Postwar Decade.* New York: The Viking Press, 1955, pp. 55-56, *et passim.* Reprinted by The Free Press, New York, 1965.

Hough, Robert L. "Crane and Goethe: A Forgotten Relationship." *Nineteenth-Century Fiction,* XVII (September 1962), 135-148.

Howells, William D. "Frank Norris." *The North American Review,* CLXXV (December 1902), 770-771, 777.

Hubbard, Elbert. "As to Stephen Crane." *The Lotos,* IX (March 1896), 674-678.

―――. *The Philistine,* XI (September 1900), 123-128.

Itabashi, Yoshie. " 'To Be a Man'—A Study of Fear and Courage in Stephen Crane's Stories." *The Tsuda Review* [Tokyo], No. 10 (November 1965), 1-48.

Ives, C. B. "Symmetrical Design in Four of Stephen Crane's Stories." *Ball State University Forum,* X (Winter 1969), 17-26.

Johnson, George W. "Stephen Crane's Metaphor of Decorum." *PMLA,* LXXVIII (June 1963), 250-256.

Johnson, Willis Fletcher. "The Launching of Stephen Crane." *The Literary Digest International Book Review,* IV (April 1926), 288-290.

Jones, Claude. "Stephen Crane at Syracuse." *American Literature,* VII (March 1935), 82-84.

Jones, Edith R. "Stephen Crane at Brede." *The Atlantic Monthly,* CXCIV (July 1954), 57-61.

Katz, Joseph. *The Poems of Stephen Crane: A Critical Edition.* New York: Cooper Square Publishers, Inc., 1966.

————. "Stephen Crane: Muckraker." *Columbia Library Columns,* XVII (February 1968), 3-7.

————. "The 'Preceptor' and Another Poet: Thomas Wentworth Higginson and Stephen Crane." *The Serif,* V (March 1968), 17-21.

————, ed. and introd. *The Portable Stephen Crane.* New York: The Viking Press, 1969.

————, ed. *Stephen Crane in the West and Mexico.* Kent: Kent State University Press, 1971.

Kauffman, Reginald Wright. "The True Story of Stephen Crane." *Modern Culture,* XII (October 1900), 143-145.

Kazin, Alfred. *On Native Grounds: An Interpretation of Modern American Prose Literature.* New York: Reynal & Hitchcock, 1942, pp. 67-72. Reprinted by Doubleday Anchor Books, New York, 1956.

Kindilien, Carlin T. *American Poetry in the Eighteen Nineties.* Providence: Brown University Press, 1956, pp. 155-161, *et passim.*

————. "Stephen Crane and the 'Savage Philosophy' of Olive Schreiner." *Boston University Studies in English,* III (Summer 1957), 97-107.

Knapp, Daniel. "Son of Thunder: Stephen Crane and the Fourth Evangelist." *Nineteenth-Century Fiction,* XXIV (December 1969), 253-291.

Knight, Grant C. *The Critical Period in American Literature.* Chapel Hill: The University of North Carolina Press, 1951, pp. 107-112, 115-117, 159-161, *et passim.*

Kreymborg, Alfred. *Our Singing Strength: An Outline of American Poetry, 1620-1930.* New York: Coward-McCann, Inc., 1929, pp. 251-252, *et passim.*

Kwiat, Joseph J. "Stephen Crane and Painting." *American Quarterly,* IV (Winter 1952), 331-338.

————. "The Newspaper Experience: Crane, Norris, and Dreiser." *Nineteenth-Century Fiction,* VIII (September 1953), 99-117.

LaFrance, Marston. "A Few Facts about Stephen Crane and 'Holland.'" *American Literature,* XXXVII (May 1965), 195-202.

Leaver, Florence. "Isolation in the Work of Stephen Crane." *The South Atlantic Quarterly*, LXI (Autumn 1962), 521-532.

Liebling, A. J. "The Dollars Damned Him." *The New Yorker*, XXXVII (August 5, 1961), 48-60, 63-66, 69-72.

Linneman, William R. "Stephen Crane's Contributions to *Truth*." *American Literature*, XXXI (May 1959), 196-197.

Linson, Corwin Knapp. "Little Stories of 'Steve' Crane." *The Saturday Evening Post*, CLXXVII (April 11, 1903), 19-20.

————. *My Stephen Crane*, ed. and introd. Edwin H. Cady. Syracuse: Syracuse University Press, 1958.

Lowell, Amy. "Introduction." In *The Work of Stephen Crane*, VI, ed. Wilson Follett. New York: Alfred A. Knopf, Inc., 1926, pp. ix-xxix.

Lucky, Robert E. "Apreciación del Poeta Stephen Crane." *Revista Iberoamericana*, V (October 1942), 317-343.

Lüdeke, Henry. "Stephen Crane's Poetry." In *The 'Democracy' of Henry Adams and Other Essays*. Bern, Switzerland: A. Francke, 1950, pp. 111-122.

Martin, Harold C. "The Development of Style in Nineteenth-Century American Fiction." In *Style in Prose Fiction: English Institute Essays, 1958,* ed. Harold C. Martin. New York: Columbia University Press, 1959, pp. 114-117, 131-133.

Martin, Jay, *Harvests of Change: American Literature, 1865-1914.* Englewood Cliffs, N.J.: Prentice-Hall, Inc., 1967, pp. 55-70.

Martin, John C. "Childhood in Stephen Crane's *Maggie*, 'The Monster,' and *Whilomville Stories*." *The Midwestern University Quarterly*, II (1967), 40-46.

Maxwell, Desmond E. S. *American Fiction: The Intellectual Background*. New York: Columbia University Press, 1963, pp. 295-299.

Mayfield, John S., ed. *Great Bugs in Onondaga: By Stephen Crane and Others.* Syracuse: Syracuse University Library Associates, 1964.

Mencken, H. L. "Introduction." In *The Work of Stephen Crane*, X, ed. Wilson Follett. New York: Alfred A. Knopf, Inc., 1926, pp. ix-xiii.

Michelson, Charles. "Introduction." In *The Work of Stephen Crane*, XII, ed. Wilson Follett. New York: Alfred A. Knopf, Inc., 1927, pp. ix-xxiv.

Miller, Ruth. "Regions of Snow: The Poetic Style of Stephen Crane." *Bulletin of the New York Public Library*, LXXII (May 1968), 328-349.

Milne, W. Gordon. "Stephen Crane: Pioneer in Technique." *Die Neueren Sprachen,* n.s. VIII (1959), 297-303.

Monroe, Harriet. "Comment: Stephen Crane." *Poetry,* XIV (June 1919), 148-152.

Morgan, H. Wayne. *Writers in Transition: Seven Americans.* New York: Hill and Wang, 1963, pp. 1-22.

Nelson, Harland S. "Stephen Crane's Achievement as a Poet." *Texas Studies in Literature and Language,* IV ((Winter 1963), 564-582.

Noble, David W. *The Eternal Adam and the New World Garden: The Central Myth in the American Novel Since 1830.* New York: George Braziller, 1968, pp. 101-105, 115-123.

Noxon, Frank W. "The Real Stephen Crane." *The Step Ladder* [Chicago], XIV (January 1928), 4-9.

Nye, Russel B. "Stephen Crane as Social Critic." *The Modern Quarterly: A Journal of Radical Opinion,* XI (Summer 1940), 48-54.

Oliver, Arthur. "Jersey Memories—Stephen Crane." *Proceedings of the New Jersey Historical Society,* n.s. XVI (October 1931), 454-463.

Osborn, Scott C. "The 'Rivalry-Chivalry' of Richard Harding Davis and Stephen Crane." *American Literature,* XXVIII (March 1956), 50-61.

Øverland, Orm. "The Impressionism of Stephen Crane: A Study in Style and Technique." In *Americana Norvegica: Norwegian Contributions to American Studies,* I, eds. Sigmund Skard and Henry H. Wasser. Philadelphia: University of Pennsylvania Press, 1966, pp. 239-285.

Paine, Ralph D. *Roads of Adventure.* Boston: Houghton Mifflin Co., 1922, pp. 162-174, 192-193, 225-238, 243-247, 251-260, *et passim.*

Pattee, Fred Lewis. *The Development of the American Short Story: An Historical Survey.* New York: Harper & Brothers, 1923, pp. 341-343, *et passim.*

Peaslee, Clarence Loomis. "Stephen Crane's College Days." *The Monthly Illustrator and Home and Country,* XIII (August 1896), 27-30.

Peck, Richard E. "Stephen Crane and Baudelaire: A Direct Link." *American Literature,* XXXVII (May 1965), 202-204.

Penn, Jonathan. "A Little Study of Stephen Crane." *The Lotus,* II (October 1896), 208-211.

Perosa, Sergio. "Naturalism and Impressionism in Stephen Crane's Fiction." In *Stephen Crane: A Collection of Critical Essays,* ed. Maurice Bassan, pp. 80-94.

Pizer, Donald. "Crane Reports Garland on Howells." *Modern Language Notes*, LXX (January 1955), 37-39.

———. "Romantic Individualism in Garland, Norris and Crane." *American Quarterly*, X (Winter 1958), 463-475.

———."The Garland-Crane Relationship." *The Huntington Library Quarterly*, XXIV (November 1960), 75-82.

Pratt, Lyndon U. "An Addition to the Canon of Stephen Crane." *Research Studies of the State College of Washington*, VII (March 1939), 55-58.

———. "The Formal Education of Stephen Crane." *American Literature*, X (January 1939), 460-471.

Quinn, Arthur Hobson. *American Fiction: An Historical and Critical Survey*. New York: D. Appleton-Century Co., Inc., 1936, pp. 532-538, *et passim*.

Rahv, Philip. "Fiction and the Criticism of Fiction." *The Kenyon Review*, XVIII (Spring 1956), 280-284.

Randel, William. "Stephen Crane's Jacksonville." *The South Atlantic Quarterly*, LXII (Spring 1963), 268-274.

———. "From Slate to Emerald Green: More Light on Crane's Jacksonville Visit." *Nineteenth-Century Fiction*, XIX (March 1965), 357-368.

Rogers, Rodney O. "Stephen Crane and Impressionism." *Nineteenth-Century Fiction*, XXIV (December 1969), 292-304.

Roth, Russell. "A Tree in Winter: The Short Fiction of Stephen Crane." *New Mexico Quarterly*, XXIII (Summer 1953), 188-196.

Schneider, Robert W. *Five Novelists of the Progressive Era*. New York: Columbia University Press, 1965, pp. 60-111, *et passim*.

Schoberlin, Melvin, ed. and introd. *The Sullivan County Sketches of Stephen Crane*. Syracuse: Syracuse University Press, 1949.

Schwab, Arnold T. *James Gibbons Huneker: Critic of the Seven Arts*. Stanford: Stanford University Press, 1963, pp. 114-117, *et passim*.

Shroeder, John W. "Stephen Crane Embattled." *The University of Kansas City Review*, XVII (Winter 1950), 119-129.

Sidbury, Edna Crane. "My Uncle, Stephen Crane, as I Knew Him." *The Literary Digest International Book Review*, IV (March 1926), 248-250.

Slote, Bernice. "Stephen Crane in Nebraska." *Prairie Schooner*, XLIII (Summer 1969), 192-199.

———. "Stephen Crane and Willa Cather." *The Serif*, VI (December 1969), 3-15.

Smith, Ernest G. "Comments and Queries." *The Lafayette Alumnus* [Lafayette College], II (February 1932), 6.

Solomon, Eric. "Stephen Crane's War Stories." *Texas Studies in Literature and Language,* III (Spring 1961), 67-80.

———. *Stephen Crane in England: A Portrait of the Artist.* Columbus: Ohio State University Press, 1964.

———. *Stephen Crane: From Parody to Realism.* Cambridge: Harvard University Press, 1966.

Solomon, M. "Stephen Crane: A Critical Study." *Masses & Mainstream,* IX (January 1956), 25-42; (March 1956), 31-47.

Spiller, Robert E. "Toward Naturalism in Fiction." In *Literary History of the United States,* II. New York: The Macmillan Co., 1949, pp. 1020-1026.

Stallman, R. W., ed. and introd. *Stephen Crane: An Omnibus.* New York: Alfred A. Knopf, Inc., 1952.

———. "Stephen Crane: A Revaluation." In *Critiques and Essays on Modern Fiction, 1920-1951,* sel. John W. Aldridge. New York: The Ronald Press Co., 1952, pp. 244-269.

———, and Lillian Gilkes, eds. *Stephen Crane: Letters.* New York: New York University Press, 1960.

———. "Crane's Short Stories." In *The Houses That James Built and Other Literary Studies.* Lansing: Michigan State University Press, 1961, pp. 103-110.

———. "Stephen Crane as Dramatist." *Bulletin of the New York Public Library,* LXVII (October 1963), 495-497.

———, and E. R. Hagemann, eds. *The War Dispatches of Stephen Crane.* New York: New York University Press, 1964.

———, and E. R. Hagemann, eds. *The New York City Sketches of Stephen Crane and Related Pieces.* New York: New York University Press, 1966.

———. "Journalist Crane in that Dinghy." *Bulletin of the New York Public Library,* LXXII (April 1968), 261-277.

———. *Stephen Crane: A Biography.* New York: George Braziller, 1968.

———, ed. and introd. *Stephen Crane: Sullivan County Tales and Sketches.* Ames: The Iowa State University Press, 1968.

Starrett, Vincent. "Stephen Crane: An Estimate." *The Sewanee Review,* XXVIII (July 1920), 405-413.

Stein, William Bysshe. "Stephen Crane's *Homo Absurdus.*" *Bucknell Review,* VIII (May 1959), 168-188.

Stewart, Randall. *American Literature & Christian Doctrine.* Baton Rouge: Louisiana State University Press, 1958, pp. 109-113.

Stronks, James B. "A Realist Experiments with Impressionism: Hamlin Garland's 'Chicago Studies.'" *American Literature,* XXXVI (March 1964), 38-52.

Tanner, Tony. "Stephen Crane's Long Dream of War." *London Magazine,* n.s. VIII (December 1968), 5-19.

Taylor, Gordon O. *The Passages of Thought: Psychological Representation in the American Novel, 1870-1900.* New York: Oxford University Press, 1969, pp. 110-135.

Van Doren, Carl. "Stephen Crane." *The American Mercury,* I (January 1924), 11-14.

Vosburgh, R. G. "The Darkest Hour in the Life of Stephen Crane." *The Criterion,* n.s. I (February 1901), 26-27.

Wagenknecht, Edward. *Cavalcade of the American Novel.* New York: Henry Holt & Co., 1952, pp. 212-216, *et passim.* Reprinted by Holt, Rinehart and Winston, New York, 1962.

Walcutt, Charles Child "Stephen Crane: Naturalist and Impressionist." In *American Literary Naturalism, A Divided Stream.* Minneapolis: University of Minnesota Press, 1956, pp. 66-86, *et passim.*

Weimer, David R. *The City as Metaphor.* New York: Random House, 1966, pp. 52-64, *et passim.*

Wells, H. G. "Stephen Crane: From an English Standpoint." *The North American Review,* CLXXI (August 1900), 233-242.

Wertheim, Stanley. "Stephen Crane and the Wrath of Jehova." *The Literary Review,* VII (Summer 1964), 499-508.

———. "Why Stephen Crane Left Claverack." *The Stephen Crane Newsletter,* II (Fall 1967), 5.

———. "Crane and Garland: The Education of an Impressionist." *The North Dakota Quarterly,* XXXV (Winter 1967), 23-28.

West, Ray B., Jr. "Stephen Crane: Author in Transition." *American Literature,* XXXIV (May 1962), 215-228.

Westbrook, Max. "Stephen Crane: The Pattern of Affirmation." *Nineteenth-Century Fiction,* XIV (December 1959), 219-229.

———. "Stephen Crane's Social Ethic." *American Quarterly,* XIV (Winter 1962), 587-596.

———. "Stephen Crane's Poetry: Perspective and Arrogance." *Bucknell Review,* XI (December 1963), 24-34.

Wheeler, Post, and Hallie Erminie Rives. *Dome of Many-Coloured Glass.* New York: Doubleday & Co., Inc., 1955, pp. 21-22, 99-101, 106-107, *et passim.*

White, W. M. "The Crane-Hemingway Code: A Reevaluation." *Ball State University Forum,* X (Spring 1969), 15-20.

Wickham, Harvey. "Stephen Crane at College." *The American Mercury,* VII (March 1926), 291-297.

Williams, Ames W. "Stephen Crane, War Correspondent." *The New Colophon,* I (April 1948), 113-123.

Wilson, Edmund. "A Vortex in the Nineties." *The New Republic,* XXXVII (January 2, 1924), 153-154.

Wright, Austin McGiffert. *The American Short Story in the Twenties.* Chicago: The University of Chicago Press, 1961, pp. 26-29, 38-39, *et passim.*

Wyatt, Edith. "Stephen Crane." *The New Republic,* IV (September 11, 1915), 148-150.

Yoshida, Hiroshige. "A Note on Stephen Crane's Use of Colloquial and Slangy Words and Idioms." *Anglica* [The Anglica Society of Kansai University, Osaka], IV (January 1961), 59-71.

Young, Philip. *Ernest Hemingway.* New York: Rinehart & Co., 1952, pp. 161-169. Reprinted in *Ernest Hemingway: A Reconsideration,* Pennsylvania State University Press, 1966, pp. 191-198.

Ziff, Larzer. "Outstripping the Event: Stephen Crane." In *The American 1890s: Life and Times of a Lost Generation.* New York: The Viking Press, 1966, pp. 185-205, *et passim.*

II. Studies of Poetry Collections and Individual Poems

The Black Riders and Other Lines

Berryman, *Stephen Crane,* pp. 113-118, *et passim.*

Cady, *Stephen Crane,* pp. 111-114, *et passim.*

Colvert, "Stephen Crane's Magic Mountain," pp. 101-103.

Cox, James M. "*The Pilgrim's Progress* as Source for Stephen Crane's *The Black Riders.*" *American Literature,* XXVIII (January 1957), 478-487.

Fryckstedt, Olov W. "Crane's *Black Riders:* A Discussion of Dates." *Studia Neophilologica,* XXXIV (1962), 282-293.

Garland, *Roadside Meetings,* pp. 193-195.

Geismar, pp. 77-82.

Gillis, pp. 74-77.

Hoffman, *The Poetry of Stephen Crane, passim.*

Itabashi, Yoshie. "The Modern Pilgrimage of *The Black Riders:* An Interpretation." *The Tsuda Review* [Tokyo], No. 12 (November 1967), 1-41.

Katz, Joseph. "Toward A Descriptive Bibliography of Stephen Crane: *The Black Riders.*" *The Papers of the Bibliographical Society of America*, LIX (Second Quarter 1965), 150-157.

————. *The Poems of Stephen Crane*, pp. xvii-xlix.

Kindilien, *American Poetry in the Eighteen Nineties*, pp. 156-160.

————. "Stephen Crane and the 'Savage Philosophy' of Olive Schreiner," pp. 99-107.

Knight, pp. 107-109.

Lowell, pp. xix-xxiv.

Lüdeke, pp. 114-120.

Miller, *passim*.

Monroe, p. 150.

Nelson, *passim*.

O'Donnell, Thomas F. "A Note on the Reception of Crane's *The Black Riders.*" *American Literature*, XXIV (May 1952), 233-235.

Schneider, pp. 69-72, 93-94.

Solomon, M., (January 1956), pp. 31-32.

Westbrook, "Stephen Crane's Poetry: Perspective and Arrogance," pp. 26-30, *et passim*.

Ziff, pp. 193-194.

A Souvenir and a Medley

Lowell, pp. xxiv-xxvi.

War Is Kind

Bassan, Maurice. "A Bibliographical Study of Stephen Crane's Poem, 'In the Night.'" *The Papers of the Bibliographical Society of America*, LVIII (Second Quarter 1964), 173-179.

Berryman, *Stephen Crane*, pp. 241-243, *et passim*.

Geismar, pp. 112-116.

Gillis, pp. 77-79.

Gullason, Thomas A. "Tennyson's Influence on Stephen Crane." *Notes and Queries*, n.s. V (April 1958), 165.

Hoffman, *The Poetry of Stephen Crane*, *passim*.

Katz, *The Poems of Stephen Crane,* pp. xlix-l.
Kindilien, *American Poetry in the Eighteen Nineties,* p. 160.
————. "Stephen Crane and the 'Savage Philosophy' of Olive Schreiner," p. 100, *et passim.*
Knight, p. 154.
Lowell, pp. xxvi-xxviii.
Lüdeke, pp. 120-122.
Marcus, Mordecai. "Structure and Irony in Stephen Crane's 'War Is Kind.'" *CLA Journal,* IX (March 1966), 274-278.
Miller, *passim.*
Monroe, pp. 150-152.
Nelson, *passim.*
Wegelin, Christof. "Crane's *A Man Said To The Universe." The Explicator,* XX (September 1961), item 9.

***

Katz, Joseph. "Cora Crane and the Poetry of Stephen Crane." *The Papers of the Bibliographical Society of America,* LVIII (Fourth Quarter 1964), 469-476.
————. "'The Blue Battalions' and the Uses of Experience." *Studia Neophilologica,* XXXVIII (1966), 107-116.
————. "A 'New' Stephen Crane Poem: An Evaluation." *Notes and Queries,* n.s. XIII (September 1966), 346-349.
Morgan, John M. *Concordance to the Poetry of Stephen Crane.* Littleton, Colo.: Libraries Unlimited, 1971.
Peck, Richard E. "A 'New' Stephen Crane Poem." *Notes and Queries,* n.s. XII (February 1965), 64-66.

III. Studies of Individual Novels

Active Service

Beer, *Stephen Crane,* p. 222.
Berryman, *Stephen Crane,* pp. 228-230.
Cady, *Stephen Crane,* pp. 148-150.
Geismar, pp. 109-112.
Gibson, Donald B., pp. 140-145.

Gullason, "The Jamesian Motif in Stephen Crane's Last Novels," pp. 77-78, 80-82.

————, ed. *The Complete Novels of Stephen Crane*, pp. 87-92.

Itabashi, Yoshie. "Comedies of Love: A Study of *The Third Violet* and *Active Service*." *The Tsuda Review* [Tokyo], No. 13 (November 1968), 34-63.

Knight, p. 154.

Quinn, p. 537.

Solomon, Eric, *Stephen Crane: From Parody to Realism*, pp. 135-144.

Van Doren, Carl. "Introduction." In *The Work of Stephen Crane*, IV, ed. Wilson Follett. New York: Alfred A. Knopf, Inc., 1926, pp. ix-xv.

George's Mother

Ahnebrink, pp. 271-272, 328-330, *et passim*.

Bassan, Maurice. "An Early Draft of *George's Mother*." *American Literature*, XXXVI (January 1965), 518-522.

Berryman, *Stephen Crane*, pp. 318-320.

Brennan, Joseph X. "The Imagery and Art of *George's Mother*." *CLA Journal*, IV (December 1960), 106-115.

————. "Stephen Crane and the Limits of Irony," pp. 186-187.

Chase, p. xv.

Colvert, James B. "Introduction." In *The Works of Stephen Crane*, I, ed. Fredson Bowers. Charlottesville: The University Press of Virginia, 1969, pp. 101-108.

Geismar, pp. 92-96.

Gibson, Donald B., pp. 40-52.

Gullason, "Thematic Patterns in Stephen Crane's Early Novels," pp. 62-67.

————, ed. *The Complete Novels of Stephen Crane*, pp. 77-82.

Itabashi, " 'To Be a Man'—A Study of Fear and Courage in Stephen Crane's Stories," pp. 23-29.

Ives, "Symmetrical Design in Four of Stephen Crane's Stories," pp. 21-22.

Jackson, Agnes Moreland. "Stephen Crane's Imagery of Conflict in *George's Mother*." *The Arizona Quarterly*, XXV (Winter 1969), 313-318.

Knapp, pp. 277-286.

Knight, p. 115.

Lavers, Norman. "Order in *The Red Badge of Courage*." *The University Review*, XXXII (Summer 1966), 287-289.

Norris, Frank. "Stephen Crane's Stories of Life in the Slums." San Francisco *Wave*, XV (July 4, 1896), 13. Reprinted in *The Literary Criticism of Frank Norris*, ed. Donald Pizer. Austin: University of Texas, 1964, pp. 164-166.

Quinn, p. 535.

Schneider, pp. 89-91, 104-105.

Solomon, Eric, *Stephen Crane: From Parody to Realism*, pp. 47-67.

Stallman, ed. *Stephen Crane: An Omnibus*, pp. 19-20.

Stein, "Stephen Crane's *Homo Absurdus*," pp. 182-184.

Wertheim, Stanley, ed. and introd. *The Merrill Studies in Maggie and George's Mother*. Columbus: Charles E. Merrill Publishing Co., 1970.

Westbrook, "Stephen Crane: The Pattern of Affirmation," p. 227.

Maggie: A Girl of the Streets

Aaron, Daniel. "Howells' 'Maggie.' " *The New England Quarterly*, XXXVIII (March 1965), 85-90.

Åhnebrink, pp. 250-264, *et passim*.

Bassan, Maurice, ed. *Stephen Crane's Maggie: Text and Context*. Belmont, Calif.: Wadsworth Publishing Co., Inc., 1966.

Berryman, *Stephen Crane*, pp. 57-64.

Bradbury, Malcolm. "Sociology and Literary Studies. II. Romance and Reality in *Maggie*." *Journal of American Studies*, III (July 1969), 118-121.

Brennan, Joseph X. "Ironic and Symbolic Structure in Crane's *Maggie*." *Nineteenth-Century Fiction*, XVI (March 1962), 303-315.

————. "Stephen Crane and the Limits of Irony," pp. 184-186.

Brooks, Van Wyck. "Introduction." In *Two Novels By Stephen Crane. Maggie: A Girl of the Streets and George's Mother*. Greenwich, Conn.: Fawcett Publications, Inc., 1960, pp. 5-6.

Bruccoli, Matthew J. "Maggie's Last Night." *The Stephen Crane Newsletter*, II (Fall 1967), 10.

Cady, *Stephen Crane*, pp. 104-111.

————. "Stephen Crane: *Maggie, A Girl of the Streets*." In *Landmarks of American Writing*, ed. Hennig Cohen. New York: Basic Books, Inc., 1969, pp. 172-181.

Cargill, pp. 85-86.

Chase, pp. xiv-xv.

Colvert, "Structure and Theme in Stephen Crane's Fiction," pp. 202-204.

———. "Introduction." In *The Works of Stephen Crane*, I, ed. Fredson Bowers. Charlottesville: The University Press of Virginia, 1969, pp. xxxiii-lii.

Cunliffe, Marcus. "Stephen Crane and the American Background of *Maggie*." *American Quarterly*, VII (Spring 1955), 31-44.

Fiedler, Leslie A. *Love and Death in the American Novel*. New York: Criterion Books, 1960, pp. 239-240.

Fitelson, David. "Stephen Crane's *Maggie* and Darwinism." *American Quarterly*, XVI (Summer 1964), 182-194.

Ford, Philip H. "Illusion and Reality in Crane's *Maggie*." *The Arizona Quarterly*, XXV (Winter 1969), 293-303.

Garland, Hamlin. "An Ambitious French Novel and a Modest American Story." *The Arena*, VII (June 1893), xi-xii.

Geismar, pp. 74-77.

Gibson, Donald B., pp. 26-39.

Gibson, William M., pp. vii-ix, xx-xxii.

Gullason, Thomas A. "The Sources of Stephen Crane's *Maggie*." *Philological Quarterly*, XXXVIII (October 1959), 497-502.

———. "Thematic Patterns in Stephen Crane's Early Novels," pp. 60-61, 62-66.

———, ed. *The Complete Novels of Stephen Crane*, pp. 55-65.

———. "The First Known Review of Stephen Crane's 1893 *Maggie*." *English Language Notes*, V (June 1968), 300-302.

Hazlitt, Henry. "Introduction." In *Maggie together with George's Mother and The Blue Hotel*. New York: Alfred A. Knopf, Inc., 1931, pp. vii-xi.

Holton, Milne. "The Sparrow's Fall and the Sparrow's Eye: Crane's *Maggie*." *Studia Neophilologica*, XLI (1969), 115-129.

Howells, William Dean. "An Appreciation." In *Maggie: A Child of the Streets*. London: William Heinemann, 1896, pp. v-vii. Reprinted in *The Works of Stephen Crane*, I, ed. Fredson Bowers. Charlottesville: The University Press of Virginia, 1969, pp. 4-5.

Itabashi, " 'To Be a Man'—A Study of Fear and Courage in Stephen Crane's Stories," pp. 9-15.

Ives, "Symmetrical Design in Four of Stephen Crane's Stories," pp. 19-20.

Jackson, John A. "Sociology and Literary Studies. I. The Map of Society: America in the 1890s." *Journal of American Studies,* III (July 1969), 105-110.

Kahn, Sholom J. "Stephen Crane and Whitman: A Possible Source for 'Maggie.' " *Walt Whitman Review,* VII (December 1961), 71-77.

Katz, Joseph. "The *Maggie* Nobody Knows." *Modern Fiction Studies,* XII (Summer 1966), 200-212.

———. "Introduction." In *Maggie: A Girl of the Streets,* 1893 ed. Gainesville, Fla.: Scholars' Facsimiles & Reprints, 1966, pp. v-xxiii.

Knapp, pp. 274-277.

Knight, pp. 109-112.

Kramer, Maurice. "Crane's *Maggie: A Girl of the Streets.*" *The Explicator,* XXII (February 1964), item 49.

Lainoff, Seymour. "Jimmie in Crane's *Maggie.*" *Iowa English Yearbook,* No. 10 (Fall 1965), 53-54.

Lenehan, William T. "The Failure of Naturalistic Techniques in Stephen Crane's *Maggie.*" In *Stephen Crane's Maggie: Text and Context,* ed. Maurice Bassan, pp. 166-173.

Linson, *My Stephen Crane,* pp. 18, 20-23.

Martin, Jay, pp. 57-59.

Martin, John C., pp. 40-41.

Matthiessen, F. O. *Theodore Dreiser.* New York: William Sloane Associates, 1951, pp. 91-92.

Maxwell, pp. 295-298.

Norris, Frank. "Stephen Crane's Stories of Life in the Slums." San Francisco *Wave,* XV (July 4, 1896), 13. Reprinted in *The Literary Criticism of Frank Norris,* ed. Donald Pizer. Austin: University of Texas, 1964, pp. 164-166.

Overmyer, Janet. "The Structure of Crane's *Maggie.*" *The University of Kansas City Review,* XXIX (Autumn 1962), 71-72.

Perosa, pp. 84-86.

Pizer, Donald. "Stephen Crane's 'Maggie' and American Naturalism." *Criticism,* VII (Spring 1965), 168-175.

———. "Introduction." In *Maggie: A Girl of the Streets,* 1893 ed. San Francisco: Chandler Publishing Co., 1968, pp. vii-xxix.

Quinn, pp. 532-533.

Sansom, William. "Introduction." In *Maggie: A Girl of the Streets,* ed. Herbert Van Thal. London: Cassell & Co., Ltd., 1966, pp. vii-xiv.

Schneider, pp. 78-79, 86-89.

Solomon, Eric, *Stephen Crane: From Parody to Realism,* pp. 23-44.

Solomon, M., (January 1956), pp. 26-30.

Stallman, R. W. "Stephen Crane's Revision of *Maggie: A Girl of the Streets.*" *American Literature,* XXVI (January 1955), 528-536.

―――. "Crane's 'Maggie': A Reassessment." *Modern Fiction Studies,* V (Autumn 1959), 251-259.

―――. "Crane's *Maggie* in Review," in *The Houses That James Built and Other Literary Studies,* pp. 63-72.

Stein, William Bysshe. "New Testament Inversions in Crane's *Maggie.*" *Modern Language Notes,* LXXIII (April 1958), 268-272.

―――. "Stephen Crane's *Homo Absurdus,*" pp. 181-182.

Tanner, pp. 6, 8.

Taylor, pp. 111-119.

Wagenknecht, pp. 213-214.

Walcutt, pp. 67-72.

Weimer, pp. 52-57.

Wertheim, "Stephen Crane and the Wrath of Jehova," pp. 503-504.

―――. ed. and introd. *The Merrill Studies in Maggie and George's Mother.*

Westbrook, "Stephen Crane's Social Ethic," pp. 590-593.

Wright, pp. 224-229.

Ziff, pp. 189-193.

The O'Ruddy: A Romance

Beer, Thomas. "Introduction." In *The Work of Stephen Crane,* VII, ed. Wilson Follett. New York: Alfred A. Knopf, Inc., 1926, pp. ix-xiii.

Berryman, *Stephen Crane,* pp. 246-247.

Cady, *Stephen Crane,* pp. 150-151.

Geismar, pp. 129-130.

Gibson, Donald B., pp. 144-145.

Gilkes, Lillian and Joan H. Baum. "Stephen Crane's Last Novel: *The O'Ruddy.*" *Columbia Library Columns,* VI (February 1957), 41-48.

Gullason, "The Jamesian Motif in Stephen Crane's Last Novels," pp. 77-78, 82-84.

―――, ed. *The Complete Novels of Stephen Crane,* pp. 92-97.

Jones, Edith R., p. 60.

O'Donnell, Bernard. "Stephen Crane's *The O'Ruddy:* A Problem in Authorship Discrimination." In *The Computer & Literary Style,* ed. Jacob Leed. Kent: Kent State University Press, 1966, pp. 107-115.

Solomon, Eric, *Stephen Crane: From Parody to Realism,* pp. 13-15.

The Red Badge of Courage

Åhnebrink, pp. 264-271, 344-357, *et passim.*

Albrecht, Robert C. "Content and Style in *The Red Badge of Courage." College English,* XXVII (March 1966), 487-492.

Anderson, Warren D. "Homer and Stephen Crane." *Nineteenth-Century Fiction,* XIX (June 1964), 77-86.

Bache, William B. *"The Red Badge of Courage* and 'The Short Happy Life of Francis Macomber.'" *Western Humanities Review,* XV (Winter 1961), 83-84.

Berryman, John. "Stephen Crane: *The Red Badge of Courage."* In *The American Novel: From James Fenimore Cooper to William Faulkner,* ed. Wallace Stegner. New York: Basic Books, Inc., 1965, pp. 86-96.

Brennan, "Stephen Crane and the Limits of Irony," pp. 187-190.

Cady, *Stephen Crane,* pp. 115-144.

Cargill, pp. 86-87.

Carlson, Eric W. "Crane's *The Red Badge of Courage,* IX." *The Explicator,* XVI (March 1958), item 34.

Chase, pp. xv-xvii.

Colvert, James B. *"The Red Badge of Courage* and a Review of Zola's *La Débâcle." Modern Language Notes,* LXXI (February 1956), 98-100.

————. "Structure and Theme in Stephen Crane's Fiction," pp. 204-207.

————. "Stephen Crane's Magic Mountain," pp. 95-100.

Conrad, Joseph. "His War Book." In *The Red Badge of Courage.* London: William Heinemann Ltd., 1925, pp. v-xii.

Cox, James Trammell. "The Imagery of 'The Red Badge of Courage.'" *Modern Fiction Studies,* V (Autumn 1959), 209-219.

Crothers, George D., ed. *Invitation to Learning: English & American Novels.* New York: Basic Books, Inc., 1966, pp. 273-281.

Dillingham, William B. "Insensibility in *The Red Badge of Courage." College English,* XXV (December 1963), 194-198.

Dusenbery, Robert. "The Homeric Mood in the 'Red Badge of Courage.'" *Pacific Coast Philology,* III (April 1968), 31-37.

Eby, Cecil D., Jr. "The Source of Crane's Metaphor, 'Red Badge of Courage.'" *American Literature*, XXXII (May 1960), 204-207.

———. "Stephen Crane's 'Fierce Red Wafer.'" *English Language Notes*, I (December 1963), 128-130.

Evans, David L. "Henry's Hell: The Night Journey in *The Red Badge of Courage*." *Proceedings of the Utah Academy of Sciences, Arts, and Letters*, XLIV (Part I 1967), 159-166.

Feidelson, Charles, Jr. "Three Views of the Human Person: *The Scarlet Letter, Walden*, and *The Red Badge of Courage*." *Reports and Speeches of the Sixth Yale Conference on the Teaching of English*, April 8 and 9, 1960, pp. 47-52.

Fraser, John. "Crime and Forgiveness: 'The Red Badge' in Time of War." *Criticism*, IX (Summer 1967), 243-256.

Free, William Joseph. "Smoke Imagery in *The Red Badge of Courage*." *CLA Journal* VII (December 1963), 148-152.

Friedman, Norman. "Criticism and the Novel: Hardy, Hemingway, Crane, Woolf, Conrad." *The Antioch Review*, XVIII (Fall 1958), 356-361.

Frohock, W. M. "*The Red Badge* and the Limits of Parody." *The Southern Review*, n.s. VI (Winter 1970), 137-148.

Fryckstedt, Olov W. "Henry Fleming's Tupenny Fury: Cosmic Pessimism in Stephen Crane's *The Red Badge of Courage*." *Studia Neophilologica*, XXXIII (1961), 265-281.

Fulwiler, Toby. "The Death of the Handsome Sailor: A Study of *Billy Budd* and *The Red Badge of Courage*." *The Arizona Quarterly*, XXVI (Summer 1970), 101-112.

Garnett, pp. 208-209, 211-213.

Geismar, pp. 82-89.

Gibson, Donald B., pp. 60-89.

Gibson, William M., pp. ix-xi.

Gordon, Caroline. *How to Read a Novel*. New York: The Viking Press, 1957, pp. 91-93.

Greenfield, pp. 562-563, 568-572.

Gullason, Thomas A. "New Sources for Stephen Crane's War Motif." *Modern Language Notes*, LXXII (December 1957), 572-575.

———. "Thematic Patterns in Stephen Crane's Early Novels," pp. 59-67.

———, ed. *The Complete Novels of Stephen Crane*, pp. 65-77.

Hart, John E. "*The Red Badge of Courage* as Myth and Symbol." *The University of Kansas City Review*, XIX (Summer 1953), 249-256.

Hartwick, pp. 25-28.

Hassan, Ihab. *Radical Innocence: Studies in the Contemporary American Novel.* Princeton: Princeton University Press, 1961, pp. 42-43.

Hergesheimer, Joseph. "Introduction." In *The Work of Stephen Crane,* I, ed. Wilson Follett. New York: Alfred A. Knopf, Inc., 1925, pp. ix-xviii.

Hitchcock, pp. iii-x.

Hoffman, Daniel G. "Introduction." In *The Red Badge of Courage and Other Stories By Stephen Crane.* New York: Harper & Brothers, 1957, pp. vii-xix.

Hough, Robert L. "Crane's Henry Fleming: Speech and Vision." *Forum* [University of Houston], III (Winter 1962), 41-42.

Howarth, William L. *"The Red Badge of Courage* Manuscript: New Evidence for a Critical Edition." *Studies in Bibliography,* XVIII (1965), 229-247.

Hungerford, Harold R. " 'That Was at Chancellorsville': The Factual Framework of *The Red Badge of Courage." American Literature,* XXXIV (January 1963), 520-531.

Itabashi, " 'To Be a Man'—A Study of Fear and Courage in Stephen Crane's Stories," pp. 15-23.

Ives, "Symmetrical Design in Four of Stephen Crane's Stories," pp. 22-25.

Johnson, Bruce. "Joseph Conrad and Crane's *Red Badge of Courage." Papers of the Michigan Academy of Science, Arts, and Letters,* XLVIII (1963), 649-655.

Katz, Joseph. "Introduction." In *The Red Badge of Courage* (1894 New York *Press* version). Gainesville, Fla.: Scholars' Facsimiles & Reprints, 1967, pp. 9-42.

Klotz, Marvin. "Crane's 'The Red Badge of Courage.' " *Notes and Queries,* n.s. VI February 1959), 68-69.

————. "Romance or Realism?: Plot, Theme, and Character in *The Red Badge of Courage." CLA Journal,* VI (December 1962), 98-106.

Knight, pp. 115-117.

Labor, Earle. "Crane and Hemingway: Anatomy of Trauma." *Renascence,* XI (Summer 1959), 189-196.

LaFrance, Marston. "Stephen Crane's *Private Fleming: His Various Battles."* In *Patterns of Commitment in American Literature,* ed. Marston LaFrance. Toronto: University of Toronto Press, 1967, pp. 113-133.

Lavers, Norman. "Order in *The Red Badge of Courage." The University Review,* XXXII (Summer 1966), 287-295.

Linson, *My Stephen Crane,* pp. 43-45.

Lorch, Thomas M. "The Cyclical Structure of *The Red Badge of Courage.*" *CLA Journal,* X (March 1967), 229-238.

Ludwig, Richard M. and Marvin B. Perry, Jr., eds. *Nine Short Novels.* Boston: D. C. Heath and Co., 1952, pp. xiii-xiv.

Lynskey, Winifred. "Crane's *The Red Badge of Courage.*" *The Explicator,* VIII (December 1949), item 18.

Marcus, Mordecai. "The Unity of *The Red Badge of Courage.*" In *The Red Badge of Courage: Text and Criticism,* ed. Richard Lettis, *et al.* New York: Harcourt, Brace and Co., 1960, pp. 189-195.

————. and Erin Marcus. "Animal Imagery in *The Red Badge of Courage.*" *Modern Language Notes,* LXXIV (February 1959), 108-111.

Martin, Jay. "*The Red Badge of Courage:* The Education of Henry Fleming." *Twelfth Yale Conference on the Teaching of English,* April 1 and 2, 1966, pp. 75-85.

McColly, William. "Teaching *The Red Badge of Courage.*" *English Journal,* L (November 1961), 534-538.

McDermott, John J. "Symbolism and Psychological Realism in *The Red Badge of Courage.*" *Nineteenth-Century Fiction,* XXIII (December 1968), 324-331.

O'Donnell, Thomas F. "John B. Van Petten: Stephen Crane's History Teacher." *American Literature,* XXVII (May 1955), 196-202.

————. "De Forest, Van Petten, and Stephen Crane." *American Literature,* XXVII (January 1956), 578-580.

Osborn, Neal J. "William Ellery Channing and *The Red Badge of Courage.*" *Bulletin of the New York Public Library,* LXIX (March 1965), 182-196.

Osborn, Scott C. "Stephen Crane's Imagery: 'Pasted Like a Wafer.'" *American Literature,* XXIII (November 1951), 362.

Pelletier, Gaston. "*Red Badge* Revisited." *English Journal,* LVII (January 1968), 24-25, 99.

Perosa, pp. 87-94.

Pizer, Donald. "Nineteenth-Century American Naturalism: An Essay in Definition." *Bucknell Review,* XIII (December 1965), 12-18.

————. "A Primer of Fictional Aesthetics." *College English,* XXX (April 1969), 575-580.

Pratt, Lyndon Upson. "A Possible Source of *The Red Badge of Courage.*" *American Literature,* XI (March 1939), 1-10.

Pritchett, V. S. *The Living Novel.* New York: Reynal & Hitchcock,

1947, pp. 173-178. Reprinted by Random House, New York, 1964, pp. 232-237.

———. "Introduction." In *The Red Badge of Courage and Other Stories.* London: Oxford University Press, 1960, pp. x-xii.

Quinn, pp. 533-535.

Rathbun, John W. "Structure and Meaning in *The Red Badge of Courage.*" *Ball State University Forum,* X (Winter 1969), 8-16.

Ross, Lillian. *Picture.* New York: Rinehart & Co., Inc., 1952.

Safranek, William P. "Crane's *The Red Badge of Courage.*" *The Explicator,* XXVI (November 1967), item 21.

Schneider, pp. 103-109.

Sewall, R. B. "Crane's *The Red Badge of Courage.*" *The Explicator,* III (May 1945), item 55.

Shroeder, pp. 123-127.

Solomon, Eric. "Another Analogue for 'The Red Badge of Courage.'" *Nineteenth-Century Fiction,* XIII (June 1958), 63-67.

———. "The Structure of 'The Red Badge of Courage.'" *Modern Fiction Studies,* V (Autumn 1959), 220-234.

———. "A Gloss on *The Red Badge of Courage.*" *Modern Language Notes,* LXXV (February 1960), 111-113.

———. "Yet Another Source for *The Red Badge of Courage.*" *English Language Notes,* II (March 1965), 215-217.

———. *Stephen Crane: From Parody to Realism,* pp. 68-98.

Solomon. M., (January 1956), pp. 33-42.

Stallman, "Stephen Crane: A Revaluation," pp. 262-269.

———. "The Scholar's Net: Literary Sources." *College English,* XVII (October 1955), 20-22.

———. "Fiction and Its Critics: A Reply to Mr. Rahv." *The Kenyon Review,* XIX (Spring 1957), 297-299.

Stein, "Stephen Crane's *Homo Absurdus,*" pp. 174-181.

Stone, Edward. "The Many Suns of *The Red Badge of Courage.*" *American Literature,* XXIX (November 1957), 322-326.

———. "Crane's 'Soldier of the Legion.'" *American Literature,* XXX (May 1958), 242-244.

———. "Introducing Private Smithers." *The Georgia Review,* XVI (Winter 1962), 442-445.

———. "Crane and Zola." *English Language Notes,* I (September 1963), 46-47.

Tanner, pp. 9-14.

Taylor, pp. 119-134.

Thomas, Donald S. "Crane's *The Red Badge of Courage.*" *The Explicator,* XXVII May 1969), item 77.

Tuttleton, James W. "The Imagery of *The Red Badge of Courage.*" *Modern Fiction Studies,* VIII (Winter 1962-1963), 410-415.

Vanderbilt, Kermit and Daniel Weiss. "From Rifleman to Flagbearer: Henry Fleming's Separate Peace in *The Red Badge of Courage.*" *Modern Fiction Studies,* XI (Winter 1965-1966), 371-380.

Wagenknecht, pp. 214-215.

Walcutt, pp. 75-82.

Webster, H. T. "Wilbur F. Hinman's *Corporal Si Klegg* and Stephen Crane's *The Red Badge of Courage.*" *American Literature,* XI (November 1939), 285-293.

Weeks, Robert P. "The Power of the Tacit in Crane and Hemingway." *Modern Fiction Studies,* VIII (Winter 1962-1963), 415-418.

Weisberger, Bernard. "*The Red Badge of Courage.*" In *Twelve Original Essays on Great American Novels,* ed. Charles Shapiro. Detroit: Wayne State University Press, 1958, pp. 96-123.

Weiss, Daniel. "*The Red Badge of Courage.*" *The Psychoanalytic Review,* LII (Summer 1965), 32-52; (Fall 1965), 130-154.

Werthcim, "Stephen Crane and the Wrath of Jehova," pp. 505-507.

West, "Stephen Crane: Author in Transition," pp. 217-219.

Westbrook, Max. "Stephen Crane and the Personal Universal." *Modern Fiction Studies,* VIII (Winter 1962-1963), 351-360.

Williams, G. L. "Henry Fleming and the 'Cheery Voiced Stranger.'" *The Stephen Crane Newsletter,* IV (Winter 1969), 4-7.

Wogan, Claudia C. "Crane's Use of Color in 'The Red Badge of Courage.'" *Modern Fiction Studies,* VI (Summer 1960), 168-172.

Wyndham, George. "A Remarkable Book." *The New Review,* XIV (January 1896), 30-40.

Ziff, pp. 195-199.

The Third Violet

Berryman, *Stephen Crane,* pp. 122-124.

Cady, *Stephen Crane,* pp. 146-149.

Follett, Wilson. "Introduction." In *The Work of Stephen Crane,* III, ed. Wilson Follett. New York: Alfred A. Knopf, Inc., 1926, pp. x-xi, xvii-xxi.

Geismar, pp. 96-98.

Gibson, Donald B., p. 140.

Gullason, "The Jamesian Motif in Stephen Crane's Last Novels,"
     pp. 77-80.

————, ed. *The Complete Novels of Stephen Crane,* pp. 82-87.

Itabashi, Yoshie. "Comedies of Love: A Study of *The Third Violet*
     and *Active Service.*" *The Tsuda Review* [Tokyo], No. 13 (November
     1968), 25-34.

Ives, "Symmetrical Design in Four of Stephen Crane's Stories," p. 19.

Knight, pp. 131-132.

Quinn, pp. 535-536.

Solomon, Eric, *Stephen Crane: From Parody to Realism,* pp. 129-135.

IV. Studies of Individual Short Stories and Short-story Collections *

"The Blue Hotel"

Berryman, *Stephen Crane,* pp. 208-214.

Cox, James Trammell. "Stephen Crane as Symbolic Naturalist: An
     Analysis of 'The Blue Hotel.'" *Modern Fiction Studies,* III (Sum-
     mer 1957), 147-158.

Davison, Richard Allan. "Crane's 'Blue Hotel' Revisited: The Illusion
     of Fate." *Modern Fiction Studies,* XV (Winter 1969-1970), 537-539.

Dillingham, William B. " 'The Blue Hotel' and the Gentle Reader."
     Studies in Short Fiction, I (Spring 1964), 224-226.

Geismar, pp. 120-123.

Gibson, Donald B., pp. 106-118.

Gleckner, Robert F. "Stephen Crane and the Wonder of Man's Con-
     ceit." *Modern Fiction Studies,* V (Autumn 1959), 271-281.

Greenfield, pp. 565-568.

Grenberg, Bruce L. "Metaphysic of Despair: Stephen Crane's 'The
     Blue Hotel.'" *Modern Fiction Studies,* XIV (Summer 1968), 203-
     213.

Itabashi, " 'To Be a Man'—A Study of Fear and Courage in Stephen
     Crane's Stories," pp. 38-44.

Johnson, George W., pp. 254-255.

---

* The listing that follows refers to a select few of Crane's short stories and short-
story collections. There are some useful discussions of other Crane short stories
and short-story collections.

Katz, Joseph. "An Early Draft of 'The Blue Hotel.'" *The Stephen Crane Newsletter*, III (Fall 1968), 1-3.

——, ed. *Stephen Crane: The Blue Hotel*. Columbus: Charles E. Merrill Publishing Co., 1969.

Klotz, Marvin. "Stephen Crane: Tragedian or Comedian, *The Blue Hotel*." *The University of Kansas City Review*, XXVII (Spring 1961), 170-174.

Knapp, pp. 268-273.

Maclean, Hugh N. "The Two Worlds of 'The Blue Hotel.'" *Modern Fiction Studies*, V (Autumn 1959), 260-270.

Martin, Jay, pp. 66-68.

Narveson, Robert. "'Conceit' in 'The Blue Hotel.'" *Prairie Schooner*, XLIII (Summer 1969), 187-191.

Osborn, Neal J. "Crane's *The Monster* and *The Blue Hotel*." *The Explicator*, XXIII (October 1964), item 10.

Roth, pp. 194-195.

Satterwhite, Joseph N. "Stephen Crane's 'The Blue Hotel': The Failure of Understanding." *Modern Fiction Studies*, II (Winter 1956-1957), 238-241.

Solomon, Eric, *Stephen Crane: From Parody to Realism*, pp. 257-274.

Solomon, M., (March 1956), pp. 37-38.

Stallman, ed. *Stephen Crane: An Omnibus*, pp. 482-483.

Stein, "Stephen Crane's *Homo Absurdus*," pp. 173-174.

Stone, Edward. *A Certain Morbidness: A View of American Literature*. Carbondale and Edwardsville: Southern Illinois University Press, 1969, pp. 53-69.

Tanner, pp. 17-18.

VanDerBeets, Richard. "Character as Structure: Ironic Parallel and Transformation in 'The Blue Hotel.'" *Studies in Short Fiction*, V (Spring 1968), 294-295.

Walcutt, pp. 72-75.

Ward, J. A. "'The Blue Hotel' and 'The Killers.'" *The CEA Critic*, XXI (September 1959), 1, 7-8.

Weinig, Sister Mary Anthony. "Heroic Convention in 'The Blue Hotel.'" *The Stephen Crane Newsletter*, II (Spring 1968), 6-7.

Weiss, (Fall 1965), pp. 147-153.

West, "Stephen Crane: Author in Transition," pp. 223-227.

Westbrook, "Stephen Crane's Social Ethic," pp. 593-595.

Wycherley, H. Alan. "Crane's 'The Blue Hotel': How Many Collaborators?" *American Notes & Queries*, IV (February 1966), 88.

"The Bride Comes to Yellow Sky"

Barnes, Robert. "Crane's *The Bride Comes to Yellow Sky.*" *The Explicator,* XVI (April 1958), item 39.

Bernard, Kenneth. " 'The Bride Comes to Yellow Sky': History as Elegy." *The English Record,* XVII (April 1967), 17-20.

Cady, "Stephen Crane and the Strenuous Life," p. 382.

Cook, Robert G. "Stephen Crane's 'The Bride Comes to Yellow Sky.' " *Studies in Short Fiction,* II (Summer 1965), 368-369.

Denny, pp. 35-37.

Ferguson, S. C. "Crane's *The Bride Comes to Yellow Sky.*" *The Explicator,* XXI (March 1963), item 59.

Folsom, James K. *The American Western Novel.* New Haven: College & University Press, 1966, pp. 91-94.

Gibson, Donald B., pp. 124-126.

Grabo, pp. 162-163.

Isaacs, Neil D. "Yojimbo Comes to Yellow Sky." *Kyushu American Literature,* No. 10 (December 1967), 81-86.

James, Overton Philip. "The 'Game' in 'The Bride Comes to Yellow Sky.' " *Xavier University Studies* [New Orleans], IV (March 1965), 3-11.

Johnson, George W., p. 254.

Martin, Jay, pp. 65-66.

Monteiro, George. "Stephen Crane's 'The Bride Comes to Yellow Sky.' " *Approaches to the Short Story,* eds. Neil D. Isaacs and Louis H. Leiter. San Francisco: Chandler Publishing Co., 1963, pp. 221-237.

Roth, pp. 191-192.

Solomon, Eric, *Stephen Crane: From Parody to Realism,* pp. 252-257.

Stallman, ed. *Stephen Crane: An Omnibus,* pp. 479, 483-485.

Stein, "Stephen Crane's *Homo Absurdus,*" pp. 184-186.

Tanner, pp. 16-17.

Tibbetts, A. M. "Stephen Crane's 'The Bride Comes to Yellow Sky.' " *English Journal,* LIV (April 1965), 314-316.

Welty, Eudora. *Short Stories.* New York: Harcourt, Brace and Co., 1949, pp. 18-20.

West, "Stephen Crane: Author in Transition," pp. 221-223.

———. *Reading the Short Story.* New York: Thomas Y. Crowell Co., 1968, pp. 17-23.

"The Clan of No-Name"

Berryman, *Stephen Crane,* pp. 253-255.
Gibson, Donald B., pp. 98-100.
Osborn, Neal J. "The Riddle in 'The Clan': A Key to Crane's Major
    Fiction?" *Bulletin of the New York Public Library,* LXIX (April
    1965), 247-258.
Solomon, Eric, *Stephen Crane: From Parody to Realism,* pp. 118-119.

"Dan Emmonds"

Gilkes, Lillian. "Stephen Crane's 'Dan Emmonds': A Pig in a Storm."
    Studies in Short Fiction, II (Fall 1964), 66-71.
Monteiro, George. "Stephen Crane's 'Dan Emmonds': A Case Re-
    argued." *The Serif,* VI (March 1969), 32-36.
Solomon, Eric, *Stephen Crane: From Parody to Realism,* pp. 149-150.
Stallman, R. W., ed. "New Short Fiction by Stephen Crane: I. 'Dan
    Emmonds.' " *Studies in Short Fiction,* I (Fall 1963), 1-3.

"Death and the Child"

Gibson, Donald B., pp. 100-101.
Itabashi, " 'To Be a Man'—A Study of Fear and Courage in Stephen
    Crane's Stories," pp. 44-47.
Katz, Joseph. "An Early Draft of 'Death and the Child.' " *The
    Stephen Crane Newsletter,* III (Spring 1969), 1-2.
Shroeder, pp. 120-121.
Solomon, Eric, *Stephen Crane: From Parody to Realism,* pp. 107-113.

"An Episode of War"

Gibson, Donald B., pp. 94-96.
Solomon, Eric, *Stephen Crane: From Parody to Realism,* p. 124.
Stallman, ed. *Stephen Crane: An Omnibus,* pp. 376-377.

"An Experiment in Misery"

Bassan, Maurice. "The Design of Stephen Crane's Bowery 'Experiment.'" *Studies in Short Fiction,* I (Winter 1964), 129-132.
Gibson, Donald B., pp. 52-54.

"The Five White Mice"

Berryman, *Stephen Crane,* pp. 108-111.
Gibson, Donald B., pp. 120-122.
Solomon, Eric, *Stephen Crane: From Parody to Realism,* pp. 249-251.
Stein, "Stephen Crane's *Homo Absurdus,*" pp. 186-187.

"The Little Regiment"

Ives, C. B. "'The Little Regiment' of Stephen Crane at the Battle of Fredericksburg." *The Midwest Quarterly,* VIII (April 1967), 247-260.
Solomon, Eric, *Stephen Crane: From Parody to·Realism,* pp. 101-102.

"The Monster"

Åhnebrink, pp. 378-381, *et passim.*
Berryman, *Stephen Crane,* pp. 191-196.
Cady, *Stephen Crane,* pp. 159-160.
Chase, p. xix.
Fiedler, Leslie A. *Love and Death in the American Novel.* New York: Criterion Books, 1960, p. 367.
Follett, Wilson. "Introduction." In *The Work of Stephen Crane,* III, ed. Wilson Follett. New York: Alfred A. Knopf, Inc., 1926, pp. ix-xi.
Geismar, pp. 116-120.
Gibson, Donald B., pp. 136-140.
Gibson, William M., p. xiii.
Gullason, Thomas A. "The Symbolic Unity of 'The Monster.'" *Modern Language Notes,* LXXV (December 1960), 663-668.

Hafley, James. "'The Monster' and the Art of Stephen Crane." *Accent*, XIX (Summer 1959), 159-165.

Hilfer, Anthony Channell. *The Revolt from the Village, 1915-1930.* Chapel Hill: The University of North Carolina Press, 1969, pp. 58-63.

Itabashi, "'To Be a Man'—A Study of Fear and Courage in Stephen Crane's Stories," pp. 33-38.

Ives, "Symmetrical Design in Four of Stephen Crane's Stories," pp. 25-26.

Johnson, George W., pp. 253-254.

Kahn, Sy. "Stephen Crane and the Giant Voice in the Night: An Explication of 'The Monster.'" In *Essays In Modern American Literature,* ed. Richard E. Langford. Deland, Fla.: Stetson University Press, 1963, pp. 35-45.

Knapp, pp. 259-266.

Levenson, J. C. "Introduction." In *The Works of Stephen Crane,* VII, ed. Fredson Bowers. Charlottesville: The University Press of Virginia, 1969, pp. xix-xxxii.

Martin, John C., pp. 41-42.

Osborn, Neal J. "Crane's *The Monster* and *The Blue Hotel.*" *The Explicator,* XXIII (October 1964), item 10.

Shroeder, pp. 127-128.

Solomon, Eric, *Stephen Crane: From Parody to Realism,* pp. 180-200.

Solomon, M., (March 1956), pp. 38-42.

Stallman, "Stephen Crane: A Revaluation," p. 258.

Walcutt, pp. 82-84.

Westbrook, "Stephen Crane's Social Ethic," pp. 595-596.

"A Mystery of Heroism"

Gargano, James W. "Crane's 'A Mystery of Heroism': A Possible Source." *Modern Language Notes,* LXXIV (January 1959), 22-23.

Johnson, George W., p. 256.

Patrick, Walton R. "Poetic Style in the Contemporary Short Story." *College Composition and Communication,* XVIII (May 1967), 79.

Solomon, Eric, *Stephen Crane: From Parody to Realism,* pp. 102-106.

Witherington, Paul. "Stephen Crane's 'A Mystery of Heroism': Some Redefinitions." *English Journal,* LVIII February 1969), 201-204, 218.

"One Dash—Horses"

Berryman, *Stephen Crane,* pp. 104-108.
Gibson, Donald B., pp. 123-124.

"The Open Boat"

Adams, Richard P. "Naturalistic Fiction: 'The Open Boat.' " *Tulane Studies in English,* IV (1954), 137-146.
Archibald, Elizabeth. "A Study of the Imagery in Stephen Crane's 'The Open Boat.' " *Exercise Exchange,* II (Winter 1954), 3-5.
Berryman, John. "Commentary." In *The Arts of Reading,* eds. Ralph Ross, John Berryman, and Allen Tate. New York: Thomas Y. Crowell Co., 1960, pp. 279-287.
Brennan, "Stephen Crane and the Limits of Irony," pp. 190-200.
Buithenhuis, Peter. "The Essentials of Life: 'The Open Boat' as Existentialist Fiction." *Modern Fiction Studies,* V (Autumn 1959), 243-250.
Burns, Landon C., Jr. "On 'The Open Boat.' " *Studies in Short Fiction,* III Summer 1966), 455-457.
Colvert, James B. "Style and Meaning in Stephen Crane: *The Open Boat.*" *Texas Studies in English,* XXXVII (1958), 34-45.
Day, Cyrus. "Stephen Crane and the Ten-foot Dinghy." *Boston University Studies in English,* III (Winter 1957), 193-213.
Dendinger, Lloyd N. "Stephen Crane's Inverted Use of Key Images of 'The Rime of the Ancient Mariner.' " *Studies in Short Fiction,* V (Winter 1968), 192-194.
Denny, pp. 39-41.
Dolch, Martin. " 'The Open Boat.' " In *Insight I: Analyses of American Literature,* eds. John V. Hagopian, Martin Dolch, *et al.* Frankfurt Am Main: Hirschgraben-Verlag, 1962, pp. 36-41.
Frederick, John T. "The Fifth Man in 'The Open Boat.' " *The CEA Critic,* XXX (May 1968), 12-14.
Gibson, Donald B., pp. 127-135.
Going, William T. "William Higgins and Crane's 'The Open Boat': A Note about Fact and Fiction." *Papers on English Language & Literature,* I (Winter 1965), 79-82.

Gordon, Caroline. "Stephen Crane." *Accent*, IX (Spring 1949), 153-157.

Greenfield, pp. 564-565.

Gullason, Thomas A. "The New Criticism and Older Ones: Another Ride in 'The Open Boat.'" *The CEA Critic*, XXXI (June 1969), 8.

Hoffman, Daniel G., *The Poetry of Stephen Crane*, pp. 271-278, *et passim*.

Itabashi, "'To Be a Man'—A Study of Fear and Courage in Stephen Crane's Stories," pp. 29-33.

Kissane, Leedice. "Interpretation Through Language: A Study of the Metaphors in Stephen Crane's *The Open Boat.*" *Rendezvous* [Idaho State University Journal of Arts and Letters], I (Spring 1966), 18-22.

Lytle, Andrew. "'The Open Boat': A Pagan Tale." In *The Hero with the Private Parts*. Baton Rouge: Louisiana State University Press, 1966, pp. 60-75.

Marcus, Mordecai. "The Three-Fold View of Nature in 'The Open Boat.'" *Philological Quarterly*, XLI (April 1962), 511-515.

Martin, Jay, pp. 68-69.

Meredith, Robert C. and John D. Fitzgerald. *The Professional Story Writer and His Art*. New York: Thomas Y. Crowell Co., 1963, pp. 107-111, *et passim*.

Metzger, Charles R. "Realistic Devices in Stephen Crane's 'The Open Boat.'" *The Midwest Quarterly*, IV (Autumn 1962), 47-54.

Meyers, Robert. "Crane's The Open Boat." *The Explicator*, XXI (April 1963), item 60.

Munson, Gorham B. *Style and Form in American Prose*. New York: Doubleday, Doran & Co., Inc., 1929, pp. 159-173, 186-189. Reprinted by Kennikat Press, Inc., Port Washington, New York, 1969.

Napier, James J. "Indifference of Nature in Crane and Camus." *The CEA Critic*, XXVIII (February 1966), 11-12.

―――. "Land Imagery in 'The Open Boat.'" *The CEA Critic*, XXIX (April 1967), 15.

Owen, Guy, Jr. "Crane's 'The Open Boat' and Conrad's 'Youth.'" *Modern Language Notes*, LXXIII (February 1958), 100-102.

Parks, Edd Winfield. "Crane's 'The Open Boat.'" *Nineteenth-Century Fiction*, VIII (June 1953), 77.

Rahv, pp. 283-284.

Reed, Kenneth T. "'The Open Boat' and Dante's *Inferno:* Some Undiscovered Analogues." *The Stephen Crane Newsletter*, IV (Summer 1970), 1-3.

Roth, pp. 193-194.

Shroeder, pp. 127-128.
Solomon, Eric, *Stephen Crane: From Parody to Realism,* pp. 158-176.
Solomon, M., (March 1956), pp. 36-37.
Stallman, ed. *Stephen Crane: An Omnibus,* pp. 416-420.
———. "The Land-Sea Irony in 'The Open Boat.' " *The CEA Critic,* XXX (May 1968), 15.
Stein, "Stephen Crane's *Homo Absurdus,*" pp. 170-173.
Stone, "Crane's 'Soldier of the Legion,' " pp. 242-244.
Tanner, pp. 15-16.
West, Ray B., Jr. and R. W. Stallman, eds. *The Art of Modern Fiction.* New York: Rinehart & Co., Inc., 1949, pp. 53-58.
———. "Stephen Crane: Author in Transition," pp. 219-221.
White, pp. 17-19.

"The Price of the Harness"

Berryman, *Stephen Crane,* pp. 230-231.
Solomon, Eric, *Stephen Crane: From Parody to Realism,* pp. 120-124.
Solomon, M., (March 1956), pp. 44-46.

The Sullivan County Sketches

Berryman, *Stephen Crane,* pp. 37-42.
Colvert, "Structure and Theme in Stephen Crane's Fiction," pp. 201-202.
Gibson, Donald B., pp. 3-24.
Gullason, ed. *The Complete Novels of Stephen Crane,* pp. 30-33.
———. " 'Four Men in a Cave': A Critical Appraisal." *Readers & Writers,* I (April-May 1967), 30-31.
Itabashi, " 'To Be a Man'—A Study of Fear and Courage in Stephen Crane's Stories," pp. 2-9.
Leaver, pp. 525-526.
Schoberlin, pp. 1-2, 5-6, 12-20.
Solomon, Eric, *Stephen Crane: From Parody to Realism,* pp. 1-3.
Stallman, ed. and introd. *Stephen Crane: Sullivan County Tales and Sketches,* pp. 3-24.

"The Upturned Face"

Berryman, *Stephen Crane,* pp. 257-258.

Dillingham, William B. "Crane's One-Act Farce: 'The Upturned Face.'" *Research Studies* [Washington State University], XXXV (December 1967), 324-330.

Gibson, Donald B., pp. 103-105.

Solomon, Eric, *Stephen Crane: From Parody to Realism,* pp. 127-128.

Stallman, ed. *Stephen Crane: An Omnibus,* pp. 375-376.

Whilomville Stories

Denny, pp. 30-32.

Herron, Ima Honaker. *The Small Town in American Literature.* Durham: Duke University Press, 1939, pp. 184-186, *et passim.* Reprinted by Pageant Books, Inc., New York, 1959.

Levenson, J. C. "Introduction." In *The Works of Stephen Crane,* VII, ed. Fredson Bowers. Charlottesville: The University Press of Virginia, 1969, pp. xi-lx.

Martin, John C., pp. 42-46.

Monteiro, George. "Whilomville as Judah: Crane's 'A Little Pilgrimage.'" *Renascence,* XIX (Summer 1967), 184-189.

———. "With Proper Words (or Without Them) The Soldier Dies: Stephen Crane's 'Making An Orator.'" *Cithara,* IX (May 1970), 64-72.

Phelps, William Lyon. "Introduction." In *The Work of Stephen Crane,* V, ed. Wilson Follett. New York: Alfred A. Knopf, Inc., 1926, pp. x-xiii.

Solomon, Eric, *Stephen Crane: From Parody to Realism,* pp. 201-228.

Stallman, ed. *Stephen Crane: An Omnibus,* pp. 533-537.

Wyoming Valley Tales

Arnold, Hans. "Stephen Crane's 'Wyoming Valley Tales': Their
    Source and their Place in the Author's War Fiction." *Jahrbuch für
    Amerikastudien,* IV (1959), 161-169.
Gibson, Donald B., pp. 101-103.
Gullason, ed. *The Complete Short Stories and Sketches of Stephen
    Crane,* pp. 34-35.